PARENTING PROFESSIONALS ENDORSE *THE PARENT'S TOOLSHOP*

This book is dynamite! It is packed with tons of practical ideas. I keep it by my bedside and recommend it to the parents with whom I work. – – Dr. Dennis O'Grady, founder of New Insights Consulting Services and author of *Taking the Fear out of Changing*

A wonderful contribution. In the fourteen years I have worked with children with emotional and behavioral issues, your presentation is unique in addressing some obvious problems and problem-solving skills parents can use. – – Linda Nicely, LSW, Supervisor, Youth Services Network of Southwest Ohio, Inc.

The philosophy and overall presentation is the most comprehensive, consistent, and impressive I've seen. It is well organized, well-received by those who use it, and conveys a sense of joy and commitment from the author. – – Pam Bonsper, M.A., Carmel, CA

This comprehensive book and its advice are built on a solid foundation of research and real-life application. I highly recommend it to any parent who wants to dramatically improve their relationship with their child. – – Deborah Critzer, Positive Parenting

An excellent resource for helping parents raise secure and responsible children. It provides an easy-to-follow guide for parenting children of all ages. I highly recommend this for all families. – – Sylvia Rodberg, Elementary School Guidance Counselor, Springboro Community Schools

It is so nice to finally find a resource that has screened and chosen ideas from other resources for me, because there are some things in other books I disagree with. I can completely trust that it is comprehensive *and* accurate. – – Marla Hurst, Adult Education teacher

An outstanding resource for practical, effective, and easily adoptable parenting methods. Anyone who is a parent, contemplating parenthood, or interested in understanding effective parenting will be richly rewarded by reading this remarkable book. – – Robert L. Seufert, Ph.D., Associate Professor, Marriage and Family Dept., Miami University

A model, a map, a guide, an organizer, a conceptual framework—by whatever name one might want to call it, this book helps parents access the wide, wide world of parenting ideas. – – Sandra Taylor, MSW, Assistant Professor, Dept. of Sociology, Anthropology, and Social Work, University of Dayton.

A valuable resource, not only for parents, but for grandparents, relatives, babysitters, teachers, care providers—anyone who influences a child's world. – – Wendy W. Gordon, Child Safety Advocate and Author of the I'm Safe! Series, published by BackYard Books

I chose this book over others, because of the clarity and consistency with which it addresses an amazing range of parenting issues. In fact, by using the universal blueprint, it addresses every possible parenting dilemma. – – Holly Anderson, M.Ed., RN, NCC, therapist

A complete and well-organized toolbox — very helpful, well organized and easy to use. I'm impressed with not only the content of the book, but also with the heartfelt writing style. – – Charlene Costanzo, author of *The 12 Gifts of Birth*

Parents Approve of *The Parent's Toolshop*

The Parent's Toolshop is great! I've looked up specific questions and found easy workable solutions. It was truly beneficial to me in dealing with my children, adult relationships and learning more about myself. – – Jacki George, mother of two children

This book is incredible. Every chapter is so comprehensive; I learn so much. When I finish a chapter I think the next one can't possibly be as good—but it always is! I've read many books by the likes of Scott Peck, Stephen Covey and Melody Beattie. *The Parent's Toolshop* pulls it all together and shows you how to *live* these revelations. This book is *not* just about parenting. – – Jeff Smith, father of two teenage daughters

I have read numerous magazine articles and books on parenting, attended lectures, and met with counselors. Yet, I have never found a resource as thorough, well-organized and interesting as *The Parent's Toolshop*. The most rewarding aspect was seeing positive results at home with my son, who is diagnosed with A.D.D. These techniques really work!!
– – Rebecca Streeter, mother of one child

No matter how skilled you think you are, this book can give you very effective ways to parent that you never thought of before. – – Rudy Thoms, father of two children

This is the most complete practical guide to human interaction I've ever read!
– – Wendy Adams, mother of two children

My wife and I have agreed more about our parenting in the past three weeks than we have in the past three years! – – Joe Hood, father of two children

I like how the book puts everything into an order that is easy to follow and speaks in a language I can understand. Plus, there are examples so we can relate to our everyday lives.
– – Karen Brooks, mother of two children

The greatest benefit of reading *The Parent's Toolshop* was self-awareness—recognizing my own feelings, speech, and actions. I now feel like I have the knowledge and hope to be able to work on our challenges. – – Elizabeth Valencia, mother of three children

Parenting is never easy, but this book makes it easy to understand.
– – Mike Lowery, father of eight teenage children

This book has absolutely changed my life. Not only have I learned more effective parenting skills, but my entire style of parenting has changed! I am so much more calm, confident, and consistent. – – Amy Reed, mother of two children

The Parent's Toolshop is my parenting Bible! I keep it close at hand and refer to it daily.
– – Cynthia White, mother of three children and home day care provider

"This 'system' *is* amazing! I thought it might prove overwhelming, but it leads you along effortlessly as you collect and put to use all that you find. The dialogues alone make the book priceless. Thanks for a tremendous resource." – – Susan Kendrick, mother of two children

THE PARENT'S TOOLSHOP

The Universal Blueprint for Building a Healthy Family

by Jody Johnston Pawel, LSW

Cartoons by Mick Wells

Ambris
Publishing

The Parent's Toolshop: The Universal Blueprint for Building a Healthy Family

Published by Ambris Publishing
P.O. Box 343
Springboro, OH, 45066
(513) 748-4541 ◆ (888) 415-1212 ◆ fax (513) 748-4620 ◆ www.parentstoolshop.com

If unavailable in local bookstores, additional copies of this and other publications by Jody Johnston Pawel, LSW, may be purchased by contacting the publisher listed above.

Library of Congress Catalog Card Number: 99-65065

Library of Congress Publisher's Cataloging-in-Publication Data

Pawel, Jody Johnston.
  The parent's toolshop : the universal blueprint for building a
healthy family / Jody Johnston Pawel ; cartoons by Mick Wells.
  – 2nd ed. – Springboro, OH : Ambris Publishing, c2000.
  p. cm.
  Includes bibliographical references and index.
  ISBN: 1-929643-34-9
  1. Parenting. 2. Child rearing   3. Interpersonal communication.   I. Title.

    HQ769 .P39 199P   99-65065
    649/ .1 – dc21   CIP

THE PARENT'S TOOLSHOP:
The Universal Blueprint for Building a Healthy Family

Table of Contents

Dedication

To Chris and Amber —

   my inspiration in the past,

      my fountain of joy and love in the present,

         and my symbol of hope for future generations.

AUTHOR'S NOTE

Ah, political correctness. To avoid offending anyone and help everyone feel included, writers must be very careful. Readers can easily misunderstand a writer's intent. For example, one editor said the use of an exclamation point (!) implied yelling—but I use it to express excitement, surprise, or to send a smile or laugh to my readers! The most difficult situation, however, is when a writer is talking about one person. Using "he" is sexist and using "he or she" is awkward and distracting. To avoid sexism and confusion, I will use plurals like "children" and "they" whenever possible. Don't be offended if you have an only child, just substitute the word "he" or "she," depending on your child's gender. Try not to get hung up on whether I use "he," "she," or "they"—the *point* is what's really important.

Similarly, the word "children" refers to all humans under the age of 18. Teens usually don't like people referring to them as "children," so I try to avoid this. The term "children" does refer to teens, however, unless the statement specifically mentions a particular age group. I know some people dislike the word "kids," since children are not baby goats. Now and then I use the term, when I want to be less formal or word something the way a parent might actually say it. I also use "people" to refer to both adults and children when the skills are useful in any human relationship. I always try (in everyday life) to be sensitive to others and not offend anyone, but I avoid using "politically correct" statements that sound ridiculous. If I accidentally exclude someone, I apologize. I trust you to be understanding and to interpret what you read in a way that applies to whatever gender or age you choose.

Every story in this book is true, including my family's personal experiences. I want others to benefit from the lessons these experiences teach, but I also want to protect the privacy of the people involved. As a result, the names have been changed.

LEGAL DISCLAIMER

This book is designed to provide information about parenting and other relationships. It is sold with the understanding that the publisher and author are not engaged in rendering therapeutic, counseling, legal, or other professional services. If you require counseling, private consultation, or other expert assistance, you should seek the services of a competent licensed professional. While this book is the basis for Parent's Toolshop^{SM} parenting classes, it is not an equivalent replacement for direct, professional instruction by a certified Parent's Toolshop^{SM} Tour Guide.

Every effort has been made to make this manual as complete and accurate as possible. However, there may be mistakes both typographical and in content. It is not the purpose of this manual to summarize *all* the information that is available to the author, but to complement, amplify and supplement other texts. Furthermore, this book only contains parenting information that was available as of the printing date. You are urged to read all available materials, learn as much as possible about parenting and healthy relationships, and to tailor the information to your individual needs. For more information about other resources, see the references in the endnotes.

For many people, the skills in this book have improved their family relationships, prevented problems from developing or worsening, and resolved long-standing conflicts. There is no guarantee, however, that these same results will occur for each reader. No one book can account for all the individual circumstances or needs of its reader so use your better judgement when applying the book's advice.

If you are attending a Parent's Toolshop^{SM} class, be sure the instructor is a certified Parent's Toolshop Tour Guide by checking to see if the instructor has a current identification badge. While Tour Guides must complete a thorough certification process, they cannot be held liable for their advice. Handle your concerns directly with them before filing an official complaint with Parent's Toolshop Consulting, Ltd. *The author, publisher, or their representatives shall have neither liability nor responsibility to any person or entity for any behavior or problems alleged to be caused, directly or indirectly, by the information contained in this book or a Parent's Toolshop^{SM} class. If you do not wish to be bound by the above, you may return this book in resalable condition to the publisher within 30 days for a full refund.*

Acknowledgments

First and foremost, I want to thank God—for giving me the honor and privilege of being raised by my parents. Without them, I would not be who I am. Thank you, also, for choosing me as Chris and Amber's mother. They have filled my life with more joy and lessons than I ever thought possible. Thank you for the endless energy and patience you have given me to complete this project. Whenever I felt discouraged, you sent me some sign that you were by my side, which spurred me to continue. I hope I can be a worthy messenger of the lessons I've learned and help even more families with this book.

To Mom and Dad — thanks for your endless unconditional love and your faith in my abilities. I trust your advice and appreciate your encouragement and support. Thanks for being such positive role models: as parents, social service professionals, amicably divorced ex-spouses, happily remarried spouses, and as loving, helpful, honest, humble people. Thanks, Connie and Jim, for being supportive, encouraging stepparents and wonderful grandparents. You *all* are terrific parenting "partners."

To Chris and Amber—thanks for being such wonderful children. Each moment with you is a precious gift. You unconditionally love and forgive me, in spite of all my imperfections. Thanks for showing me the value of these skills through your behavior and examples. I appreciate your permission to share our personal stories with others. I especially appreciate your understanding of the importance of my work and my need to be gone so much, teaching parents. Thanks for giving me the extra time and space I needed to finish this book. I hope I've been there for you when you needed me most and also when nothing special is going on and we just hang out together and talk. Thanks, Chris, for the late night shoulder rubs and Amber, for bedtime hugs and angel stories.

To my husband, Steve—thanks for being my best friend and partner in this lifetime journey of self-improvement. You're always there to give me support when I'm ready to give up and to remind me of the value of this book. I appreciate your sound business advice and your sense of what's *really* important in life. Thanks for understanding my driven nature and for *making* me take breaks, to smell the flowers, see the birds, and watch the garden grow.

To the thousands of parents I've met through my parenting programs—thanks for your excitement and encouragement. Through you, I realized the possibilities of the Universal Blueprint's application in all areas of life. Thanks for asking tough questions that cause me to stretch my knowledge and skills to the limit. Thank you, also, for your evaluations and suggestions, which helped me develop a program that is practical, user-friendly, and highly successful. Thank you for allowing me to share a part of your lives and to be a positive source of change. And thanks to all of you who have shared your stories—which make me think, laugh, and cry—and for allowing me to share them with others.

To the thousands of professionals who have participated in Parent's Toolshop continuing education training programs—thanks for your commitment to giving accurate advice to the parents with whom you work. Thanks for sharing *The Parent's Toolshop* with parents and enthusiastically encouraging me to produce other products to help professionals and meet the needs of the parents you serve.

To Elaine Jelly, Ron Eckerle, and Carrie Morris of Catholic Social Services of the Miami Valley—thanks for your enthusiasm and support of the Families Count Project. The United Way outcome evaluation mandates helped prove what parents kept telling us—the skills work and improve families' lives. Thank you for family-friendly work policies that help me balance work and parenthood. A special thanks to the late Denny Breidenbach, my mentor, for suggesting I venture on my own as an author and speaker and for his support and faith in my potential.

To the other Parent's Toolshop℠ Tour Guides—thank you for your belief in *The Parent's Toolshop* and for teaching the parents I can't reach. I highly value *all* your suggestions for program and leadership development. Thank you for showing me the many ways to adapt the program for diverse populations, while remaining true to its universal principles. I appreciate your sense of commitment to the preservation of the integrity and quality of the program. Thank you, also, for expressing your unique teaching styles; you've shown me the potential I have for self-improvement as a leader.

To Nancy Shockey, my content editor—thanks for helping me tame this monstrous manuscript. You have just the knack I needed: getting to the point, cutting length, but keeping the heart and soul intact. Thanks for all the extra read-throughs you've done, to help this book be as comprehensive, user-friendly, and as short as possible. Your suggestions have taught me to be a better writer. I especially appreciate your occasional notes and funny comments. They were a refreshing break as I waded through pages of edits.

To Cindy Lanning, my editor, proofreader, and formatter–thanks for your dedication to this project, despite computer problems, summer break distractions, and personal obstacles. Thank you for enlisting help from DPS Associates to help meet our deadlines. A special thanks to Crystal Chapin for coordinating your troop of editorial and layout experts–you all are true miracle workers.

To Mick Wells, my cartoonist—thanks for taking my ideas and turning them into cartoons. I especially appreciate your patience with this project. I had no idea just how long the process would take.

To Tom Helmers at EPIC Printing—thanks for helping me keep up with the local demand for the book. I appreciate your expertise in pulling all the parts together and keeping a stock of books flowing. We would have never kept up the pace without your hard work.

To The Jenkins Group, Inc., especially Susan Howard, Nikki Stahl, and Barb Hodge—thanks for your sound publishing advice and for coordinating this production project. I appreciated your patience throughout the many decisions I had to make and your expert advice, which helped create a professional high-quality book.

To MarketAbility, especially Tami DePalma, Bradley James, and Kim Dushinski—thanks for reading *The Parent's Toolshop*, in full, so you could put the right *twist* on its promotion. Thanks for your patience a I pulled together the production and distribution details. Most of all, thanks for arranging magazine, TV, and radio interviews before the book was even in print.

And thanks to everyone who has enthusiastically spread the word about *The Parent's Toolshop*. Whatever success comes from this book, I owe it all to you.

– – Jody Johnston Pawel, LSW

INTRODUCING YOUR TOOLSHOP TOUR GUIDE

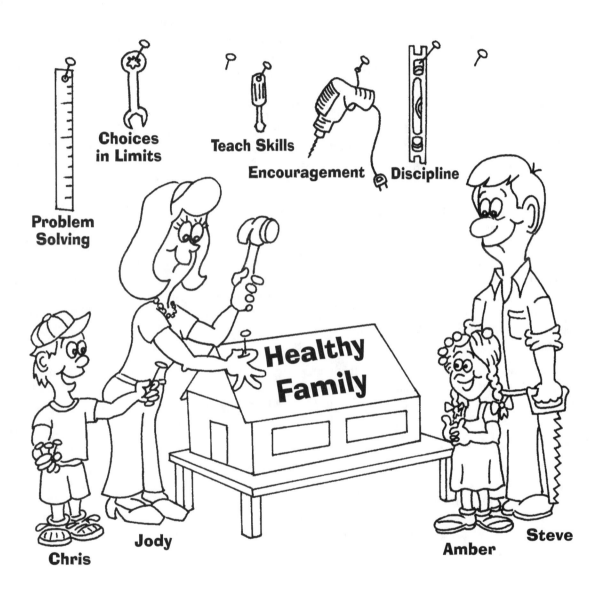

Problem Solving

Choices in Limits

Teach Skills

Encouragement

Discipline

Healthy Family

Chris

Jody

Amber

Steve

INTRODUCING YOUR TOOLSHOP TOUR GUIDE

Welcome to *The Parent's Toolshop*. I'm Jody, your Parent's Toolshop "Tour Guide." This book is part of who I am and it reflects my personal and professional life. I want to share a bit about myself so you understand my perspective and why I believe so passionately in what I teach.

My Childhood Experiences with Parent Education

I've been *involved* in parent education since I was eight, when my parents took a parenting class. I was old enough to remember what my parents were like before the class and to recognize the positive effect their new skills had on me. Both of my parents taught parenting classes for ten years and my mother continued teaching parenting in Christian* settings for over 30 years. I helped my parents make audio-tapes for their classes. I'd play the role of a snotty-nosed, bratty kid and they'd use a communication or discipline skill to respond. This was my first realization that some parenting techniques are more effective than others and parenting classes can be a fun place to learn these skills.

My parents, like parents today, took a parenting class because they wanted to do the best job they could. They wanted to bring up their children differently than their parents raised them. They wanted their children to have a strong sense of self-worth and values and be responsible and self-disciplined. They wanted to have open, trusting communication with their children and resolve problems in healthy ways. My parents succeeded in all these areas. As a child and teen, I listened to friends' stories about their parents. I realized my parents were not typical and counted my blessings. Even as a teen, I could talk to my parents about almost anything. I trusted them and they trusted me. They weren't perfect parents, but I always had tremendous admiration and respect for them. Although I was not a perfect child, they always showed me unconditional love. When they needed to correct me, I was often both surprised and impressed by their positive, helpful responses. My parents taught me life skills such as decision making, problem solving, effective communication, budgeting, and time management. Through their words and examples, they taught me values such as honesty, self-discipline, accountability, compassion, and faith in God. I will share some of my experiences as a child raised with the skills this book teaches.

Because of my upbringing, people think that I am an exception—that parenting skills come naturally to me, that I had perfect parents, and we had a perfect family. None of this is true. Each member of my family is imperfect, and we have learned important lessons and skills through very trying experiences.

My Personal Family History

Effective parenting skills help many families avoid and solve problems—but children also interact with people outside the family. These people can traumatize children from even the best of families, which is what happened to my family. I want you to know what happened to my family so you know that I *can* understand the frustration *every* family member experiences in a troubled family. I can attest from *personal* experience, that the skills I teach *can* improve situations that seem hopeless.

---

*While this book teaches ideas that are *consistent* with Christian beliefs and values, it is written for the general public, which represents many religions and nonbelievers. Many people use this book to provide parenting programs in a variety of religious and non-religious settings. There are a few references to God, but these could apply to almost any religion, not just Christianity. If Biblical references are important to you, feel free to do your own research or call Ambris Publishing's toll-free number to request our free handout "Guidelines for Christian Parents," which has scriptural references correlated with *The Parent's Toolshop* toolsets.

Each member of a family can have a different family experience. It's all a matter of perspective. Many things influence this opinion: one's personality, experiences, and interpretations of events. My parents viewed our family from an adult perspective. From my perspective, my relationship with my parents and childhood was ideal (with a few exceptions). My brother, who is five years older than I, experienced a totally different childhood.

When my brother was nine, he was playing with a friend deep in the woods behind our house, when a teenage boy grabbed and molested him. In the early 1960s, children didn't learn about good and bad touches or telling grownups about inappropriate advances. The shame and trauma my brother felt caused him to keep this event a secret. He could not, however, forget what happened. He had difficulty concentrating in school, his grades went down, and his teacher held him back in the fourth grade. My parents were concerned about his school problems, but didn't realize a deeper problem might be the cause. (Parents were not informed then about warning signs or symptoms of child sexual abuse.) They followed the teacher's advice, but over the next several years his problems only worsened.

My parents took their first parenting class in the late 1960s, when my brother was about 13. Drugs, sex, rock 'n roll, long hair, and permissiveness were everywhere. The society in which they were raising children was drastically different from anything they expected. In his teen years, my brother became involved in a rock group that exposed him to drugs as a popular lifestyle. Since my brother denied his drug use, my parents and the professionals they consulted were unable to accurately diagnose this problem. Drug addiction was a new phenomenon; professionals knew little about specific drugs, the symptoms of addiction, and treatment methods. When my parents consulted psychologists, they received unhelpful or inadequate advice. My parents' new parenting skills worked well with me, because I was a younger child who had never been traumatized. With my brother, however, the skills brought limited improvement. Although my brother and parents received counseling, we never received family counseling, which was a relatively new treatment back then. I realized then, that siblings are often the forgotten "patients" in family problems.

My brother's problems started when I was four, so we had only a brief positive relationship. Seeing his behavior and my parents' concern, I subconsciously decided that my role in the family was to be the good child. (My parents didn't compare us this way. I put myself in this role.) I tried to do everything I could to be the perfect child. I did my best to put on a perky, chipper front and not burden others (including my parents) with my problems. I thought we had to appear to be a perfect family, and often I felt like I was leading a double life, public and private.

At home, my brother teased me, belittled me, and played cruel jokes on me. If I told my parents, he'd treat me even worse when they were gone. I found I could get revenge on him by rubbing in my successes. We were in a vicious cycle and either ignored each other or argued when we were together. Most of our arguments occurred at breakfast and dinner, when we ate as a family. I tried to hold in my emotions, but they'd spill out unexpectedly. If I watched *Lassie* on television, I'd cry for hours. When I was 13, I had stomachaches that were so painful I was hospitalized for a week. Holding in my feelings had literally made me sick—even I didn't realize how deeply things were bothering me.

By the time I was a teenager, my brother's behavior and emotional problems had worsened to the point that there was obviously something serious going on. Since his sexual abuse and drug addiction were still secrets, efforts to help him had only a limited effect. When he tried to detoxify himself, he experienced severe withdrawal symptoms and became violent. Not knowing he was addicted, doctors diagnosed these symptoms as a mental illness, but medication that should have helped only made him more withdrawn and depressed. The doctors and therapists told my parents to give up any hope of him being well again. They said he'd never hold gainful employment and suggested he claim a disability and live off government support. Now he was not only dealing with the pain of childhood sexual abuse, drug addiction, and being the "problem child," but he also had to overcome the stigma of being labeled mentally ill. While my parents had no choice but to believe the diagnosis, neither they nor my brother were willing to accept the hopeless prognosis. Fortunately, they believed he could be healed and whole again and continued seeking new treatments. Remarkably, the first breakthrough came when my mother's college professor offered two suggestions: "get him out more and involve him in meaningful activity" and "see that he gets good nutrition." Massive doses of vitamins balanced and restored his depleted body chemistry, which improved his depression and recovery from drugs. His involvement in Bible studies and a Gospel music group brought joy into his life again.

At the age of 23, my brother finally told his therapist, and then my parents, about his molestation and drug addictions. With this new information, it was clear what the *real* problems were and why previous efforts had not been successful. By combining spiritual, psychological, nutritional, and behavioral treatments, my brother started rebuilding his life. Only then did the parenting skills seem to have a greater positive affect. His progress was steady, with occasional setbacks. The real turning point in his life and the key to his total healing was his spiritual conversion.

My brother's adult life has focused on becoming totally healed and whole again. Today, he has a master's degree in pastoral counseling and counsels other victims of sexual abuse or drug addiction. Faith, hope, love, courage, and my brother's hard work and determination helped make possible what others said was impossible. Whatever guidance my parents and God provided, my brother deserves the credit for turning his life around.

My Professional Training

During our family's healing years, we all learned a lot about psychology, healthy families, and good mental health. Our efforts to heal our family resulted in each of us changing (or starting) careers as helping professionals. (My mother is a therapist and the Founder/Executive Director of a Christian counseling center. My father is the retired Executive Director of a juvenile diversion program and an accomplished artist.) When I was 17, I attended my mother's parenting class—the only teen in a class for parents of teens. This experience gave me an early insight to a parent's point of view and helped the parents see a teen's perspective. I was impressed with my mother's teaching style and the way the skills helped me in *all* my relationships. It was then I decided to become a family social worker.

I have a special sensitivity to sibling, teen, and parenting issues, because of my life experiences and training. In college, I researched sibling violence and learned how to prevent, identify, and treat all forms of abuse and unhealthy family relationships. I worked my way through college at a teenage runaway shelter and campus counseling center. On summer breaks, I worked with inner city teens. After graduation, I received my social work license and worked with abusive and neglectful families in a unit that specialized in sexual abuse. It was the early 1980s and there were few parenting classes available. Because of my background and experience, several employers asked me to teach parenting classes, although I wasn't a parent yet. (You can guess how much credibility I had with parents!)

The Birth of *The Parent's Toolshop*

I married in 1983 and our first child, Chris, was born in 1984. When my maternity leave ended, I couldn't bring myself to leave my son, so my husband and I made a difficult financial decision—I would become a mom-at-home and pursue my career from home-based businesses. The next year, a local newscaster asked me to be the co-producer and on-air child care expert for a weekly television series featuring safety tips for parents. It only required me to be away from home several hours a week. When the series ended, my son was still young and I was starved for adult companionship. I started a mom-at-home discussion group called The Family Network, which is still going strong more than ten years later.

I wrote *Shared Blessings: Creating and Facilitating Stay-at-Home Parent Discussion Groups* to help other parents start similar groups around the country.

To help myself be a better parent and to share my knowledge with other parents, I taught parenting classes for the next eight years, in my home and other parents' homes, using several popular parenting curriculum kits. While I agreed with everything these curricula taught, I continually experienced two problems. First, parents had difficulty learning certain skills, because they hadn't learned foundational skills that the curricula said to teach later in the class. For example, parents had a difficult time disciplining effectively if they hadn't dealt with their own power and control issues. I was constantly jumping around the chapters so parents could better learn and understand the skills. Second, I kept finding other resources that had valuable suggestions, so I kept adding extra reading assignments to help parents get the most comprehensive parent education possible. I was constantly searching for—and frustrated at never finding—*one* resource that had *all* the skills parents needed to learn that was presented in a logical order that made their learning easier and more effective.

My daughter, Amber, was born in 1989. When she entered preschool in 1992, I began a job at Catholic Social Services of the Miami Valley, in Dayton, Ohio, teaching parenting classes to inner city families. I needed one comprehensive resource but still hadn't found one on the market. Plus, the program had no funds for books but was told I could make copies of any notes I wrote on my own time. That's when I began writing *The Parent's Toolshop*, although I didn't know it would turn into a book at that point. At night, after the kids were in bed, I'd write down the practical tools I had found over the years and organize them in a logical, useful order. For each, I'd add suggestions to help parents use the tools to their greatest potential and avoid common mistakes. Over the next four years, the parents in my parenting classes (through CSSMV and my private classes) field tested the program and its tools, offering suggestions for improvement and testimonials of its effectiveness.

I learned through trial and error that the tools were especially effective if parents learn and used them in a particular order. I designed the Universal Blueprint flow chart in 1990 and the house diagram in 1992 to provide easy *visual* ways for parents to remember these steps. During the four year field-testing stage, I taught the Universal Blueprint to over two thousand parents and professionals in a variety of settings. After several weeks of using the skills, many parents were bursting with excitement because of their success. Many said, "These skills have helped my marriage" or "I even use the tools at work!" I realized that this Universal Blueprint was a useful guide for *any* relationship. When I needed to develop a new presentation, for teachers, businesses, or group leaders, I simply referred to the Universal Blueprint and developed new programs faster than ever before.

Requests for my programs were so great I couldn't meet the demand, so I trained more leaders before the first edition of this book was complete. Within six months, there were over a dozen certified Parent's Toolshop[SM] Tour Guides throughout the state of Ohio and people were calling from around the country, because they'd heard about the success of Parent's Toolshop programs. All this happened strictly by word-of-mouth, with no publicity, *before* I had finished the final revisions to the first edition of this book. By 1999, when the second edition was complete and ready for national distribution, there were over two dozen Tour Guides throughout the United States.

I know that there will always be parents and professionals who want to learn about *The Parent's Toolshop*, but can't take a class. I wrote this book especially for these people. I have included everything I say in class and tried to answer all the questions parents frequently ask. Yet, my goal is not to give parents all the answers, although I do give hundreds of ideas to try. My goal is to empower parents with the knowledge and skills they need to think for themselves.

In Summary

I have spent most of my professional life researching and writing this book. I have devoted more years to its development than I have been a parent. The process has felt like a *very* long pregnancy: I've been pregnant for over ten years (researching and developing the program), in labor for three years (writing at all hours of the day and night), and pushing for two years (making final revisions and changes). After putting so much of myself into this creation, I feel just as protective and rewarded as a mother feels when she holds her newborn in her arms for the first time.

I know how hard it is to be a parent. I want to offer ideas and support from an educated, experienced, and practical perspective. While my personal experiences have affected my opinions, I don't select tools that simply fit *my* beliefs. I include those tools that are accurate, healthy, and proven effective over time for the families who use them consistently and appropriately.

I am *not* a perfect parent. I have old habits and personality traits that are a challenge to my effectiveness as a mother, wife, and person. I still struggle to master some of the skill I teach and keep trying to improve myself. (I will share some of my parenting mistakes and successes and what I learned from them.) Although sitters and strangers often comment on my children's good behavior, they are still learning and growing, which provides me with my fair share of challenges.

While many of the tools are now second-nature to me, it is because I was raised with them and get constant practice from teaching parenting classes almost every day. Any parent who works with these tools and practices them daily can feel they are second-nature, too. Whether you are looking for a miracle or a boost of confidence, these tools will be an important part of your efforts to be a positive, effective parent.

Parental love might come naturally, but effective parenting skills are *learned*. It takes constant practice to develop and maintain them.

CHAPTER 1
TOURING THE PARENT'S TOOLSHOP

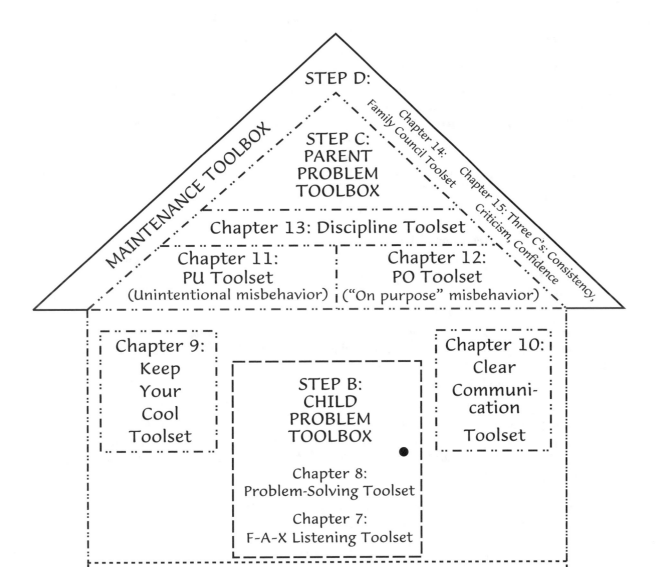

STEP D:

MAINTENANCE TOOLBOX

Chapter 14: Family Council Toolset

Chapter 15: Three C's: Consistency, Criticism, Confidence

STEP C:
PARENT
PROBLEM
TOOLBOX

Chapter 13: Discipline Toolset

Chapter 11:
PU Toolset
(Unintentional misbehavior)

Chapter 12:
PO Toolset
("On purpose" misbehavior)

Chapter 9:
Keep
Your
Cool
Toolset

STEP B:
CHILD
PROBLEM
TOOLBOX

Chapter 8:
Problem-Solving Toolset

Chapter 7:
F-A-X Listening Toolset

Chapter 10:
Clear
Communi-
cation
Toolset

STEP A: PREVENTION TOOLBOX

Chapter 6: Independence Toolset

Chapter 5: Cooperation Toolset

Chapter 4: Self-Esteem Toolset

Chapter 3: The Universal Blueprint

Chapter 2: Foundation-Building Toolset

BUILD
UP!

CHAPTER
1 TOURING THE PARENT'S TOOLSHOP

When we want to build a house, we don't call a bunch of workers, give them a pile of wood, and say, "Go to work!" We need a blueprint to follow and skilled workers who know when and how to use specific types of tools to build or repair the house. To build a stable family, parents also need a plan—a blueprint to follow. We need to know how to use several types of parenting tools, when to use them, and how to use them to their maximum effectiveness.

*The Parent's Toolshop is a comprehensive, step-by-step plan that uses the most effective tools available to parents. Its "Universal Blueprint" helps us build healthy relationships, prevent problems, and respond effectively to situations that occur. Beyond parenting, we can follow this Universal Blueprint and use its skills to improve **any** relationship.*

ANOTHER PARENTING BOOK?

Of all the jobs and professions in the world, parenting is the most important, difficult, and potentially rewarding. It is the only job that never ends; we are parents 24 hours a day, 7 days a week, 12 months a year, every year. Even when children are adults, we are still their parent. We don't make money by having children; we spend it. Our paychecks can't be measured by material standards; they are hugs, thank-you's, smiles, and seeing our child grow and mature. We need skills, not luck, to reach our parenting goals. Yet, despite its importance, parenting is one of few professions that does not require a license, degree, or any special training.

Anyone can have a dramatic influence on a child's life because children record every experience, positive or negative, in their memory. Their minds replay these tapes over and over, influencing their entire lives. Thus, each adult who interacts with a child has a profound responsibility to fulfill—yet often few guidelines to follow.

Since the beginning of time, family and friends have been the primary source of parenting advice. Only in the twentieth century have professionals researched child-rearing, educated parents, and developed parenting expertise. While many of us were growing up, parenting pioneers were testing and refining many theories about the different styles of child-rearing. Some techniques provided short-term successes but had negative long-term effects. For over four decades, one general parenting style has proved to be most effective in producing self-sufficient, well-balanced adults and healthy family relationships. Within this style, there are several types of skills parents need to use, and within each skill area there are dozens of options from which to choose.

Common Problems with Parenting Resources

We are one of the first generations of parents to have a multitude of resources easily available to us. In each of our homes, we can probably find some evidence of parent education—a flyer from a maternity ward, a newspaper advice column, a parenting magazine or book. Throughout my 20-plus years of working with families, and especially after becoming a parent myself, I have read hundreds of these resources. Like many parents, I found a lot of helpful, accurate information, but also had frustrations and concerns. This book is my attempt to correct the following problems with parenting resources:

- **Some books are philosophical, with few practical applications. *The Parent's Toolshop* is practical, not just philosophical.** Chapter 2, "Foundation-Building Toolset," presents a balanced parenting philosophy that is the foundation of effective parenting. Subsequent chapters briefly explain the philosophical basis for each set of tools and why they are more effective than other common parenting techniques. The bulk of each chapter explains nearly a dozen skills in simple terms and applies each tool to sample situations. Plus, there are opportunities to practice using the special language and actions that are a part of effective parenting.

- **Some authors focus on what *not* to do, without offering positive alternatives.** *The Parent's Toolshop* **focuses on what parents *can* do.** I promise to avoid telling you *not* to do something unless I offer one or more positive alternatives. We learn the universal guidelines and the options available within those limits. This is how we create individualized plans for our own families.

- **Many books have good ideas, but no one book seems to have them all; they are spread throughout hundreds of resources.** Parents must buy several books and find the good ideas to get all the information they need for an effective parenting plan. *The Parent's Toolshop* **is a one-stop resource that equals dozens of books combined.** It represents ten years of researching literally hundreds of resources. Consequently, it teaches over one hundred practical skills and addresses over one thousand issues or problems parents could face. Best of all, we can use the Universal Blueprint to file ideas from other resources and know how and when to use them most effectively.

    A Graduate's Comment. Of all the books and magazines I've devoured regarding parenting skills, this one put them all to shame. I learned more from one chapter in this book than I could have learned from one hundred books put together. — Debbie Klein

- **Many books discuss only one skill area, one developmental stage, or one type of relationship.** When our children mature or we want to improve an adult relationship, we must read a whole new series of books. Many parenting skills can be slightly adjusted to improve adult relationships. It's less confusing and more consistent to use similar effective relationship skills at work *and* at home to improve *every* area of our lives. **The tools in *The Parent's Toolshop* are useful in any relationship—with children of any age and in adult relationships.**

    A Professional's Comment. The Parent's Toolshop is absolutely excellent. It is appropriate for all human relationships. It is amazing to me how I can see organizations in all this. There's great value in relating to people at work the way we do with families. The tools are very practical, so we can use them every single day at home and at work. — Donna Lehner, lay counselor

- ***Books that have many helpful ideas often present them randomly.*** This makes it difficult to understand, properly select, and use the skills to their full potential. *The Parent's Toolshop* **organizes parenting tools in a logical step-by-step format that helps us plan the most helpful response to any relationship situation.** The order of the chapters is specific and follows each step of the Universal Blueprint.

    A Professional's Comment. I've been teaching parenting classes for almost 30 years and The Parent's Toolshop is the best resource I've found. It's so comprehensive, like dozens of parenting books rolled into one. I like the way the toolsets put the whole parenting process into a logical sequence that's so easy to use. — Millie McCarty, M.A., L.P.C., President & Executive Director, Lighthouse Counseling Inc.

- **Few resources explain how to avoid common misuses or abuses of effective skills.** Some people learn a little about effective parenting skills, but not enough to use them to their full potential or in the most helpful way. **With every tool, *The Parent's Toolshop* explains *why*, *when*, and *how* to use it, and how to avoid common misuses.**

- **Parenting advice is often contradictory.** One book says to do one thing while another says the complete opposite. **Every tool in *The Parent's Toolshop* has passed a stringent screening process.** They are consistent in philosophy, and can be cross-referenced with other reliable parenting resources.

- **Many books teach quick-fix methods that are not effective over time.** We want to choose a parenting plan that resolves current problems *and* helps us reach our long-term parenting goals. **The Universal Blueprint and its tools often provide quick fixes, but more importantly, the long-term results are always positive.** For over 40 years, these tools have helped parents build healthy families, prevent problems, and effectively solve problems that arise. In addition, four years of field testing proved *The Parent's Toolshop* is a highly effective resource for improving parenting skills. Here are the results:

  - From 1992 to 1996, over 2,000 parents and professionals of all backgrounds field tested *The Parent's Toolshop*. Of those, nearly 1,000 parents participated in an eight-week parenting class in the Dayton (Ohio) area, which is a representative cross-section of the cultural, racial, and socioeconomic makeup of the United States. In addition, more than 100 professionals received training in using *The Parent's Toolshop*'s Universal Blueprint in their business, teaching, and counseling professions.

  - Almost 900 parents received a pre/post-class skill assessment, using an outcome-focused evaluation tool specifically designed for *The Parent's Toolshop* that assesses participants' knowledge and skill mastery in 11 parenting skill areas.

  - *Every* parent who completed a Parent's Toolshop parenting class (100%) showed improvement in their parenting skills. On a scale of 11 points, the average improvement in skills was 3.13 points, from below the midpoint (5.66) to well in the skillful range (8.67). Demographic research showed skill improvement was consistent, regardless of socioeconomic or other background factors. (Parents who had reading comprehension difficulties showed improvement from classroom participation, not just reading the book.) During a 6-month follow-up assessment, the average graduate not only maintained the post-class skill level, but showed continued improvement.

  - Program evaluations, which determine participant satisfaction, showed 92% rated the program "excellent" (the other 8% rated it "good"), 94% said they had learned new information, and 100% said they'd recommend the program to others.

    > *A Professional's Comment. Each year, since 1992, our agency receives dozens of requests from agencies and community groups to provide Parent's Toolshop programs to parents of all economic and cultural backgrounds. The programs are very popular and successful in achieving significant parenting skill improvement. The Parent's Toolshop is a helpful resource for people of all skill levels. — Ronald Eckerle, Ph.D., LISW, Executive Director, Catholic Social Services of the Miami Valley*

- **Many books have helpful ideas, but also foster myths or include inaccurate information.** Due to my personal and professional background, I can easily recognize inaccurate but commonly accepted information. **The Parent's Toolshop weeds out common myths and misinformation that confuse parents or result in less than effective parenting.** We learn a common language and universal guidelines for evaluating information from other resources so we can recognize inaccurate advice we find in other resources.

To give you a sense of the mixture of accurate and inaccurate information experts give parents today, take the true/false quiz on the next page.

Myth or Truth?

_____ Parents should attend parenting classes when having problems with their children.

_____ Parent educators tell parents what they are doing wrong and how to raise children the right way.

_____ Whenever parents use an effective parenting skill, they should see it work right away.

_____ Children should not be the center of the family; the parent should.

_____ Democratic parenting is too permissive and only works with certain kinds of children.

_____ It is the parent's job to control children's behavior.

_____ Parents need to immediately react to a problem to effectively resolve it.

_____ When parents stop children's misbehavior, the problem usually goes away.

_____ Parents can encourage children by giving them lots of praise and rewards.

_____ When parents let children know they are proud of them, children feel parents are giving them credit for their accomplishments.

_____ Sometimes it's helpful to offer constructive criticism to help children improve.

_____ Children should obey their parents because they are adults in authority. When children ask "Why should I?" parents only need to say, "Because I said so."

_____ Behavior charts with stars or rewards foster internal motivation.

_____ When parents give children choices, children think they should have a choice about everything.

_____ All toddlers go through a "no" stage; it's a normal part of childhood.

_____ Parents should give children more independence when they show they can handle it.

_____ When children struggle with simple tasks, it helps to say, "You can do it if you try harder."

_____ When children have problems, parents should help solve them.

_____ When children aren't doing their homework, parents should set up a homework schedule, make sure they stick to it, supervise their work, and sign off on it every day.

_____ People get angry because other people and events are out of their control.

_____ Children know how to push their parents' buttons because they program and control them.

_____ When children misbehave, parents should show their disappointment so the children will want to change.

_____ When parents repeatedly tell children to stop misbehaving and they don't stop, parents can assume their children know how to behave better.

_____ Children misbehave to get what they want or sometimes just to get on their parents' nerves.

_____ When misbehaving children need to "learn a lesson," parents should make sure they suffer a little, to drive home their point.

_____ When parents want children to behave, they should threaten to punish the children.

_____ Time-outs should be one minute for every year of age. Children should be isolated in an unpleasant or boring place and not allowed to play.

_____ Parents should call a family meeting when there is a problem.

_____ Every family member votes on decisions in family meetings.

_____ Parents should be consistent. If they say they are going to punish their children, they need to follow through, even if they realize later they overreacted.

_____ Inconsistent parenting is damaging. Effective parenting partners do things the same way.

WHAT *THE PARENT'S TOOLSHOP* DOES

The Parent's Toolshop and its Universal Blueprint offers parents three major benefits:

1. A *universal plan* for effective parenting.

2. A way to apply this plan in ways that meet the *individual needs* of each individual family, even when these needs (such as personalities or backgrounds) differ from other families or among family members.

3. The freedom for parents to express their *unique personal style,* while using the Universal Blueprint and its tools.

Universal Purpose

Building a healthy family is similar to building a stable house. All houses need certain things, no matter where or by whom they are built: a sturdy balanced foundation, protective walls that are not imprisoning, doors and windows for healthy ventilation, repairs to problems in the structure or its contents, and a roof to protect the inhabitants from the harsh outside elements. These are the universal, common factors necessary for quality human shelter.

Healthy families also have certain universal features:

- A stable foundation of love and respect.
- Flexible boundaries that are protective yet not imprisoning.
- Doorways that invite rather than inhibit helpful communication.
- Outlets for healthy ventilation of feelings and concerns.
- Effective responses to problems that affect the whole family or individual family members.
- A sense of security and togetherness that provides support in times of crisis.

The Universal Blueprint and its tools provide a universal plan for building a healthy family. They offer parents clear guidelines to follow and a means for knowing when they have stepped over the line into ineffective or unhealthy practices.

You can use the Universal Blueprint and its tools with any age child—and even in adult relationships—because they are consistent with the universal laws of human behavior, feelings, and thoughts. The tools are so valuable, we want to use them in every relationship and model and teach the skills to children and others.

Individual Needs

A house that meets the universal guidelines for quality shelter must also address the specific needs of the people living within. In swampy marshlands, the foundation of a house might be supported by stilts to protect the house from flooding. Still, the stilts must be balanced and sturdy. Many factors influence how a particular house is built. These individual needs must be met while meeting the universal qualities of stability and quality shelter.

While our families are similar in some ways, they are different in even more. To build a stable family, we need to address these individual needs while following the universal process of effective parenting.

When you look at all the factors that could play out in a particular problem, there are an infinite number of individual problem combinations. Each of these combinations, however, will fit within one of six problem "types" identified with the Universal Blueprint. Once you know which type of problem you are dealing with, it narrows down which group of skills or toolsets you want to use. This is how you take the Universal Blueprint, the universal effective parenting plan, and tailor it to the individual needs of each person in a specific situation at any point in time.

Within the Universal Blueprint, there are many options (tools) parents can use to meet the individual needs of each family member and each relationship. In each situation, we use the Universal Blueprint to identify the steps we need to take. At each step, we choose specific tools based on the individual circumstances or people involved.

Unique Personal Style

A stable, quality house that meets an individual family's needs differs in one final way—personal style. Whether a simple hut or Tudor mansion, a house is a reflection of the builder's personal taste. Even the interior decorations, whether simple or ornate, reflect the creativity of its dwellers. It's the finishing touch that makes a house a home.

Each of us has a unique personality; some of us are loud and goofy (like me), others are soft-spoken and reserved. We can each follow the Universal Blueprint's guidelines and still feel comfortable and genuine in our responses and expressions. **We can also use our imagination and resourcefulness to add to or adapt the tools to fit our unique style, while still remaining true to the universal principles.**

THE UNIVERSAL BLUEPRINT

Whether building a new house or remodeling an existing home, we start with a plan. What type of house or change do we need? What features are important? What steps do we need to take and in what order?

When we build or remodel our family we need a plan with clear-cut guidelines. Otherwise, it is confusing to receive too many ideas. Many parents fly by the seat of their pants, learning as they go from trial and error. These parents are more likely to emotionally react to problems rather than follow a plan that gives them the results they want. ***The Parent's Toolshop* is the only book available to parents that provides a decision-making guide, organized in a specific logical order that helps us respond effectively to any situation in any relationship.** We can even add tools from other resources if they fit the universal guidelines in *The Parent's Toolshop*.

Just as there are four major steps to building houses, there are also four major steps to building healthy relationships and responding to problems. The bold italicized words below show how each step, called a *toolbox*, deals with a different type of problem. The bold and underlined letters show the universal response formula, called PASRR (pronounced "passer"), which we'll learn in Chapter 3, "The Universal Blueprint."

Step	Building a House	Building Healthy Relationships	Universal Blueprint
A	Lay the foundation.	***Prevent problems* from starting or worsening** by developing positive qualities in self and others and teaching skills.	Prevention Toolbox
B	Build the external structure.	***When children (or other adults) have a problem,* <u>A</u>cknowledge their feelings** and guide them through the process of finding their own solutions.	Child Problem Toolbox
C	Install the internal systems.	***When you have a problem,* <u>S</u>et limits and express your concerns** assertively and respectfully. This may include <u>R</u>edirecting misbehavior and/or <u>R</u>evealing discipline.	Parent Problem Toolbox
D	Add the finishing touches.	***Maintain the progress you've made*** in your personal growth and family relationships.	Maintenance Toolbox

Every *second*, each of us is at one of these steps in every relationship we have. The Universal Blueprint shows us the step we are on and which skills we can use. If we follow the steps of the Universal Blueprint, *in order,* it greatly improves the quality and effectiveness of our response. Since the blueprint is a step-by-step process, we start by setting a balanced foundation and work our way up to maintaining progress.

Most parents lack guidelines for choosing the best tool for a particular situation and using it correctly. When problems arise, we often use the first tool that comes to mind, even if it is not the most appropriate. This is like using carpentry tools to fix a plumbing problem, simply because the carpentry tools are the only tools we have or know how to use. *The Parent's Toolshop* is a common-sense, logical method of correctly identifying problem types and choosing an appropriate response. This sets *The Parent's Toolshop* apart from all other parenting resources. This problem-solving method is straight-forward and really quite simple, once we get used to stopping to think before we respond. The more difficult tasks are using the tools to their maximum potential and avoiding common misuses.

A home builder uses electrical tools to install wiring. Similarly, parents use specific groups of skills, called *toolsets,* located in the appropriate toolbox. To prevent problems, for example, we can use any of the toolsets in the Prevention Toolbox—the Cooperation Toolset and the Independence Toolset are just two possibilities. Since there are several ways to build cooperation or independence, each toolset contains about a dozen individual techniques that meet the toolset's special purpose. For example, the Cooperation Toolset houses the individual tools that promote cooperation. Offering children choices within limits is just one of nearly a dozen tools parents can use to build cooperation. Once we know the *type of problem* we are facing (the toolbox) and the *type of tools* we need (toolset), we can choose individual tools based on the needs of the people or situation involved.*

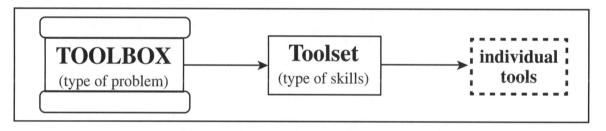

In summary, the blueprint is the **universal** plan. We can solve certain types of problems (the toolboxes) by following specific steps (the universal PASRR response formula), using different groups of skills (the toolsets). We choose specific tools from these toolsets, based on the **individual needs** of the situation and people involved. If we follow the basic universal guidelines, we can apply the tools in ways that express our own **unique style**.

The Toolboxes and Toolsets

The Universal Blueprint contains four toolboxes; each addresses four major problem "types." Each toolbox houses the toolsets (types of tools) that can prevent or best resolve that type of problem. Each toolbox is one of the four major steps of our universal response formula:

   Step A. Prevention Toolbox
   Step B. Child Problem Toolbox
   Step C. Parent Problem Toolbox
   Step D. Maintenance Toolbox

* This tool graphic appears next to individual tools.
▶ Triangular bullets flag examples of the tools in use.

Together, these four toolboxes contain 12 toolsets. Each chapter (toolset) of *The Parent's Toolshop* describes the following:

- *Why* certain tools are more effective than others.
- *When* to use the tools.
- *How* to use the tools appropriately and avoid common misuses.
- *Which* tools to use when specific problems arise.
- We also *practice* using the tools in real-life situations.

Here is an overview of what we learn on our detailed tour of *The Parent's Toolshop*.

PREVENTION TOOLBOX

These are the themes of the Prevention Toolbox:

- Prevent problems from starting or worsening.
- Develop skills and positive qualities in self and others that enhance relationships.

These practical tools are useful *anytime* so we want to use them 24 hours a day, 7 days a week. First, we learn how to use these tools to prevent problems. In later chapters, we learn how to use these same tools to respond to problems.

We start our tour with Chapter 2, **"Foundation-Building Toolset." The foundations of parenting are the beliefs and attitudes that influence our parenting choices.** First, we set healthy long-term parenting goals, so we know what we are seeking to achieve. Then we look at the different styles of parenting and how effective each is in reaching these goals. We will see that "balanced" parenting helps children develop the qualities and life skills they need to succeed in adulthood. Next, we get a few tips for working cooperatively with other parenting partners and how to avoid unhealthy seesawing between imbalanced approaches. Then, we examine some attitudes and beliefs that influence parenting. We can *choose* the beliefs, attitudes, and perceptions that lead to more positive responses and maintain a balanced approach.

Once we've laid the foundation, we need to review our blueprint, the general plan we'll follow. Chapter 3, **"The Universal Blueprint,"** is different from all the other chapters, because it is an overview of how *The Parent's Toolshop* is logically organized.

Your Mission

When you experience a problem you will know how to . . .

STOP and

1. **THINK** for 1–10 seconds
2. **PLAN** a helpful response
3. **DELIVER** it effectively

In this chapter, we learn two critical skills: how to identify the six general types of problems and how to apply the universal response formula to each. These two skills help us arrive at the most appropriate response to *any* situation that arises in *any* relationship. This meets the first two mission goals. Each chapter thereafter takes us, step by step, through the Universal Blueprint, learning what tools we can use and how to use them to their maximum effectiveness. This meets the third mission goal of delivering our response effectively. Throughout our tour of the remaining chapters, we will refer often to the Universal Blueprint, as we build our comprehensive parenting plan step by step. We immediately use what we learn and begin to see rather quickly how all the pieces fit together.

The first toolset that details specific, practical tools is Chapter 4, **"Self-Esteem Toolset." This chapter teaches us how to use descriptive language to encourage positive behavior and stimulate** *internal* **motivation in others (not just children).** We learn the difference between self-esteem and self-image, encouragement, and praise. We learn how to prevent discouragement, which is the root cause of most problem behaviors. These tools help others see themselves as unique and valuable, without feeling conceited, pressured to perform, or dependent on others' opinions for their self-worth.

The next chapter in the Prevention Toolbox is Chapter 5, **"Cooperation Toolset***.*" **This chapter teaches us how to build teamwork and cooperation, which helps avoid most power struggles, rather than demanding blind obedience, which causes rebellion and resentment.** We learn how to word requests so others *want* to cooperate. The Cooperation Toolset is many parents' favorite because it contains many eye-opening and practical four-star skills.* Most parents see immediate changes in their approach and their children's behavior, especially if their children are into testing and defiance.

> *A Graduate's Comment. I like this book because it gives me power—not over my children, but over the situation and myself. It also empowers my children to be in control of themselves. I saw immediate results the first week! I'm spending less time being in power struggles and they're learning to make choices. I know, now, that there is going to be a solution to every problem. I especially like the fact that the book tells me what* **to** *do, instead of what not to do. — Bonnie Sessley*

The last stop in the Prevention Toolbox is Chapter 6, **"Independence Toolset." This chapter focuses on teaching children life skills so they can handle more freedom responsibly.** We learn how to foster independence through every separation stage, from weaning to leaving home. As we teach children tasks, behavioral skills, and family values, children develop responsible behavior. Then, we can increasingly trust them with more freedom, instead of overprotecting or abandoning them. This healthy balance allows children room to grow and mature.

CHILD PROBLEM TOOLBOX

These are the themes of the Child Problem Toolbox:

- Open the door of communication by acknowledging the other person's perspective first.
- When others have problems, keep the ball in their court and guide them through the process of discovering their own solutions.

Chapter 7, **"F-A-X Listening Toolset," helps us respond helpfully when someone else has a problem, without taking over and solving the problem** *for* **them.** We cover the basics of effective communication, how misunderstandings occur, and how we can better understand our child's perspective. We learn how to listen effectively, which can peel off defensive layers and reveal the core of a problem. Often, this alone helps others figure out how they feel and what action they want to take.

If, after listening, someone is still unsure about a solution, we can move on to Chapter 8, **"Problem-Solving Toolset,"** to help the person explore possible options. **These tools teach children independent, responsible problem-solving and decision-making skills.** This chapter also offers specific suggestions for dealing with dozens of common problems that can arise between a child and siblings, peers, or people at school. The conflict mediation tools can help any group of people, adults or children, work toward a solution that is agreeable to all. By the end of this chapter, we know *when* to intervene in others' problems and *how* to help them resolve their *own* problems independently and responsibly.

---

* Every tool is helpful or it would not be included in a toolset. **Four-star skills, however, are** *exceptionally* **effective.** We want to use four-star tools regularly, as part of our daily parenting style. A four-star skill has four open stars (☆☆☆☆) next to it when it is first introduced and on the summary page for that toolset. One solid black star (★) appears next to important points to remember.

PARENT PROBLEM TOOLBOX

The Parent Problem Toolbox contains the largest number of toolsets. It provides parents with the tools they need to deal with problems they find the hardest to respond to—those that affect them.

The themes of the Parent Problem Toolbox are consistent with the Universal Blueprint's effective-response formula:

- Think before you speak.
- Speak before (or while) you act.
- Take action instead of reacting.

First, Chapter 9, **"Keep Your Cool Toolset,"** focuses on understanding *our* feelings and reactions. We learn what *really* causes anger and stress and how to manage it. We can use these tools to develop individualized anger/stress management plans for ourselves and our children. If we have emotional trigger buttons, this chapter teaches us how to reprogram them. **The Keep Your Cool Toolset is the first and most important step in responding to Parent Problems because we can turn all the other tools in this toolbox into weapons if we use them in anger.**

Next, Chapter 10, **"Clear Communication Toolset," helps us express our feelings and concerns without blame, criticism, lectures, nagging, or hidden messages that cause others to tune us out.** We learn how to communicate in simple, clear, respectful, and assertive ways. Many parents are surprised how well their children listen when they use these tools. By combining the Communication, Listening, and Problem-Solving Toolsets, *any* relationship can improve, including those with spouses (or other partners), relatives, friends, colleagues, bosses, or employees.

The Keep Your Cool Toolset helps us *think* clearly and the Clear Communication Toolset helps us plan what to *say*. The last three toolsets in the Parent Problem Toolbox help us plan what to *do* when responding to problem behavior.

The first step in responding to misbehavior is recognizing the difference between *unintentional* and *intentional* misbehavior that serves a purpose. Chapter 11, **"PU Toolset (Parent problem, Unintentional misbehavior)," redirects misbehavior resulting from children's lack of skills or maturity by teaching them appropriate behavior skills.** Rather than excusing age-appropriate problem behavior, children can move through troublesome developmental stages in healthy ways while learning important life skills. This toolset also addresses other causes of unintentional misbehavior, such as personality traits and medical conditions such as Attention Deficit Hyperactivity Disorder (ADHD).

Chapter 12, **"PO Toolset (Parent problem, 'On purpose' misbehavior),"** deals with children who have mastered the skills to behave properly but *intentionally* misbehave. **We learn *why* children (and adults) misbehave and how to avoid common reactions that either give a payoff or make matters worse.** This information helps us choose the most appropriate tools (from previous toolsets) that help meet the child's purpose through positive behavior. When misbehavior no longer achieves its purpose, it usually stops.

Chapter 13, **"Discipline Toolset,"** is the final chapter in the Parent Problem Toolbox. It's the toolset you are probably most anxious to see, but don't jump ahead to this chapter. **This toolset is located farther into the Universal Blueprint for four specific reasons:**

1. **We need to reserve the discipline tools for serious situations or use them after or in combination with other tools.** By the time we get to this toolset, we have dozens of other tools that might resolve a problem before it gets to the point of discipline.

    A Graduate's Story. I don't need to discipline as often as I thought I did. Before the class, I used discipline this much (holding his arms wide apart) and the rest of the skills only this much (holding his hands in front of his chest). Now, I only need to use discipline this much (his hands in front of his chest) and I use the rest of the tools this much (holding his arms wide apart). — Bryan Belden

2. **Discipline is most effective when we use it to teach children how to behave properly.** For this, we use the Prevention Toolbox, Clear Communication Toolset, and PU Toolset (Parent problem, Unintentional misbehavior) before or with the discipline tools.

3. **Discipline is only effective if we first break negative behavior patterns such as power struggles or revenge cycles.** This is what the PO Toolset (Parent problem, "On purpose" misbehavior) does. If we don't use the PO Toolset before discipline, there is a good chance the discipline will escalate the misbehavior or give it a payoff, which is ineffective or even harmful.

4. **It is easy to misuse the discipline tools.** To discipline effectively, we use everything we've learned up to this point *with* the discipline tools.

These are the three themes of the Discipline Toolset:

- Teach children self-discipline, by revealing the effects of their behavior choices and holding them accountable for poor behavior choices.
- Decide what *you* will do, not what you will make *others* do.
- Help children *learn* from their mistakes and be involved in solving the problems their mistakes caused (discipline), rather than making them *suffer* for their mistakes (punishment).

These changes in attitude prevent us from misusing effective discipline tools as weapons that destroy relationships. There are many commonly accepted myths and inaccurate information about discipline. In this chapter, we dispel each myth so we can respectfully, helpfully, and effectively discipline. It might be hard to wait, but trust the experience of other parents who learned about discipline too early and became more confused and ineffective as a result. By using the other tools, many problems will have already improved by the time we get to this chapter. With the tougher problems that remain, it is especially important to make sure we use the discipline tools appropriately.

MAINTENANCE TOOLBOX

The Maintenance Toolbox builds on and uses almost every tool in *The Parent's Toolshop*. These are the two themes of the Maintenance Toolbox:

- Prevent new situations from becoming problems.
- Maintain progress in personal growth and family relationships.

Chapter 14, **"Family Council Toolset,"** teaches us how to effectively consult the entire family when decisions or problems affect the family. Effective family councils develop each family member's communication skills and leadership qualities. They help each person feel like an important, contributing member of the family team. **Family councils enrich family relationships and help us make decisions and resolve conflicts in ways that meet everyone's needs.** This chapter presents several council formats we can use, based on the ages of the children and what we want to accomplish. There are several myths about conducting family councils and many ways family councils can turn sour. This chapter has a troubleshooting guide that can keep our family councils a sweet experience.

Finally, Chapter 15, **"Three C's: Consistency, handling Criticism, and Confidence,"** details the reasons we can stray from our parenting plan and offers suggestions for maintaining the progress we've made. We learn how to be the kind of parent we want to be, without feeling the need to bend or sway to the demands of well-meaning, but unhelpful, advice-givers. We learn how to apply the Universal Blueprint and its tools in non-parenting relationships, when others criticize us or exhibit troublesome behavior. We also learn how to recognize inaccurate advice and use the universal guidelines to select tools from other resources. By the end of this chapter, we realize how far we have come in our growth and establish a positive vision for our future.

SUGGESTIONS FOR USE

Before we begin our full tour of *The Parent's Toolshop*, a few suggestions will help you know what to expect and what *not* to expect from your tour. These tips will help you get the maximum benefit from your tour and remember all you learn.

1. **The first time you read the book, read each chapter** *in order*. Each chapter builds on information and skills from earlier chapters and follows the Universal Blueprint step by step. You need to understand the tools from the Prevention Toolbox to use the more difficult tools, later in the book, to their full potential. If you are dealing with a tough problem, you might be tempted to jump ahead to whatever chapter you think will solve it best, such as the Discipline Toolset. This approach skips over skills that could prevent the problem or resolve it without a last resort response. The only exceptions are Chapter 9, "Keep Your Cool Toolset," Chapter 11, "PU Toolset," and the consistency and criticism sections of Chapter 15, "Three C's." You can read these chapters anytime.

   Don't worry if you don't remember everything you learn the first time you read the book. There is *so* much information it can realistically take us a lifetime to master all the skills in all our relationships. Each time you read *The Parent's Toolshop*, you will get what you need at that time.

   > *A Graduate's Comment. I can't wait to read the book again—and again. There's so much in it, I want to digest it all. Every time I read it, new things jump out at me that I didn't notice the first time. There were some sentences and sections that were so profound that I just had to think about what was said for awhile. That's how awesome some of the concepts are. This book and class have changed my life, every area of it, for the better. — Rita James*

   It is best to read no more than two toolsets (chapters) at a time and reflect on the ideas. After practicing those skills for a week, you are ready to build on that knowledge. Schedule a time each week to read, so you can keep moving forward through the book. Many parents read the book several times or every few years, as their children reach new developmental stages. Use the detailed house diagram (a summary of the entire book that is on the last page of this book and on the color poster you can order), summary sheets and index as quick refreshers or to deal with a particular problem.

2. **Use** *all* **the tools and steps in the Universal Blueprint.** They are interrelated and reach their full potential only when we use them together. Discarding tools or foundational beliefs weakens the effectiveness of *all* the tools, because each toolset is dependent on the others.

3. **Do the practice exercises in the book.** Simply thinking about a behavioral technique is not as effective as actually doing it. People learn by *hearing* or discussing the information, *seeing* the information, and *using* the information. Reading this book or attending a class led by a certified Parent's Toolshop Tour Guide are ways to *hear* the ideas explained. The house diagram and examples are ways to *see* the information. The practice exercises help you *use* the tools you are learning. The more ways you learn and process the information, the better you will remember it.

   Since you are learning a new parenting language, it is important to practice forming effective responses. Written practice lets you think about and *plan* the most effective response. This helps you later when you need to respond quickly to real-life situations. After giving your answers, read the answer key; it offers additional insights and suggestions for common problems. Remember that the answer key usually lists *possible* answers, not the *only* correct answers.

   > *A Graduate's Comment. I'm so glad you gave us practice exercises. The first time I skipped the practice exercises I had a harder time using the tools that week. When I used the practice exercises, I realized how helpful it was to actually think of the words on my own. I especially like the detailed answers you give. Your answers helped me realize where I was on track and where I still needed to improve. — Kathy Bellar*

THE BIGGEST SECRET ABOUT *THE PARENT'S TOOLSHOP*:
The most common real-life parenting problems are posed in the practice exercises. In the answer key, there are specific suggestions about exactly what to say and do. If you see a problem in the practice exercises you are dealing with at home, think about your answers first, then **read the answer key.**

4. **Use the tools in an individualized way.** At each step of the Universal Blueprint and its effective-response formula, we can choose many options. We use the guidelines and our knowledge of the person and situation to choose the most appropriate response. There is no one right way to respond to a situation. If one response doesn't seem to work, don't abandon the blueprint. Instead, select a different tool from the toolsets available at that step or reexamine the situation to make sure you have correctly identified the type of problem.

The Parent's Toolshop describes the tools in general ways, the way we apply them to most children most of the time. **Sometimes, certain tools need to be applied in special ways if children are very young or much older. The chapters explain these exceptions in a special *Tips for Tots and Teens* section or in separate paragraphs with the age range in bold type. If you don't have a child of that age, feel free to skip over these sections.** You can benefit, however, from doing all the exercises, even if they don't apply to your child's age.

5. **Practice the skills in *all* your relationships.** The tools in *The Parent's Toolshop* work to the extent we practice them. Since the tools are *human* relationship skills, they are useful in any setting—at work, with friends, relatives, strangers, a spouse or other partner. Instead of shifting from one approach in one setting, to another in other settings, choose particular tools based on the individual circumstances of the relationship or situation. You will be more consistent and effective in *all* your relationships and will see just how effective the tools are. *The Parent's Toolshop* uses terms that fit parenting relationships, but you can change the words *parent* and *child* to make the Universal Blueprint fit any relationship.

> ***Two Graduates' Comments.** I learned some of these communication and listening skills in training programs at work. I can't believe it didn't occur to me to modify them for use at home with my kids! — Bill Stanley*
>
> *I started using the F-A-X Listening process with my employees and was amazed how well it works! I kept the ball in their court and asked questions that helped them solve their own problems. My employees are showing increased self-confidence, motivation, and self-reliance. These skills are G–R–E–A–T! — Bryan Belden*

6. **Be willing to change first.** This course stresses *your* self-improvement, but you must be willing to change. Don't say, "When my child (or someone else) does _____, then I will change." The only person you can really control or change is *you*. Take responsibility for your own growth and start using the skills. This will set the wheels of change in motion. If you control *your* emotions, actions, perceptions, and words, others often respond in more positive ways. This is called the ripple effect. When you drop a pebble into a pond, ripples start at the middle, expanding outward. **Any time one person in a family changes, it is like dropping a pebble in the family pond. There is always some change; it's the natural law of cause and effect.**

> ***A Graduate's Story.** The first night of a parenting class, a mother was upset that **she** had to come to a class, because it was her **son** who was misbehaving. She stayed for the class and tried to have an open-minded attitude. The following week, she arrived for class with a personal letter for me:*
>
> *Dear Jody,*
>
> *When I left class last week, I felt rather discouraged. Andrew and I had been having communication problems for the last couple of years and they seemed to be escalating. I wanted **him** to take the class so he could see that I was not the "bad" person and that my point-of-view was for his own best interests. What a surprise! I was the one who had to adjust!*

After I arrived home, Andrew started asking me about the class, which somehow got on to a discussion of curfew and other rules. Rather than get angry and tell him what he had to do (my normal response), I listened to him and asked a few pertinent questions. All week long I did this, rather than argue with him and try to win. Amazing! He not only started opening up to me, but also did chores around the house that I never told him to do! My son is a good kid and is very capable. I just needed to trust him more and give him the chance to show me just how capable he is. Thanks.

Two weeks later she gave me another letter:

*For the past three weeks, my son and I have had the most peaceful times in years! I **was** the one that needed changing! But it hasn't been as great an adjustment or as hard as I thought it would be. I know that I basically am teaching myself the concepts, but if you hadn't had the forethought or the ideas to begin with, I wouldn't be this much further ahead. Thanks for all your efforts, from the bottom of my heart. — Mary K.*

7. Have realistic expectations. To prevent discouragement, there are several things you can expect and not expect:

   a. *Expect temporary setbacks.* Human growth and development involves testing and mistakes. Whether children learn from their mistakes and correct their behavior often depends on the reaction they get. The tools in *The Parent's Toolshop* help us prevent or quickly redirect these normal problem behaviors. Don't be surprised, however, if you think you've stopped a particular behavior, only to have it reappear later. Children often forget what they've learned, especially when they are busy learning other skills at a new developmental stage. These regressions are normal and usually temporary if handled appropriately.

   b. *Expect to develop more patience.* Patience is not something we can buy off a shelf, nor is it a skill that can be taught. However, after learning the tools in *The Parent's Toolshop*, most parents feel they have more patience. Why? When we understand *why* a problem exists and we have more tools to use, it takes longer to run out of patience.

   c. *Expect to develop "healthy paranoia."* I often joke that I have a contagious virus that people catch once they start learning the language of effective parenting. They become infected with a condition I call healthy paranoia. They are more aware of their words, attitudes, thoughts, and actions. They start catching their mistakes when they make them, or even before the words get out of their mouths! This awareness is a positive sign that we are becoming *conscious* parents. Healthy paranoia not only reveals negative habits; it also shows us the many positive habits we already have. This, too, is important to know because it provides us with a foundation on which we can build.

   d. *Expect to develop response-ability.* Being a conscious parent also means responding in a planned or thought-out way. Reactions allow children to control situations and the parent's emotions. Then, parents feel justified in blaming children for causing their emotions. Response-ability means we consider our options and *choose* a response.

   e. *Don't expect perfection.* Once healthy paranoia sets in, you become aware of mistakes you made in the past and in the present. Don't be too hard on yourself. Remind yourself that you did the best you could at the time, with the knowledge and skills you had. Use your past mistakes to increase your present effectiveness. Ask yourself, "What did I learn from this?" and "What would I do if it happened again today?" At whatever point you catch yourself, put the Universal Blueprint to work. Eliminate the discouraging words *right*, *wrong*, *good*, and *bad* from your vocabulary. Instead, view choices as *more effective* and *less effective*. Remember, mistakes are a natural part of any learning process, and everyone makes them when learning new skills, including you and your children.

Accept the fact that you are not a perfect parent, will never be a perfect parent, and don't want to be a perfect parent. Perfect parents believe they have nothing new to learn. Children don't want perfect parents. They want human parents who are honest about their mistakes and can model what to do to correct them. What we do *after* a mistake often makes a greater impression on others than the mistake itself. If you tend to expect perfection of yourself, read the following affirmation. If you are alone, read it out loud. The spoken word is far more powerful than a thought.

Declaration of Imperfection

I, now, allow myself to be an imperfect parent; one who makes mistakes and is sometimes wrong. I know I have made mistakes in the past and am sure to make more in the future. That's okay. While I am not happy about my mistakes, I am not afraid of them. Instead, I strive to learn what I can from the experience to improve myself in the future. When I catch a mistake, I correct myself respectfully. I pick myself up and don't put myself down. As I become a better and better parent, I won't make the same mistakes too often—but, I still won't be a perfect parent. That's okay, because my goal is continual improvement, not perfection.

★ **8. If at first you don't succeed, figure out why and try again.** Parents often see immediate results when they use the Universal Blueprint and its tools, but there are never any guarantees when human behavior is involved. Most of the tools in *The Parent's Toolshop* have been used by parents, recommended by professionals, and have proven their long-term effectiveness for several decades. **If you don't see results, consider the six reasons a tool might not work immediately. Apply the following suggestions and try again.**

   a. ***Choose** the best tool for the job.*

   It's important to have more than one tool at our disposal. A hammer and screwdriver are both effective, useful tools. If we want to put a nail in a wall, a hammer is the best tool to use. If we use a screwdriver, we are choosing an ineffective tool for the job.*

   Some parents only have one tool and use it for every problem. Parents of toddlers tend to use spanking or timeout for every misbehavior. When a child spills milk, the parents says, "Go into timeout" instead of handing the child a towel to clean up the mess. Parents of teens tend to use restrictions or grounding for every misbehavior. Whatever happens, the parent declares, "That's it! You're grounded for a week!" This may not resolve the problems the misbehavior caused and having a teen stuck in the house for a week may be punishment for the *parent*!

   Each tool in *The Parent's Toolshop* accomplishes a certain goal. To achieve the best results, we use the tool in situations where we are trying to accomplish that goal. The Universal Blueprint is a decision-making process for identifying the type of problem we are facing so we can choose the most appropriate tool. If a tool doesn't work, we refer to the Universal Blueprint to make sure we have properly identified the type of problem and chosen the best tool for the situation.

   b. *Use the tools in the proper **order**.*

   *If we choose a hammer for this job but don't put the nail on the wall **first**, we will only hit the wall, since the nail isn't even there! The proper order of the steps is to put the nail on the wall, **then** hit it with the hammer.*

---

* This analogy refers to hitting a nail with a hammer to illustrate similar mistakes parents may make. It in no way implies that we hit children.

While this tool analogy seems ridiculous (who would ever forget to put the nail against the wall first?), this is a common mistake in parenting responses. Some tools work best if parents use them *after* other tools. For example, if we express our concerns without acknowledging the other person's perspective first, we often get defensive reactions. Before we discipline, we must break any power or revenge cycles, or the discipline will escalate the cycle.

c. *Use the tool <u>properly</u>.*

> *If we try to use the claw side of the hammer, it will be harder to get the nail in quickly and straight. The proper way to use the hammer is to use the flat head.*

Many parenting tools are easy to misuse, so every tool has instructions for its most effective use. If we select the most appropriate tool for a situation but it doesn't seem to work, we consider *how* we used it. Our attitude, body language, and tone of voice all influence the effectiveness of a tool. Look at your behavior and listen to your words the way the other person would.

d. *Use the tools consistently, <u>long enough</u> for change to occur.*

> *To hammer a nail into a wall, we must hit it several times before it is completely in the wall. If the nail doesn't go in after the first strike, it doesn't mean the hammer doesn't work or the nail is defective. Our first attempts made progress, but it takes time to reach our final goal.*

While people often see results from using these tools, change is not always quick. Usually, small changes come before more obvious changes, just as the small ripples in a pond occur before the larger ones. Change can take place on the inside, without any obvious change on the outside. If it has taken some time for a problem to develop, it is realistic to expect it to take some time to resolve. Be patient and consistent. The other person may need time to rebuild trust, break old habits, and learn proper behavior. If this approach makes sense to you and you believe in the value of the skills, give the tools a chance to work. Look for small changes to reassure yourself that you're on the right track.

e. *Examine your <u>beliefs</u>; they can change the effectiveness of the tool.*

> *It is harder to hammer a nail into wood than plasterboard. If we believe the nail is being stubborn, we might feel angry or frustrated and pound the hammer more wildly. In reality, wood is more difficult to penetrate. Knowing this, we make more firm, controlled impacts.*

Many of us have commonly accepted, but inaccurate, beliefs. Here are three examples:

- If parents believe discipline has to make children feel bad, their tone of voice and behavior will be hurtful. This will turn the discipline into punishment, which is ineffective and causes resentment.

- If parents believe all toddlers' misbehavior is intentional, they may angrily punish children who display age-appropriate misbehavior. Since the parents didn't teach the children better skills, the children don't improve their behavior as quickly and the parents get more frustrated and angry—a negative behavior cycle continues.

- If parents believe all teens are rebellious, they may be impatient and critical of the teens' efforts to become their own persons. Teens sense this distrust and feel more discouraged and resentful, which can lead to rebellion—a self-fulfilling prophecy.

Expect to have some of your current beliefs about parenting challenged. Once we are more conscious of our beliefs, it's easier to tell if they are interfering with our effectiveness.

f. *Look for a <u>deeper problem</u>.*

> *If we are trying to hammer a nail into a surface that is hiding a brick wall, we might not understand, at first, why the nail won't go in. Until we look for the reason the nail won't go in, we won't know the brick wall even exists! Once we know the brick wall is there, we can change the type of nail we are using.*

Immediate change is unlikely when a problem behavior is severe, has lasted a long time, or is the result of a medical condition or deep emotional hurt. (My brother's problems are a good example.) Ineffective parenting methods only make matters worse. Effective parenting skills can prevent the problem from getting worse and help the child slowly work through the real issues causing the problem. This process takes time, but it is the only way any true, final healing can take place. In these cases, you may want to seek professional help. Therapy is helpful for issues such as deep emotional hurts, violent or self-destructive behavior, or problems that seem to persist despite your efforts to use these skills consistently for a significant period of time.

Keeping these suggestions in mind, we are ready to begin our detailed tour of *The Parent's Toolshop*. Take things one step at a time and enjoy the tour!

ANSWER KEY

Myth/Truth quiz: Each statement is a common myth about parenting, so each is either totally or partially false. By the end of the book you will know why each statement is false and how to change it into a true statement. You will have a chance to rewrite each statement in the last chapter.

WHAT'S NEXT?

If you are ready to begin the full tour, turn the page to "Step A: Prevention Toolbox" and begin reading Chapter 2, "Foundation-Building Toolset." There, we discuss our parenting goals, different parenting styles, and which parenting approach will best meet our long-term goals. Here we can make an attitude adjustment: from negative to positive, from controlling children to teaching children self-control, from doing too much for children to fostering children's independence. We consider our own upbringing and the advice we get from others. Once we have accurate definitions, clear goals, and consciously choose our parenting style, we have a stable, positive, balanced foundation on which we can build a healthy family using the effective parenting tools throughout the rest of the book.

STEP A
PREVENTION TOOLBOX

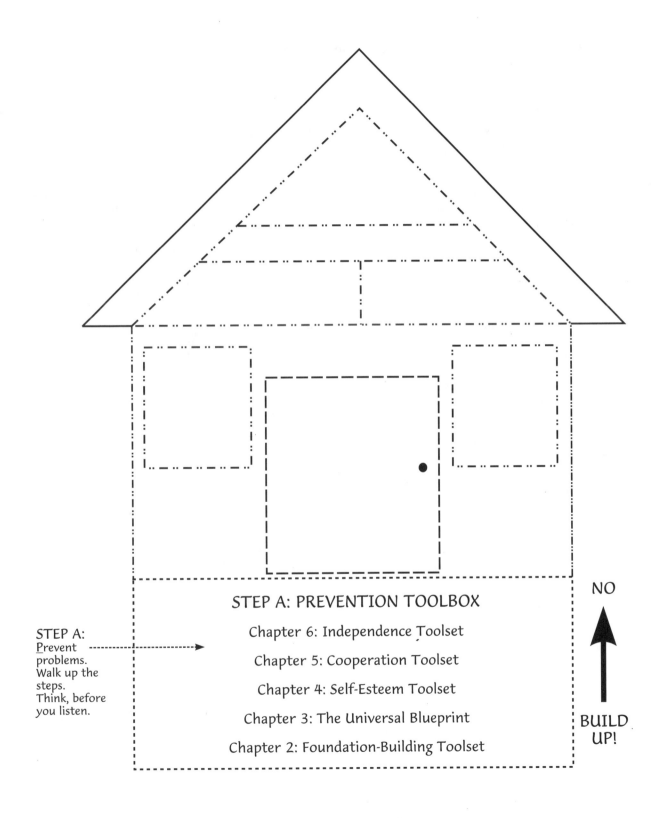

STEP A:
Prevent
problems.
Walk up the
steps.
Think, before
you listen.

STEP A: PREVENTION TOOLBOX

Chapter 6: Independence Toolset

Chapter 5: Cooperation Toolset

Chapter 4: Self-Esteem Toolset

Chapter 3: The Universal Blueprint

Chapter 2: Foundation-Building Toolset

NO

BUILD
UP!

A PREVENTION TOOLBOX

Builders can use some sets of tools for almost any task, while other sets of tools have special uses. In parenting, the Prevention Toolbox contains the toolsets we can use any time. We can use them to prevent problems from occurring, worsening, or at any time in our response.

IN THIS SECTION

Step A of the Universal Blueprint is the Prevention Toolbox. In this section, we learn how to use five different toolsets:

- Chapter 2, "Foundation-Building Toolset," suggests several healthy long-term parenting goals and describes a balanced parenting style to help us reach them. In this chapter, we identify our current parenting style and consider replacing any negative beliefs and attitudes we might hold with positive, healthy alternatives.

- Chapter 3, "The Universal Blueprint," explains the process of identifying the six general types of problems we encounter in human relationships and the universal response formula we can use for each.

- Chapter 4, "Self-Esteem Toolset," describes the difference between self-image and self-esteem, and praise and encouragement. We learn a descriptive language that builds internal motivation and self-worth, without creating dependency on others' opinions. We also learn how to avoid unhealthy competition and to free children from unhelpful roles and labels.

- Chapter 5, "Cooperation Toolset," discusses the problems that result when we demand obedience or use rigid or negative commands. We learn how to foster internal motivation without bribes or incentives, offer flexible choices within clearly defined limits, and nearly a dozen tools that engage cooperation without starting power struggles. Many parents say this is their favorite chapter.

- Chapter 6, "Independence Toolset," describes the balance between maintaining reasonable limits, teaching life skills, and letting go enough that children can grow and develop independence. We also learn how children develop responsibility and effective ways to use allowances.

WHEN TO USE THE PREVENTION TOOLBOX

We can use the Prevention Toolbox anytime with anyone, to bring out the best in others, have a positive attitude, teach important life skills, and prevent problems from developing or worsening. These are the all-purpose parenting tools we want to use constantly—24 hours a day, 7 days a week—to develop and maintain positive, healthy relationships.

CHAPTER 2
FOUNDATION-BUILDING TOOLSET

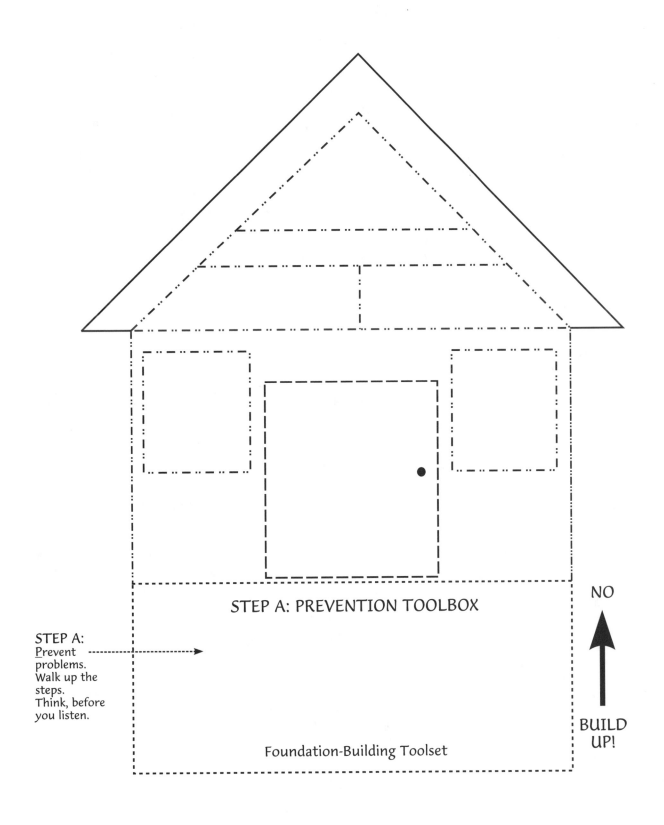

STEP A: PREVENTION TOOLBOX

STEP A:
<u>P</u>revent
problems.
Walk up the
steps.
Think, before
you listen.

NO

BUILD
UP!

Foundation-Building Toolset

CHAPTER
2 FOUNDATION-BUILDING TOOLSET

The first step in building a house is to lay a foundation that is stable and balanced. If a house's foundation sits partly on rock and partly on sand, the house will eventually sink into the weak sand. The people in the house may not realize the foundation is imbalanced until problems start to develop, such as cracked or crooked walls. A beautiful house is worthless if the foundation is sinking and it's a difficult and expensive problem to fix.

*Effective parenting tools won't work as well if parents' beliefs are unhealthy, imbalanced, or inconsistent. As the imbalances increase, more damage occurs and problems worsen. Unfortunately, some parents don't realize they have an imbalanced parenting style until they see problems. Fortunately, balancing our parenting style is much easier than fixing a sinking house's foundation. Ideally, we want to set and maintain a balanced parenting style **before** problems develop, to prevent problems.*

One of our parenting goals is to provide a solid, balanced base from which children can get a firm launch into adulthood. Children of negative, over-controlling parents will try to launch before they are ready, to escape this restrictiveness. Children of overly permissive parents will not get a firm launch because the foundation is too unstable and soft. Children from balanced families get a solid, healthy launch.

IN THIS CHAPTER

The tools in the Universal Blueprint only work to their full potential if we also choose healthy beliefs and attitudes. Before we learn about the Universal Blueprint and how to use specific tools, we need to do three important tasks:

1. Set long-term parenting goals and then choose a parenting style that will best meet these goals.

2. Identify our current parenting style (from the five general parenting styles) and decide whether it is the most effective style for reaching our long-term parenting goals.

3. Balance our parenting style by replacing unhelpful beliefs and attitudes with positive alternatives.

WHEN TO USE THE FOUNDATION-BUILDING TOOLSET

Our beliefs are the foundation of our parenting, so they *constantly* affect our responses—even if we are not aware of them. To have a balanced parenting style, we need to choose healthy, helpful beliefs. Therefore, we use this toolset constantly. At first, we need to examine beliefs carefully and consciously, to set a balanced foundation for our family. Then, we make a stronger effort to look at our beliefs when we are responding to problems, to maintain our balance. If our responses backfire, we review the six reasons the tools might not work (See the section entitled "Suggestions for Use" on page 13 in Chapter 1, "Touring The Parent's Toolshop"), since unhelpful, inaccurate beliefs are one of those reasons.

ESTABLISHING A COMMON LANGUAGE

To prevent misunderstandings caused by different advice we've heard, we will occasionally need to clarify words that might have more than one definition. When we work with other parenting partners, establishing a common language can be a major step in resolving what we *think* are our disagreements.

A Graduate's Story. After our first child was born, my husband and I often disagreed about the proper way to handle parenting situations. When we took the parenting class together, it gave us a common language. We realized we agreed on our parenting goals, but sometimes disagreed about how to accomplish them. The class taught us more effective parenting skills, which helped us work as a team toward our common goals. While we don't always agree, we first eliminate the possibility that we are using different definitions to say the same thing. Often, we actually agree, but are using different words to explain our beliefs. We then use the problem-solving skills we learned in the parenting class to resolve our differences and plan a consistent response.

We want to be sure parenting advice will help us reach our long-term goals *before* we follow it. Some parenting resources make unhelpful, inaccurate advice sound appealing. Other resources use terms that some people consider negative to describe accurate, helpful advice. *The Parent's Toolshop* uses accurate, original definitions to explain and compare effective and ineffective parenting skills. These definitions describe the *qualities* of effective and ineffective parenting, so parents can easily recognize other sources of trustworthy, accurate advice, regardless of the terms they use. Chapter 15, "The Three C's: Consistency, Criticism, and Confidence," page 416, offers specific suggestions for screening parenting advice. (Remember, you can read the first two sections of that chapter out of order.)

WHAT ARE OUR PARENTING GOALS?

Some parenting experts base their advice on what worked for their families. Others take a logical theory and test it, noticing the effects. These methods sometimes result in interesting findings, but the suggestions aren't reliable for most people. The most valuable information comes from studying adults who display the behaviors and qualities parents strive to develop in their own children. When researchers ask these adults questions about their upbringing, they discover what worked, why it worked, and develop guidelines for parents to follow.

Ask yourself, "What skills and qualities do I want my children to develop?" Your list may include:

- self-confidence
- emotional and social maturity
- self-motivation
- independence
- responsibility

- cooperation and helpfulness
- self-discipline
- assertiveness, conflict-resolution skills
- respect for self and others
- problem-solving and decision-making skills

Most parents are realistic; they don't expect perfect children who get straight A's and become famous super-achievers. They simply want their children to be well-adjusted, responsible adults. If you share the goals listed above, we can establish these as our *individual goals* for our children.

Since *The Parent's Toolshop* teaches a "universal blueprint for building a healthy family," we must also define what a "healthy" family is. Dolores Curran, author of *Traits of a Healthy Family*,[1] studied hundreds of families who produced children with the skills and qualities we've listed as individual goals. She found these families had 15 common characteristics.

A healthy family . . .

1. communicates and listens.
2. affirms and supports one another.
3. teaches respect for others.
4. develops a sense of trust.
5. has a sense of play and humor.
6. exhibits a sense of shared responsibility.
7. teaches a sense of right and wrong.
8. has a strong sense of family in which rituals and traditions abound.

9. has a balance of interaction among members.
10. has a shared religious core.
11. respects the privacy of one another.
12. values service to others.
13. fosters family table time and conversation.
14. shares leisure time.
15. admits to and seeks help with problems.

Do these qualities describe your family? Would you like your children to have a family like this? If so, we can establish these as our *family goals*, the qualities we want our family to have.

Whether we grew up in a healthy family or not, we can establish one for our children. When parents want to be different from their own parents, some do the opposite of what their parents did. This approach, however, is usually just as unhealthy. Once we are parents, we can *choose* how to raise our children.

Conscious parenting is the process of *choosing* our parenting style and responses. It differs from trial-and-error parenting or seeking quick fixes, which often create long-term problems.

A Graduate's Story. My father was an abusive alcoholic. I knew I didn't want to raise my children the way my parents raised me, but didn't know any other way to parent, so I guessed and tried to learn from my mistakes. The Parent's Toolshop and the Universal Blueprint have given me a plan and specific tools that will help me reach my goals. There's little guess work, I'm making fewer mistakes, and I feel so confident about my parenting. I know now that I will reach my goals of raising a well-adjusted child and being a loving, effective father.

Next, we want to look at our long-term goal of preparing children for self-sufficient adulthood, which is our *societal goal*. Ask yourself, "What kinds of skills and qualities does my child need to succeed as an adult, work in the business world, and contribute something positive to our society and world?" Most people include the following traits and skills:

Personal Traits or Qualities

- Self-discipline
- Self-motivation
- Cooperation
- Honesty
- Reliability
- Confidence
- Willingness to take "healthy" risks
- Respectfulness toward self and others
- Commitment to community service

Skills Needed in the Business World

- Decision-making
- Effective communication
- Time and stress management
- Conflict-resolution and problem-solving
- Organization
- Cooperating as a team player
- Following rules, yet recognizing unethical requests
- Creative thinking, offering suggestions and ideas for improvement

Now that we have individual, family, and societal goals, we want to choose the parenting style and techniques that best accomplish these goals.

We can tell if a particular parenting style or tool will help us reach our parenting goals by asking two questions:
1. How well will this style or technique develop the skills and qualities I want my children to have?
2. How does this style or technique prepare my children for adulthood in the society in which they need to succeed? Does it develop the skills and qualities businesses look for in their employees and leaders?

A Graduate's Comment. At work, I have weekly, quarterly, and yearly goals. To achieve these goals, I develop a plan. I read books and attend workshops to learn better methods to work my plan. The Parent's Toolshop helps me do the same thing with my parenting plan.

PARENTING STYLES

Family studies have identified three general types of parenting styles. Two are imbalanced and ineffective in the long-run: *over-controlling* and *under-controlling*. Only one general style is most effective in raising children who have the positive qualities and behaviors we identified as our goals. We will call this style *balanced* parenting.

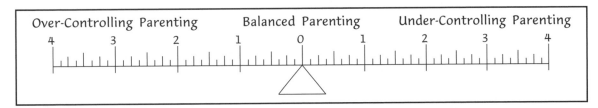

Consider the laws of physics when you look at this scale. Where would you need to put a weight on the scale to balance the scale the quickest? The closer the weight is to the middle, the quicker the scale will balance. Moving the weight slightly, within the balanced area, creates only small imbalances. The farther the weight moves to either end, the more imbalanced the scale becomes. It is humanly impossible (and impractical) to always stay right at the zero. Balanced parenting is a *range*, between the two 1s. We can *choose* more flexible or more firm responses within that balanced range, based on the individual needs of the child, parent, or circumstances of the situation.

> **If our general, daily parenting style and techniques are within the balanced range, the effects (short- and long-term) are healthy and balanced. The degree to which we experience negative and unhealthy effects (short- and long-term) depends on how *frequently* and *extremely* we use imbalanced styles or techniques.**

The following sections detail five styles of parenting—three general styles and two specific categories within each of the two imbalanced styles. For each style, we ask similar questions about parenting and show how the answers might differ based on the parenting style.

Each style has positive qualities, but if taken too far, the extremely imbalanced forms of these qualities become harmful. In the general descriptions, we might recognize traits we have, yet disagree that we have other traits common to that style. In truth, each of us might use a little of all three styles, but one is usually our main parenting style. We usually have an everyday parenting style and another style we fall back on when we are under pressure, frustrated, or angry. We also might use one style at work or with adults and another at home or with children. As you read the descriptions, consider how they can apply to adult relationships, such as those involving spouses, supervisors, leaders, or teachers.

Before we look more closely at the three major parenting styles and the subgroups within them, take the Parenting Styles Quiz on pages 26 and 27 to determine your current parenting style. This will help you focus throughout the rest of the chapter on those skills and beliefs you might choose to replace with healthier, more balanced alternatives.

Parenting Styles Quiz

What type of parenting style do you use? Find out by taking this quiz. Answer the questions honestly, based on your beliefs and what you would really say or do, not how you *think* the questions "should" be answered:

1. What is the parent's job?
   a. To make children behave and to obey authority and rules.
   b. To provide constant supervision/structured rules so children will act/choose "right."
   ✔c. To teach children the life skills they need to be self-disciplined, responsible adults.
   d. To make sure children have a happy, carefree childhood.
   e. To let children learn the proper skills and behavior on their own.

2. Who is responsible for controlling the child's behavior?
   a. Parents must stay in charge and children should obey their rules.
   b. Children should do what the more experienced and knowledgeable parents say.
   ✔c. Parents are responsible for teaching children behaviors and skills they need for self-control.
   ✱d. Parents should explain to the children why they should behave and ask for their cooperation.
   e. Children can figure out their own limits through trial and error.

3. Who has rights?
   a. The parents have all the rights, just because they are adults; children have few or no rights.
   b. Parents have superior knowledgeable and experience; therefore they have more rights.
   ✔c. Parents and children both have the right to be treated with dignity and respect.
   d. Children's rights and needs are more important than the parents.
   e. Children have rights as long as the parents aren't inconvenienced.

4. Who gets respect?
   a. Children are expected to respect parents, but parents are not obligated to respect children.
   b. Children have to earn their parents' respect before they will receive it.
   ✔c. All people deserve to be treated respectfully, regardless of age or position.
   d. Parents should respect their children so the children will be happy.
   e. Children act disrespectful now and then, it's no big deal.

5. How are mistakes handled?
   a. Children must be punished if they break the rules. The punishment must either make the child feel bad or inconvenience the child somehow.
   ✔b. Parents can correct children's mistakes by expressing disappointment, offering constructive criticism, urging children to try harder, and telling them how to fix the mistake and prevent it later.
   ✱c. Children can learn lessons from mistakes and how to fix them or prevent them in the future.
   d. It is a parent's responsibility to fix children's mistakes or protect children from the negative effects.
   e. Others (besides the parents and children) are probably to blame for the children's mistakes.

6. How are problems solved and decisions made?
   ✔a. Choices are made within limits that respect the rights and needs of others.
   b. The problems will go away on their own; if not, the parents can deal with it later.
   c. Parents have the right answers, so the children should follow their advice.
   d. Parents should monitor their children's activities, set goals for the child, and offer rewards or incentives for reaching the goals.
   e. Parents should try to find out what the children want and make them happy.

Co-written by Jody Pawel and Pam Dillon of the *Dayton Daily News* (for 4/6/98 article). Permission granted to reprint **only** in *The Parent's Toolshop*, © 2000 or by PTC personnel.

7. How are negative feelings handled?
 ✓ a. Parents shouldn't try to change their children's negative feelings but can teach them how to express them appropriately.
   b. Everything will go smoother if children keep their negative feelings to themselves.
   c. Children should not express negative feelings because it shows defiance and disrespect.
   d. Children should think and feel what their parents think and feel is "right."
   e. Parents should protect or rescue children from negative feelings.

8. Who decides how children should behave, which interests they pursue and the goals they set?
 ✓ a. Parents can teach children positive behavior skills so children can set and reach healthy goals.
   b. Children can figure out how to behave and what interests/goals to pursue through trial and error.
   c. Parents should tell children what to do and the goals to pursue and make them follow through.
   d. Parents should set high standards for children and choose interests/goals that will help the children succeed as adults.
   e. Children should be allowed to do whatever interests/goals they want so they'll be happy.

9. Who makes the rules and how are they enforced?
 ✓ a. Children can have choices, within reasonable limits, and understand the value of the rules.
   b. If parents set and enforce limits, their children will feel too constricted and rebel.
   c. Parents should tell their children what to do, and children should obey without question.
   d. Parents can set structured rules and correct children with constructive criticism and advice.
   e. If parents politely remind children to behave, they eventually will.

10. How can parents motivate children?
 ✓ a. Parents can teach their children the value of tasks so they are self-motivated to do them.
   b. Children should be responsible for motivating themselves.
   c. Children can be motivated through commands and threats.
   d. Children can be motivated by rewards and incentives, acceptance and praise.
   e. If parents do enough for their children, the children will be happy and motivated.

11. How do parents discipline?
 ✓ a. Parents can explain children's behavior choices and hold them accountable for their decisions.
   b. Children can monitor their own behavior.
   c. Punishment should be uncomfortable or inconvenient so misbehavior will stop.
   d. Parents should make their children feel bad for misbehaving and take away special privileges.
   e. Parents shouldn't punish their children too often or they will lose their children's love.

Scoring:

You will have five totals—one for each of the five parenting styles. Your highest score shows your dominant parenting style.

- **Power Patrol:** Add 1 point for every (a.) answer on questions 1 through 5, and 1 point for every (c.) answer on questions 6 through 11.
- **Perfectionistic Supervisor:** Add 1 point for every (b.) answer on questions 1 through 5, and 1 point for every (d.) answer on questions 6 through 11.
- **Balanced:** Add 1 point for every (c.) answer on questions 1 through 5, and 1 point for every (a.) answer on questions 6 through 11.
- **Overindulger:** Add 1 point for every (d.) answer on questions 1 through 5, and 1 point for every (e.) answer on questions 6 through 11.
- **Avoider:** Add 1 point for every (e.) answer on questions 1 through 5, and 1 point for every (b.) answer on questions 6 through 11.

The Over-Controlling Parenting Style (Autocratic)

Over-controlling parents are also called autocratic parents. The over-controlling parenting style seems the most extreme and negative. There are two types of over-controlling parenting styles, Power Patrols and Perfectionistic Supervisors. One is more extreme and negative than the other, but there are some traits that are common to almost all over-controlling parenting styles.

ANSWERS TO COMMON QUESTIONS

What is the parent's job?

Over-controlling parents believe a parent's job is to control their children. (We detail, later, *what* they want to control and *how* they try to control.)

Who has rights?

Over-controlling parents stand up for their rights, but often at the expense of their children's rights. Winning is important, even if it means the children "lose." The family revolves around the parents' needs or wants, without considering their children's feelings or needs.

Over-controlling families have a pecking order: parents are superior to children, older children are superior to younger children, and younger children are at the bottom of the ranks. If there are two parents present, both are superior to children or one parent is considered superior to the other.

Who gets respect?

Children are expected to treat their parents with respect, but parents are not obligated to treat children with respect.

How are mistakes handled?

Because parents are adults, they are always right. When someone points out their mistakes or offers a different opinion, over-controlling parents feel defensive, rather than admitting to and learning from their mistakes or considering other points of view.

How are problems solved and decisions made?

Over-controlling parents make the decisions and solve the problems that arise in the family, even problems or decisions that don't directly affect them. They believe they have the right answers and want their children to do the right thing, so they do what they can to *make* their children follow their advice.

Who decides how children should behave, which interests they pursue, and the goals they set?

Over-controlling parents want their children to have the behaviors, opinions, personality traits, feelings, goals, and values the *parents* think their children should have.

Who is responsible for controlling the child's behavior?

It is the parents' responsibility to do whatever it takes to *make* children behave the way *they* think children should behave.

Who makes the rules and how are they enforced?

Over-controlling parents want their children to unquestioningly obey all authority figures and their rules. They tell children what to do and how to do it. Sometimes, parents expect children to obey their commands even when they are unreasonable or beyond their children's ability.

Over-controlling parents use "power tools" to control their children. It *is* important for children to follow rules, but over-controlling parents emphasize the superiority or power of the enforcer, rather than the *value* of the rule. Instead of fostering respect for *all* people, over-controlling parents emphasize adults' authority. Children behave and do what *others* tell them to do so they can *avoid* harsh punishment or criticism.

How do parents discipline?

Over-controlling parents use punishment that imposes suffering of various degrees and types—mental, emotional (shame), or physical suffering. If something goes wrong, it is somehow the child's fault.

SYMBOL FOR OVER-CONTROLLING PARENTING

In the book, *Active Parenting*, author Michael Popkin calls over-controlling parenting "autocratic." He uses the symbol of an empty circle to represent limits with no choices. We use his symbol to represent the over-controlling parenting style.

Over-controlling

LONG-TERM EFFECTS OF OVER-CONTROLLING PARENTING

- When children are denied all power and control, they miss important opportunities to make decisions and learn valuable life skills. They take little initiative because they lack confidence and are afraid of making mistakes or not being perfect.

- Children from over-controlling families usually wait for others to set limits for them, rather than setting limits for themselves. If they do something wrong, they are more inclined to lie, to avoid harsh punishment. When they are punished, they either seek revenge or give in out of fear and become blindly submissive to any authority figure. Hence, they don't learn to think for themselves.

- Children and young adults from over-controlling families function well in controlled, structured settings, unless they are rebelling against authority. They have difficulty, however, functioning in permissive settings where no one sets limits for them. When they have excessive freedom, they take advantage of it or can't decide what to do. When they are away from the controlling parent, they frequently engage in excessive behavior (eating, drinking, sex, television-watching, or partying).

- Over-controlling parenting poorly prepares children for today's business world, where employers need adults who can take initiative, think for themselves, and perform independently, with little outside guidance. Adults who were reared in over-controlling families often have difficulty in these areas because they rely on others to tell them what to do and are afraid of making mistakes.

TYPES OF OVER-CONTROLLING PARENTS

The two types of over-controlling parents are Power Patrols and Perfectionistic Supervisors. The following descriptions detail the ways these two parenting types expand on the general traits of the over-controlling parenting style.

Power Patrols

The Power Patrol parenting style, in its most extreme form, is physically or emotionally abusive. Power Patrols are not, however, always abusive. They are simply more concerned with the love of power than the power of love. They want to be in control of situations and the people in them.

Personality Traits of Power Patrols

Power Patrols make strong leaders, but can be bossy, have little patience or flexibility, and want to see immediate results. They expect unquestioning obedience and want things done their way, because it is the *right* way. They view compromising as losing or giving in, and often get into power struggles with their children and other adults.

Power Patrols often have difficulty establishing warmth and closeness in their relationships. They often appear angry and resent anyone who tries to control them. Their insensitivity to others' feelings usually shuts down communication. Power Patrols are often argumentative and take different viewpoints just to stay in control. They don't realize (or don't care) what it's like to be on the receiving end of their demands, orders, and criticisms.

What Power Patrols Believe

A parent's job is to make sure children always follow the rules and to punish them if they break the rules. Children must obey all rules and authority figures or they will grow up to be delinquents. (Studies of delinquent teens have found, however, that angry, aggressive children are often from families where at least one parent is rejecting, hostile, critical, controlling, or revengeful.)

How Power Patrols Handle Negative Feelings

Power Patrols usually think in black and white, right and wrong, my way and the wrong way. They don't allow children to express negative feelings, because they fear they won't be able to control the situation, the child, or themselves. They usually think their children's opinions and negative feelings are wrong so they should not express them. When children speak their minds, Power Patrols usually think they are being disrespectful and defiant.

The Power Patrol's Tools

Power Patrols use commands and threats to motivate children. When children misbehave or challenge their authority, Power Patrols fear they are losing the battle for control. If verbal threats, shame, or blame don't work, they might resort to physical punishment. They believe that if negative behavior brings emotional or physical suffering, children will stop.

Long-Term Effects of Power-Patrol Parenting

- Children of Power Patrols often feel discouraged, have little self-respect, and have a poor relationship with that parent. It is difficult to trust someone you fear, so children build walls to protect themselves from being hurt by the Power Patrol's rejection, criticism, judgment, and harshness. Power Patrols are often unaware of how hurt others are by their actions and words or the unhealthy lessons they are teaching.

- Children don't respect the Power Patrol's authority; they fear it. Children obey rules so they won't get punished, not because they respect the parent's judgement, see value in the rule, and *choose* to follow it. Children of Power Patrols are *other*-disciplined; they often behave only when adults are watching. They wait for the next command, taking little initiative, since they fear mistakes.

- Children of Power Patrols are often impressed with the power their parents have over them and seek ways to have power over others. When they are in positions of power, they often try to control others, get their way, and prove they are right. Since children don't learn assertive, respectful communication skills, they often have negative relationships with others.

- If children (and adult children) don't rebel or strive to be in control, they are likely to blindly follow orders from those they perceive as superior (including bossy peers).

- If Power Patrols tell their children they are controlling or hurting them because they love them, the effects can last a lifetime. As adults, they may equate love with pain, physical or emotional, and stay in abusive relationships. They often believe they deserve to be abused and that the abuse is somehow their fault. As adults, children can make a choice to repeat the errors of their upbringing or break the cycle of physical, verbal, or emotional abuse.

Perfectionistic Supervisors

Perfectionistic Supervisors are the more positive but still imbalanced, type of over-controlling parent.

Personality Traits of Perfectionistic Supervisors

Perfectionistic Supervisors are usually highly capable adults—self-disciplined, organized, scheduled, and responsible—and they expect children to be that way, too. Perfectionistic Supervisors are the ultimate super-achievers—they hold down a job, volunteer at school or the family's religious group, coach a team, assume most household responsibilities, and write a book in their spare time. (Have you guessed that this is the way I become imbalanced?) People admire their accomplishments, so they pressure themselves to achieve more and never disappoint others.

I HAVE YOU SCHEDULED TO DO YOUR HOMEWORK NOW. I WILL CHECK YOUR WORK IN HALF AN HOUR.

Some professions, such as teaching or management, require qualities that come naturally to Perfectionistic Supervisors. They must be organized, manage large groups, point out mistakes, and keep to a schedule. These qualities, if not extreme or critical, can be helpful. At home, however, children can feel pressured or controlled and believe their efforts are never good enough.

What Perfectionistic Supervisors Believe

Constant supervision and structure will prevent children from misbehaving. They also believe their children's behavior is a reflection of whether they are good parents, which influences some of their parenting decisions.

How Perfectionistic Supervisors Handle Negative Feelings

Perfectionistic Supervisors overuse the word *should.* When they listen, they often judge feelings and opinions as right or wrong and try to make their children fit the mold of what *they* think people or children should think, feel, believe, or be like.

The Perfectionistic Supervisor's Tools

Perfectionistic Supervisors often go beyond taking an active interest in their children's activities and identities. They take responsibility for scheduling and monitoring the child's responsibilities. They try to *improve* their children through rewards, incentives, and goal-setting. They reward their children for their compliance by telling them they are proud and happy to have such "good" children. They try to correct their children's mistakes and weaknesses through suggestions, nagging, criticizing, lecturing, and guilt trips ("I'm disappointed in you"). If these techniques don't work, Perfectionistic Supervisors increase their control by taking away special privileges, even if they have no logical relation to what the child did.

Long-Term Effects of Perfectionistic Supervisor Parenting

Children of Perfectionistic Supervisors are usually on time, perfectly dressed, well-mannered, and finish their school work promptly—because the *parent* makes sure of it. Their parents are often unaware, however, that their short-term successes have many negative long-term effects and unhealthy hidden messages:

- Children of Perfectionistic Supervisors often express resentment, frustration, and discouragement because their parents have unrealistic expectations. They usually lack self-confidence and think they are a disappointment to their parents, because nothing they do is ever good enough. They try to please other people, so no one will ever be disappointed in them. This inhibits their curiosity, creativity, individuality, and problem-solving or decision-making skills.

- Children behave and do their work because they get rewards—material payoffs, acceptance, and conditional praise—not because they are *self*-motivated.

- Separation issues are often difficult for Perfectionistic Supervisors because they think they are losing control of their children. When their children try to spread their wings, these parents often have difficulty letting go. The children resent this ongoing control and struggle to control their own lives. As teens, their children might rebel, to prove they can't be controlled.

- As teens, children of Perfectionistic Supervisors frequently display obsessive, over-achieving, or perfectionist habits. They practically kill themselves (sometimes literally) trying to live up to unrealistic expectations. If they are not obsessed with trying to prove their worth and don't rebel, they might simply give up trying.

- As adults, children of Perfectionistic Supervisors often have strict rules about what is right and wrong. They usually see things in black and white and having difficulty operating in gray areas.

HISTORICAL TRENDS IN AUTOCRATIC PARENTING

Until the 1950s, most parents used an over-controlling (autocratic) parenting style, which fit the structure of society and most families. Back then, there was a pecking order of superiors and inferiors. At home, the father was the supreme ruler, the mother was expected to obey him, and the children were supposed to obey both of them. To succeed in the workplace people said, "Yes, Sir. No, Sir. What do you want me to do next, Sir?" If someone in authority told people to do something, they did it—without question. Autocratic parenting was the style that best prepared children for the real world *then*.

The 1960s brought a major shift in American society, from a superior/inferior structure to one of equal worth and rights. Civil rights, women's rights, laborers' rights, minority rights, and children's rights forever changed American society. Only when children believe adults are superior and infallible do they believe adults have the right to punish or hurt them.

Teenagers in the 1960s resented adults telling them what to do and rebelled against their autocratic control: how to wear their hair, what clothes to wear, which profession to enter, whether to go to college or be drafted into war. They believed they had a right to voice their feelings, opinions, and make decisions about issues that affected them. Autocratic parenting did not allow for such individuality. Drugs and "the sexual revolution"

> **Did you know . . .**
> *In America, there were laws and agencies to protect animals from abuse and neglect long before children received the same protection? If children were abused, people called the local animal shelter to intervene!*

provided a temporary escape and a new way to rebel. Parents saw they were losing control. The professionals who tried to help these parents recognized this rebellion against authority and encouraged parents to loosen their reins. So began a new trend—permissive parenting.

The Under-Controlling Parenting Style (Permissive)

Parents who don't control their children *enough* are also called permissive. At first glance, it may seem to be a positive parenting style because there is no harshness, criticism, or punishment. It is, however, as equally imbalanced as the over-controlling style, but in the opposite way, and also has many negative long-term effects. There are also two kinds of under-controlling parenting styles, the Avoider and the Over-Indulger. They are more different from each other than the two kinds of over-controlling parenting styles. There are some common traits, however, to most under-controlling parenting styles.

ANSWERS TO COMMON QUESTIONS

What is the parent's job?

It is the parent's job to avoid conflict and make or keep children happy. This usually includes protecting children from disappointment, frustration, and getting in trouble.

Who has rights?

Most permissive families revolve around the children; their rights and needs are more important than the parents'.

Who gets respect?

Under-controlling parents try to treat their children with respect, hoping they will feel happy and, therefore, behave better. Since parents put their needs and rights below children's, they are more willing to accept disrespectful behavior from their children. While it's clear most parents aren't getting respect in these families, the children are also not getting real respect.

How are mistakes handled?

When children make mistakes, permissive parents might listen to the child's feelings, but not hold them accountable for the results of their actions. Children have unlimited chances to correct their behavior, with few or no consequences for misbehavior. Some under-controlling parents are overprotective so the children will not make mistakes. Most under-controlling parents rescue their children from mistakes by making excuses for the child's behavior or by blaming others (including themselves).

How are problems solved and decisions made?

Most under-controlling families solve problems and make decisions based on the children's demands or what will make the children happy. Some under-controlling parents solve problems *for* their children. Most let their children make whatever decision they want, even if it is impulsive or irresponsible. When a problem arises, these parents deny it exists, hope the problem will go away, or view it through filtered lenses. They only acknowledge a problem's existence when it gets so bad that they can no longer ignore it.

Who decides how children should behave, which interests they pursue, and the goals they set?

Children make behavior, interest and goal decisions. The parents are usually willing to let the children do whatever makes them happy.

Who is responsible for controlling the child's behavior?

Being responsible means "to be *accountable* for" our behavior. We consider our options, the possible risks, make the best decision we can, and accept the positive or negative effect of the choices we make. Therefore, children from under-controlling families are not *responsible*, but are definitely *controlling* their behavior choices (even if their choice is to behave irresponsibly).

Who makes the rules and how are rules enforced?

Children can usually do as they please, since under-controlling parents rarely set limits or enforce rules. They use reminders and polite pleading to convince children to behave properly. If they set limits, they rarely enforce them. If the children don't like others' rules or experiencing the effects of breaking rules, their parents often request special treatment or rescue their children.

How do parents discipline?

Under-controlling parents rarely discipline because it's too inconvenient or because they fear losing their children's love. When repeated pleading doesn't work, parents often say, "I've had it. I'm tired of being ignored." They either give in or jump to the other extreme and try to regain control through over-controlling means.

SYMBOL FOR UNDER-CONTROLLING PARENTING

Under-controlling

In *Active Parenting,* author Michael Popkin calls under-controlling parenting "permissive." He uses the symbol of a zigzag line, which symbolizes freedom and choices, without any limits. We use his symbol to represent the under-controlling parenting style.

LONG-TERM EFFECTS OF UNDER-CONTROLLING PARENTING

• An under-controlling parenting style poorly prepares children for the real world. Most societies offer some freedom, but within consistent, reasonable limits that protect the rights of others. Since these children can usually do what they want and experience few discomforts, they have little motivation for changing or improving themselves and are unprepared for the harsh realities of the real world. Children who lack self-control, self-discipline, and respect for others have difficulty operating within the rules of structured settings like school and work. They test limits, hoping they can manipulate others into loosening the reins. When their efforts to change others or their environment fail, they often quit, saying "School (or the job) was too hard (or restrictive)."

• Children from under-controlling families are used to others rescuing them or excusing their behavior, so they don't accept responsibility for their actions. They seek out rescuers and blame everyone—parents, teachers, employers, spouses—for their problems and failures. Because they've been pampered, they can't handle criticism or suggestions for improving themselves. They use their energy and creativity to manipulate others into taking care of their needs and desires. They spend more time trying to get *out* of responsibility than in developing responsible independence.

TYPES OF UNDER-CONTROLLING PARENTS

Under-controlling parenting can involve two extremes—not doing enough (avoidance) or doing too much (over-indulgence) for children. The following descriptions detail the ways these two extremes expand on the general traits of the under-controlling parenting style.

Avoiders

Some under-controlling parents are Avoiders. In these families, the parent's needs are most important. Parents don't teach skills, set limits, supervise, or follow through because it takes too much time; they are either too busy or too tired (lazy?) to be bothered. Extreme Avoiders are physically or emotionally neglectful.

Personality Traits of Avoiders

Avoiders are into comfort—their own comfort. They are often easy going, undemanding, and let their children do for themselves. They avoid responsibility and commitments because they are too busy or too relaxed to be inconvenienced. They often break promises at the last minute, because they no longer feel like doing it. They are often emotionally detached and rarely take the time to talk or listen.

What Avoiders Believe

Children will learn skills and proper behavior on their own, just from trial and error. Children should not inconvenience parents. Problems (and problem behavior) will eventually go away if parents ignore them or pretend they don't exist.

How Avoiders Handle Negative Feelings

They avoid stress, negative feelings, and conflict. Even if people are upset, they should not express it. They often perceive even healthy disagreements and assertiveness as fighting or arguing and insist on eternal family peace.

The Avoider's Tools

Avoiders have a hands-off approach to parenting. They let their children do whatever they want, as long as it doesn't inconvenience them. Parents who are into their own comfort are often preoccupied with adult conversations and activities. They don't pay attention to children, allowing them to do whatever they want, even if it is inappropriate or hurts others.

Long-Term Effects of Avoidance Parenting

- Letting children learn by trial and error has its merits, but Avoiders don't take the time and effort to teach their children good decision-making skills or help children process what they learn from their mistakes. If children are unsupervised or alone a much of the time (e.g., latch-key kids), they become bored and often make impulsive, poor decisions.

- The children often respond to problems and mistakes as the parent does—they deny responsibility, make excuses ("I'm too busy" or "I don't feel like it."), and expect special treatment. When the real world holds the children accountable and they fail, their parents want to avoid further disappointment, so they often give up on the children and "write them off."

- Children of Avoiders usually have a poor sense of self-worth because their parents didn't make an effort to show they cared.

Over-Indulgers

Over-indulgence is the more common, positive, yet still imbalanced, type of under-controlling parenting style. Here, the parents don't set limits because it might make their child unhappy.

Personality Traits of Over-Indulgers

These parents are usually sensitive and understanding people, in touch with others' feelings and desires. These are positive traits, if used properly. Over-indulgent parents want to be loved, liked, and appreciated. They try to please others to earn this approval. They sacrifice their own needs and rights to keep the peace or make others happy.

What Over-Indulgers Believe

Children should have a happy, carefree childhood. Over-Indulgent parents want their children to have the things they didn't have and protect them from negative experiences, even if these experiences could offer valuable lessons.

How Over-Indulgers Handle Negative Feelings

They do whatever it takes to keep others happy and rescue them from their negative feelings. These parents usually sense what their children want or need and are afraid to disappoint or frustrate them. So they give in or give undue service, hoping that if their children are happy, they'll cooperate more.

The Over-Indulger's Tools

Too often, these parents give and serve too much, at the expense of their own rights and needs. They suffer from "affluenza," doting on their children, emotionally and materialistically. They usually take on too many responsibilities, becoming maids, cooks, toy stores, tutors, financiers—and doormats.

Over-indulgers are great rescuers, protecting children from even healthy hardships. They often volunteer their time to the child's activities so they can intervene or prevent problems from occurring. They deliver forgotten lunches and retrieve homework left at school so their children won't experience disappointment. Perfectionistic Supervisors are overly involved so they can *control* the situation or child and look like good parents. Over-indulgers are overly involved so they can *protect* children and *serve* their children's whims.

Long-Term Effects of Over-Indulgent Parenting

- Children from under-controlling homes develop a distorted perception of reality—they think the world revolves around them. At first, they may feel powerful, because they can take advantage of others. Eventually, they resent the people who don't have the courage to set limits. Because they've been protected and rescued, they have trouble coping with the normal struggles of adult life. They expect success, but aren't willing to work for it.

- Over-Indulgers, who bend over backwards to keep their children happy, are often shocked when their children become ungrateful, demanding, and disrespectful in return. But the children know who's really in control—them! Children learn to manipulate by using "please," promises, and logical arguments to get their parents to give in.

- Young adults from under-controlling families have difficulty operating within the limits of a job, its rules, and with authority figures. They often drift from job to job, trying to find the perfect job. When they can't support themselves, their parents welcome them home, offering the standard of living to which they are accustomed. The parents think this is their job and they like feeling needed.

> ***A Personal Story.*** *When I was in college, I worked at a runaway shelter. I expected most runaway teens would come from negative, controlling families. I was surprised to find just as many who ran away from perfectionist-controlling families and permissive ones. Runaways from permissive homes thought their parents didn't care about them. They tested how far they could go before their parents would set limits. I rarely saw a child who had run away from a family that wasn't over-controlling or under-controlling.*

HISTORICAL TRENDS IN PERMISSIVE PARENTING

The angry teens of the 60s blamed their parents and authority for their problems and vowed to raise their children differently. Instead of keeping what their parents did well (such as setting limits and teaching respect for authority) and rejecting what they did poorly (such as demanding blind obedience and trying to control children's individuality), they went to the other extreme. These changes tipped the scale to the other extreme—permissive parenting.

In 1970, Thomas Gordon developed *P.E.T.: Parent Effectiveness Training,* the first parenting curriculum that was widely accepted in America. It taught effective communication skills such as problem-ownership, active listening, I-messages, and problem solving. These skills greatly improved family relationships by fostering effective communication. In fact, *P.E.T.'s* communication skills are so effective, nearly every major institution still uses and/or teaches them, including business, education, counseling, human relationships, and parenting. Parents and professionals eventually became frustrated with *P.E.T.* because it contained no guidelines for discipline—and they labeled it "permissive." Today, a few popular parenting resources encourage parents to throw out all the important valuable skills *P.E.T.* taught, simply because it was missing one important skill area. *P.E.T.* was *not* a permissive parenting program, just an incomplete one.

By the 1980s, problems that started in the 60s had reached epidemic proportions. Many families were touched, in some way, by problems such as widespread drug use, teenage pregnancy, AIDS, gangs and violence, child abduction, and sexual victimization. Many people rightly blamed permissiveness for most of these problems. Other problems, such as abduction and sexual victimization, had their roots in abusive parenting and autocratic practices that taught children to blindly obey any authority at the expense of their own rights. Some people said parents should go back to autocratic methods to regain control. They had obviously forgotten, or didn't know, the reason permissive parenting became popular in the first place— because autocratic parenting had a long-term rebound effect. The pendulum was swinging away from permissive, but was going too far again into the autocratic zone, without finding and maintaining a healthy balance. Since autocratic and permissive parenting both resulted in negative results for children and society, it is wise to avoid both of these extreme, imbalanced parenting styles.

The Balanced Parenting Style ☆☆☆☆

Any time our parenting style is extreme, so are the long-term effects. The balanced parenting style is based on a healthy, balanced philosophy and uses effective parenting techniques. Therefore, the long-term effects are almost exclusively positive.

ANSWERS TO COMMON QUESTIONS

What is the parent's job?

Balanced parents share the individual, family, and societal goals we listed earlier. They believe their job is to *teach* children the life skills they need to be self-sufficient, responsible members of society.

Who has rights?

In balanced families, parents and children are equal but different. They each have equal human worth and deserve to be treated with equal dignity and respect, even when their individual needs are different. Parents try to balance the needs of the adults and their

relationships and also the children's individual needs and the parent/child relationship. While this is a difficult balancing act, they also realize that they can't (and shouldn't) meet each member's every need. Their goal is to teach children how to meet their own needs. They strive to maintain appropriate boundaries—they are available to their children, without fostering unnecessary dependency.

In balanced families, the adults aren't superior to children, just different—they are older, more experienced, and usually more knowledgeable. Increased privileges result from increased responsibility, not just one's age or position.

Who gets respect?

Balanced parents believe that *all* people deserve to be treated respectfully, regardless of their age or position. Parents teach respect to their children and earn respect from their children by treating their children and others respectfully, as role models.

Balanced parents set rules that are mutually respectful. They show self-respect by setting limits and they show respect for their children by offering choices. Children have some freedom and choices, within limits that show respect for others' rights. Balanced parents are socially responsible, teaching their children the positive and negative effects of their behavior choices.

Over-controlling parents treat children like objects, doing things *to* them. Under-controlling parents treat children like royalty, doing things *for* them. Balanced parents treat children like assets that have worth by doing things *with* children and involving them in decisions and activities.

How do balanced parents handle negative feelings?

Balanced parents show empathy and understanding for their children's negative feelings and differing opinions. They don't try to *change* them or label them right or wrong. They recognize that feelings and opinions are a part of life, so they teach their children *how* to express those feelings appropriately. In a balanced family, "We can agree to disagree, if we disagree respectfully."

Balanced parents regularly practice the healthy communication skills they teach to their children. They express their concerns in respectful, assertive ways. The stand up for their rights, but don't violate their child's right to be treated with respect. They avoid using blame or guilt to motivate others. When their anger is about to erupt, they disengage and calm down so they don't direct their anger at their children.

How are mistakes handled?

Balanced parents encourage their children to learn from their mistakes. They know that mistakes are part of life and learning, so they avoid blame and criticism. Instead, they hold children accountable for making amends for the effects of their choices and learning better skills.

Balanced parents are gentle with their own mistakes, willing to admit when they are wrong, and consider others' viewpoints. Through their words and actions (role modeling not lecturing), balanced parents show children how to make responsible decisions, accept responsibility for their mistakes, learn and grow from them, and still maintain their self-respect and sense of self-worth.

How are problems solved and decisions made?

When problems arise in a balanced family, parents take responsibility and ownership for their contribution to the problem. They shift the focus to what there *is* a choice about, within limits that respect the rights and needs of others.

Whenever possible, balanced families strive to reach win/win solutions to problems. *Balanced families do not vote* because there are always losers—and discouraged losers will usually sabotage the decision. While mutual agreement is their goal, it isn't always possible. On occasion, parents need to make an executive decision. Balanced parents listen to their children's ideas and opinions and consider them in their decision. Children can have a say about an issue, but might not always get their way.

Who decides how children should behave, which interests they pursue, and the goals they set?

Balanced parents view their children as unique individuals, not carbon copies of themselves or balls of clay to mold into whatever forms *they* think the children should become. They teach their children *how* to set and reach goals, rather than setting goals *for* their children and then pressuring them to meet unrealistic expectations. They may not share their children's interests, but they strive to understand them so they can increase their own knowledge and better support their children.

Who is responsible for controlling children's behavior?

The balanced parent's job is not to *control* their children; their job is to guide and teach children how to control their *own* behavior. As children develop the skills and qualities they need to be healthy, well-balanced, fully-functioning adults, they naturally make increasingly responsible decisions that positively affect their lives.

> Sometimes balanced parents are more firm than flexible or more flexible than firm. These are *conscious* choices, based on the needs of the situation, the parent, and child. They are not the result of their personality issues. Such slight, temporary, conscious imbalances, within the balanced range, are often quite appropriate.

Who makes the rules and how are they enforced?

Balanced parents tell children what they *can* do, instead of what they *can't* do. Their rules focus on the *value* behind a rule, rather than the power of the rule-maker. Balanced parents offer some choices or freedom within reasonable rules or limits. They provide limited privileges to see how responsibly their children can handle them. Over-controlling parents use privileges to bribe and control children. Under-controlling parents offer unlimited privileges without any responsibility.

How do balanced parents discipline?

Balanced parents try to *prevent* the need for discipline by telling children what they *can* do, teaching behavior skills, revealing children's behavior choices and the possible outcomes of those choices. When children choose to misbehave, balanced parents consider the children's point of view and their possible goals. They show their children how to meet these goals through positive behavior. If children still *choose* to behave inappropriately, balanced parents allow the revealed outcome to occur. They may also need to use discipline in unexpected situations in which behavior is so inappropriate that parents must set immediate boundaries.

The actual discipline balanced parents choose depends on the situation. Balanced parents use the most logically related discipline for the misbehavior. Balanced parents do not add suffering to their discipline, because this distracts children from the lessons they need to learn. It builds resentment and invites revenge, instead of focusing on how children can make amends for their mistakes.

SYMBOL FOR BALANCED PARENTING

Active Parenting calls balanced parenting "democratic" and uses the symbol of a zigzag, representing choices or freedom, inside a circle, which represents reasonable limits. We refer to this symbol often as we learn how to set and maintain a balanced parenting style.

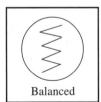
Balanced

Balanced parenting got the label "democratic" when authors compared the qualities of a balanced parenting style to a democratic *society*.[2] Here are just a few examples:

- Citizens have certain basic rights (free speech, for one) and privileges they can earn (a driver's license, for example). They must balance these rights and privileges with the responsibility of using them appropriately and not violating other people's rights in the process.

- All people have equal human worth, even when they are different or have individual needs. "All men are created equally." ("Men" refers to humankind.)

- Citizens are involved in decision-making whenever possible. When they cannot make the final decision, they can express their opposing opinions and their representatives will consider them in the decision.

Balanced parenting is no longer called "democratic," because parents and professionals confused democratic parenting with a liberal political belief. (Someone can be a conservative Republican and still practice balanced, "democratic" parenting.) As a result, a few authors have criticized "democratic parenting" as being liberal and permissive. These authors inadvertently discourage parents from using accurate, healthy, effective parenting resources, simply because the resources use a label that has lost its original meaning. They usually present only two extreme styles of parenting, permissive parenting and autocratic parenting.

When you read criticism about "democratic" parenting, carefully read the explanation. If you use the guidelines and accurate definitions in this book, you can recognize imbalanced parenting advice, whatever its label. (See the "Screening Advice" section of Chapter 15, "The Three C's," page 416, for more suggestions.)

LONG-TERM EFFECTS OF BALANCED PARENTING

Research and decades of experience have proven that children from balanced families learn the life skills and develop the qualities we listed as our individual, family, and societal goals. Over the past 40 years, each generation has had a growing number of children raised in healthy, balanced families. Even when these children (and later, adults) are the minority, they make a significant impact on their corner of the world.

- Children and young adults from balanced families know how to operate within rules and limitations. They find the *value* of a rule (even when it is not stated) and the choices they have within those limits. They also act responsibly in permissive settings because they are *self*-disciplined. They usually only resist a request if doing so defies logic or would violate someone's rights, ethics, or a higher law.

- As teens and adults, children of balanced parents usually make responsible decisions. They have been making choices their entire lives—to varying degrees, based on their age, maturity, and the situation. Children from balanced families often want more independence and are usually skilled and responsible enough to handle it.

- Children from balanced families are self-motivated. They are more likely to take the initiative to do tasks, simply because they see that it needs done. They also know when they need to ask permission first. These are valued qualities in the business world.

- Children and young adults from balanced families have excellent leadership and communication skills. They know how to motivate people without bribes or threats. They promote teamwork and bring out the assets in each team member. They know how to resolve problems, learn from their mistakes, and accept responsibility for their behavior choices.

- Children raised in balanced families learn *how* to be responsible—for their jobs, emotions, bodies, and behavior. They have good time-management and organizational skills. Whatever profession these children choose as adults, they are active members of the work team and resolve problems professionally and maturely.

- Children from balanced families are less likely to rebel against authority. Their relationships with authority figures are usually positive because they don't see them as a threat or symbol of power and control. They see them as people—and people have different personalities and needs. Because their parents respected their individuality and taught them important life skills, they know how to tolerate or work *with* people who are different. When someone treats them disrespectfully or tries to manipulate them, they know how to respond appropriately. They might reach a win/win agreement or voice their opinion assertively, which are both respectful options.

Some parents comment that the military's autocratic style of training develops some of the qualities they want their children to develop. They suggest, therefore, that similar tactics will develop these traits in their children. There are several reasons why this is an incorrect assumption.

(1) The military *must* be autocratic. A general cannot assemble the massive troops and ask "Which field should we attack? What strategy should we use?" The military's goal is to develop soldiers who will unquestioning obey their orders. Therefore, autocratic leadership fits the goals of the military. (Military *leaders*, however, often use peaceful negotiation to prevent conflict or brainstorm options before passing on orders to the troops.) Healthy parents, on the other hand, strive to meet a broader range of goals. To develop positive traits and skills in children, they must choose a parenting style that is most likely to help them meet *all* their goals, not just a few.

(2) The military trains *adults*, who undergo the harsh training necessary to serve their country. Children are affected much differently by such harsh training. There may be obedient children who would thrive in a military career, but the military also needs soldiers who are emotionally stable. Autocratic parenting does not develop or nurture emotional stability. An over-indulgent family might develop children with emotional stability because it is nurturing, but it doesn't develop children who operate well within strict limits. Balanced parenting, however, is the style most likely to develop emotional stability *and* a broad range of skills that produce well-balanced adults who can succeed in *any* career.

HISTORICAL TRENDS IN BALANCED PARENTING

Since the beginning of time, there have always been healthy, balanced families. They were often in the minority and there was no label for that parenting style. In 1976, Donald Dinkmeyer and Gary McKay wrote *S.T.E.P. (Systematic Training for Effective Parenting)*. *S.T.E.P.* took the effective communication skills of *P.E.T.* and added guidelines for understanding and disciplining problem behavior. These additional skills came from Rudolf Dreikurs, who coined the terms "The Four Goals of Misbehavior" and "logical and natural consequences."

Today, most parenting resources teach balanced parenting, including *The Parent's Toolshop* and the many resources it references. Only a few parenting authors encourage parents to exert their power by using quick fixes that are unhealthy and ineffective in the long-run. These authors feed on parents' fears of losing control of their children and offer few helpful, healthy suggestions. Since there are so many accurate, healthy parenting resources available to parents, parents are wise to simply avoid parenting authors whose advice is so questionable.

Most people have healthy, positive parenting goals. They want their children to learn how to think for themselves and make decisions *and* follow rules that respect the rights of others. Parents, children, and society have already proven, for several generations, that a balanced parenting style is most effective in producing well-balanced, fully-functioning, mature, responsible, independent adults who make positive contributions to society. We are now at a critical turning point in family history—only time will tell if parents (and society) will repeat the mistakes of the past or learn from them to improve the future. Now, more than ever, parents and professionals need to know how to use balanced parenting (and teaching and leadership) skills, so we can work together to reach the healthy individual, family, and societal goals we share.

THE ULTIMATE EXAMPLE OF A BALANCED PARENT

Balanced parenting is not only psychologically and emotionally sound, it is also spiritually healthy. Consider the three common philosophies people believe about God as a heavenly parent. One is balanced and the other two are extreme. These three sets of beliefs are similar to the three styles of parenting. If you disagree with the religious interpretations presented here or don't believe in God, simply view them as interesting analogies to consider.

> **God is a balanced parent.** God is loving and forgiving, yet has clear expectations and laws. God understands the emotional nature and difficulties of human existence. God reveals rules and guidelines, through the writings and living examples of godly men and women, to help us live responsible, enriching lives. God gives us the information we need to make responsible decisions and

reveals the effects of our positive and negative options. Then, because God also gave us free will, we are allowed to live our own lives and make our own decisions. One universal law states, "As you sow, so shall you reap," which means "what you give, you get." (This law of cause and effect is obvious when we consider the long-term effects of the different parenting styles.) People may choose to ignore the teachings, examples, and their conscience (God's intuitive nudging) to violate the universal laws. God does not stop us from making these choices—or the positive and negative effects that result. The results are not God's subjective, personal revenge; they are objective, natural consequences. God shows us unconditional love, when we are good *and* when we stray. It is as though God embraces us and says, "I will always love you. You knew my rules and the effects of your choices before you decided to do this, so *I* am not doing this *to* you. It is happening because of the *choice you made.* You will soon have another chance to show you've learned this important lesson and choose differently. I am always here for you, to love you and guide you, if you choose to allow me." When we see others are on the wrong path, we can share the values of virtuous behavior in non-judgmental ways, serve as role models of godly living, and unconditionally love others, even if they don't immediately change.

One extreme belief is that God is a permissive parent who is *only* loving and forgiving—no matter how often we sin, whether we feel regret, or if we ask for forgiveness. God is always watching over us, to catch us when we fall and to pick us up. Because we don't always immediately see the effects of violating God's laws, it must be okay to break them. We don't need to take personal responsibility for our actions, because God will forgive us anyway.

The other extreme belief is that God is an autocratic parent who hovers over us, watching every move and judging every mistake, so we will get our rightful punishment on Judgment Day. We must follow the rules of our *religion,* rather than discovering the wonders and revelations of deeply spiritual experiences. Anyone who doesn't follow the same denominational rules or share our beliefs is wrong and bound for hell. Since God tells us the right way to live and judges our actions, we must do the same to others, to try to convince them to follow what we know is right. If we point out others' faults, they will feel shame and want to improve. If we can make them fearful, by describing the horrible punishment that awaits them, they might change their ways.

When parents use religious beliefs to intimidate, shame, and control their children, it emotionally traumatizes their children. The clinical term for such parental treatment is called "religious abuse."

> *A Graduate's Story. My girls, ages 4 and 6, were playing at a neighbor's house with her children, a boy age 3 and a girl age 7. It was during a scorching heat wave and her house had no air conditioning. The children went to an upstairs bedroom to play and closed the door. When they got hot and sweaty, they took off their shirts and continued playing. When my neighbor saw them she screamed at them, saying they were "naked, sinful children and God would punish them." She locked each child in a different room for a half an hour and told them they had to stay on their knees and pray for God's forgiveness. When my children returned, they were **very** upset and confused. They didn't understand what they did wrong.*
>
> *I don't want my children to be ashamed of their bodies, but also want them to be modest and sexually responsible—although they are still too young to even understand these concepts. My girls don't usually take off their shirts, but that wasn't even my issue here; I could understand a parent's disapproval of girls taking off shirts, although I knew these children weren't doing anything sexually inappropriate. My problem was with the way my neighbor treated my children. I've taught my children about a loving God and that our bodies are beautiful creations we are to respect and protect. My neighbor undermined these values. Now I wonder what my children think about God, the purpose of prayer, and healthy, appropriate sexuality.*

A belief in a "balanced" God is a *healthy* belief, but is it an accurate belief? To answer this, consider the following questions. When people do something wrong or commit a crime does God reach down from the sky and physically slap them? Does God shoot a bolt of lightning? Does God yell at us in a harsh, critical, discouraging voice? No. Just because this doesn't happen, does it mean people are getting away with their crime? No! Sooner or later, there are consequences for their actions, even if we don't see them. People may experience emotional or spiritual pain (in life or the afterlife), or physical problems (depression, drug addiction, etc.).

Of the thousands of people who have had near death experiences, none have reported meeting an angry, wrathful presence. While some details of near-death experiences vary among cultures and religions, almost all people encounter a similar spiritual presence who is warm, loving, teaches them lessons, and sometimes even has a sense of humor. Another common trait of near-death experiences is a life review. Here, the person re-experiences *every* thought, word, and deed from their lifetime—and the effects these had on others, from *that* person's perspective. They see every mistake they made, whether small or severe, and the value of their other options. People who attempted suicide or lived a criminal, disrespectful, or irresponsible life before their near-death *still* experienced complete joy, peace, and love in the afterlife. Their life review, however, sent additional, strong messages: God is Love, all human life is sacred, life's hardships can help us grow, and we *will* be held accountable for *everything* we do in life. As a result of their near-death experience, many people who didn't believe in God dramatically changed their beliefs. They embraced a God that loves them intensely and unconditionally, but also holds them personally accountable for every choice they make.

As human parents to human children, we can follow God's example. We can show unconditional love toward others. We can teach positive values and behavior and reveal the possible effects of straying from that path. We can be disciples, who model appropriate words and deeds. When our children make mistakes, we can teach them how to choose more wisely in the future. If their behavior isn't dangerous, we can allow the natural consequence to occur and help them learn from the experience. When there are no natural consequences, we can discipline in loving ways that don't impose additional suffering that can traumatize them.

We do not often explore religious parallels in *The Parent's Toolshop*. Nevertheless, you can feel assured that if you believe in a loving but firm "higher power," the teachings in this book will be consistent with your beliefs.

> **Balanced parenting principles are based on the universal laws of human behavior, so the positive and negative effects of our parenting choices *will* occur whether we believe this philosophy or not.**

PARENTING AS A TEAM

Many of us have a variety of parenting partners: spouses, ex-spouses, teachers, day care workers, religious educators, relatives, and neighbors we regularly visit. Each partner can have a parenting style that differs from ours. When parenting styles clash, resist the urge to overreact, interfere, rescue the child, or control the partner.

If we have a parenting partner with an opposite style, we can fall into an overcompensation cycle; one partner thinks the other is too strict, so he or she becomes more lenient to counteract the other. As this partner becomes more lenient, the other gets more strict. Each tries to compensate for the imbalances of the other and they seesaw back and forth. (Consider the balancing scale again. If you put *two* weights on the scale, where would you need to put them so the scale balances the quickest? Opposite ends create a seesaw effect. When each weight is close to the middle, the scale will balance more quickly.) Overcompensation cycles damage parenting partnerships and children learn how to manipulate better.

Many of us, upon learning effective, balanced parenting skills, are concerned when others parent our children in ineffective ways. We often judge or criticize the person and preach about all we've learned. This causes the criticized person to become even more defensive and closed to learning new ideas. Whoever your parenting partners are, there are some ways you can work together as a team.

• Talk to your partner about the parenting approach you have *chosen.* Explain that you want to work *cooperatively.* Ask your partner to read the book, just to "see what you think." If it makes sense to both of you, you can use the information as a common language and starting point.

• If your partner isn't interested or is resistant and defensive, back off. Your main purpose in reading this book is to improve *your* relationship with your child. Your child will benefit from that improvement alone. When only one parent changes, it still changes the family system and each member adjusts. (Remember the ripple effect?) Often, the changed parent serves as a role model for the partner, which avoids criticism, lectures, and interference. When parenting partners see a positive change, they might try the skills, without even realizing they are changing. If not, their behavior choices are not your responsibility. Do what *you* believe is best for you and your child; don't make it a divisive issue between you and your parenting partners. If your differences persist, be careful not to fall into old habits of overcompensating. (In Chapter 15, "The Three C's," there are additional suggestions in the "Inconsistent Parenting Partners" section, page 414. You can read these suggestions anytime.)

If you and your parenting partners can agree on a common style, discuss situations and options regularly. Talk often and encourage each other. Recognize times when each of you used the skills, rather than pointing out times when someone missed the mark. If you do discuss mistakes, focus on what was learned and brainstorm ideas for more effective responses, in case the situation arises again.

> *A Graduate's Story. My sister and I attended the parenting class together, since we had our firstborn children within six months of each other. At the time of the class, our daughters were both two-years-old and we needed help just to survive the experience of child-rearing. Discussing the ideas and skills with her was very helpful, especially in times of crisis. We would observe the situation between our two girls, such as fighting over a toy, and put our heads together to plan the most effective response we could find, then do it and evaluate our results. If one of us fell back into an old habit, such as yelling, using guilt trips, or spanking, the other one would offer support and remind her that our children keep giving us chances to try again.*

> *We felt silly huddling in a corner and talking "strategy" for a few extra seconds while our children were fighting in the next room, but we were so excited by the success of our new skills that it was well worth it. Now our girls are four years old, and we have adopted the strategies we learned over two years ago. We frequently receive comments about how delightful our children are and how well they play with others. We know that we owe it to the parenting skills we learned.*

ATTITUDE ADJUSTMENT TOOLS

The first step in balancing our parenting style is to *identify* our imbalances. The next step is to become aware of and change the beliefs that *cause* the imbalances. Our beliefs are the result of what we were told, what we saw, and how we interpreted events as we were growing up. They are the little tapes that play in our minds, influencing our interpretation of situations and, therefore, our responses to them. Beliefs can be positive or negative, accurate or inaccurate. Consequently, what we *believe* about a situation influences our perceptions, feelings, and reactions more than the *reality* of the situation.

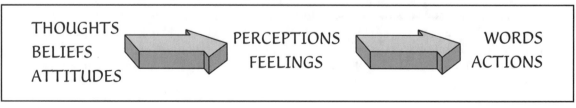

THOUGHTS BELIEFS ATTITUDES → PERCEPTIONS FEELINGS → WORDS ACTIONS

Beliefs also affect our children's attitudes, thoughts, feelings, words, and actions. Children observe the world around them and don't always interpret situations accurately. These mistaken beliefs can affect them into adulthood. Consider this example: A child makes her bed, leaving lumps in the sheets. Later, she finds her mother smoothed out the lumps. If this is a daily occurrence, the child might conclude, "My way is never good enough. Everything always has to be perfect" or "Why should I even bother making my bed if she's going to make it again?" If you asked the mother, she'd probably say she was *helping* the child. Nevertheless, it is the *child's* interpretations, not the parent's intentions, that program the child's beliefs. Throughout life, the child will occasionally hear a little voice inside, saying her best is never good enough. Did her mother ever say this? No! But the child *believed* this was the message behind her mother's actions.

There is always more than one way to look at a situation. Once we are aware of an unhelpful belief, we can choose to replace it with something more positive. The power and choice are ours.

> *A Personal Story. When my son, Chris, was eight, I encouraged him to try baseball. He was afraid he wouldn't be one of the best players, since some children had been playing longer. I pointed out that four years wasn't a big disadvantage at that age and he was very coordinated so he'd probably catch up quickly. He argued with all the praise, logic, and explanations I offered. He dug his feet in and wouldn't budge. I even resorted to bribing him, if he'd at least try it for one season. "No," was his firm response. He only wanted to play soccer and maybe track when he was older. I realized I couldn't **make** him try it.*
>
> *I finally looked at why this was so important to me. After all, I don't even like baseball, was never involved in any sports, and the rest of our family is not athletic. I realized **I** saw his potential and wanted him to reach it. I also saw the value of "giving it a shot." I decided to look at the positive side of the situation: He knew what he wanted and wouldn't be swayed. This was a quality I admired—if he were applying it to a situation where someone was pressuring him to do something negative. He was committed to one sport and focused on doing it to the best of his ability. I would only have to drive to one sport's practice. When I looked at it from this perspective, I realized there was nothing wrong with his decision and backed off.*

While we teach life's lessons to children, children teach *us* life lessons, too. They teach us about unconditional love and forgiveness. They watch what we say and do, so we try harder to set a good example. Parenthood sometimes forces us to explore parts of ourselves that we have not looked at before. It can raise buried issues about our own childhood, which we might not have resolved had we not become parents. When we reprogram our beliefs, we have a chance to "re-parent" ourselves. We can free ourselves from the past and develop our potential as parents—and people.

Replace Unhealthy Beliefs

If we consciously choose our parenting beliefs, it is easier to develop the skills that are consistent with those beliefs. By now, you have probably decided that "balanced" parenting sounds like the style you'd like to have. To achieve this balance, use the styles quiz to identify the style(s) of imbalance you might have. Consider replacing the common, unhealthy beliefs of that style with the healthier alternative beliefs you read in the "Balanced Parenting" section. You can write the helpful beliefs on index cards and repeat them out loud or in your mind throughout the day. Read them all each day or focus on one statement each day. If you do this for at least 21 days, the healthier beliefs will become a new habit.

Believe It and You'll See It ☆☆☆☆

Have you ever watched an Olympic athlete prepare for a performance? Many of them close their eyes and rehearse their moves—and success—in their minds *before* they start. They know that believing in success can bring success. Most people operate on the idea, "When I see it, I'll believe it!" When it comes to change, however, we usually have to believe "it," before seeing it. It's never too late to change or improve a relationship. When we believe we have the potential to change, we start seeing the change in ourselves. Once we change, it affects other people and situations in positive ways. Start picturing the qualities and skills you want to have. Believe that you already possess them. Believe that your relationship with your children can be full of joy and love. You will soon start noticing that reality is growing closer to what you have pictured in your mind.

> *A Graduate's Story. I took the parenting class so I could help my four-year-old grandson. I found myself using the communication skills with my adult children and people at work. People commented on how my attitude and behavior changed. I had a new sense of joy in my life and soon saw positive changes in all my relationships. My adult son and I had never really gotten along. After changing my attitude and beliefs, he started opening up to me and we resolved some hurts we were both hanging on to. I guess it's never too late to change! Every area of my life has improved—and I really believe a lot of it is because I changed my perspective from negative to positive!*

Avoid Double Standards

The old saying, "Do what I say, not what I do" was designed to steer children in the right direction. It was proven, however, to produce the opposite result. Parents' *actions* impress children. Double standards confuse children. Children quickly detect their parents' inconsistencies. "If you slap my hand when I reach for something you don't want me to touch, why can't I slap the kid who grabs my toy?" "Why do I have to knock on your door, but you can walk into my room without knocking?" We need to act and speak the way we want our children to act and speak.

Ideally, we want to have few or no double standards. Apply rules to everyone in the family: "Everyone hangs up their coats when they come home." "In this family we don't hit." "We respect each other's privacy."

When we can't avoid a double standard, we set guidelines that explain *when* and *why* the rule can change.

For example, a child leaves a mess after eating in the family room, where both parents and children often eat snacks. The parent can say, "People may eat in the family room *if* they clean up their messes. Tomorrow you'll have another chance to eat there and show you can remember to clean up your mess." That night, if the father eats in the family room, the child might ask, "Why does Daddy get to eat there?" The parent can respond, "Because Daddy has shown he will clean up his mess." If the father *also* doesn't clean up his mess, it would be difficult for the mother to "discipline" him as she did the child. She'll need to rely on her communication skills, to reveal the consequence of the double standard: the children will test the rules more. Therefore, double standards need to be the exception, not the rule.

> *A Parenting Class Discussion. During the last session, I asked if anyone still had any behavior problems they wanted to discuss. Jean spoke up saying, "My four-year-old still cusses. I tell him he shouldn't talk that way and try to teach him what to say instead, but nothing is working." My first reply was, "Do you cuss?" She admitted that she had only recently started making an effort to control her tongue, but her husband still cursed regularly and was unwilling to stop. He expected his son to hear cussing, but not repeat it. Her three sisters, in class with her, commented on the number of negative role models her son encounters at home and at school. Given the situation, a double standard seemed unavoidable. I asked her, "When **can** he cuss?" She thought a second and answered, "Thirteen." "Okay," I responded, "tell him he can cuss when he's thirteen!" Surprised, she said, "But I don't want to hear that in my house!" "Well," I said, "tell him he can cuss when he's thirteen if he's outside the house!" We all laughed at how ridiculous the idea sounded, but agreed she had few other options.*

Be a Role Model ☆☆☆☆

Children are sponges; they imitate what they see and hear, more than what they are told to do. We are their first example of how to speak, act, think, and believe. As they grow older, their positive changes are sometimes *in spite of* our example and their negative behavior is sometimes *because* of our example.

> *A Graduate's Story. When my little girl was only a year old, I began babysitting and I noticed something interesting: Children who can speak give a babysitter a good glimpse at what goes on at home. I heard four- and five-year-old children playing house with statements like, "Do you want a whipping? Then STOP!" and "Now, young lady, I told you a thousand times . . ." and "Fine. I don't care. Go out and play." I'd see them spank the dolls for spilling milk and sit them in time-out for falling off their chairs. I recognized in their actions some of my own responses, only* **they** *seemed to be* **unreasonable** *"parents" while I considered myself a decent one.*
>
> *I decided to learn more about how to parent so that some day, when my baby could talk and play, I would be proud to have the babysitter hear her play house. I took the parenting class when my girl was two and worked hard at practicing the skills. I was rewarded for my efforts when she was three-and-a-half, and I heard her playing house. She was putting her doll to bed, saying, "Now, honey, I know you don't feel sleepy, but it's bedtime. You can lay quietly in your bed and look at a book, or just close your eyes. You decide." Since then, I have heard her playing often, and I don't worry at all what a babysitter might hear.*

The best way to learn effective people skills and impart them to our children is to live them, rather than preach them. In short . . .

Become the kind of person you want your child to become.

Balance Your Parenting Style ☆☆☆☆

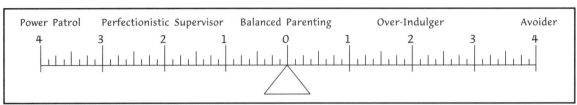

OVER-CONTROLLING	BALANCED	UNDER-CONTROLLING
demands sole power	shares power	gives up power
inflexible, few choices	flexible choices, within limits	too flexible few limits
teaches obedience to any authority	teaches respect for others and life skills	teaches self-centeredness
focuses on rules and compliance	focuses on respect and earned privileges	focuses on freedom and happiness
parents' rights and needs are most important	all rights and needs are equally important, but different	children's rights and needs are most important
rules apply to children	rules apply to all, usually	rules aren't applied or enforced
uses punishment, children suffer for mistakes	uses discipline, children learn from mistakes	rescues from mistakes or denies children are wrong
negative feelings are not allowed	negative feelings are expressed and resolved	rescues children from negative feelings
parent solves problems	parent teaches children how to solve problems	parent rescues from or avoid problems
rigid consistency	consistent, based on needs of situation	wishy-washy, inconsistent
parent makes all decisions	children learn to make decisions, within limits	children do what they want, no "decisions"

SUMMARY SHEET
FOUNDATION-BUILDING TOOLSET

BALANCE YOUR PARENTING STYLE ☆☆☆☆

Over-controlling: many limits with few choices or freedoms.

Power Patrol, Perfectionistic Supervisor

Under-controlling: many choices and freedoms with few limits.

Avoider, Over-indulger

Balanced: choices and freedoms within reasonable limits.

REPLACE UNHELPFUL BELIEFS WITH HEALTHIER ALTERNATIVES

CHOOSE YOUR ATTITUDES AND PERCEPTIONS ☆☆☆☆

"When you believe it, you'll see it."

ELIMINATE DOUBLE STANDARDS

Apply rules to the whole family.

BE A ROLE MODEL ☆☆☆☆

"Become the kind of person you want your child to become."

PRACTICE EXERCISES

A. Identifying Parenting Styles. In each of the following situations, identify each parent's parenting style (Power Patrol, Perfectionistic Supervisor, Avoider, Over-Indulger, Balanced) and answer the questions that follow each scenario.

1. Mr. Jones was offered a promotion at work, but it would involve moving. He calls his wife and tells her he has decided to take the job. She isn't happy about having to move, but since he's the father, she must comply. She decides to do what she can to make the children agree and make things go smoothly.

    That night at the dinner table, Dad informs the children of his decision. They are not happy about the idea—at all! Dad holds up his hands to quiet the mob and says, "This is a good opportunity and I'm not going to pass it up. You'll adjust." Mrs. Jones says, "Your father and I know what's best for you. You'll see, this move will be for the better." Then she tells the children her plan for making the move go smoothly. She has lists and schedules the children can use to help them get organized. When the children continue to protest, she stands up, starts clearing away the half-eaten plates of food, and says, "Now that's enough. Go to your rooms and start cleaning. We need to get the house ready to sell."

    What is Mr. Jones' parenting style? What is Mrs. Jones' style? What were their goals? How did they try to accomplish them? How did the children respond? What was the result?

2. Mr. Smith was offered a promotion at work, but it would involve moving. He wants to accept the position and calls his wife to tell her the "good" news. She isn't very happy about having to move, but knows how much it would mean to her husband. She wants him to be happy, so she agrees to the move. That night, at the dinner table, Mr. Smith tells the children the news. The children are not happy about the idea—at all! Mr. Smith starts to feel angry and confused, so he leaves the table to watch TV. Mrs. Smith, left with the angry mob, listens to the children's fears and reasons for not wanting to move. She tries to explain, "But this job would make your father so happy." When the children say *they* won't be happy, Mrs. Smith replies, "I'll talk to your father and explain how hard it would be on all of us. I'm sure he'll understand. Maybe another promotion will come along that doesn't require a move."

    When Mrs. Smith tries to talk Mr. Smith out of taking the job, he is amazed! "I thought you wanted me to take the job." Mrs. Smith explains, "I wanted you to take it so *you* would be happy. But then I realized how miserable the children would be." "Fine!" Mr. Smith snaps, "I'll turn it down. Now leave me alone!"

    What is Mr. Smith's parenting style? What is Mrs. Smith's style? What were their goals? How did they try to accomplish them? How did the children respond? What was the result?

3. Mr. Brown was offered a promotion at work, but it would involve moving. He wants to accept the position, but knows it will affect his wife and family. He calls his wife, tells her about the offer and his desire to accept it. They discuss it over the phone and decide this is an opportunity he should accept. Both know that the rest of the family will probably have concerns. They decide to schedule an "emergency" family council after dinner, to discuss the decision.

    After dinner, at the family council, Mr. Brown explains the job opportunity and the move it would entail. When the first child interrupts him, he says, "I really want to hear *everyone's* feelings and concerns. Let me finish and each of you can have a turn to be heard." He concludes his explanation by saying, "This job is a great opportunity for me and I think there could be some benefits for all of us. Your mom and I have already discussed it and I plan to accept this offer. I want your support, too. What do you each think? How do you feel about moving?" Each child expresses only negative comments. Mrs. Brown says, "Each of you has very valid concerns. Your dad and I can't imagine leaving either. *We* need to make this decision, but we care about your feelings and needs and want to consider them as we work out the details." Mr. Brown adds, "Right now, we just want you to know what's going on. We'd like to hear and discuss your concerns more at this week's family council. We are also willing to listen to your feelings and concerns privately. Until then, will everyone try to think of some positive things the move will bring as well as your concerns?"

The children aren't happy about moving, but they know they will have a chance to talk about their concerns. A few share their feelings with their parents throughout the week. Mr. and Mrs. Brown listen with respect and help them work through their concerns. When they ask questions about specific details, their parents suggest writing them down, so they can involve the entire family in future planning.

At the next family council, the children are beginning to think a little more positively but still don't like the decision. They realize they can't change the decision to move, but want their opinions and concerns to be heard. The family brainstorms ideas for making the move easier for each person and makes a list of questions, decisions, and ideas to discuss at future family councils.

What is Mr. Brown's parenting style? What is Mrs. Brown's style? What were their goals? How did they try to accomplish them? How did the children respond? What was the result?

B. Rewriting Unhealthy Beliefs.

1. In addition to the imbalanced beliefs you identified while reading this chapter, listen to your self-talk. Record the positive and unhelpful thoughts.
2. Re-write the negative beliefs into positive affirmations. Some good formulas are:
   I will . . .   I can . . .   I want to . . .   I choose to . . .
3. Notice how the changes in your thoughts and beliefs change your responses and perceptions.

One graduate did this exercise for a month and found 75 negative thoughts or statements she made to her children! (Don't worry, you don't have to come up with that many!) Here is one example.

Negative Thought or Statement	*Positive Alternative*
I don't understand my son; he never listens to me.	I can better understand my son, if *I* listen to *him* first.

Activity for the Week

Choose a situation involving your child that seems negative and answer the following questions:

1. What am I telling myself about the situation and how I "should" respond?
2. Is there a positive side to this behavior or situation?
3. Is there a more helpful way to respond?

Here is one example of a positive interpretation of a behavior parents often view negatively:

Negative Behavior	*Positive Perspective*
A child is argumentative.	Being logical and analytical are traits that are helpful as an adult. Children express their individuality by voicing opinions. At least my child has the courage to speak up. I can teach my children how to voice their opinions assertively *and* respectfully. I can choose not to argue and acknowledge my *child's* perspective. If my child just wants to argue, I can walk away.

Detailed Answers

1. Mr. Jones is a Power Patrol. He has a demanding attitude and puts his needs above others'. *He* makes the decision, although it affects the rest of the family. He doesn't consider or address their feelings. Mrs. Jones is a Perfectionistic Supervisor. She tries to control through organizing and doesn't listen to the children's feelings, either. The Jones' are trying to force the decision on the children, thinking that if they just tell them "That's the way it is," the children will cooperate. The children think their feelings and opinions don't count. They have no healthy outlet for their concerns. The family will move, but the children will probably feel angry and resentful. Once they get to their new home, one or more might even try to sabotage the move, to prove the move was a bad idea. Score: parents won, children lost.

2. Mr. Smith is an Avoider. He avoids conflict by shutting everyone out. Mrs. Smith is an Over-Indulger. She tries to please everyone, except herself, and gets caught in the middle trying to please her husband *and* the children. She won't let the children be temporarily unhappy, even if the move might be good for the family in the long-run. The children have learned that if they complain and push hard enough, their parents will give in to their wishes. The family doesn't move. Score: children won, parents lost.

3. Mr. and Mrs. Brown are both balanced parents. They recognize that a family move is an executive decision that is ultimately up to the parents. Since it will affect the entire family, they want to deal with everyone's feelings, so the move will go smoothly. They hold a family council meeting, but not to take a vote on *whether* to move. They discuss everyone's feelings about moving. The children still aren't happy about the news, but they have a healthy outlet for their feelings. This will prevent resentment and revenge in the long run. They can also have *some* choice about the move, such as whether they move before or after summer break. By offering choices within limits, the family will still move, but each family member's feelings and ideas will receive equal respect. Score: parents won, children won.

WHAT'S NEXT?

Take the knowledge and skills you just learned and use it daily with children *and* adults. Be observant; you can find many examples of these styles at home, at work (leadership and teaching styles), and in the world around you.

If you have decided that balanced parenting is the style you want to use in your family, this is the book for you. You are ready to start touring the Universal Blueprint and the actual toolsets. The next chapter, "Chapter 3, The Universal Blueprint," is different from all the other chapters; it is an overview of our parenting plan and explains a logical thinking process. In it, we learn how to look at *any* situation and ask three questions to identify what type of problem it is. We also learn the steps that are part of our universal response formula. Once we understand the general steps we will take, the rest of the book will go through each step, toolset-by-toolset, telling us exactly what tools we can use and how to use those tools effectively. If you are ready to read Chapter 3, then (as my elementary school teachers used to say) put on your thinking cap!

REFERENCES

1. Dolores Curran, *Traits of a Healthy Family*, (Winston Press, 1983. Ninth printing, Ballantine, 1988.) pp. 26–27.

2. Rudolf Dreikurs, M.D. (*Children: The Challenge,* with Vicki Soltz, R.N.: E.P. Dutton, 1964) discussed how a democratic *society influences* parenting. *S.T.E.P.* and, later, *Active Parenting* labeled a balanced parenting style "democratic" and further defined the democratic analogies.

CHAPTER 3
THE UNIVERSAL BLUEPRINT

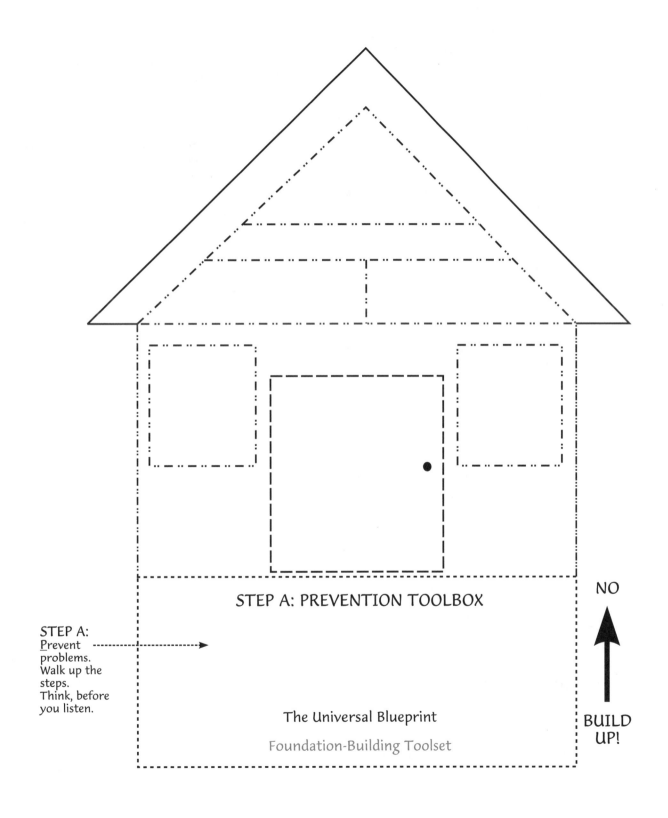

STEP A: PREVENTION TOOLBOX

STEP A:
<u>P</u>revent
problems.
Walk up the
steps.
Think, before
you listen.

NO

BUILD
UP!

The Universal Blueprint

Foundation-Building Toolset

3 THE UNIVERSAL BLUEPRINT

Once our foundation is set and balanced, we are ready to build our house. We first review the blueprint with the workers, so they know the general plan they are following. "First, the carpenters will build the structure, then the electricians will install the wiring . . ." If the details of the blueprint seem overwhelming, we reassure the workers that we are going to build the house one step at a time. Later, when the workers are focusing on specific tasks, they can refer to the blueprint to see how all the different parts fit together.

Parents also need a blueprint for child-rearing—a general plan that tells them where to find the specific tools they need and what steps to take. "First, we want to prevent problems. Then, if problems arise, we first identify what type of problem it is . . ." Parenting can seem overwhelming, so it helps if we summarize our general plan before focusing on each part. Later, when we focus on specific problems and their solutions, we can refer to the blueprint to better understand the details of each step we are taking.

IN THIS CHAPTER

This chapter teaches us the tools we need to meet our first two mission goals (see page 9 in Chapter 1): **STOP and THINK for 1–10 seconds** and **PLAN an effective response**. We learn two important skills in this chapter:

1. Countless situations can occur in a relationship, but each individual situation will fall within one of six general problem "types." This chapter explains how to identify each problem type.

2. There is a basic flow to effective responses. Once we know what *type* of problem we are facing, we follow certain steps in this universal response formula. Within each step, there are a variety of tools we can choose.

When we combine these two skills, we can take *any* situation, identify what type of problem it is, and follow the universal response formula in an individualized way, using tools we learn in later chapters. As we look at examples of the different types of problems, we refer to some of the individual tools, but you do not need to remember them. **The only skills you need to learn now are the two listed above**. Don't worry if you get to the end of this chapter and don't have the fine details of the Universal Blueprint memorized. The rest of the book follows the Universal Blueprint, step by step, repeating and reinforcing the problem-identification process and universal response formula.

WHEN TO USE THE UNIVERSAL BLUEPRINT

At any point in time, in every relationship, we are in one of the "problem areas," because one type of problem is a "NO problem." Therefore, **we use the Universal Blueprint all the time.** We make a *special* effort to use the Universal Blueprint, however, before we respond to problems. The Universal Blueprint helps us correctly identify what type of problem we are facing so we will choose the most effective tools for our response. ***With each problem, the steps we take and tools we choose depend on the type of problem and the individual needs of the situation or child.*** When we use the Universal Blueprint regularly, this process becomes a quick, natural step in our response.

A Graduate's Story. *Knowing how to identify problem types and when to use each toolset are the most important skills I learned in* The Parent's Toolshop. *As an emergency room nurse, I have* *found that deciding how to choose a parenting response is similar to the basic ABCs of emergency assessments: airway, breathing, and circulation. Each emergency room staff member memorizes these ABCs until they are ingrained and second-nature. Then, if a person with a spectacular injury comes in and the staff becomes embroiled in the crisis, they won't overlook these key areas of the patient's treatment. If someone walks into the emergency room and tells me he has a broken finger, I can quickly assume he's breathing and has a clear airway. I'm not skipping or overlooking these steps, I'm just moving through them quickly, hardly noticing the steps I take mentally. With practice, I've found that using the Universal Blueprint also takes only a split second. I might go through the steps fast, but I'd never want to skip them altogether. I've avoided making many problems worse because I stopped to think before I responded.*

BALANCING LOGIC AND EMOTION

People are not used to viewing parenting, relationships, and communication logically. Human behavior can seem unpredictable and overwhelming, but there *are* somewhat predictable patterns to it. Once we see the patterns in one relationship (parenting) we start seeing similar patterns in *all* our relationships.

Many people also find it difficult to respond to problems logically. Instead, they do the first thing that comes to mind to get a quick fix. Gut reactions are usually ineffective. If they *do* give a quick fix, they often have negative long-term effects. For example, when children have a problem and parents offer a quick solution, the children don't learn how to solve the problem independently. In the long-run, parents spend more time solving their children's problems than it would have taken to teach the children problem-solving skills. Plus, the children *still* don't know how to solve their *own* problems so they make poor decisions.

To respond to problems as effectively as possible, we need to balance emotions with logic and common sense. Planned responses increase our consistency and our chances of handling situations helpfully.

Because we are looking at the "bigger picture" in this chapter, your learning style will influence how easily you will learn and remember the Universal Blueprint the first time it's presented.

- *Whole-to-part learners* need to see the bigger picture and how all the pieces fit together before they learn the different parts. They usually understand the Universal Blueprint the first time it's presented, but need to refer to the Universal Blueprint (the bigger picture) now and then. (Look at the last page of this book for a quick reference).

- *Part-to-whole learners* need to learn a process step by step. They are overwhelmed with the big picture if they haven't learned the separate parts that go into it. These learners might not remember the entire Universal Blueprint the first time it's explained because it is a formula with missing pieces. **Remember, when you first read this chapter, you *only* need to understand how to identify types of problems and the basic steps of the universal response formula.** Since we use these two skills throughout our tour, every chapter brings an increasingly better understanding of how all the pieces fit together.

  *A Graduate's Comment. When I first looked at the Universal Blueprint it seemed complicated, but as I used it, I quickly realized it was simple common sense. Before long, a light bulb went off in my head and I realized just how profound the Universal Blueprint really was. Now, I use the Universal Blueprint in **all** my relationships, to help me resolve **any** problems that arise.*

Problems Are Like Onions

Problems, like onions, have many layers. Negative behaviors and emotional outbursts are often the symptoms of deeper issues. If we only respond to the negative behavior, we might get a temporary quick fix. However, the deeper issue *causing* the problem is still there and usually erupts again, sometimes through different behavior. This surface approach to problems is like using bandages to treat a disease. We can treat the symptoms (problem behavior), but also need to diagnose and cure the disease (the real issue). When we have a problem and follow the universal response formula, *in order,* we will always address the child's feelings or perspective *first.* This step "peels onions," revealing the real issue behind the behavior. When we resolve the *real* issue, the symptoms (misbehavior) often disappear.

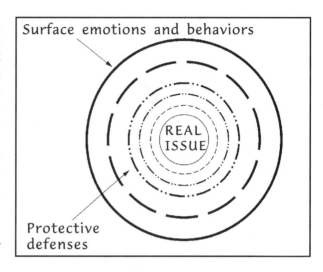

Change often occurs from the inside-out. If we don't see an immediate change, there might be change occurring inside that isn't observable, yet. For example, one common parenting goal is to help children develop *self*-discipline. If the parent or child is in the habit of using power struggles to deal with problems, the prevention tools might not work immediately. When we follow the Universal Blueprint, we might have to reach the discipline step only once or twice. Since discipline helps children *learn* from mistakes, the next time we might only need to give a simple reminder, acknowledge the child's feelings, or offer choices within limits to prevent or stop the problem behavior. Step by step, with each response, we eliminate specific problem behaviors. Soon, the child is *self*-disciplined in these situations.

> **The universal response formula not only addresses problem behavior, but also the issues and emotions that *cause* misbehavior. Consistently following the Universal Blueprint's steps can eliminate misbehavior and reduce the need for stronger responses.**

TYPES OF PROBLEMS

In this section, we learn how to identify each of the six types of problems and apply the universal response formula to each. The sample situations reinforce the *general* steps and offer a few examples of useful tools. We do *not* learn exactly what to say and do at each step with each example, nor are *all* the possible responses listed. Our purpose is to learn how the Universal Blueprint works, in general.

In *The Parent's Toolshop,* there are no standard responses to particular *behaviors.* The appropriate response depends on the *type* of problem or the *reason* the child is behaving that way. For example, children might not do chores for several reasons—they don't think the chore is important, don't know how to do the chore, feel overwhelmed, want help, or are exercising their power by refusing to do the chore. Each of these reasons could be the "core of the onion." To respond most effectively, we must identify and resolve the correct *cause* of the behavior we are facing (the type of problem) in *that* particular situation.

Although parents might seem to face an infinite number of possible problems, each individual problem will fit into one of six categories. Throughout our *Parent's Toolshop* tour, we use the following symbols to represent these six general problem types.

Symbol	Type of problem	Description
NO	No problem	There is no problem or a problem could develop.
C	Child problem	The child has a problem that doesn't involve/affect the parent.
P	Parent problem	The parent has a problem that does not involve misbehavior.
PU	Parent problem, Unintentional misbehavior	The parent has a problem with misbehavior that results from the child's lack of maturity, skills, or knowledge.
PO	Parent problem, "On purpose" misbehavior	The parent has a problem with misbehavior that seems intentional, to serve a purpose.

C/P
 	
C/PU
C/PO
	part **C**hild problem and part **P**arent problem	The problem involves/affects *both* child and parent. C/P problems do *not* involve misbehavior. If misbehavior is involved, add the appropriate symbol to the end.
		    The **P**arent problem involves **U**nintentional misbehavior.
		    The **P**arent problem involves **O**n purpose misbehavior.

★ **We can use the Universal Blueprint and problem identification process in *any* relationship.** Simply replace *parent* with *I* and *child* with *other person:*

NO = Things are going well and I want to build a better relationship.

C = The other person has a problem.

P = I have a problem.

PU = I have a problem with the other person's behavior, but the other person doesn't realize how the behavior affects me or it's just the way he or she is.

PO = I have a problem with the other person's behavior, and the person seems to be acting this way on purpose. I wonder why?

C/P = *We* have a problem.

THE UNIVERSAL RESPONSE FORMULA

There are five ways to remember the steps of the universal response formula:

    1. **The letter/number of the step.** For example, "Step B."

    2. **What you do; the PASRR formula.** For example, "**A**cknowledge feelings."

    3. **The tools you use.** For example, "Child Problem Toolbox."

    4. **A visual reminder of the house diagram.** For example, "Open the door."

    5. **A quick reminder.** For example, "Listen, before you talk."

The two-page table on pages 78 and 79 lists the different reminders for each step. Choose the one that is easiest for you to remember. In this chapter, we'll list all of them to help you learn them. Throughout the remainder of the book, we will mostly use method #2, which we will call the "PASRR formula" (pronounced "passer").

PASRR Response Formula
(pronounced "passer")

Prevent the problem from starting or worsening.

Acknowledge the other person's feelings or perspective.

Set limits or express concerns.

Redirect misbehavior (PU or PO).

Reveal discipline or take action.

★ **At any step, we can use tools from previous steps.**

* There is actually one last step, *Maintain progress*, but we don't include it in the "PASRR" formula, since it isn't usually part of our verbal response. It simply reminds us to follow-up with the Maintenance Toolbox.

Using the PASRR formula may take only two or three sentences in all—and each part of the statement serves a specific purpose. Use your better judgment to decide if you need a quicker, firmer response or can give each step time to work.

Sometimes we move through the steps with each attempt to resolve a problem. Other times, we take the steps quickly, with each sentence (or half sentence).

When we flow through the steps using two to four sentences in all, it sounds something like the following example. The partial sentences in this example are just *one* choice of many that we might make when filling in the blanks of this formula. We might also use fewer or simpler words.

Step A: Prevent the problem with the **Prevention Toolbox.** Walk up the stairs. Think before you listen.
  "You can (one acceptable option) or (another acceptable option). You decide."

Step B: Acknowledge the other person's feelings or perspective with the **Child Problem Toolbox.** Open the door. Listen before you talk.
  "It (looks/sounds/seems) like you are feeling/wanting _____."

Step C: Parent Problem Toolbox. Address your part of the problem. Enter the house.

  C1: Set limits or express concerns with the **Keep Your Cool and Clear Communication Toolsets.** Open the windows. Talk before you act.
  "(Negative behavior) can (state the negative effect/rule/value)."

  C2: Redirect misbehavior with the **PU *or* PO Toolset.** Choose a bedroom. Redirect, before you react.
  "If you want to (what the child wants), you can (acceptable alternative) instead."

C3: <u>R</u>eveal discipline or take action with the **Discipline Toolset.** Move to the attic. Take action, without a reaction.

> *"If you choose to <u>(negative behavior)</u>, I'll know you've decided to <u>(reveal discipline)</u>."*

Step D: Maintain progress with the **Maintenance Toolbox.** Check the roof regularly. Follow-up.

> *"Since this affects the whole family, let's bring it up at our next family council and see if we can decide how to handle this situation in the future."*

At this point, you don't have to remember exactly what to say or do at each step, only *what* each step is. With each chapter, we reinforce and practice the Universal Blueprint's steps. Soon, you will flow through the process and hardly think about the steps.

To help you memorize the steps of identifying problem types and using the PASRR formula, review the two-page table on pages 78 and 79. *Start at the bottom* of the first page and read each row from left to right, crossing from the first page to the next page. It may be helpful to refer to these pages while you are reading this chapter.

IDENTIFYING PROBLEM TYPES

Identifying problem types involves a simple process of elimination. By asking three questions, we narrow down what specific type of problem we are dealing with. The type of problem determines the steps we take (or stop at) and the toolsets we use. As we learn to use the Universal Blueprint, remember the following four rules:

★ **Answer the three questions based on who is involved and the situation you are facing** *at that moment.* Your answers might vary from other parents' answers in a similar situation. Your child's abilities might be different from what they were last month or from another child's abilities. *Your* individual answers decide the course *you* want to take at *that* moment with *that* child. This is how we apply the Universal Blueprint to individual situations.

★ **Regardless of the type of problem, follow the PASRR response formula's steps** *in order.* The location of each toolset is specific, according to the order in which it is most effective. Decide whether and when to take each step by the type of problem it is or if the problem continues.

★ **Every response can begin at Step A, but may not have to go further, depending on the type of problem or response we get.** Once we know what type of problem we are dealing with, we know which toolsets to use and which step is our final "stop."

★ **At each step, we can use any toolset from previous steps.** Since the Prevention Toolbox is Step A, we can use it *anytime* in our response.

Now let's look at each problem type separately. We'll review how we answer the three problem-identification questions, which PASRR steps to take, and offer two examples of each type of problem.

Overview of Problem Type Identification ☆☆☆☆

When there is NO problem, <u>P</u>revent problems *from starting or worsening with the Prevention Toolbox (Step A).*

When there is a problem, look at the smaller issues and identify the problem type for each.

QUESTION #1: Is this a Child problem (C) or a Parent problem (P)? (Narrow it down.) Consider whether the problem involves any of the following "SHARP RV" parent issues.

Safety   **H**ealth   **A**ppropriateness   **R**ights   **P**roperty   **R**ules   **V**alues

"No" to each* SHARP RV *issue = Child problem. <u>A</u>cknowledge the child's feelings or perspective. (Stop at Step B: Child Problem Toolbox.)

"Yes" to any one* SHARP RV *issue = Parent problem. <u>S</u>et limits or express concerns. (If there is no misbehavior, stop at Step C1: Keep Your Cool, Clear Communication Toolsets).

If the Parent problem involves misbehavior, ask QUESTION #2: Is the misbehavior Unintentional (PU) or "On purpose" (PO)? (Narrow it down.) Consider the following questions:

1. Is this behavior the result of the child's **immaturity** or developmental stage?
2. Is this behavior part of the child's **personality** (it doesn't come naturally)?
3. Is this an **accident** or could a **medical** condition be influencing the child's self-control?
4. Does the child **lack the information** to know better?
★ 5. **Has the child** *not consistently shown* **that he or she has** *mastered* **the skills to behave properly in this situation?** (This one often covers the first four issues, which might explain *why* the child hasn't mastered the skill.)

"Yes" to any one* question = PU problem** (**P**arent problem, **U**nintentional misbehavior). **<u>R</u>edirect the misbehavior* using the PU Toolset (Step C2) *before* **<u>R</u>***evealing discipline* (Step C3).

"No" to all questions = PO problem (**P**arent problem, "**O**n purpose" misbehavior). Ask Question #3.

QUESTION #3: If the misbehavior is "On purpose" (PO), what is the purpose? (See Chapter 12.) **<u>R</u>***edirect the misbehavior* using the PO Toolset (Step C2) *before* **<u>R</u>***evealing discipline* (Step C3).

Combination types: Identify the problem type for each part of the combination problem. ***Address the Child problem first.***

C/P   =   Part **C**hild problem *and* part **P**arent problem involving no misbehavior.

C/PU   =   Part **C**hild problem *and* part **P**arent problem involving **U**nintentional misbehavior.

C/PO   =   Part **C**hild problem *and* part **P**arent problem involving "**O**n purpose" misbehavior.

Follow-up with the Maintenance Toolbox (Step D). For family decisions/problems, use the Family Council Toolset. For personal maintenance, use the Three C's: Consistency, handling Criticism, and maintaining Consistency.

NO = No Problem

WHAT'S HAPPENING?

Neither parent nor child is experiencing a problem. Nevertheless, there are tools we can use to prevent situations from developing into problems.

WHAT WE DO

Stay at Step A: Prevent problems (**Prevention Toolbox,** walk up the stairs, think before you listen.) Maintain a balanced approach, build self-esteem, promote cooperation, and foster independence.

★ **The Prevention Toolbox is useful *anytime,* whether there is a problem or not.**

EXAMPLES OF NO PROBLEMS

1. *A child wants to do something that is difficult.*

Step A: Prevent problems (Prevention Toolbox). Encourage the child's efforts (Self-Esteem Toolset). Offer helpful tips and allow the child to try, rather than taking over and doing the task for the child (Independence Toolset). These tools increase the child's skills and prevent discouragement.

2. *A child has had difficulty in the past making transitions from one activity to another. It will soon be time to leave a fun party.*

Step A: Prevent problems (Prevention Toolbox). Using the Cooperation Toolset, plan ahead by giving a five-minute notice to the child before leaving. If the child resists, the parent can offer choices about how to leave. **If the child *still* resists, it is no longer a "No problem."** It is either a PU or PO problem. The parent needs to figure out which type of problem it is to know what will be the most helpful response.

```
                    NO PROBLEMS




....................................................
: STEP A: PREVENTION TOOLBOX:  N O
:      Independence Toolset      :
:       Cooperation Toolset      :
:       Self-Esteem Toolset      :
:      The Universal Blueprint   :
:    Foundation-Building Toolset :
....................................................
```

When There Is a Problem, STOP and . . . THINK for 1-10 Seconds

During that time, begin asking yourself the three questions to identify what *type* of problem you are facing.

QUESTION #1: IS THIS A <u>C</u>HILD PROBLEM OR A <u>P</u>ARENT PROBLEM?

(Narrow it down.)

This question is not as easy to answer as we might think; it's easy to misidentify Child problems. Without guidelines, we might simply ask ourselves, "Who does it bother?" or "Who is it a problem *for*?" These questions might help us recognize *some* Child problems, but consider situations such as children not doing their homework. Is the child upset about not doing homework? Usually, it bothers the parent more. If we look beyond the surface of this onion, we find that the *reason* the child isn't doing homework. For example, the child might not understand the work, is overwhelmed, doesn't share the value of homework, or hasn't established good study habits. If parents conclude homework is a Parent problem, they might take over and children won't learn how to take responsibility for solving the problem on their own. If parents exert too much control, doing homework can turn into a power struggle. Since it is easy to confuse Child and Parent problems, consider the following issues.

Does the Problem (or any part of it) Involve Safety, Health, Appropriateness or Protection of Property *or* Violate Someone's Rights, Rules, or Values?

Remember these "parent problem areas" with "SHARP RV."

Safety   Health   Appropriateness   Rights   Property   Rules   Values

---

"No" to *each* **SHARP RV** issue = **A Child problem.**

"Yes" to *any one* **SHARP RV** issue = **A Parent problem.** (If there *is* misbehavior, move on to Question #2.)

Let's take a closer look at Child and Parent problems, before moving to Question #2.

"No" to *Each* SHARP RV Issue = A Child Problem

WHAT IS HAPPENING?

The child (or other person) has a problem that does not directly involve or affect the parent.

WHAT WE DO

Step A: Prevent problems (Prevention Toolbox). Offer encouragement, teach skills, and prevent sibling and peer conflicts.

Step B: Acknowledge feelings (**Child Problem Toolbox,** open the door, listen before you talk.) Offer supportive guidance, without taking over. **Use the F-A-X Listening Toolset** to better understand children's thoughts and feelings about the problem. **Use the Problem-Solving Toolset** to mediate sibling/peer conflicts and guide children through the process of resolving problems to the degree they are able.

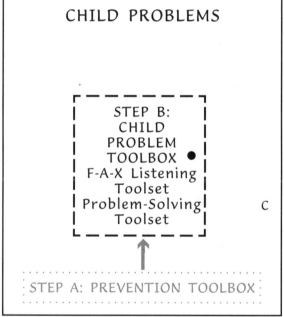

★ **In Child problems, we work *exclusively* from the Child Problem and Prevention Toolboxes.** Alternate between these two steps (toolboxes) as necessary.

★ **If the situation is a Child problem, do not take over or solve it *for* the child.** This deprives children of important learning experiences. When people get angry about our attempts to help, it is a clue that we might be trying to solve a problem that belongs to someone else. We can still care and be involved, by using the Child Problem Toolbox to offer support and guidance as others resolve their *own* problems.

The most commonly misdiagnosed Child problems are school, sibling, and peer issues. When problems involve these issues, keep the ball in the children's court and *guide* them through the problem-solving process.

EXAMPLES OF CHILD PROBLEMS

1. *Two children are having a disagreement. They are not being disrespectful or physically fighting.* This problem is between the children. They need to learn how to resolve such conflicts.

Step A: Prevent problems (Prevention Toolbox). Encourage the children, expressing faith in their ability to work out the problem. Use the Independence Toolset to teach conflict-resolution skills.

Step B: Acknowledge feelings (Child Problem Toolbox). Use the F-A-X Listening Toolset to empathize with the children's feelings and thoughts about the situation. Do not give advice. Instead, use the Problem-Solving Toolset in the Child Problem Toolbox to help them generate ideas for resolving the conflict. If their ideas are inappropriate, ask them to consider the effect of that approach. This is how parents can raise their concerns without criticizing ideas or taking over.

2. *A child feels left out at school.* It's difficult to see children feeling hurt or being treated unfairly. It's natural to want to rescue or protect them. If we solve the problem, children might feel incapable of solving the problem. They might also have information we don't have, which would make our solution less effective. Children need to learn how to handle such situations on their own.

Step A: Prevent problems (Prevention Toolbox). Use the Self-Esteem Toolset to point out the child's positive qualities. Use the Independence Toolset to teach skills for making friends or dealing with rejection.

Step B: Acknowledge feelings (Child Problem Toolbox). Use the F-A-X Listening Toolset to recognize the child's feelings of rejection. Then use the Problem-Solving Toolset to explore alternatives for how the child can resolve the problem.

"Yes" to *Any One* SHARP RV Issue = <u>P</u>arent Problem

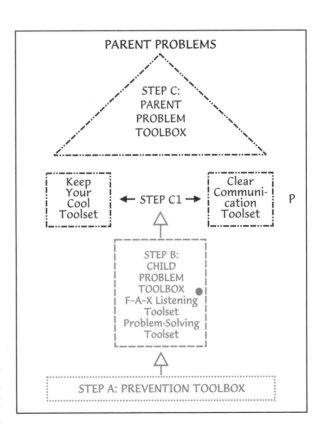

WHAT IS HAPPENING?

The parent has a problem or concern that does not bother the child.

WHAT WE DO

Step A: Prevent problems (Prevention Toolbox). Make requests in positive words and offer choices within limits (Cooperation Toolset). Teach children the skills they need to comply with the request (Independence Toolset). Express faith in their ability to figure out a solution, based on the information and skills they've learned (Self-Esteem Toolset).

Step B: Acknowledge feelings (Child Problem Toolbox). Often, just acknowledging children's feelings reduces their defensiveness and they cooperate. Other times, we need to bring the problem to their attention. Here, we recognize the children's feelings in the first part of our sentence and finish the sentence with tools from the next step.

Step C1: Set limits and express concerns (**Parent Problem Toolbox: Keep Your Cool and Clear Communication Toolsets,** open the windows, set limits and express concerns, talk before you act.) Stop, take a deep breath (keep your cool), and respond assertively. Describe the problem, briefly and respectfully.

★ **If we have already taken the first two steps (A and B) in the past and the same situation occurs,** we can jump right to Step C1 and offer a quick one-word reminder. This is a time when skipping steps is appropriate, because the parent already took the other steps first, in the past.

★ **If *no* problem behavior is involved (P), stop at this step.** Alternate between the steps, choosing the appropriate tools to work through differences of opinions, values, or needs until you reach an agreement.

★ **Just because a situation is a Parent problem does *not* mean the parent is always responsible for *resolving* the problem.** Consider the example of a child not doing a chore. Children don't care if their chore isn't done. Yes, they may care that they won't get to play if it's not done, but this is how they feel about one possible *effect* of the problem, not the problem itself. This is a Parent problem, because it violates a family rule, value, or the parent's right. The parent is responsible for bringing the problem to the child's attention, but the child is responsible for doing the chore.

EXAMPLES OF PARENT PROBLEMS

1. *The children are playing loudly and it's distracting you from your work.* The noise violates the parent's right to work in a peaceful setting. The children are not misbehaving, just playing loudly. Therefore, it is strictly a Parent problem.

Step A: Prevent problems (Prevention Toolbox). The Cooperation Toolset suggests telling children what *to* do, instead of what *not* to do. Parents can offer choices within limits, "You can play quietly inside or play loudly outside—you decide." Another option is to combine the next two steps into one sentence:

Step B: Acknowledge feelings (Child Problem Toolbox). "I can tell you are having lots of fun . . ." (Listening Toolset)

Step C1: Set limits or express concerns (**Clear Communication Toolset**). ". . . but I can't concentrate on my work when there is so much noise." If it happens again, you can say one word, "Quiet!" (Any further disruptions suggest problem behavior, which is a PU or PO problem. Since you've already taken these first few steps, go right to Step C2, using the PU *or* PO Toolset.)

2. *Your son's soccer practice was rescheduled to the same time as your daughter's gymnastics lesson.* Trying to drive both children violates the parent's *right* to manageable schedule. Being in two places at once is simply impossible. The parent and children have a conflict of needs. The child has not misbehaved in any way, so this is strictly a Parent problem. Our response could have three sentences that quickly move through the steps.

Step A: Prevent problems (Prevention Toolbox). "I've seen a lot of improvement in your coordination since you started gymnastics . . ." (Self-Esteem Toolset)

Step B: Acknowledge feelings (Child Problem Toolbox). ". . . and can tell how much you enjoy going."

Step C1: Set limits or express concerns (**Clear Communication Toolset**). "Your brother's soccer practice was moved to the same day and time as your gymnastics lessons. I can't be in two places at once, so we need to look at some ways you both can do what is important to you." At this point, the parent and children can brainstorm possible solutions. The first sentence (Steps A and B) prevents the child from jumping to conclusions, such as "You're going to make me quit gymnastics." If there is no risk of this, the parent could say the last sentence (Step C1) first and, at some point, say the other statements. Remember, at any step, you can use the toolsets from previous steps.

If the P̲arent Problem Involves Misbehavior, Ask QUESTION #2: Is the Misbehavior U̲nintentional or "O̲n Purpose"?

(Narrow it down.)

To tell the difference between PU and PO behavior, consider the following questions:

1. Is this behavior the result of the child's **immaturity** or developmental stage?
2. Is this behavior part of the child's **personality** (it doesn't come naturally)?
3. Is this an **accident** or is a **medical condition** influencing the child's self-control? (Illness, mental retardation, ADHD, autism, food allergies, etc.)
4. Does the child **lack information** to know better?
★ 5. **Has the child *not consistently shown* that he or she has *mastered* the skills to behave properly in this situation?** (This one often covers the first four issues, which might explain why the child hasn't mastered the skill.)

"Yes" to *any one* question = PU problem (**P**arent problem, **U**nintentional misbehavior).

"No" to *all* questions   = PO problem (**P**arent problem, "**O**n purpose" misbehavior).

★ **When in doubt, assume the behavior is PU.** The child's reaction to your response will confirm whether their behavior is unintentional (PU) or on purpose (PO). Give information or teach skills. If the child masters the skill and *still* repeats the misbehavior, you *know* it's PO behavior.

★ **Remember the difference between PU and PO with these simple analogies.** PU reminds us of something stinky, like a dirty diaper. Situations, such as toilet training accidents, are frustrating but a normal part of development. They are problems that may involve safety or health (**P**arent issues), but the problem behavior is **U**nintentional.

> *A Personal Story. I took Amber and her friend, Emmy, both two, to an indoor playground with some friends and their children. It was hard to keep an eye on both of them every second. Amber was still in diapers, so I didn't remember to tell Emmy to go to the bathroom, as her mother did. A man walked up and asked me if that little girl was mine, as he pointed to Emmy. Emmy was squatting on the floor, with her pants pulled down to her ankles and a pile beneath her! I was tempted to say I'd never seen this child before, but said, "Yes, she's with me today. Thank you." I took Emmy to the bathroom and cleaned her up while another mother cleaned up the mess. (I've got great friends, don't I?) I felt so bad for Emmy. She didn't know to ask to go to the bathroom and I had not reminded her. I had a problem (P), but her behavior was Unintentional.*

PO problems involve misbehavior (a **P**arent problem) that seems to be **O**n purpose. When it seems a child is misbehaving on purpose, we usually feel "PO'd"—you know, p - - - ed off! (You did fill those blanks with p-e-e-v-e-d off, right? I want this to stay G-rated!)

> *A Parent's Story. My son, age four, is fully potty trained and can hold it when he needs to. But if he is mad at me, he does something to get my attention, gives me a defiant look, and then pees on the floor, furniture, bed, or whatever is close! (Clearly, this Parent problem involves behavior that is "On purpose," to get revenge—and the mother feels quite PO'd!)*

"Yes" to _Any One_ Question = PU (Parent Problem, Unintentional Misbehavior)

WHAT'S HAPPENING?

The parent has a problem (P) that involves "unintentional" misbehavior (U). In PU problems, the reason we say "yes" to one of the SHARP RV issues (Question #1) is usually _because_ the child doesn't know any better or hasn't developed appropriate behavior skills (Question #2). For example, "I'm worried about my child climbing the jungle gym (safety issue) _because_ she hasn't had much experience and isn't very coordinated (child has _not_ shown mastery of the skills)." We learn more about the five issues in identifying PU behavior (developmental stages, etc.) in Chapter 11, "PU Toolset."

★ **Even if you've "told them a million times," it does not mean children _know_ better.** "Knowing better" means children _fully_ understand the information. Until children _master_ a skill, PU behavior can still occur.

★ **"Unintentional" is _not_ an excuse.** Medical conditions, such as Attention Deficit Hyperactivity Disorder (ADHD) or learning disabilities, can influence a child's self-control and behavior. These conditions, however, should not become a crutch or excuse for a child's behavior, "He has ADHD, so don't expect him to _____." Identifying these behaviors as PU diagnoses the _cause_ of the behavior and what skills we need to teach.

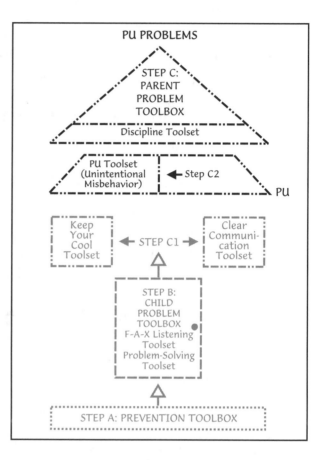

★ **PU behavior can turn into PO behavior _if_ we react to it or respond unhelpfully.** The classic example is a child who repeats a cuss word, without knowing what it means. The first time this happens, it is PU behavior. If the parent gives a shocked, extreme reaction or laughs, the child might repeat the behavior later, to get a similar reaction. _Then,_ the behavior is PO, to serve a purpose.

WHAT WE DO

Step A: **P**revent problems (Prevention Toolbox). This step is _vital,_ because these tools can prevent _or_ respond to unintentional misbehavior. These tools can increase a child's confidence, engage cooperation, and teach appropriate behavior skills. Until these skills and behaviors become habits, parents often need to take additional steps.

Step B: **A**cknowledge feelings (Child Problem Toolbox). Notice the child's feelings, thoughts, or perspective about the situation. (Sometimes this can be the first half of your first sentence, for example "You seem (feeling) . . .")

Step C1: **S**et limits or express concerns (**Clear Communication Toolset**). Be clear and respectful. (This can be the second half of the sentence, ". . . but (the negative behavior) can (give information.")

***Step C2: Redirect misbehavior* (PU Toolset).** (Choose the PU bedroom, redirect problem behavior before you react.) These tools help us correctly identify PU problems and redirect the behavior until children master the necessary skills. For example, a possible second sentence can be, "If you want (or feel) _____, you can (describe appropriate behavior) instead."

★ **If the behavior continues or action is necessary, use the PU Toolset *before* moving to the Discipline Toolset.** (Step C3, **R**eveal discipline, move to the attic, take action without a reaction.) The PU Toolset teaches children skills and the Discipline Toolset helps children *learn from* their mistakes. Together, they can eliminate similar PU behavior in the future. Our last sentence could be, "Until I see you can (describe positive behavior), I'll know you need to (reveal discipline)."

EXAMPLES OF PU PROBLEMS

1. *A high-spirited child.* Children are born with certain personality traits. Sometimes, skills that might come easily to many children (such as the ability to adjust to change or handle noise and activity) are more difficult for other children to learn—it just doesn't come naturally to them. Their behavior is often inappropriate (P), but unintentional (U). These children need to build on the positive strengths of their personality, while learning skills to balance these difficulties.

Step A: *Prevent problems* (Prevention Toolbox). Look at your beliefs using the skills in the Foundation-Building Toolset. Recognize that there is nothing wrong with spirited children and that their difficult behavior is not an intentional attempt to irritate others.

Step B: *Acknowledge feelings* (Child Problem Toolbox). Recognize the child's feelings (frustration, hunger, etc.).

Step C1: *Set limits or express concerns* **(Clear Communication Toolset).** State rules and realistic expectations in simple, positive words.

***Step C2: Redirect PU misbehavior* (PU Toolset).** Model and teach appropriate behavior. Until children master the skills, use distraction or environmental engineering. (These tools are in Chapter 11, "PU Toolset.")

***Step C3: Reveal discipline* (Discipline Toolset).** When necessary, discipline can help children make amends, learn self-control or other important lessons from the effects of their behavior choices.

2. *A teenager who is individuating.* A parent might think that the *way* the teen is individuating involves a SHARP RV issue (P), such as driving too fast or wanting to stay out past curfew. It is normal, however, for teens to want more freedom (U). "Individuation" is the process every teen goes through on the way to adulthood. It is the process of becoming an individual: deciding who I am, who I want to be, and what I believe about the world and myself. Teenage individuation is as normal and age-appropriate as an infant learning to walk or a toddler wanting to touch everything. Individuation is different from rebellion, which is a reaction to control. ***Every teen individuates, but not every teen rebels.*** If teens do not have positive, appropriate ways to express their individuality and have some control in their lives, they may choose more negative, defiant ways to *prove* their parents can't control them (PO). This is one example of how PU behavior can turn into PO behavior, depending on the parent's reaction. (The Independence and PU Toolsets explain individuation in more detail.)

Step A: *Prevent problems* (Prevention Toolbox). Educate yourself about adolescent development, so your beliefs and expectations are realistic and you don't take their behavior personally. Make requests using positive words that offer choices within reasonable limits (Cooperation Toolset).

Step B: *Acknowledge feelings* (Child Problem Toolbox). The F-A-X Listening Toolset opens the door to communication (and keeps it open). Empathize with the teen's perspective, frustrations, and desire to be an independent individual. Deal with the feelings as soon as possible. If parents only address *their* concerns (moving directly to Step C1), teens will think the parents are trying to control them, which *increases* their resentment and invites rebellion.

Step C1: Set limits or express concerns (Clear Communication Toolset). Voice concerns about any SHARP RV issues. Use parent/child problem solving to help teens see the long-term effects of their behavior choices.

***Step C2: Redirect PU misbehavior* (PU Toolset).** Generate ideas for more acceptable ways to assert their independence. These steps often result in solutions and agreements that help teens feel more independent, without violating any SHARP RV issues.

***Step C3: Reveal discipline* (Discipline Toolset).** Make agreements that reveal the effect of the teen (or parent) breaking the agreement. When teens have options for appropriate behavior, they can make better behavior choices in the future-and know what to expect if they don't.

"No" to *Any One* Question = PO (Parent Problem, "On Purpose" Misbehavior)

WHAT'S HAPPENING?

The **P**arent has a problem *and* the child *has* consistently shown he or she has mastered the skills to behave properly but seems to be misbehaving **O**n purpose.

WHAT TO DO

Step A: Prevent problems (Prevention Toolbox). This step is *vital,* because these tools can prevent *or* respond to intentional misbehavior. The Self-Esteem Toolset can prevent attention-seeking behavior and the Cooperation Toolset is the best toolset for preventing power struggles. The Independence Toolset helps children learn skills, so they don't get so discouraged they give up. (Remember, the Prevention Toolbox is useful *anytime,* even when responding to problems.)

Step B: Acknowledge feelings (Child Problem Toolbox). This step reveals the *real* issue beneath the misbehavior. Try to understand the child's feelings, wishes, and viewpoint. (This does not mean we *agree* with the child.) F-A-X-

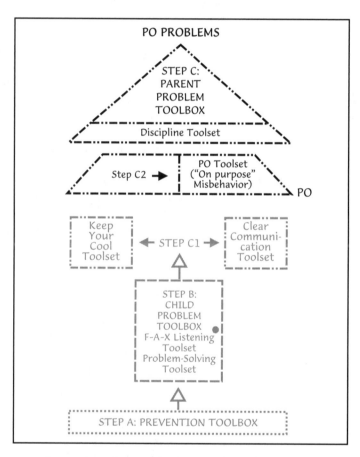

Listening can prevent revenge cycles *or* respond to revengeful behavior by building trust.

Step C1: Set limits or express concerns (Clear Communication Toolset). These tools help parents avoid gut reactions, which usually escalate the situation or give PO misbehavior a payoff.

(You'll learn what to do instead, when we get to the PO Toolset.) Our goal is not to *control* children, but to maintain our *self*-control, which increases the effectiveness of our response.

***Step C2: Redirect PU misbehavior* (PO Toolset,** PO bedroom, redirect problem behavior before you react.) Use the PO Toolset to identify the purpose of the behavior (Question #3), avoid escalating the problem or giving a payoff, and show children how to meet the purpose with positive behavior. (You'll learn the specifics of identify the purpose of PO behavior in Chapter 12.) If the problem behavior continues or action is necessary, move to the next step.

★ **In a PO problem, use the PO Toolset (Step C2)** *before* **moving to the Discipline Toolset (Step C3:** move to the attic, reveal discipline, take action without a reaction.) Skipping this step can turn the discipline into punishment and escalate the problem. Once PO cycles are broken, discipline can help children learn from their mistakes, take responsibility for their actions, and make amends for the effects of their decisions—which leads to *self*-discipline.

★ **Some parents ask, "Why do I need to take all these steps when yelling or threats get children moving?"** There are two answers to this question.

1. When most parents are "PO'd," they nag, remind, or threaten two to three times before following through with action. If we are going to say two to three sentences, we want to make each part of each comment to be as effective as possible and account for the real reasons the problem developed. This is how our responses can prevent future PO behavior.

2. Quick fixes might get children to comply, but often have negative long-term effects. Competent responses often solve the problem in a similarly short time, but have positive long-term effects.

EXAMPLES OF PO PROBLEMS

1. *A child makes up "lame" excuses at bedtime to delay the inevitable "goodnight."* Who cares that the child goes to bed or sleep? The **P**arent. Since the excuses are "lame," it implies the child doesn't have a real problem and is making excuses **O**n purpose.

Step A: ***P****revent problems* (Prevention Toolbox). Plan ahead and have pleasant, consistent bedtime routines. Offer choices within limits—the limit is how much time you are willing to spend at bedtime and the choice is how the child chooses to spend that time. More choices are, "You don't have to go right to sleep. You can (list quiet activities), but need to stay in bed and be quiet." Avoid threats or catering to the lame excuses, since this gives the behavior a payoff. Parents can also teach children skills (Independence Toolset), such as how to relax when they aren't tired and how to put themselves to sleep.

Step B: ***A****cknowledge feelings* (Child Problem Toolbox). Show that you understand the child isn't tired or doesn't want to go to sleep. (This might be the first half sentence.)

Step C1: ***S****et limits or express concerns* (Clear Communication Toolset). Express your concerns about the child's health and assert your right to have some quiet time. (This could be the second half of the sentence.) If the child balks or expresses negative emotions, it is now a C/P problem. Go back to the Child Problem Toolbox to acknowledge the child's feelings, then move back to the Parent Toolbox to restate your expectations.

Step C2: ***R****edirect PO misbehavior* **(PO Toolset).** If the child refuses to stay in bed, the lack of cooperation is intentional, because the previous three steps have covered the possibility that it is PU. Use the PO Toolset to identify whether the purpose of the child's behavior is power or attention. If it's power, shift the focus of the choices, maybe to *how* or *when* to go to bed. If children try to keep the parent involved by procrastinating, remind them of the positive activities the parent already did during the bedtime routine. Ignore further requests.

Step C3: ***R****eveal discipline* **(Discipline Toolset).** If necessary, reveal the natural effect of not getting enough sleep; children will be tired the next day. Also let children know that if they choose to delay bedtime tonight, they are choosing to go to bed that much earlier the next night. When following through the next night, remind them that they will have another chance tomorrow night, to *show* they can go to bed at the regular time and in a cooperative way. Remember, if we discipline without breaking the negative behavior cycle, our discipline will be less effective and might make the situation escalate into revenge, more intense power struggles, or attention-seeking behavior.

2. *A child eats food while playing on the family computer, knowing this violates a family rule.* The last half of the sentence confirms that this is a PO problem.

*Step A: **P**revent problems* (Prevention Toolbox). Use the Cooperation Toolset to offer choices within limits or state rules in positive words, such as "You can play on the computer or take a break to eat. You decide."

*Step B: **A**cknowledge feelings* (Child Problem Toolbox). In the first part of your next sentence, recognize that your child wants to keep playing on the computer. Move to the next step to finish the sentence.

*Step C1: **S**et limits or express concerns* (Clear Communication Toolset). Explain the negative effect of eating near the computer; it can ruin the electronic components. Then make your expectations clear. Post a sign as a reminder for *everyone* who uses the computer. If the child still eats at the computer after understanding the rules, move to the next step.

*Step C2: **R**edirect PO misbehavior* **(PO Toolset, "On purpose" misbehavior).** These tools help you identify the purpose of the child's misbehavior as power. Threats or punishments invite testing, sneaking, or rebellion. Offer choices within limits in a firm, but friendly, tone of voice. "People who want to use the computer need to keep food away from it." Make sure any power struggles are diffused before moving to the next step.

*Step C3: **R**eveal discipline* **(Discipline Toolset).** If they choose to break the rule, they are choosing to *give up* their computer privileges. If this is revealed ahead of time and the parent follows through, it is clear that the child *chose* this outcome.

Combination Problems = C/P (Part **C**hild Problem, Part **P**arent Problem)

WHAT'S HAPPENING?

Problems can get complicated when more than one type of problem occurs at the same time. When this happens, **look at the smaller issues and identify the problem type for each part of the bigger problem.** Often, both people have a problem. It could be more than one problem or different perspectives of the same problem. Part of the problem involves/affects the child (**C** problem) and part of the problem bothers the parent (one of the three types of **P**arent problems).

The type of parent problem decides the final diagnosis:

C/P   Part **C**hild problem *and* part **P**arent problem with no misbehavior, just a difference of opinion or needs.

C/PU   Part **C**hild problem *and* part **P**arent problem with Unintentional misbehavior.

C/PO   Part **C**hild problem *and* part **P**arent problem with "On purpose" misbehavior.

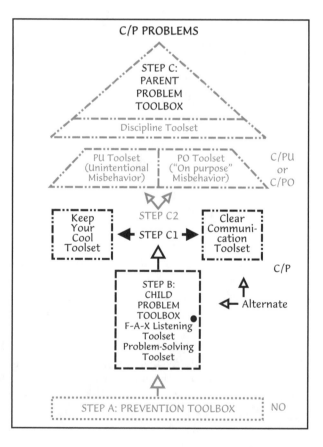

WHAT WE DO

*Step A: **P**revent problems* (Prevention Toolbox). These tools provide encouragement, teach skills, and promote teamwork. We can use these tools any time in our response.

***Step B: Acknowledge feelings* (Child Problem Toolbox).** Work exclusively from this and the Prevention Toolbox when addressing the Child problem.

★ **In a C/P problem, always address the Child problem *first*,** unless the Parent problem poses real or immediate danger. When parents voice *their* concerns first, children often conclude that the parents don't understand or care about the children's feelings or opinions. They usually shut down or defend themselves. When we acknowledge children's feelings first, they are more likely to listen when we express *our* concerns. When we use the Child Problem Toolbox, we might find that our children already understand our concerns, or we may only have to use one or two sentences to express our values or concerns. Applying the tools in this order helps keep the lines of communication open. Remember the quick reminder, "listen before you talk!"

The house reminder is also a good way to remember this rule. The best way to come into a house is through the front door. This reminds us that the door, the Child Problem Toolbox, is the first step of *every* response. When parents state their part of the problem first, it's like they are climbing into the house through the window. If parents use discipline as a *first* response, the parents have climbed a ladder into the attic! The door, not the windows or attic, is the best way to enter a house.

***Step C1: Set limits or express concerns* (Clear Communication Toolset).** Use these tools to address *only* the parent's "SHARP RV" concerns, respectfully and assertively. If it is a C/P with no problem behavior, alternate between the F-A-X Listening and Communication Toolsets (Steps B and C1) to reach a mutual agreement.

*Step C2: **R**edirect misbehavior* (PU or PO Toolset). If misbehavior is involved, choose the toolset for that type of behavior. Teach skills (if PU) or break misbehavior cycles (if PO), to redirect the behavior.

*Step C3: **R**eveal discipline* (Discipline Toolset). If necessary, build discipline into the agreements you make. By revealing discipline in this way, children understand they must keep agreements and *they* are responsible for part of the solution.

★ **Select tools from the Child or Parent Problem Toolbox according to how much of the problem is the child's and how much is the parent's.**

Mostly a **C**hild problem.
Mostly use the Child Problem Toolbox
Only use the Parent Problem Toolbox
for the **P**arent part of the problem.

Mostly a **P**arent problem.
Still start with the Child Problem Toolbox,
but mostly use the Parent Problem Toolbox.
Go back to the Child Problem Toolbox
for the **C**hild part of the problem (feelings).

EXAMPLES OF C/P PROBLEMS

1. *A child wants to quit music lessons.* Children need to be involved in making decisions about their extracurricular activities; they are Child problems. If this problem didn't involve quitting a commitment (a Parent problem that violates *rules* and *values*), it might be a 100% Child problem. Thus, the smaller part of the problem (not to be confused with its importance) is the Parent part.

*Step A: **P**revent problems* (Prevention Toolbox). Before children make the commitment to take music lessons, parents can confirm that children are agreeing to finish the series.

Step B: *Acknowledge feelings* (Child Problem Toolbox).** Listen to the child's reasons for wanting to quit. Perhaps the child is reacting to another problem, such as feeling overwhelmed, discouraged, or embarrassed. F-A-X Listening helps children feel comfortable revealing these underlying issues.

Step C1: *Set limits or express concerns* (Clear Communication Toolset).** Use these tools *only* to address the value or rule of fulfilling commitments. In this situation, parents would probably need to go no further than Step C1: Clear Communication Toolset and use parent/child problem solving to resolve the problem.

Step B: Go back to the Child Problem Toolbox to help children generate ideas for fulfilling the current commitment and consider the effects of quitting. By asking helpful questions, children can realize the consequences *on their own,* without parental lectures. Since the major part of the problem is a Child problem, the final decision must be the child's, as long as he or she considers commitments already made.

2. *A young girl bites another girl when she doesn't get what she wants.* The biter's part of the problem (C) is her frustration about not getting what she wants. Biting, which involves safety and health issues, is the parent's part of the problem. Since the girl is young, she probably doesn't have the skills to express herself appropriately (PU). With dangerous behavior, the parent needs to *act* immediately, but still follow the PASRR steps for the *verbal* statements made *during* the action.

Step B: *Acknowledge feelings* (Child Problem Toolbox).** While physically separating the children, the parent acknowledges the biter's angry feelings. "I can see you are *really* angry."

Step C1: *Set limits or express concerns* (Clear Communication Toolset).** State limits firmly, yet respectfully. "Biting hurts!"

Then: Go back to the Child Problem Toolbox and tend to the victim. Recognize her feelings. "Biting hurts your arm and your feelings, huh?" Offer a hug, stroke, or pat on the back.

*Step C2: **R**edirect misbehavior* (PU or PO Toolset). *Focus again on the biter.* If she doesn't already know acceptable anger management skills (PU), teach them. If the child knows not to bite and has consistently shown that she can control her anger, use the PO Toolset instead. Show the child how to get attention, power, or justice through positive behavior. Only give the biter enough attention to stop the biting, but not so much that it rewards the behavior.

Then: Shift back to the Child Problem Toolbox and tend to the victim. Use problem solving to discuss options for what she can do in the future if someone tries to bite her. (The bully/victim section of the Problem-Solving Toolset offers suggestions.)

*Step C3: **R**eveal discipline* (Discipline Toolset). Let the biter know that if she wants to play with other children, she must show she can treat other children respectfully. The child has shown she's not ready to do this, so she needs to take a break from playing until she has calmed down. Before the child returns to play, use the Prevention Toolbox to get agreements and review the child's options in future conflicts. Use the Discipline Toolset to reveal what will happen if biting occurs again. The child will give up play privileges for a longer, but still reasonable, period of time. The child can practice the skills the parent just taught while the lesson is fresh in her mind.

★ **Whenever possible, resolve the issues closer to the "core of the onion" first.** (Unless it would be dangerous to do so.) Complicated problems have several problems occurring at once, with some closer to the core of the onion than others. Identify each part of the bigger problem. If you know what the "real issue" is, address it first. If not, follow the PASRR response formula. At "Step B: Child Problem Toolbox," the F-A-X Listening Toolset can help reveal the deeper issues.

> *A Parenting Class Discussion. A parent shared a rather complicated scenario in class. When her eight-year-old son came home from school, she reminded him that he had his first religious education class that night and would need to get his homework done before leaving. He threw his books down, saying "I want to play with Ryan! I'm not going to do this stupid homework and I'm not going to that stupid religion class." The mother reacted to the son's behavior and things deteriorated quickly. She knew she didn't handle it well, but wasn't sure what she could have done instead. The class helped her see that there were several problems happening at once. I drew the following onion diagram and we helped her come up with a general plan that might have resolved each part of the bigger problem.*

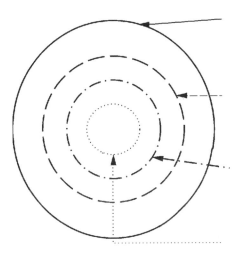

Presenting Problem: Son threw down books, refused to do homework and complained he couldn't play. *Type of Problem:* C/PO, the child complained, which means he has a problem. Throwing books is intentional misbehavior, a PO problem. *Important Question:* Why is he so upset? The answer determines the response.

Problem: Child **thinks** he can't play. *Type of Problem:* PU, because he doesn't know for sure that he can't play, he is assuming this. *Response:* The parent first lets him know he can play, *if* he comes up with a plan to get his homework done before he needs to leave.

Problem: Child is overwhelmed by homework. *Type of Problem:* C, because homework is his responsibility and he has a problem with the amount. *Response:* The parent acknowledges his frustration and uses problem solving to guide him.

Real Issue: Child doesn't want to go to religion class. (The mother thought this was the core issue, more than the child feeling overwhelmed.) *Type of Problem:* C/P, because the child doesn't like something the parent values. *Response:* The parent listens to the child's reasons for disliking it, **briefly** states her values, and uses problem solving to arrive at a win/win solution.

Use the Maintenance Toolbox (Step D) for Family Decisions and Problems or to Follow-up.

WHAT IS HAPPENING?

There is no problem and we want to maintain progress. We also might need to make decisions or solve problems that involve or affect the entire family.

WHAT WE DO

Step D: Maintenance Toolbox. (Check the roof regularly, maintain progress, follow-up.) When we are in the No problem zone,

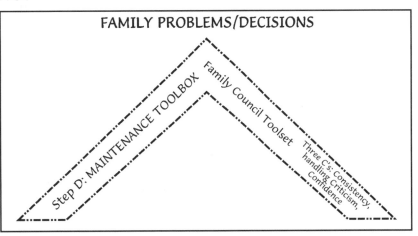

we can use the Family Council Toolset to build teamwork, discuss issues, teach healthy communication skills, and build the self-esteem of all family members. When decisions or problems affect the entire family, we can use the Family Council Toolset to involve family members in the problem-solving process. When family members agree on solutions, they are more likely to follow through with them. We can also use the Three C's (Consistency, Criticism, Confidence) to maintain our *personal* progress.

FINAL POINTS TO REMEMBER

★ **One type of behavior can be more than one type of problem, depending on how we answer the decision-making questions.** We decide which tools to choose at each step of our response by the type of problem it is at *that* time with *that* person. A good example is temper tantrums. People of any age can have "tantrums." Teens and adults might yell, stomp, or slam doors. Young children might throw themselves on the floor, kicking and screaming. The *type* of tantrum decides our response.

Frustration tantrums (C) usually occur after a build-up of emotions. We first want to offer comfort and recognize the difficulty of the situation (Child Problem Toolbox). Then, we can offer encouragement and teach skills, without taking over the problem (Prevention Toolbox).

Over-stimulation tantrums (PU) usually occur when young children are hungry, tired, or overwhelmed. They don't know how to handle these physical changes and "fall apart." **P**revent problems by establishing regular routines and teach children how to listen to their bodies (Step A). Parents need to repeat these lessons often and be patient, until children mature and master these skills. During over-stimulation tantrums, **A**cknowledge the child's feelings (Step B). Give children information to help them better understand what's happening (Step C1: **S**et limits or express concerns). **R**edirect the child by offering acceptable options that meet the child's immediate need (Step C2). Until children's skills improve, we can either remove the source of stimulation (which might be the parent) or gently but firmly remove children from the source (Step C3).

Attention tantrums (C/PO) usually occur when children use extreme behavior (PO) to get their parents to notice them (C). If attention tantrums have paid off in the past, children will escalate their behavior, until the parent *must* notice them. We can avoid some attention tantrums by spending regular quality time with children and involving them in activities that help them feel important and noticed (Step A: **P**revent the problem). When responding to attention tantrums, we recognize the child's desire to spend time with us (Step B: **A**cknowledge the feelings). We keep our cool and state our needs (Step C1: **S**et limits). Teach children positive ways to ask for attention and offer activities they *can* do, until we can give them our full attention (Step C2: **R**edirect misbehavior). If these responses don't stop the behavior, any further attention will only reward it. Selectively ignore the negative behavior long enough to make it clear that we do not pay attention to this type of behavior. If necessary, briefly remove the source of attention, which might be the parent (Step C3: **R**eveal discipline). After a brief period, suggest an activity that will result in positive attention (Step C2).

Power tantrums (C/PO) occur when children use resistance (PO) to get what they want (C). We can **P**revent many power tantrums by offering children choices about what they can have or do (Step A). When children resist, **A**cknowledge what *they* want (Step B), keep cool, and offer choices within the bottom line limits (Step C1: **S**et limits). If the tantrum continues, arguing will escalate the tantrum and giving in will give it a payoff. Instead, restate their choices, then disengage (Step C2: **R**edirect misbehavior).

If tantrums involve destructive behavior (P), we firmly but gently guide children to a place they can safely calm down (Step C3). *As we do this,* we acknowledge the child's feelings (Step B) and use controlled, calm communication (Step C1) to de-escalate the situation. Then we provide appropriate anger energy outlets (Steps C1 and C3).

★ **If you misjudge the problem or it shifts from one type to another, adjust your skills accordingly.**

> *A Personal Story. When I was a teen, I went on a camping trip with my church group. On the way home, our bus broke down and we were stranded for over two hours without a phone. It was important for me to get home on time because my mother needed help preparing for a dinner party. As I raced home, I planned my apology and how I could clean up and fulfill my duties.*
>
> *When I walked in the door, I hardly opened my mouth when my mother explained how worried and pressured she was because I was late. I started to explain what happened, but she was too overwhelmed to listen. Tired, dirty, and frustrated, I burst into tears and ran to my room.*
>
> *I'll never forget what she did next. She stopped what she was doing in the kitchen (she was already terribly behind and didn't really have the time), calmed down and came to my room. She apologized for not letting me explain what happened. I told her about the events that were totally out of my control, how I knew she was counting on me, and my plan for getting things done. She let me clean up and we worked together, finishing everything on time.*

Before I arrived, my mother thought this was a PO problem and prepared her response accordingly. When I started crying, she immediately shifted gears and dealt with my part of the problem. She realized, by the time I was done with my explanation, that it was really a C/PU problem (unintentional misbehavior). My comments addressed her concerns, so we moved on to a solution, instead of arguing.

TIPS FOR TOTS TO TEENS

Infants, Toddlers, and Preschoolers. Parents of young children find that most of the problems they encounter are PU problems, due to the child's immaturity and lack of skills. Parents need to be careful not to do too much for young children (taking over responsibility for a problem). Parents of infants and toddlers mostly use the Prevention Toolbox (Step A) and PU Toolset (Step C2). The Child Problem Toolbox (Step B) helps parents show empathy, teach children appropriate ways to express their feelings, and guide children to their own solutions. Use the following "rule of thumb" with young children.

> **Let toddlers help solve problems, moving gradually from small challenges to more difficult ones. When young children are close to solving a problem on their own, let them try and try again, offering skills, encouragement, and empathy at every step.**

"Tweens," elementary school-aged children and preteens. Parents of tweens experience a variety of problem situations and use every tool in this book. As children mature, they have more ideas, opinions, and values of their own. It is important that they have increasing opportunities to practice making decisions and resolving different types of problems. Use the following "rule of thumb" with tweens.

> **As children mature, we want to use tools that help them resolve their own problems and involve them in generating ideas for resolving problems that affect us.**

Teens. Parents of teens need to work primarily from the Child Problem Toolbox (Step B). When parents are concerned about SHARP RV issues, they need to use open-ended questions (Child Problem Toolbox) to help teens realize *on their own* the potential problems or parents' concerns. If potential mistakes are not serious or dangerous, let teens experience these trials and errors. These events, rather than a parent's moral lectures and rescuing, will prepare teens for adulthood. Use the Child Problem Toolbox to help teens process the lessons they learn from these mistakes. We can handle most of the problems our teens encounter as either C or C/P problems. Use the following "rule of thumb" with teens.

> **Let teens resolve problems independently whenever possible. Teach decision-making skills while offering supportive guidance. When problems affect the parent, involve teens in two-party problem solving, which will result in win/win solutions teens are willing to follow.**

NOBODY SAID PARENTING WAS EASY

Quick fixes often have negative long-term results. The Universal Blueprint offers a simple, reliable process for planning effective responses to problems that not only work in the short-run, but help us reach our long-term parenting goals. The hardest parts of using it are stopping to think, using the tools appropriately, and following through consistently until we see results.

In every problem situation, ask first, "What type of problem is this?" The logical thinking may be difficult now, but it *will* get easier the more you practice it.

> ***A Parent's Story to Her Class.*** *I had an interesting experience after learning the Universal Blueprint last week. My twelve-year-old daughter never confides anything to me. This week she came home, upset about a problem with her friends at school. I stopped to think about what type of problem it was. I could tell the problem was a Child problem and knew I didn't want to do what I always did—tell her what to do about the problem. I didn't know exactly what to do, so I just listened. I said, "umm-hmm" and "I can see why you'd be upset by that." To my surprise, she shared more with me than she ever had before! Although I haven't learned exactly what to do at each step, the Universal Blueprint worked anyway!*

At this point in the book, just practice stopping to think before you respond. Use the PASRR formula as best you can with your current level of knowledge and skills. Figure out what you are already doing that is effective and what doesn't work. As you learn to use the individual tools, use them to replace those you've discarded. By the time you've finished the book, you will have *many* tools at your disposal. Soon, you will move through the decision-making process in a split second.

SUMMARY SHEET
THE UNIVERSAL BLUEPRINT ☆☆☆☆

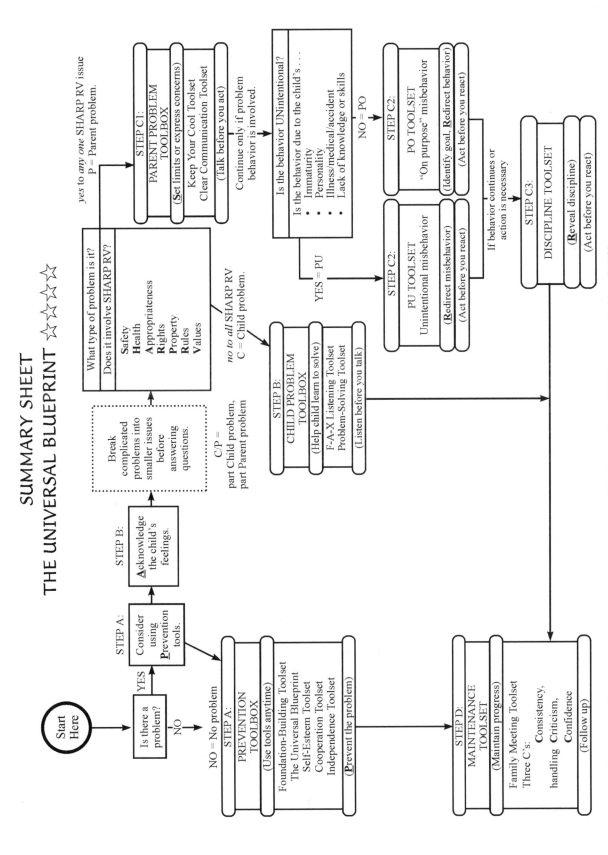

Start Here

Is there a problem?

YES

NO

NO = No problem

STEP A:
Consider using **P**revention tools.

STEP B:
Acknowledge the child's feelings.

Break complicated problems into smaller issues before answering questions.

What type of problem is it?

Does it involve SHARP RV?

Safety
Health
Appropriateness
Rights
Property
Rules
Values

yes to any one SHARP RV issue
P = Parent problem.

STEP C1:
PARENT PROBLEM TOOLBOX
(**Set** limits or express concerns)
Keep Your Cool Toolset
Clear Communication Toolset
(**T**alk before you act)

Continue only if problem behavior is involved.

Is the behavior UNintentional?

Is the behavior due to the child's . . . .
• Immaturity
• Personality
• Illness/medical/accident
• Lack of knowledge or skills

NO = PO

YES = PU

STEP C2:
PO TOOLSET
"On purpose" misbehavior
(Identify goal, **R**edirect behavior)
(**A**ct before you react)

STEP C2:
PU TOOLSET
Unintentional misbehavior
(**R**edirect misbehavior)
(**A**ct before you react)

If behavior continues or action is necessary

no to all SHARP RV
C = Child problem.

STEP B:
CHILD PROBLEM TOOLBOX
(Help child learn to solve)
F-A-X Listening Toolset
Problem-Solving Toolset
(**L**isten before you talk)

C/P =
part Child problem,
part Parent problem

STEP C3:
DISCIPLINE TOOLSET
(**R**eveal discipline)
(**A**ct before you react)

STEP A:
PREVENTION TOOLBOX
(Use tools anytime)
Foundation-Building Toolset
The Universal Blueprint
Self-Esteem Toolset
Cooperation Toolset
Independence Toolset
(**P**revent the problem)

STEP D:
MAINTENANCE TOOLSET
(Maintain progress)
Family Meeting Toolset
Three C's:
Consistency,
handling Criticism,
Confidence
(Follow up)

THE UNIVERSAL

(Read each row from left to right,

Identifying Problem Types

Problem Type[1]	Questions to Ask to Identify the Problem[2]	Toolbox/Toolset to Use	When to Use It
NO	If the problem or decision affects the entire family, use family councils to solve.	**MAINTENANCE TOOLBOX:** Family Council Toolset & Three C's	To prevent or resolve **problems that affect the entire family**
PU/PO	If action is necessary, discipline is indicated.	**PARENT PROBLEM TOOLBOX:** Discipline Toolset	**PU/PO problems.** Use last, after PU/PO Toolset or in combination with other toolsets
PU/PO	**Q2: Is the misbehavior PU or PO?** Has the child *not consistently shown mastery* of appropriate behavior? **Q3: If PO, what *is* the purpose?**	PU *or* PO Toolset	**PU or PO problems,** when misbehavior *is* present
P	Yes to *any one* SHARP RV issue *and no* misbehavior involved = P If misbehavior is involved = PU *or* PO. Go to Question #3.	Keep Your Cool & Clear Communication Toolsets	**Parent problems, with *no* misbehavior,** to express parents' concerns/feelings
C	**When there is a problem, identify the problem type: Q1: Is it a Child or Parent problem?**[3] A: No to *all* SHARP RV issues = C <u>S</u>afety, <u>H</u>ealth, <u>A</u>ppropriateness, <u>R</u>ights, <u>P</u>roperty, <u>R</u>ules, <u>V</u>alues	**CHILD PROBLEM TOOLBOX:** F-A-X Listening & Problem-Solving Toolsets	**Child problems,** when problems directly affect or involve the child ***and*** as the first step in response to all types of parent problems
NO	If there is no problem, we can still teach skills and develop positive qualities.	**PREVENTION TOOLBOX:** Independence Cooperation Self-Esteem Foundation-Building	**NO problems,** to prevent problems or ***anytime*** in response to a problem

1   C/P combination problems: Break problems into smaller parts and identify type for each part. Always address Child problem first. Select tools according to how much of the problem is C or P.

2   Answer the questions for *that* moment with *that* person in *that* situation.

BLUEPRINT

from the bottom, up.)

Universal Response Formula (PASRR)

Step[4]	What We Do	Quick Reminder	House Reminder	House Graphic
D	Maintain progress.	Follow-up.	Check the roof regularly for maintenance.	STEP D: / MAINTENANCE TOOLBOX / Family Council Toolset / Three C's: Consistency, Criticism, Confidence
C3	**Reveal discipline,** the outcome of poor behavior choice.	Take action, without a reaction.	Go to the attic.	STEP C: PARENT PROBLEM TOOLBOX / Discipline Toolset
C2	**Redirect** misbehavior.	Redirect, before you react.	Choose a bedroom.	PU Toolset (Unintentional misbehavior) / PO Toolset ("On purpose" misbehavior)
C1	**Set limits** or express our concerns and feelings.	Talk before you act.	Open the windows.	Keep Your Cool Toolset / Clear Communication Toolset
B	**Acknowledge feelings** or the other person's perspective.	Listen before you talk.	Open the door.	STEP B: CHILD PROBLEM TOOLBOX / Problem-Solving Toolset / F-A-X Listening Toolset
A	**Prevent problems** from starting or worsening.	Think before you listen.	Walk up the stairs.	STEP A: PREVENTION TOOLBOX / Independence Toolset / Cooperation Toolset / Self-Esteem Toolset / The Universal Blueprint / Foundation-Building Toolset

3   In adult relationships, C = the other person and P = me.
4   Follow the steps in order. At any step, you can use tools from previous steps.

PRACTICE EXERCISES

A. Sample Situations. Here are some common situations. For each, ask three questions:

- *What type of problem is this?* (Use the six symbols)

  NO = No problem

  C = Child problem

  P = Parent problem

  PU = Parent problem, Unintentional misbehavior

  PO = Parent problem, "On Purpose" misbehavior

  C/P = Part Child problem, part Parent problem. If it involves problem behavior, add the appropriate symbol: C/PU or C/PO.

- *Why?* (How did you answer Questions 1 & 2 to identify the type of problem?)

- *What toolbox or toolsets can you use?* Use the summary sheets in this chapter, the color poster, or the house diagram on the last page of the book to help you select the toolboxes and toolsets that are most appropriate. You don't have to include specific tools or responses, since we haven't learned them yet. After you give *your* answers, read the detailed answer key. It offers some specific suggestions and shows how some problems can be more than one type of problem, depending on the individual answers people might give to the three problem-identification questions (SHARP RV, PU or PO, etc.).

1. Your daughter, 2, is grabbing another child's toy, but won't to share her toy.

2. You are at a restaurant with your son, 4, waiting for your food. Your son is being loud and climbing around. It's starting to bother the people around you.

3. Your son, 7, delays getting ready in the morning.

4. Your daughter, 8, says she feels left out at school.

5. Surprise! An old childhood friend just called. He's in town for the day and would like to drop in and visit. The house is a bit cluttered and you have a half hour to clean it up. Your children, ages 4, 9, and 13 are outside playing.

6. Your daughter, 10, doesn't want to set the table because she's in the middle of a video game.

7. Your daughter, 13, brought home a note from her teacher, saying she is missing three homework assignments. This is unusual, since she normally completes her work on time.

8. Your son, 16, peels out of the driveway, squealing the car tires and speeding down the street.

B. Personal Application. List several problems you have experienced. Identify the problem type for each. Decide what toolbox or toolsets you could use next time. Notice if answering these questions offers insight to the *real* cause of the problem or a more effective way to respond.

C. Practice for Home. As problems arise at home or work, practice identifying the type of problem it is before responding. You can also observe others and how they handle problem situations. It's easier to stay objective when you aren't emotionally involved. When you see others experiencing a problem, decide what type of problem it is and which toolbox or toolsets *you* would use. Don't judge others or interfere. It is *their* problem and they are probably responding the best they can with the knowledge and skills they have. (The only exception is if you witness child abuse, which you should immediately report.) Practice the PASRR steps in your mind in case *you* ever have to respond to a similar situation.

Detailed Answers

Look at the poster, flow chart, or two-page table to see the logic in the following answers. As we go through the individual toolsets, you will learn about the tools that are mentioned in the answers.

1. Your daughter, 2, is grabbing another child's toy, but won't to share her toy.

Type of Problem: C/PU

Why?   Your daughter wants something she can't have and doesn't want to share or trade her toy (the Child part of the problem). Several SHARP RV issues are present (the Parent part of the problem): Grabbing is *inappropriate* behavior that violates the other child's *rights* and family *rules* or *values*. Since the child is immature, she doesn't understand or have the skills to share properly (PU). Although this behavior is considered "normal" for children this age, it should not be *excused.*

What toolbox or toolsets can you use?

Step A: **P**revent the problem by closely supervising and guiding young children. Allow them to have *some* toys they don't have to share. Let them put away these toys before playing with other children. Encourage young children to "parallel play," playing independently near each other. Teach sharing skills, such as asking permission to borrow toys, trading toys for ones she wants, and taking turns. Don't expect young children to make progress quickly. It takes time for their skills and maturity to develop. When property disputes arise, continue the PASRR process.

Step B: **A**cknowledge the child's desire to play with the other child's toy.

Step C1:   **S**et limits and express your rule or value about sharing, *while* taking the next step.

Step C2:   **R**edirect the behavior by teaching the skills and exact words she can say, "If you want that toy, you need to say 'May I please have . . .' or 'Can we trade toys?'"

Step C3:   **R**eveal the outcome of grabbing or not sharing toys: one or both children will be upset and have hurt feelings. If she can't share, she may need to play elsewhere.

2.   You are at a restaurant with your son, 4, waiting for your food. Your son is being loud and climbing around. It's starting to bother the people around you.

Type of Problem: C/PU or C/PO

Why?   Your son is bored and hungry (C). His inappropriate behavior is interfering with other people's rights (P). At four, children often fall apart when hungry or still lack good manners (PU). If he can usually handle being hungry and bored, but is trying to get attention, it is intentional misbehavior (PO).

What toolbox or toolsets can you use?

Step A: **P**revent or respond to this problem by using the Cooperation Toolset. Tell children what they *can* do while they wait, offering choices within limits. Use the Independence Toolset to teach manners, public behavior skills, and how to entertain oneself. Do activities *with* them, instead of reading a paper and ignoring them. If there aren't any activities, flip over the paper placemat and take turns drawing pictures, letters or words and guessing what they are. Play tic-tac-toe or connect the dots.

Step B: **A**cknowledge the child's boredom or hunger. Recognize the difficulty in keeping quiet and still for a long time. (You can take this step first, if you choose.)

Step C1:   If you do these first two steps and the problem continues, quickly **S**et limits, "When we are in a restaurant, we need to be quiet so other people can enjoy *their* dinner."

Step C2:   Decide whether the behavior is intentional and use the appropriate toolset to **R**edirect the negative behavior. Take a walk, look at paintings on the wall, or trees outside as a distraction.

Step C3:   When misbehavior is severe or previous attempts fail, it's time for action (**R**eveal discipline). Temporarily leave the room or restaurant. Go to the parking lot or car. (There are several ways this action could escalate the situation, so there are step-by-step guidelines in Chapter 13, "Discipline Toolset.") If you leave completely, you are violating your right to occasionally eat out. If it comes to this, as it might, go alone next time.

3.   Your son, 7, delays getting ready in the morning.

Type of Problem: NO, PU, or PO, depending on your answers.

Why?   It is a NO problem if you don't need to go somewhere or have a flexible schedule. It is a PU problem if you need to go somewhere, but the child is still learning the skills to perform his morning routine. It is a PO problem if you are in a rush and your child is skilled and mature enough to understand and perform his morning routine, but is purposefully delaying.

What toolbox or toolsets can you use?
If it is a NO problem:
Step A: Use *only* the Prevention Toolbox. Allow more time in the morning, plan the night before, offer choices, or make requests in positive words. Teach skills and offer encouragement for his efforts.

If it is a PU problem:
Step A: **P**revent the problem with the Prevention Toolbox (same as above).
Step B: **A**cknowledge the difficulty of doing so many tasks in a short time.
Step C1:   If necessary, **S**et time limits and state your concerns.
Step C2:   **R**edirect the behavior by teaching skills and/or structure the environment, such as rearranging the order of the routine.

If it is a PO problem:
Step A: Use the Prevention Toolbox first.
Step B: **A**cknowledge that the child doesn't want to wear particular clothes.
Step C1:   If necessary, **S**et limits and describe your expectations and feelings.
Step C2:   If the child resists, use the PO Toolset to identify the purpose. It could be attention, to keep you involved or power, to exert independence and control in the situation. **R**edirect the misbehavior by helping him accomplish this goal in a positive way.
Step C3:   If this is not enough, **R**eveal the natural consequences that will occur. (Children can go hungry, but not naked!)

4.   Your daughter, 8, says she feels left out at school.

Type of Problem: C

Why?   Although you certainly care about what your child experiences at school, it doesn't involve any SHARP RV issues. (*She* isn't violating anyone's rights). If others are violating *her* rights, this is a problem for her (a Child problem). It's important for children to learn how to handle such situations on their own and work through their feelings of rejection. If you solve these problems *for* children or offer solutions, they might not feel understood or capable of solving the problem.

What toolbox or toolsets can you use?
Step B: **A**cknowledge your daughter's feelings of rejection and hurt. Use F-A-X Listening and problem solving (the Child Problem Toolbox) to empathize and explore options for how she can prevent or deal with the problem at school. At any point in the conversation, you can offer encouragement and teach skills (Step A: **P**revent the problem from starting or worsening.)

5.   Surprise! An old childhood friend just called. He's in town for the day and is visiting in a half an hour. The house is a bit cluttered and your children, ages 4, 9, and 13 are outside playing.

Type of Problem: NO or P, depending on your values.

Why?   If you don't care whether your house is cluttered when company visits, this is a NO problem. Go fix some iced tea. If you want the house to be clean, that's *your* issue. Since you were not already planning to clean, you could choose, in *this* situation, not to ask your children for help. Normally, household duties are the *family's* responsibility and it violates your *rights* to do all the work. If you choose to ask for help, plan a helpful way to gain their cooperation, which will prevent a power struggle.

What toolbox or toolsets can you use?

Step B: Acknowledge their needs and perspective up front. "I see you are all having a lot of fun."

Step C1:   Explain the problem and own your issues. "An old friend will be here in a half hour. We should have cleaned the house already and some of the messes aren't mine, so I'd like everyone to pitch in."

Step A: Add one last sentence (from the Cooperation Toolset) to prevent resistance. "If we all work together we could get it done in 20 minutes. You can go right back to playing when we are done."

If they still resist or complain, *they* have a problem (C/P).

Step B: Shift back to the Child Problem Toolbox, "I know, it really isn't fair that I'm asking you to do this on such short notice. I feel bad interrupting you when you're having so much fun."

Step C1:   "It also isn't fair if I clean up other people's messes."

Step A: Don't get stuck in a back and forth negotiation; the clock is ticking. Use your creativity and the Prevention Toolbox to move forward. "We don't have to dust, mop, or vacuum. All you need to do is pick up stuff and put it in your rooms. Let's play music and see how much we can get done."

★   Did you notice we didn't go PASRR this time? In this situation, we knew the children would probably resist, so we tried to prevent a power struggle by acknowledging their feelings *first*. Since we can use the Prevention Toolbox *any time,* this was the most flowing way to say what we wanted to say.

6.   Your daughter, 10, doesn't want to set the table because she's in the middle of a video game.

Type of problem: C/PO

Why?   The parent cares that the table needs to be set. There is not much time flexibility, and it would violate the parent's *rights* to do all the work for a family dinner. The child's problem (the smaller, but not less important part) is that she is still playing her game.

What toolbox or toolsets can you use?

Step A: **P**revent the problem by planning ahead.

Step B: Use the Child Problem Toolbox to **A**cknowledge her perspective. "I see you're in the middle of your game . . ."

Step C1:   Use the Clear Communication Toolset (Parent Problem Toolbox) to **S**et limits and state your needs. ". . . but the table needs to be set in five minutes."

Step C2:   Use the PO Toolset ("On purpose" misbehavior) to **R**edirect a power struggle, offering choices within limits. "You can either pause the game or turn it off. It's your choice."

Step C3:   If she doesn't come in five minutes, **R**eveal discipline. Either the child can turn off the computer or the parent can. The child's behavior will show her choice. (Remember, don't move to discipline, unless you present it as a choice. If you don't, it will turn the discipline into a power play.)

7.   Your daughter, 13, brought home a note from her teacher, saying she is missing three homework assignments. This is unusual, since she normally completes her work on time.

Type of Problem: C

Why?   Homework is *her* responsibility and this problem is between her and the teacher (C/T?). Naturally, the parent will be concerned and want to discuss the problem with the child. Since this is a Child problem, the parent must keep the ball in her court and hold her accountable for the solution. If this were an ongoing problem, then it would violate rules or values (C/P).

What toolbox or toolsets can you use?

In Child problems, we only use the Prevention and Child Problem Toolboxes. Ask a few *helpful* questions, pausing between each, to listen respectfully to her answers. "What happened?" "How do you plan to make up this work?" (No blaming or criticizing!) Use problem solving to finalize the details of her plan. Express faith in her ability to handle this situation promptly.

8.   Your son, 16, peels out of the driveway, squealing the car tires and speeding down the street.

Type of Problem: PO

Why?   Who cares about speeding? Probably not the teen. Since the behavior endangers safety (SHARP RV), it is a **P**arent problem. Although taking risks is a common developmental behavior of teens, this teen is aware of the laws and rules regarding driving. (He *did* pass a driving exam to have the *privilege* of driving.) This makes the misbehavior intentional, "**O**n purpose."

What toolbox or toolsets can you use?

Step A: **P**revent the problem from worsening or happening again by *planning* a helpful response. Express faith in the teen's ability to be a safe driver and describe his past efforts.

Step B: **A**cknowledge the teen's natural desire to experiment with the thrill of speeding (or wanting to impress his friends). Then listen carefully to the teen's perspective; it will reveal the purpose of the misbehavior.

Step C1:   **S**et limits and state your concerns about the dangers of speeding and his agreement to abide by the driving laws. Focus on driving being a privilege. To have the privilege, one must show responsibility. Get agreements for the conditions of maintaining the privilege. *Avoid lecturing.* Be ready to shift gears between the Clear Communication Toolset (Step C1) and the Child Problem Toolbox (Step B).

Step C2:   **R**edirect the behavior by identifying the purpose behind it. Is the child speeding to impress his friends (attention) or to prove he has power? If we listen effectively, he will give us the clues to know the difference. When problem solving, brainstorm more appropriate ways to meet this purpose.

Step C3:   **R**eveal the effects of violating the driving laws by building discipline into your agreements. If he chooses to speed or drive dangerously, he is showing he is not ready for the privilege of driving. He will be temporarily giving up his driving privileges or could be forced to give them up by getting a speeding ticket. Should it happen again, follow through, reminding the teen that his behavior and the resulting effects are *his* choice.

WHAT'S NEXT?

Let the information from this chapter sink in for a week and then read the next chapter. Observe the world around you. Practice identifying problems and rehearsing the PASRR formula flow in your mind.

The rest of the book teaches us the tools we need to meet our third mission goal: **DELIVER it [the response] effectively.** Beginning with the next chapter, we will go through each step of the Universal Blueprint and explain exactly how to use each individual tool available at that step.

When you are ready to start learning about specific tools and how to use them, begin your tour of the toolsets with the next chapter, Chapter 4, "Self-Esteem Toolset." We discuss unconditional love, seeing the positive side of every situation, comparisons and competition, internal and external motivation, and how to handle mistakes (ours and our children's). We learn the special language of descriptive encouragement, which builds self-esteem without unintentionally pressuring or discouraging our children.

CHAPTER 4
SELF-ESTEEM TOOLSET

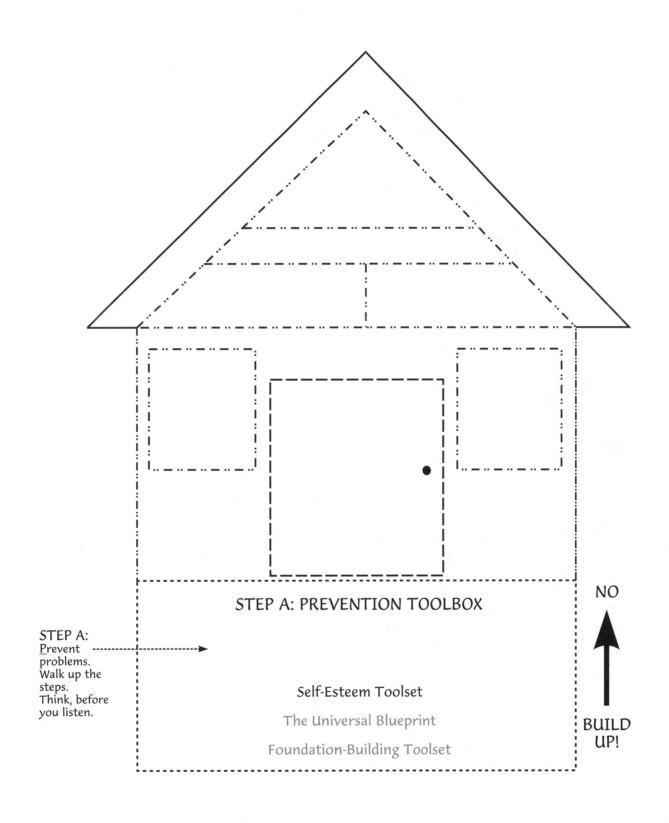

STEP A: PREVENTION TOOLBOX

STEP A:
Prevent
problems.
Walk up the
steps.
Think, before
you listen.

Self-Esteem Toolset

The Universal Blueprint

Foundation-Building Toolset

NO

BUILD
UP!

CHAPTER
4 SELF-ESTEEM TOOLSET

We can build a beautiful house and decorate it with expensive, fashionable furniture, but if the structure itself is of poor quality, its beauty is simply a disguise. We will be continually frustrated with the problems resulting from its inferior quality. On the other hand, we can build a house that is plain and simple but of high-quality workmanship. This house, while not as pretty or expensive, is more valuable in a different way. While we might occasionally be disappointed by the external appearance, we can feel satisfied that the house is worthwhile and will experience fewer problems.

Likewise, healthy parents help their children feel good about their inside qualities, even when their outside appearance is less than perfect. To do this, healthy parents use specific attitudes and tools, such as those in the Self-Esteem Toolset.

IN THIS CHAPTER

This chapter encourages us to consider three important parenting ideas:

1. There is a difference between self-esteem, self-image, and ego-esteem.

2. There is a difference between praise and encouragement.

3. The attitudes and language of descriptive encouragement are the most effective tools for building self-esteem.

WHEN TO USE THIS TOOLSET

We can build self-esteem *anytime*, when people work hard on a task, do something well, feel frustrated, make a mistake, or accomplish a goal. We can use these tools with *anyone*, with children, adults, and ourselves.

WHAT IS SELF-ESTEEM?

> **Self-esteem refers to our *feelings* about our *inside qualities*. This includes our worth as a human being, sense of purpose in life, and how lovable we think we are.**
>
> **Self-image refers to our *thoughts* about our *outside appearance*, what we think others see. This includes our looks, talents, popularity, or accomplishments.**

When people appear to have a positive self-image, we often assume they have high self-esteem. Having a positive self-image is important, but it is only superficial. We can have a positive self-image, but still feel we are no good inside. Likewise, we can feel worthwhile and lovable even when we are insecure about our looks or popularity.

A Personal Story. Throughout my childhood, I had a bad underbite. Wearing braces for over five years still didn't correct the problem. It was difficult not being pretty, and my self-image was always low. Nevertheless, I felt confident and capable and knew I had a lot of positive qualities—inside. I did not love my looks, but I loved who I was. As an adult, I had reconstructive surgery and could see some prettiness for the first time. I still avoid mirrors, but the experience helped me realize that outside appearances are helpful, but inside qualities are what really count.

There is a myth that if parents praise or compliment children, they will become conceited. Conceit is a belief that I am better than others. This type of self-image is called "ego-esteem." People with high ego-esteem build themselves up by putting others down. Their defensiveness is a disguise for their real insecurity.

> **People with high ego-esteem often compete with others, trying to be the *best* or always *win*. Egotistical people believe they are *better than* others.**

True self-esteem comes from within. When we have a healthy self-esteem we are confident, independent, and willing to try new things. We strive for excellence and try to do our best. We accept ourselves as we are, recognizing both our strengths and weaknesses. We work to improve ourselves, but are not perfectionists; we have realistic expectations for ourselves.

Our job as parents is to raise fully functioning adults, not just adults who appear to be well-adjusted. We are often surprised when children or teens who appear confident run into problems. We thought they *were* well-adjusted, because they *appeared* so. When we use effective parenting skills, we might not have children who are always on time or never argue, because they are human, but we *will* reach our goal of raising well-balanced adults.

ENCOURAGEMENT VERSUS PRAISE

Encouragement is the most effective tool to build self-esteem. If we want to help build positive internal qualities, such as courage, confidence, a sense of purpose, or self-worth, we need to use words and phrases that focus on these positive, internal qualities.

Parenting advice often tells us to *praise* our children, but *praise* and *encouragement* are very different. When we read advice that tells us to praise our children, we need to look closely at how they define or explain praise. Often, what they call *praise* is actually *encouragement*. When we understand the difference, we can avoid common mistakes and use the tools to their full potential.

> • *Encouragement* uses descriptive, non-judgmental terms that cause others to say positive things to themselves.
>
> • *Praise* uses judgmental labels that can accidentally cause discouragement or add negative pressure. It focuses on others' opinions of our worth.

The way we word statements influences what others say to themselves. Encouraging words cause good feelings, so children naturally *want* to do better. Even when we disapprove of children's behavior, encouragement lets them know we still unconditionally love and accept them as worthwhile human beings. Praise is a conditional reward and motivates children to do better *if* they can please others or get a reward. This causes children to become dependent on others' opinions for their self-worth.

> **Encouragement has two parts:**
> 1. What we say.
> 2. What others say to themselves as a result of our statement.

First, let's summarize the eight major differences between praise and encouragement. Then we'll take a closer look at the specifics of each.

PRAISE . . .	ENCOURAGEMENT . . .
1. Gives approval or love if people are acting "good."	1. Gives approval and love unconditionally.
2. Focuses on what other people expect or think. It can be insincere and superficial. It fosters praise "junkies."	2. Focuses on what the *receiver* feels or thinks. It is sincere and fosters trust in one's inner voice and judgment.
3. Rewards a job completed or done well. People can use it to control or manipulate.	3. Points out any effort made, even if a task is still in progress. It focuses on what is right or positive.
4. Uses "constructive criticism" to improve others. Expectations are sometimes unrealistically high. It adds pressure to perform or to be perfect.	4. Describes improvements already made. Expectations are realistic. There is no pressure to be perfect, just to do one's best and strive for excellence.
5. Uses judgmental words that label people or their acts.	5. Uses words that describe the value of the job or the internal qualities displayed while doing it.
6. Is based on competition, being *better than* others.	6. Focuses on cooperation and building on the strengths of each family member.
7. Is only given when people do what the praiser wants.	7. Is given any time, even when people are discouraged.
8. Mistakes are reflections of internal worth.	8. Mistakes are opportunities to learn.

SELF-ESTEEM TOOLS

Some parenting resources say self-esteem is overrated; they are confusing self-image and ego-esteem with self-esteem. Most credible parenting resources talk about the importance of self-esteem. Few, however, offer clear, specific guidelines for how parents can think, talk, and act, without accidentally praising, pressuring, or discouraging children. Here are some specific tools and suggestions to help us meet our goal of building self-esteem in ourselves and our children.

Show Unconditional Love

People can use praise as a reward or to control others. Praise sends the message, "If you do something I consider 'good,' I will reward you by showing you love, recognizing you, and valuing you." While people don't actually say these words, their attitude implies this hidden message.

When we use love to manipulate, our children think we love them or they are lovable only if they are "good." Children are human beings, however, and occasionally make mistakes and behave unacceptably. A more encouraging attitude is to genuinely *accept* children as they are, with all their imperfections, even if we don't *approve* of their choices. Later, we can teach them the skills they need to improve.

Unconditional love is possibly the most important factor in feeling a sense of self-worth. It says, both verbally and nonverbally, "You are lovable. You may be different from me, but I respect you simply because you are worthy of respect. Whatever you accomplish or whatever you do, I will still love you." When people receive unconditional love, they think "If someone can love me even when I make mistakes, I can more easily love myself. Since I love myself, I want to do my best." Receiving unconditional love brings a deep sense of security and reassurance that a few mistakes cannot erase.

Consider God's example of unconditional love. Imagine if God judged and loved us as conditionally as we do others. Would any of us ever be deserving of His love? No matter how hard we tried, we'd probably feel discouraged. Fortunately, God loves us despite our imperfections and mistakes. God supports us but does not rescue us from our mistakes. God is an eternal presence that says, "I'm here and I love you. I won't force you to grow and change, but I will provide guidelines and examples and be here to guide and encourage you when you are ready." We can follow God's example by looking beyond human flaws to the eternal beings inside, who are constantly growing. All people have positive special qualities, though these qualities are sometimes hidden. Inside, people are usually flowers, not weeds. They may be wilted, but they will thrive, if given the warmth of unconditional love to nurture their growth. Only in a safe environment can they learn from their mistakes and begin to see their own potential.

NOTICE THE CHILD'S SPECIAL, UNIQUE QUALITIES

We can show our children, through words and actions, that we love them just because they are and no other reason. This can be difficult if we don't *like* a child's personality or behavior. We can love someone even if we don't always agree with or like the person. It's difficult, but *we* grow when we love unconditionally and let go of our unrealistic expectations to change others.

When our children ask us "Who do you love more?" they really want reassurance that we love *each of them* specially. We can list the qualities that make *that* child special to us. If one child's personality is more compatible with ours, we need to be careful not to show favoritism. Instead, we can focus on each child's special, positive traits.

AVOID THE FAIRNESS TRAP

Trying to always be fair or give equally is an easy trap to fall into. Many parents do this when purchasing items, serving food, or giving time. Being fair or equal develops a score-keeping attitude. Children learn to measure their worth by comparing their treatment to that of others. Children really appreciate our recognizing and meeting their special needs, even if we occasionally treat them unequally.

For example, if your son needs a jacket and his sister complains, don't feel you have to buy her a jacket or spend the same amount of money on her. Let her know that her brother needs a jacket today and when *she* needs something, you will provide for her, too. Don't worry about spending the same exact amount of money on gifts or adding junk to one child's loot just to even the score. Base gifts on the child's individual needs or interests and stay within a general budget.

Instead of measuring amounts of food, give children as much as they are hungry for. Reassure them that if they want more, they can have more. There are two other options: Let children serve themselves, understanding that they must eat what they take. Or have one child serve, such as cutting pieces of cake, and let the other child pick first. The cutter will be sure to make the pieces equal, since the chooser is sure to pick the larger piece!

Instead of interrupting time with one child just because we haven't spent an equal amount of time with other children, remind them that we will spend time with them, too. Base the amount of time on individual needs that might be quite different, but equally important. For example, it might require more time to review spelling words with one child than to play a game or read a book. Avoid giving time and attention to children *only* when they ask for it, either verbally or through their actions. If there is one high-need child, be careful to also spend time with the low-need child. Our efforts can go a long way in preventing low-need children from believing they have to be sick or misbehaving to get our attention.

It can be difficult, for both parents and children, to change beliefs about fairness and equality. If children are conditioned to keep score, they may question a parent's new approach—for a while. Stick with it and help each child feel special and important.

A Personal Story. *When I was growing up, we had two rocking chairs in a little nook of our dining room. When two people wanted to talk about a problem or share the events of the day, they'd sit in this conversation area with a cup of anything and relax. I viewed this area as the heart-to-heart corner, and each chair was half a heart. When we sat in those chairs together, they formed one heart and left us with a warm, glowing feeling. Many times, I said, "Mom, if you ever get tired of these chairs and I have my own place to live, let me buy them from you."*

Recently, when she was preparing to move to a new home, she said she had decided to give my brother and me one rocker each. To my mom, the chairs were just pieces of furniture and she wanted to treat us equally. I was heartbroken—not because I wasn't going to get the set, but because the set, the heart, might be split.

I told her that as much as I loved and wanted those chairs, I'd prefer she give my brother both of them than split them for the sake of fairness. We talked about the hurt feelings that can result from treatment that is "equal, but less." She said that when we were young, parents were told to make every effort to be equal and fair. I dropped the issue and told her I'd respect whatever decision she made. She chose to give me the chairs and we now have a heart-to-heart nook in front of our fireplace.

MAKE TIME FOR FUN

Spend daily one-on-one time with each child. Make sure the time is positive and enjoyable. (No lectures or discussions about Parent problems.) Offer encouragement. Be there to listen to *their* troubles, joys, and detailed stories. Get to know and understand each child better. Laugh together and have fun simply sharing their company.

Schedule "dates" with each child. If other children seem jealous, remind them when their date is planned. Alternate parent-child combinations so each child can count on some special time to be alone with Mom or Dad. Single parents can hire a sitter, trade sitting with a friend, or schedule a date when the other child is participating in another activity. We do not have to spend money to spend time with our children. Here are just a few examples of activities we can share. Ask your child for more suggestions.

- Work on creative projects.
- Have a picnic in the backyard or local park.
- Let them teach you a sport or skill.
- Do activities they plan.

- Take time off from work to "do lunch" and clear your schedule for one hour.
- Bring lunch to their school and eat on the playground.

DON'T USE LOVE AS A REWARD

"Positive and negative reinforcement" is a practice professionals have promoted over the past few decades. This theory teaches children to behave the way adults want them to, to get positive reinforcements, such as praise, rewards, love, and approval. (Chapter 5, "Cooperation Toolset," offers alternatives to rewards as well as guidelines for using behavior charts.) If children misbehave, the adults give negative reinforcement, such as withholding praise, love, and approval or applying punishment.

It's easy to encourage children who are behaving well. But when they disappoint, embarrass, or disobey us, we often say things like "Go to your room. I don't want to be around you if you can't behave," or "Nobody will like you if you behave like that." If we withdraw our love when children are too difficult, they learn we won't stick with them when times get tough. It is during rough times that children most need encouragement. Our attitude and tone of voice can say, "While I am frustrated or disapprove of something you *did,* I still love *you.*"

Like any of the prevention tools, *encouragement is useful any time.* When people are frustrated with themselves, we can send the message "I believe in you and love you no matter what." This message is different from "I know you can do better." The latter implies "You didn't do well enough" and is discouraging. It is also different from "whatever you do is okay," which says that we agree with the person's choice. We don't have to agree with children's feelings or perceptions to understand and accept them. We may need to set limits on how they express those emotions, but we allow the emotions themselves. (Chapters 7 and 8, the Child Problem Toolbox, have more information about responding to negative emotions.)

Most importantly, give encouragement and show love for no apparent reason. An unexpected hug or "I love you," a pat on the back, a back rub while sitting together or standing in line, or a smile from across the room express love and a sense of appreciation. Such physical touches can cure depression, reduce stress, and replenish energy. In basic psychology, students learn about an experiment in which researchers raised three baby monkeys with three different "mothers": a real mother monkey, a monkey-shaped object covered with fur, and a plain wire monkey-shaped object. The baby with the real mother monkey thrived, grew, and bonded. The monkey with the fur-covered object was very insecure and clung to it. The baby monkey with the wire object died. It is common knowledge among brain researchers that physical, emotional, and intellectual stimulation during the first three years of life are critical, because it stimulates brain growth and development. Neglected children, who have not been regularly held and talked to, have less brain matter than children who receive this stimulation. In severe cases, neglected children's brains actually shrunk. The first three years set the stage for the child's personality, emotional bonding or attachment, and ability to learn.

> **Touch is a basic biological need. We need it to survive, and it is most fulfilling when there are no strings attached.**

Focus on Self-Motivation, Not People-Pleasing ☆☆☆☆

Many parents were raised with the belief that children should want to please their parents and that this desire is an important motivator. We act on this belief when we make statements such as, "I'm so proud of you," "You make me happy when you get good grades," or "Your teacher said you're a good speller." Most parents see nothing wrong with children trying to please others, especially if they are trying to please the parents. But let's look at the long-term effects:

- **Praise creates "praise junkies"** because it's addictive. Over time, some children do things just for the praise and recognition they get, rather than the value of the act or the good feelings *they* get. They come to expect praise and appreciation for everything they do. If they don't get praise, they question their worth and whether they did a good job. Others may feel they have no reason to cooperate if they won't get praise or a reward. They think "What's in it for me? If nobody notices what I do, why should I bother?" While these children may behave well, their motivation is to seek approval from others.

- **Praise promotes unhealthy pride.** Praise often shifts the focus from the pride or pleasure *children* feel in their accomplishments to pleasing someone else. Saying "I'm so proud of you" may be misinterpreted by children in several ways: "You make *me* look good," "Your job is to make *me* happy," or "You please me by doing what *I* want." While children may be glad they pleased someone else, pleasing others deflates what *they* feel. Instead, use words that focus on how *children* feel. "I bet it feels great to get a good grade after putting such hard work into it" or "You've really come a long way! It's exciting to see you do that on your own."

  > *A **Graduate's Story**. It took my son, Mark, age 4, many months to learn how to swim. He'd hesitate for nearly 5 minutes before he jumped in the water and took 2 weeks to get his face wet. Months later, when he swam across the pool all by himself, stroking and breathing correctly, I was thrilled! I waited for him at the pool's ladder, ready to give him a hug. As he rose out of the water, he had the biggest grin of satisfaction on his face. I said, "Oh Mark, I'm so*

proud of you!" He immediately stopped smiling and looked disappointed, as though I'd taken away his hard-earned accomplishment! Until that moment, I didn't understand (or believe) why those words were so discouraging. It's really important to Mark to do things on his own and he often resists doing things just to please me. While I'm often proud of Mark's accomplishments, I am careful to focus on his feelings about what he did.

Children need to learn how to handle discouragement well. We want our children to say to themselves, "Maybe I didn't do as well as I hoped I would, but I know I did my best and improved. If I keep trying, I will eventually get it." Our children will say these things to themselves, if we focus on the value of their deeds, rather than whom they pleased.

> *Unhealthy pride* is thinking we are *better than* others.
>
> *Healthy pride* is an *inner* sense of accomplishment and satisfaction that we've done our best.

- **Praise can bring on resistance.** Praise can be manipulative and controlling, as in "You're a big boy now. You should be able to go on the potty by yourself!" When some children catch on to their parent's hidden motive, they refuse to cooperate, viewing it as giving in. Instead of feeling more motivated, they feel resistant and resentful.

- **Praise increases the risk that children will follow negative peer pressure.** When children try to please us, their parents, we usually don't mind. As children approach their teen years, however, they give greater value to what their friends think. This is a healthy and necessary part of becoming an adult. Children who make decisions to please others are more likely to try pleasing their peers by going along with the crowd. We want our children to *resist* negative peer pressure. We hope our children will have the courage to say "I don't care if you think I'm not cool or won't be my friend, I'm not going to do that!"

If we want to avoid these pitfalls and develop self-motivation in our children and others, there are several things we can do.

ASK THE CHILD'S OPINION

Encouraging statements use words that focus on children's opinions or feelings about their efforts, instead of relying on others' approval. When children think their ideas are important and they have something to contribute, they feel useful and valued. Ask questions such as "What do you think?" or make comments like "I can tell you're pleased with it." These statements tell children that their opinions are important and they are capable of judging their own work. If we value their opinions and skills, they are more willing to trust their *own* judgment and abilities.

A Personal Story. When I was a teen and struggling with a decision, I would sometimes ask my parents what I should do. They would first ask me what I thought and listen to my ideas. They might offer advice, if I asked for it, and end by saying, "Well, I know you have a good head on your shoulders. I trust your judgment. I know you'll work it out." I would think to myself, "If they think I have good judgment, they must see something I don't see. If they see it, it must be there! If they trust my judgment, then so can I." When faced with tough decisions, especially as a teen, I always tried a little harder to use that "good head on my shoulders." It saved me from many mistakes and I learned to trust myself, my opinions, and my inner voice.

When children ask, "Did I do a good job?" first ask, "What do you think?" Or "Tell me what you like about it." If children are persistent in wanting your opinion simply describe what you like. "Well, I think _____, but you can decide for yourself."

See the Positive ☆☆☆☆

There will always be events or behaviors that we have little or no control over. We learned in Chapter 2, "Foundation-Building Toolset," that our beliefs and interpretations of these events greatly affect our response. We can view situations negatively or positively—the choice is ours. It's like looking at our cup as half full, instead of half empty.

What we see (and look at) is what we get. If we spend 75 percent of our time and energy noticing negative behavior, that will soon be all we see. If this is the only behavior we comment on, children begin to see themselves as bad people. On the other hand, if we spend our time and energy looking for and pointing out positive behavior, we begin seeing more of it. This does not mean we do nothing about negative behavior; we just make an extra effort to notice positive behavior. As we point out the positive and choose our reaction to the negative, children see themselves more positively. Feeling encouraged, they try harder to avoid mistakes and learn from those they can't avoid. They feel like worthwhile people who occasionally make mistakes.

It usually takes more time and effort to look for positive behavior than to notice negative behavior. When all is going well, we don't want to rock the boat or distract children from their good behavior—so we say nothing. We need to make a conscious effort to pay more attention to positive behaviors and choose how we interpret negative behaviors. Here are some suggestions:

FOCUS ON WHAT IS RIGHT

Always point out what children do right, even if part of what they did was "wrong." Consider carefully whether the negative is important enough to even comment on. Often, when we simply notice the positive and ignore the negative, the negative disappears. If the negative is too difficult to ignore, downplay it, focusing mostly on the positive. For example, if your daughter is chattering away in church as she draws a picture, say "You're having fun *and* keeping yourself busy. Just remember to whisper."

> *A **Graduate's Story**. Since I learned about encouragement, I have been trying to focus on the positive with my son. His teacher, however, grades papers by putting how many points he missed. Instead of seeing a 95% grade, he sees –5. He gets really upset, can only focus on his mistakes, and is becoming more discouraged. I have tried pointing out what he did right and even re-marked papers in more positive ways. Finally, I talked to the teacher. I pointed out how discouraged my son feels when his mistakes are pointed out, without giving him credit for all he did right. I explained what I do to be more encouraging and how I marked his papers with a positive grade. She didn't realize such a small thing was making such a negative impact. She changed her grading and my son immediately changed his attitude. He's enjoying school again and isn't being so hard on himself for his mistakes.*

SEND POSITIVE MESSAGES TO CHILDREN

Even when children are doing nothing in particular, positive or negative, send positive thoughts their way or give an unexpected positive stroke. Notes of encouragement are very powerful. If children save the letter or note, they can refer to it anytime they want to remind themselves of their good qualities. We can use special cards, sticky notes, or stickers. We can leave them in lunch boxes, on a mirror, next to phone messages, on the refrigerator with a magnet, or on bed pillows. If we use the tips and tools from this toolset, we can create special reminders of how much we love them and how special they are to us.

RECOGNIZE WHAT CHILDREN DO WELL

We can show interest in areas that our children are interested in, even if these interests aren't important to us. If our children have a special skill or talent, we can find ways to let them help the family and ask for their opinions and advice.

> ➤ "I need someone with a small hand to reach behind the couch. Could you help?"
> ➤ "I can never seem to balance my checkbook. Would you look at my math and see if you can find the mistakes? I am amazed at the way you do math in your head so well."
> ➤ "You have such rhythm. Could you show me a few steps I can use when Daddy and I go dancing next weekend?"

DESCRIBE HOW CHILDREN'S EFFORTS HELP OTHERS

We need to give children responsibilities that are age-appropriate and build on their strengths. When children are helpful, avoid thanking them for *pleasing* you (their job is not to make us happy) and point out how it *helped* you, the family, or others.

> ➤ "The bathroom faucets really shine! I bet our guests will enjoy using such a clean restroom. Thanks for being so thorough."
> ➤ "Thanks for collecting all the trash and carrying out the cans. I didn't realize how heavy they were! My back appreciates your help!"
> ➤ "I'm so glad you were here when baby Mikey came to visit. He would have been into everything if you hadn't kept him so busy. He likes playing with you. You're so patient with him."

NOTICE EFFORT

When children put forth effort and think they've failed in spite of their efforts, they feel discouraged. Acknowledge any effort children make, even if they or their efforts aren't totally successful.

> *A Personal Story. When I was about 13, I decided to bake biscuits for my parents while they were at a meeting. The recipe called for cream of tartar, but I couldn't find any ingredient by that name. I thought, "Here's some tartar sauce! Maybe they make it by adding water to cream of tartar. If I use this and less water, it might be a good substitute."*
>
> *When my parents came home, they were pleasantly surprised that I took the initiative to cook something for them. Then they tasted my creation. They controlled their facial expressions as they tried to swallow their first bite. (I'm impressed they could do it!) Without a hint of disappointment or disapproval my mother politely asked me "What recipe did you use?" I told them the problem and my logical substitution. My mom put her arm around my shoulder and showed me the cream of tartar in the cabinet.*
>
> *She said, "I can see how you thought tartar sauce might work. Have you tasted the biscuits to see if your theory worked?" "Why no!" I proudly stated with a smile, "I wanted you to be the first to taste them." "Here," she said, "try one." It was awful! I spit it out immediately and threw the remaining biscuits in the trash. While I was embarrassed by my mistake, I was more impressed that my parents appreciated the thought behind my gift and handled my mistake so tactfully.*

By showing children we believe in them, they picture themselves having a quality and naturally develop more of that quality. We can point out times when we've seen our children handle a situation well, even if only part of their decision was responsible. For example, "I can see you regret going to that party, but you showed good judgment by leaving when those kids started trouble."

NOTICE IMPROVEMENT

Parents can give praise only after children complete a task and only for the part that was successful. We can give encouragement, however, at each step of the process, with or without any sign of improvement.

> ➤ "Wow! You got to touch the basketball three times this game!"
> ➤ "I can tell your trumpet playing has improved. That song is so smooth and clear."
> ➤ "You might not feel comfortable driving on the freeway yet, but look how well you handled the left turn back at that busy intersection."

Sometimes, the *absence* of negative behavior is the very behavior we want to notice. Don't hesitate to comment at these times.

> ***A Parenting Class Discussion.*** *A foster mother and her teenage daughter took my Parents and Teens—Together class. I asked what positive behaviors the parents had noticed that week. The mother said she hadn't noticed her daughter behaving positively. The daughter said, "But we haven't argued in three weeks!" The mother acknowledge this was true. The daughter's eyes welled up with tears as she added, "You have no idea how hard I've been trying to avoid arguments." I commented that positive behavior isn't always obvious. Sometimes the absence of negative behavior is a sign of effort and improvement. When we don't notice this positive behavior, children feel more discouraged. The daughter nodded. The mother looked surprised and then got an "Aha!" look on her face. "I never thought about it that way before," she said. She put her arm around her daughter and said "Thanks for trying so hard." The foster daughter relaxed as tears ran down her face. "Thanks for noticing," she said.*

AVOID REMINDING CHILDREN OF PAST MISTAKES OR WEAKNESSES

If we give encouragement, but add a negative comment, it cancels the positive effect. Focus on the child's strength, without mentioning past failures:

▶ Change "Your room *finally* looks clean" to an encouraging statement by taking out finally and describing how clean it is.

▶ Don't say, "The lawn looks nice. I can't see any spots you missed *this time*." Show your appreciation without the criticism, "Thanks for mowing the lawn, it looks nice and even."

▶ Don't say, "You really worked hard on that project. If you put that kind of effort into all your work, you'd be an 'A' student!" Instead, say "I bet it feels good to know your hard work paid off."

▶ Surprisingly, it's discouraging for children to hear, "You did it! See what you can do *if you try*?" The last part of the sentence implies they haven't tried in the past. Eliminate the last sentence, simply saying, "You did it! You tried and tried, and didn't give up."

AVOID "CONSTRUCTIVE CRITICISM"

Constructive criticism is a contradictory term—constructive means to build up; criticism tears down. Parents often think if they point out mistakes, children will want to improve. "Maybe if I keep pointing out how sloppy her writing is, she'll take the time to be neater." This approach is rarely effective. When we remind people of their mistakes, they don't feel like improving. They feel more discouraged and resentful. Focus, instead, on what the child is doing well. If we need to teach skills, our approach and timing are critical.

1. **Always start with encouragement, pointing out what others did well.** Avoid the words *right* and *wrong*. Use words like *effective, less effective, helpful,* and *unhelpful.* Describe the possible outcome of making the mistake again, so they can use the information later.

2. **Allow children to experience their pleasure and satisfaction.**

3. **Decide how important it is to point out the negative now.**
   a. If they know how to do the task but didn't do it well, notice their efforts and any progress they made. Reassure them that they'll continue improving with practice.
   b. If they don't know how to do the task well or lack information, wait to teach another time (if you can). Don't cancel the positive effort and feeling of encouragement by adding criticism. Later, use the "teaching skills" tool from the Independence Toolset (Chapter 6), which builds encouragement into the teaching process.
   c. Ask children how they feel about their work. If *they* are dissatisfied, ask them if there's anything they would do differently or to improve. If they have no ideas, ask if they want suggestions. If they say "no," let them learn on their own. Show faith in their ability to figure out a way to do their best.

A Personal Story. I took my kids to the pool on the last day of summer. There was only one family there. The father repeatedly told his children how to spend their time, instead of allowing them to freely enjoy the last few minutes of summer. Every time his son jumped off the board, the father commented on how he could have improved his technique. He was impressed with his own knowledge about swimming and diving. The boy said he was going to do a "half gainer." (I don't even know how to spell it, let alone do it!) Instead, he did a cannonball. His father criticized his choice, "That wasn't a half gainer!" The boy, obviously discouraged and tired of the constant pressure and corrections just said, "Well, I changed my mind." He ignored his father's next few comments. The father explained the technical features of half gainers to his wife and anyone else who was willing to listen. I'm sure this father was trying to help, but the boy obviously wanted to play without the diving lesson.

Describe, Don't Judge or Label ☆☆☆☆

It is a common misconception that people like praise. If we look at how we react to compliments, we'll see that we often feel uncomfortable or embarrassed. Why do we make excuses or deny compliments such as "You're hair always looks so perfect" or "You're such a good singer"? We feel good, but we also doubt their judgment. We might say, "Well, I wouldn't say it's *perfect*" or "*Good* singer?" Praise often sounds insincere.

Sometimes our discomfort comes from feeling pressured to perform well the next time, since someone is judging us. Compliments like "You're such a good cook, you should open a gourmet restaurant" might leave us focusing on our weakness (which is really our human nature). "Great! Now every meal has to be a gourmet one! I was planning beans and franks tomorrow night!"

What all these compliments have in common are their judgmental words: *best, good, perfect,* or labels like *gourmet*. These words add pressure and make people (children included) think others have unrealistic expectations of them. People who give compliments usually don't mean to pressure or judge. They are trying to make the person feel good. Nevertheless, the way we word a compliment or encouragement greatly influences how others receive it. Here are some examples of common statements of praise and the resulting self-talk:

COMPLIMENT	SELF-TALK
"You're such a good boy!"	"Am I really good?" "Do I have to be good all the time?" "What if I'm not good? Will you still love me?"
"You did a good job."	"You might think it's a good job. I know I didn't do this . . . and this . . ." "I wonder what I did that was good so I can do it again."
"You got an 'A'! You're such a good student."	"What would you have said if I didn't get an 'A'?" "Am I only a good student or person if I get good grades?"

To use the language of encouragement, remember one word—*DESCRIBE*.

Describe children's feelings, efforts, progress or improvements, skills or qualities shown, the value of the act, or how it was helpful.

When we use descriptive words, there's no question about our sincerity. It's factual, so there's nothing to dispute. It doesn't add unrealistic pressure because we aren't judging or labeling. As a result, people are more likely to take the comment in a positive way, feeling good about themselves and their efforts. Using this skill, let's look at three praise statements, the child's self-talk, an encouraging alternative, and the likely result for the child.

1. *Praise:* "You're such a big boy! You can go potty all by yourself!"
   Child's self-talk: "Gee, I don't know if I can always be a 'big boy.' Sometimes I like to keep playing without stopping to do this potty thing!"

   Encouragement: "Hey! You made it to the potty, got your pants down by yourself, and remembered to flush the toilet! I bet it feels good to be able to go potty all by yourself!"
   Child's self-talk: "I really did do a lot this time! I'm getting better at this potty thing!"

2. *Praise:* "You did a good job on your project."
   Child's self-talk: "Well, I won't know that until I get a grade."

   Encouragement: "Gee! I can tell you spent a lot of time on your project! The writing is neat and easy to read and the color codes on your map make it easy to follow."
   Child's self-talk: "Yeah, I did a pretty good job on that project! I'm glad I decided to use color. I'll have to remember that next time."

3. *Praise:* "That was a great game even though your team lost. You played really good today."
   Child's self-talk: "Right, you think it was great. It wasn't a great game—we lost! You must not have been watching or you would have seen me miss that goal in the second quarter."

   Encouragement: "Boy, you really played your heart out, didn't you? You came so close to getting that goal in the second quarter and really poured it on at the end! I can tell you're disappointed the team lost, but I could really see how much you've all improved! You're passing the ball more, taking the ball further up the field, and working together as a team."
   Child's self-talk: "I can't believe I missed that goal, but I did do my best. I didn't notice before, but we were passing more. We are improving! If we keep it up, maybe we'll do better next time."

If you doubt that people make these self-talk comments, pay attention to *your* self-talk the next time you receive praise and encouragement. When we give others a compliment and they argue or deny it, chances are we used unhelpful praise. If we use descriptive encouragement and they disagree, don't argue, just say, "Well that's how I saw it. You don't have to agree."

> ***A Personal Story.*** *When Amber was about 4, she showed me an art project she had just finished. When I saw it, I said, "Wow! Look at that! You found the construction paper on your own, cut all those triangles out by yourself, and glued them in that neat shape! Did you have fun?" She replied, enthusiastically, "Yeah! I'm going to make another one!" As she skipped down the stairs I could hear her singing a song to herself: "I'm a good artist. I'm a good artist." I was so pleased she was telling this to herself, instead of needing me to tell her.*

Encouragement usually takes more effort and more words. We have to be observant and sincere. It's a lot harder than tossing out halfhearted one-word judgments. Unlike other wordy statements, such as criticism and lectures, others don't grow tired of hearing positive comments that don't add pressure. They keep listening.

EXPRESS APPRECIATION

Always say, "Thank you." Even if people are just doing their job or are expected to do something anyway, don't take their cooperation or helpfulness for granted.

► "I bet Brian had fun playing with you. You gave him lots of turns playing with your toys."
► "Thanks for playing quietly while I took a nap. I feel more rested and happy."
► "Thanks for helping with the dishes. I know it's not your favorite thing to do. I don't like to do it either. It really helps us finish quickly so we have more time to do what we really want to do."

NAME THE QUALITY[1]

At the end of a descriptive encouragement state-ment, we can add one or two words that sum up the *quality* it took to accomplish that act.

*Notice and **describe** positive behavior.*

> "What a day! We've been on the road for hours! You kept yourself busy with puzzles, cards, and coloring. What a trooper!"

> "When Tony was here you let him play with your toys even though he doesn't know how to share. You taught him how to ride your little bike. And you were gentle with him, even when he pulled your hair. Now that's *tolerant!*"

> "That little girl didn't seem to know anyone. I bet it made her feel really good when you asked her to play on the seesaw. That's what being *friendly* is all about!"

Remember, we aren't *judging* the behavior, pres-suring, or labeling the child; we are *describing* a skill, value, or quality the behavior showed.

RELEASE CHILDREN FROM ROLES AND LABELS

Labeling children is common. Because children act a certain way, we label them as though they *are* the behavior. Labels, whether positive or negative, are limiting and discouraging. Labels influence how others think about children and, therefore, how they treat them.

When children hear a negative label, they see the label as their identity or the role they *should* play. People often recognize only behaviors that fit the label. "See, there you go again. You're so mean." Since everyone expects them to act this way, what motivation do they have to change or improve? Even normal behaviors can be turned into negative labels, such as "the terrible two's," "rebellious teen," or "shy." When such normal behaviors get negative labels, children think there is something wrong with them. Discouraged, they give up and live *down* to the label.

But let's not ignore positive labels, such as *bright, athletic, angel,* or *big girl.* Any label, even a positive one, limits a child. The *bright* child be devastated by an average grade. *Athletes* might hesitate to pursue academics or music or feel pressured to be good in all sports. An *angel* might fear making mistakes, having a bad day, or expressing natural, negative feelings. A *big girl* probably feels pressure to always act grown up and guilty when she acts like a baby, which is normal at times. ("If she feels guilty then she'll change her behavior," you say? Yes, guilt can change behavior, but there are effective ways to change behavior without unhealthy guilt. We learn effective alternatives in Chapter 5, "Cooperation Toolset," and the definition of unhealthy guilt in Chapter 10, "Clear Communication Toolset.")

Labels are something we carry throughout life. When we believe a label, we *become* the label. We feel pressure to live up or down to the expectation, which limits our potential to improve or be hu-manly imperfect. When we get to this section in my parenting classes, we discuss our experience as a sibling or only child and the roles or labels we accepted. While some of us overcome these labels once we leave home, the label often reappears every time we are around our family. Parents have said, "I'm 50 years old and everyone still calls me 'the baby.'" "My brother was always Mom's favorite. They always show pictures of his kids and brag about his wonderful career. Our kids hardly even get a holiday greeting, let alone any attention when they come to visit. I feel like a constant disappointment to them, no matter how successful I am."

A Graduate's Story. *"I was talking to my sister about the sibling class I was taking. I told her that I realized how much my upbringing affected my self-esteem. I had always scored well on intellectual tests, but was never able to succeed academically. I told her how much I admired her for finishing college. She told me that she had always admired my popularity. Then she told me something I hadn't remembered. She said our mother used to tell us that I was the "pretty" one and she was the "smart" one. Suddenly, it was clear to me. We each felt it was our "role" to be pretty or smart. We were expected to fit those roles, even if we had the potential to be different.*

"Okay," we might say, "I guess I've been guilty of occasionally labelling my children." Maybe our children have put themselves in roles or perhaps others (peers or teachers) have. What can we do to help our children become more than their role—to become whole again?[2]

- **Point out times when people behave differently from their role or label.** Instead of saying "*For once* you weren't bossy," describe what the child did, "I noticed the way you let Brad pick the game he wanted to play."

- **Create situations that can show children their full potential.** Say "Sure, you can walk on the curb," instead of "No, you're such a klutz, you'll probably fall." Instead of rolling our eyes as we watch her stumble and fall while playing hopscotch, say "I was watching you play hopscotch! How do you play? . . . It's hard to hop on one foot like that, huh?"

- **Speak positively about them to others.** Many parents talk about their children as though they weren't there. If children hear what we say to others, it makes more of an impact because they think they weren't supposed to hear it. Make an extra effort to tell a positive story to others about times when they behaved differently from their label. When Grandma calls, skip the story of Mark getting sent to the principal's office—again. Be sure to tell her, though, about something positive Mark did that week (even if it's the only time you can remember). We might tell others about the problems we have, but *not* when our children can hear. Also, be careful only to share this information with people who will treat the child with unconditional love and not judge or criticize. We don't want to reinforce labels others have for our children.

- **Restate the labels/roles you hear others use.** Other children and adults may use labels that limit our children. Or our children might put themselves in roles or label themselves. We can respond in ways that put the quality in a positive context. For example, when a lady at the store says, "My, isn't she shy," we can respond, "Sue speaks up when she feels comfortable talking."

- **Model the behavior you want to see.** If a child is a "smart mouth," be sure to speak in respectful ways, even when angry. If children lie, share your feelings the next time you are tempted to lie but choose not to.

- **Remind children of times they didn't behave according to their role.** If children have a hard time resolving conflicts without aggression, remind them of a time when it took a lot of effort, but they worked things out. Be careful not to word this like a guilt trip: "Why did you hit him? You know better than that! Can't you be civil?" Instead, we can reassure them when they're getting aggressive: "Hey! I know you're really angry with John. So angry you feel like punching him! It's hard, but I've seen you control your anger before. When Tom took your toy and broke it you were so angry! But you didn't deck him. You left before you did something you would regret. What can you do now?" We can physically direct the children while we speak, not just stand there commenting while they pound each other. (For more ideas about "bullies and victims," see the "Common Sibling Issues" section of Chapter 8, "Problem-Solving Toolset.")

- **Watch your thoughts.** Even if parents never use labels and roles in their speech, their thoughts can still affect their children. Words, looks, attitudes, and tone of voice can express parents' expectations and beliefs. The first step in changing children's roles is to change our thoughts. Believe children can be different, whole, and can reach their potential. Look for the positive qualities a negative label can have. Use positive words when talking to children or about them. We will be more encouraging, our children will feel less discouraged, and will start displaying the positive qualities more often. Here is a list of negative labels and their positive qualities:

LABEL	POSITIVE QUALITY
Bossy	Knows what he or she wants, has leadership potential
Loud	Enthusiastic, outspoken
Messy	Carefree, busy, creative
Picky	Knows own likes and dislikes, has specific tastes
"Into everything"	Curious, eager to learn
Spacey	Internal, imaginative
Stubborn	Committed, opinionated, knows what he or she wants, sticks to it
Wild	Energetic, enthusiastic, vivacious

When we release children from roles, we help them see their full potential and teach them skills that help them feel whole and valuable.

> **Sticks and stones may break our bones and names really *can* hurt us. Our words can have a powerful effect on another person's life.**

 ## Stress Personal Achievement, Not Competition

Praise and ego-esteem are based on unhealthy competition—comparing oneself to others and trying to be better than them. When we compare ourselves to others, someone will always be better and someone will always be worse. Encouragement focuses on doing one's best, even if that best effort isn't perfect or even better than another's efforts. There are two ways parents can be more encouraging: (1) avoiding comparisons and (2) promoting only healthy competition.

AVOID COMPARISONS

Parents often praise children by comparing them to another child. Negative comparisons can make children feel inferior and can discourage them. For example, "You should save your money the way Jack does. He saved enough to buy a video game." This child might now believe he is a poor saver and probably *always* will be. He may resent his brother for outdoing him and for having a prized toy he doesn't have. Even if the brother did not contribute to this exchange, it still increases the competition and rivalry between them.

Positive comparisons can also be problematic. "It sure is nice to have at least one neat kid. Your sister is such a slob," can leave the praised child with one of several unhelpful feelings. She could feel sorry for her sister or feel better than her sister in a conceited way. Or she could feel pressure to always be better than her sister. Adele Faber and Elaine Mazlish, in their book *Siblings Without Rivalry,* offer the following rule of thumb:

> **Whatever you want to tell this child can be said directly, without any reference to another child. The key word is *describe*.**

Encourage the child's effort instead of comparing the child or the effort to another. Using descriptive encouragement in the above situations, we might say the following:

➤ "If you'd like a video game, you can save some of your money."

➤ "Your room looks so neat. Not only did you pick up all the dirty clothes, but you even dusted and organized your shelves. I bet it feels good to spend time in there."

Even when parents don't compare them, children may compare themselves as they compete for a place in the family or peer group. If one child is good in athletics, another child might believe that role is taken and pursue another talent. If one child is better than another in athletics, music, dance, or academics, it doesn't mean another child shouldn't pursue that interest. When children compare themselves, respond without validating the comparison:

Child: "Susan's such a good violin player. I'll never be as good as she is."
Parent: "How Susan plays has nothing to do with whether you should play or not. If you want to keep playing the violin, do it! You seem to enjoy it and you've improved a lot this year . . . I remember when you first tried that hard sonata. Last night when I heard you playing it, I actually stopped drying the dishes and just listened. It sounded so beautiful."

Child: "My kite didn't break because I took care of mine. Jimmy's is broken already!"
Parent: "Jimmy knows how to take care of his things, too. Jimmy, you must be disappointed your kite broke. What happened? . . . Oh . . . I bet you'll avoid those trees next time, huh?"

It is natural to notice differences between children. One child's strength can be another's weakness. Instead of trying to make children the *same* as each other or into what *we* consider ideal children, we can appreciate their differences.

> **Families who focus on competition actually *increase* the differences and resentment among family members. Families who value individuality and model cooperation have children who are more confident and cooperative with each other.**

PROMOTE ONLY HEALTHY COMPETITION

Comparisons are never helpful; competition, when used in healthy ways, can be. Many people think the only way to prove they are *good* is to compete and win. In the workplace, some adults compete with cutthroat tactics. At home, parents encourage their children to race, to motivate them into action. "The first one to _____ wins!" Of course, the youngest or weakest children usually lose, which only discourages them more. Racing differs from seeing if we can do something fast with no winners. "Let's sing the clean-up song and see how many toys we can pick up before we're done." If children insist on racing, encourage them to level the playing field by giving less-experienced children a head start or encouraging them to do their best without racing.

A Personal Story. Chris, being the fast runner that he is, likes to race. He likes to challenge himself and have some reference for how fast he ran. When we take walks, he'll say, "I'm going to run around the block. I'll see if I can get back to you by the time you get to the corner."

Amber is four years younger and dislikes racing. But she has a healthy, noncompetitive, self-motivated attitude and is usually willing to try new things. I've handled Chris' racing challenges several ways. I have always focused on the process of an activity, rather than the outcome. If Chris wants to race, I sometimes say, "A race takes two people. Amber, do you want to race?" If she declines, I suggest Chris just run by himself. Other times, I'll say, "If you want to run, Amber, go ahead. You don't have to race, just have fun."

When Chris gloats or teases her for losing, I tell him I expect him to be a good sport and be respectful and encouraging to the other players. "If you want Amber to keep racing with you, give her some encouragement." He usually describes her improvements and thanks her for racing.

Competition can be healthy or unhealthy. In unhealthy competition, the pressure to win is more important than the fun of playing or the value of the skills we learn in the process. The motivation to win reinforces the desire to be the *best* or *better than* others. It is discouraging to lose, because winning is the goal. Consequently, unhealthy competition promotes selfishness and poor sportsmanship.

> ***A Personal Comment.*** *A local newspaper reporter did a feature story about select sports teams and how some emphasize winning at the cost of equal participation.[3] I was shocked at some of the comments made by coaches and the clubs' official rules. For example, a third-grade team's coach said, "We don't want to lose a ball game because we played kids equally. It's sort of like a business: I'm trying to put the best product on the floor." He views these eight- and nine-year-old children as **products**! The official statement of that ball club says, "While the commitment of [the club] is to develop talent, the parents and players must realize that [the club] will play to win . . . there is no guarantee regarding playing time." Parents enroll their children, who are obviously good enough to make the team, so the children can improve their skills. Instead, some children warm the bench, which doesn't improve their skills at all! The coach's response to this comment was, "At some point in time, kids have to understand they're not good enough." Can you imagine how many children would give up a sport before their prime after hearing this! When the reporter interviewed a dozen children, they seemed to have their priorities much more in line than the adults. They all said they favored playing over winning. One girl said, "If I had my choice of playing five games or winning one, I'd rather play five. I think it's more fun to play than it is to win." It makes me wonder, "Who are these kids playing for—their coaches' reputation and prestige (or maybe their parents') or to build skills, self-confidence, and a healthy attitude about competition?"*

Healthy competition focuses on doing one's best. We only need to compete with ourselves. Those who give a strong effort and strive to improve themselves will often advance without taking someone else down in the process. If learning or improving is the goal, we always reach it. If we happen to win, it's icing on the cake. Healthy competition in work or team sports promotes teamwork, working together for a common goal—to participate and do one's best. Team members learn to support each other, work together, and do one's individual best to help the team.

> ***Unhealthy competition.*** **Winning, being the best, or being better than others is more important than having fun or learning skills. It adds pressure.**
>
> ***Healthy competition.*** **Doing one's best, having fun, and learning skills in the process.**

In their enthusiasm, some parents model poor sportsmanship when they stand on the sidelines yelling insults at referees who penalize their children. These parents teach their children to make excuses or to find someone to blame for their mistakes. Parents who yell negative advice such as "Come on! Wake up!" or "It's about time" are a pain in the neck to their children and an irritation to other parents who want to be encouraging.

> ***A Personal Story.*** *At one of Chris' soccer games, a father kept yelling criticisms at his son, thinking he would motivate the boy. His father's nitpicking continually distracted the boy and irritated the other parents. Finally, in the middle of a play, the boy stopped and yelled, "Just leave me alone!" The father probably thought his son was "talking back," but many of the other parents silently appreciated **someone** speaking up to the father.*

If we must yell during a game, let's make it encouraging: "Yes!" "Way to go!" "That's it!" "Nice kick!" "Keep it up!" If we see something that needs improvement and just can't keep quiet, tell children what to do in a positive way: "Spread out!" "Work together!" "Center it!" "Run!" After an event, let's restrict our comments to descriptions of how the child or team did well, made an effort, or improved. Don't focus on the score or outcome. If children bring this up, acknowledge their positive or negative feelings and include some comment about effort or improvement.

*A **Personal Story**. Sometimes it is **really** hard to find something positive to say in our comments. Amber only played soccer for one season. It was obvious, with each game, that this was probably not her cup of tea. She was clueless about the purpose of the game and her foot never touched the ball through the first half of the season.*

Over time, she improved, but very little. She ran a little faster each game. She still planted herself in her defensive position and didn't move—but she did stick her foot out, now and then, when the ball came near. It was painful to watch these games from the sidelines. My husband, my parents, and I wanted so much to cheer her on, but struggled to find anything positive to say. We were thrilled if she did something we could encourage. After each game, I tried to offer several positive (but honest) descriptive comments. My father still chuckles when he reminds me of my comments after one game. I enthusiastically said, "Your foot touched the ball three times today! You almost caught up with the pack! And I saw how well you defended your spot. No one was going to get the ball into your space!"

Be Gentle with Mistakes

The biggest difference between perfectionists and healthy achievers is the way they view and handle mistakes. Perfectionists are rarely satisfied because their best is never perfect. Most had perfectionist parents, who wanted to be perfect parents with perfect children. Now as adults, these parents may not realize how their comments reinforce a child's insecurities or add pressure. When they say things like "You could do better if . . ." or "I know you can do it," their children believe that they are never good enough, no matter how hard they try.

*A **Graduate's Story**. My mother would always remake my bed and rehang my clothes after I left for school. I could never figure out what was wrong with it. To me, my bed looked like an army bunk, tight enough to bounce a coin. I tried doing it the way she said, but despite my efforts, my mother was never satisfied. I finally figured, "What's the point, it's never good enough anyway," and stopped trying. To this day, I hate to make beds and have to force myself to hang up clothes.*

One of the scariest trends facing parents today is the frightening number of teen suicides. Teens who seem to have it all are literally killing themselves because they can never reach unrealistic goals (their parents', society's, and their own). Teens see how specialized jobs have become. They think they must quickly find their niche—one way they can be perfect. If they have a failed love affair, they wallow in despair. But who has found the perfect love or the perfect niche in their teens? Teens who are naturally smart and don't have to work hard to succeed can actually be a high suicide risk. Because they rarely fail, they might fall apart when they make mistakes.

Children who have to work hard for their achievements, making mistakes and occasionally failing along the way, often handle disappointment better. Their mistakes and struggles strengthen their character. They are healthy achievers: good self-starters, ambitious, courageous, and willing to take risks. They build on their strengths and work to improve their weaknesses. They try to do their best and strive for excellence, but don't expect perfection. If their best only warrants a "C" grade, they might be disappointed, but they know they did their best and learn ways to improve the next time. So what can we do as parents to avoid perfectionism or help a child who is too critical?

So what can we do as parents to avoid perfectionism or help a child who is too critical?

LET CHILDREN MAKE MISTAKES AND LEARN FROM THEM

I often hear teens complain, "I want to make my own decisions and learn from my own mistakes. My parents are always telling me about what *they* learned, instead of letting me learn lessons myself." A teen's desire for independence is a healthy sign of maturity and confidence—"I can do it myself." When our babies wanted to walk, did we stop them? We couldn't protect them from every fall and thank goodness we didn't! (We further discuss parents' legitimate concerns about the dangerous risks that come with teenage independence in Chapter 6, "Independence Toolset.")

We need to be careful that we don't protect our children from non-dangerous mistakes or go around behind them correcting what they've done. It is discouraging when others point out and correct mistakes. If we are always there to rescue our children, they will never learn to stand on their own. Mistakes show us what *not* to do in the future, which is often a valuable lesson.

When children make a mistake, don't belittle their emotions, "It's no big deal. You'll get over it." Recognize what they might be feeling, "It can be frustrating to work on a project so long and not have it turn out like you hoped." Help them view the mistake as an important part of the learning process. Don't lecture or point everything out for them. Instead, ask questions to help them see what they learned. "What happened? Do you have any idea why?" "How do you feel about it?" "What did you learn?" Reassure them, "Hey, we still love you—a lot."

> **Some mistakes are unavoidable. Correcting and learning from our mistakes is most important. In truth, there are no mistakes—*everything* is a lesson.**

HELP CHILDREN DEVELOP COURAGE

In the book *Active Parenting,* author Michael Popkin defines courage as "the willingness to take a *known risk* for a *known purpose.*" The known purpose is what we hope to accomplish. The known risk is the worst that could happen. Often, the risk is simply to try, possibly fail, but learn some valuable skills in the process. Courage is different from impulsiveness or disregard for the risks; courage is not blind. The key element of courage is knowing that the purpose *is* worth the risk. Truly courageous people are not without fear; they just don't let the fear prevent them from taking educated, planned risks. Courageous people ask themselves, "If I fail, what will I have accomplished in trying?" Even if they don't get the expected results, they realize they have gained knowledge and have stretched themselves further than they thought they could.

When I think of someone who was not afraid of mistakes and knew how to learn from them, I think of Thomas Edison. He never viewed his failures as mistakes, because they always taught him some piece of information that was helpful later. Had he not been willing to take risks, we would be without many modern inventions.

> *A **Personal Experience.** At a conference I attended, H. Stephen Glenn, author of* Developing Capable People, *shared a story about Thomas Edison and the risks of letting mistakes affect another person's self-esteem. The night before Edison was to present his new invention, the electric light bulb, to the press and public, his assistant accidentally broke the only working bulb. They had spent all day making this bulb and stayed up all night remaking a new one. The next day, he handed the bulb to his assistant for safe keeping. "Why did you let him hold it?", others asked him, "Weren't you afraid he'd break it again?" Edison responded, "There was more at stake than a light bulb; affirmation and trust are more important. After what he did, who could I trust more to hold on tight?"*

IS PRAISE EVER OKAY?

Okay, by now your healthy paranoia is in full bloom. You are probably saying, "I've been praising my children their whole lives! I had no idea that my efforts to make them feel better could be making them feel bad!" Whoa! Take it easy. First, if the worst thing you ever do in parenting is to praise rather than encourage, you still get a gold star. Remember, we are looking at *more effective* and *less effective* methods, not *right* and *wrong*. Praise isn't bad, it's just less effective at building self-esteem than descriptive encouragement and has potential negative side effects.

Knowing the pitfalls of praise, there will still be times when praise is natural and necessary. Praise *can* be encouraging, depending on the following factors:[4]

- We are accepting of our children, despite their behavior.

- We can be proud of our children just because of who they are.

- Our genuine intent is to encourage rather than control.

- Children are not expecting or demanding praise to get attention.

- Children are not dependent on other's opinions for their self-worth.

Use praise with encouragement, not as a tool by itself. If you're feeling genuinely enthusiastic and find yourself exclaiming "Good!" don't feel guilty. Just follow it up with an encouraging, descriptive statement so the child knows *why* it was good.

To tell whether our statements are praise or encouragement, ask:

- Am I inspiring self-evaluation or dependency on others' opinions?

- Am I being respectful or patronizing?

- Can I see their point of view or only my own?

- Would I make this comment to a friend?

ENCOURAGE YOURSELF

Raising your self-esteem as a parent strengthens the self-esteem of the entire family. You are worthwhile because you are you. You do not have to earn your worth by being an effective parent.

Use Positive Self-Talk

It's easy to criticize ourselves. Self-encouragement takes much more effort, at least at first. We can consciously *choose* what we tell ourselves about events and our abilities. The self-esteem and serenity we gain make it worth the effort.

Pay attention to the dialogue that goes on in your head. Many negative thoughts are leftover baggage from childhood. "You shouldn't do that . . ." "That was somehow my fault." If you had an unhappy childhood, it's not too late to give yourself what you need. Encourage yourself now, the way you wish your parents had.

Give yourself credit for what you are doing well. List, on paper, what you do well and your strengths as a person and parent. If you notice a negative thought about your abilities, decide if it is accurate. "I am a bad parent" is not accurate. You are judging, criticizing, and labeling yourself. Ask yourself, "What, specifically, do I think is so bad?" As you list your weaknesses, view them as areas to work on. Take each negative quality and create a positive statement out of it.

When writing positive affirmations, use words that are constructive and reassuring, as though you already have the quality.

- Instead of saying, "I will try . . ." say "I will . . ."

- Instead of "I will stop (old action)" say "I will (new action)."

- Instead of "I wish I could be . . ." say "I am . . ."

- Avoid words that compare. Instead of "I will _____ more than _____," say "I will _____."

Repeat the statements out loud throughout the day. Say them to yourself in the shower, while driving or jogging, when relaxing, or when looking in the mirror in the morning. By telling yourself you have positive qualities, you begin to believe in yourself. What you believe, you will see. The truth here is that you *do* have all the positive qualities you want to have. You just have to be willing to believe you are worthy of your own love. Program your thoughts and speech in the positive and the negative will begin to disappear.

Love Yourself Unconditionally

Value, accept, and appreciate yourself as you are, with all your imperfections. Parenting is a challenging task; both you and your children will make mistakes. When you do something you wish you hadn't, be kind to yourself. Remember, what's important is that you learn something from the mistake and make amends if you've hurt someone. View your mistakes with a sense of humor. Laugh at yourself in a friendly, loving way. (Reread the Declaration of Imperfection in Chapter 1, "Touring The Parent's Toolshop.")

Divorced parents can face difficult challenges to their self-esteem. When a relationship fails, the partners often feel like *they* are failures. Even if a separation or divorce is an improvement, family members can experience a temporary dip in their self-esteem. If either parent uses the children to hurt the other, it affects the self-esteem of both parents and children. Self-blame and blaming the other spouse create a negative and unhelpful attitude. Parenting after divorce is a time of healing and establishing new, revised family relationships.

Children have a higher need for security and affirmation during and after divorce. Some children wrongfully blame themselves for the divorce. Children are frightened to see the adults in their life acting like children—arguing, blaming, yelling, or being revengeful. Children can have temporary regressions in behavior or start behaving negatively. Since misbehavior is the result of discouragement, encouragement at these times is critical.

You can regain or improve the self-esteem your family had before the divorce. Focus on strengths, encourage yourself, use positive self-talk, and visualize yourself meeting your goals. Offer your children encouragement and reassurance. You can live and thrive after divorce. You have a choice, however, as to the quality of that life. Whatever the financial or material resources you have, your inner resources are what matter most to your recovery.

IMPORTANT POINTS ABOUT ENCOURAGEMENT

- **Encouragement is the one tool that most directly builds self-esteem.** Several other toolsets build self-esteem in indirect ways. The Independence Toolset teaches children skills, helping them feel more capable and confident to try new things. The Cooperation Toolset prevents power struggles, which are discouraging to parents and children and can lead to misbehavior. The F-A-X Listening Toolset helps us acknowledge children's feelings, giving them the courage to face and overcome their problems. While the specific toolset we choose will differ according to the situation, follow the basic guidelines outlined in this chapter when using encouragement.

- **Descriptive encouragement is a powerful tool.** When we describe what our children do in an appreciative or enthusiastic way, they will often repeat the behavior. So be careful what you encourage. If your child is playing with a loud, obnoxious toy, and you want him or her to stop, don't say, "Boy! You look like you're having fun!" The child is sure to show you just how much fun by making noise for another hour!

- **Don't just use encouragement *on* your children, *teach them* how to use the skills, too.** Show them how to give compliments that increase self-esteem rather than ego-esteem. Restate their comparisons to other children. Give them positive statements to replace negative self-talk. Help them turn their mistakes into important learning experiences they can feel good about.

> **When people hear encouragement, it boosts their self-esteem, without increasing their ego-esteem. There is no pressure, because the judgments and evaluations come from within. Best of all, no one can erase the good feeling with criticism later, because encouragement is a gift from yourself.**

SUMMARY SHEET
SELF-ESTEEM TOOLSET

SELF-ESTEEM is how we feel about our inside qualities.
SELF-IMAGE is how we think we appear to others on the outside.
EGO-ESTEEM is thinking we are (or are trying to be) better than others.

PRAISE uses judging labels that focus on pleasing others.
ENCOURAGEMENT uses descriptive words that foster internal motivation.

SHOW UNCONDITIONAL LOVE
- Give encouragement when children aren't expecting or demanding it.
- Don't use love as a conditional reward.
- Describe each child's special qualities.
- Give according to individual needs, not equally.
- Spend one-on-one time with each child; have fun!

FOCUS ON SELF-MOTIVATION ☆☆☆☆
- Show trust in children's judgement. Ask children their opinions.
- Help children trust their inner voice and not rely on others' opinions.
- Focus on children's feelings about their accomplishments.

SEE THE POSITIVE ☆☆☆☆
- Focus on what's right. Point out positive behavior and qualities.
- Give credit for any effort children make.
- Describe how children's efforts help themselves or others.

POINT OUT ANY IMPROVEMENTS CHILDREN MAKE
- Avoid "constructive criticism" and reminding children of past mistakes.

DESCRIBE, DON'T JUDGE ☆☆☆☆
- Don't judge or label. Instead, describe what makes it "good," etc.
- Express appreciation.
- Name the quality.
- Free children from roles and labels, both positive and negative.

AVOID COMPARISONS
- Describe what that person did, without any reference to others.
- Discourage unhealthy competition. Focus on doing one's best.

BE GENTLE WITH MISTAKES ☆☆☆☆
- Let children experience mistakes and focus on what they learn.
- Help children develop the courage to try.
- Have realistic expectations. Encourage children to do their best.

THE LANGUAGE OF ENCOURAGEMENT

I love you just because you're you.

You are special, because . . . (list qualities).

Your needs are important.

I like spending time with you.

Let's do something together, just you and me. Any ideas?

What do you think?

You have a real talent/ skill for . . .

Can you help the family by . . .?

I trust your opinion.

I believe in you.

It's okay to feel that way.

Even if I'm upset about something you *did,* I still love *you.*

I know you did the best you could.

I can tell you're pleased with it.

Tell me what you like about it.

You've really come a long way!

I bet it feels good to be able to. . .

You can be proud of yourself . . .

I trust your judgment.

I know you'll work it out.

You have a good head on your shoulders.

You showed good judgment by. . .

I can see you did (describe what's "right").

Thanks for helping with . . .

Thanks, that helped a lot.

It was thoughtful of you to . . .

Thanks, I really appreciate ____ because it . . .

I need your help with . . .

I admire your . . .

That's it! You (describe)

Try again.

I can tell you have improved (describe).

You might not feel ____, but look how well you . . .

You really worked hard on that.

Your hard work really paid off.

You tried and tried and didn't give up.

You'll get it with practice.

How do *you* feel?

I have faith in you.

You spent a lot of time on . . .

The way you ____ is especially ____.

Hey! You made it!

You came so close!

I could really see how much you improved. (Describe how.)

Look at that!

I know it's not your favorite thing to do. Thanks for doing it anyway.

You sure (describe).

You ____ and ____ That's what I call ____.

I bet it made (person) feel (feeling) when you (describe).

Did it feel good to ____?

I noticed the way you . . .

I really appreciate the way you . . .

Remember when you . . .

Go ahead! Try!

What (person) does has nothing to do with you. If you want to ____, do it!

Not only did you ____, but you even ____.

Just do your best.

Way to go!

That's it!

Keep it up!

Work together!

Even if it isn't perfect, that's okay. You did your best.

I know you'll learn something from it.

What happened?

Do you know why?

What did you learn?

Is there anything you might do differently?

PRACTICE EXERCISES

Write an encouraging response to these statements or select the multiple-choice answer you think is most encouraging. There's not one right answer to most, but there are some clues to help you choose certain helpful tools you just learned. It's still up to you to plan the actual words to use. (Possible answers are at the end of the chapter, but give your answers first, before looking at them.)

1. Child: "Who do you love more? Me or Jessica?"

2. Child: "He got more than me!"

3. Your child has been in her room for an hour and says she's finished cleaning her room. When you look, it's still cluttered and disorganized.

   (Finish this sentence.) I see you've . . . (describe, list)

   If you haven't taken time to teach what "clean" is or how to do it, what would you do?

   If you *have* taught what "clean" is and how to do it, what would you say?

4. Your daughter was pulling weeds, but accidentally pulled up flowers. (Show understanding for her mistake and give information.)

5. Your preschool child got dressed by himself. His shoes are on the wrong feet and his shirt is on backwards. (Describe what's "right" and how this effort was an improvement.)

6. Your son finally said "Excuse me," instead of laughing, when he burped at the dinner table. What would you say?

7. Your daughter scored in the 99% range in math on a placement evaluation, but only got a B– on her report card. What do you say?

8. Your son cooked macaroni and cheese by himself. Thank him by describing the steps he took.

9. Your daughter is an accident-prone "klutz." Write statements to help free her from this label.
   a. Ask her to do something that takes coordination.
   b. Describe a time when she didn't fall.
   c. Describe what she did well.

10. Your children are arguing in the back seat. As usual, it's the same one picking on his favorite victim, his older sister. Help free both of them from their roles.
    a. Express confidence in the "bully's" ability to get along.
    b. Encourage the "victim" to be assertive.

11. Name the quality, using the formula: "You (describe). That must have taken (quality)."
    a. Your child returned your tools to the toolbox, for once.
    b. Your daughter styled her hair in a fancy braid.

12. Your son and daughter are cleaning their rooms. Your son finishes first and did a good job. Your daughter is getting distracted and hasn't accomplished much. Say something to each, without comparing to the other.
    a. What would you say to your son, who's done?
    b. What would you say to your daughter, who's not done?

13. At a baseball game, your child is daydreaming in the outfield. If you shout something, what will you say?

14. Your child wants to run for class office. Encourage her without focusing on winning.

Activity for the Week

Use your family members' names and information to fill the blanks. Tell them these statements sometime this week.

"I like the way you _____ . Will you help us by _____?"

"Thanks for doing _____ . It _____."

(describe how it helped you or the family)

Something _____ does well is_____.

(name) (describe)

Something _____ accomplished this week is _____.

(name) (describe)

Something _____ did that helped someone is _____.

(name) (describe)

Something _____ did that took courage is _____.

(name) (describe)

One way _____ has improved in _____ is _____.

(name) (skill) (describe)

A good habit _____ has is _____.

(name) (describe)

Something _____ did for me this week that I never thanked him/her for is _____.

(name) (describe)

Possible Answers

1. "I love you both in very special ways. You are special to me because . . . (describe qualities)."

2. "Would you like more? If you're still hungry when you finish that, you can have more."

3. "I see you put your dirty clothes in the laundry basket and your books on the shelf." If you haven't taught them what "clean" is, drop it, for now. Plan to teach your definition of "clean" another time. If you have taught them, ask "What else do you see that you might have forgotten?"

4. "I appreciate all the hard work you did here. I can see how you might mistake these for weeds, but they're flowers. Next time, you can tell the difference by looking at (show and describe)."

5. "Wow! You got dressed all by yourself! You got your head and arms in your shirt, pulled your pants up all the way, and even got your socks on! They can be pretty tricky!" Unless you are going someplace special, don't even comment on mistakes. Spend time later teaching skills. You could make a suggestion, like "Sometimes it helps if . . ." or ask a question that will help the child realize *on his own* that he made a mistake. For example, "How did you decide which foot to put your shoes on?"

6. "Thank you for saying, 'Excuse me'."

7. "Look at this 'A' you got in spelling! How do you feel about your grades? Are you satisfied with your math grade? Do you want to bring up the grade? How could you do that?"

8. "Thanks for fixing this! It will be so nice to be able to relax before dinner. You really did a lot, didn't you? You got out the right size pan, cooked the macaroni nice and tender, and the cheese is just the right consistency. Did you do anything special to make it so creamy?"

9. (These are just my ideas, did you come up with some?)
    a. "Here, will you carry this for me?" (Select a non-breakable object for this.)
    b. "Remember how you stepped off the escalator at the store the last time? We can count 1-2-3 again, if you like."
    c. "Thanks for putting that bowl of mashed potatoes on the table. It's pretty heavy. You must have used those muscles of yours."

10. To the "bully": "I know you are can play quietly and respectfully. Why don't you suggest something you can do together, or maybe you'd rather sit in the other seat." To the "victim": "If you don't like what Tom is doing, say, 'Stop it!' You can speak up for yourself."

11. a. "You returned my tools! I'll appreciate being able to find them quickly. That was a conscientious thing to do!"
    b. "Wow! Did you braid your hair all by yourself? That must have taken fancy finger work!"

12. To your son, who's finished cleaning, describe what you see, without comparing him to his sister. To your daughter, who's not done, describe what she has done so far and ask what she plans to work on next. Don't point out or remind her that her brother is already done or the quality of work he did.

13. "Go Mark!" "Eyes up, Bud"! "Here it comes!" "Get ready!" (Pick one. I bet you had some more!)

14. "What would you like to accomplish as class officer? What would your responsibilities entail? It takes courage to run for office. I admire your willingness to make an effort to take on a leadership role. Whether you win or lose, I'm sure you'll learn a lot from the experience."

WHAT'S NEXT?

Use descriptive encouragement in your daily interactions with children *and* adults. You can find many ways to build self-esteem in your children, other family members, co-workers, friends, and even strangers. When you notice the good in others and point it out to them, they blossom before your eyes. Feel free to work with these skills for a week before reading the next chapter.

Chapter 5, "Cooperation Toolset," is most parents' favorite chapter. In it we learn many four-star tools that can prevent the power struggles most parents face. Life is smoother when we work *with* our children as members of the family team. We reach win/win solutions by offering choices within the limits we set using positive words. Most parents see immediate results from these tools—their attitudes change and so does their children's behavior.

REFERENCES

1. *How To Talk So Kids Will Listen and Listen So Kids Will Talk,* by Adele Faber and Elaine Mazlish (Avon Books, 1982) p. 181–183.

2. For more information on freeing children from roles and labels, see *How to Talk So Kids Will Listen and Listen So Kids Will Talk* (Avon Books, 1982) and *Siblings Without Rivalry* (Norton Books, 1987), by Adele Faber and Elaine Mazlish.

3. "Select Teams' Goals Bench Some Kids," by Susan Vinella, *Dayton Daily News,* July 7, 1997.

4. *The Parent's Handbook (S.T.E.P.: Systematic Training for Effective Parenting),* by Donald Dinkmeyer and Gary D. McKay, (American Guidance Service, Third Edition 1989) p. 39.

CHAPTER 5
COOPERATION TOOLSET

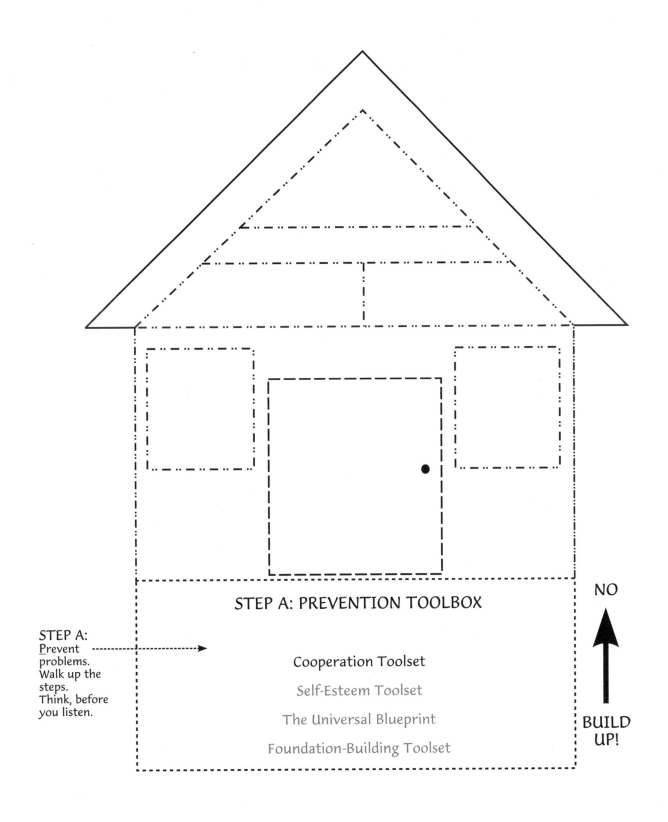

STEP A: PREVENTION TOOLBOX

STEP A:
Prevent
problems.
Walk up the
steps.
Think, before
you listen.

Cooperation Toolset

Self-Esteem Toolset

The Universal Blueprint

Foundation-Building Toolset

NO

BUILD
UP!

CHAPTER
5 COOPERATION TOOLSET

To build a house, a contractor needs a team of workers and the master blueprint. The team includes specialists and assistants who have assigned tasks. Together, they build the house. The contractor oversees the work and assures quality and timeliness. If the contractor orders people around and treats them disrespectfully, the discouraged and unappreciated workers might not perform their duties well. They might cut corners just to say they are finished, complain about their treatment, argue, and in some cases, refuse to cooperate. Getting fired might not even matter, for there are times when unemployment seems better than having a job where one is repeatedly mistreated.

In families, parents are the contractors who have the master blueprint. They need the cooperation of their team, the children, to help the family function in healthy ways. Sometimes children have special talents or skills to offer the family, while others help with tasks as their skills develop. If parents bark orders and treat children disrespectfully, as though they are inferior people, the children become discouraged and uncooperative. They may do as little as possible, complain about unfair treatment, and resist the parent's requests for cooperation. While children can't quit the family, they might resist participating in family activities if they think they will be repeatedly mistreated. Some children would rather argue or fight for some control than be blindly submissive.

IN THIS CHAPTER

This chapter encourages us to consider three important parenting ideas:

1. Promoting cooperation is more effective, both short-term and long-term, than demanding obedience.

2. Internal motivation is healthier and more effective than external motivation.

3. We can promote cooperation and internal motivation by using the special language of cooperation—using positive words to make requests or set limits and offering positive choices within those limits.

WHEN TO USE THIS TOOLSET

We want to use the Cooperation Toolset as part of our permanent, daily style of parenting. When children say "no," test limits, and make smart remarks, they usually get into power struggles with their parents. We can use the Cooperation Toolset to avoid or stop these power struggles. When we use the Cooperation Toolset, we usually notice an immediate change in both our attitude and our children's responses. We work together with our children as a team, instead of working against each other.

THE DIFFERENCE BETWEEN COOPERATION AND OBEDIENCE

There is a big difference between demanding obedience and promoting cooperation. First let's look at the negative effects of demanding obedience and compare them to more cooperative attitudes. Then we can learn the specific tools to use when we want more cooperation from our children.

Demanding Attitudes

Children usually want to be helpful, but our attitude or tone of voice can unintentionally discourage cooperation or start a power struggle. If we want more cooperation, we must change the negative attitudes that start power struggles: demanding power, wanting to control others, needing to win, or wanting children to obey commands. Dogs are trained to obey commands. People can be motivated to voluntarily cooperate with respectful requests.

When parents feel superior, giving orders to inferior family members, they often speak to their children disrespectfully. "I set the rules and you follow them." These attitudes create resentment and parents are more likely to get disrespectful attitudes and replies in return.

Healthy families value each person's role in and contribution to the family, despite age or ability. When children feel their contribution is important, they naturally want to cooperate more. They learn "We cooperate and help each other, not because someone makes us, but because we are a family who works together. We need each other." This approach differs from permissiveness, where children have few responsibilities and parents do too much for their children. A team theme helps the household run smoother and makes it easier to uphold family rules and practices.

DEMANDING OBEDIENCE CREATES RESISTANCE

It is a natural reaction to resist someone who is trying to control us. Most children and adults don't like being told what to do, how to do it, and when to do it in a rigid or demanding way. Most of us are willing to do what others ask, unless they speak disrespectfully and *demand* that we do something. Allowing others to treat us disrespectfully lowers our self-respect and self-esteem.

DO PARENTS ALWAYS KNOW BEST?

When asking a child to do a task, we usually think we know the best way to get the task done. Often, we are in such a hurry that we don't stop and listen to the child's ideas. Our children's stubbornness is often an effort to get us to listen to their ideas or let them be more involved in planning *how* to do a task. If children are more involved in the planning, it increases their motivation to cooperate.

Most of us think that if others need our help, we should have *some* say about how, where, or when we do the job. Children are no different. When we focus on cooperation, a task doesn't have to be done *exactly* the way we might do it, but must meet realistic time and quality guidelines. When we allow some flexibility, people are more likely to cooperate and put forth greater effort.

If we insist our children do something our way, stop and ask, "Why?" If we have simply pictured in our mind how we want it done, we can look for ways to offer choices within those limits.

WINNING AND LOSING

Demanding obedience is a win/lose game. Both parent and child try to win, but eventually one or both lose. Ultimately, the relationship always loses. Cooperation finds win/win solutions. Parents and children work together to meet both their needs.

> *A Graduate's Story.* We were leaving to have our pictures taken and my four-year-old son was piddling around (as usual). I was late (as usual) and told him to get his shoes on so we could go. He started into this long explanation, "I want to wear my old shoes in the car and then change when we get there and have my pictures taken with my new shoes, then change into my old shoes again . . ." I was too impatient to listen and didn't want to be tying shoes all day, so I said, "Pick a pair of shoes and put them on; you can't keep changing shoes all day." He started his litany again, and I completely lost my patience and said, "Just get your shoes on, NOW!"
>
> This, of course, caused the tears to flow and he tried again to explain. "Mom, they're my feet, and I don't tell you what shoes to wear. Why can't I wear what I want to wear?" I took a deep breath, thought about it, and said, "You're right, they are your feet, and you can choose whichever shoes you want. I will tie your shoes once. If you decide to change shoes, you will need to either wear them untied or choose your Velcro shoes."
>
> He put his tie shoes in his bag and his velcro shoes on his feet. On the way he explained to me that he didn't want his new tie shoes to get dirty and that's why he wanted to change into them at the studio. He actually had a very good reason for the whole thing! I "won," because I didn't have to tie shoes more than once and he "won," because he could wear the shoes he wanted for his photos. When I focus on win/win solutions, I often prevent power struggles and long negotiations.

LONG-TERM EFFECTS

Demanding obedience sometimes works in the short run, but it usually breeds resistance. We can punish or overpower children until they obey orders, but eventually children become discouraged. They either give up or fight back. Most importantly, children obey out of fear, not because they *want* to cooperate or understand the *value* of the request.

Cooperation, on the other hand, is effective in both the short and long run. The short-term result is more helpful behavior with less resistance and fewer power struggles. In the long run, it promotes an atmosphere of teamwork and self-responsibility. Children become *self*-disciplined, because they understand the value of rules and requests and feel their contributions are important.

THE DANGERS OF BLIND OBEDIENCE

Some professionals advise parents to say "Because I said so" or "Because I'm an adult and you are a child." While parents get their way by pulling rank, children do not learn to think for themselves. This type of power play might cut off a child's disagreement—but undermines healthy long-term parenting goals. The most competent way to handle a situation is not always the easiest or quickest route!

Many parents were taught as children to obey *anyone* in authority. In today's society, it is not safe for children to do something just because someone in authority tells them to. We've all heard about authority figures who have victimized children by using their position to gain children's trust and obedience. These abusers often succeed because adults and children are less likely to question people in authority.

Demanding obedience usually results in one of these outcomes: children either rebel or become submissive. Submissive teens often seek out peer leaders to guide them—and may not choose their leaders wisely. Clique and gang leaders try to impress others with their power and popularity. Teens who feel rejected, lost, or powerless often seek membership in these peer groups to gain acceptance and a sense of power. Children who feel unconditionally loved and accepted by their families and already have some power in their lives are less likely to join these negative peer groups.

Today, children need to judge whether they should obey a *request*, rather than the *person* giving the order. It is important for children to treat *all* people with respect (adults *and* children) and *cautiously* obey orders. A balanced parenting style helps children find the value behind requests, so they *want* to cooperate more. They seek win/win solutions that respect everyone's needs. If children need to refuse a request to protect themselves, they learn to do so assertively and respectfully.

DEMANDING OBEDIENCE	PROMOTING COOPERATION
Rigid limits with few or no choices.	Some choices within reasonable limits.
Superior parent gives orders to an inferior child.	Team theme—work together and each person's role is important.
"My way or the highway."	Children have *some* choice, such as when or how to do something.
Children obey out of fear.	Children understand the *value* of the request.
Children *have to* do what they are told.	Children are *self*-motivated to cooperate.
Win/Lose game.	Win/Win solution.
Short term—it sometimes works.	Short term—it almost always works.
Long term—creates resentment, rebellion, or blind obedience.	Long term—creates teamwork, self-responsibility, cooperation, and mutual respect.

If we wait to see cooperation before we stop demanding obedience, we continue to see the results of ordering children around—resistance. If we change our attitude first, we begin to see other people's attitudes and behavior change. The difficulty for most parents is taking the first step: adding choices or flexibility to their firm limits and rules—or simply wording our requests in more respectful terms. Many parents are surprised at how cooperative their children become when the children are no longer *forced* to obey.

COOPERATION TOOLS

I could fill an entire book of testimonials from parents who rave about the effectiveness of the Cooperation Toolset. Many parents begin seeing immediate changes in their attitudes and their children's willingness to cooperate. The following story is similar to comments many parents make after learning the Cooperation tools.

> ***A Graduate's Story.*** *As parents arrived for the Cooperation session, a young mother wiggled in her chair with a grin on her face. I asked the group if anyone had any success stories to share. The mother almost leaped out of her chair to tell the following story.*
>
> *All day long I've been telling the people at work how anxious I was to come to class tonight. I could hardly wait to tell you about my week. You all have heard about my daughter and how headstrong she is. We argue day and night. Every time I ask her to do something, try to do anything for her, or tell her to stop something, we get into a power struggle. After I read the Cooperation Toolset, I started using the tools immediately. **Everything** has changed! We haven't had a single argument for five days and I'm still counting! Our whole home atmosphere is more peaceful. She's more cooperative and I feel so much better about how I'm handling situations that used to lead to arguments.*

 Avoid Bribery

> ***Bribes*** **are tempting rewards, designed to manipulate, control,**
> **or influence someone to take a particular action.**

When children are slow to cooperate, parents often use bribery. They offer their children something enticing, like a toy for good behavior, payment for good grades, or a cookie to finish their veggies. Parents are usually trying to distract the children from what *they* want to do so they will do what the *parent* wants them to do. Bribes sometimes work in the short run, but they quickly become addictive for the child and ineffective for the parent.

Bribery teaches children to cooperate so they will get something in return. Most parents would prefer their children do something because there's some value behind the request.

> ***Bribes*** **are offered by the person seeking *control* and focus on *external* payoffs.**
> ***Cooperation*** **focuses on the *value* of the request or rule and the *internal* payoffs.**

When parents state the value of a rule or request, children cooperate because they understand *why* the request is important, even if they don't get a payoff. As children mature, they can figure out the value of a request on their own, even if it's not spelled out for them. Bribes are always external payoffs, so children get used to looking outside themselves for motivation. Bribes send hidden messages that are often different from the value of the request. Here are a few examples.

FOOD BRIBES

If we say to children, "If you eat your peas, I'll give you a cookie," why would they eat their peas? To get a cookie! But we *really* want them to eat their peas because they're nutritious, right? That's not the message the bribe sends. Food bribes can result in children developing unhealthy habits or overeating. If we want children to eat better, we teach them about nutrition, limit the unhealthy snacks that are available, and set consistent rules about when they can eat unhealthy food. "Unhealthy food can make you sick if you don't already have healthy food in your stomach. When you've given your body enough healthy food to grow, you can have a little unhealthy food just for fun."

Another type of food bribe is to give children food for comfort and stress relief. If children are upset, we need to teach them stress management skills and healthy ways of dealing with negative emotions. "I can tell you are really upset. Let's sit, so you can tell me what happened." Human comfort eases stress and upset feelings; food pacifiers simply offer a temporary distraction.

MONEY BRIBES

If we pay children for their grades, why are they motivated? For the money? If we pay one dollar for good grades in the third grade, what will we pay when one dollar no longer motivates children? Five dollars? What will children expect when they graduate? A car? And what if they try their hardest, but can never earn as much as another child who naturally excels at academics? Will they be motivated to try harder or give up, feeling their best is never good enough? We want children to get good grades so they will learn important information and skills. We can instill a love for learning by asking, "How do *you* feel about your grades?" We can offer encouragement, "Your hard work really paid off." If children want a reward, we can present it as a celebration, not a payoff.

> ***A Personal Story.*** *My son came home from school one day and said, "Jack just bought a new video game with the money his parents paid him for his grades!" "Really?" I asked. "Yeah, but you know what really stinks? I got better grades than he did!" For a second I was tempted to pull out my wallet, but stopped myself. I said, "I bet it seems unfair to know you worked harder than he did but didn't get that kind of a payoff." He nodded his head in agreement. "You know I don't agree with paying for grades," I said. "Why do you think Jack tries to get good grades?" I asked. "So he can get more money," Chris replied. "And why do you try to get good grades?" I added. He thought for awhile and said, "Because it feels good to put things in my 'proud portfolio' at school." "How long does Jack's money last?" I asked. "A couple days," Chris answered. I continued, "And how long do your good feelings last?" Chris looked at me, smiled, and said, "I get the point." I gave him an understanding look and a big hug.*

THE DANGERS OF BRIBES

Bribes are addictive. Children *only* do something *if* they get a reward. If we have been using bribes and try to change our approach, it might take some time to break their addiction to bribes. If we consistently use these tools, however, our children learn to cooperate without payoffs. The inner values they learn are far more lasting than any tangible payment they could receive.

Bribe junkies are more likely to follow abductors or peers of negative influence. Today, parents are more aware of the need to teach children to resist bribes, since adults and other children might use bribery, rewards, and threats of punishment to trick children. Many parents tell their children, "If someone offers you money, candy, or toys to do something, chances are you don't want to do it. The person thinks he has to pay you something to get you to go against your better judgement." If parents teach this rule of self-protection and then use bribery themselves, it's confusing and dangerous.

APPROPRIATE REWARDS

Bribes are different from spontaneous gifts, signs of appreciation, or celebrations. These bonuses are only bribes *if* parents present them ahead of time as a *reason* to do the task. If children do the task because they understand the value and don't know there is any payoff, the gift is a surprise. Children do not need to always get paid or rewarded if they cooperate. We can express our appreciation by returning a favor or saying "thank you" with our actions.

HOW TO TELL IF WE ARE BRIBING OR MOTIVATING CHILDREN

If we aren't sure if we are offering a bribe, conditional reward, or simply pointing out the natural positive consequence of cooperating, we look at four factors:

1. **Motive.** If we are "dangling a carrot" to motivate them, it is a bribe.

2. **Emphasis.** Bribes emphasize the *reward,* rather than the *value* of the request.

3. **Timing.** When parents use bribes *they* present the idea of the reward. "I'll give you a snack if you finish cleaning your room." If the *child* presents the idea of the reward and the parent wants the child to know when he can have it, it's not a bribe. For example, if children ask for snacks to delay finishing their work, parents can say, "When you're finished cleaning your room, you can have a snack." Here, the parent is teaching a value, rule, or explaining conditions the child must meet to get what he wants.

4. **Words or tone of voice.** Children usually (but not always) interpret *"If you _____, then I'll _____"* statements as bribes. "If you clean the house, I'll take you swimming!" Here the bribe is presented first, as an exchange for doing the task. *"When (or "As soon as") _____ then _____"* statements present the task first, emphasizing its value or the conditions children must meet to receive the reward *they* requested.

   ▶ *"As soon as* we finish cleaning the house, we *can* go swimming."

   ▶ *"When I see you are* finished cleaning your room, *I'll know you're ready to* play outside."

These statements teach the rule or value of "work before play." Even these small changes in wording and tone of voice can change a bribe into an appropriate motivating statement.

BEHAVIOR MODIFICATION PROGRAMS

Weight loss programs, employee incentives, and sticker charts for children are all examples of "behavior modification" programs. These programs are a result of scientific studies in which researchers rewarded subjects for desired behavior and withheld rewards or imposed punishments for undesirable behavior. They had great success training rats. (I've seen them play basketball for a food pellet!) They tried it on children, who responded well, too. So, the scientists concluded that rewards and punishment motivate people—which may be true—for a short time.

Instead of buying children's cooperation . . .　　　　*. . . focus on the value of the behavior, not the reward.*

Long-term studies of all types of behavior management programs have found that they foster dependency on external motivation and material payoffs.[1] People will do a task long enough to get the reward, but lose motivation if a payoff is absent. There are many tasks and behaviors people need to perform that have great value, but no material payoff. It is a sign of maturity to do something because it is helpful to others, improves our skills, or offers intangible benefits.

> *A Personal Story. I attended a seminar with a teacher who works in an SBH program (Severely Behavioral Handicapped). The SBH program used a token system (earning tokens to buy privileges) to motivate the children to attend school and change their behavior. Often, the children's behavior improved enough to return to a regular classroom. But the regular classroom didn't have the same reward system, so their progress deteriorated. These children learned **how** to behave but not **why** they should behave. They only behaved well when they got a payoff. They hadn't understood or accepted the **value** and **natural** positive benefits of cooperative behavior.*

Modified Use of Behavior Charts

Parents and professionals are now seeing the long-term consequences of incentive programs—a generation of reward junkies. Rewards work well on rats, but humans need deeper motivation. *The Parent's Toolshop* has plenty of tools to motivate children without rewards, so throw away your stickers and use these skills instead. Despite your efforts to foster internal motivation, some professionals may insist on using behavior charts with your child (in a classroom or therapy situation, for example). You can choose whether to state your philosophical objections before using one of the following options:

a.   Say you do not want your child to participate and offer an alternative approach;

b.   Grant limited permission for your child to participate in certain parts of the program (track progress but not receive "prizes" from an adult, for example); or

c.   Take action and make comments only at home to counter or reduce the inherent side effects of the incentive program.

If your child will participate at all in any incentive program, remember the following suggestions:

- **Explain the value of the task or behavior. Help children see it is a meaningful, worthwhile contribution** to the family, others, or themselves.

- **Involve children in developing the chart.** Creative ideas, like gluing pictures of tasks or desired behavior to a poster, can make this a fun project. Ask open-ended questions to help children set goals and decide how *they* want to celebrate reaching these goals.

- **Focus on learning new skills, instead of getting rewards.** When children reach their goal, comment on how good *they* feel about it and the skills they learned. Avoid referring to the reward as the goal or *reason* they did the task. Let children reward *themselves* if they feel good about what they did.

- **State the intangible rewards of doing the task.** Children will have more play time, know a new skill, and/or develop a new positive habit if they do the task.

- **Use the chart as a reminder of agreements or routines,** not a tally of rewards or payoffs.

- **Keep it positive.** Instead of giving demerits for *not* doing something, have each mark be a record of something positive the children accomplished. Use descriptive encouragement, not praise. (See Chapter 4, "Self-Esteem Toolset.")

- **Focus on doing one's best, not competing.** Competition destroys teamwork and damages relationships. Children are discouraged if they work twice as hard to earn points that other children can earn with less effort. This especially applies to siblings.

- **Gradually phase-out charts,** as children learn skills and change habits. Wean children off the rewards before they become addicted.

*A **Personal Story***. *Our elementary school introduces a homework reminder sheet in the second grade. It helped Chris learn good study habits. Amber's teacher used the sheet as part of a reward program. If a parent signed the reminder sheet every day, the child got a raffle ticket for a toy at the end of the week. We didn't forbid Amber from participating in the raffle program, but we never asked her about the prizes. Instead, we focused on the **value** of doing homework, **her** responsibility for accurately recording her assignments, and how she could use self-reminders to improve her memory skills and study habits.*

Later that year, on "Take Your Kids to Work Day," Amber attended my parenting class for the first time. As the class discussed homework routines, I asked Amber several questions.

Me:	*What time do you do homework?*
Amber:	*At seven o'clock, for 20 minutes.*
Me:	*What if you don't have homework?*
Amber:	*I read a book.*
Me:	*What do you do if you bring home a paper with a mistake on it?*
Amber:	*I fix it.*
Me:	*What do you do if there is a blank worksheet that you don't have to do for school or homework?*
Amber:	*I do the paper anyway.*
Me:	*Why do it if the teacher doesn't say you have to?*
Amber:	*Because it gives me extra practice.*

*As I looked up at the parents in the group, many had their mouths and eyes wide open. They were surprised that even an 8-year-old could understand and voluntarily accept the values and habits of homework. I noticed that she made no mention of the incentives her teacher offered. Amber will continue improving her study habits in the years to come, but it won't be the result of bribes and rewards or stickers and toys, which someday will end. She'll improve because she understands the **value** behind the task, has learned the **skills** she needs to do the task, and feels good knowing she's done her best, which are all better, longer-lasting rewards.*

Plan Ahead ☆☆☆☆

One of the most effective prevention tools is to anticipate a problem and take steps to avoid it. If you experience a recurring problem or expect a problem, here are several steps you can take:

- **Discuss the behavior you expect.** Describe the behavior you want to see in positive, specific terms that your child understands. "We need to leave the playground in five minutes. You have time for two more rides. After two more rides I'll say it's time to go. I expect you to come right away and walk with me to the car."

- **Teach skills so your expectations are realistic.** Simply saying, "Don't talk to strangers," is often ineffective. Children are either scared to talk to strangers even when their parents are present (to store clerks, for example) or when a "safe" stranger could help them (asking a security guard for help when lost). They might also mistakenly think strangers must look scary and trust someone who looks friendly, but is an unsafe stranger. Define the difference between safe and unsafe strangers and what types of conversations are acceptable. For example, "If you are with Mom or Dad and someone talks to you, you can say 'Hello' and answer questions like 'How old are you?' But if *anyone* asks you to go somewhere, come and tell me right away, even if you know them."

- **Agree to a rule or plan for potential problems.** For example, once parents and teens have negotiated a time, pick *a* clock. *That* clock's time is the time they use. Get an agreement that children will call whenever they are late. Make sure they have spare change so they can call from a pay phone if there is an emergency. Many teens today carry beepers and cellular phones. If they can leave signals on their friends' beepers to say "Hi," they can call parents to say "I'll be late."

Offer Choices Within Limits ☆☆☆☆

This is one of the most effective and useful four-star tools in *The Parent's Toolshop*. We learn several different ways to use this tool throughout our tour. When we use choices within limits, we shift the focus from giving commands to possible options within our rules or limits. Here are a few guidelines for offering choices effectively.

Don't give a choice if there is no choice. "Do you want to take your medicine?" sounds like the child has a choice. The child could say, "No, I don't want to take my medicine." Also avoid saying "The trash cans need to be brought in, *okay*?" "Okay" sounds like we are asking children if they *agree* with our request. We need to say what we really mean, "Do you understand?" or "Did you hear me?"

State your bottom line or what needs to be done, then offer choices within those limits. "We are having guests Saturday, so your room needs to be clean by Friday. You can either clean it all up at once or do it a little each day." "If you stay in the sun any longer, you'll get sunburned. You can either put on a shirt or play in the shade. You decide."

"Bottom line" limits are the minimum standards that must occur, what is non-negotiable. We balance limits by offering choices within our bottom line.

Choices involve the following types of statements:

- "Which would you like?"
- "How many do you want?"
- "Are you going to _____ or _____?"
- "When do you plan to _____?"

- "You can _____ or _____, you decide."
- "How do you plan to _____?"
- "Do you want to _____ or_____?"

Using this tool in the previous examples, we can say, "Do you want to take chewable medicine or liquid?" "The dogs need to be fed before you play. *When* will you feed them?"

Make the choices respectful to both parent and child. If we say "Either quit throwing the ball in the house or I'll take it away," we are making a threat, not offering a respectful, fair choice. This is called a power play. An effective, mutually respectful choice would be, "You can either play with the ball outside or with another toy inside. You decide." Here, parents address their safety concerns *and* respect the child's need or desire to play.

Allow the child to offer choices. "We can have meatloaf or fish for dinner, unless you have an idea for something nutritious and delicious." Remember to state your bottom line. Don't be too open-ended unless there are truly unlimited choices. Otherwise, children will suggest pancakes, pop, and donuts. If children suggest something different, go with the idea if it meets your bottom line. This is *not* giving in. If children say, "I want spaghetti" and that's okay, say, "Well, spaghetti is quick and nutritious. Good idea!" (If it's not okay, use the "No No's" tool described later in this chapter.) Don't be overly rigid about forcing children to pick one of *your* choices; it could lead to a power struggle. Remember, your goal is to *share* power and reach a win/win solution.

Continue to focus on what the child can control.

If there is not a choice about *if* something will happen, offer a choice about *how* or *when* it can happen.

Think about the circle symbol for over-controlling parenting in the Foundation-Building Toolset. When parents debate *if* something will happen, they can go in circles debating and it often turns into a power struggle. These are win/lose battles. Now, think about the symbol for balanced parenting, a circle with a zigzag inside. The circle represents the bottom-line limits, the parent's "win." The zigzag represents the choices children have within these limits, their "win."

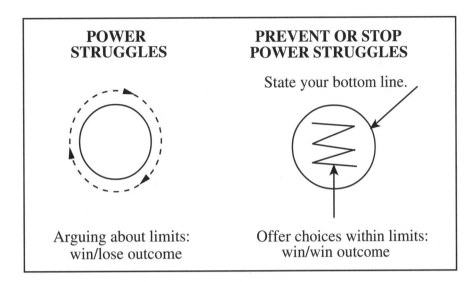

When we set reasonable limits and then shift the focus to *how* or *when* they can meet these limits, children still have some power—their choices. When facing a win/lose game or having some control in a win/win situation, most people choose win/win. We can use choices to prevent resistance at every step of a task.

A Personal Story. When Amber was 5, she often got distracted while getting dressed. (I once saw her playing with only one leg in her pants.) One day I realized just how much I used choices to keep her moving from one step to the next.

"Your body and hair look dirty. Do you want to take a bath or shower?" Whether she wanted a bath or not, I shifted the focus to her choices again. Knowing she prefers baths, I said "Do you want to take your bath before I take my shower or after me so you'll have more time to play?

"Okay, get your clean clothes while I'm in the shower. You can play with your dolls until I'm done." As her water filled, I said, "Are you going to get in now or wait until the tub is full? . . . Okay! Be careful stepping in!"

After a few minutes, I said, "Do you want to wash your own hair or do you want me to wash it?" As she shampooed, I offered suggestions such as, "If you tip your head back you'll get all your hair wet." I planned ahead, saying "Daddy needs to take a shower, too. You have until I'm done with my makeup to finish washing and playing."

When I finished my makeup, I said, "Go ahead and let the water out. You can get out now or wait until the water is all gone." She decided to stay and a few minutes later I said, "Daddy needs to take a shower. Do you want to get dressed in here or in your room?" She got out of the tub.

Amber was clean, dressed, and ready in the time it took me to dry my hair, put on makeup, and get dressed (about 20 minutes). By using choices, she improved her ability to move from one step of a task to the next. By age 7, she could get ready on time all by herself with no input from me.

ACCOUNT FOR INDIVIDUAL PERSONALITIES

***"Strong-willed"* children need lots of choices.** If we order and command, they debate with the skill of union negotiators. When we provide choices within reasonable limits, these children learn that rules are a natural part of life and following them does not always mean giving up personal power. If we say "Do you want milk or juice" and children say, "I want both," we can say, "Which one *first*?" If we offer a choice and children respond with "neither," we can say, "That's not one of your choices."

If children persist, we can say, "You can decide or I'll decide for you. It's up to you." We need to focus on what children *do* have a choice about or we might start a power struggle. Usually, children who are this logical and persistent can handle more open-ended choices. Try stating the bottom line and allowing *them* to figure out their options.

***Pleasing* children sometimes feel overwhelmed by choices.** They try to anticipate what the parent wants and can't decide what *they* want. With these children, we need to keep choices simple and use them less often. We must be careful, however, to not always tell pleasing children what to choose. These children need permission to make decisions, try new things, and take risks.

***Indecisive* children are afraid that if they choose one thing, they'll miss out on the other option.** Always point out that they'll have another chance to try other options later. They often play the "I can't decide" game. This game drives even the most sane parent up a wall. It goes like this: "Do you want milk or juice?" "Juice." "Okay, juice it is . . ." "No! Milk!" "Milk?" "No! Juice!" Get the picture? You want to avoid going in circles trying to please children who have no idea what they want. To promote cooperation without getting sucked into this game:

1. *Use choices less often if the child is going through an indecisive phase.* (These periods come and go, often unexpectedly.) During these times, offer only two choices. More choices might overwhelm and confuse the child.

2. *Teach indecisive children simple decision-making tricks*, like "eenie, meenie, miney, moe." They will usually make their finger land on their favorite item or will do it again until they select the choice they really want.

3. *When children finally choose, confirm their choice.* Say "Okay, you want cereal, right? Once I pour the milk on the cereal, I expect you to eat it." Be clear that you are unwilling to be a short-order cook, throw out food, or make multiple meals, because this violates *your* rights and makes children think the world revolves around them.

4. *When they change their answer* say, "Think carefully! You will need to stick with your next answer!" Then give them a minute to think about their options and decide.

5. *If they still can't decide, add "Either you decide or I'll decide for you."* This can be a short-term, sanity-saving measure. Still, remember that these are the children who need practice at making choices, so you want to give them opportunities to make choices about other issues.

6. *Follow through with the choice.* You may still have an upset child who throws a tantrum. (See the section on tantrums on pages 74–75.) You might still get the I-can't-decide-game, but stick with your plan. Eventually children learn that when they have a choice to make, they need to think about their options and be sure of their choice before answering. Learning this decision-making skill is much more important than the actual choices the child makes.

7. *If children don't like the choice they made,* acknowledge their disappointment and remind them that they can choose another option next time.

Young children need limited choices. Two simple choices are usually enough. The number of choices can increase as the child's intellect and maturity develop. ***Older children*** need broader choices or it starts power struggles or long negotiations. ***Teens*** need open-ended choices. State your bottom line and ask them to come up with a plan. Express your confidence in their ability to make an appropriate decision. Remember to get agreements with specific time frames if the time limit isn't open-ended.

Children of all ages love choices. They quickly catch on to the change in language. In fact, many parents report that their children start offering *them* choices! At first, the choices children offer aren't always fair to the parent. Some parents feel threatened when their children offer them choices, as though parents should only be allowed to come up with options. Instead, encourage children to keep thinking of options and teach them how to offer choices appropriately.

> *A **Graduate's Story**. My son offered me an interesting choice when it was time to leave the playground. I planned ahead, offering him choices about leaving. He calmly and firmly said, "But I don't want to leave! You can either let me stay or I'll scream and cry." I tried hard not to laugh! I said, "Choices have to meet both people's needs. I know you are having a lot of fun and don't want to leave. I also know that Janey will be home from school soon and someone has to be home when she gets there. We can't stay much longer, but you can choose how you spend the time you have left. You can go on two more rides and have fun or we can leave now. If you decide to scream and cry when it's time to leave, I'll know you don't want to come to the playground the next time we have a free sunny day. It's up to you."*

Here, the parent not only taught her son how to present appropriate choices, she also revealed the positive and negative effects of his behavior choices (which is part of the Discipline Toolset). Remember, you can teach children how to use the tools you are learning, so they can improve the relationships they have with others.

One final note about choices: Some parents have so much success using choices within limits that they use it in *every* situation. They forget that in some situations another tool may be more appropriate. Don't overuse choices or feel you have to give children a choice about *everything*. Use them within reasonable limits.

Don't Say "Don't" ☆☆☆☆

This is a favorite tool among parents because it is logical, positive, and usually has immediate results.

People learn by hearing, seeing, and doing. When we hear something, we see it in our minds and then try to do what we see. We also do what we see others doing. When children hear "don't," "stop," or "quit" before a description of negative behavior, they picture the negative behavior the parent is trying to prevent or stop. For example, if a parent says "Don't spill your milk," the child pictures the milk spilling. For children to obey this command, they must:

1. Figure out the opposite,
2. Picture it in their mind,
3. Think of the different options for accomplishing it,
4. Evaluate each option,
5. Select one, and
6. Do it.

They must do all this in about five seconds, or the parent might get impatient, angry, and louder. ***Older children*** and adults have had many years to practice this process of taking a negative image and figuring out what to do instead. ***Younger children***, however, simply do what they see. If they see the milk spilling in their minds, they are more likely to spill their milk.

> *A **Graduate's Story**. I was volunteering at my daughter's preschool Valentine party. I heard the parent at the other table say "Don't spill your drinks!" I remembered what you said about "Don't Say Don't" and told the kids at my table "Keep your drinks in your glass!" Almost immediately, a kid at the other table spilled a drink—and it was like dominoes. Almost every kid at that table spilled a drink and then it spread to the other tables on that side of the room! Not one kid spilled a drink on my side of the room. "Don't say Don't" really works!*

Sometimes children want to find out *why* they aren't supposed to do something, so they do it to see what happens. These are I-want-to-learn-for-myself children. Their frustrated parents say, "Didn't I just tell you *not* to do that?" Saying "don't" and describing negative behavior offers no helpful information about the value of the request or the behavior we want to see.

We *all* respond better to positive directions. Do good track coaches say to their runners, "Don't fall over the hurdles"? No! They describe how to run and extend their legs, so the runners will clear the hurdles. This creates a picture of success in the runner's mind. If we watch athletes on TV, we often see them closing their eyes and moving their bodies. They are picturing what they want *to* do. In the military, a parent once told me, instructors only explain the correct way to do something. They see no value in mentioning the incorrect way.

> *A Personal Story. When my daughter first played soccer, at age four, she had difficulty understanding the rules. When she played with her team, she'd stand there, confused. But when she practiced with us and my son's coach, she played better. I finally understood why, when I overheard her coach reviewing the rules before a game. She said, "Now remember, don't touch the ball with your hands, don't run in the wrong direction, and don't **not** listen to the coach."*
>
> *My husband and I were shocked! No wonder our daughter was confused! How many kids could figure out those rules? Clearer directions would be "Kick the ball with your feet, run toward **that** goal [pointing], and listen to me if I call you."*

Sometimes, children (and adults) rebel when they hear "stop" or "don't." They resist, simply because they don't like being told what to do. Or they enjoy getting a reaction by misbehaving.

> *A Graduate's Story. I was at a barbecue at Carol's house, my next door neighbor. Her son began shooting us and the grill with his water pistol. Carol kept saying, "stop it" and "don't do that." I shared the idea of "Don't say Don't" and suggested a different way to say what she meant. Carol scoffed at the idea, "Right! Like he's going to listen any better to that!" I simply said it had really worked for me and dropped the issue. When her son squirted his father, who was standing at the grill, Carol said **to me,** "What am I supposed to say, 'Squirt the water on the grass'?" Although she said the statement to me, her son immediately turned and squirted his water pistol in the grass! Carol's jaw dropped in amazement and she said, "Wow! That really does work!"*

Whenever possible, we want to flip our attitude, thoughts, and words from negative to positive. Instead of telling people what *not* to do, we describe the behavior we *want* to see, so they will see it in *their* minds. Tell children what they *can* do and let them test what happens when they do it. Here are some examples of flipping negative commands into positive requests:

NEGATIVE COMMANDS	POSITIVE STATEMENTS
"Stop fighting!"	"Use words, not fists," or "People aren't for hurting."
"Stop arguing!"	"Find out what you both need and make an agreement."
"Don't play so loudly!"	"Use your inside voices," or "Play quietly."
"Quit whining."	"Talk so I can understand you."
"Don't talk back to me."	"In this family we talk to each other respectfully." (Then make sure you honor this rule, too!)
"Don't forget your lunch."	"Remember your lunch box."

If you don't have "healthy paranoia" yet, you are sure to have it after learning this skill! Many parents say "don't" or "stop" dozens of times a day. One mother insisted, "I *can't* stop saying 'don't'!" On the other hand, some parents try to completely erase the words "don't" and "stop" from their vocabulary. They are afraid to say "I want to stop at the store" or "I don't like broccoli." Just avoid the words *don't* and *stop* when trying to redirect or prevent unwanted behavior. If you hear yourself saying an unhelpful "don't" or "stop," just think about what you want your child *to* do and describe it.

Using this tool is awkward at first. It's easier to point out what others *shouldn't* be doing than to point out what they *should* do. If we have trouble flipping a "don't" around, imagine how difficult it is for children. With practice, you'll catch yourself *before* the "don't."

A Personal Story. I have countless success stories from parents and my own life about the effectiveness of "Don't say Don't," but there's one last story I must share. When Amber was four, she was playing in a small pool with Brian, our neighbor. My son, Chris, who was eight, asked if he could play too, ". . . but don't splash me" he added. As if on cue, Amber and Brian stopped splashing each other, took a bucket of water and chased him all over the yard. Chris came to me, dripping wet, and said, "I shouldn't have said 'don't'—I gave them the idea!" That's when I knew "Don't say Don't" really makes sense to kids!

No "No's" ☆☆☆☆

Every parent needs to set limits or refuse a request at times. The most common and seemingly simple way is with the word "no." But this small word often results in dramatic, uncooperative responses from children. If parents can get what *they* want by saying "no," children think, "Hmm, 'no' equals power." It's only natural for them to then imitate this behavior when *they* want control.

"No" might bring short-term success when setting limits, but more often it starts a power struggle. Now, let me be very clear. I am *not* saying "don't set limits" or *mean* "no." Parents have the right and the responsibility to set reasonable limits and need to do so. But we can state those limits with positive words, without the word "no," to prevent a power struggle. This switch, from negative to positive words, actually accomplishes more with less resistance.

Toddlers and preschool children are still developing self-control and learning how to influence the world around them. Therefore, they may say "no" when they really mean "yes." This is a test to see if they can have control with this word, too. When parents think children are challenging their authority and react by exerting more power, the child learns it is important to have power over other people and "no" is the way to get it. This is one way a toddler's "no" phase begins.

Most parents believe that every child goes through a "no" stage, that it's inevitable. Dozens of parents who use this skill, however, can tell you that it is *not* a certainty. It depends on how the people in his life handle power and control issues and whether they use negative or positive words to set limits.

A Graduate's Story. I am so glad I learned these skills when my kids were still young. I have a lot of friends who ask, "What do you do when your kids do (this and that)?" I realize I haven't had a real problem with those behaviors. I know the parenting class is the reason I avoided these common problems. In fact, neither of my boys ever went through a bad "no" phase. This is not to say I never experience resistance or conflicts. They just seem less severe and I know I have the resources to respond to them quickly and productively.

Older children, from school-aged to teens, value independence and want more choice about issues involving them. When parents use the word "no" or lay down the law in negative, inflexible ways, these children think the parent is challenging *their* power and rebel. When parents make a power play, they are practically asking for defiance. Then the cycle starts. As parents exert their authority to say "no," these children try to show parents they aren't willing to be controlled. (In Chapter 12, "PO Toolset," we learn how to stop power struggles once you are in them. Right now, let's learn how to avoid them!)

Many resources offer suggestions for setting limits in positive words, without the word "no." Most of these ideas fit within one of the following tool groupings:

GIVE A CONDITIONAL "YES"

When some children hear "no," they start planning their strategy to change our minds. Their loud protests usually drown out our explanation. If we say, "No, you can't have a snack, because we are getting ready to eat," when do they tune us out? After the "no." If we say, "Yes, when . . .," they are still listening when we explain the conditions they need to meet.

This tool does not allow unwanted behavior. It simply tells the child under what circumstances the answer could be a "yes." For example, instead of saying "No, you can't go to the movies. You haven't finished your homework yet," say "Sure, when your homework's done."

Sometimes, there is no way the answer could be a "yes," such as, "Yes, you can play in the street . . . when you're twenty years old!" In these cases, a conditional "yes" is not an appropriate tool to select.

> ***A Personal Story.*** *My son and his friend (then ages nine and ten) asked if they could eat a popsicle. I said, "Yes, if you stay in the kitchen or take it outside to eat." When I checked on them, they were sitting in the living room with their feet propped up on chairs in the kitchen. This was their interpretation of "staying in the kitchen." This time, I stated more clearly my bottom line, "I want the popsicle to be in the kitchen, over the tile floor and away from the carpet and chairs." They put down their feet and leaned over in their chairs so any drips would go on the tile. I guess the lesson here is to be clear about what you ask for; they might take you literally.*

OFFER AN ACCEPTABLE ALTERNATIVE

When parents take something dangerous away from a baby, they usually trade it for an acceptable toy. We can use this approach in any situation with children of any age (and adults). In fact, I was using this tool when I promised in the first chapter to ". . . avoid telling you *not* to do something unless I offer at least one or more positive alternatives." When we want to redirect children without saying "no," we can say, "You can do ____" or "Well, you can ____ instead," or "I'd prefer you . . ."

GIVE INFORMATION

Children can't read our minds. We often have a good reason for denying a request, but if our children don't have this same information, they may balk when we say "No." For example, if a child with a cold asks to play outside, the parent can say, "If you play in the rain, your cold could get worse. When your fever goes away, you can play in the rain again." This gives children information they can use in the future. Try using the previous suggestions to give information with positive words. For example, if your child asks you to take him to the toy store to get a friend's gift, avoid saying, "No, I don't have time." Instead, say "I need to leave for a meeting in an hour. We could go tomorrow, though." Long explanations are not necessary, nor is repeating yourself. If we don't really have a good reason, this skill might not be appropriate.

There may be times when we sense that the child's request isn't a good idea, although there is no tangible reason for that opinion. We can actually state this as our reason, "I know you really want to go to Joe's party but I have this uncomfortable feeling that I can't explain. Maybe if I knew more about Joe or his party I could figure out if my concern is valid."

TAKE TIME TO THINK

Children are great at pressuring us for a quick response—and we can get ourselves into agreements we wish we hadn't made. Tell children you *will* answer them, after you have a moment to think over their request. Respond in a timely manner, out of respect for the child, instead of using this response to avoid or delay the issue. If we delay too often, children will only pressure us more strongly for a quick answer.

RECOGNIZE FEELINGS

When we acknowledge feelings first, before denying a request, our children know we understand how they feel and are more likely to listen to us. This reduces the chances of an Oscar-winning performance to convince us of their position. (This is also consistent with the PASRR formula: **P**revent the problem and **A**cknowledge feelings, then **S**et limits and **R**edirect problem behavior.)

Remember that children's priorities are often different from ours. Sometimes, our goal is not to make our children *like* doing the things we ask them to do or agree with our priorities. Sometimes we simply want them to agree to do a task, even if they don't really want to do it. If children ask to stay up late, we can say, "I know you might not feel tired now" or "It's hard to go to bed when you don't feel like it." This could be all we say. We don't even have to say "no" or "you have to go to bed anyway," because our sentence implies it. We can add choices, "You don't have to go right to sleep. You can read, work puzzles, or do some other quiet activity. That's your choice." Notice how this statement shifts the focus away from the firm limit to what the child *can* do.

GIVE WISHES IN FANTASY[2] ☆☆☆☆

While we can use this skill any time we want to recognize feelings, it is particularly effective to use it when children can't have what they want. When children get in fantasy what they can't have in reality, it helps them move on. At least they know we understand that they "wish" it could happen. Wishes and fantasy can take many forms, depending on the situation and the age of the child. Here are a few examples:

➤ "I bet you wish you could stay at the pool all day and not get sunburned!"
➤ "I know you'd like to have that sword. What would you do with it?"
➤ "If you had a magic wand and could change this situation in any way, how would you change it?"
➤ "Let's erase this argument and start over fresh."

Don't be afraid that you will have to grant the wish. Most children understand it is just a wish. The point is that we show we understand their heart's desire. We can also have fun with this tool, creating exaggerated fantasies that helpfully redirect the conversation. I gave this tool a four-star rating after other parents raved about it and I had the following experience.

> *A Personal Story. When Chris was three, we went to a shopping mall. I quickly realized I would have to pass a toy store. Fortunately, I had my wits about me that day. As we approached the toy store, Chris said, "I want to play with the train!" I moved to his other side so he couldn't see the store, locked eyes, smiled and said, "We won't be able to play with the train today. It sure is a neat train, isn't it? It's nice that they let us play with it when we have extra time. What's your favorite part of the train set?" As he described the train set, I escorted him past the store.*
>
> *Soon he asked, "Can we buy a toy on the way back?" I was tempted to give my usual prerecorded reply of, "I don't have the money today, besides, you have too many toys already." Instead, I said, "That's a pretty neat toy store isn't it? What are some of your favorite toys in there?" I listened and responded as he listed them.*
>
> *By this time we were well past the store, but we were enjoying the fantasy so I said, "If you had all the money in the world, what would you buy?" He named several things and then asked me, "What would you buy?" I pointed to an outfit in a store window and mentioned a car, etc. He asked, "Mom, where would we put all that stuff?" I enthusiastically said, "Well, if we had all the money in the world, we could buy a house as big as a castle, and fill it up with all our toys!" He was quiet for a minute and then said, "Mom, that sounds like too much stuff. We'd never play with it all!" He paused, then added, "Maybe we're better off with just the toys we have." I had to watch my step so I wouldn't trip over my jaw, which was now dragging on the floor! Without giving my prerecorded excuse, my son had figured out **on his own** that it is sometimes better not to get everything we want!*
>
> *Several weeks later, he was watching TV and saw an advertisement for a toy. He said, "I wish I could have that." I didn't have my wits about me this time and blurted out, "It's too expensive. Besides, you already have enough toys." In a matter-of-fact voice, he said "Mom, all I said was, 'I wish.'" **That's** when I knew this "wishes and fantasy" skill really worked. Even a three-year-old could understand the difference between **wanting** something and **having** to get it!*

This tool usually brings great satisfaction to both children and parents, but there are a few exceptions. When children are too reality-based or insistent on getting their way, choose a different way to say "no" in positive words. Some wishes can never be granted and may unnecessarily expose deep wounds. If so, avoid using this tool or use F-A-X Listening (Chapters 7 and 8) to help children work through their pain.

> *A Graduate's Story. Nina attended the parenting class to help her grandson, who was living with his abusive mother. Nina had cancer, so she was unable to take custody of the boy, but he visited with her every weekend. One weekend, he asked why he had to go home. Nina used wishes and fantasy in her response, "You wish you didn't have to go home, huh?" The boy started sobbing— and so did Nina—for she realized just how hard it was for both she and her grandson to deal with the pain and impending loss of their situation.*

SAVE "NO'S" FOR DANGEROUS ISSUES

There will be times when "no" is the first thing that comes out of your mouth, such as, "No! The iron is hot!" There will also be times when a request, such as "Can I stay out all night?" is just too dangerous to grant. When our children's moral or physical well-being is at stake, it is certainly worth taking a stand, even if we have to say a firm "no." Whether a "no" accidentally escapes our lips or is quite deliberate, always try to use one of the other skills before or with the "no." When we use "no" sparingly, our children really take notice and usually respond appropriately.

> *A Personal Story. I learned "No No's" when Chris was an infant. With some creativity, I was usually able to come up with a positive way to set limits. One day, I was visiting my parents. I walked into the kitchen and saw Chris, then two, dangling my expensive camera over the tile floor. I squealed, "No!" as I rushed over to grab the camera. As I explained what could happen, my father rushed into the room. He said, "I've never heard you say 'no' like that so I figured there must have been something really wrong."*

When we first try to flip our negative statements into positive ones, it usually takes longer to think and respond. But it's well worth our time to choose positive words. We can prevent power struggles, tantrums, or having our children pester us for 15 minutes with negotiations and explanations. If we are willing to make the investment of time and effort, we *will* start seeing results.

Use Humor ☆☆☆☆

Children usually listen and cooperate more when we make funny, light-hearted requests. This can be difficult, especially when we are tired, but humor can prevent many power struggles. Here are a few suggestions, but I'm sure you can add more.

- Use a funny voice, impersonating a celebrity or robot.
- Use sign language or charades to get your point across.
- Act like a media announcer calling the plays of a game or interviewing your child.
- Sing your request or set your request to a familiar tune. (When my children were young, I made up lyrics to dozens of familiar tunes. It really got my kids moving—and lightened up the moment. Be careful, though, because children may repeat the song. . . .)

> *A Graduate's Story. One parent, teasing her husband about his vasectomy pains, changed the name of the body part in the song, "Do your ears hang low." She sang it once and didn't think the kids heard her. Six months later, the principal from her child's school called to say her son had been singing an inappropriate song. The principal had the child call his mother, to tell her what he was singing. In front of the principal, her son said, "You should know the words, Mom! You made them up when you sang it to Dad!"*

Make It Child-Friendly

Sometimes we only need to make a task or item sound more appealing to a child, by using our creativity. For example, encourage picky eaters to try new foods by making fruit-kabobs, dips, and food shakes, such as fruit smoothies. Use creative packaging such as ice cream cones. Let children create food art, such as faces and animals out of food.

> *A Personal Story. In my house, plain milk became "Slimer® milk" by adding green food coloring. "Snow trees" were much more interesting to eat than cauliflower. To get Amber to sit still while I fixed her hair, I called a French braid a "Barbie® braid" after the dolls whose hair I braided to prevent tangles. Pigtails were "Dorothy pigtails," after the girl in her favorite movie.*

 Be Polite, But Don't Plead

Saying "Please" is appropriate when making simple requests like "Will you please get the mail?" It models manners and avoids ordering children around with "Go get the mail." "Please" can sound like pleading, however, if our request is more important, like "Please don't hit your sister," especially if we've already asked nicely and the child hasn't complied. Using "please" politely, once, can be appropriate when there is no problem going on. If we don't get cooperation using the tools in this toolset, we have a problem (a Parent problem) and need to use more firm, yet respectful, statements from Chapter 10, "Clear Communication Toolset."

 Follow the Rules for Setting Rules

Sometimes our efforts to set rules can backfire on us; we get defiance, are pressed to follow through *to the letter* by a child who takes everything literally, or realize a child has found the exception to the rule. While our rules may still hit snags, we can reduce these frustrations by incorporating some previous skills when setting rules:

1. State the bottom line.
2. Present it as a choice.
3. Credit a "higher authority" or inanimate object with the rule, if possible.
4. Use general terms.
5. Use positive words.

> *A Personal Story. I figured out these rules the hard way (Is there any other way for most parents?) when I had to set rules about climbing the tree in our front yard. This tree invites every neighborhood child to climb it. I didn't want to wait for a disaster or be a party-pooper by forbidding children from scaling the only decent climbing tree on the block. I invented the "Rules for Setting Rules" while trying to avoid loopholes and vague, negative, discouraging restrictions.*
>
> *My bottom line for kids climbing our tree was safety and legal liability. I said, "Remember, safety first!" Instead of saying, "You can't climb my tree" and explaining why, I said, "If you want to climb this tree . . . ," which made it clear they had a choice. I finished the sentence, ". . . you need to agree to the tree's rules. The tree doesn't want anyone to get hurt in its branches!" This made the rule more neutral and you can't argue with a tree!*
>
> *Instead of measuring and testing each child for ability, I said, "Only kids who are tall enough to reach the lowest branch can climb the tree." When the tall, uncoordinated children asked my help to climb the tree, I amended the rule, "Only kids who can get up in the tree by themselves can climb it." This kept me from standing in the yard giving boosts to the kids and spared children embarrassment if I had to single out the uncoordinated children. I also noticed that the children were more motived to learn tree climbing, instead of feeling discouraged.*
>
> *When my daughter tried to climb the tree in her tights and patent leather shoes, I realized I needed another rule. I didn't want to sound negative and sexist, so I used general terms. I said, "Only kids wearing pants and shoes can climb the tree."*

I've seen so much value in flipping a "don't" into a positive statement, I used the same idea when I set my tree rules. I didn't want to give the kids any vivid ideas by saying, "Don't climb too high in the tree, you could get stuck." Someone said this to me as a kid and I got stuck in a tree for nearly an hour. That's why I'm not willing to climb a tree to get them down! Instead, I said, "You can only climb as high as you can get yourself down."

Once, when a child got stuck at the top, I reminded her of the rule and that I don't climb trees. I told her I knew she could get herself down, since she did such a good job climbing up! I then offered suggestions such as, "That's it! Now put your foot on that branch down there and grab that branch with your other hand."

To date, I have never had to rescue anyone from my tree. All have come down in one piece and each child has developed extraordinary tree-climbing abilities.

Parents often comment on the negative words schools, churches, preschools, and other child-focused institutions use in their rules. Several have rewritten them, using the "rules for setting rules."

***A Personal Story.** My son's fifth-grade teacher was wise. She just had one general rule, instead of many rules about everything. To this day, my son remembers this rule: "Respect yourself, others, and your environment." If you think about it, it covers everything!*

In most settings, parents or other adults set the rules and then tell children what they are. The adult's tone of voice and attitude, however, can turn rules into orders and commands. **Teens** are especially likely to rebel when adults talk down to them. If teens don't agree with a rule and adults can't enforce it, they might sneak to do it anyway. It is far more effective, especially with teens, to use two-party problem solving (Chapter 10, "Clear Communication Toolset") to negotiate rules.

Establish Routines

Children are more cooperative when it's time to do chores, clean up after themselves, or go to bed if there is a special routine. Younger children adapt especially well to routines. Older children may need time to break poor habits. It's important to involve children in planning new routines, instead of *telling* them what they will do. Routines increase parental consistency, eliminate power struggles, and help each family member feel his contribution is important to the family.

Here are some examples of routines to use. Some are more elaborate than others. You can tailor your routines to fit the ages, abilities, structure, and schedules in your family.

Meals. Whoever isn't cooking can either set the table or help clean up. People can volunteer or make a schedule.

Laundry. Divide laundry duties at family councils—sorting, washer/dryer loading, folding, and ironing. The family can decide whether to rotate these duties or keep regular voluntary assignments. Only wash clothes that are in the hamper by sorting day. Family members put away their own basket of clean clothes.

Bedtime. For many families, bedtime battles are routine. Most parents know about the basic "5 B's: bath, brush teeth, bathroom, books, and bed" routine. To prevent bedtime struggles and delays, offer choices about these steps. For example, children can choose whether to take a bath at night or in the morning, brush teeth before or after bathroom duties, and how many or which books to read. Invent fun, but not too physical, games as options to bedtime books and tapes. These games can have time limits. Each person gets one turn or you play the game until the time is up. The following games have helped our family turn bedtime into precious, loving memories.

▶   *Twenty questions.* Think of a person or thing. Others ask yes and no questions to guess what it is.
▶   *Guess the feeling.* Someone acts out an emotion while others guess the feeling.
▶   *Guess that animal.* The same, except you act like an animal.

- *Finish that story.* One person starts a story and, at some point, passes the story on to the next person, who continues it however he wants.
- *Tell a family story.* Write in a journal and read the stories occasionally. Or tell stories from your childhood.
- *Guess the story.* Tell a familiar story without identifying the characters, such as a movie or family adventure. The rest of the family tries to guess who the story is about.
- *Build forts and tents* on weekends or school breaks—with an agreement for when the children will clean up. Let them camp out on the floor in sleeping bags or in each others' rooms.
- *Back rubs and scratches.* Draw letters, pictures, and words on their backs and have them guess what you drew.

House Cleaning. Pick a time each week to clean the house together. Besides family members cleaning their own rooms, they can choose one or two rooms to clean or one or two activities, such as dusting, vacuuming, or cleaning sinks. Play music or make a game of it, but not a competitive game, such as racing, which would have a loser. I have catchy names to specify levels of cleaning:

- "Litter control" means to just pick up.
- "Vacuum path" means the floor has to be ready to vacuum.
- "Organize" means things need to be put in their place, rather than just thrown in the general area where they belong.
- "Hotel quality" means everything needs dusted and to look like it's ready for guests. I try to be realistic, reasonable, and not overuse "hotel quality," or my children are tempted to check into one to get a break from me!

Keeping one's bedroom clean is a *routine* many parents wish their children would develop. This especially applies to parents of **teens.** Teens' bedrooms are an extension of their identity and a symbol of one area of their life that is theirs to control. It's very difficult to start this routine once a child has already reached the teen years. If parents start the routine when children are young, they can develop positive habits.

> ***A Graduate's Story.*** *Jack and I are both very organized. Everything has a place and we always take a few extra seconds to put things away. Ever since our kids were young, we have taught them to pick up after themselves. We've never had a problem with them being messy. I guess they have never known any different. I didn't realize how many other parents had a problem with getting their kids to clean up. I guess our neatness has some advantages.*

FINAL COMMENTS

All the tools in *The Parent's Toolshop* are great, but this toolset is a favorite. Many parents and children make a complete change in their attitudes and behavior within weeks of using these tools. If you can honestly look at your power and control issues, focus on cooperation rather than demanding obedience, and consistently use these tools, you will also have fewer power struggles and more teamwork.

SUMMARY SHEET
COOPERATION TOOLSET

AVOID BRIBES

PLAN AHEAD ☆☆☆☆

OFFER CHOICES ☆☆☆☆
If there's not a choice *if* something happens, give choices for *when* and *how* it can happen.

DON'T SAY "DON'T" ☆☆☆☆
Describe what they *can* do.

NO NO'S ☆☆☆☆
Give a conditional "yes."
Offer an alternative.
State a reason.
Give information.
Recognize feelings. Use wishes and fantasy.
Save "no" for dangerous issues or emergencies.

USE HUMOR ☆☆☆☆

MAKE IT CHILD-FRIENDLY

BE POLITE, BUT DON'T PLEAD

FOLLOW RULES FOR SETTING RULES
Use general, simple, positive terms that state your bottom line.

ESTABLISH ROUTINES

PRACTICE EXERCISES

(Possible answers are at the end of the chapter.)

A. Choices. Find a way to offer choices within limits in these situations.
1. Your toddler wants to play in the sand box in his good clothes.
2. Your preschooler resists having her hair washed.
3. Your elementary school-aged child needs to work on a book report.
4. Your preteen wants to plan a party.
5. Your teenager is trying to decide where to apply for jobs.

B. Don't Say "Don't." Flip these negative orders into positive requests.
1. "Quit pulling the dog's tail."
2. "Don't run away from me in the store!"
3. "Quit being so bossy!"
4. "Stop teasing and calling people names! It's not nice."
5. "Don't be late!"

C. Personal Application. List three things your children do that you tell them to "stop" or say "don't." Now say each with positive words.

D. No "No's." Write an alternative to saying "no" in the following practice situations. Your choices are:

a. Give a conditional "yes"
b. Give a reason
c. Give information
d. Recognize feelings
e. Offer a positive alternative

1. "Can we go out to eat tonight?" (You don't have the time or money.)
2. "Can I borrow the car?" (The last time the car was returned with an empty gas tank.)
3. "Can I go to the park with Tom and John?" (You are concerned about three 10-year-old boys walking through the woods to the park.)
4. "Can you take me to the library to do research for my book report? It's due tomorrow." (You don't have time tonight, but would have, had you known sooner.)
5. "Can I have this toy?" (You are in the toy store shopping for someone else.)

E. Personal Application. List three things your child might ask for and to which you would say "no." Now, word your refusal with positive words instead.

Activity for the Week

Practice using these tools at home for one week. Then list a situation (or more, if applicable) where you are having difficulty in getting your child to cooperate. Now review the summary page to see if there are any tools you could use in that situation.

Possible Answers

The following answers are just *one possible* response. Different answers are not wrong answers. See if your answers also fit the guidelines for using the Cooperation Toolset.

A. Choices
1. "Clothes get dirty in the sand box. You can either change into play clothes for the sand box or keep your nice clothes on and play inside. You decide."

2. "I know you don't like getting your hair washed. Would you like a wash cloth to cover your eyes or would you rather tip your head way back?"

3. "Will you work on your book report before dinner or after?"

4. "I only have three rules for having a party here: (1) There are no drugs, alcohol, or cigarettes. (2) You know that the people attending are responsible. (3) There is an adult at home during the party. If you agree to those rules, I'd love to hear your ideas for the party."

5. (Pause between each question.) "What are you interested in doing? What kind of jobs appeal to you? What is your class schedule? How will you balance school and work?"

B. Don't Say "Don't"

1. "Be gentle and kind to the dog. Pet him like this." (Guide child's hand.)

2. "Stay where you can see me." Or "Stay with me." (If you say, "Stay where I can see *you*," children don't realize when *you* have lost sight of *them*!)

3. "When people are ordered around, they might not want to play anymore. Can you give your friends some choices or ask what *they* want to do?"

4. "Teasing hurts people's feelings. Treat others with respect."

5. "You need to be home by five o'clock," or "Be home on time," or "Keep track of the time."

D. No "No's"

1. "Maybe we could go out to dinner Friday night. We don't have any plans and I get my paycheck."

2. "You can borrow the car, if you put gas in it before you return it.

3. "I know how much fun you have together at the park, but I worry about you walking through the woods without an adult." If you can't go with them, ask if an older sibling could go with them.

4. "I am always willing to take you to the library to do your research, if I have a couple days notice. I have a meeting tonight, so you'll need to find another way to get there."

5. "It's fun looking at toys, isn't it? Today we are buying a toy for Suzy. Can you find a toy *she* will like?"

WHAT'S NEXT?

Use the Cooperation Toolset everyday to prevent the struggles most parents face. We will refer to them often when we get to the Parent Problem Toolbox and learn how to redirect children's intentional misbehavior and reveal discipline.

In Chapter 6, "Independence Toolset," we talk more about balancing parental limits—as it relates to children's independence. We discuss ways to develop responsibility, teach skills (such as tasks, behaviors, and values), and dozens of other ideas to prepare your child for self-sufficient adulthood.

REFERENCES

1. Two resources that offer strong arguments that behavior charts cannot be used "appropriately" because incentives are counterproductive are *Punished by Rewards: The Trouble with Gold Stars, Incentive Plans, A's, Praise and Other Bribes,* by Alfie Kohn (Houghton Mifflin, 1993) and *Kids Are Worth It!* by Barbara Coloroso (Avon Books, 1994).

2. *How To Talk So Kids Will Listen, And Listen So Kids Will Talk,* Adele Faber and Elaine Mazlish (Avon Books, 1982) pp. 17, 44.

CHAPTER 6
INDEPENDENCE TOOLSET

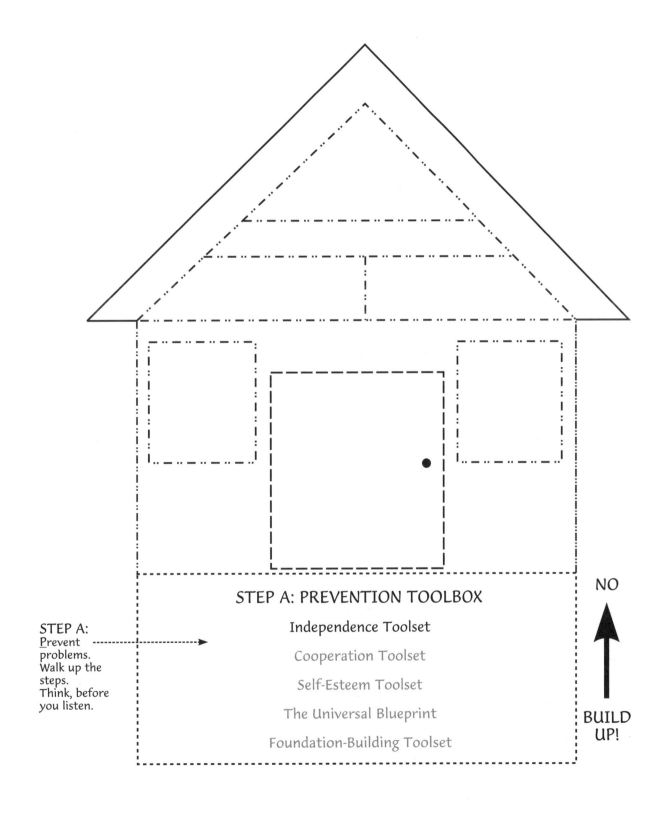

STEP A: PREVENTION TOOLBOX

Independence Toolset

Cooperation Toolset

Self-Esteem Toolset

The Universal Blueprint

Foundation-Building Toolset

STEP A:
Prevent
problems.
Walk up the
steps.
Think, before
you listen.

NO

BUILD
UP!

CHAPTER
6 INDEPENDENCE TOOLSET

We want our house to have the features and internal supports it needs to stand independently. We might use temporary supports, but our ultimate goal is to have a house that stands on its own and is strong enough to weather storms. If our children ask to help build the house, what should we do? Tell the children to leave? Wait until they learn the skills before we let them practice? Let them watch? Explain how to use the tools? Let them try simple steps?

Similarly, our ultimate parenting goal is to build internal qualities within our children so they are strong enough to independently weather the storms in their lives. To do this, children need to know how to do certain tasks and adopt helpful behaviors and values. Parents need to teach children these important life skills and let them practice using the skills by gradually increasing their freedom and responsibilities. This maintains a healthy balance that gives children room to grow and to separate from their parents in healthy ways.

IN THIS CHAPTER

This chapter encourages us to consider three important ideas about independence:

1. Parents *and* children can resist responsibility and block children's need for more independence.

2. There is a delicate balance between expanding limits and teaching skills so children can responsibly manage their increasing freedom.

3. Parents can use specific tools to foster responsibility and self-sufficiency.

WHEN TO USE THIS TOOLSET

We often think of independence when talking about young children, who are learning skills for the first time, and teens, who are on the brink of adulthood. In reality, we foster independence every day, from birth through adulthood. Every day, month, and year we have many opportunities to teach values such as responsibility and allow our children to practice the life skills they need as adults. Therefore, we constantly use these skills *with* children and *teach* the same skills *to* children.

THE BALANCE OF INDEPENDENCE

Parents may hinder their children's independence because they have difficulty letting go or are afraid the children will make mistakes. Our job is not to control children or do things *for* them, but to teach them to be self-responsible. We face a constant balancing act of guiding our children without demanding so much control that we get into power struggles with them. To build independence, we need to deal with our children's power and control issues *and* our own.

> **The key to healthy independence is to teach skills while expanding limits, staying one step ahead of our children's abilities.**

Using the symbols we learned in the Foundation-Building Toolset, we can illustrate this delicate balancing act and the imbalances that can occur.

Zigzag = child's skills and abilities Circle = parent's limits and child's freedom		
Over-Controlling	**Under-Controlling**	**Balanced**
Children have the skills, but little freedom to use them. They resent these unreasonable limits and push for more freedom.	Children have few skills and too much freedom. They can't handle the freedom responsibly.	As children increase their skills, parents expand the limits, staying one step ahead. Balance is maintained, so children can handle the freedom responsibly.
Parents believe: "When he has the skills, I'll give him the freedom."	*Parents believe:* "When I give him the freedom, he'll develop the skills."	*Parents believe:* "I must provide enough freedom for my child to grow and practice the skills I am teaching."

It takes more time, patience, and skill to foster healthy independence, but there are many positive benefits. As children learn more skills, we don't have to do so many things *for* children, remind them as often, and feel frustrated with their slowness. Children learn skills that help them throughout their lives—as youngsters, teens, and as adults. Children who learn they can do things on their own develop self-confidence. We feel more trusting when our children are away from us, because we know they have the knowledge and skills to avoid or effectively deal with potential problems.

DEVELOPING RESPONSIBILITY

Most parents include "responsibility" in the list of qualities they want their children to develop. Often, however, the definition of responsibility and how to achieve it are unclear. When most people think of responsibility, they think of chores. Actually, there are three kinds of responsibility.

1. **Personal responsibility**—being responsible *for* and *to ourselves.*
   a. Self-care (getting dressed, personal hygiene).
   b. Taking care of our own property (keeping room clean, treating belongings with respect).
   c. Making decisions and choices.
   d. Being responsible for the consequences of decisions (admitting mistakes, making amends).

2. **General responsibility**—being responsible *to* the *family* and *society.*
   a. Contributing to the daily operation of the family (setting the table) or society (peaceful conflict resolution).
   b. Helping without being asked (emptying the trash when we see it is full, replacing the toilet paper when we use the last piece).

3. **Specific responsibility**—being responsible *for* specific *tasks.*
   a. Accepting chore/job assignments that include ongoing or one-time tasks with or without payment. These tasks are performed within school/work schedules and within reasonable quality guidelines.

We can't wait until our children reach adulthood to begin transferring responsibility to them. Children mature when they learn to accept increasing responsibility for their choices and actions. Many adults, however, struggle with their own response-ability.

> *Response-ability* **is the ability to accept the consequences of the choices we make.**

We all know people, adults and children alike, who avoid responsibility. It's natural to want to be right. It's more difficult to admit when we are wrong, make a mistake, or to respond to blame and criticism. So we try to justify our failures and mistakes, giving away our personal power and self-responsibility in the process. To teach our children responsibility, we need to model it.

> *A **Personal Story.** A co-worker entered my office to apologize for something she did that could have upset me. She asked for my forgiveness. I didn't remember her doing anything and wasn't the least bit upset. I was quite impressed by the inner strength it took for her to accept responsibility for her actions and the possible consequences. I decided, then and there, that I wanted to have the kind or integrity it took to own up to my mistakes and earn respect from others. It isn't easy. I'm often tempted to defend myself or blame others, but try to accept responsibility for my actions whenever I can.*

No one can avoid making choices, but our attitude toward the *consequences* of our choices shows whether we are responsible. If the consequence is positive, we know how to make a similar choice in the future. If the consequence is negative, we can learn from the experience and choose better next time. This is how children and adults learn and grow. Being a role model and teaching responsibility through our responses is sometimes surprisingly effective.

> *A **Graduate's Story.** I told my six-year-old daughter to give me something for safekeeping. I assured her I would keep track of it. Later, when she asked for it, I searched the house, but couldn't find it anywhere! I said, "Maybe when Dad gets home we can ask him if he's seen it." My daughter replied, "Mom, it was **your** responsibility, not Dad's."*
>
> *I was taken aback, being put in my place by a six-year-old, but was more impressed by her understanding of the need to accept responsibility for one's actions and mistakes. I responded, "You're right. It **was** my responsibility. I'll keep looking until I find it." Looking back, my daughter might have done a better job keeping track of it in the first place!*

Sometimes, a child's irresponsible behavior is really just a difference in priorities. A **preschooler's** creativity and desire to play is often incompatible with our expectations for neatness and organization. A fort, still in progress, can look like an abandoned mess of blocks. A tired child might conveniently drop books on the floor, because he's supposed to stay in bed. Neatness is a gradual process that evolves with age and a change in priorities. We need to keep our expectations realistic, teach skills, offer encouragement when they improve, and hold them accountable when they forget.

Older children, especially **teens,** can have different priorities from their parents. Neat children sometimes turn into messy teens, as their priorities change to issues more important than cleaning: career goals, friends, romance, trying on identities, and keeping up with busy schedules. We can focus on the skills they are learning and qualities they are developing, even if they are not the particular skills or means of learning that we would choose for them.

> *A **Group Discussion Story.** A mother in one of my parenting classes was concerned about her teenage son's involvement in a body-building competition. As the day of the final competition approached, he became more focused on his training. One evening when it was time to attend his teen group at the Jewish Community Center, he chose to miss the group rather than skip his workout. His mother was concerned that his priorities **might** be on the wrong track. She was afraid he **might** be more concerned with a beautiful body than socializing with his friends. She worried that he **might** start wanting others to accept him for his body, rather than his mind and personality. She thought he **might** be obsessed with the competition. (I emphasize the word "might," because she was assuming this and had not checked out these perceptions with her son.)*

*The other parents in the class knew the parent and her teen. They pointed out some positive lessons her son was learning from the competition. They saw that part of her conflict was that she didn't value body-building and felt the teen group should be a priority. Her son seemed to feel that, during the competition, his workout should take priority over socializing. The other parents didn't think he was being obsessive about the competition, since he wasn't using steroids or neglecting his home and school responsibilities. Had he already worked out that day, he probably **would** have attended the teen group.*

*Another parent asked her, "If you had a work project, were behind on your deadline, and were invited to a party, would you miss the party to fulfill your commitment?" The mother could see that, in his own way, he **was** being responsible and self-disciplined. She started seeing the lessons her son was learning, although he was learning them through an activity she didn't value.*

Attaching Privileges to Responsibilities

Many children earn their privileges through responsible behavior. This is a valuable approach which can motivate children to accept responsibility or explain why a parent denies or restricts a privilege. (We will explore restrictions more in Chapter 13, "Discipline Toolset.") Parents need to be careful, however, that they don't use privileges as bribes or to control children.

A Graduate's Story. My teenage son is so irresponsible. His idea of summer break is to sleep until noon, watch TV, and hang out with his friends. He argues with us every time we ask him to do chores and then turns around and wants us to grant him privileges we don't think he's ready for. When we say, "No," he compares himself to his older sister, who is in college. For example, he wants his own car and points out that we purchased a car for our daughter when she graduated from high school. I told him that we will purchase a car for him, too, when he shows us he can handle the extra responsibilities that go along with having a car: a job to drive to that would provide money to pay for gas, repairs, and insurance.

Recently, we had an argument about what he was going to do with his life. I own a business and he said he would just work for me, assuming that when I'm ready to retire I would pass the business on to him. I told him, "When I retire, I will sell my business to the person whom I think will manage it the best. Whoever the person is, he (or she) will have a college degree, so I know he has the self-discipline to work hard for his accomplishments. If you happen to be interested and qualified, I will consider selling the business to you—but not just because you are my son. You would have to meet the same requirements as anyone else who wants to buy it.

This son is focusing only on the privileges, a car or employment in the family business. The father is focusing on the internal qualities necessary to *earn* those privileges. The father provides opportunities for his son to develop responsible driving behavior whenever he lends his car to his son. His son can develop responsible work habits when he does chores at home or with his school work. It is the son's choice whether to take advantage of these opportunities. The father did not use the privileges as bribes. He simply detailed the conditions under which the son could obtain the privilege.

Parents can send the message, "When you have chosen to handle your current privileges responsibly (and detailing what this means), I will know you are ready for more privileges." There is a delicate balance here, however, and parents frequently set up no-win situations for their children. They say the child isn't responsible in a particular area, but don't provide opportunities to develop that responsible behavior. Or they say children must show the ability before giving any level of the privilege. This is similar to the experience of applying for our first job or when starting a new career. The employer says, "Sorry, you don't have enough experience." But you can't get experience if no one is willing to hire you!

ALLOWANCES

Allowances are a controversial practice for developing responsibility. Some parents view allowance as a privilege children earn, while others view it as each family member's right.

When parents pay children for chores, children often do the chore only for the money, not to help as a family member. Consequently, money is the value, not cooperation. Then, if parents ask the child to do an extra job or accept more responsibility, the child may ask, "How much will I get for it?" Soon, the parent becomes a labor negotiator, paying increasing amounts of money just to get basic chores done. If children don't complete a chore and don't care about money, the chore still doesn't get done. (Yes, there really are children who don't care about money, especially if someone uses it to control them.)

Parents want their children to learn that jobs can earn money, since that's the way the real world works. There are many jobs in the real world, however, that require work without pay. (Do you get paid for washing your dishes or doing the family's laundry? If so, I want to live in your house!)

Allowances and chores each teach life skills.
- *Allowances can teach money management:* how to earn, save, budget, and prioritize purchases.
- *Chores can teach cooperation and responsibility:* pitching in as a member of the family, following through on agreements, and doing quality work.

Separately, each is a valuable teaching tool. When combined, problems often arise.

Three-level Allowance Plan

Parents can meet their goals for teaching responsibility, money management, and cooperation, without negative side effects, by following a three-level plan for chores and allowances.

- **Level 1: Base allowance.** Give a base allowance for money management purposes. If children don't manage their money, let them experience the consequences. Children often spend their money carelessly for a couple of months. If parents don't criticize or rescue them when they run out of money, children usually realize they must save their money for nicer purchases and naturally change their spending habits.

  Have children do base chores simply because they are part of the family to make the household run more smoothly. Do not connect their base allowance with their base chores. If they do not do their base chores, they can experience a loss of a social privilege, not money. This teaches the value of work-before-play. Level 1 chores might include making one's own lunch, keeping one's room neat, and a regular chore such as vacuuming or dusting. Chores such as doing the dishes or setting the dinner table can rotate among family members. The effects of not doing these chores are logical: no lunch that day, unable to have friends in the house because it's too messy, not eating until the table is set, and no cooking until the previous meal's dishes are clean. (We'll learn more about discipline in Chapter 13, "Discipline Toolset.")

- **Level 2: Earning more money.** Children can earn extra money if they accept additional responsibilities beyond self-care and base chores. These chores are usually more difficult or need to be done less often than daily chores. Level 2 chores might include laundry, weeding, washing windows or cars, and mowing the lawn.

- **Level 3: Saving for purchases.** If children want to save money for a large purchase, they can do Level 3 jobs. These are large, one-time or several-times-a-year chores such as cleaning a closet, raking leaves, or helping a parent with a large project like landscaping or painting. Since Level 2 and 3 chores teach children the value of earning money through increased responsibilities, consider having children do chores for relatives or neighbors. This will prevent extra money always coming out of your pocket.

  A Personal Story. A note about allowances and credit—use caution. Chris had been asking for a video game system for several years. I was philosophically opposed to them and really couldn't afford such an expensive purchase. Chris was not much of a saver, so I suggested a compromise. If he saved half the cost, I'd pay the rest. I assumed he would probably not reach the goal, but this was the motivator Chris needed to discipline himself to save. He volunteered for extra jobs, but I often didn't have the extra cash to pay him. He knew it would be too tempting to have the cash anyway, so I agreed to record what he had earned. When he finally earned half the cost of the system and his birthday was near, I could not put off the purchase any longer. In the end, I still had to foot the whole bill and he only had to do extra work but not actually save anything. I learned my lesson the hard way and stopped all credit plans. Now, my children have to decide if they want something enough not only to do extra work but also resist the temptation to spend the money they are saving.

Budgeting Options

The amount of an allowance depends on what children need to buy with it. Parents' budgets may be such that parents could give larger allowances, but overindulging children robs them of the experience of saving. When children receive their allowance, they can divide it into budget categories. Experts and parents hold differing opinions about *making* children budget their money or allowing them to freely spend it. Older children want to be in control of their own money. If parents suggest new budget requirements, it often leads to power struggles. If parents establish budget requirements when children are young, they get used to the routine, but still might resist this control as they grow older. You'll need to test this plan and decide whether mandatory budgeting works for your family. If you decide to try it, consider the following budget items. Involve children in choosing the categories and percentages they will contribute:

- Charitable donations such as religious offerings.
- Long-term savings.
- A family fun fund. Family members contribute to a general fund that is used for special outings.
- Free spending money.

Some parents provide *saving incentives*. For example, the parents match any money the child saves or they pay interest on the total savings balance. The parents might only require the children to put a small percentage of their allowance in long-term savings, but the incentive offers a bonus if children save more. It is still each child's choice to save. While this plan works for many families, I've heard horror stories of parents going broke so money-hungry children can increase their bank accounts without having to do any extra work. Think about the long term money figures you might have to pay as your children's savings increase. Also consider teaching your children about investment options that could increase their bank accounts without breaking yours. **Beware, once you start a saving incentive plan, it can be addictive like any other bribe or incentive plan.** Money is power, so use caution or it can rule (and ruin) your family.

*A **Graduate's Story**. My sister is divorced and her children live alternate weeks at her ex-husband's house. She and her ex-husband are caught in a vicious cycle of trying to outdo each other. They each take the children on expensive vacations and give the children expensive gifts like VCRs, camcorders, and computers. To encourage her children to save, my sister started a savings incentive program; whatever the children save, she puts half that amount in the savings account. This policy applies to any money the children get—allowances, gifts from relatives, and job earnings. Not to be outdone, the father agreed to also contribute half the amount to the savings account they keep at his house (they must use this money to buy items they use at his house). It doesn't matter which account the children make their deposit to; each parent will add half that amount to the savings account the child keeps at that house. These kids get a 100% return on their money! If they deposit Grandpa's $100 Christmas check, they get a total of $100 from their parents. Whatever they deposit automatically doubles!*

These children are nice, sharing, good kids caught in the middle of this competition. My nine-year-old niece even said to me, "I'll be able to buy a Volvo when I'm sixteen!" These parents are caught in a trap that is very unhealthy for their children, but neither will stop because it would make them look bad. Although the children are learning how to save money, they are also learning how to be more manipulative.

Whatever allowance plan you choose, it is best to decide or change family-wide plans in a family council meeting. Here, the entire family can weigh the options, decide the details and consequences, and get a commitment to the plan from *everyone*. (See Chapter 14, "Family Council Toolset.") You can also use one-on-one problem solving. (See Chapter 8, "Problem-Solving Toolset.") If only parents decide and enforce allowance and chore plans, it turns chores and money into bargaining chips, which usually leads to more power struggles.

INDEPENDENCE TOOLS

There are some basic tools we use to build independence, but the independence issues differ greatly at each developmental stage. While we can't address all ages and issues, use these guidelines and suggestions to get ideas for applying the tools to your child's individual needs or issues.

 ## Openly Model Behavior ☆☆☆☆

When we model behavior, we simply "practice what we preach" through observable behavior. *Openly* modeling behavior is particularly useful for internal (logical or emotional) processes that are difficult for children to directly observe. When we openly model behavior, we make these internal processes something the child can *hear and see*, usually by talking our way through the steps we normally take in our mind. This way, children can learn the steps to take in their own minds when responding to similar situations.

For example, if children often respond to frustrating situations in aggressive ways, we can talk aloud to ourselves when *we* are frustrated, knowing a "sponge" is soaking up what we say. When another driver cuts us off in traffic and we say nothing, children assume that nothing happened. What actually happened was a very quick, but internal process of experiencing a rush of frustration and aggravation, talking ourselves through our feelings, and deciding not to say or do anything about it. This inside process is what we want to say aloud, not *to* our children, but *to ourselves in front of* them, for their benefit. We might say out loud, "Geez! I can't believe that guy just cut in front of me! That was dangerous! I feel like honking my horn or calling him a name. But that won't help me or him. I just need to take a deep breath and calm down. Maybe he's in a rush to get somewhere and isn't thinking about what he's doing." By revealing our internal thoughts, our children have a model to follow the next time they need to talk themselves through a frustrating situation.

 ## Teach Skills ☆☆☆☆

If we do too much for children, they miss opportunities to learn how to do these things for themselves. If we teach them skills instead, they learn independence. It's like the old saying, ***"Give a man a fish and he'll eat for a day. Teach him to fish and he'll eat for life."***

In the past, children had many opportunities to learn independence and responsibility. Parents and children worked side-by-side, feeding animals and planting crops. Today, children still need to work *with* their parents, receiving on-the-job training while contributing to the family.

The ideal time to teach skills is when children are young, but it's never too late. We *can* teach older children "new tricks," but it's harder to break bad habits than to prevent them. We need to be patient and to understand our children's surprise at their new duties or our sudden unwillingness to do things for them.

When teaching children values, tasks, or behavior, there are ten tips we can follow. We don't have to use all ten suggestions every time or use them in the order they are listed below. When teaching difficult skills or children are hesitant, we can use more tools. If we take the extra time to work together and teach skills, both parents and children can benefit.

1. **Plan Ahead.** Make a mental note that your child needs to work on a particular skill. Set aside a time when you won't feel rushed and can spend time teaching your child. Other times you will "teach on the fly," looking for teachable moments as they arise.

2. **Explain the value the skill has for the child, the family, others, or society.** What is the benefit of learning this skill? Acknowledge that your children might not share your values, such as tidiness.

3. **Break the task into smaller steps.** Do the task one step at a time or concentrate on the different skills you use to do the task. Offer suggestions for safety, quality, and convenience as you explain each step.

4. **Let children watch.** If this is the first time you are teaching your children a skill, show them *how* to perform the skill, explaining slowly as you do it.

5. **Let children try.** Let children practice the skill while you watch for safety and quality assurance. Don't hover, pressuring children. Instead, sit back and watch with patience and encouragement. Or you can work on a related task, keeping an eye on them and offering helpful hints as you go along. Your children's efforts will probably be imperfect. Instead of pointing out inadequacies or rescuing children when they are discouraged, remind them that it takes practice and time to improve.

6. **Let children do things their way.** The result does not have to be perfect; it just needs to meet your bottom line. Children might find a way that's better for them. Don't insist on perfection or expect it to look the way it looks when you do it. Just let them try their best and get practice. Avoid the urge to step in, out of impatience, and do it for them or "show them the right way." Coach and teach instead. In fact, if your children devise a unique way of doing a task, ask them to teach *you*! This is a real confidence booster and helps them learn teaching skills.

   > *A Personal Story. After teaching Amber, who was 7, how to clean the bathrooms, she took pride in doing the task alone. She would shut the bathroom door and instruct everyone to stay out. Once, she accidentally splashed water all over her shirt, which then stuck to her body. She asked me to help her take it off. When it got stuck on her head, we both laughed. She decided to keep her new "hat" on while finishing the job. It really didn't matter that she was half naked while in the bathroom alone. What mattered was that she kept working. The next time she cleaned, she pulled her shirt onto her head and made her "cleaning hat," which was part of her cleaning "routine" for several months. Whenever I saw her in her "cleaning hat" and carrying a bottle of bathroom cleaner I knew she was busy working.*

7. **Offer choices.** Encourage your children to take ownership of the task. They will be more willing to do something if they feel *they* are doing it, rather than following someone's specific directions.

8. **Work together.** As children learn skills, work together as a team. Do one part while your children do another part. Let them bring their work to where you are, if they can. (For example, they can get dressed where you are or make their lunch while you fix breakfast.) This provides more opportunities for descriptive encouragement and offering helpful tips.

Be careful if you have older children teaching younger children as apprentices. Older children are often easily frustrated with younger siblings, have unrealistic expectations, or give younger children an unfair share of the work. If *you* work with your children it provides many rich memories and opportunities to learn more about their thoughts, motivations, and interests. It also provides more chances to give positive attention and have quality one-on-one time. Only allow older children to teach younger siblings if they will be respectful, encouraging, and patient.

You may be trying to develop behaviors or establish habits, such as better anger control or healthier eating habits. Share *your* desire to work on these things and the value the new skill will have for you or others. Invite your children to join you in your efforts. "I'm going to work on this . . . do you want to join me so we can support each other?" Don't tell them to join you, simply invite them and let them choose. If your children choose to join you, make these times together a rewarding experience. Share your frustrations, triumphs, and challenges with each other. Most of all, support and encourage each other.

9. **Make it fun.** Play music, dance, sing a song, or make a game of it. Do not, however, race or compete, since these pressure children and there is always a loser. (See the section on competition, pages 101–103 in Chapter 4, "Self-Esteem Toolset.") No one has to *win*, be the fastest, or do the "best" job. If you can use your children's interests (e.g., music, sports) to teach the skill, your children will be more interested in learning.

   Another variation is to make the task more **child-friendly.** When you are doing something dangerous or requiring a high level of skill, find ways children can imitate you in an age-appropriate, safe way. For example, when you are painting, give them a paintbrush and let them paint with water on the sidewalk or with paint on another section of a wall. Give your children toy tools or safe adult ones and let them practice on sample projects. If buying toys is not an option, use your creativity to find other safe ways for your children to help.

10. **Offer encouragement at every step.** Describe your children's efforts and progress. Avoid words like *good* or *perfect*. (Remember what we learned in Chapter 4, "Self-Esteem Toolset"?)

We can apply the "teaching skills" tool to physical tasks, appropriate behavior, or values, since these are all learned skills. Let's look at one common example of each:

TEACHING A PHYSICAL TASK

Organizing Belongings

- *Plan Ahead.* Figure out *why* children are disorganized. Are they overwhelmed by too many toys? Do they lack convenient places to put things? Are they easily distracted? Is cleaning at the bottom of their priority list? Is organization simply not part of their personality? Once we identify the cause, we can adjust our approach. Plan a special time to de-clutter, make shelves with boxes, or think about ways your children can build self-reminders into their plans.

- *Explain the value of the skill.* Acknowledge the difficulty of being organized and that it doesn't come naturally to most people. Show understanding for their lack of interest. Point out the benefits of being more organized—we find things quicker, the floor is safe to walk on, and toys won't get broken. If they pick up toys regularly, it doesn't take as much time to organize and clean, which leaves more time to play.

- *Break the task into smaller steps.* Make the job easier by classifying objects and discussing options for organizing their belongings. Avoid vague commands like, "Clean up this mess," which is overwhelming. The child looks at the mess and wonders, "Where do I start?" Instead, focus on one area at a time, "You could start by putting the books in the bookshelf." This statement gives some direction to get children started. Don't teach all the steps in one session. This gives children a chance to remember what they have learned before learning something new.

- *Let children watch.* The first time you sort the toys, do it with them and explain as you go along. For example, say "book" (as you slide the book toward the bookshelf), "pencil" (as you toss it near the desk). Do a couple items from each category and invite them to help.

- *Let children try.* Help children decide where to put miscellaneous items. If they get distracted and start to play with a toy, ask "Where does that go?" This helps them refocus.

- *Let children do it their way.* It doesn't really matter *how* a child cleans, as long as it is safe, fairly quick, and effective. They can roller skate to the different locations, use a robot-hand toy to lift items, or put a basketball hoop over their clothes hampers to make that task more fun.

- *Offer choices.* "Do you want to pick up the toys or dirty clothes first?" "You can to start at one end of the room and put away each thing you find or make piles before you put them away. You decide."

- *Work together, gradually doing less each time.* Offer to do one group of items while your children choose another. Eventually, you can work on another chore at the same time. It is always preferable to do *some* kind of work, instead of relaxing with a book, because children feel alone and resentful. Working at the same time, even if not together, promotes teamwork.

- *Make it fun and child-friendly.* In addition to singing and making games out of a job, look at the room from your children's perspective. Can they easily reach everything? The more accessible you make their rooms, the less you will have to help in the future.

- *Offer encouragement at every step.* When your children are busy working or when you check on them, describe the progress they've made and how hard they're working. When children get distracted, keep your comments to one-word reminders or a few words. (See Chapter 10, "Clear Communication Toolset," for specific suggestions.)

TOO MANY TOYS?

- Organize toy storage and play areas at least twice a year. Involve children in identifying broken and outgrown toys.
- Plan a garage sale. Let children keep any money they make from selling their toys. This motivates them to let go of a toy. Remind them that they can buy new toys with the money they earn.
- Clean out toys before gift-giving holidays. Remind children that they need more room to store their new gifts. Suggest they give their old toys to needy children.

If children don't want to give up their toys:
- Have children select certain toys to box and rotate boxes every one to three months.
- Instead of rotating entire boxes of toys, some parents have a one-in-one-out rule. For every toy children want to take out, they need to trade one in.

If children never play with a toy, they may not be as upset about getting rid of it. If they do play with it, let them keep it and get agreements for putting it away. (If this doesn't work, there are other options, in later chapters, for getting children to clean after themselves.)

*If children are attached to their toys, **never** sneak and throw it out.* If children don't want to give an outgrown toy to a younger sibling or neighbor, make the donation a ceremonial event.

- Reminisce about the fond memories children have about their toys and how sad it is that they've outgrown them.
- Explain how much another child would appreciate the toy.
- Offer the choice of giving the toy directly to another child or offer to pass it on for them. Sometimes, putting a toy up for a short time can help make a transition of ownership easier for the child who's giving.

TEACHING BEHAVIOR SKILLS

Assertive Respectful Communication

- *Plan Ahead.* We notice children need to work on this behavior when they respond to people in passive or disrespectful ways. We usually teach this skill "on the fly," as situations arise, leaning down to whisper our comments and suggestions, so we don't embarrass children in front of others.

- *Explain the value of the skill.* Disrespectful or rude behavior causes problems in relationships and leads to arguments and hurt feelings. If children are shy or afraid to speak for themselves, others may take advantage of them or not realize what they want or need. Assertive communication, as we learn in Chapter 10, "Clear Communication Toolset," is speaking out for one's rights, without violating another's. It resolves problems in healthy, helpful ways that improve relationships.

- *Break the task into smaller steps.* There are several steps to assertive communication. For children, we can help them work on several areas: realizing what they want, having the courage to speak out, and wording requests, opinions, or concerns in respectful, clear ways. Teach children the language of assertiveness. We learn this in more depth in the Clear Communication Toolset.

- *Let children watch.* When you complain about poor service or respond to a rude comment, practice respectful, assertive communication. Afterward, share with children how difficult it was to control your anger, think before speaking, and how you talk yourself through the experience (self-talk to control your anger and speak respectfully). We simply share our experience as we would if we were talking to ourselves or a friend who happened to be with us.

- *Let children try.* Provide opportunities for children to practice speaking out and making requests in non-threatening situations. Give older children or teens a chance to change their rude or disrespectful comments, instead of reacting to them in equally aggressive or disrespectful ways. Let them know they are certainly allowed to have negative feelings and opinions, but you (and others) are more willing to listen to them if they express those ideas respectfully.

- *Let children do it their way.* Children don't have to word things exactly as we do, although they tend to mimic what they hear. As long as children are speaking out for their needs or opinions without offending others, they can develop their own personal style of communication.

- *Offer choices.* When we brainstorm ideas for responding to conflicts, discuss the options and possible effects of each. You will learn more about this problem-solving process in Chapter 8.

- *Work together.* As children become more skilled at assertive communication, stand further in the background, giving them space. If children are hesitant to speak to others, offer to go with them, but they must speak for themselves. Assure them that if the cashier asks them a question they aren't expecting, you will coach them, but will not speak *for* them.

- *Make it fun and child-friendly.* Role-play possible scenarios. With young children, play store and practice being polite and responding to small-talk. Play restaurant; when children are the waiters, share a concern about your food in a respectful way and then reverse roles. Play with character figures; when they get into conflicts, model and encourage children to practice respectful responses and alternatives to fighting, which is usually how children make their characters resolve problems.

- *Offer encouragement at every step.* When children try their new skills, others sometimes respond unhelpfully or unpredictably. At this point, many children (and adults) throw their skills out the window and revert to power and control tactics, like grabbing a toy or shoving a child in anger. Give them credit for their effort and describe any improvement you see. Do some brief problem solving (see Chapter 8) to plan possible responses they can use if this happens again. Carefully consider whether you should discipline the aggressive action, if they gave their assertive communication skills a fair try and are still in the process of learning (a PU problem). You will probably be more effective if you use the experience to teach skills, rather than simply punishing them for trying and failing.

    > *A **Personal Story.** When my children were young, both were hesitant to talk to adults. I remember one summer my son offered another child money, if she would buy candy for him at the pool's refreshment stand. I immediately nixed that idea! We rehearsed his request, but he still refused to speak, even when I stood by him! It was embarrassing and frustrating, as the line of hungry children grew longer. Since the pool was a small, safe place and I could watch him from afar, I finally told him that if he wanted candy at the pool, he would need to buy it himself. I didn't rescue him or allow his friends to bail him out. Finally, he did it. Each time after that, he seriously considered how much he wanted something. Over time, he became more skilled and confident about speaking up for himself. By his early teens he was regularly handling tasks like placing orders, calling stores for inquiries, and making purchases on his own.*

TEACHING VALUES

(For general information about teaching values see Chapter 10, "Clear Communication Toolset.")

Appreciating Diversity

- *Plan Ahead.* There are countless opportunities everyday to teach children an appreciation for diversity. We see people in our community, on television, or in public who are "different"— people with physical or mental challenges and from different races, cultures, and religions. Children naturally ask questions, but sometimes at awkward times or in loud embarrassing ways, like "Why is that kid in a chair with wheels?" Tell children they can ask you any question or make any comment, but they need to whisper it in your ear or wait until you are alone. Let them know you understand their curiosity and explain that some comments hurt other people's feelings.

- *Explain the value of the skill.* It is natural for people to compare others to themselves; we see ourselves as the norm and anyone different seems "abnormal," until we understand, respect, and appreciate these differences. Intolerance for people's differences is the root of many world conflicts. In our own lives, we can benefit from learning how to get along with others who are different. We acknowledge the differences, instead of *denying* they are there. If we get to know people as individuals, appreciating their unique talents, skills, or qualities, we avoid prejudging people and break common stereotypes.

- *Break the task into smaller steps.* The different steps in appreciating diversity are understanding the causes of the differences, knowing how to accept differences and use them to enhance relationships, and tactful ways to treat others who are different—with the same dignity and respect we need to give *everyone.*

- *Let children watch.* Openly model respect for diversity. If you are surprised, offended, or uncomfortable with someone because of their differences, model respectful behavior toward them. If children ask questions, discuss your feelings. Reveal to them your first impressions and thoughts, which might be negative, how you came to understand more about the person or their differences, and how (or why) you responded respectfully. Thoughts are not observable, unless we share them. Sharing our thoughts helps children know how to respond when they have similar thoughts.

- *Let children try.* Fine-tune children's skills as situations arise. For example, if children see another child in a wheelchair and whisper to you, "Why is that kid in a wheelchair?" offer a factual explanation, not a label. Say, "His legs probably don't work well and it's hard for him to walk." Don't say, "He's handicapped"—physical and mental disabilities are challenges, negative attitudes make them handicaps. Encourage children to smile at the child in a friendly way and say "Hello," if that is how they would respond to any other child. Encourage children to go beyond distant politeness, befriending other children, regardless of their differences. They should not, however, go out of their way to baby a child with a mental or physical challenge, which is demeaning and implies the child is incapable.

- *Let children do it their way.* As children establish friends of different religions, races, backgrounds, and physical abilities, they will find ways to compensate for any difficulties those differences raise and build a closer relationship. Encourage their efforts and describe how valuable the other child's relationship is to your children.

- *Offer choices.* When differences pose difficulties (they want to play a computer game with a partially blind child, play on a playground with a physically challenged child, or can't understand someone who speaks with an accent), explore options for working or playing together. Allow partially blind children to put their nose on the screen, adjust playground equipment to make it more accessible or encourage children to ask the challenged child's parent for suggestions. Teach children how to ask others for clarification tactfully and respectfully.

- *Work together.* Look for or create opportunities to learn and practice acceptance skills. Volunteer together at a mental or physical rehabilitation clinic, attend services of another religion, and visit playgrounds where there are children of diverse backgrounds.

> ***Diversity in life is the norm.*** **It would be *abnormal* if everyone were the same.**

- *Make it child-friendly.* There are more creative and effective ways to teach values than lecturing: read or tell stories that illustrate the value and ask your child thought-provoking questions. "How did (character's name) feel when . . .? Why did (character's name) do . . .?" Role-play situations, "What would you do if someone . . .?" Play games that develop values such as honesty, good sportsmanship, teamwork, and respect for other people's feelings. With diversity, describe differences to young children in simple, factual, accepting ways.

- *Offer encouragement at every step.* When children make efforts to be respectful, accepting, and helpful to others (whether or not they are "different"), describe how good that can make the other person feel. If they don't talk down to a physically/mentally challenged person or treat them differently, point out how much that person probably appreciates their friendliness. When they control their stares and nonverbal reactions, notice their efforts and the positive effect. Encourage mostly during the early years or stages of the learning process, to reinforce children's efforts. Once these attitudes and behaviors are their natural way of perceiving others, don't point out others' differences or children's reactions, since that would only draw more attention to the differences.

> *A **Personal Story**. When Amber was 4, she asked why her friend's skin tanned so darkly and hers stayed so light (she's a redhead). I explained that everyone's skin has a different amount of pigment, a chemical that makes skin lighter or darker. I gave her several examples. Referring to our neighbor who has albinism, I explained, "Byron has no pigment, so his skin and hair are very white. You have more pigment, but not much. Emmy has olive-colored skin, so she has more pigment than you, and Barry (an African-American child in her class) has even more pigment." Amber wondered why people aren't all the same. I offered both a scientific and spiritual explanation. (Sunnier climates develop more pigment, so our ancestry determines our skin color, and God created us each to be special and unique.) I explained that even though people might look or act different, we are all very similar on the inside—we are all children of God and are deserving of love and respect. We all have feelings that can be hurt, want to feel accepted by others, and want to have friends.*
>
> *Byron, our neighbor, has severe vision problems, so Amber has learned how to modify their play to fit their mutual needs. She points out hazards he might not see. She knows he needs to hold objects closer to his eyes to see them and gives him the extra time he needs to adjust to new situations. He shares his braille books with her and has her close her eyes to test how "sharp her fingers are." Amber doesn't overprotect him; she respects and understands he needs to do things in a way that is best for him.*

Give a Quick Tip

Offering a quick tip or giving children information is a simple tool for building independence. Present suggestions in a *tentative* way. Don't *tell* them what to do, simply offer a suggestion they can take or leave. Children can often figure out the information if we ask it as a question. For example:

▶ "If you don't rinse the sink after you spit out your toothpaste, what happens?" (Wait.) "Yeah, the toothpaste dries on the sink and looks yucky."

▶ "Do you know how to save your computer game? If you save your game now and then, you don't have to go back to the beginning each time."

Instead of telling children what to *do,* it is often more helpful to give them information they can use later. This should be information they do not already know. Here are a few examples:

▶ "When milk is left out too long, it spoils."

- "When food is left out, the dog (or ants/bugs) will get into it."
- "If you put on your socks first, they'll stay pulled up when you put on your pants."

If you've found one way of doing things to work well for you, offer your personal style as one possible way to do things. Again, don't insist that the child has to do it your way, simply point out that it works for you and the child can try the idea. Here are a few examples:

- "Sometimes I _____. You can do it however you want, but that's what works best for me."
- "Would you like to know a secret?" If they say yes, say, "I usually do _____." If they say no, let them discover their own best way to do something.
- "Sometimes it helps me if I do _____."

Let Children Be Responsible for Their Own Mistakes ☆☆☆☆

Many parents try to help their children avoid mistakes by offering advice or rescue them by stepping in. While we might succeed in protecting our children from pain or mistakes, we might also rob them of self-confidence, a positive attitude toward mistakes, and an opportunity to learn important life skills.

Think about experiences when you learned a valuable lesson. Chances are, you learned the lesson firsthand or directly saw the effects of someone's mistakes. These firsthand experiences always teach lessons that last longer and have a greater impact than secondhand advice. Whenever a potential mistake is not dangerous, we want to guide children, without taking over or rescuing them.

> *A Personal Story. I am a coach for a worldwide program that teaches children creative problem solving. A team of up to seven children works together to solve problems: one long-term and many on-the-spot problems. The coach's most important task is to guide the team by asking questions and teaching them skills—we are not allowed to offer **any** ideas, advice, or help. The children must do **everything**: decide the plot, write the script, and make the props. If any team receives outside assistance, the judges will disqualify the team. I use **all** the tools from The Parent's Toolshop, but not interfering is the most difficult. If the team wants to try an idea that probably won't work, I can only ask questions to help them realize **on their own** whether the idea is worth pursuing. Ultimately, the choice is theirs. "Failure" is an important part of the learning process. It helps the children devise a better solution. This process is more time consuming and frustrating than telling them the answer, but the **process** of allowing children to learn lessons on their own is what's important. Being a coach for this program also helps me as a parent. When I'm tempted to rescue my children, I am better able to guide them without taking over, too.*

Many people (both adults and children) don't like to be told what to do, they would rather experience it themselves. When I work with groups of *teens,* they often complain "I wish my parents would let me make my own mistakes. I'm capable of learning from them." If children make a poor decision that is not life-threatening, let them experience the effects. Later, ask them questions that will help them figure out *for themselves* what to do differently next time. Ask helpful questions, such as "What happened?", "What did you learn from that?", "What did you do that worked?", and "What could you do differently next time?" Use encouragement to point out when they used good judgment or made a responsible decision, no matter how small. We can also help children learn from other people's mistakes. Discuss news events and ask them questions. "Why do you think this happened? How could it have been avoided? What would you do?"

> *A Personal Story. When I was young, I had red curly hair, which was out of style back then. Other children sometimes made fun of my hair and I always wished I had straighter hair (I even tried ironing it). Once, when I was in elementary school, I had saved up enough money to buy roller skates. My mom took me to the mall and we passed the wig department on the way in. I asked if I could try on one wig, just to see what I would look like. I found a strawberry-blonde, straight-haired wig that was less than the price of the skates. I asked my mother if I could buy the wig with my money. She acknowledged my feelings about wanting to have different hair and pointed out the disadvantages of having a wig and no skates. She did not, however, forbid me from buying it. She suggested we look at skates before I made my decision.*

After looking at the skates, I still wanted to buy the wig. My mom was very hesitant to say "yes." We went back to the wig department so I could try the wig on one more time. As I did, my mom talked to the clerk. She was probably making sure I could return the wig if I changed my mind.

I bought the wig and took it home, excited to wear it for the first time. I left immediately, to show my friends down the street. When I was still two houses away, they realized I was wearing a wig and began to laugh and make fun of me. I turned around and went home. My mom asked me helpful questions about the decision I had made. She provided the option of exchanging the wig for the skates, which is what I did.

My mom could have forbidden me to buy the wig, but I'm glad she didn't. I had always wondered what I would look like with different hair. I was excited about making an independent decision about spending my money. Had she forbidden me to buy the wig, I probably would have gotten into a power struggle with her. Did I make a poor decision? Yes. Was I embarrassed and disappointed? Yes, but only slightly. Mostly, I learned to appreciate the hair God gave me. I learned a lot from making a decision and experiencing the effect, even though it was negative.

Let Children Do Things by Themselves ☆☆☆☆

Parents today are busy and usually in a hurry. It seems easier and faster to do things *for* children, rather than wait for them to do things. If *we* do it, we know it is done the right way (our way). This might be a reflection of our need for control or perfection. While it may be quicker now, in the long run it takes longer to do two people's jobs. Our goal is to teach children life skills and how to use them wisely. We can be supportive and encouraging, giving children chances to practice and improve their skills.

If children take a long time to do tasks on their own, plan ahead by allowing more time. Make things accessible and child-friendly. With young children, for example, put bite-sized chunks of veggies and fruit on a lower refrigerator shelf. Let them make their own snacks, however imperfect. Whatever the age, remember that practice makes better, not perfect.

It's difficult, as children grow older, to realize they don't need us as much. We have mixed feelings about giving up the tasks we gladly do for our children out of love. Acts such as feeding and dressing our children aren't usually difficult to give up. It's much harder, however, to let children solve their own problems, learn from their mistakes and have different opinions. It's hard to see them struggle and make mistakes, when we know we could protect them from pain or disappointment. So we give our advice, sure that we have the answer.

Adults (and older children and siblings) often wait until children are older to teach or involve them in more difficult tasks. Unfortunately, when children are older, they often don't want to help. We've

*Instead of doing tasks **for** children . . .*   *. . . make tasks easier for children to do themselves.*

missed our chance to teach skills to a younger but more motivated and interested child. Usually, there are small ways young children can help with more difficult tasks.

Sometimes, parents don't realize their efforts to help children actually encourage their dependency or rescue them from responsibilities. Continual reminders to get up, remember coats and books, and eat their food are all ways we take on children's responsibilities. When we protect children from the effects of their mistakes, we prevent them from learning on their own. When we offer advice or tell them how to solve problems, we rob them of important opportunities to learn problem-solving skills. These are just a few ways we keep children dependent, so we can feel indispensable and protect them from disappointment. Dependency creates negative feelings and unhealthy beliefs, such as the following:

Common Statements	Resulting Feelings/Thoughts	Alternative Statement
"Let me do it for you"	Inadequacy. "I *can't* do it."	"You try."
"Do it *this* way."	No control. "My ideas are no good."	"How do you think you could do this?"
"You don't want to . . ."	Confusion. "I don't know what's best best for me. Others need to tell me what I want."	"Would you like to . . . ?"
"Don't play with those friends (pick those clothes, etc.)."	Uncertain. "They don't trust my judgment, so I shouldn't."	"How do you feel when . . . ?" "What do you think?"
"It's time to do _____."	"I don't have to be responsible for remembering. They'll remind me."	"When do you plan to do _____?"

Notice the Difficulty[1]

When we tell children something is "easy" to do, it can discourage them. If they succeed, they feel they haven't accomplished much, because the task was easy. If they can't do it, they feel like a failure for not being able to do something simple. If, on the other hand, we say, "That can be difficult," children feel good about accomplishing something difficult. If they can't do it, they at least know that the task was tough, not that they're inadequate. If we feel phony saying "t-   ard," look at the task from an inexperienced child's point of view. The first few times we do anything new, it usually *is* hard. Also, avoid saying, "That must be hard for *you*." Children might think, "It's only hard for *me*."

There are times when it *is* okay to do something for children that they can do for themselves. We need to use discretion to decide when our children are tired or in need of extra attention. Just try to maintain a balance. Nudge, but don't push. Guide, but don't rescue. Coach, but don't control.

Ask Their Opinions ☆☆☆☆

Involve children in solving problems by asking questions like "What do *you* think we could do?" Allow them to make decisions about things that directly affect them, such as selecting their own library books or deciding how to spend their allowances.

When people speak about your children like they aren't there, show respect for your children by involving them in the conversation. If the cashier asks, "What grade is he in?" let your child answer the question. Encourage children to describe their symptoms to the doctor, explain to the dentist how they brush their teeth, order their own food in restaurants, or buy their own candy.

As children mature, they naturally develop individual opinions. These opinions are obviously less experienced views than adults have, but no less valid or important. Our job as parents is not to create carbon copies of ourselves, with identical beliefs and preferences. It is much healthier to encourage and respect our children's opinions and preferences, even if we don't agree with them. If we don't force our values and opinions on children, but simply share *our* opinions, children are more likely to consider them. Don't assume that the opinion or value children or teens have today is what they will always believe. Trust the growth and maturation process. Get to know your children as unique human beings, with individual opinions. We can learn much from their perceptions and grow more ourselves.

Wait Before Answering Questions

Children are famous for asking questions: "When will the pool be open?" "Why do I have to study? I got all my work done at school." We often think we need to immediately respond with an answer.

> *A Graduate's Story. My friend, Diane, was watching TV with her two girls, 9 and 7. They saw a commercial about a feminine pad with "wings." The nine-year-old asked, "What's that about?" Diane had been waiting for a "teachable moment" to have this talk and explained the menstrual cycle to her daughters. When she finished, the daughter said, "So do the pads really fly?"*

Usually, when children ask a question, they've already thought about the answer. Find out what your children are thinking, first. "Why *is* the pool still closed during the winter?" "Why do *you* think your teacher asks you to study at home?" When we take the time to listen to children's ideas, they often reveal the real reason they asked the question.

> *A Graduate's Story. My son came home from school one day and asked, as he had before, "Why is Daddy only home on the weekends?" I was tempted to give him the answers I always gave, "Daddy has to travel all week for his job" and "So we have enough money to live in this house and so I can stay home with you." This time, I used my new skills and asked him, "Why do you think Daddy is gone all week?" He said, "Well, Joey's parents are divorced and he only sees his dad on weekends. Are you and Daddy getting a divorce?" I was floored! I never would have guessed that my son had doubts about our marriage! I quickly reassured him that all was fine and that Daddy wished he **could** be home more, to spend more time with **all** of us. I was so grateful I learned this skill. Otherwise, my son could have gone on misinterpreting our family situation for something it wasn't.*

Usually, the process of finding an answer to a child's question is as valuable as the answer itself. Don't feel you or your children need an immediate answer. If you do answer your children's question, be brief, use words your children understand, and answer only what they asked.

> *A Graduate's Story. When I was pregnant with my second child, my son Denny, who was four at the time, was very curious about the reproductive process. I answered his questions honestly and factually. He'd think about the answers, sometimes for days, and then ask another question, often out of the blue. We'd gotten to the part about the male's sperm fertilizing the female's egg. (I hoped I wouldn't have to explain any further!) One day, as we were driving in the car, he asked, "How does the sperm get from the man to the woman?" I explained in general terms and he thought about the answer. "So did Daddy . . . ?" Now, I was getting nervous and uncomfortable. I matter-of-factly said, "Yes," and added my values of sex within the context of love and marriage. He excitedly asked, "Can I watch the next time you do it?" . . . I tried to not laugh or react in shock and quickly, calmly said, "No, it's a very private moment between husband and wife." That was it! He knew all the facts and never asked any other questions.*

Show Children How to Use Outside Resources

We can develop our children's independence by showing children the other resources available to them. You can get a book on insects to find out what kind of bug your child found. Encourage your daughter to have a beauty make-over, to learn appropriate ways to apply makeup. Have a teacher recommend a tutor to help with problem subjects. If children are concerned about being overweight, buy books or encourage them to attend a special class to learn how to lose weight in healthy ways. Aside from children learning to be resourceful and relieving parents from being know-it-alls, advice from outside sources usually carries more weight than lectures from Mom or Dad.

Respect Their Privacy

- **Privacy is a two-way street; parents expect privacy and need to extend the same courtesy to their children.** Older children, especially *teens,* have a strong need for privacy. Teens live in two rather unrelated worlds—the world of friends and the world of home. They try to maintain boundaries between these worlds by not talking about parents to their peers and not talking about peers to their parents. Teens often view their parents' questions about their friends as an intrusion into their private world and may lie to maintain their privacy. (See Chapter 12, "PO Toolset," for more information on lying.)

- **Set priorities about what qualifies as a "need to know" issue and what children can keep private.** Make these "need to know" issues clear to children, along with the reasons for this need. We can reassure them that they still have areas of privacy they do not have to share. For instance, their telephone conversations and letters are their private concerns as long as there has been no sign that the child has been harassing people. A "need to know" list might include[2]:

COMMON "NEED TO KNOW" ISSUES	
• Friends' behavior	***For older children, we might add:***
• Whereabouts in free time	• Sexual behavior of/with peers
• Snacking behavior	• Use of drugs or alcohol
• TV, Internet, computer, and electronic game usage	• People/behavior at parties
	• Transportation arrangements
• Behavior at school	• Behavior driving/riding in cars
• Homework accomplished	

- **Let children take charge of their own bodies, such as their hair styles or clothes.** Young children frequently choose clothes that don't match or style their hair in imperfect ways. We can offer our opinions, but let children make the final decision. For a special occasion, such as a wedding or picture day, get agreements in advance to let you style their hair or pick the outfit *that* day. Remind them that they can usually decide these for themselves. (If you still get flack, follow up with the suggestions from the Cooperation Toolset.) Avoid fussing with your child's hair, shirt tails, or posture. It's embarrassing and implies that they didn't do a good enough job and you are following behind correcting them.

- **Respect children's physical and emotional space, and their property rights.** This can prevent many sibling/peer conflicts. (The Sibling/Peer section of Chapter 8, "Problem-Solving Toolset," details specific ways to mediate such disputes.)

 Let Them Dream[3]

Children often have dreams or expectations that seem unrealistic to adults. When children share these dreams or hopes, don't rush to pop their bubbles. Ask questions that help them explore the pleasure of the fantasy, and only if necessary, the truth of reality. If children say they want to be a sports superstar, ask, "What would you like the most about being a star?" Or "What would it take to do that?" Avoid discouraging comments, such as "Everyone wants to be a star, but only a few will make it. Don't put all your eggs in one basket." While this statement might be true, it doesn't necessarily mean the goal is impossible. Most professional athletes had to work extra hard to achieve their dreams—and their dreams were what motivated them to stick with it.

> ***A Personal Story.*** *When Amber was 4, she would say "I want to be a doctor when I grow up." When I asked her why, she said, "so I can help my friends when they're sick. "When Amber needed a blood test for kindergarten, I explained what would happen and that it would hurt a little bit. I didn't add that I used to pass out at the sight of blood. To my amazement, she watched the nurse take her blood and didn't flinch or cry! I started to think "Maybe she would be a good doctor or nurse."*

Several months later, my 17-year-old dog had to be put to sleep. We had already discussed death with the children when another pet died. Despite my squeamishness about such procedures, I decided to be present when Punkin was put to sleep. Amber asked if she could go with me. I was very hesitant. I explained the procedure in detail and what "putting to sleep" really meant, but Amber still wanted to go. At the vet's, I offered her the option of leaving if she felt uncomfortable. She helped me hold and caress Punkin as she left us. I cried the whole way home, but Amber was much more matter-of-fact about the experience. She viewed it like a veterinarian.

Later that year, Amber said her desire to be a people doctor had changed into a desire to be a veterinarian. When our other dog had dozens of tumors removed, I could hardly stand to look at her stitches without getting squeamish. When Taffy chewed out one of the stitches on her paw, Amber helped my husband wrap it and he gave her a close inspection of the wound, explaining the different skin layers.

The next day, Amber wanted to come with me to the vet's office. I was feeling light-headed just thinking about the sight of watching the vet put in new stitches. When we spoke to the vet, he explained the options, with all the skin-layer alternatives. I felt seriously faint. I told him to do whatever was best for Taffy and that I'd wait in the lobby. Amber said, "Mom! Someone has to be here for Taffy! I want to stay and hold her." I knew she would be well-behaved and helpful, and the vet said her presence was no problem. I reminded her that she could come to the lobby if she changed her mind. I sat down and hung my head between my knees, while my six-year-old watched with fascination as Taffy got her stitches. I felt like a such a wimp. Later, Amber performed pretend surgery on her stuffed animals, with rubber gloves, soapy water, and a pretend needle and thread.

I am now convinced Amber really would make a fine vet or doctor. She taught me a big lesson about allowing a child to dream and not underestimating a child's abilities. Any dream is possible, if someone is willing to believe enough in the dream to do what it takes to make it happen.

Nudge, but Don't Push ☆☆☆☆

> **Nudging** is a firm and gentle encouragement to take the next step.
> **Pushing** is an unrealistic pressured expectation to reach the final goal all at once.

Some children are naturally more independent, always wanting to do things by themselves. Others are more dependent, frequently asking for help and hesitant to try new tasks. As parents, we need to respect our children's temperaments and respond accordingly. When children are naturally daring, we can teach skills for taking safe risks and supervise them until they have mastered the skills. When children are hesitant and truly scared of new experiences, we can nudge and encourage them to take the next step. We can read their reactions and be ready to back off a bit or slowly ease them into a new situation.

At times, children want to do something very much, but aren't emotionally or physically ready. They want to go swimming, but are still afraid of the water or want to ride a two-wheeler, but still aren't coordinated enough to remove the training wheels. Instead of forcing, urging, or pressuring children, we can express our confidence in their growing abilities and reassure them that some day they *will* do these things. At these times, offer quick tips and lots of encouragement. Here are three behaviors parents often push their children too quickly to do and how they can nudge instead:

▶ *Toilet training:* "You wanted to play longer so you didn't get to the potty on time. I'm sure you'll stop sooner next time so your pants stay clean and dry."

▶ *Getting ready on time:* "You had your lunch and backpack ready, but couldn't find your shoes. Where could you put them so you can find them quickly next time?"

▶ *Getting a job:* "You'd really like to be able to buy _____. Where could you earn the money?"

Let Go and Trust

Every stage of life presents separation issues. First children are weaned, then potty trained, they start school, begin to date, drive a car, move out, maybe get married, and before we know it we could be grandparents! Some stages of separation are easier for us to deal with. Each of these stages of separation, however, prepares both our children and us with the inner strength and confidence necessary for our children to become responsible, independent adults. As hard as it may be, we must work though our conflicting feelings, so we can do what is best for our children—to let go, lovingly and with support.

The key ingredient for building independence is to let go—let go of our need to control, desire to be needed, and temptation to rescue. Our children will always *need* us, but the ways they need us change over the years. Letting go does not mean parents cut the reins and allow total freedom. As you are letting go, teach them the skills they need to be responsible, independent adults. By replacing unhelpful habits with helpful responses, we maintain a healthy balance between freedom and limits.

TIPS FOR TOTS TO TEENS

In my parenting classes, we brainstorm ideas for building independence at each stage of childhood. Here are just a few suggestions from other parents. You can probably think of even more.

Let *infants* reach for objects, instead of scooting them closer. Child-proof their environment, so they can safely explore their world. Don't immediately rush to your crying infant—walk or finish going to the bathroom first. It is important to respond faithfully, so our children learn to trust us and feel secure. But we can pause a few seconds to see if they can calm themselves down or resolve their own problems.

> *A **Personal Story**. Like many parents, I used to believe infants aren't capable of solving their own problems. At a conference I once attended, the instructor asked a group of nearly a hundred parent educators, "At what age are children capable of solving their own problems?" Some of us answered, "Two, when children can think logically." "Earlier," the instructor responded. Several classmates answered, "At birth," remembering that infants cry when they are wet or hungry. "Earlier," was the instructor's reply. We looked puzzled. Then she asked, "When you are pregnant—men, imagine a woman you know—what do babies do when they're cramped in a tummy?" We all replied in unison, "They kick!" "Right," she replied, "when babies have a problem, like being cramped, they solve the problem by stretching their legs! Humans are innately capable, from the time of conception, to resolve problems. Their ability is dependent on their intellectual and physical abilities, but they are nevertheless capable to some degree."*

Let *toddlers* try. Let them feed themselves—put a mat under the high chair, use finger foods, and get easy-to-use utensils. Supervise their teeth-brushing by pretending you are a dentist who is checking or counting their teeth when they are done. As they learn to put on their clothes, teach skills without taking over. Stay nearby, guiding and coaching, but let them do as much as they can.

Let *preschoolers* help. They can sort dirty clothes, fold towels and wash cloths, and match socks. In the kitchen, let them measure, pour, and stir. Teach them how to dust furniture, removing any breakable items for them, at first. Outside, let them water plants or spray-clean lawn furniture. They can gather sticks before mowing or help rake leaves. Promise to let them play in the pile before you dispose of the leaves. At the grocery store, let them carry non-breakable items to the cart. Give them coupons and see if they can match them with the right items. Let them choose their clothes and get dressed, teaching skills when you help. Don't expect perfection; they will improve with more practice.

Hold *elementary school children* accountable for their responsibilities and let them discover their own way of doing things. Let them get ready and out the door on time, *on their own*. (We discuss in Chapter 13, "Discipline Toolset," what to do when children are running late.) Remember that school and homework are their "jobs." We can teach skills when we intervene, without doing everything for them.

> *A **Personal Story.** If we take the time to teach skills, these are realistic expectations. By first grade, both of my children were totally self-sufficient in the morning. They set their own alarms, took a shower and got dressed, made their own breakfast, packed their own lunches, found and filled their own backpacks, and found ways to know when it was time to go to the bus stop. They had practiced and refined these skills during their preschool and kindergarten years, when they only attended half days and had more time to get ready. Back then, I taught parenting classes most evenings and got home late. I was bumping into walls at 6 a.m. and could hardly think straight. My **only** task was to give the children milk money—and I regularly forgot to do it! By planning ahead, teaching skills, and being patient, I now have two self-sufficient children who rarely need my help.*

If we take the time to teach skills, elementary-age children can be solely responsible for certain family chores and earning and budgeting money. As they mature, let them try riskier activities with your supervision: using sharper scissors and knives or crossing a not-too-busy street. By late elementary school, we can expand their boundaries, letting them go to a friend's house around the corner by themselves (this depends on your neighborhood, of course). Let your children be responsible for re-membering their after-school activities. Get agreements for the responsibilities that come from extra privileges, such as calling you when they arrive at the friend's house.

Preteens (junior high) and teens (high school) can have even more expanded boundaries and responsi-bilities. Hold them accountable for planning and managing their home, work, and school schedules and budgeting their finances. Have open discussions about *their* opinions and values. They appreciate our efforts to better understand them and know us well enough to know our opinions on almost any topic. As we show our willingness to listen to their differing opinions, they actually ask for our advice more often.

Let teens indulge in harmless clothing or hair fads. Each generation has some fashion fad that parents dislike—it's their way of expressing of their independence and individuality. Most fads are harmless and will pass quickly. If a fad, such as body piercing, raises healthy or safety risks, use parent/child problem solving in the Clear Communication Toolset to get agreements that allow teens a safe way to express their independence.

Recognize that teenagers need separate identities from their parents or their childhood identities. This process is called individuation. It starts at birth, but really blossoms in the teen years. As teens strive to become unique individuals, they *try on* different identities. These are usually temporary, unless we overreact and push them to fit our mold of who they should be. Such pressure only causes teens to rebel and make even stronger statements of independence.

Individuation **is the natural, necessary process of becoming an individual, with ideas, identity, beliefs, and values all one's own.**

Rebellion is a reaction to control.

Every **teen is individuating, but** *not* **every teen rebels. Individuation can turn into rebellion—if parents try to control children's efforts to express their indepen-dence and individuality.**

When a four-year-old dresses in a Superman cape and jumps off the couch, we say, "Isn't that cute?" We might address the dangers of jumping off couches, but we humor the act of trying on a different identity. When teenagers wear outlandish clothes and put glitter in their hair, many parents flip out! Jane Nelsen, the author of *Positive Discipline for Teenagers*, suggests parents also develop an "isn't that cute" attitude with teens. We can express our concerns about dangerous acts, but need to remember that part of a teen's "job" is to try on different identities, to figure out who they are separate from their parents.

In my T.I.P.S. for Teens class, we discuss individuation. I share an analogy with the class that helps explain the values clarification process children go through.

> Children are born with an invisible backpack on their backs. As they go through life, people put things in their backpacks—rules, roles, identities, values, and beliefs. Some examples are "Look

both ways before you cross the street," "You're the minister's child so you have to set a good example," or "Change your underwear every day in case you are in an accident."

Some children examine and question each belief that goes into their backpack. They want control over their backpack from the toddler years on. When we give orders, make requests, or say "no" without any reason, it is like stuffing something in their backpacks without their permission. These children resist such control and test these rules or values before accepting them into their backpacks.

Other children misunderstand what is put into their backpack. If a parent says "education is important," as the parent takes over responsibility for getting homework done, children might inaccurately conclude, "Education is important to *them*," or "It is *their* responsibility to make sure I remember my homework." Later in life, problem behaviors can arise from these inaccurate beliefs. These parents will wonder why their children aren't developing self-responsibility but don't realize it is partly because there is a rule or belief in the backpack that the child misunderstood.

Finally, there are some children who don't question what others put into their backpack, until it becomes heavy or they realize people are sticking things in without the children knowing what they are. By the teen years, their backpacks are getting rather heavy and teens figure, "If I have to carry this thing around the rest of my life, I want to know what's in it." They begin to go through their backpacks, examining the rules, values, and beliefs. They might accept some beliefs right away: "I know I need to look both ways before I cross the street, because the risk of not doing it is dangerous." Others they might reject or accept on their own terms, "I'll change my underwear every day, because I want to be clean, not because I fear an accident." Some they might reject, "I don't care if I'm the minister's child, I'm tired of people expecting me to be perfect. I'll do what I want to do, just to prove I'm my own person." Others they may need to question and test, before accepting, "Well, education is important to my parents, but sometimes it seems like a waste of time to me." They need to wrestle with these values and beliefs, before settling into what *their* beliefs will be.

The individuation process is very healthy and normal. In order to be a fully-functioning, well-balanced adult, one must have a sense of individual identity. Although children may test or seem to reject their parents' values or beliefs, the process is usually short-lived. If parents don't get into power struggles with their children, forcing their beliefs on them, children and teens usually consider the options and settle on beliefs, rules, and values that are very close to their parents'.

The teen years are a time when parents must readjust how much they teach skills and how much they listen to their children's opinions and decisions (see Chapters 7 and 8, "Child Problem Toolbox"). As we learned in Chapter 3, "The Universal Blueprint," teenagers "own" most of the problems they experience. We don't want to rescue them from these problems, so we use the skills in the Child Problem Toolbox instead. These tools help teens resolve their own problems or make decisions. We explore the details of *how* to do this in the next chapter.

LET GO

Letting go does not mean to stop caring,
    it means I can't take responsibility for someone else.

Letting go is not cutting others off,
    but the realization I can't control others.

Letting go is not enabling,
    but allowing others to learn from natural consequences.

Letting go is admitting powerlessness,
    which means that the outcome is not in my hands.

Letting go is not to try to change or blame another,
    it is making the most of myself.

*Letting go is not to care **for**, but rather it is caring **about** others.*

Letting go is not to diagnose, but to support.

Letting go is not judging others,
    but is allowing them to be fallible human beings.

Letting go refuses to arrange or guarantee results
    and allows others to make choices that determine their own destinies.

Letting go refuses to protect others from reality
    but encourages one to face the facts.

Letting go refuses to nag, scold, or argue
    but instead searches out my own shortcomings and corrects them.

Letting go is not regretting the past but growing and living for the future.

Letting go is fearing less and loving more.

                                                        Anonymous

SUMMARY SHEET
INDEPENDENCE TOOLSET

OPENLY MODEL BEHAVIOR ☆☆☆☆

TEACH SKILLS ☆☆☆☆

1. Plan Ahead.
2. Explain the value of the skill.
3. Break the task into smaller steps.
4. Let children watch.
5. Let children try.
6. Let children do things their way.
7. Offer choices.
8. Work together.
9. Make it fun and "child-friendly."
10. Offer encouragement at every step.

GIVE A QUICK TIP

LET CHILDREN BE RESPONSIBLE FOR THEIR MISTAKES ☆☆☆☆

LET CHILDREN DO THINGS BY THEMSELVES ☆☆☆☆

NOTICE THE DIFFICULTY

LET CHILDREN HELP YOU

ASK THEIR OPINION ☆☆☆☆

WAIT BEFORE ANSWERING QUESTIONS

SHOW CHILDREN HOW TO USE OUTSIDE RESOURCES

RESPECT CHILDREN'S PRIVACY

LET CHILDREN DREAM

NUDGE, BUT DON'T PUSH ☆☆☆☆

LET GO AND TRUST

PRACTICE EXERCISES

A. Use the Tools. Change each statement to one that will encourage a child's independence, using the suggested independence tools. (Possible answers are at the end of the chapter.)

1. A child says, "I'm hungry." The parent is tempted to say, "I'll fix you a peanut butter and jelly sandwich." How can the parent *teach skills*?

2. A parent is tempted to say, "I wish you weren't such a procrastinator. You always put things off until the last minute!" How can the parent *openly model behavior*?

3. A parent is tempted to say, "Let me sort the dirty laundry. They have to be separated properly." How can the parent *give a quick tip*?

4. A parent is tempted to say, "That game is too hard to set up. Pick a different one." What can the parent say or do to *let the children do it by themselves*?

5. A parent is tempted to say, "Your make-up looks terrible! You look like a clown!" How can the parent *notice the difficulty* of applying make-up?

6. A child asks, "Can I color these invitations for your [adult] party?" The parent is tempted to say, "These invitations have to be colored in just right. Let me do them." How can the parent *let the child help*?

7. A parent is planning to plant a vegetable garden. How can the parent *involve the children*?

8. A child asks, "Why do you work, and work, and work?" The parent is tempted to say, "So I can afford this house and all your toys!" What can the parent say *before answering this question*?"

9. A child says, "I want hair like Emily's." The parent is tempted to say, "Don't dye your hair. Your shade is so unique!" How can the parent *show the child how to use outside resources*?

10. A child complains, "Patty keeps messing up my tower." The parent is tempted to say, "Why don't you let Patty help you build it?" What can the parent say or do to *respect this child's privacy*?

11. A child says, "I want to be a park ranger when I grow up." The parent is tempted to say, "There's no money and hardly any jobs in forestry. Get a real job and go to the park on your days off." What can the parent say or do to *let the child dream*?

12. A child who still wets the bed asks to spend the night at a friend's house. The parent is tempted to say, "You can't, because you still wet the bed at night." How can the parent *nudge, but not push*?

B. Encourage Independence. In this exercise you'll see a series of situations that often frustrate parents or tempt them to take over. As you read each situation ask yourself, *"What could I say or do to encourage my child's independence?"* Draw on *all* the techniques you just learned.

1. A child calls from school to say, "I forgot my lunch. Will you bring it to me?"

2. A child says, "I can't work this zipper."

3. A child resists wearing a coat, saying "I get hot on the way home from school!"

4. A parent offers his child a choice between eggs or cereal for breakfast. The child chooses eggs. When the parent serves the eggs, the child says "I changed my mind. I don't want these eggs. I want cereal instead."

5. A preteen says, "I want to invite Jimmy to my birthday party, but I also want to invite Scott and they hate each other. What should I do?"

6. A teen says, "I'm going to save my allowance for a motorcycle."

Activity for the Week

List things you now do for your children that they could do themselves. Some examples are picking up clothes, buttoning shirts, buying expensive toys or clothes for them. Now look at the list and brainstorm ideas for transferring responsibility to your children.

Possible Answers

These are just possible answers. Give your own answers before you read these.

A: Use the Tools

1. "You can fix a peanut butter and jelly sandwich. . . You don't know how? Here's what you do. Take two pieces of bread. Use a butter knife to spread the peanut butter . . . Yeah, that's tricky . . . That's it! . . . Then the jelly . . . Now put the other piece of bread on top. You did it! Your very own peanut butter and jelly sandwich!"

2. When parents have a project to do that they don't feel like doing or that has a deadline, they can say aloud to themselves, "I really should (whatever the task or project is). I really don't feel like it, but if I do it now, (the positive consequence or benefit of getting it done.) Then I can do (something the parent likes)."

3. "When dark clothes are washed with the light ones, they get dark colors all over them, so I separate them into different piles. This is the basket for the whites, this is the basket for the darks. Let me know if you aren't sure which basket to use."

4. "That's a tricky game to set up! You've got the board and cards in the right place. If you take the pieces and look at the picture, you can sometimes see where they belong."

5. "It can take awhile to get the hang of how much make-up to put on. Sometimes, if I blend my eye shadow with this brush, it doesn't seem so strong."

6. There are three possible options: (a) "I'd like to do the coloring, but you can help me with the folding and licking the stamps and envelopes. Here are some envelopes to do." (b) Plan ahead and make a few extras so you can say, "Here's one you can color." Chances are it will take the child a longer time to color it. (c) Allow the child to color a few and send those invitations to people on your list who would appreciate your child's coloring.

7. "Summer is coming soon. Do you have any ideas for vegetables you'd like to grow?" (Later) "Tell me which seeds you would like to plant and I'll show you how to do it."

8. "I wish I didn't have to work so much. Why do *you* think I have to?" (My daughter asked me this question and I replied this way. Her answer was, "Because you help lots of people?" I thought it was neat that she understood the importance of my work.)

9. "The next time we get your hair done, ask Lory how much it costs to color hair, what shades there are, how often people have to keep dying it, and what could happen to your real hair color if you dye it." (This was my daughter's question and my response.)

10. "John, you can build that tower up in your room with the door shut. Or Patty, you can play with something else." (When Amber was a toddler, I borrowed a large play gate. When Amber bothered Chris or he played with small toys that Amber could choke on, *Chris* played inside the play gate and Amber roamed the child-proofed house.)

11. "You really like being in the woods, don't you? What else would you like about being a forest ranger?" (This was my husband's dream when he was younger. His parents thought he'd be better as an engineer. Now, he's an environmental engineer.)

12. "One of these days, you'll be able to stay dry all night. Then you can stay all night at Susie's."

B: Encourage Independence

1. "I bet you'll remember your lunch tomorrow! What can you do about lunch today?"

2. "Zippers are really tough. Here, you take this side and I'll take the other. Put your side into this spot right here. I'll hold this side. Now pull! . . . There you go!"

3. "Go look at the thermometer. If it is 50 degrees or higher, you can go without a coat." (A great idea is to cut out pictures of clothing, such as a winter coat, hat, bathing suit, and sweater. Paste to an outdoor thermometer by the appropriate degree markers. For example, 30 degrees = hat and mittens, 40° = winter coat, 50° = sweater, 60° = long-sleeved shirt, 70° = shorts, 80° = bathing suit.)

4. "Since you asked for the eggs today, you'll need to eat them. I only cook breakfast once. Tomorrow you can have cereal." Or "After you eat the eggs you asked for, you can fix yourself cereal."

5. "Well, that's a dilemma. *You* are friends with both Jimmy *and* Scott, but don't want them to ruin your party. What do you think your options are?"

6. "You'd like a motorcycle, huh? What do you like the most about motorcycles?" "Are there any extra dangers of owning a motorcycle?" "How much would you have to save? What other expenses are involved, like a license or helmet?"

WHAT'S NEXT?

We have completed our tour of the Prevention Toolbox. Practice using these skills daily. As we move through the rest of the toolsets, we refer to these tools often.

Chapter 7, "F-A-X Listening Toolset," is the first stop on our tour of the Child Problem Toolbox (Step B of the Universal Blueprint). We review the process of identifying Child Problems and keeping the ball in the child's (or other person's) court. We learn about the first step in the F-A-X communication process—Focus on feelings. We discover which responses can accidentally shut down communication. Then we practice the art and skill of effective listening.

REFERENCES

1.   "Notice the Difficulty" is a paraphrasing of the skill, "Show Respect for their Struggle," in *How to Talk So Kids Will Listen and Listen So Kids Will Talk,* by Adele Faber and Elaine Mazlish (Avon Books, 1982) p. 155.

2.   *Why Kids Lie: How Parents Can Encourage Truthfulness,* by Paul Ekman, Ph.D. (Penguin Books, 1989) p. 123.

3.   "Let Them Dream" is an expanded description of a skill called "Don't Take Away Hope," which I first read in *How to Talk So Kids Will Listen and Listen So Kids Will Talk,* by Adele Faber and Elaine Mazlish (Avon Books, 1982) pp. 145, 153.

STEP B
CHILD PROBLEM TOOLBOX

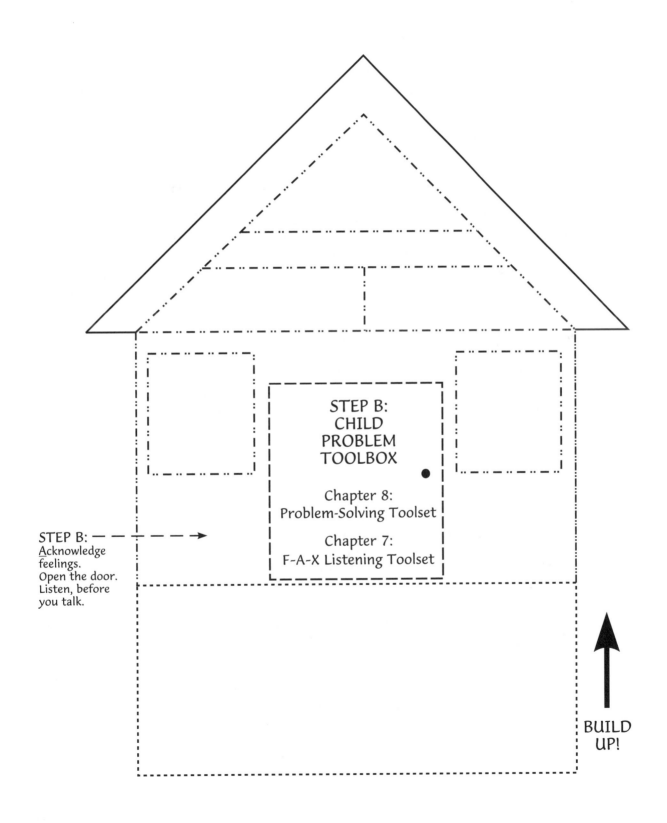

STEP B: Child Problem Toolbox

STEP B: – – –→
Acknowledge feelings.
Open the door.
Listen, before you talk.

STEP B:
CHILD
PROBLEM
TOOLBOX

Chapter 8:
Problem-Solving Toolset

Chapter 7:
F-A-X Listening Toolset

BUILD
UP!

B CHILD PROBLEM TOOLBOX

Secure houses protect us from nature's storms and other outside threats by controlling who enters our house. Likewise, people build emotional walls and doors that protect them from emotional storms and outside threats by controlling who enters their private world of feelings. The Child Problem Toolbox is represented by a door, because it contains the tools that help others feel trusting enough to open their emotional doors, share their thoughts and feelings, and weather the stormy problems that can happen in life.

IN THIS SECTION

Step B of the Universal Blueprint is the Child Problem Toolbox. In it, we begin learning about "F-A-X Communication." One part of F-A-X Communication is *sending* messages to others, which we learn in Chapter 10, "The Clear Communication Toolset." In this section, we learn the other part of F-A-X Communication, *receiving* messages. The Child Problem Toolbox contains two toolsets that help us respond effectively to Child problems or the child's feelings and perspective of Parent problems.

- *Chapter 7, "The F-A-X Listening Toolset,"* teaches us the first step of F-A-X Listening, "**F**ocus on feelings." These tools let others know it is safe to open their emotional doors to their private world of feelings. When people feel understood, they work through feelings and problems quicker.

- *Chapter 8, "The Problem-Solving Toolset,"* teaches us the last two steps in F-A-X communication, "**A**sk helpful questions" and "**X**-amine possible solutions." These are the real "power" tools in *The Parent's Toolshop*, because they em-power people to resolve their *own* problems.

Many of the explanations in the Child Problem Toolbox are presented in general terms, referring to *people*, not just children, because these tools are useful in *any* human relationship. Wherever you see the word *child* you can replace it with *the other person*.

WHEN TO USE THIS TOOLBOX

We can use the Child Problem Toolbox when others want to do any of the following:
- Tell a story, express strong feelings (positive or negative), or share a problem.
- Have others understand their thoughts, feelings, or opinions.
- Clarify or resolve a problem.

As we learned in the Universal Blueprint chapter, the first step in resolving problems is to identify what type of problem we are facing:

- If children have a problem (C) *children* are responsible for solving it.

- If parents have a problem (P, PU, PO), *parents* are responsible for starting the problem-solving process by bringing the problem to the attention of those involved.

- If there is a problem that bothers or affects *both* parents and children, *each* has a shared responsibility for finding the solution.

We can use the Child Problem Toolbox as part of our response to *any* type of problem.

No Problems (NO)

The *Self-Esteem Toolset* taught us to listen to children's feelings and opinions, so they know they are important.

The *Cooperation Toolset* taught us to acknowledge feelings when setting limits with positive words.

The *Independence Toolset* taught us to use listening and problem solving when children want information or help. This helps us avoid taking over *their* problems.

Parent Problems (P, PU, PO)

When Parent problems occur we "come into the house" to respond (Step C: Parent Problem Toolbox). It is *vital* that we take Step B, **A**cknowledging the other person's feelings or perspective, *before or while* we take Step C, **S**etting limits, expressing our concerns and redirecting misbehavior. If we only focus on our issues, other people usually feel defensive and stop listening or are distracted because they are waiting for their chance to talk. Either way, we lose our audience. When *we* have a problem (Parent problems), we briefly bring up the issue and quickly shift to our listening skills, allowing others to express their feelings. We can also acknowledge feelings *while* we are redirecting misbehavior. When we include Step B, **A**cknowledging feelings, others can work through their emotions, which is the real issue beneath their behavior.

We need to make a clear distinction, at this point, that allowing negative feelings and opinions is different from allowing hurtful actions. *Feelings are okay, they are there and they are real.* If hurtful actions are involved, that part of the problem is a Parent problem (SHARP RV). Listening is the first step (Step B), which could only involve a half-of-a-sentence, followed by steps C1 and C2, which set limits and redirect the misbehavior. Once parents and children understand the problem, the parents can come back to the Problem-Solving Toolset to get agreements for future behavior.

> **Effective communication is the key to resolving problems and F-A-X Listening is *the* most important communication tool.**

Child Problems

Let's quickly review what Child problems are and how to diagnose them. Then, we will learn the specific tools for resolving them.

When a problem arises, we stop to consider the SHARP RV issues. We ask, "Does the problem involve Safety, Health, Appropriateness, Rights, Property, Rules, or Values?"

- *If we answer "no" to each SHARP RV issue,* the problem is *only* a Child problem. We *only* use the Prevention and Child Problem Toolboxes.

- *If more than one problem or issue is involved*, we want to also ask ourselves, **"Is *any* part of this situation a problem for the child (other person)?"**

  - If the answer is "no," we *briefly* use the Child Problem Toolbox, maybe only a half sentence, to **A**cknowledge children's feelings or perspective, as we bring the problem to their attention.

  - If the answer is "yes," this is a C/P combination problem. We *alternate* between the Child and Parent Problem Toolboxes, depending on which part of the problem we are addressing.

In this section, Step B, the Child Problem Toolbox, we are *only* going to focus on resolving Child problems. Once we know how to use these tools to their full potential, we can also use them to help resolve Parent problems.

TAKING OVER CHILD PROBLEMS

Imagine a problem being like a ball. When people show us a ball (a problem), they are not saying, "take this ball." They are really saying, "Look at this ball I have." When adults see a child's ball (problem), many take it away and say, "I know this ball! I had this ball once! What I did is . . ." This is taking the ball and running with it. We need to "keep the ball in their court." Notice the ball and find out how the child feels about having it. "Look at that ball! Is it heavy? I see some spikes there, does it hurt to hold it? What do you plan to do with that ball?" If we always take a child's ball (problem), the child will stop showing it to us. Instead, we want children to learn how to handle different kinds of balls (problems) on their own.

The difference between being responsible *for* others and being responsible *to* them:

Taking responsibility *for* others involves fixing, protecting, rescuing, controlling, and taking on their problems, feelings, and responsibilities.

Being responsible *to* others **involves listening, showing empathy, offering encouragement, and guiding others, side-by-side (not dragging them), through the problem-solving process.**

Parents are often confused about the difference between being responsible *for* others and being responsible *to* them.[1] When we take responsibility *for* our children's problems, we offer solutions, give answers, and worry about whether our children will "do the right thing." This approach suggests children are not capable of making good decisions for themselves. Many parents think adults have better ideas than children—and if we deny them opportunities to grow and develop problem-solving skills, these beliefs become self-fulfilling prophecies. If we, instead, support and guide people as they figure out solutions to their own problems, their creativity and independence blossom. This is being responsible *to* others.

When other people have a problem or are experiencing strong emotions, we can do one or more of the following:

1. *Let them figure out the solution on their own* by showing respect for their struggle and giving encouragement.

2. *Use the F-A-X Listening Toolset* to help them work through their emotions, but leave the final decision up to them.

3. *Use the Problem-Solving Toolset* to help them explore alternatives and plan a solution to the problem.

REFERENCES

1   *Listening for Heaven's Sake*, by Dr. Gary Sweeten, Dave Ping, and Anne Clippard, (Teleios Publications, 1993).

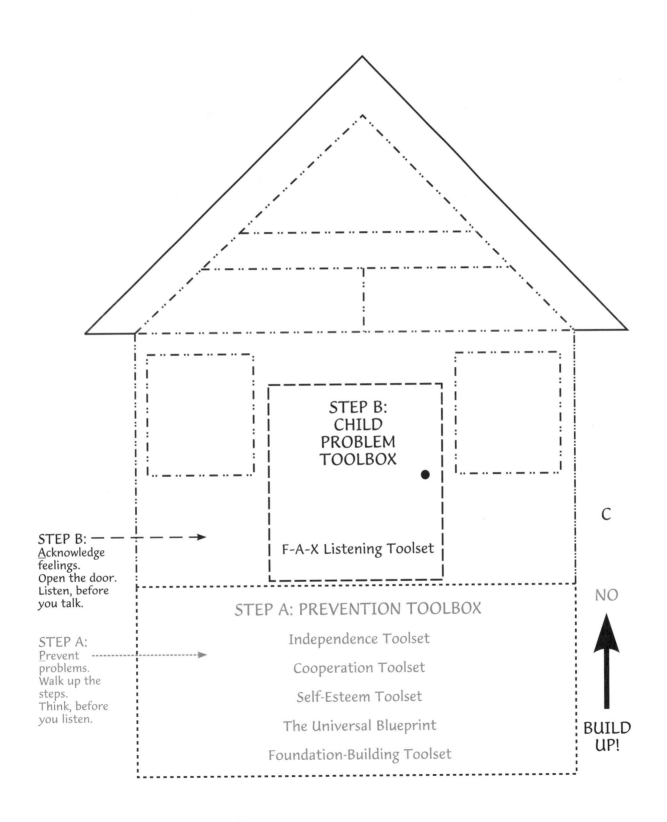

STEP B:
Acknowledge feelings.
Open the door.
Listen, before you talk.

STEP A:
Prevent problems.
Walk up the steps.
Think, before you listen.

STEP B:
CHILD
PROBLEM
TOOLBOX

F-A-X Listening Toolset

STEP A: PREVENTION TOOLBOX

Independence Toolset

Cooperation Toolset

Self-Esteem Toolset

The Universal Blueprint

Foundation-Building Toolset

C

NO

BUILD
UP!

CHAPTER
7 F-A-X LISTENING TOOLSET

*If the door to our house looks like a six-inch-thick steel bank vault, just its appearance will deter most people from coming in. Even those who might be welcome will get the message that **no one** is welcome. The ideal door is one that opens when we choose, but is sturdy enough to protect us when necessary. If we want to enter another person's house, we don't barge into their house. If we did, they'd feel unsafe and lock their doors. Instead, we knock on their door and let them know we are safe people to let in their house.*

*Similarly, if we feel threatened or have been hurt in the past, our emotional doors and walls are thicker and we are less likely to open them. If we want others to open their emotional doors to us, we don't barge in by probing or telling them what they are feeling or what to do. This would only cause them to get defensive and build thicker walls. We ask permission to come in and show them it is safe to share their feelings and thoughts with us. When they open their emotional doors to us, even by a crack, we treat them respectfully. We do this even when **we** need to discuss a problem, so we can continue communicating.*

IN THIS CHAPTER

This chapter explains the first step in F-A-X Listening, "Focus on feelings," and teaches us four important tasks:
- Encourage others to share their feelings without accidentally shutting down communication lines.
- Understand the different problem-solving styles.
- Identify the *real* issues or feelings others are facing.
- Help others work through troubling or confusing feelings without taking over.

WHEN TO USE THIS TOOLSET

Use the listening tools when others are experiencing feelings, positive or negative. If *we* have a problem, we acknowledge others' feelings or perspectives *before* we share ours. When children misbehave, these tools help us recognize and resolve the underlying feelings that are *causing* the behavior. In their book, *How to Talk So Kids Will Listen, And Listen So Kids Will Talk,* authors Adele Faber and Elaine Mazlish say, "There is a direct connection between how kids feel and how they behave. When kids feel right, they'll behave right. How do we help them feel right? By accepting their feelings." In *Siblings Without Rivalry* they add, "The very emotions we want to close the door on and lock out, need to be invited in, made welcome, and treated with respect."

PEELING ONIONS

Remember in Chapter 3, "The Universal Blueprint," we learned that problem behavior and negative feelings are like onions. Young children are like pearl onions, which are small onions with few layers. Sometimes they react to small events. When we listen to their feelings and connect it with what happened, young children experience great relief and usually move on to something else. Many parents who are used to their children going on and on with their emotions are surprised at how quickly their young children stop fussing once their feelings are noticed and parents show they understand.

Teens and adults are like white salad onions. They have more layers because they experience more complex problems and emotions and have more complicated personalities. Unless they feel safe and trusting (which we promote with these skills) they will not allow others to see their inner layers. Remember, privacy is very important to teens.

Troubled teens and adults are like Bermuda onions, which are the largest onions with many thick layers. These layers are from years of hurt feelings, bad experiences, and unhelpful communication habits. These layers are *not* all from the parent/child relationship. *Any* experience can add a layer to their defensive walls. Just as peeling onions causes us to cry, troubled teens and adults are more hesitant to relive their hurt feelings because of the pain stored inside. When parents of troubled teens use these listening skills, they don't always see immediate changes in their teens' behavior or a willingness to open up. Whenever we listen, however, layers *are* dissolving and doors are opening, even if it's not obvious. The thicker the onion, the longer it takes to peel. Likewise, people with many deep hurts and defensive layers take longer to work through their feelings.

When people are upset, their actions and words can be irrational. This is the surface of the onion. Denying feelings sends the message that we don't understand or can't handle their true feelings (the core of the onion). In return, people shut their emotional doors. Their feelings, however, don't go away! They either build a new or thicker wall to hide them or express them later through misbehavior. If we want our children to trust us enough to shed their outer layers and reveal their inner emotions, we need to build trust and show we understand their emotions (by listening).

If children express strong emotions or behave irrationally, we can recognize it as an onion and know we need to look deeper. Listening helps us find clues to the feelings that are at the heart of the problem. We want to acknowledge what children are feeling and thinking *at that point in time* and connect it to whatever we know about the situation they are dealing with. This lets children know we understand where they are *now*, so they can move on and resolve whatever's bothering them.

Often, when we realize something is bothering someone under the surface, we are tempted to drill down to the core. This is too intimidating and intrusive. People are sure to put up walls to protect their vulnerable hurt. They wouldn't be protecting themselves with layers if they felt safe enough to reveal their true thoughts and feelings. Instead, we need to help people make connections with where they are at that level and just beyond it. Once they feel understood or have insight to what caused the feeling, they release that layer, exposing the next.

> *A Graduate's Story. My 13-year-old son has not confided in me for over three years. I always get "Nothin'" and "I dunno" answers to my questions. When I started using the listening tools this week, my son came into my bedroom and started talking to me! He has **initiated** heart-to-heart talks almost every night! I had to bite my tongue a lot, because I didn't want to shut the door on our communication. The results I got were so immediate, it gave me the patience and motivation to keep trying.*

People often begin a story with a simple or straightforward comment, but something in their nonverbal cues shows there might be more to their comment. Listening helps them connect with those complex, deeper, or hidden thoughts and feelings. The F-A-X Listening Toolset helps people resolve superficial issues and also those that are deep within.

> *A Personal Story. My parents were true artists at the listening and problem-solving skills. Their attitudes helped me feel safe enough to talk to them about almost anything. Even when they weren't sure of the problem, their responses helped **me** figure out what was really going on. They asked me questions that got me thinking about how **I** could solve my problem. I'd usually say, "Thanks, Mom (or Dad)" and they'd reply, "All I did was listen, honey, **you** figured it out for yourself." And they were right! This boosted my self-confidence and self-esteem. As a teen and an adult, I have used the problem-solving skills to resolve my own problems and the listening skills to support others who were experiencing conflicts.*

FAX COMMUNICATION ☆☆☆☆

Human communication is like a fax machine. A fax machine takes a message and turns it into a code to send across telephone lines. The other fax machine receives these codes, decodes them, and creates an exact copy of the original message. When people express emotions, their thoughts and feelings are turned into verbal and nonverbal codes, which they send to others. When we hear these messages we decode the message so we can understand it. While fax machines have a precise formula for decoding messages, people don't. We take the coded message and filter it through our own code—our beliefs, thoughts, experiences, and

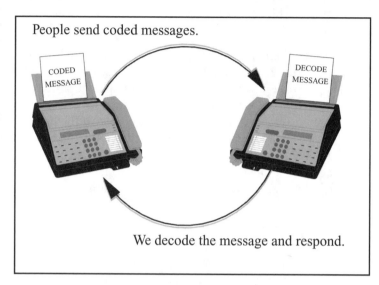

emotions. As a result, we often misunderstand someone's message. Usually, when we hear a message, we react to what someone *said*. Often, however, we have misunderstood what that person *means*. Before we respond, we must first check whether we correctly understood the message. There are ways we think, speak, and act that disconnect communication lines. The next few sections identify these barriers and how to avoid them.

PROBLEM-SOLVING STYLES

We block communication when we make assumptions about *why* people are sharing their problems with us. If we assume they are bringing the problem to us to solve *for* them, we respond differently than if we think they are simply sharing information with us. We must understand how different people solve problems if we are to respond helpfully to everyone.

When people experience a problem, they move through a three-step process to resolve it.
1. They must work through their feelings *first*,
2. Logically understand the problem,
3. *Then* plan possible solutions.

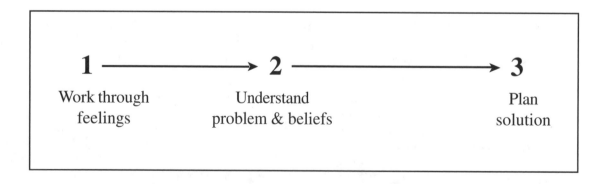

While this three-step process is universal, people differ in two ways:
- Whether they prefer to work out their problems *alone or with others*.
- The *pace* they move through the steps.

Internal Problem Solvers prefer to do their problem solving alone. To be most helpful to these people, we need to give them space and respect their privacy. Assume they can solve their problem unless they suggest, verbally or nonverbally, they are having difficulty. Offer empathy and let them know your "door is open" if they choose to talk. (Don't say "I'm willing to *talk*." Say, "I'm willing to *listen*.")

External Problem Solvers work out their problems with others. These people are relationship-oriented. They tend to be open about their feelings and we can see where they are at each step of the problem-solving process. Just because these people seek others when they have a problem does *not* mean they feel incapable of resolving their own problems. They need to *hear* their ideas, rather than just think them. They need people to show they understand and not take over their problem.

The other difference in problem-solving styles involves the pace people move through the three-step process and where they spend most of their energy. There are two styles: Conquerors and Venters. If we were to compare the problem-solving process to a road trip, Conquerors would take the quickest route possible. Venters would stop to experience each place before moving on to the next.

Conquerors want to get to the bottom of problems and solve them. They tend to be logical people, so they quickly move through the feeling phase of the problem-solving process (step 1). They may not experience emotions strongly or think feelings don't accomplish much. When they talk about problems, they usually comment on the facts (step 2) or possible solutions (step 3).

Venters are usually emotional people who need more time to work through their feelings (step 1) before they can think logically about the problem (step 2). Sometimes their emotions can seem irrational or illogical, but venting releases the emotional energy that is blocking their logic. Once they release this energy, they can think more clearly about solutions (step 3). When Venters talk about problems, they usually mention their feelings and are not necessarily seeking a solution.

Neither problem-solving style is right or wrong. Nor is one style emotionally healthier than the other. People often assume that Conquerors aren't in touch with their emotions. This may not always be the case. At the other extreme, there are Venters who become so consumed by emotions they can't get beyond them to reach a solution.

We usually have one dominant problem-solving style. However, our problem-solving style can change, depending on the type of problem we are facing. For example, we might be a Conqueror at work and a Venter at home or in personal relationships.

If we take these two sets of problem-solving styles, Internal (I) versus External (E) and Venters (V) versus Conquerors (C), we see there are four individual problem-solving styles.

PROBLEM-SOLVING STYLE COMBINATIONS		
	Internal	**External**
Venter	**I/Vs** want to be alone before they release their emotions. For example, they might go to their room, cry, and then write in a journal. When people give them advice, it is an intrusion into their private world.	**E/Vs** seek out others to discuss their feelings and possible solutions, but get frustrated by advice, unless they've had a chance to work through their feelings.
Conquerors	**I/Cs** think through solutions on their own. They usually don't talk much about their problems. If I/Cs have enough time to think, they might be open to advice. Otherwise, it violates their privacy.	**E/Cs** talk to others about the facts of the situation and the ideas they are considering. They might be open to advice, since they think logically and like to hear ideas.

Many communication problems are the result of different problem-solving styles. Knowing your problem-solving style and identifying other people's problem-solving styles can prevent these problems. When problem-solving styles clash, each person assumes the other person solves problems the way they do and responds accordingly. The mistakes usually involve timing or approach.

Timing conflicts are the most common clash in styles. They usually happen when Venters share feelings with Conquerors. Since Conquerors rush through feelings, they mistakenly assume Venters should do the same. They try to "fix" the Venter's problem as quickly as possible by offering solutions (step 3, the Conqueror's strength). Venters think it's probably unwise to accept someone's advice if that person doesn't fully understand the problem (step 1 or 2), so Venters wait for some sign of understanding *before* they move on. When Conquerors try to solve the problem too soon, Venters get frustrated and think the Conquerors still don't understand the problem, so they repeat themselves. Then, Conquerors get frustrated because the Venters are getting *more* upset, repeating themselves, and *still* haven't solved the problem.

Approach conflicts often occur when logical Conquerors ask fact-finding questions, which is frustrating for Venters. Venters can't think about details until they release their emotional energy. When Venters share irrational thoughts, like "I feel like ripping his head off," Conquerors may say, "Why do you let him get to you like that?" and "Why don't you just . . .?" The Venters think the Conquerors are denying their right to be upset and get defensive. Venters are rarely serious when they fantasize, but the fantasy helps them vent faster. When Conquerors think Venters are irrational and are rejecting their advice, they see no point in discussing the issue, because the Venter "won't listen to reason."

Conquerors must bite their tongues when they get the urge to offer solutions or try to change how someone feels. They need to develop more effective listening skills, so they can help Venters move through the problem-solving steps faster, which is the Conqueror's goal.

Venters can usually read other people's nonverbal cues and respond accordingly. Unfortunately, they often assume others can read such hints, so they aren't clear about what they want. When groups of Venters are together they reinforce each other's ineffective communication. For logical Conquerors, interpreting such hints is a foreign passive language. Venters need to be more clear about what they want. They need to explain, "When I come to you with a problem, let me blow off steam. Just try to understand my frustration and feelings. When I *ask* for help or ideas, *then* you can give me advice." Venters also need to learn how to "vent in a nutshell" and get to the point.

While reading this, you were probably thinking about style clashes you have in your adult relationships more than your parent/child relationships. Remember, these skills are useful in *all* human relationships!

> *A **Personal Story**. When my husband and I were first married, I was a Venter and he was a Conqueror. My long stories drove him nuts, so he taught me how to tell a story in a "nutshell." Feelings were a foreign language to him so I modeled listening and empathy skills when he had problems and suggested more helpful responses when I had problems. (We found marriage communication tapes and books[1] after we had figured this out the hard way!) After fifteen years, my husband is more in touch with his feelings, a better listener, and sometimes talks more than me! Because I do so much listening in my profession, I work through my feelings faster and have less need to vent on and on. We have balanced our differences and met in the middle!*

Many parents, even Venters, try to "conquer" children's problems. This is because most adults believe they are better at solving problems than children and parents should be responsible *for* solving their children's problems. When others have problems, remember it is *their* problem. Join them where they are, instead of trying to push or pull them down the path you think is best. Support them as they try to resolve their own issues and concerns. When people discover their own solutions, they are more likely to follow through on them and remember their lessons.

COMMUNICATION BARRIERS

Problem-solving style clashes are one reason communication can break down, but there are many others. Think about times when you have a problem or are upset. What helps you feel understood and safe to open up? What causes you to feel defensive and shut your "emotional door"? Most people say they want others to give them their full attention and show they understand how they feel. How do you feel when you get advice? Most people say, "It depends on *when* and *how* people give the advice. If I'm still upset, I get frustrated and defensive. If they tell me I *should* do something I feel like they are trying to control me, but not if they offer it as a suggestion." The same things that help us open our door are the same attitudes and responses that help children feel free to express their opinions and feelings to us.

> *A **Graduate's Story**. As a day care worker, I listen to kids all day long. But when I come home, I throw all my skills out the window! (She is in her "professional" role at work and has parent/child trigger buttons with her own children.) After I read the Universal Blueprint chapter, I realized I wasn't listening to my teenager. I promised to try harder. Since we hadn't gotten to the Child Problem Toolbox yet, I just listened quietly. She really opened up! Then she started telling me things I didn't really want to hear. I started getting upset and telling her what to do. She shut down immediately.*
>
> *I was mad at myself. I realized that if I invited her to open up, I had to be ready to handle whatever facts and feelings came up. The next time, I bit my tongue and didn't jump in. I'm anxious, now, to learn what I can say when I have concerns, without taking over or getting upset. (We cover this in the Clear Communication Toolset, since our concerns are Parent problems.)*

This mother saw how her attitude and responses caused her daughter to open or close her "emotional door." Many parents, of teens especially, want their children to confide in them and don't understand why they don't. In my "Teens and Parents—Together" class, I ask teens to list the reasons they don't open up to their parents. Here is one list, exactly as they wrote it:

1. Afraid will use against us.
2. I don't have much in common.
3. Don't want them to get mad at me for what I feel or did.
4. If we open up, they will interrupt us and preach.
5. Keep bringing up the past.
6. They try to make us learn from their mistakes, instead of letting us learn from our own mistakes.

If we want our children to confide in us, there are certain attitudes and responses we want to avoid and others we need to adopt.

Door Slamming Attitudes

Distractions. When people are talking, we don't always give our full attention. Our minds wander and we think about what *we* want to say or how we feel about their problem. Sometimes our body language says we aren't paying attention. When we play with objects, look out the window, yawn, or look at our watch, we send the message that we'd rather be somewhere else.

> *To give your full attention, STOP, LOOK, AND LISTEN—*
> **STOP what you are doing,**
> **LOOK in their eyes (the "windows to the soul"),**
> **and *really* LISTEN.**

Bend or sit at their eye level. Offer a gentle touch (if they are comfortable with this). Lean forward; about one arm's length is ideal. Be relaxed but attentive. Our body language and facial expressions can show warmth and interest, even if we say nothing. We can also use statements such as "Oh?" "Um-hmm," or "Wow!" to show we are listening.

If direct eye contact seems to intimidate or pressure someone, we can wait until we are doing something together, side by side, and are mostly focusing on the activity. These low-pressure, nonchalant conversations are particularly effective for getting teens to open up.

> *A Personal Story. My mom and I often had discussions while fixing dinner. Although she wasn't always looking right at me, her verbal responses made it clear that she was paying attention and was trying to understand what I was saying or feeling.*

Impatience. Listening takes time and effort. We often become impatient, hoping others will "get to the point." Sometimes we assume we know what they are going to say and interrupt. If we think we already have the answer, we want them to be quiet so we can tell them what to do. Such hurried attitudes are arrogant and disrespectful. They also cause us to take over problems, which deprives children of opportunities to learn problem-solving skills.

It can be difficult to listen to lengthy, detailed stories that are not problems. It's important, however, to listen to these "trivial" things. They are the small tests children give us to see whether they can trust us to handle the bigger problems and more difficult feelings that might arise later. When people go on and on, summarize and clarify what they are saying, "Let me get this straight. First . . . then . . ."

If you are genuinely too busy or distracted to listen, say so, "I can see you're (feeling) and want to tell me more. I'd really like to listen to everything you want to say, but right now I'm (what you're doing). At (give a time) I can sit and hear all about it." Give a specific time and *follow through*. Don't wait for *them* to bring the subject to you again.

Imposing our world on their world. Sometimes, when others express emotions, it triggers unpleasant memories from *our* past. If we don't face and work through these unresolved issues, we get overwhelmed by other people's problems or have difficulty separating our feelings from theirs. If we assume that people are trying to get us to *agree* with their perceptions, we might explain and defend ourselves. This shifts the focus to *us*. There are also times when we simply can't relate to their world. We mistakenly assume that our children (and others) will feel and behave the way we do. We minimize what is important to them or overreact to simple problems. Either extreme causes us to lose our perspective and focus, which needs to be on the person with the problem.

When listening to others, allow them to have different feelings, thoughts, and opinions. If we think about it, every person comes from a slightly different, unique world. People's individual personalities, experiences, beliefs, and interpretations influence their viewpoint. We may not *agree* with people's feelings or perceptions, but we can show we *understand* them.

To really listen, we must consciously work on these unhelpful attitudes. Effective listening involves putting everything else out of our minds to concentrate on what others are saying. We need to put our own feelings and thoughts on hold and put ourselves in the other person's shoes, seeing the situation from their viewpoint. Don't belittle what is important to others. *Their* perceptions are what counts. If we talk, we want to talk about *their* perspective. We need to discipline ourselves to slow down and listen to people *at their pace.*

Door Slamming Responses

People often respond unhelpfully to someone's feelings when they think the person is overreacting or the negative feelings are directed at them. Other times, we are trying to help, but accidentally take over or say something that shuts down communication. Unhelpful comments usually ignore people's feelings or overlook their real meaning. There are several types of responses to avoid, to help others feel safe to open up or express feelings.

Advising or giving solutions. *"You need to . . ." "If I were you, . . ."* When people share problems or express feelings, they are not asking us to take over or give *advice.* When we give advice, it implies others can't solve their own problems. Advice also causes parents to take responsibility for solving children's problems. And if our advice fails, guess who they blame?

Sometimes advice sounds like an order. *"You must . . ." "You have to. . ." "You will . . ."* No one likes to be ordered around. It makes them feel as if they know nothing. Orders can also start power struggles. By doing the opposite, children prove parents can't control them.

Analyzing. *"What's really going on here is . . ." "You must be tired . . ." "You're feeling that way because . . ."* Analyzing focuses on facts, which is frustrating for people who are expressing feelings. They don't want their feelings analyzed. Nor do they want predictions such as *"You'll probably . . . Then they'll . . . You could end up . . ."* These responses sound like we know it all.

Blaming and judging. *"What did you do to make them . . .?" "What did you expect?" "This wouldn't have happened if . . ."* These criticisms treat others as though they are stupid and have poor judgment. People shut their doors to avoid further criticism. When we judge children's feelings and ideas as right, wrong, good, or bad, they conclude their feelings are wrong and they shouldn't trust them. They might even memorize our opinions and not share anything that goes against them. If people trust us enough to share their thoughts and feelings with us, it's important to treat them with respect.

Denying feelings. *"You don't feel that way!" "Don't worry, be happy!"* These responses try to change negative feelings to positive feelings. When we tell people not to feel what they are feeling, they may conclude their feelings are wrong and unimportant—and so are they.

Parents especially want to stop negative feelings when children criticize siblings or parents. Our natural impulse is to defend the person and tell children they must always love their family members. We don't have to agree *or* defend anyone. We can simply acknowledge that right now this is how the person feels. If we start where they are and let them vent their feelings, they will usually to move on to solutions. Later, we can discuss other ways of viewing the situation and responding.

When children react negatively to our requests, we often assume they are *refusing* to cooperate. Usually, children are *willing* to cooperate, they just aren't *happy* about it and want us to know. If we deny children's feelings, they often become more dramatic, to get their feelings across. We can acknowledge how children feel, without agreeing or disagreeing—or changing our mind. Once we show we understand children's feelings, they are more likely to move on.

Diverting and distracting. *"Don't think about it." "Oh, come on, you look so pretty when you smile." "You think that's bad! Did you hear . . ."* These statements try to distract people from their feelings by changing the subject. They encourage people to avoid problems and feelings, rather than deal with them. They imply that the person's problems are unimportant. Not thinking about a problem, however, does *not* make the problem disappear.

Quick fixes. *"I'll do . . . and then I'll . . . That will make it better." "All you have to do is . . ." "Just hang in there!"* Quick fixes rescue people from their problems by offering simplified solutions. Clichés also fall in this category. Superficial solutions help *us* avoid spending the time and energy it takes to really listen. They also insult others, implying their problems aren't really important or they aren't capable of solving them..

Journalistic questioning. *"Why did you do that?" "Who did it?" "Where . . ."* If we want to know all the details about a problem, we are probably trying to figure out the solution. Such questions leave people feeling like they are getting the "third degree." Fact-finding questions avoid feelings—and until people deal with their feelings, they can't focus on solutions.

People feel especially defensive when we ask "Why" questions. They think we are asking them to justify their feelings. Sometimes, we get non-answers, such as, "I don't know" or "Nothing." These answers are usually true! Often, people *don't* know why they are feeling a certain way or even what they are feeling. They may not have a large feeling vocabulary. Amazingly, when we focus on feelings, people know we want to understand the problem, so they usually volunteer the facts!

> *A Self-Reminder.* **I need to know the facts only if I am going to solve the problem. If this is not my problem, I do not need to know the facts, unless they help me better understand this person's feelings or perspective.**

Labeling or name-calling. *"Quit being a cry-baby." "Oh yeah, Mr. Smarty-pants?" "You're acting like a spoiled brat."* These responses are most common when children have negative feelings about us or they are misbehaving (which is an expression of their emotions). No one likes to be called names and the names can create labels that stick. Name-calling hurts people and brings on revengeful behavior.

Telling stories or lecturing. *"When I was your age . . ." "The last time I . . ." "I remember when . . ."* Stories and lectures shift the focus from the speaker's experience to the listener. Stories are helpful *only* if they convey empathy, "I think I may understand how you feel because I've experienced something similar." It is most helpful *after* people have vented their feelings and if the story is brief. The story should show compassion, not impose our ideas on others. Any ideas we share are simply for others to think about and we want to quickly refocus on the person with the problem.

Logical debates. *"That's not how it happened." "Yes, but . . ."* Debating is never helpful. People feel inferior, inadequate, and defensive. Debates cause arguments because people think the listener is trying to change their feelings, opinions, or values. People feel misunderstood and shut down. Allow others to have different interpretations or opinions about the same situation or facts.

Minimizing. *"You'll get over it." "Be tough!" "It's not worth getting upset over." "It's no big deal."* Sometimes, listeners try to avoid dealing with problems by being overly optimistic and pressuring people to change their feelings. If something *is* important to others and we minimize it, they can become very angry, "That's easy for *you* to say!" Thinking we didn't understand, the person either gives up or gets more upset, trying to show us that it *is* important.

Moralizing and preaching. *"You should . . ."* *"It's your responsibility . . ."* *"You know better."* The word "should" carries a heavy load of guilt and obligation. People have to feel or handle the problem a certain way or they're wrong. When we give moral sermons, we are talking down to others, which creates resentment. It also implies that people can't figure out the problem or trust their own values and morals. Sometimes we're right, they probably *should* do something. But until people work through their feelings and catch up to us, they won't see the answer for themselves.

Warnings and threats. *"If you don't . . . you'll . . ."* *"You'd better . . . or . . ."* When we want people to see the negative possibilities of an idea, we sometimes word it like a threat. The power and authority in our tone of voice causes people to feel defensive. Sometimes, when we tell children to stop feeling what they're feeling, they persist—then we threaten to punish them for their insistence. For example, "If you don't stop crying, I'll give you something to cry about." Now the child is upset *and* scared and might cry even harder. These power plays produce fear, submissiveness, resentment, rebellion, and challenge children to test the threatened consequences.

If you've identified unhelpful comments you've made when your children are upset, don't beat yourself with guilt. Remember, we always do the best we can with the information and emotional resources we have at the time. The rest of this chapter explains how to respond helpfully.

F-A-X LISTENING ☆☆☆☆

Communication is a surprisingly complex process—it isn't easy. Hearing a message is different from understanding it. People don't always say what they mean. Their body language can contradict their words. Our brains work so fast, that we can easily misinterpret a message. We need to slow down our thinking, which takes energy and focus.

Effective listening is really a simple process. (Not easy, but simple.) Each step of the F-A-X Listening process matches the three problem-solving steps we just learned. We learn step 1 in this chapter and steps 2 and 3 in the Problem-Solving Toolset. (The Summary Sheet at the end of the Problem-Solving Toolset summarizes *all* the steps of the Child Problem Toolbox.)

- *Focus on feelings.* (Step B1) The first step of F-A-X Listening is, quite simply, how to check whether you decoded a person's message correctly. The secret to decoding messages is to know how to listen to what others *mean,* rather than just hearing words. This process is more of an art and an action skill than an exact science or passive process. We listen with our eyes, ears, brain, and heart (intuition). By using warmth, empathy, respect, and effective listening tools, we encourage people to share their thoughts and feelings and show we understand. People connect with deeper feelings that they might not be aware of yet. This step brings great relief from overwhelming feelings, which may be all someone needs.

- *Ask helpful questions.* (Step B2) We can use helpful questions to better understand people's feelings. They still might be upset, though, because they are confused or have inaccurate beliefs about the situation. We can *also* use helpful questions to help them realize, on their own, that there is another way to view the situation. This brings new insights, greater self-understanding, and a readiness to resolve the problem.

- *X-amine options.* (Step B3) If people need to plan a response or choose a solution, "Ask helpful questions" (Step B2) *and* "X-amine options" (Step B3) to guide them as they set goals and choose the best solution to meet those goals.

LISTEN

When I ask you to listen to me
        and you start giving advice
        you have not done what I asked.

When I ask you to listen to me
        and you begin to tell me why I shouldn't feel that way
        you are trampling on my *feelings*.

When I ask you to listen to me
        and you feel you have to do something to solve my problem
        you have failed me, strange as that may seem.

Listen! All I asked, was that you listen,
        not talk or do, just hear me.
Advice is cheap: 35 cents will get you both Dear Abby
        and Billy Graham in the same newspaper.
And I can do for myself; I'm not helpless.
        Maybe discouraged and faltering, but not helpless.

When you do something for me *that I can and need to do
        for myself,* you contribute to my fear and weakness.

But, when you accept as a simple fact that I do feel what I feel, no matter how irrational,
        then I can quit trying to convince you
        and can get about the business of understanding
        what's behind this irrational feeling.
        And when that's clear, the answers are obvious,
        and I don't need advice.
Irrational feelings make sense when we understand what's
        behind them.

Perhaps that's why prayer works, sometimes, for some people
        because God doesn't give advice or try to fix things.
        He just listens and lets you work it out for yourself.

So please listen and just hear me. And, if you want to
        talk, wait a minute for your turn; and I'll listen to you.

Author Unknown

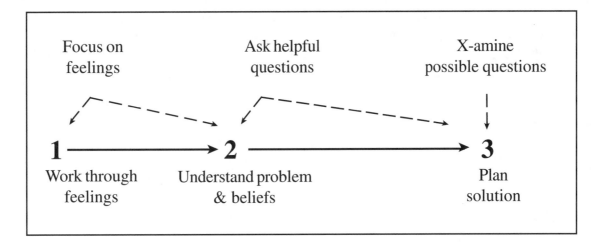

Step B1: Focus on Feelings ☆☆☆☆

> **When people are sharing their feelings, use the following three-step process to respond helpfully:**
>
> **Step B1: Focus on Feelings**
>
> a. *Identify the feeling.* In our minds, we look for clues to what people are feeling.
>
> b. *Identify the thought, belief or event.* In our minds, we look for clues about why people are having those feelings and how they are interpreting the event.
>
> c. *Summarize, in your own words, what you think they mean.* We take the clues and use them in our spoken response, to check whether we understood them correctly.

a. IDENTIFY THE FEELING

When children misbehave or express emotions, we ask ourselves, "What are they feeling?" If we aren't sure, we can ask, "How would I feel if that happened to me?" Think of a word that describes the feeling.

- **Don't worry about making children *more* upset by calling attention to their feelings.** Children feel reassured to know their feelings have names—it means they are normal and it must be okay to feel them. When we use feeling words, children learn how to express themselves with words, rather than misbehavior.

- **It's okay to use big words.** If we use feeling words in context, children learn "This feeling is called ___." This is the same way they learn "this feeling in my stomach is called hunger." (My son's first feeling word, at age two, was "embarrassed"—and he was not very verbal.)

- **If we are unsure what others are feeling, it's okay to guess.** If we are wrong, they usually correct us—and by correcting us, they better understand what they are really feeling. "Well, I'm not really *scared*, just *careful*."

★ **If you identify more than one feeling, go with the feeling that is closest to the center of the onion.** "Secondary" emotions come *after* another feeling. For example, sadness is usually the result of something else—loneliness, inadequacy, anger, or depression. All these feelings can appear on the surface to be sadness. It is important to find out the *cause* behind someone's sadness, because it is the feeling that's closer to the core of the problem. This is the feeling we want to reflect back to them, since it helps them feel understood and work through whatever is causing them to feel sad.

> *A "secondary emotion"* **is an emotion that comes after another feeling. The first feeling, which is closer to the real issue, causes the second feeling they are expressing.**

There are two difficulties we often face when focusing on feelings (besides the temptation to use the communication barriers mentioned before):

i. Responding to Nonverbal Messages

When people aren't *saying* anything, we want to tune in to their behavior. Here are some examples of nonverbal clues and their possible meanings[2]:

NONVERBAL CLUE	POSSIBLE MEANING
sagging shoulders	discouraged, exhausted, despair
arms folded tightly across the chest	defensive, impatient, or rejected
clenched hands and jaw	angry or tense
quivering chin	struggling with intense emotion
fidgeting and foot tapping	nervous or anxious

Tone of voice is another clue to the real meaning behind people's words. Emphasizing different words can change the meaning of the same statement. Here is an example from *Listening for Heaven's Sake*[3]:

Actual words: "*I* didn't say your outfit looked silly."
Interpretation: "Someone else said it was silly."

Actual words: I didn't **say** your outfit looked silly.
Interpretation: I may have thought it was silly, but I didn't say so.

Actual words: I didn't say **your** outfit looked silly.
Interpretation: It wasn't you I was talking about.

Actual words: I didn't say your **outfit** looked silly.
Interpretation: It wasn't your outfit that looked silly, it was you.

Actual words: I didn't say your outfit looked **silly**.
Interpretation: I didn't say silly exactly, I said it looked unusual.

Sometimes people hide or deny their feelings as a defense mechanism. For example, "It doesn't hurt that bad" or "It doesn't really bother me." Don't assume they aren't really bothered. Instead, lightly acknowledge the underlying feeling in a matter-of-fact way and give them permission to feel that way. For example, "I know you're trying to be *tough*, but it's okay to admit it hurts."

ii. Tuning into Feelings

Many people have difficulty getting in touch with feelings. Feelings can seem like a foreign language if we have any of the following traits:

- Logical and analytical
- Raised in an over-controlling family where negative feelings weren't allowed (learned to stuff or ignore feelings)
- Taught not to express *any* strong emotion, positive (tears of happiness) or negative

Don't view these last two statements as blame or criticism of your parents. Remember, before the 1960s effective listening skills were not commonly known to parents or professionals. There was little information about the mind and emotions. If the information was not available to our parents, they could not have taught it to us. They, too, did the best they could with the resources they had.

If you struggle to find a name for feelings, the cartoon on the next page might be helpful.

b. IDENTIFY THE THOUGHT, BELIEF, OR EVENT

Usually, a person's statement includes one of the following clues:
- The event that caused the feeling.
- The person's beliefs or thoughts about the situation, which influence their perceptions and feelings.

If we are confused about *why* a person has these feelings, we can clarify facts without using journalistic questions. We do this by tying the facts to the feeling they caused. For example, "Let me get this straight. First this happened . . . then you felt . . . so you did . . ."

Be careful not to confuse thoughts and feelings. For example, "I feel the teacher shouldn't give us so much homework." The *belief* is that the teacher is giving too much homework. The *feeling* might be "overwhelmed" or "frustrated." We learn in Chapter 9, "Keep Your Cool Toolset," that our feelings are a direct result of our beliefs about an event. If our beliefs are inaccurate or unhelpful, we experience misguided or unhelpful feelings. As we listen to others, their statements often reveal these inaccurate or unhelpful beliefs. For example, a child might say, "My coach doesn't like me because she told me I could do better." The child is *assuming* the coach said this because she didn't like her, which might not be accurate.

Try to balance thoughts and feelings. If we overemphasize thoughts, we tend to forget about people's feelings and start analyzing or judging. If we focus only on feelings, however, we might feed into inaccurate beliefs. We need to maintain our objectivity while remaining in touch with the other person's feelings and perspective.

c. SUMMARIZE WHAT YOU THINK THEY MEAN

First, we listen intently, identifying (in our minds) the speakers' feelings and thoughts. Then we check whether we understood them accurately by restating *in our own words* what we think they mean.

So we don't come across like a know-it-all, we can end our statement with a questioning tone of voice. Even if we're sure we are correct, we are usually better received if we sound like we are "checking this out," rather than *telling* them what they are feeling.

Here are some possible responses:

- "You sound like you're feeling . . ."
- "So you believe/think/feel . . .?"
- "Correct me if I'm wrong, but . . ."
- "Let me get this straight. You think/feel . . ."

- "Are you saying . . .?"
- "From your point of view . . ."
- "I wonder if you're thinking/feeling . . ."
- "Do you wish . . .?"

Important Points to Remember
- **If you identify inaccurate beliefs, do not *tell* people their viewpoint is wrong.** In the example about the coach, it is accurate, but unhelpful, to say,"You're overreacting. Your coach likes

you. She probably just wants you to try harder." Many children would think or say, "No she doesn't! I was already trying as hard as I could!" Now the child thinks we are siding with the coach and gets more upset because we don't understand. Instead, we can *repeat the belief in a slightly different way* so the child hears what was really said. We might say in a questioning tone of voice, "So she wants you to do your best because she doesn't like you?" When people hear their beliefs restated, accurately but differently, they see *on their own* that they might be misinterpreting the situation.

If they are too upset to see this, don't pursue the belief any further until they work through their feelings. Examining beliefs is a logical process. When they move to the next step, "understanding the problem or beliefs" (B2), we can ask helpful questions to explore this area again.

- **Use the word "I" cautiously; use "you" whenever possible.** If this is a Child problem, we want to keep the ball in the child's court. When we say "I," we are talking about us, not them. "I" often leads to personal opinions or advice, so it is usually a barrier. Likewise, be careful using the word "we," especially when talking about the other person's responsibilities, such as school, work, or chores. "We" implies that the task is partly our responsibility. This might result in people accepting less than total responsibility for the solution or fostering dependency on others to solve their problems.

- **Don't repeat names people call themselves or others.** If children say they're stupid or ugly, don't use the names in your response. You don't want to give the negative more power or seem as if you are agreeing with them. Instead, get in touch with what happened and how they feel about it. For example, "I bet it was really *frustrating* to have to spend a whole hour on your homework, when you thought it would only take 20 minutes" or "Do you feel *self-conscious* in your bathing suit?"

- **Match your tone of voice with their emotional intensity.** Don't overreact to what people say, "I bet you *hated* the teacher calling on you." The child might have felt just slightly embarrassed. On the other hand, if someone is furious, don't calmly say, "You're angry." Instead, say with emphasis, "You're *furious*!" We don't have to *act* furious, just emphasize the word so people know we understand how strongly they feel the emotion. If they are out of control, we can use our words and tone of voice to show we understand, but control our own emotions. This helps people regain control, without dismissing their feelings.

- **Our words, tone of voice, and body language** *combined* **communicate whether we understood someone.**

  A Personal Story. When I was selecting my son's preschool, I visited a school that taught S.T.E.P.[4] classes to their teachers and parents. Since I knew the skills and philosophy would be consistent with mine, I was optimistic. I observed a young child who was sitting at a table crying. Her teacher walked up to her, remained standing, put her hands on her hips, and said in a deadpan voice, "You're sad because you can't play with the blocks right now." While her words were constructed according to all the rules, her body language said she didn't really care how the child felt. She looked irritated to have to deal with the child's feelings. Had she knelt down next to the girl, put an arm around her, and sounded more empathetic, she would have been much more effective.

Universal Formula for Effective Listening

When we combine the three steps for focusing on feelings, we get a simple formula for responding to people's problems.

"<u>You sound like (or similar opening)</u> you're feeling <u>(feeling)</u>, because <u>(event, thought, or belief)</u>."

As you become more comfortable responding to feelings, you will develop your own personal style. Just remember to include the three a-b-c steps: (a) identify the feeling, (b) identify the event, then (c) summarize what you *think* they mean in your own words. In the following statements, the feeling and event words are emphasized, so you can see how they fit together in various, more comfortable statements.

➤ That *math problem* is really *frustrating*!
       (event)   (feeling)

➤ It's *irritating* to *be bothered* when *you want time alone*, huh?
   (feeling)   (event)   (thought)

➤ I can tell you're really *excited* about *the pool opening* tomorrow!
               (feeling)   (event)

To respond to nonverbal clues, match a feeling word to the behavioral clue, like the following examples.

➤ When I *see you smile* like that, I can tell you're *having fun*!
     (behavior)   (feeling)

➤ I *see you wandering around*, like you *don't know what to do*. Are you *bored*?
      (behavior)   (event)   (feeling)

➤ You seem *quiet*. Is anything *bothering* you?
    (behavior)   (feeling)

Sometimes people have contradictory or confusing feelings. It can be helpful to let them know this is natural and normal.

➤ Sometimes you *like* playing with Tommy, but not *when he's bossy*.
    (feeling)   (event)

➤ In some ways you are *glad* you *weren't invited to her party*, because *you don't really like her*,
          (feeling)   (event)   (thought)

but you feel *left out* too."
   (feeling)

What Do I Say Next?

When we first start using these listening skills, we can usually think of a first-response, but don't know what to say next. Our first response opens the door and children usually start sharing more. Many parents panic at this point. We just continue reflecting the thoughts and feelings we hear.

Continue reflecting the thoughts and feelings you hear, until:

1. The person vents the emotions, feels better, stops sharing, and *moves on.*
2. The person expresses *confusion* about why the problem happened or talks about logical facts. At this point, move on to the next step, "B2: Ask Helpful Questions."

Here is an example of a listening conversation between a mom and her 13-year-old son.

A Graduate's Conversation.

Adam: Dad wouldn't let me talk in the car tonight.

Mom: You sound hurt that he told you not to talk.

Adam: Yeah, he said, "Mike, don't say anything," right in front of the girls, like it's all my fault.

Mom: Do you feel like Dad is blaming you for the squabbles in the car, the teasing?

Adam: Yeah, he thinks it's my fault, but they always start it. They're always saying something.

Mom: It's rotten to take the blame for stuff like that.

Adam: I just shut up. I didn't say anything.

Mom: So you didn't say anything at all?

Adam: No, I didn't say anything the whole way home.

Mom: What happened?

Adam: Dad just talked to them.

Mom: How did that go?

Adam: Okay. They just talked and I didn't say anything.

Mom: Were there any fights?

Adam: No.

Mom: Does that work okay for you?

Adam: I guess.

Here, Mom didn't want to defend Dad or the girls, or offer a solution. She felt it was more important to **F**ocus on her son's feelings and leave the "ball" in his court. She could have taken the next two steps, **A**sking helpful questions and **X**-amining possible options, which she might do if the same problem occurs again.

When <u>Not</u> to Use Listening Skills

- **Sometimes we can overdo reflecting statements.** You don't have to respond to every frown or comment—use discretion. You will learn to recognize when people want to talk and when they don't. You'll also learn when it's best to give a nod, a comment, or say nothing at all.

- **Don't try to force people to share their feelings.** A power contest could result if you push the matter. Let them know you are willing to listen and they are free to talk or not talk. Don't be discouraged if people don't open up to you quickly. This is a new experience which may be uncomfortable for them. If you've had unhealthy communication in the past, they might be hesitant to open up. Give them time and space, to rebuild trust.

- **Turn complaints into requests and ask people what they want.** For example, "You think the carrots look dirty when the skin's on. Would you like them peeled?"

- **If someone is trying to involve you in unhealthy or inappropriate interactions**, such as gossip, simply nod your head or give a dull "um," then refuse to discuss the topic further. Change the subject or stop making eye contact.

TIPS FOR TOTS AND TEENS

Communication is a skill that can take young children some time to develop. Older children who can speak quite well, sometimes express their feelings and opinions quite bluntly, which can trigger parents' reactions and shut down communication. The following tips will help you adjust the skills we just learned when listening to younger children or teens.

Young Children

- **As children mature, their ability to express emotions appropriately can be inconsistent.** One day children may manage a situation or emotion well and the next day fall apart over the same incident. This is normal. If adults have difficulty at times handling their emotions, just imagine what young children, with their limited experience and vocabulary, face when coping with their feelings. Remember that "three steps forward, one step back" is still progress.

- **Young children don't usually verbalize feelings well, they act them out instead.** Learn to watch their body language. Their facial expressions and body language will offer clues to what they are feeling and trying to say.

- **Respect the importance of security objects.** One way young children cope with emotions is to depend on objects. Sucking a thumb or hugging a blanket is not a sign of weakness. It is usually a temporary means of managing their emotions. Respect children's needs as you teach them to use feeling words. Be there to offer hugs and an empathetic ear, so they learn how to get human reassurance instead of always looking to objects for security. As children improve their emotional vocabulary, they will use words more often to express their feelings.

  > *A Graduate's Story.* I took Adam, my three-year-old son to the dentist, who told me he was developing an over-bite. The dentist suggested Adam give up his pacifier (which he calls a "sucky.") I asked the dentist to tell my son, so he would hear it from someone other than me. He told Adam, "You might want to start thinking about not taking it anymore because . . ." and explained why. On the way home, Adam held the pacifier, saying, "I really like my sucky." I said, "Yeah, it's really nice to have that sucky. What did the dentist say would happen if you sucked it?" I was careful to let Adam own the problem. My past efforts at weaning him told me I could easily get into a power struggle if I tried to take over the decision. I just kept acknowledging his feelings and the difficulty, "It must be hard not to use something you really like to use." Adam never used his pacifier again. For several days, though, he still held the pacifier for security. I know that if I hadn't learned how to reflect feelings and keep the ball in my child's court, I would have started lecturing him and forcing him to give up his pacifier. While I might have made Adam give up a bad habit, it would have been in an unhealthy way. Instead, Adam weaned himself, which showed him the inner strength he possessed.

- **Use listening skills with even the youngest infants.** Infants are born with the ability to communicate; at first, they use crying and nonverbal cues. The understand *our* words before they can speak clearly. The especially understand the meanings of our tone of voice and facial expressions. Responding to infants' nonverbal language and acknowledging their feelings builds trust, promotes bonding, and increases intellectual, emotional, and language development. If we practice listening to infants, we feel more comfortable with the skills when they begin to use words.

- **Listening skills also increase young children's vocabulary.** While our children are learning words like "ball" and "cup," they can also learn words for their feelings. When we play with young children, we can give their dolls, stuffed animals, or puppets feelings that children or others might have. As they develop their feeling-word vocabulary, they are more able to talk about their own feelings.

- **Don't expect young children to understand another person's perspective.** Statements such as, "How would you like it if someone took your toy?" are probably meaningless. Young children are "egocentric," which means they are the center of their world. They are learning about the world from *their* perspective at this age. As they mature, they will naturally become more aware of others' feelings and needs. (In Chapter 10, "Clear Communication Toolset," there are specific tools for helping others understand your feelings or viewpoint.)

Teens

- **It is important for teens to separate from their parents and have individual opinions.** Such independent thinking is a strength that will help them as adults. If we try to make teens do what *we* think is best, we end up preaching and they become argumentative. Instead, we need to talk *with* our teens, not *at* them. We need to let our teens know we are on their side. We can support their individuality (thoughts, feelings, beliefs) and listen with respect to their ideas. If they seem to go astray, we can use the other F-A-X Listening steps (B2: Ask helpful questions and B3: X-amine possible options) to guide them to their own revelations and solutions.

- **Ask teens if they *want* to discuss their experiences with you, but don't be offended if they don't.** Teens usually handle crises within their peer group, so it is important for teens to have assertive, respectful communication and conflict-negotiation skills they can use. If we stay on the fringes of their activities, we are not invading their privacy but are available for discussions that build trust and open communication.

- **Teens can think logically *and* abstractly.** They seem to understand human behavior better than many adults. They are usually also searching for spiritual truths during these years. Discuss logical, psychological, and spiritual topics in impersonal ways, as a general conversation to understand each other's opinions better. These are opportunities to contribute "pearls of wisdom" and learn more about your teen's values and perceptions. These conversations build trust and give you insight to their inner world.

- **Teens do not want instant understanding and pat answers to their problems.** When they experience a conflict, they feel unique, as though they are the only ones who have experienced this exact problem before. While many teens experience common problems, each person lives in an individual world and their experience, to some extent, *is* unique to them. Comments such as, "I know just how you feel" or "I went through the same thing when I was your age" can sometimes be reassuring, but more often they frustrate teens. It makes their problems and their feelings seem so simple, when the problems feel so complex and mysterious to them.

- **When teens are upset, don't belittle their distress.** Acknowledge how important and confusing it is to them. Help them view their mistakes and problems as opportunities to learn skills and develop strength of character. Let them know that there is *no* problem too big to handle. Tell them that no matter what, you will be there for them and support them.

FINAL POINTS

Trouble-Shooting Guide for Listening to Feelings

If your attempts to listen seem less than successful, ask yourself these questions:
- Did I use a feeling word in my response?
- Did I *tell* the child how to feel or did I guess how the child *might* be feeling?
- Did I simply repeat the child's words or did I summarize in my own words?
- Did I reveal anything that might be closer to the real issue than what the child presented?
- Did I offer a quick solution, brush off the feelings, or use any other communication barriers?

Dealing with feelings is an art, not a science. It is a process, not a procedure. Knowing the exact words to say is not as important as conveying warmth and empathy. It is normal to feel uncomfortable with this new way of speaking and listening. After a while, we sense what is helpful to an individual (child, partner, co-worker, etc.) and what isn't. We discover what frustrates them and what calms them. Soon, we find ourselves using the tools without thinking.

When we accidentally shut the door on someone's feelings, we can always go back to repair the damage. Just say, "I've been thinking about what you said about . . ." Don't give up on the tools if they don't seem to work right away. Give yourself and others time to adjust to these new ways of communicating. Focus on the quality of your long-term relationship, not the immediate response to a single situation. You are making a life-long investment in your relationship when you take the time to listen.

SUMMARY SHEET
F-A-X LISTENING TOOLSET

F-A-X COMMUNICATION ☆☆☆☆

Parent problems: Listen before you talk. Double-check the message.
Child problems:
    Avoid taking over their problem.
    Start where others are—don't push your views or solutions.

Problem-solving styles

- Internal problem-solvers need space and time.
- External problem-solvers need to bounce ideas off others.
- Conquerors rush through feelings and focus on facts and solutions.
- Venters need to express feelings before thinking rationally about solutions.

Avoid communication barriers

Unhelpful Attitudes:

- Distraction
- Impatience
- Judging feelings
- Imposing our world on theirs

Unhelpful Responses:

- Advising or giving solutions
- Analyzing
- Blaming and judging
- Denying feelings
- Diverting and distracting
- Quick fixes
- Journalistic questioning

- Labeling or name-calling
- Telling stories or lecturing
- Logical debates
- Minimizing
- Moralizing and preaching
- Warning and threatening

F-A-X LISTENING ☆☆☆☆

Focus on feelings ☆☆☆☆

a. Identify the feeling
   Stop, Look, and Listen.
   Avoid reacting to surface emotions and behaviors.
   Look for clues to feelings underneath (including nonverbal signals).
   Choose a feeling word.

b. Identify the thought or the event causing the feeling.

c. Summarize in your own words what you think they mean. ☆☆☆☆
   Give wishes in fantasy.

Keep reflecting until people move on, express confusion, or are ready to discuss possible solutions.

PRACTICE EXERCISES

Read each child's statement. Acknowledge the child's feelings by following the three steps we learned for planning a helpful response:

Step B1: Focus on feelings
a.   Identify the feeling.
b.   Identify the event, thought, or belief causing the feeling.
c.   Respond by summarizing, in your own words, what you *think* the child *means*, to show you were listening and understand.

(Plan *your* response before reading the answer key, which offers *one possible* response and extra pointers to keep the lines of communication open.)

1.   "Emily is spending the summer at her grandmothers! She's my best friend!"
     (What is this child feeling? Why? Check this out with your response.)

2.   "I'm scared to go to bed. There's a monster under my bed that comes out in the dark!"
     (What is this child feeling? Why? Check this out with your response.)

3.   "I don't feel like cleaning the toilets! I'll do it after I play."
     (What is this child feeling? Why? Check this out with your response.)

4.   "I played soccer at recess. Brandon and Chris were the captains and I was the last one to get picked." *(What is this child feeling? Why? Check this out with your response.)*

5.   "I can't believe I missed that catch. We lost the game because of me."
     (What is this child feeling? Why? Check this out with your response.)

6.   "Why do I have to get my picture taken? I hate to smile with these braces on."
     (What is this child feeling? Why? Check this out with your response.)

7.   Your preteen daughter says, "I'm not sure if I'm going to Tom's party. John will be there."
     (What is this child feeling? Why? Check this out with your response.)

8.   "Finals are next week and I've got to work every single night!"
     (What is this child feeling? Why? Check this out with your response.)

Possible Answers

While you probably identified similar feelings, thoughts, beliefs, and events, the following answers might vary from your answers. There is no one right response. If your answer differs, look at the trouble-shooting guide.

Imagine how the conversation would go after our first response. At the end of the next chapter, we continue the conversation using the next two steps of F-A-X Listening, **A**sk helpful questions and **X**-amine possible options.

1.   "Emily is spending the summer at her grandmothers! She's my best friend!"
     Child's feelings, thoughts, beliefs: sad, because the friend will be gone a *long time* and the child will *miss* her.
     Listening response: "You're really going to *miss* her, aren't you? (pause) All summer sounds like a *long time*, doesn't it?"

     Avoid glossing over the problem with a quick fix, "She'll be back at the end of the summer. You'll see, time will fly." If the child nods her head after our first response, we can ask helpful questions. (We'll continue this conversation in the next chapter.)

2. "I don't want to go to bed. There's a monster under my bed that comes out in the dark!"
   Child's feelings, thoughts, beliefs: scared, because she *believes* there are monsters or that things are *different* in the *dark*.
   Listening response: "It must be scary to think there is a monster there."

Notice how this possible response acknowledges the child's fear and the possibility that things look different in the dark, but does not feed the inaccurate belief in monsters? Once we've acknowledged the child's feelings, we can ask helpful questions. (We'll discuss fears more in the next chapter and continue this conversation in the answer key there.)

3. "I don't feel like cleaning the toilets! I'll do it after I play."
   Child's feelings, thoughts, beliefs: torn between work and play.
   Listening response: "I know it's *hard to work* when you'd *rather be playing*."

This is a trick question, because this was really a Parent problem—until the child refused. Then it became a C/P problem. We need to back up and acknowledge their feelings *before* setting limits. Often, if we notice their feelings, they move on and do as we request. If not, we can use the Cooperation Toolset, "When you're done with the toilet, you can go out and play." If children persist, we can use helpful questions or problem solving to resolve the problem without a power struggle. (See the next chapter for specific ideas.)

4. "I played soccer at recess. Brandon and Chris were the captains and I was the last one to get picked."
   Child's feelings, thoughts, beliefs: left out or *rejected, disappointed,* or *discouraged,* because he was the *last child chosen* for the team.
   Listening response: "It *hurts* to be *rejected*." Or "It's *discouraging* to be the *last one picked*."

Children might assume that Brandon and Chris didn't pick them because they don't like them or aren't their friends anymore. If we bluntly point out false beliefs, we sound like we are criticizing or disagreeing that there is a reason to feel bad. If we listen effectively, children might share their reaction to being chosen last. Perhaps they decided to sit out the rest of recess. We can use helpful questions and problem solving to help children see that this is not their only option and plan a better response if it happens again. (See the next chapter for ideas.)

5. "I can't believe I missed that catch. We lost the game because of me."
   Child's feelings, thoughts, beliefs: disappointed, sad, and *blames self* for *missing* the catch.
   Listening response: "I can tell you're really *disappointed* you *missed that catch.* It's *hard to make a mistake* at such an important time."

When children are being hard on themselves, we often try to cheer them up with logical explanations, such as "You might have lost the game anyway," or "Lots of people miss catches." While these might be true statements, children think we don't understand how rotten they feel. Beyond the actual loss, children probably think they let down the team and that the other teammates are angry with them. Or maybe they are so embarrassed they can't face their teammates. Avoid smoothing over their concerns with, "I'm sure they still like you." Their concerns might be valid! Once they are thinking logically, you can start asking helpful questions. (See the next chapter for ways to help the child consider a different point of view.)

6. "Why do I have to get my picture taken? I hate to smile with these braces on."
   Child's feelings, thoughts, beliefs: self-conscious or unattractive *wearing braces* for the photograph.
   Listening response: "Are you feeling *self-conscious* about *wearing braces* in your pictures?"

Avoid the temptation to say, "But you look nice with braces." Even if this is true, children will rarely believe it. Start where they are, but don't agree they look "ugly." Also avoid smoothing over their feelings, "You'll see, your teeth will look nice when your braces come off." Again, this is probably true, but that's not how they feel *now*. Even if children's perceptions are inaccurate, acknowledge how they see things. Once children know we understand, we can use questions to help them consider different viewpoints and options for solving the problem. (See the next chapter to continue this conversation.)

7. Your preteen daughter says, "I'm not sure if I'm going to Tom's party. John will be there."
    Child's feelings, thoughts, beliefs: hesitant to see John, so *unsure* whether to go to Tom's party.
    Listening response: "You sound like you *aren't sure* you want to *see John.* Any particular reason?"

    Don't ask, *"Why* do you want to avoid John?" We would be assuming she wants to avoid him or that he's been mean. She could have a crush on him! If we jump to conclusions and we are wrong, she will conclude we aren't listening or get defensive. If we listen effectively, she will probably reveal the *real* reason she doesn't want to see John (he's mean to her, she has a crush on him, or another reason). Then we can ask helpful questions to help her explore options. (See the next chapter to continue this conversation.)

8. "Finals are next week and I've got to work every single night!"
    Child's feelings, thoughts, beliefs: pressured or *overwhelmed,* because finals and work schedule conflict.
    Listening response: "Wow, you're under a *lot of pressure* right now. You have *extra studying* you need to do, but they *need you at work,* too."

    If you have a teen who has a job *and* cares about studying—count your blessings and don't offer any advice! Make sure you give this teen credit for being a responsible worker, who doesn't want to let the employer down, *and* a responsible student who thinks about schedules in advance. Then move to the next step by asking a few helpful questions. (See the next chapter to continue this conversation.)

WHAT'S NEXT

If we practice these listening skills often, in *all* our relationships, others will start sharing more with us. We will feel more comfortable with the language of effective listening and see how our attitude and skills promote greater understanding in our relationships.

"**F**ocus on feelings" is just the first step of F-A-X Listening. In Chapter 8, "Problem-Solving Toolset," we learn what to do, beyond listening, to guide people through the problem-solving process. We learn the last two steps of F-A-X Listening: "**A**sk helpful questions" and "**X**-amine possible solutions."

REFERENCES

1   Two helpful resources for more information on male/female communication styles are *Hidden Keys to a Loving Relationship*, by Dr. Gary Smalley (a videotape series, 1993) and *Men Are From Mars, Women are From Venus,* by Dr. John Gray (HarperCollins, 1992).

2   *Listening for Heaven's Sake,* by Dr. Gary Sweeten, Dave Ping, and Anne Clippard (Teleios Publications, 1993) p. 89.

3   Ibid. p. 91.

4   *S.T.E.P. (Systematic Training for Effective Parenting),* by Donald Dinkmeyer and Gary McKay (American Guidance Service, 1982).

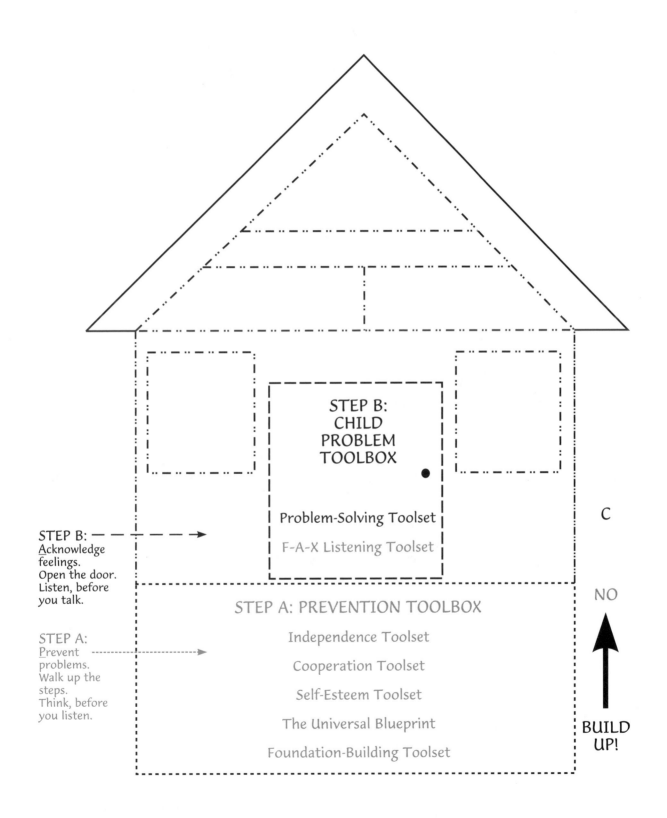

STEP B: — — — — — →
Acknowledge
feelings.
Open the door.
Listen, before
you talk.

STEP A: - - - - - - - - - →
Prevent
problems.
Walk up the
steps.
Think, before
you listen.

STEP B:
CHILD
PROBLEM
TOOLBOX

Problem-Solving Toolset

F-A-X Listening Toolset

STEP A: PREVENTION TOOLBOX

Independence Toolset

Cooperation Toolset

Self-Esteem Toolset

The Universal Blueprint

Foundation-Building Toolset

C

NO

BUILD
UP!

8 PROBLEM-SOLVING TOOLSET

We usually experience some problems with our house that are frustrating but need no repair. All we can do is vent our frustration, "I wish we had more room." Other times, there are problems we need to solve, "That darned sink is clogged up again!" If we simply do the first thing that comes to mind, we might grab a hammer and start banging out our frustration. A better approach is to look at the different options and decide which is the best plan to resolve the problem.

*Likewise, people are sometimes frustrated or aggravated about a problem and simply need to vent, "First this happened, then that . . ." There isn't anything they need to do about the problem, they just want to be heard and have their feelings understood. Other times, people need to **do** something about their problem. The first idea that comes to mind might be irrational or poorly thought out. It can be helpful to look at the possible options and decide the best plan for responding to the problem. In these cases, the Problem-Solving Toolset is most useful.*

IN THIS CHAPTER

When we use the Problem-Solving Toolset, we don't solve problems *for* our children. We help children look at different ways *they* can solve their own problems. The problem-solving process is a universal decision-making method we can apply to *any* type of problem. This process begins with the first step of the F-A-X Listening process that we learned in Chapter 7:

Step B1. *F*ocus on feelings.
Invite people to share their feelings about the problem. Listen carefully and let them know you heard and understood them. ***The most common mistake is to rush this step.*** We stop at this step when people simply need to vent.

The last two steps, **A**sk helpful questions and **X**-amine possible options, require logical thinking. In these steps, we help people correct mistaken beliefs, consider the possible solutions and make a final decision. This chapter teaches these last two steps. In it we consider several important points:

Step B2. *A*sk helpful questions.
• There is a difference between helpful and unhelpful questions.
• We can ask a series of questions that lead people to a conclusion or point that we want them to consider—*without* offering advice or shutting down communication.

Step B3. *X*-amine possible solutions.
• There is a basic problem-solving process we can use in *all* types of relationships and problems.
• We can apply this problem-solving process to all types of Child problems.

Flowing through the steps of F-A-X Listening.
• There are specific times when we stop at a step or move to the next step.
• We can shift gears between the listening steps and between the Child Problem Toolbox and other tools, depending on the child's needs or the situation.

WHEN TO USE THIS TOOLSET

We can ask helpful questions *if* we have first acknowledged feelings or if the questions clarify the other person's feelings, thoughts, or beliefs. Once people have worked through their feelings, we can also ask helpful questions to examine different perceptions of the problem or as a bridge to problem solving. *Only* move to problem solving when the person with the problem seems ready to think logically about solutions.

STEP B2: ASK HELPFUL QUESTIONS

Helpful questions are a bridge between listening and problem solving, because they help us accomplish each goal of the 1-2-3 problem-solving process we learned in the last chapter. Helpful questions can help the listener and talker (person with the problem) clarify feelings and meanings, reveal inaccurate beliefs, and examine options—*all* without taking over the problem.

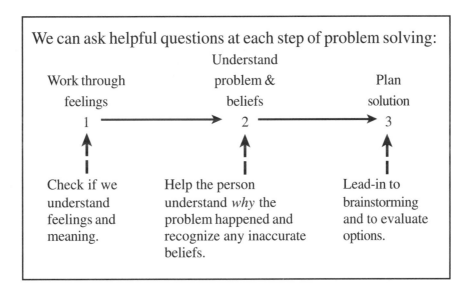

Asking questions at the <u>listening step</u> is the riskiest, because we may want to ask probing questions about facts. <u>Questions at this step should only relate to feelings.</u> Once people understand their feelings, they still might be confused, however, about *why* the problem happened. This shift to logical thinking is a sign to move to the next step. Here, we use questions to help people gain new insights by looking at the problem from different perspectives. Some questions are more helpful than others.

Unhelpful Questions

Unhelpful questions usually have yes or no answers or shut down communication. We especially want to avoid questions that involve any of the following communication barriers.

- Questions that analyze, criticize, or judge, because people feel defensive. "Why do you feel that way?" "I don't know!" "Why did you do that?" "Because I felt like it!"

- Asking too many questions, prying, or "giving the third degree," because we usually get non-answers. "So, how did it go last night?" "Okay." "Did you have a good time?" "Yeah." "Where did you go?" "Around." "What did you do?" "Nothing."

Many parents have had these exchanges with their children (especially teens). Children use vague responses to protect their privacy, to avoid criticism, or when they simply don't feel like talking.

Some parents think they aren't being good parents if they *don't* ask their children questions. If their children don't come home and immediately spill out a long detailed story, parents often feel impatient and could make one of the following inaccurate assumptions:

- "If I don't ask them, they'll never tell me what is going on in their lives." This is not true. Usually people talk more when they can volunteer information and aren't *forced* to talk.

- "If I don't ask questions, they'll think I don't care." If we listen, they'll know we care.

- "They must be hiding something." Wanting privacy is different than covering up something bad.

> *A Personal Story. My son is a very private person. When he started attending school, I was naturally curious about what he was doing. If I asked him what he did in school, he'd say "Nothing" and "I dunno." I tried simply saying, "Hi! It's great to have you home. Did you have a good day?" If he didn't volunteer information, I'd drop the issue. But he still wasn't sharing much. Finally, I discovered several options that worked well.*
>
> *I said, "I'm really curious about what you learn in school and how your teachers teach things. I know you don't always feel like talking right after school. I can understand that. Will you tell me more about school at bedtime?" He said "Yes" and sometimes did, but sometimes weeks would go by and he had not told me a thing.*
>
> *One day, I said, "There are times when I am so curious about your day that I have a hard time waiting until you feel like talking. Can we make a deal for those days? If I hold up three fingers will you tell me three things you did that day if I promise not to ask any more questions?" He agreed. The first time, he said, "I rode the bus, ate lunch, and had recess." When I asked what happened during those activities, he said, "The same thing that happens every day, nothing new." So I amended the agreement. Now three fingers meant "any three things besides lunch or recess and one specific thing about each." I kept my agreement not to use the three-finger signal very often and he told me more specific information. I still didn't get information every day, but it was a great improvement. By junior high, he readily shared specific information about school **and** his social life. He knew I wouldn't overreact or judge his friends. Occasionally, I had concerns, but I asked questions that didn't put him on the defensive and helped him consider my concerns, without giving him a lecture.*

Helpful Questions

Helpful questions invite more feelings or information. People can't simply answer yes or no. "What" and "how" questions develop thinking and judgment skills. "Why" questions are *only* appropriate *if* they are totally void of judgment and express a sincere desire to understand the child. Here are some examples of helpful questions:

- "You look (feeling). What happened?"
- "How did you feel?"
- "Could you give me an example of . . . ?"
- "What do you mean when you say . . . ?"

- "What do you think caused that to happen?"
- "What did you think at the time?"
- "What did you learn from that?"
- "Is there anything else bothering you?"

We must have a respectful tone of voice that says "I really want to know" or "I'm not angry" when we ask these questions. If our tone of voice is intimidating or disrespectful *at all*, it doesn't matter what words we use—people will close their emotional doors.

Give Information

While clarifying the problem and understanding *why* it happened, offering information or pearls of wisdom can be helpful, *if* we avoid lecturing or shifting the focus to us. When we give information, timing is everything. We want to wait until people have had a chance to share their feelings. If they seem confused or ask "Why?" we know they are open to the information. Our purpose in sharing information is not to play the one-upmanship game, "Well I went through something even worse than that!" Our purpose is to express empathy and understanding, "I've been there. This is what I did and what I learned from my decision (positive or negative)." ***Keep it brief*** and quickly shift the focus back to them, "Is that how you feel? What do *you* think you might do?"

We can also give information that explains other people's behavior. Use general words to describe people's behavior, rather than the person's name, which could sound like we are taking sides or judging the person. For example, instead of saying "(Sister's name) is too young to know how to share," explain, *"Two-year-olds* still don't know how to share. Your sister's learning, but it might take her awhile to share as well as you do." Remember to keep it brief—these are small pearls of wisdom, not giant rocks. Just plant the seed of an idea, don't try to grow the whole plant at once. Here are examples of common behaviors children might not understand and how to explain them.

▶ *Bullies:* "Sometimes people are mean because they don't know how to use words when they are angry." "Some people try to get what they want by being mean or feel important if other people are scared of them."

▶ *Cliqués:* "Some people need to be part of a group before they believe others like them." "Some groups make others feel left out so they can feel that their group is special and important."

Keep the Ball in the Other Person's Court

It is difficult to "keep the ball in the other person's court" when we have a concern, opinion, or idea we want to share. If we don't, it can easily turn into a lecture or sound like advice. It's also difficult, but important, to hold children accountable for their problems even when *they* aren't taking responsibility for them. The most skillful way to use helpful questions is to walk people through the logical thought process that leads them to our point, without actually telling them what to do. Our questions help them realize and choose, *on their own*, to do what we would have told them to do. Because they think of the idea on their own, they act on it. If we told them to do it, we could easily get into a power struggle.

> ***A Graduate's Story.*** *It was time for Robert, (age 11) to get ready for a softball game but he was still watching TV. In the past I'd remind him and try to motivate him, but he usually says I'm nagging, argues, and we get into a power struggle. I wanted to help him realize **on his own** what he needed to do.*
>
> *Mom: What time is it?*
> *Robert: I dunno. About five, I guess.*
> *Mom: What do you have going on tonight?*
> *Robert: Umm. Oh yeah, my softball game.*
> *Mom: What time is your game? (I already knew the answer.)*
> *Robert: Six o'clock.*
> *Mom: When do **you** plan to get ready?*
> *Robert: After this show.*
> *Mom: (I knew that wasn't enough time.) Will that give you enough time to eat?*
> *Robert: (He thought.) No, I guess not. I'll just skip dinner.*
> *Mom: (I wasn't crazy about that solution.) Will you have enough energy to last all seven innings?*

Robert: Probably not. I guess I'd better start getting ready now.
Relieved inside, I pleasantly said, "Good idea." I knew he could figure it out himself; he just needed a little guidance without pushing.

Here, the mother had to say more sentences than if she were reminding and nagging her son, but she knew that approach didn't work and was tired of him depending on *her* to remind him of *his* responsibilities. She wisely spent her time and energy using open-ended questions to lead her son through the logic that helped him realize her point. Because he decided *on his own,* it made more of an impression than her lectures, which he would have tuned out and resisted. It also gave him experience in remembering a commitment, which will help him in the future.

Build a Bridge to Problem Solving

There are times when both parties understand *what* happened and *why,* but the remaining issue is *how* the person can resolve the problem. When we reach this phase and are still trying to use reflective listening statements or clarifying questions, we often feel like we've reached a block. At this point, we want to ask one of the following questions that lead to problem solving:

▶   "Would you like to think of some ideas for dealing with that problem?"

▶   "So what do you think you can do about this?"

STEP B3: X-AMINE POSSIBLE SOLUTIONS

If people seem ready to discuss solutions or start offering ideas on their own, begin the five-step problem-solving process:

a.   Brainstorm ideas.
b.   Evaluate each idea.
c.   Choose a solution.
d.   Make a plan.
e.   Commit to a trial period.

In the Child Problem Toolbox, we learn one-on-one problem solving, when another person has a problem that doesn't directly affect us. Later, in the sibling section, we learn how to use this process to mediate conflicts between children, siblings or peers. In the Parent Problem Toolbox, we add a few steps to account for our part of the problem. In the Family Council Toolset, we use problem solving to resolve conflicts and make decisions that affect the entire family.

> **Problem-solving sessions include the people the problem affects and those people must all agree on a solution.**

Let's learn the general steps, then we'll apply them to several types of Child problems.

a. Brainstorm Ideas

Once we ask a bridging question to start problem solving, we allow others to suggest as many ideas as they can think of. Ask, "What else?" until they can't think of any more ideas. Remember these important points when brainstorming.

All ideas are okay. During brainstorming, don't evaluate or judge ideas. Allow *all* ideas, even if they sound bad, silly, or stupid. There are several important reasons to do this.

- Ideas get the creative juices flowing.
- People are rarely serious about acting on irrational ideas, but the fantasy is a final way to vent.
- If we criticize or judge people's suggestions, they are less likely to offer more suggestions. These other suggestions are usually the better ideas.
- A bad idea can contain the seed of a good idea. If we allow all ideas, we might see (at the next step) that there is some value in an idea that we were first tempted to throw out.

Write down the ideas whenever possible. Older children can write down the ideas themselves. Writing down ideas serves several important purposes:

- Children feel their contributions are important when someone takes the time to actually write them down. It encourages them to share more ideas.
- It is easier to *look* at all the options, instead of trying to remember them.
- Children learn a valuable tool for sorting through their feelings, thoughts, and ideas.

Get as many ideas from the other person as possible. Keep *your* suggestions to a minimum so children don't always depend on you to solve their problems. If children cannot generate ideas (they may not have much practice thinking for themselves) allow a few seconds of silence before offering your ideas. Present your idea as a suggestion, not advice. For example, "Could you . . . ?" "What about . . . ?" "Have you considered . . . ?"

> **Whenever you are tempted to give an idea, turn your statement into a question that will help the other person think of your idea.**

b. Evaluate Each Idea

For each idea, ask "What would happen if you (whatever the idea is)?" Help children consider the possible effects of inappropriate or unhelpful ideas, which also teaches children to think before they act. We need to be careful giving *our* opinion of *their* ideas—we don't want to label the ideas *good* or *bad*. Instead, we want to acknowledge their feelings and ask questions that help them consider the possible effects. For example, "You are so angry with him, I can see how it might feel good to bop him in the nose! But what do you think would happen if you did that?" If you get no response, "Do you think it would help the problem or make him more angry?" A question can lead people to the points we want them to consider if we offer clues in the question. For example, "If you hit him, would you be doing the same thing he did to you? If it was wrong for him to do that, is it wrong for you to do it?" Judgments, lectures and preaching close the door on communication. If children figure out the answers themselves, they are more likely to use the information to avoid or resolve problems in the future.

c. Choose a Solution

After evaluating the ideas and eliminating some, look at the ideas that remain. Ask, "Which idea do you think is your best option?" We want to be careful not to push *our* favorite idea. The person (or people) affected by the problem needs to choose or agree to the solution. Take a broad view on choosing solutions—there are always choices; even doing nothing is an option! Even if their choice doesn't seem best, the insight children gain from the experience teaches them important lessons.

d. Make a Plan

Discuss the specifics of their solution, asking who, when, where, and how questions. Ask them what they plan to say and how they can say it. Teach children effective communication skills. Role playing the solution is helpful to teach effective body language. Ask, "What's the worst that could happen," then plan for it. If they know how to handle the worst, anything less is manageable, too.

e. Commit to a Trial Period

Once children have a plan, get a commitment from them to try it for a specific time period. This leaves the door open to discuss unsuccessful attempts to use the plan. We want children to learn that no single solution is the *only* possible way to solve a problem. They can always adjust their plan later, once they see where the flaws are. Children are more likely to try solutions if they know there are other ideas to try later.

> ***A Personal Story.*** *As a creative problem-solving coach (which I described in Chapter 6, Independence Toolset), I cannot offer **any** suggestions or advice that might directly affect my team's decision. I **must** rely on questions to guide and support them through the problem-solving process.*
>
> *There are many times we spend the entire practice time solving **one** problem. Do I get tired and frustrated? Yes. Do I get a headache? Yes. Am I excited when the children solve a problem on their own? Yes. Is it worth the time and effort? Yes! Even if they don't make perfect props or make mistakes along the way, it is okay. The only thing that counts is that they do **everything** on their own—and learn first-hand lessons in the process. Since I've been a coach, I notice I wait longer before offering suggestions to my own children and ask more questions to help them plan their own solutions.*

WHEN TO MOVE FROM STEP TO STEP

When we are unsure when to move from one F-A-X step to the next, we simply look at the clues the speaker gives us. We can ask ourselves certain questions at each step.

Step B1. *F*ocus on feelings. Is the person still expressing *emotion*?
- If the answer is "yes," continue using warmth, empathy, and listening skills.
- If the answer is "no," move onto the next step.

Step B2. *A*sk clarifying questions. Is the person talking about *facts, thoughts or beliefs*? Is the person confused about what happened or why it happened? Are the perceptions inaccurate or unhealthy?
- If the answer is "yes," use open-ended or leading questions and give information.
- If the answer is "no," move to the next step.

Step B3. *X*-amine possible options. Is the person talking about *solutions or ideas*? Is the person considering unhealthy goals or options?
- If the answer is "yes," do problem solving to set healthy goals and get commitments.
- If the answer is "no," you may need to return to a previous step if the person is still emotional or talking about feelings (B1) or is expressing beliefs or confusion (B2).

While we generally follow the F-A-X, 1-2-3 steps in order, we might shift between the skills to respond to people's comments. For example, if we are discussing options and people share feelings, we temporarily shift to our listening skills (B1) to show we understand what they said. Then we can ask a helpful question (B2) to help them resolve the feeling or reconsider their options (B3). Remember the Universal Blueprint's rule: At whatever step we are on, we can always use tools from previous steps.

*A **Personal Story**. Several weeks after Chris started junior high, he came home upset.*

Chris: *I failed my reading test today.*

Me: *(with surprise) You did?*

Chris: *We were just starting to take a test and the kid next to me said something to me. I told him to be quiet. The teacher heard me and gave us both an automatic F.*

Me: *Did you explain you were telling him to be quiet?*

Chris: *It wouldn't matter, we just get in worse trouble if we say anything.*

Me: *Oh? (I paused, letting my mind process the situation.) I guess I can see why. Can you imagine if teachers listened to every child's reasons?*

Chris: *Yeah, we'd never get to the test.*

Me: *(with a smile) Can you imagine some of the excuses they'd hear? (He nodded.) So what did you learn?*

Chris: *Not to sit next to **that** kid again!*

Me: *(Since he suggested a solution, I moved to problem solving.) So what can you do the next time someone tries to talk to you? Can you just say Shh?*

Chris: *(Tears welled up in his eyes and he raised his voice.) That's what I did! I gave him a dirty look, did this (he put his finger to his lips) and said, "Shh!"*

Me: *(He was upset again, so I moved back to focusing on feelings.) I bet it was discouraging to get in trouble when you were trying to **avoid** getting in trouble! (He nodded. I went back to problem solving.) So if you can't even say "Shh," what **can** you do?*

Chris: *(He thought before he answered.) Just ignore him, I guess.*

Me: *And not even look at him or make a sound, huh? (He agreed. I ended with a bit of encouragement.) Most of us have made the same mistake, but we usually only make it once—'cause it's a hard lesson to learn.*

Chris: *Yeah, really.*

VARIATIONS OF PROBLEM SOLVING

We can always use the F-A-X process to respond to Child problems. There are certain points we want to remember, however, when dealing with children of certain ages or certain types of Child problems. This section details some of these important points.

Young Children

Give young children time to think of ideas—don't rush them. They haven't had much practice. If they can't think of any ideas, combine the brainstorming and evaluating steps by saying, "What would happen if you . . . ?" Start with one idea. Use an **abbreviated format** with young children by saying only one sentence at each step: "You didn't like it when Bryan took your truck. You wish he would ask you first, huh? What do you think you could do?" If they don't offer any ideas, continue, "Could you try saying, 'Bryan, ask me first'? Are you willing to try that?" (Teach young children the exact words to say, instead of giving vague suggestions like, "Use words.")

With young children, writing ideas has advantages and disadvantages, depending on the child. Most children like us to record their ideas. It's like writing a gift list and they become more involved. Young children with short attention spans might lose interest. Some children even get upset when we write their ideas (especially the irrational ones) because they think we are carving it in stone. They don't understand it is just *one* idea of many. Try writing ideas and see how children react. If we get a negative reaction, wait until they are a little older and try again. We don't want to give up the idea, though. There are tremendous benefits to teaching children this process. If they learn to write down their ideas, it will be a process they can use on their own in the future.

Older Children

The problem-solving process can move in spurts or extend over weeks. Older children and internal problem solvers usually want to solve their problems on their own at their own pace. Give them space. If they share a problem, just acknowledge their feelings. They will probably feel better, disengage, and go within again. Just take the process at their pace.

Avoid offering suggestions to teens. They are usually quite capable of solving their own problems, if we give them some time and encouragement. If we have an idea or see a possible problem with an idea, we use helpful questions to help *them* realize the point on their own.

Sibling/Peer Mediation

When more than one child is involved in a problem, our role is to be an objective middle-person, not a referee who takes sides. Our goal is to involve each child in the problem-solving process. We will explore sibling conflicts in greater depth later in this chapter. If you have an only child, that child still interacts with other children and may experience similar conflicts. As you read the sibling section, substitute the word *peer* wherever you see *sibling*.

Problem Solving "On the Run"

We can use the abbreviated format of problem solving or mediation mentioned above in the "Young Children" section when conflicts involve any of the following factors:

- It is a minor problem.
- Children have short attention spans.
- The problem does not occur often.
- We don't have enough time to do thorough problem solving. (Don't use this factor as an excuse to *skip* problem solving, just postpone it.) Problem solving and mediation usually *save* us time in the future, because children learn how to work out problems on their own.

USE A PROBLEM-SOLVING WORKSHEET

If you would like an outline to follow or a worksheet to write ideas on, use the "Problem-Solving Worksheet" on page 205. You can use it for Child problems, mediation between two people, C/P problems, or family councils. Here are directions for its use.

1. **Feelings and Perceptions.** Write the person's feelings and perception of the problem—almost exactly as the person states them. If it is a Child problem, write only the child's feelings. If you are mediating, write each person's feelings. If it is a C/P problem, write your feelings as "Person #2."

2. **Summarize the problem.** Once we've listened to the description of the problem and the person's feelings, we want to sum up the problem in our words. Check the accuracy with the other person first, which will help identify the "core of the onion."

3. **Options.** Write *all* the ideas that are mentioned during brainstorming.

4. **Comments (+ or –).** Evaluate the positive and negative points of each idea.

5. **Plan.** Decide the details of the plan. Role play or teach skills so the child can put the plan in action.

6. **Next time it happens.** If this is a Child problem, have the child select a backup plan. If the problem is a C/P problem or it affects the family, decide the consequence of breaking the agreement. (Chapter 13, "Discipline Toolset," details specific possibilities.)

7. **Signed.** Signatures are optional, but are useful when mediating between two people or emphasizing an agreement between parent and child. Signatures are not proof of guilt or innocence if agreements are broken. They are tangible ways to emphasize agreements and commitments to try a plan.

PROBLEM-SOLVING WORKSHEET

FEELINGS AND PERCEPTIONS:

PERSON #1:_____

_____

PERSON #2: (if it applies)_____

_____

SUMMARIZE THE PROBLEM:_____

_____

_____

<u>OPTIONS</u>	<u>COMMENTS (+ OR -)</u>
_____	_____
_____	_____
_____	_____
_____	_____

PLAN: (Who, What, When, How, Other)_____

_____

_____

_____

NEXT TIME IT HAPPENS: Backup plans (or reveal discipline for Parent problems)

_____

_____

_____

SIGNED:_____   _____
            (Person #1)   (Person #2)

COMMON CHILD PROBLEMS

This section describes the four most common Child problems that parents tend to take over: fears, sibling/peer conflicts, school issues, and parents' concerns about children's friends.

Fears

When dealing with fears, it is particularly important to start where children are in the problem-solving process. They are usually stuck at the first step, being overwhelmed with feelings. Some fears are valid and helpful. For example, a fear of heights or mean dogs will cause people to be extra careful. When fears start to *control* people, they need to look at what's really going on and learn how to take control of their fears.

Children often have *imaginary* fears, "There's a gorilla in my closet!" Don't tell children their fears are silly or to simply stop feeling that way. To them, it is very real. You can notice and name the feeling without agreeing that the imaginary object exists. "It must be scary to think there's a gorilla in your closet." After naming the fear (B1), you can ask a helpful question (B2), "I'm going to turn on the light. Can you show me what looked like a gorilla and where you saw it?"

If children have a hard time talking about their fears, have them draw a picture or act out their fears with play characters. If they have fears that are caused by something that has really happened to them, they may benefit from seeing a therapist. Young children are best helped by play therapists, who help children express and work through their emotional issues through play.

When dealing with common fears, ask helpful questions, to reveal children's thoughts and beliefs. Give them factual information to explain anything they misunderstand. Tell children that they have control over their thoughts and feelings. Teach them how to talk themselves through their fears. Examine possible options that help children take control of the situation and calm their fears. If they practice and rehearse their response, they can use these skills to face their fears.

A Personal Story. Several years ago, I was helping my mother sort through old toys in her attic. We found my old Raggedy Ann doll, scorched and brown, which triggered my earliest memory, a childhood nightmare.

I was sleeping in my crib when an evil witch appeared in my room. She commanded me, "Say you hate your brother!" "No!" I said. She set a corner of my room on fire. She continued this pattern, "Say you hate your father . . . mother . . ." Each time, my fear intensified and I hesitated longer, but still said "No." Each time, she set another part of my room on fire. By now, the entire room was in flames and she was leaning over my crib, pointing her fire wand at **me**! *She yelled, "Say you hate God!" I knew if I agreed to do this she would set me on fire and I would die. I hesitated, knowing I would be lying if I agreed, closed my eyes and prepared to die as I yelled, "NO!" She fired her wand, but only hit the Raggedy Ann doll I had in my arms. I woke up as the smoke cleared. I looked around my room and everything was exactly as it was before she had appeared—except my doll. My Raggedy Ann was truly scorched from head to toe. I was very upset, but was too young to tell my parents about the dream. By the time I was old enough to speak well, I had put the dream in the back of my mind.*

When I found the doll in the attic, I told my mother (for the first time) about the nightmare. She had no logical explanation for the burns on the doll's body. Suddenly, this memory became a puzzle piece that finally explained my lifelong fear of sleeping alone. As a child, my parents used a pleasant, loving bedtime routine. Nevertheless, I hid under my blankets, slept with the door open, and kept a night light on. I slept on the floor with the dog, outside my parents' closed bedroom door, since this was the closest I could get to them at night. I'd sneak back into my own bed before they awoke. I slept with a doll until I was 12 and snuggled with pillows until I was married. Although my adult mind has rationalized that there is no reason to fear sleep, I still have many of these deeply ingrained habits. The memory of the nightmare helped this all make sense.

*If you have goose bumps after reading this story, you can only imagine how freaked out I was as a young child. Take my word for it, children's "imaginary" fears can be **very** real to **them.** If they can remember and tell us their fears, we can help children work through them. Fearful children need our reassurance and understanding, not pressure to "grow up" and to "stop being so child-ish." They'll only stop being afraid when they feel secure and more in control of their thoughts and feelings. We can best help them by using the F-A-X process.*

Sibling Conflicts

UNHELPFUL RESPONSES

The best way to increase sibling conflicts is to interfere in unhelpful ways. Some parenting advice says to let children work out problems by themselves. If children have never learned healthy conflict reso-lution skills, this approach can result in harmful, unfair resolutions. On the other hand, if parents always get involved in sibling conflicts, children get the payoff of our attention and don't learn how to resolve conflicts independently. Here are some common unhelpful responses to avoid:

- **Telling children to stop fighting or arguing.** They might stop, but the conflict is unresolved. The resentment that's left over crops up again, with the same issue or another.

- **Taking away the item they are fighting over*.** The child who didn't want to share "wins" because he doesn't have to share and the other child resents this child for winning.

- **Sending them to their rooms*.** Children don't learn how to work out the problem because they are separated. In their rooms, they spend their time thinking about how to get revenge on each other or how unfair you are. One or both feel more discouraged and angry.

- **Punishing *all* the children, because one or two children are misbehaving or arguing.** This increases resentment between the siblings and toward the parent. Revenge is sure to follow.

- **Offering a solution and making them use it.** Children might go through the actions, but they didn't learn how to find a solution on their own and follow through with the resolution process. If the suggestions don't work, they can blame the parent. Use problem solving instead.

- **Finding out who started it.** This keeps parents going in circles for some time without resolving the core issue. If the parent is wrong, the parent's solution will be unfair to someone. F-A-X listening reveals this information, without the negative side effects.

- **Taking one child's side.** One child loses and resents the parent and sibling. When parents take the youngest child's side, older children resent the parent and sibling. Youngest children learn they can get away with anything.

- **Voting or flipping a coin to decide the solution.** Whatever the outcome, there is a loser—and the loser may sulk about the solution or try to sabotage it. Use this option only if both parties agree to it and always acknowledge the loser's feelings.

HEALTHY PARENTING GOALS FOR SIBLINGS

Many parents want their children to love each other and be best friends. We can't *make* children do either of these. What we *can* do is teach them how to get along with people who are different from them and live or work together peacefully. As children learn how to work through their differences respectfully, they usually have fewer sibling/peer conflicts and naturally develop feelings of friendship and love for other children. The healthy goals for parents of siblings are to help children learn how to do several things:

---

*There are helpful variations of these responses—under certain circumstances and *if* they are presented in specific ways. As we detail sibling/peer conflicts, we learn these variations.

- Listen to each other's needs.
- Respect each other's differences.
- Learn ways to resolve differences respectfully, even if they never become close friends.

WHEN TO INTERVENE

If we are unsure whether to step into a sibling conflict, we can ask ourselves the following questions:

- Is one child being emotionally or physically hurt?
- Is their problem disrupting the entire household?
- Does this problem keep coming up and they can't seem to resolve it?

HOW TO INTERVENE

Sibling and peer conflicts are always Child problems. When the conflicts involve a SHARP RV issue, they are combination Child/Parent problems. In these C/P sibling conflicts, "keep the ball in their court" as much as possible. Only use the Parent Problem Toolbox to address the parent's part of the problem. Once you've interrupted the dangerous behavior, shift back to the Child Problem Toolbox to guide the children as they resolve their conflict.

1. *Listen to each child's feelings and side of the conflict with respect.* Repeat what you heard, to check out the accuracy. **We are not searching for the *truth* about the facts.** We may get two very different stories and could go in circles without resolving anything. Instead, we want to hear and acknowledge each person's feelings and perspective. "So you want _____ and you want _____." This alone might calm them down. If children are blaming or calling names, we can restate their feelings or opinions in more tactful ways. If children are still upset, keep reflecting feelings and asking helpful questions.

2. *Summarize the problem in your own words.* Show appreciation for the difficulty of the problem. Look through the surface issues to what is really going on. For example, the surface problem might be one toy and two kids. The *real* issues might be one child's ownership of the toy and the other child's boredom. *These* are the core issues you want to state and resolve.

The next step depends on the children's ages and their skill at problem solving.

3a. *If children know effective conflict management skills,* tell them you believe they can work out a fair, agreeable solution and leave the room.

   - *If they keep arguing,* say, "If you can't work it out, we will need to sit together and work out some agreements for what to do when this problem comes up again."

   - *If their solution always results in the same child giving in,* discuss this issue with each child individually. Teach the one who always gives in how to be more assertive. Ask the one who always wins to consider the positive feelings that come from win/win solutions and whether resentment and hurt feelings from losing may create more conflicts later.

3b. *If children haven't mastered conflict management skills,* mediate by saying, "So what do you two think you can do that is fair and respectful to both of you?" Continue mediating until they reach an agreement.

Sibling/Peer Mediation

When conflicts continue or the same issue keeps coming up, take the time to guide the children through a more thorough problem-solving session, using the Problem-Solving Worksheet. Mediation applies each step of the F-A-X process, back-and-forth, to the two parties. We can use this process with *any* two people: siblings, children and their friends or two adults.

1. ***Set a time to discuss the problem.*** Allow a cooling-off period first, if children are too upset to calmly discuss the problem. Before you start, set some ground rules, such as no interrupting or name-calling. Tell the children that they *both* will have an equal chance to be heard and respond to what the other child says.

2. ***Allow each child a turn to share his or her feelings and side of the conflict.*** Write each child's feelings and concerns on the worksheet, then *read them* aloud to make sure they are accurate. Allow differences of perceptions and opinions.

3. ***Let each child respond to the other child's comments.*** At this step, they can add new information or state their disagreement. Be careful not to get sidetracked with debates about who did what. Quickly move to the next step.

4. ***Summarize the problem in your own words,*** trying to focus on the *real* issues of the conflict.

5. ***Brainstorm solutions.*** Write down all ideas. Do not evaluate the ideas, yet. Don't label the idea as "his" or "hers." *Once an idea is suggested, it doesn't belong to anyone.* It is simply *one* idea. This prevents hurt feelings if the idea is rejected or someone says "See, *I* was right!"

6. ***Evaluate the ideas,*** asking each child's input on a particular idea. As they evaluate the ideas, get specific details for how that plan would actually work.

7. ***Decide on the solutions everyone can live with.*** If discipline is necessary, wait to discuss those options at this step. There are several problems if you discipline earlier:

   • Children think we don't respect their feelings or understand their perspective.
   • Children misinterpret the discipline as punishment, because it seems like a reaction, not a planned response.
   • The parent has taken over the problem.
   • One or both children will resent you *and* the other sibling for getting them in trouble.

8. ***Encourage them to try the solution for a trial period.***

9. ***Follow-up*** later or remind them of their agreement if the problem comes up again. Ask if the agreement is working. Let them know you will *mediate,* but *they* are responsible for solving *their own* problems. Encourage them to try resolving problems on their own, *before* bringing them to you.

It may seem like the mediation process has too many steps, but each step teaches important skills and has specific benefits. As we mediate more often, the process flows more quickly and smoothly and children come up with more ideas. As we see their skills increasing, we can stay more on the fringes of their conflicts. We need to be patient as they move from where they are now to being independent problem-solvers. After awhile, we can streamline the process for younger children, more skilled children, or when we need to solve problems on-the-run. Our ultimate goal is to say "I have confidence the two of you can work this out," believe it, and walk away. When children know we will not take sides and referee fights, but put the responsibility back in their court, they are less likely to use us in inappropriate ways.

COMMON SIBLING ISSUES

Many parenting resources offer helpful suggestions for dealing with sibling conflicts. Few actually tell parents specifically *what* to say, because there are so many issues siblings fight over. While the following suggestions still might not cover every possible sibling issue, we can apply these basic suggestions in similar situations.

Personal Space

Most of the time, *my* children's sibling conflicts boil down to this issue, but rarely do they realize this is the core of their problem. I will use a problem-solving session with my children to show how sibling mediation actually sounds as the discussion flows through the nine steps.

1. Set a time to discuss the problem.

    My kids had been arguing more than usual. When this fight occurred, it was more aggressive and hurtful and I could no longer ignore it. Both children were so angry they couldn't think, speak, or listen. I told them both to go somewhere alone to calm down and meet me in the living room when they were ready to resolve the problem. Amber, four, was ready within several minutes and sat with me in the living room. We waited for Chris, who was eight, and took much longer to calm down. When I heard him playing, I said that if he was calm enough to play in his room, he was ready to join us.

    Me: *The two of you have been fighting a lot more lately and it seems you can't work things out on your own. I want you both to have a chance to explain what is going on and see if you two can agree on a solution.*

2. Allow each child a turn to share his or her feelings and side of the conflict.

    Me: *I can tell you are both very angry. Amber, can you tell me your side of what happened.*
    Amber: *Chris pushed me . . .*
    Chris: *(interrupting) No I didn't! (I realized I had neglected to set the ground rules.)*
    Me: *Chris, you'll get a chance to tell me your side next. Let Amber finish and you'll have a chance to say whatever you want, too.*
    Amber: *. . . and he called me a baby.*
    Me: *(I wrote all this down.) Anything else? (Amber shook her head, "No." I turned to Chris.) Okay. Chris? What about you?*
    Chris: *I did push her, but only after she tried to grab the remote control while I was watching TV. I only called her a baby because she made me mad. (I asked him, "What else bothers you?") She bites me and doesn't stop when I tell her to. She calls me names, sticks her tongue out, screams in my face, and goes in my room without permission. (I quickly wrote each complaint as he spoke.)*

3. Allow each child to respond to the other child's comments.

    Me: *Amber is there anything you want to say about what Chris said?*
    Amber: *Yeah, I want to play with him but he pushes me away! (She got teary-eyed again.)*
    Chris: *I don't mind playing sometimes. It's just that she mostly bothers me when I first come home from school.*
    Me: *Okay. (I wrote down their comments.)*

4. Summarize the problem in your own words, trying to focus on the *real* issue of the conflict.

    Me: *So Chris, it sounds like you want to be left alone and have Amber respect your privacy. And Amber, you want to play with Chris. When he won't, it hurts your feelings and you want to hurt him back. Does that sound right to both of you?*
    Both: *Yeah.*
    Me: *Amber, do you miss Chris when he's gone at school all day? (She nodded her head.) Are you happy to have him home to play with? (She again nodded and I turned to Chris.) And Chris, do you want to be alone for a while when you get home?*
    Chris: *(insistently) Yes!*

5. Brainstorm solutions to their problem.

Me: *So, what can you two do when Amber wants to play but Chris wants privacy?*
Amber: *We could make a deal!*
Me: *What kind of deal?*
Chris: *When we feel like hurting we could use* **words!** *(He looked at Amber as he stressed this last word.)*
Me: *(I didn't want them to start blaming again, so I refocused on solutions.) What else?*
Chris: *I could go to my room and close my door.*
Me: *Okay. I'll add that and "walk away." (I wrote down their ideas.)*

6. Evaluate ideas.

Me: *(Reading back their list of ideas.) Okay I have "make a deal, when you feel like hurting use words, go to room, or walk away." How do you both feel about those ideas? (They nodded their heads in agreement. Since they agreed with <u>all</u> the ideas, I confirmed each child's willingness to abide by the solutions.) Amber, if you want to play, are you willing to use words to ask Chris? (She said, "Yes.") And, Chris, if you want to be alone, will you use words to tell her you want privacy?*
Chris: *I do use words, but she won't listen!*
Me: *(I moved back to exploring alternatives.) So what can you do if words don't work?*
Chris: *(in a questioning voice) Walk away and go to my room?*
Me: *That's right, and Amber, when Chris wants to be alone, what can you do?*
Amber: *(in an "I know" tone of voice) Go play somewhere else.*
Me: *(Knowing Chris could play in his room all day just to be alone, I thought we'd better have some time limits on this idea.) Amber, how much time would you be willing to give Chris to be alone when he comes home? (She shrugged her shoulders, "I don't know.") Chris, knowing that Amber has been home alone all day long, what's the smallest amount of time you need to be alone before you would be willing to play?*
Chris: *An hour?*
Me: *I think a four-year-old would have a hard time waiting an hour. If you played with her for a bit, she might be more willing to leave you alone. Would you be willing to settle for 15 minutes, play for a while, then ask for more time alone?*
Chris: *I guess.*

7. Decide on the solutions you can all live with.

We seemed to have a plan, all we needed was a final summary of their decision.
Me: *So Amber, are you willing to give Chris 15 minutes alone when he first comes home and find something else to do?*
Amber: *Yeah, but what will I do?*
Me: *I'd be willing to help you make a list when we are done here, okay? (She agreed.) And Chris, will you play with Amber if she leaves you alone for a while when you first come home? (He agreed.) Are you* **both** *willing to make a deal that when you feel angry and like hurting each other you will use words or walk away? (They agreed in unison.)*

8. Encourage them to try the solution for a trial period.

Me: *Okay, you have a deal. Try your plan. If there is a problem later, we can always sit and work things out some more. Okay? (Both agreed.) Are you willing to shake on your deal or sign the agreement I wrote here on my notes? (They chose to do both.)*

9. Follow-up later or remind them of their agreement if the problem comes up again.
    After *this session, I only needed to remind them about their agreement a few times. I explained recharge styles to Amber (which we learn in Chapter 9, Keep Your Cool Toolset) and her activity list helped her stay busy when Chris needed privacy.*

Property Disputes and Sharing

When we resolve fights over property, someone usually loses. If the property owners win, they are less likely to share because they know they don't have to. If we force them to share, they resent the other child and the parent. They are less likely to share because it is something the parent is *making* them do. There are some universal rules about property disputes.

In the following examples, notice how the parent's responses teach values or suggest options without taking over.

*   **Personal property:** The owner has the right to decide whether to share. Others must ask first. Back up the owner's decision and teach others to ask first. Acknowledge the nonowner's disappointment if the owner chooses not to share the item and redirect them to another activity.

    > *A **Personal Story.** Amber, age 3, took her water toys to the baby pool. I knew if she saw another child playing with her toys, she would think the child was taking her toy home and get very upset. When children asked permission first, she almost always said "Yes." I saw a little boy playing with one of her toys and said, "That toy belongs to the little redheaded girl over there. I bet if you ask her, she'll say you can play with it for a while." He asked her and she said "Yes." This suggestion usually prevents an unnecessary conflict and teaches other children to ask before using others' belongings. No parent has ever gotten upset with me when I say this to their child. I am polite, respectful, and encouraging to both children.*

*   **Community property:** Whoever has possession first has the right to decide whether to share. Others must ask for a turn instead of grabbing the item. State this rule without actually taking sides, "Janet had it first, so she can decide whether to share it now or tell you when she will give you a turn to play with it." By offering these two choices, we make it clear that "hogging it" is not one of the options.

In either case, suggest that sharing would be the respectful and kind action, but don't force the decision.

Steps in responding to property disputes:

1. *Acknowledge both children's feelings.* "You don't want to share it because (it's special to you or you had it first) and you really want to borrow it because _____."

2. *State the rule about property rights.* You can support one side, but leave final decision up to the children. "Well it's your (item) and your decision, but if you want to work something out with your brother/sister, I'm sure it would mean a lot to him/her."

3. *Put the ball in their court and see what happens.* It could go in a dozen different directions, depending on the children, who we'll call Jan and John:

    a. *The property owner chooses not to share.* To the child who wants to borrow, we can say, "I know you're disappointed and upset. Maybe next time she'll decide differently. John, have you ever had a toy first and Jan wanted to play with it, but you didn't want to share it?"

        Remember that young children have difficulty considering another person's feelings. They can't imagine being in that person's shoes or simply don't care. Don't say "How do you think Jan feels when . . ." Instead, describe the problem and put them in the owner's position. "Can you remember a time when . . . ?" "I remember when ____ happened to you."

b. *The other child asks nicely, but the child with possession still doesn't share.* To the child who asked nicely, we can say, "You asked very politely. I guess right now Jan is not ready to share. It can be disappointing to try to be nice and still not have things work out your way."

Often, by simply validating the owner or possessor's rights and not forcing them to share, they change their minds and decide to share. If they don't change their minds and it's personal property, ask John, "Can you think of something else you can play with in the meantime?" If it's community property, say, "John, can you ask Jan *when* you can have a turn?" While redirecting John to another activity, say, "I'm sure Jan won't be playing with it all day. Why don't you wait awhile and see if she puts it down. Then you can have a turn and it will be your turn to decide if you want to show Jan how good it feels to share."

c. *The child is not using the item but doesn't want anyone to play with it either.* If it's personal property, ask the owner, "If you don't want to share it, where could you keep it so John can't see it?" If it's community property, acknowledge each child's feelings, negotiate agreements for the item's use, and teach children how to negotiate, ask to share, and take turns.

d. *The property owner says "I'm afraid he's going to break it!"* We can say to the property owner, "Would you be willing to let him use it if he promises to take good care of it or replaces it if it breaks?" If the borrower has a record of breaking borrowed items, be careful not to reinforce a negative label. This might be an opportunity for the borrower to show he can be more careful this time. Don't force the other child to share. Explain to the borrower that her unwillingness is the natural effect of having her property broken. "Maybe you can show her how well you take care of *your* belongings so she might decide differently another time."

e. *Tug-of-wars and broken property:* Don't fall into the referee trap, trying to figure out who is doing the most grabbing or who should get their way. If one child damages the item, that child is responsible for fixing or replacing it. If the property owner cries or is aggressive because the toy is broken, acknowledge the owner's feelings and give the child some space. Sit with each child and work through feelings individually before coming together in joint mediation. To the one whose toy was broken, say "You have a right to be upset. You trusted your brother to take care of your toy." To the one who broke it, say "I know you feel bad and surprised that it actually broke! What do you think you two could have done instead of tugging? (Pause.) What needs to happen now?" If the "breaker" is defensive and blames the owner, "It's not my fault because she ____," you can ask "Does that make it okay to break the toy?"

Say this last statement as a question. Lecturing, "Well that doesn't make it okay to . . . " makes them feel worse. Ask other questions, waiting for a response to each: "So when you're hurt one day, is it okay to hurt him the next? How does that help? Do you think now that he's mad at you he might do something to one of your toys later? So when does all this end?" Take them by steps through the logic so they can see the answer on their own and choose more helpful responses.

If we can't tell who broke the item, the bottom line is, "The ____ got (broken, ripped) because two people were fighting over it instead of using words. One person lost a ____ and the other person lost a chance to use it. What can you do next time to prevent this from happening?" Use children's poor decisions to help them learn how to make better decisions in the future.

Ownership issues are greatly affected by developmental stages. Children who are three and younger won't understand ownership, sharing, and taking turns very well or follow-through consistently. We need to repeat ourselves often and consistently. We can help them move through these difficult stages by carefully choosing the messages we're sending and skills we're teaching. As they logically understand the concepts, they will master the skills. By age four, children better understand sharing.

Beyond age, however, skills have a greater impact on property disputes. We could have a 15-year-old who has no respect for property owners' rights and a 3-year-old who is verbal enough to ask permission. It depends on their life experience and what they have been taught. When we intervene, we want to teach these skills, so we can eventually get to the point of saying, "Gee, I bet if you two put your heads together you can come up with a plan that is respectful and fair to both of you"—and they will!

Territory

Territory issues involve people's physical space and their right to have others respect it. Handle these issues using the same steps described for property disputes and personal space.

If children share a room, it can be particularly difficult to reach agreements that are respectful to both children. It is important to make sure each child has some personal space in the room—an area that belongs only to that child to have some privacy or personal space. Allow them to decorate or use this personal territory as they choose, as long as their choices don't interfere with others' rights or personal space. Let each child choose another location, besides the room they share, where they can go if they want privacy or space. Then encourage others to respect the child's need to be alone when he or she is in that space. Crowded quarters are never ideal; just try to work out the best possible solution.

Tattling

There is a difference between *tattling* and *telling*:

- Children *tattle* when they are trying to get another child in trouble or to get unnecessary attention from the parent.
- Children *tell* an adult when another child is doing something that is dangerous or someone is hurt and an adult needs to know.

Tattling can destroy sibling and parent/child relationships, so parents need to decide if learning the truth is important enough to undermine the siblings' loyalty to each other. Make it clear that children can bring complaints to you but you will not take sides. We never know if the version we hear is accurate and could make an unfair decision. Also, don't play the "who did it" game. What *is* important is that the two of them resolve it respectfully. You can say, "I don't listen to tattling" or "I can see you're (feeling) about (event). What do you think *you* can do about it?" Don't bite the bait—put the ball back in the child's court.

> *A Graduate's Story. We were late for the bus and I ran into the house to get something while the kids waited at the curb. When I came out, T.J. said, "Mommy, Tony stepped on my foot!" I said, "Gosh! I bet that hurt!" He said, "Yeah," with a shocked look on his face, because he's not used to my acknowledging his feelings. I said "I hope you have a better day at school!" He looked back at me like I was an alien mother and then called out, "Love you mom!" I was shocked! He rarely says this, 'cause it's not cool anymore. That's when I realized that sometimes just acknowledging their feelings is enough and I don't have to go any further trying to solve the problem **for** them.*

Bickering

Bickering **is when people argue about petty issues and no physical or emotional harm is occurring. These disagreements can serve the positive purpose of practicing conflict-resolution skills.**

Anyone in a relationship, living in the same space, will have petty arguments now and then. We've all had this experience with a spouse or friend. To us, children's issues seem petty because they are issues we've grown out of, but to our children, these issues are very important. They have not yet resolved the issue nor learned and refined their verbal negotiation skills. Their bickering doesn't always sound like negotiation, just a round robin disagreement. As long as no one is getting physically or emotionally hurt, allow them time to work things out on their own.

If one sibling responds respectfully and assertively and the other doesn't, use descriptive encouragement to notice the child using respectful words. Restate your expectation that family members treat each other with respect. Offer the other child the choice of acting respectfully or leaving. If you are in the car, the respectful child can move to the front seat. Don't move the disrespectful child to this honorary position. If changing seats is not an option, the child can remain silent rather than move. It's like the old saying, "If you can't say something nice, don't say anything at all."

If we do get involved, we want to mediate in a way that teaches children the basics of respectful communication (the universal PASRR formula and problem-solving steps): Listen to the other person's feelings and opinions before you offer yours. State your feelings and opinions respectfully. Brainstorm ideas for what you can each do differently. Make an agreement for how you will both handle the situation in the future.

When we are not available to mediate, children need to know the following nonviolent options for resolving conflicts with siblings or peers:

- ignore the comment
- walk away
- do something else
- apologize
- tell them to stop
- count to ten

- talk it over respectfully
- agree on a win/win compromise
- try again
- listen to the other person

- make an agreement for handling the situation in the future.
- ask for help from a mediator

Teasing/Taunting

> *Teasing* **is meanspirited and hurtful. It often involves put-downs or name-calling.**

To tell the difference between bickering and teasing, ask yourself, "Are they dealing with the issue or just being hurtful?" Comment if they start calling each other names or are disrespectful. We can do this with one sentence, "I hear name-calling" or "Use respectful words." They know we are listening but often appreciate the fact that we didn't take over or lecture.

If children are being teased by a sibling or peer, acknowledge their hurt feelings. It helps to explain the teaser's motive. There are several reasons children tease:

- Children make rhymes at another's expense, as in "Billy, Billy, so Silly."
- Children find something different about a child and use teasing to establish their membership in a peer group. "You don't have brown eyes, so you can't play with us."
- Children tease just to see if they can get a rise out of the victim.
- Children put others down to make themselves feel more important.

Sometimes there is a reason the child is being teased. If the child has a loud voice and is very talkative, they might invite the name "Big Mouth." If children have a personality trait that might offend others, be cautious pointing it out. Describe the behavior in general terms. "When someone interrupts others, people can get angry and not want to be around that person. Do you think there are ever times you might do this?" We might know the child does this, but we want to word the statement carefully so the child doesn't feel like we are joining the crowd. If children aren't doing anything to bring on the teasing, they can use one of the ideas in the list of nonviolent options in the bickering section or the bully/victim section below.

Roughhousing

> *Roughhousing* is when both children *want* to play rough and no one is getting hurt. It is different from real fighting.

1. Teach children the difference between roughhousing and real fighting.

2. Have children agree on a code word like "Ouch" "Stop" "Uncle" or "Pickles" that means, "I'm not having fun anymore" or "I'm getting hurt." Both children must agree to stop if either child says the code word. If one or both children still need to get out their energy, brainstorm less hurtful ways.

3. If you are unsure whether they are really fighting, ask, "Are you both having fun?" or "Are you playing or fighting?" To roughhouse, both children must agree to play fair and safe.

4. Use environmental engineering (Chapter 11, "PU Toolset"). Let them wrestle on a mattress or pull cushions off an old couch so they can roughhouse without anyone getting hurt.

Physical Fights

If the situation is dangerous, physically intervene. Dive into the action, block blows with your body or hands, stand between them, or place a hand on their arms. Take these actions *while* you say the following statements.

1. **A**cknowledge feelings. "I can tell both of you are really angry . . ."

2. **S**et limits. ". . . but fighting hurts feelings and bodies." Teach them the proper words if they don't have good verbal skills.

3. If this de-escalates the situation, continue mediating. If the situation is still hot, everyone (including you) separates for a cooling off period (see Chapter 9, "Keep Your Cool Toolset" and self-control timeouts in Chapter 13, "Discipline Toolset"). Make it clear that whenever conflicts come to the point of separation, mediation is automatic. During the cooling-off period, review your plan (see the Problem-Solving Worksheet on page 205).

Bullies and Victims

The most common roles that children adopt, especially siblings, are the bully and victim roles. When bullying starts, try this time-tested (and parent-tested) process[2]:

1. **Avoid giving bullies extra attention, which gives them a payoff for their aggression.** When bullies are scolded, labeled, and punished, it proves to them that they really are mean people and deserve to suffer. Discouraged and angry, they get revenge on their favorite victim for getting them in trouble. (Bullies usually don't accept personal responsibility for their actions, they justify them with excuses. "She made me . . . ") Don't confuse an unwillingness to give *immediate* attention with ignoring the bully's behavior. We *will* make it clear, as we move through the steps, that bullying is unacceptable, *without* giving the bully a payoff.

2. **Tend to the injured victim first.** This shows that meanness does not get attention. Be careful not to overreact to victims, coddling or rescuing them. Just tend to their needs and acknowledge their hurt. As we talk to the child who was hurt say, "Ow! That really hurt, didn't it? People are not

for hitting! Your brother (or sister) needs to use words to get what he wants, even when he's angry." The bully hears this statement, although we don't say it directly to the bully, which would give the bully extra attention.

3. **When we shift the focus back to the bully,** we say, "I can tell you are really angry. Hitting hurts and there are ways to tell your brother (or sister) how angry you are without hurting him (or her). You can say (give the exact words to say, if you know what the conflict was about). Your brother (or sister) is hurt. What can you do to help him (or her) feel better?" *Do not* force children to say they're sorry. "Sorry" is a word that people can say insincerely to erase their responsibility and guilt. Instead, encourage children to *show* they're sorry by taking responsibility for any harm they caused. They can get ice, look at the wound, say they're sorry, or do nothing—and live with whatever self-imposed guilt they might have.

4. **Later, talk with the bully.** Teach anger management skills (from Chapter 9, "Keep Your Cool Toolset") and use problem solving to brainstorm other options for resolving conflict.

5. **Also, problem-solve with the victim.** We often reinforce victim roles by rescuing them, reinforcing their belief that they can't handle their own problems. We confront the bully on the victims' behalf, which tells bullies the victims need their parents to fight their battles for them. Instead, help victims brainstorm options for handling bullies. Teach them how to stand up for themselves, using assertive verbal and nonverbal skills and the following defensive (not aggressive) physical moves:

Nonverbal responses

Teach children to carry themselves confidently and walk with bold steps. They don't have to walk like pompous bullies themselves, but they want to send the message that "I can take care of myself. Don't mess with me."

Parents often tell victims to ignore bullies. Children, however, often think this means they should be passive, which creates a more wimpy attitude. To ignore effectively, they need to use strong body language. Stand up straight and look the person in the nose (it's too scary to look them in the eyes), smile, shrug the shoulders and walk (or run) away. This response tells bullies, "What you said didn't affect me in the least. You are not worth my time." Children don't have to say this, their attitude says it for them.

It is also helpful for victims to keep their distance from bullies by avoiding situations that will bring them into unnecessary contact with the bully. If they can't avoid the bully, they could stay in a group of friends or in view of (but not clinging to) an adult, since the bully is less likely to pick on them.

Verbal responses

Most children spend so much time defending or explaining themselves that they only reinforce the power of bullies' words. If they insult bullies, the bullies get ticked off more and seek revenge. Instead, children can use self-directed humor. For example, if someone calls them a chicken, they can pretend to be a chicken. This tells bullies they know the comment is ridiculous. Others who are watching will usually laugh with the "victims" and join their side.

Victims can also exaggerate their responses, which also uses humor. If the bully says, "Your Mama wears army boots" the victim can add, "Yeah! And she wears a helmet and wakes me up with a reveille each morning." This tactic not only defuses, but helps victims take control of the situation.

If children have time to plan ahead, they can think of nice, honest things to say to the bully. They don't want to kiss up to bullies, which keeps bullies in power. They can, however, say sincere, true, flattering statements. "That was a great touchdown you made at the game last night. You really saved the day!"

Physical defense moves

- *Windmills.* When children are grabbed, they rotate their arm from the elbow to wrist in a "windmill" motion. (Down, in toward the other shoulder, up, and out away from the body.) They do this in the direction that goes against the thumb that's grabbing them. If they are grabbed from behind, they move both arms, fully extended—down, cross, up, out, and away—to break the grip. If someone starts to push them from the front, they can use this motion to deflect the arm.

- *The bite defense.* If a child is coming toward them to bite, they can extend their hand an arm's length in front and put the palm of their hand on the biter's forehead, locking their elbow. This gives them time to free their legs and make a getaway.

- They can *block* punches by bending their arm at the elbow and placing it in front of their face, or other target-area.

These are temporary, self-protective moves that buy time for victims to either get away or use verbal conflict resolution skills. These moves are not aggressive, but will protect children in nonviolent ways. It is better to teach children these skills instead of encouraging them to return punches. This usually escalates the revenge cycle and sends the message that violence is okay.

If you live in a high crime area or there's a lot of gang harassment, it is tempting to teach violent responses. In this day and age, you never know who might have a hidden weapon. Violence needs to be a last resort, used only to *defend* ourselves, when leaving the scene and other options are impossible, or in life and death situations.

We may have to get involved, after trying these other responses first. We can volunteer on the school playground or wherever bullies usually attack. Other adults might not believe our children, but if we say we witnessed it, they are more likely to take our concerns seriously.

> *A Personal Story. When Chris was in the fourth grade, he and his friend, a fifth-grader, had a problem with a bully on the bus—a second-grade girl. The bus driver would not believe their complaints of her kicking, taunting, and tripping them as they walked through the bus, because she was a younger girl. When they came home from school, they'd tell me what happened, and we'd do problem solving. Eventually, they tried every idea the three of us had. I was considering writing a letter when I happened to be in my car behind the bus one day and witnessed her behavior first-hand. In my letter to the transportation director, I simply described the girl's behavior and the boys' attempts to resolve the problem respectfully. I didn't tell the director what to do, but wanted him to be aware of the problem. I only mentioned my eyewitness account at the end as a side-note. The bus driver changed the seating arrangement—moving the **boys** to the front of the bus instead of the bully.*

Whenever possible, we want our intervention to empower victims and teach bullies better ways to handle conflicts. This helps free them both from unhelpful roles and boost their self-esteem and skills. Since victims feel incapable and helpless, assertiveness skills help them feel more capable. Since bullies are often stuck in a negative role, nonviolent alternatives give them a way out.

School Problems

School problems are touchy issues. Often, parents are more concerned than children and it's hard to get involved without taking over or exerting too much control, either of which can backfire.

HOMEWORK

Homework is a child's responsibility—we need to be careful how much we help. We need to be aware of what our children are doing and be involved in helpful ways, but not help too much. Keep the ball in the child's court. Avoid the word "we"—it implies that school issues are partly our responsibility. Say, "When are *you* going to do *your* homework?" If they require assistance, say "I am willing to look at what *you* are doing." If they are having problems with their homework, use listening skills to figure out *why*. We don't want to assume the child is lazy or incompetent.

- **If children have a time management problem,** have *them* schedule their time, instead of telling children when to do homework. Ask questions such as, "How much time do you need for homework each night? Would you like to play after school and study after dinner? Or study after school and play until dark? How can you remember when it is time to stop playing and do your homework?"

  *A Personal Story. One of Amber's teachers required the children in her class to use a homework journal that was so complicated it took **me** three weeks to learn! Amber and I did some problem solving and found a way to use the school's basic system with symbols Amber chose and could more easily follow.*

- **If children don't understand the homework,** ask questions that help *them* figure out the answer. "What are you supposed to do here? How can you find the answer? Where in the book does it talk about this? What does it say?" If the information is there, but children don't understand it, we can try to explain it. We do not have to understand what children are learning to be helpful. All we really need to know are the skills for helping our children figure it out for themselves. If children seem to need daily help, they may benefit more from a tutor than from our taking so much responsibility for helping them. It's a delicate balance to help, without fostering dependency, rescuing, or helping too much.

  A Personal Story. In high school, my husband took honors calculus. When he was stuck on a problem, he'd ask his mom for help. She didn't have the slightest clue about calculus, so she'd say, "Show me what you are working on." As he explained the problem, the answer would suddenly come to him. He'd say "Thanks Mom!"

Instead of taking on children's responsibilities . . .   *. . . guide them to their own solution.*

Children who have given up on school are experiencing a deeper problem. Use the Child Problem Toolbox to find out the real issue. *This* is the issue that needs to be resolved. You may want to enlist professional guidance, if indicated. The "real issue" and improving poor school performance will take longer to improve than other school problems.

If children forget a book, lunch, or homework, teach skills (Chapter 6, "Independence Toolset.") and use problem solving to have children chose self-reminders. Children are responsible for getting themselves off to school, so avoid being their reminder or rescuer. If the problem occurs often, it usually affects parents, so we cover these issues in more detail in Chapter 13, "Discipline Toolset."

PROBLEMS WITH SCHOOL PERSONNEL

When children have a problem with a teacher or principal, it is a Child/Teacher problem. We can offer support to either party and do problem solving with children to see if they can resolve the problem directly with the teacher. Brainstorm ideas and help children practice what to say to the teacher. Try to anticipate the various responses the teacher might have, positive or negative, and how children can respond. Emphasize that it is *their* problem and we want them to give it their best shot before we get involved.

> *A Personal Story. When Chris was in fourth grade, his teacher outlined the rules for turning in schoolwork. She said they had until recess to finish their work. If it was not done by then, they had to stay inside for recess. Recess was a top priority to Chris.*
>
> *One day, he waited to turn in a paper until right before recess. The teacher told him it was late and he'd have to stay inside for recess, even though the work was already done. She said the paper was due an hour before recess and this had always been the rule. Chris thought the teacher had changed the rules without telling him. He didn't see the logic of staying inside to work on a paper that was finished.*
>
> *When he told me about the situation after school, I acknowledged his feelings. I could see how the teacher's actions would seem unfair if the rules had actually changed. I encouraged him to double-check the rule with the teacher, but he didn't want to talk to her directly. I told him it wasn't my place to step in, if he hadn't talked to her first. He was afraid of how she might react, so we role-played the possibilities. He agreed to follow whatever rule the teacher set, even if it wasn't what he thought it should be.*
>
> *The next day, he asked the teacher to clarify the rule. She said the deadline was one hour before recess. He wasn't happy, but at least he knew which rule to follow. He had also taken a giant step forward by having the courage to talk to the teacher directly. He never missed the deadline again.*

When we meet with teachers to discuss problems and children are present, don't talk about them like they aren't there. Involve the children and serve as a mediator between them and the teacher. Use problem solving to address the teacher and child's feelings, ideas, and needs. Only make commitments to be responsible for tasks that are truly a parent's responsibility. We *can* agree to teach the child skills or use problem solving to develop plans. We need to maintain a balance; we want to be responsible, supportive parents, without overstepping boundaries and solving the problem for children or teachers.

Peers/Friends

In most situations, we use the same skills with our children's peers and friends that we would if the other children were their siblings. If other children do not have the skills our children have, we can coach them through the problem-solving process.

PARENTAL CONCERNS ABOUT A CHILD'S FRIENDS

When children are young, through early elementary school, we have more influence over their choice of friends. If we don't like a friend's influence, we can invite the friend to play at *our* house, where our rules apply, and keep an eye on their interactions. If the friend's behavior is unintentional, for example not sharing or being bossy, we can redirect the behavior by offering helpful suggestions for positive behavior. When conflicts arise, we can handle the problem as we would any other parenting problem. If we use a balanced, respectful approach, other parents will not object to anything we do. If the friend's behavior is detrimental to our children, either physically or by exposing them to values and behaviors we cannot tolerate, we need to set more firm limits. The friend can choose to abide by the rules in our house or choose not to play there.

As children get older, ***junior high through teens***, parents have less influence over their decisions. If we don't like a teen's friends, we can first try the approach described above. Usually, though, teens socialize away from home. If we forbid our teens from seeing particular friends, they will usually rebel. They may defend the friend more strongly and make an extra effort to keep the friend, just to prove we can't control them and our opinions about their friends are wrong.

> ***A Parenting Class Experience.*** *Toni, age 15, and her father were angry when they arrived at the Teen and Parents—Together class. They had gotten in a huge argument because Toni knew her father had to meet her friends before she could go out with them and intentionally defied this rule.*
>
> *Toni told the group that she **was** willing to bring her friends to the house but her father was always rude to them. He criticized the way they dressed and "gave them the third degree." She was so embarrassed and angry she decided she'd rather be disciplined for breaking the rule than put herself and her friends through that humiliation.*
>
> *All Toni's father could hear was "I am willing to do it but won't." The group helped the father focus on what Toni **meant**. I mediated, helping them listen to each other, state their needs, and negotiate an agreement. They agreed that if Toni brought her friends home, her father would treat them with respect. Because the father had broken this promise in the past, they agreed to practice specific questions he could ask to address his concerns respectfully. It was a temporary role reversal, but Toni had a better grasp of respectful communication and her father was willing to improve his skills by listening to her suggestions.*

Instead of lecturing, accusing, and restricting children from seeing their friends, use F-A-X communication. The goal is to help children see *for themselves* that this friend might not be a good influence. We can ask questions now and then, not all at once like an interrogation. For example, "Have you noticed John sometimes ___? Has he ever done this to you? How did you feel? What did you do?" After one of these discussions, back off for a bit and give children time to think about the points they realized through our questions. Often, if we express our concerns respectfully, listen to their concerns, and express trust in their judgment, children realize on their own that this friend may not be a good influence. This process may not be quick. While we wait, we need to trust our child's judgment and pray—for guidance, patience, and for our child's protection.

If our children's friends are involved in dangerous or extremely inappropriate behavior, we need to take a stand and risk a power struggle—but we must carefully plan our strategy. Our concerns are Parent problems, while peer relationships are Child problems. We can use the Clear Communication Toolset to describe what we've seen, instead of judging or labeling their friends. Instead of singling out one friend, we set bottom-line limits with general rules, "You can only go to someone's house if a parent is there and I have met the friend." Once we set limits, we need to listen to and acknowledge our child's feelings of frustration, resentment or anger toward us. If we use F-A-X communication, we can usually get agreements that address our concerns *and* teach teens the skills they need to handle more freedom responsibly. We discuss this type of parent/child problem solving in Chapter 10, "Clear Communication Toolset" and appropriate disciplines for breaking agreements in Chapter 13, "Discipline Toolset."

> ***A Personal Story.*** *I've never had a serious concern about any of Chris' friends, but Amber has had problems with other girls' being bossy, rejecting, lying and trying to take advantage of her since she entered preschool. (Imagine trying to explain cliqués to a four-year-old!)*
>
> *When problems arise with Amber's friends, I first do problem solving to see if there is anything Amber can do to resolve the problem herself. I teach her the language skills she needs to stand up for herself respectfully and to offer win/win choices to the other child. Sometimes, the problem continues. If Amber has tried every reasonable option, I ask her whether playing with this friend is worth being mistreated. Amber usually has enough self-respect that she says she would rather not play with the child. I back up her decision and we brainstorm other options for playmates.*
>
> *There have been only two friends that I have had to restrict her from seeing. One girl was a chronic liar and Amber was picking up the habit. The girl also engaged in sexually inappropriate activities that made Amber feel uncomfortable and shameful. Another girl repeatedly teased, criticized, and humiliated Amber. I also had intuitive gut feelings that Amber might not be safe at this girl's house. Only in these two cases have I felt strongly enough about the emotional, physical, moral risks to my daughter to put my foot down and forbid Amber from being friends. In one case, Amber agrees and is grateful I've given her an "easy out" for not playing with the girl. The other girl, however, lives close by and Amber wishes she could still play with her. She disagrees that there is a continued risk. At these times, we have another discussion, in which I acknowledge her feelings of disappointment and disagreement. I ask questions instead of lecturing, to help Amber see why I still have concerns and what her other options are.*

The most extreme case of choosing bad friends is joining a gang. The most common reasons teens join gangs are to gain acceptance, have a sense of identity, feel secure (protected), and have more power and control. These are all age-appropriate teen issues, but gang membership is a very negative way to meet these needs. Because gangs require a strong commitment, their members develop intense loyalty; the gang then becomes their new "family." When we look at the gang member's real family, we often find it lacks many of the qualities the teen is seeking. When the teen's only obvious choices are to have the needs go unfulfilled or to meet the needs in negative ways, some teens will choose the latter.

If you live in a gang-infested community, prevention is the key. Give children love and acceptance, emotional support, loving protection (setting reasonable limits in respectful ways), and offer appropriate ways to develop independence and a positive identity. Develop healthy listening and communication skills. If children grow up in a healthy, loving family, there is less chance they will seek a substitute "family"—a gang.

If your teen is already in a gang or deeply involved with extremely negative friends, you'll need to work even harder to develop the personal skills and family qualities that will encourage the teen to "come home." Trying to separate teens and their friends is always difficult, no matter what you try, but there are several options. Involve the teen in meaningful activities (youth groups, sports teams, volunteer work, summer camps). When teens are involved in purposeful activities, they have less time, desire, and opportunity to get into trouble. Have the teen spend the summer with relatives. The change can offer the break the teen needs to make a fresh start. Change schools. This option may not be financially feasible, but don't automatically rule it out. It may be worth the financial sacrifice to give your teen the chance to see that there *are* teens who enjoy life without engaging in antisocial behavior. If all the above fail, don't give up. Be firm and keep open lines of communication. If we alienate teens in the process of protecting them, we may win a few battles but lose the "war," which is our desire to reach our healthy long-term parenting goals.

It's hard to trust teens who are exposed to negative influences (they *all* are). Things are so different and more dangerous than when we were teens. Parents have to do what is best for their children and their family. Most teens can be trusted more than their parents think they can. If teens respect themselves and have the courage, determination, and *skills* to resist peer pressure, other teens will not necessarily influence them. If parents express unconditional love, show trust and keep the lines of communication open, their teens are more likely to conduct themselves in trustworthy ways. As teens mature and come into their own identity, negative friends usually have less influence on them.

FINAL COMMENTS

Trouble-Shooting Guide

If you try F-A-X Listening and things don't go well, ask yourself the following questions:

- Did I focus on facts *or* did I acknowledge their feelings?
- Did I minimize or overreact to the problem *or* did I respond appropriately?
- Did I interrupt or talk about myself *or* did I give them a chance to talk freely?
- Did I tell them they were interpreting the situation wrong or did I ask questions so they would figure this out on their own?
- Did I give advice or did I ask what *they* could do?
- Did I criticize their ideas or ask "What would happen if . . . ?"

When we have faith in our children, it is easier to support them in respectful, empowering ways. The F-A-X process teaches children valuable skills they need when they have problems and we aren't there.

A Personal Story. My mother, in her parenting class, used to tell a story that I had forgotten. She reminded me of it and we compared notes on our perspectives of the situation.

When I was 16, my mother found me at the kitchen table at three in the morning. I told her that my boyfriend (who was 19 and traveled for his job) had invited me to visit him in California. I hadn't decided whether I was going to go and was writing down the pros and cons of my options.

Inside, my mother thought, "You'll go over my dead body!" To me, she said, "Well, I know you'll think through all the things that could happen if you go, good or bad, both there and here. I'm sure you'll make a responsible decision." She went back to bed and stayed awake for some time, praying. The next morning, she asked me what I had decided. I told her I had decided not to go.

Now a parent myself, I asked her, "What would you have said if I had decided to go?" Inside, she would have said, "Over my dead body!" To me, she probably would have said, "I have some serious concerns about you going and want to discuss them before you make a final decision." She would have asked me questions that would have led me to decide, on my own, that I shouldn't go.

*Looking back, I have even greater appreciation for my mother's parenting skills. Had she **told** me I couldn't go, I might have been tempted to rebel and go anyway. (Although I doubt I would have followed through.) She was wise to keep the ball in my court and give me a chance to make my own decision. I also realized how my problem-solving skills helped me make a responsible independent decision instead of an impulsive one.*

**The *process* of solving a problem
is often more important than the solution we reach.**

Whenever your kids are out of control, you can take comfort from the thought that even God's omnipotence did not extend to God's kids.

After creating heaven and earth, God created Adam and Eve.
And the first thing He said to them was: "Don't."
"Don't what?" Adam replied.
"Don't eat the forbidden fruit," God said.
"Forbidden fruit? We got forbidden fruit? Hey, Eve . . . we got Forbidden Fruit."
"No way!" she replied.
"Yes, WAY!"
"Don't eat that fruit!" said God.
"Why?"
"Because I'm your Father and I said so!" said God, wondering why he hadn't stopped after making the elephants.

A few minutes later, God saw the kids having an apple break and was angry.
"Didn't I tell you not to eat that fruit?" the First Parent asked.
"Uh huh," Adam replied.
"Then why did you eat it?"
"I dunno," Eve answered.
"She started it!" Adam said.
"Did not!"
"Did so!"
"DID NOT!"
Having had it with the two of them,
God's punishment was that Adam and Eve should have children of their own.
Thus the pattern was set and it has never changed.

But there is a reassurance in this story.
If you have persistently and lovingly tried to give your children wisdom and they haven't taken it, don't be hard on yourself. If God had trouble handling children, what makes you think it would be a piece of cake for you?

- - From the Internet, Author Unknown

SUMMARY SHEET
PROBLEM-SOLVING TOOLSET

F-A-X COMMUNICATION

B1: Focus on feelings

a. Identify the feeling (in your mind).
b. Identify the thought or event (in your mind).
c. Summarize in your own words what you think they mean.

If the child is confused or misinterpreting the situation, move to next step.

B2: Ask helpful questions ☆☆☆☆

- Ask open-ended questions to invite sharing, avoid yes/no answers.
- Clarify details so others understand why something happened.
- Restate possible mistaken beliefs so others can gain insight to the lessons involved.
- Give pearls of wisdom, not lectures.
- Guide others through their logic, to consider important points—without giving advice

If you and the child understand the problem, but need a solution or plan, move to the next step.

B3: X-amine possible solutions ☆☆☆☆

a. Brainstorm ideas. All ideas are okay. Simply list them.
b. Evaluate each idea. "What would happen if you did this?"
c. Choose a solution.

PRACTICE EXERCISES

Take the response you gave to the practice situations in the F-A-X Listening Toolset and continue the conversation. Practice the back and forth flow of listening, asking helpful questions, and moving into problem solving. In real life, the other person does not respond according to a script; each person will have different feelings or reasons that are hiding beneath the surface. So the best way to practice conversational problem solving is to find someone to role-play the child. Role playing also helps us practice reading nonverbal clues such as body language and tone of voice.

1. "Emily is spending the summer at her grandmothers! She's my best friend!"

2. "I'm scared to go to bed. There's a monster under my bed that comes out in the dark!"

3. "I don't feel like cleaning the toilets! I'll do it after I play."

4. "I played soccer at recess. Brandon and Chris were the captains and I was the last one to get picked."

5. "I can't believe I missed that catch. We lost the game because of me."

6. "Why do I have to get my picture taken? I hate to smile with these braces on."

7. Your preteen daughter says, "I'm not sure if I'm going to Tom's party. John will be there."

8. "Finals are next week and I've got to work every single night!"

Possible Answers

I am not going to detail an entire conversation for any of the situations. I have, however, done dozens of role-plays in my parenting class and have seen the variety of directions they can go. Here are some suggestions for common communication barriers you want to avoid and important points to remember.

1. *Child:* "Emily is spending the summer at her grandmothers! She's my best friend!"
   Parent: "You're really going to miss her, aren't you? (pause) All summer sounds like a long time, doesn't it?"

   Ask helpful questions. Don't rescue the child by offering suggestions, "We could . . ." Use helpful questions and *problem solving* to allow your child to come up with the ideas. "Can you think of a way you could keep in touch while she's gone?" "Would you like to do something special with her before she leaves?" The child might think of ideas like a calendar to count the days until Emily returns, writing letters, and planning a going-away party. If not, the parent can offer these suggestions and see if the child wants to use any of them.

2. *Child:* "I'm scared to go to bed. There's a monster under my bed that comes out in the dark!"
   Parent: "It must be scary to think there is a monster there."

   Ask helpful questions. Sit together in the dark and ask the child to point to the things that scare them when you aren't there. Then turn on the light and ask what the shape really is. Teach them how to talk themselves through their fear, "That's really my coat rack." *X-amine possible options.* Give them a flashlight or night light. If children refuse to believe the monsters aren't real, tell them that any monsters that enter their room have to obey their orders. They can talk to the monsters, make friends with them and ask them to play. They can tell the monsters to get out and leave them alone. Since their imagination is creating the problem, use their imagination to solve the problem. For example, give them some magic monster spray (a water spritzer) that scares monsters. Have them draw a picture of the monster and then change the picture to control the outcome. This is especially helpful with nightmares. As we tuck them in at night, we can describe a peaceful scene they can visualize. We can also pray with them, asking guardian angels to watch over them.

3. *Child:* "I don't feel like cleaning the toilets! I'll do it after I play."
   Parent: "I know it's hard to work when you'd rather be playing."

   Ask helpful questions that maintain your bottom-line limits. For example, you could offer choices, such as "Do you want to clean the toilet before you play and stay out until dinner? Or go play and come inside a half-hour earlier to clean the toilet?" *X-amine possible options* for a win/win solution. For example, the child might be willing to trade a job with the parent. These are not the only skills available to parents. In Chapter 10, "Clear Communication Toolset," we learn some quick and effective responses we can also use.

4. *Child:* "I played soccer at recess. Brandon and Chris were the captains and I was the last one to get picked."
   Parent: Listening response: "It hurts to be rejected like that." Or "It's discouraging to be the last one picked for a team."

   Ask questions that help children realize *on their own* that people have different reasons for making choices and we can get our feelings hurt when we incorrectly assume someone's motives. In this situation, here are some possible questions to ask: "If you were the captain, how would you decide who to pick?" "How do you think Brandon and Chris decided?" "Do you think that not picking you means they don't like you or that they just wanted to win?" If the child continued to play soccer, but was feeling discouraged, you can probably stop at this step. If the child quit when he was rejected, use *problem solving* to help the child consider other possible responses. "What else could you have done? What do you think would have happened?"

5. *Child:* "I can't believe I missed that catch. We lost the game because of me."
   Parent: "I can tell you're really disappointed you missed that catch. It's hard to make a mistake at such an important time."

   If we have discussed children's feelings and shown we understand, but they are wallowing in self-pity, we can *ask helpful questions*. "Is it possible your team might have lost the game anyway?" "Has anyone else missed a catch like that? How did you feel about the person? How did the other teammates treat the person? What did the person do?" Timing is everything, here. If the child is still caught up in his feelings, he will get more frustrated with these kinds of logical questions. If he has released most of those feelings, however, this will help reveal any unhelpful or inaccurate beliefs and can lead to *problem solving*. "What do you think you'll do at practice tomorrow?"

6. *Child:* "Why do I have to get my picture taken? I hate to smile with these braces on."
   Parent: "Are you feeling self-conscious about your braces?"

   Ask helpful questions to help children consider different viewpoints. Here are some possible questions: "Are there other students who have braces? How do you think they feel when they get their picture taken? Have you noticed how they smile in their pictures?" Use *problem solving* to help children plan a solution that meets their (and your) needs. Here are some possible options: children can practice smiling in a mirror, they can not get pictures taken that year, or, if parents want the pictures, they could agree to only give the pictures to relatives.

7. *Child:* Your preteen daughter says, "I'm not sure if I'm going to Tom's party. John will be there."
   Parent: "You sound like you aren't sure you want to see John. Any particular reasons?"

   If we have listened effectively, the daughter has probably revealed the *real* reason she doesn't want to see John (he's mean to her, she has a crush on him, or another reason). Depending on her reasons, it might be helpful to offer a few small pearls of wisdom about people's defensive reactions when they are mad or how people can act uninterested even if they have a crush on someone. If we *tell* someone, "don't let it bother you," we are minimizing the problem. We also need to be careful not to offer advice unless she asks. We can use helpful questions to clarify the problem and evaluate possible solutions, "What would happen if you . . . ?" "What do you think John would do?" "If you didn't go to the party, how would you feel? If you go and John (possible behavior), what could you do?" Practice any communication or anger management skills that would help her when she carries out her plan.

8. *Child:* "Finals are next week and I've got to work every single night!"
    Parent: "Wow, you're under a lot of pressure right now. You have extra studying you need to do, but they need you at work, too."

    Ask helpful questions that can help the teen *X-amine possible options*, "What do you plan to do?" "Would you get in trouble at work if you asked for one night off?" "Do you have any extra time you can spend studying for finals?" If the teen gets defensive with these questions, stop. Show respect for the teen's ability to work out a plan.

WHAT'S NEXT?

We have completed our tour of the Child Problem Toolbox. Practice the F-A-X process daily. When we take the time and make the effort to *really* listen and understand others, we accomplish so much: We open the lines of communication and build trust. Others learn problem-solving skills through first-hand experience. We also discover just how capable our children (and others) are of solving their *own* problems.

Chapter 9, "Keep Your Cool Toolset," is the first stop on our tour of the Parent Problem Toolbox (Step C of the Universal Blueprint). We review the process of identifying Parent problems and the toolsets we use to resolve problems that affect us. In the Keep Your Cool Toolset, we discuss healthy anger and stress management skills we can use every day in any setting—at home, work, or social settings —and can teach these skills to our children. It is critical to manage our anger before using any of the other tools in the Parent Problem Toolbox or it turns the tools into destructive weapons.

REFERENCES

1. For more information about fostering healthy sibling relationships and dealing with bullies and victims, read *Siblings Without Rivalry*, by Adele Faber and Elaine Mazlish (Norton Books, 1987).

STEP C
PARENT PROBLEM TOOLBOX

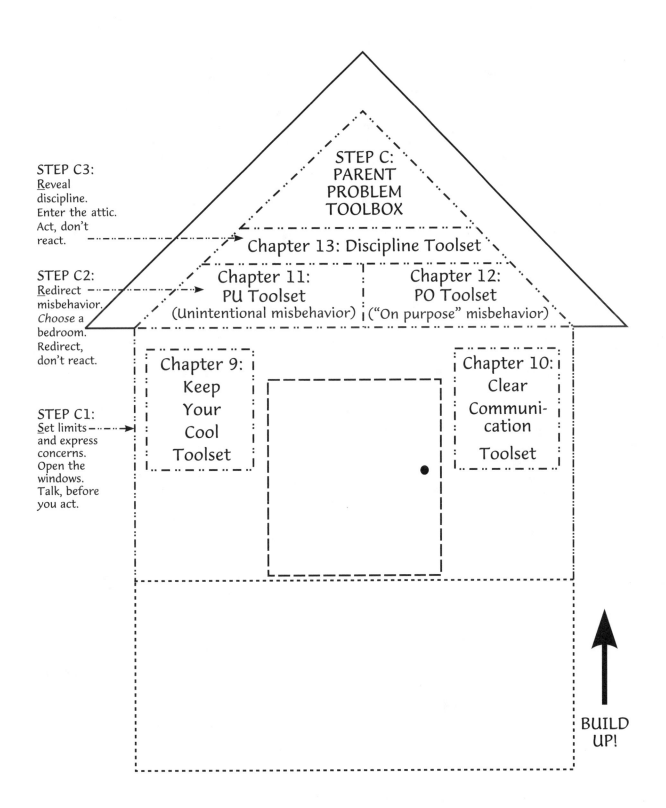

STEP C3:
<u>R</u>eveal
discipline.
Enter the attic.
Act, don't
react.

STEP C2:
<u>R</u>edirect
misbehavior.
Choose a
bedroom.
Redirect,
don't react.

STEP C1:
<u>S</u>et limits
and express
concerns.
Open the
windows.
Talk, before
you act.

STEP C:
PARENT
PROBLEM
TOOLBOX

Chapter 13: Discipline Toolset

Chapter 11:
PU Toolset
(Unintentional misbehavior)

Chapter 12:
PO Toolset
("On purpose" misbehavior)

Chapter 9:
Keep
Your
Cool
Toolset

Chapter 10:
Clear
Communi-
cation
Toolset

BUILD
UP!

STEP

C PARENT PROBLEM TOOLBOX

Once we enter a house, we can open the windows to let in fresh air and light or go to a bedroom. We can even explore the attic, where we store items that we don't use every day but don't want to throw away. Each part of the interior serves a specific purpose.

The inside of the Universal Blueprint's house contains several toolsets that serve specific purposes. One window is the Keep Your Cool Toolset; we open it to release the toxic fumes of anger and let in fresh healthy feelings. The other window is the Clear Communication Toolset; it helps us communicate with others so they can see and understand our feelings and concerns more clearly. The two bedrooms contain the tools we need to redirect problem behavior; the PU Toolset responds to unintentional misbehavior and the PO Toolset redirects misbehavior that seems to be on purpose. Finally, the attic contains the Discipline Toolset; the tools we don't use very often but can't throw away. When we have a problem, we walk up the stairs (Prevention Toolbox), open the door (Child Problem Toolbox), and come into the house (Parent Problem Toolbox). We walk step-by-step through the house to find all the tools we need to resolve our part of the problem.

IN THIS SECTION

Step C: Parent Problem Toolbox. The last three steps of the PASRR formula are within this toolbox.

Step C1: **S**et limits and express your feelings or concerns.

- Chapter 9, "Keep Your Cool Toolset," teaches us healthy anger and stress management skills that we can also teach to our children.

- Chapter 10, "Clear Communication Toolset," teaches us assertive, respectful, effective verbal responses. When children misbehave, we take the next step.

Step C2: **R**edirect misbehavior.

- Chapter 11, "PU Toolset" (**P**arent problem, **U**nintentional misbehavior), details the differences between PU and PO behavior and the options we have to redirect PU behavior.

- Chapter 12, "PO Toolset" (**P**arent problem, "**O**n purpose" misbehavior), teaches us how to identify the specific purpose behind PO behavior and which tools can prevent or stop it.

Step C3: **R**eveal discipline.

- Chapter 13, "Discipline Toolset," teaches us the difference between punishment and discipline, the four important parts of effective discipline, and the options available to us.

WHEN TO USE THE PARENT PROBLEM TOOLBOX

We *only* use the Parent Problem Toolbox when *we* have a concern or problem. When problems involve *any* of the SHARP RV issues (safety, health, appropriateness, rights, property, rules, or values), we use the Parent Problem Toolbox to plan our verbal response and any action needed. As with all the other tools in this book, we can use the Parent Problem Toolbox in adult relationships, too.

CHAPTER 9
KEEP YOUR COOL TOOLSET

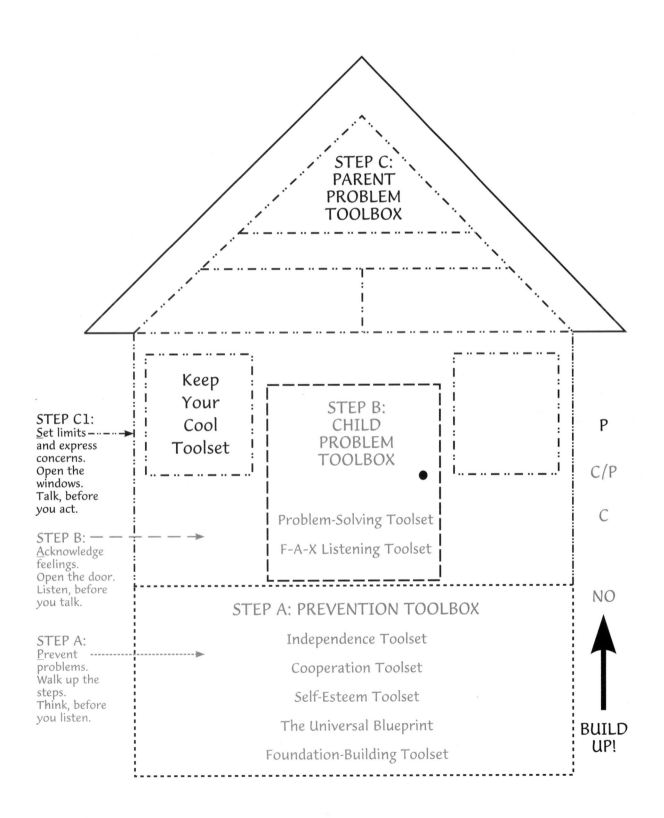

STEP C:
PARENT
PROBLEM
TOOLBOX

Keep
Your
Cool
Toolset

STEP C1:
Set limits
and express
concerns.
Open the
windows.
Talk, before
you act.

STEP B:
CHILD
PROBLEM
TOOLBOX

Problem-Solving Toolset

F-A-X Listening Toolset

STEP B:
Acknowledge
feelings.
Open the door.
Listen, before
you talk.

STEP A:
Prevent
problems.
Walk up the
steps.
Think, before
you listen.

STEP A: PREVENTION TOOLBOX

Independence Toolset

Cooperation Toolset

Self-Esteem Toolset

The Universal Blueprint

Foundation-Building Toolset

P

C/P

C

NO

BUILD
UP!

CHAPTER

9 KEEP YOUR COOL TOOLSET

Most houses have windows that provide fresh air and sunlight. A house without windows is a dark and dreary place. It is hard to see where we are, where we're going, and what we're doing. Windows also let out extra heat and toxic fumes that can build up inside. Without ventilation, these poisons can cause discomfort, illness, or even death.

People need a different kind of light—a clear vision of what's going on inside us. We need to see clearly what we are feeling, what we are doing, and where we are going. Without this sense of direction, we bump into obstacles and become lost. We also need a way to rid our bodies of toxic emotions. When there are no healthy outlets for angry emotions, the chemicals and energy they produce can bring emotional or physical discomfort, illness, or even death. We need to learn how to control our bodies and minds so we can release chronic anger and stress in healthy ways.

IN THIS CHAPTER

When dealing with a problem, we control our anger first, so we can keep our logic on-line and respond helpfully. This chapter encourages us to consider seven important ideas:

1. Anger is a natural human emotion—but there are healthy and unhealthy ways to express it.
2. Events and other people do not *cause* our anger and stress. Our *beliefs* about the people and events affect our feelings and responses.
3. We can stop or control the anger cycle by *choosing* to control our reactions.
4. We can have different styles of "recharging" our energy and learn techniques, consistent with our style, that prevent and relieve stress buildups.
5. There are healthy, assertive ways to relieve the energy anger causes—verbally and physically.
6. Once we can identify someone's individual anger and stress style, we can design an individualized anger and stress management plan for ourselves and our children.
7. We can use these skills to defuse others' anger and teach children healthy stress and anger management skills.

WHEN TO USE THIS TOOLSET

It is important to use the Keep Your Cool Toolset before any of the other tools in the Parent Problem Toolbox, because anger can turn our tools into weapons—to blame or get revenge. These tactics only cause more defensiveness and rebellious behavior. As with all the tools, we can use the Keep Your Cool Toolset in *any* relationship, because we can feel angry and stressed in situations that have nothing to do with parenting.

WHAT IS ANGER?

Anger is a physical and emotional reaction to a perceived threat.

In prehistoric times, humans faced many dangerous situations (like large animals), so the body developed the ability to generate extra strength and energy to stay and fight or quickly escape the danger.

When this fight-or-flight response kicks in, adrenaline dramatically increases, the heart pumps faster, blood pressure rises, and blood flows faster. The body releases chemicals that make muscles tense, stronger, quicker, and prepared for action (either fighting or fleeing). These chemicals also cause people to lose some of their self-control, which could cause them to wait before acting. (A dangerous thing to do when a large animal is attacking!)

As the human brain developed, people learned how to better control their environment. They had less need for fighting or fleeing and learned to use their brains to analyze and solve problems. Nevertheless, our bodies still have this automatic fight-or-flight response, which we still need in emergencies.

Busy lifestyles can frequently trigger the fight-or-flight response. Traffic jams, hectic schedules, annoying interruptions, and conflicts with others are just a few of the events that can trigger chemical reactions in the body. If the body triggers these reactions daily, the extra tension and stress chemicals can seem normal, but their damaging effects can go unnoticed—until it's too late.

If people don't use these extra chemicals for action, the buildup hurts the body. Fat, which is sent to the blood for energy to fight or run, turns into cholesterol, which causes heart disease and eventual death. Chronic anger and stress can also cause high blood pressure, headaches, stomachaches, skin irritations, digestive problems, and eating disorders. Nonphysical problems can develop, too. People can become accident-prone and their hostility, sarcasm, and critical attitudes can destroy their relationships with others. Without healthy outlets for these extra emotions and chemicals, the body acts like a car going 9000 r.p.m. in neutral—eventually, it burns out.

Healthy Anger

Conflicts are unavoidable when two or more people with individual opinions and personalities live together. *How* people handle these conflicts depends on their skills and choices.

Destructive anger destroys relationships and hurts the body.
Constructive anger uses the extra energy from conflicts to resolve them peacefully and respectfully.

Destructive anger hurts others by trying to control them, win arguments, or get revenge. It gets results because angry reactions get attention. The strength and tension in someone's face can cause fear and obedience. However, anger may lose its effectiveness over time. People build walls to protect themselves from the angry person and their own feelings and reactions. What once only took a raised voice can later take yelling, threats, or even punishment to get the same results. This cycle has serious long-term consequences on the relationship and the self-esteem of the people in it.

When parents try to control their children, they often forget to control their *own* behavior. Self-control is more difficult when we are angry. Emotions are high, which lowers our ability to think straight. To respond effectively to problems, we need to ease our physical reaction to stress *and* increase our ability to think clearly. Instead of *losing* our temper, we can *use* it in positive ways to solve the problem.

Constructive anger separates *feeling* angry from *acting* angry. It releases the energy created by anger and stress in healthy ways, using it to help resolve the conflict. It is possible to be angry *and* respond assertively and respectfully. Healthy conflict can provide opportunities to practice anger management, negotiation, and problem solving.

STEPS OF CONSTRUCTIVE ANGER/STRESS MANAGEMENT

The abc's of Constructive Anger/Stress Management

Step C1:
a. *Become aware of your anger/stress cycle.* **(Keep Your Cool Toolset)**
b. *Relieve the pressure of the anger/stress.* **(Keep Your Cool Toolset)**
c. *Plan an assertive response to the problem.* **(Clear Communication Toolset)**

In this chapter, we learn how to do steps a and b, using the Keep Your Cool Toolset. These two steps get our emotions under control and our logic on-line. Once we have calmed down enough to think clearly about how we want to handle the situation, we can move to Step c and use the Clear Communication Toolset to formulate our response. This a-b-c process can take a split second, unless we are *extremely* angry. In that case, we control our anger long enough to respond to the problem helpfully. Then we take time to deal with our remaining feelings in a healthy way.

a. Become Aware of Your Stress/Anger Cycle ☆☆☆☆

If we understand how anger eruptions happen, we can recognize unhealthy anger, unhelpful beliefs and responses, break unhealthy reaction habits, and replace them with healthier alternatives for relieving stress and expressing anger.

WHAT *REALLY* CAUSES ANGER?

Think about a situation that sometimes makes you angry, such as a traffic jam. Most of us can remember a time when we got frustrated and angry and a time when we handled the same situation calmly. Most people mistakenly believe that other people and events *cause* their anger and stress. If this was true, our reaction would always be the same—we would *always* get angry. Since this doesn't happen, there must be another factor.

The process of getting angry can take a split-second, but if we slow down and look at what's really happening, we see there are actually four steps involved[1] :

First, an event happens. Then, in our minds, we tell ourselves something—it could be accurate or inaccurate, rational or irrational, helpful or unhelpful. The feelings we experience are a direct result of what we tell ourselves—what we *believe* the event means. We actually talk ourselves into believing we *should* feel a certain emotion. Finally, based on our feelings and beliefs, we respond. We actually *choose* our feelings, but are rarely aware of this amazingly quick process.

Remember in the Child Problem Toolbox, when we learned that anger is a secondary emotion? It is important to remember this now. Anger can result from a build up of other emotions—frustration, hurt, annoyance, or harassment. If we get in touch with these *primary* emotions, we can tap into the *real* cause of our anger.

The Anger Cycle

EVENT what happens → BELIEF what you think | FEELING how you feel | RESPONSE what you do

Our belief about the event causes our feelings—and our feelings influence our response. If our beliefs are inaccurate, our feelings will be irrational and so will our response. If we view the event in rational, helpful ways, we see our primary feelings more easily. This helps us respond more effectively.

Here's an example of how positive and negative beliefs can influence a parent's response to the same situation:

Negative Outcome

Event:	Joey complains about the food his father serves for dinner.
Negative Belief:	The father thinks, "He is so *ungrateful!* After all the time I spent cooking dinner, *the least he could do* is show some appreciation. If *I* had ever complained about food *when I was a kid*, I would have gotten *no* dinner!"
Feelings:	Put out, taken advantage of, resentful, and angry.
Response:	The father calls Joey "ungrateful," lectures him about starving kids in Africa, and tells him "when I was a kid . . ." stories. The father sends Joey to bed without dinner, then stews about it through the rest of the meal. He has indigestion all evening and blames Joey for making him sick.

Positive Outcome

Event:	Joey complains about the food his father serves for dinner.
Positive Belief:	The father thinks, "*I wish* he wouldn't complain after I've taken the time to cook a meal. *I'd like* him to appreciate my efforts, even if he doesn't like it. *I can* use this to *teach* Joey about good manners."
Feeling:	Unappreciated, offended by impolite comment, motivated to prevent similar behavior in the future.
Response:	The father says, "People don't like it when others criticize their cooking. It hurts their feelings, especially since they made the time and effort to cook something. We don't have to like what people fix, but we can still be polite to the cook. We can take small servings and say 'no, thank you' to more."

As you can see, the key step in anger control is how we choose to interpret events. That is where the chain reaction *really* starts.

CHOOSE YOUR BELIEFS

If we can identify and change our self-talk, we can better manage our anger. When we *choose* our beliefs, we put things in perspective. We get in touch with our primary, rational feelings, instead of getting hooked into the anger trap.

Unhelpful beliefs:
- *Use absolute words,* such as *should, must, have to, need, always,* and *never.* These words lock us into all-or-nothing thinking which keeps us from thinking about other perspectives, feelings, and responses.
- *Make assumptions* about the other person's motives or how people are *supposed* to feel and act in similar situations.
- *Judge others' feelings/beliefs* as wrong or take their comments and actions personally.

Helpful, assertive beliefs:
- *Use flexible, positive words* such as, *I can, I choose, I wish, I hope, I don't like,* and *I would prefer.*
- *Consider other points of view.*
- *Are objective* and nonjudgmental.
- *Focus on solutions,* rather than blame.

Since our choice of beliefs directly affects our feelings and response, let's look at the four styles of anger and the beliefs behind each style. People usually develop these beliefs in childhood when they see and hear others expressing anger.

STYLES OF ANGER

Passive anger is unexpressed. People stuff their anger or only hint at it.
Aggressive anger explodes and hurts people (physically or emotionally).
Passive-Aggressive anger hurts others (aggressive) in passive ways.
Assertive anger is healthy and honest without hurting others.

Passive Anger

Passive anger, or stuffing feelings, is usually the result of believing that anger is bad. It can have one or more of the following beliefs:

- If I express my anger, I might upset the other person and then that person won't like me anymore.
- Expressing anger is childish and bad. I must always be in control of myself.
- I must be a perfect parent—who is always calm, cool, and collected.
- I must avoid conflict at all cost. To do this, I must avoid expressing my feelings, or ignore what is happening, even if others violate my rights.

People who stuff their anger were often taught as children that anger is an unacceptable emotion. If they expressed anger, they got sent to bed or to a corner. This taught them to not show their anger. The anger, however, didn't just disappear. They learned ways to deny and avoid their feelings or cover them up with other thoughts, feelings, and actions. Some people turn their anger inward, which can lead to harmful habits such as drug or alcohol abuse, eating disorders, depression, sleep disorders, and physical illnesses. Instead of trying to stuff the anger altogether, these people can learn to express it in nondestructive ways.

Aggressive Anger

Aggressive anger explodes at targets. It is the result of believing that other people *make* us angry so they should be punished for upsetting us. Aggressive people control their anger by trying to control the *person* they blame for causing the anger. Aggressive anger can have one or more of the following beliefs:

- People who hurt me should be punished and controlled. It's their fault I'm angry. If they are wrong or treat me unfairly, I must do something to make them stop or change.
- I am the boss and my children must not forget that.
- If my children do not act properly at all times, they're bad and should be punished for making me look bad.

People who act out their anger aggressively often feel relief after the outburst, but those on the receiving end usually feel hurt or scared. People who express their anger aggressively usually pass on blame to others. This eases their load and helps them avoid responsibility. "It's not *my* fault!" Sometimes they hold their anger until they can find a target. Children, who naturally misbehave at times, are often targets for a parent's blame. Parents who save their anger, waiting for a target, often erupt when their children misbehave and overreact to the child's misbehavior. They let out not only their valid concerns, but also their stored up anger and blame from previous events.

Passive-Aggressive Anger

Passive-aggressive anger is a less obvious form of aggression. The most common form is to outwardly deny anger, but do hurtful things that only angry people would do. A few examples are the silent treatment, conveniently forgetting, or ignoring. Defiant compliance is obeying a command in a hurtful way to get revenge. (For example, cutting the grass *and* all the flower beds.) Passive-aggressive anger can also be outwardly passive and inwardly aggressive, as in putting ourselves down to others. Passive-aggressive anger can have any of the beliefs listed so far *and* any of the following beliefs:

- If my children really loved me, they would want to please me. I shouldn't have to ask them.
- I am sacrificing the best years of my life for my children. They should show more gratitude.
- I can't help how I feel and act. It's all because of my past. It's their (the event's) fault.
- I don't want anyone to know I'm angry, but I've got to say or do something to get revenge on this person for hurting me.

Assertive Anger

Assertive anger expresses emotions honestly without hurting our self or others in the process. It appropriately expresses feelings after deciding how to best express the anger. Assertive anger tries to fix the problem, not fix the blame. It can have one or more of the following beliefs:

- While things might happen or people might do things I don't like, they don't *make* me angry. I have a *choice* about my feelings and whether to be angry.
- I can choose my beliefs and find healthy ways to express my feelings and needs.
- I can focus on win/win solutions, instead of blaming or trying to change others.

REWRITING UNHELPFUL BELIEF STATEMENTS

Change	*To*
I need	I want
I have to	I'd like to
I should *or* I must	I choose
They should	I wish they would
I must *or* I want	I would prefer
I can't	I can
This must happen	I wish *or* I'd like this to happen
I expect	I hope

PUT THINGS IN PERSPECTIVE

When we stop to examine our beliefs, we become aware of our primary feelings. But we can still get hooked into looking at the conflict from our personal, biased view. To grasp and maintain an objective perspective, try asking the following questions:

1. **Is this a situation I can change?** Even if we are only two percent of the problem, we can change that two percent. If the situation is out of our control, we may need to adjust to the situation and accept it. To do this we can step over it or find some humor in it (which is usually best in these situations). We may need to shift our focus from resisting what is happening to planning how we can live with it.

*A **Personal Story.*** *When I worked at a runaway shelter, there were frequently parents who were unwilling to change in order to resolve the problems with their teens. There wasn't any blatant abuse or neglect (so removal from the home was not an option), but it was clearly difficult for these teens to get along with their parents. In these situations, our case plans often focused on helping the teens accept that their parents might not change and find a way to love their parents in spite of their behavior. We'd help the teens plan ways to live in their home environment, until they turned 18. Beyond independent living skills, we taught them how to choose helpful attitudes, beliefs, and behaviors that might help them do their part to improve the family, whether their parents ever met them halfway.*

2. **How important is this?** Is this issue really important in the scheme of life? Is it worth getting upset over? Is a higher principle involved? Is serious danger present? If we can't answer yes to one of these questions, we've probably lost our perspective and our anger is causing us to blow things out of proportion.

   If we weigh the importance of the problem against the consequences of our anger to the person and our relationship, we can pick our battles carefully. Major issues usually involve physical, emotional, or moral danger: serious SHARP RV issues. Minor issues are usually a matter of preference: food, clothing, hair styles, and housecleaning habits. We can still address these problems, but not make the *issue* more important than our relationship or inner peace.

   For example, if children refuse to use safety gear (such as a bicycle helmet or car seat), we need to stand our ground more firmly than if children refuse to bathe, but are not filthy. The cost of arguing about safety gear is worth the benefit; it could save their lives. The cost of forcing a bath, which could increase power struggles, damage the relationship, or create a hatred for baths, is not worth the benefit; children are more clean than they already were.

   > **If we experience more than two or three unhealthy anger episodes per day, our anger could be greatly affecting our body or relationships. And if more than a fourth of our angry events are not worth the cost, we are probably having too many of them.**

3. **Is there another way to solve this problem besides getting angry?** What are our goals? Are we trying to win or make someone lose? Are we really interested in solving the problem with a win/win solution? If we aren't ready to let go of our anger, we go to Step b, Relieving the Pressure of Anger/Stress, before we respond. Once we get the anger out of our system, we can do something constructive to solve the problem. If we *are* ready to respond, we skip the next step and go to Step c, Plan an Assertive Response (Clear Communication Toolset).

b. Relieve the Pressure of the Anger/Stress

Each of us has a volcano inside us that can angrily erupt. While it may seem our volcano could erupt for many reasons, there are two basic types of eruptions.

> **There are two types of anger eruptions:**
>
> - *Smoldering embers* are slow buildups of stressful situations that eventually spill over or erupt.
> - *Flash fires* are caused by events that push an emotional trigger button that sets off a sudden eruption.

Whether we are experiencing a stress overload or a trigger-button eruption, taking a time-out is recommended. Time-outs can be as short as ten seconds or last an hour. It depends on how much time we need and how much time we can reasonably take. Unless we are dealing with a life or death situation, we can usually spare three to five minutes. While we may want more time, we can learn to squeeze a half an hour of relaxation into five minutes. This helps us hang on until we can take a longer time-out later.

During our time-out, we can either emotionally withdraw or physically remove ourselves until we regain control. (When children are very young, we need to make sure they will be safe and occupied while we are gone or stay with them and tune out distractions we can't avoid.) If the timing or circumstances of a situation don't allow us to take an immediate time-out, we can give a quick, controlled, effective response and disengage. Once we calm down, we can resolve the problem further.

SMOLDERING EMBERS NEED STRESS MANAGEMENT

Smoldering embers are a result of built-up stress. Any change, whether positive (the birth of a baby) or negative (a divorce) can be stressful. Even everyday irritations (a baby's constant crying) and frustrations (a curious toddler) can cause stress to build. Children occasionally do things that are annoying, irritating, and even infuriating. It's part of the parenting territory. There are certain stages of development that will test our patience more than others. While most parents have felt like hurting their child at some time, *acting* on that feeling is totally off limits!

Sometimes our stress has nothing to do with our children, such as marital or work conflicts. We can explain to our children that we're dealing with a problem (we don't have to go into details) that has made us angry, sad, or frustrated. Reassure them that we are *not* upset with them. If we say nothing, children pick up on our stress, which increases *their* stress level. As children feel more stressed, they are more likely to misbehave. As their misbehavior increases, our stress increases and we are more likely to blow our tops. See the vicious cycle?

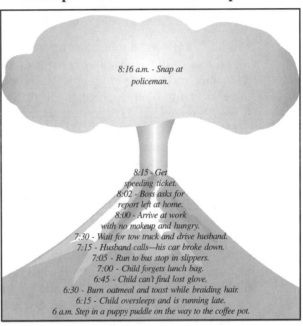

Example of Stress Overload Eruption

8:16 a.m. - Snap at policeman.

8:15 - Get speeding ticket.
8:02 - Boss asks for report left at home.
8:00 - Arrive at work with no makeup and hungry.
7:30 - Wait for tow truck and drive husband.
7:15 - Husband calls—his car broke down.
7:05 - Run to bus stop in slippers.
7:00 - Child forgets lunch bag.
6:45 - Child can't find lost glove.
6:30 - Burn oatmeal and toast while braiding hair.
6:15 - Child oversleeps and is running late.
6 a.m. Step in a puppy puddle on the way to the coffee pot.

Smoldering embers build when we handle several small or big problems well, but don't take the time to calm down and regroup. As a result, our stress level increases with each new event. Soon, our overall stress level increases so much that even a small irritation can trigger our wrath—the straw that breaks the camel's back.

The real key to managing stress overloads is to prevent them. Our bodies send us signals, such as shaky hands, rapid and shallow breathing, sweating, or knots in the stomach or neck. We can become more aware of our body signals and take time for a calming activity (even ten seconds) to prevent a stress overflow.

There are several common stress management techniques. Some of these calming activities can be done any time, anywhere. Others require some planning:

- **Deep breathing** is the simplest relaxation technique. It involves paying attention to how and *where* we are breathing. We breathe shallowly from the upper chest when we are stressed. Deep breaths come from the diaphragm (which makes the stomach expand) and release tension. When we take a breath, we want to hold it for several seconds. When we exhale, we imagine blowing out all our tension or anger. When we realize we are breathing quickly and shallow, we remind ourselves to breath more, talk less.

- **Muscle relaxation** is helpful for tense muscles. Simply start at the toes and work up to the head. With each deep breath, we focus full attention on a muscle group—toes, then ankles, calves, knees, thighs, and so on. As we exhale, we imagine all the tension flowing out, like melting wax. Tension from the lower body (below the chest) flows out the toes and tension from the upper body flows out the fingertips. Our goal is to become as relaxed as a rag doll. Sometimes we don't realize how tense our muscles are until we do this exercise.

- **Meditation** helps us let go of all thoughts and tension. We choose a word or phrase and focus our attention on it. We repeat the word or phrase in a slow, rhythmic way, either mentally or out loud. As distracting thoughts come to mind, we simply refocus on the word or phrase and our breathing. We allow the distracting thought to pass by, like a floating cloud, instead of holding on to it.

- **Prayer** is a powerful relaxation technique. Whatever our religion, contacting the universal consciousness or our higher power brings inner strength and serenity. There are many books and resources, such as prayer groups, which help us learn to pray and share the insights we gain from it. Learn to pray? Yes. A common mistake people make when praying is to plead or fill their prayer time talking *to* God. This helps us *share* a concern—but we must truly and completely *release* it and trust in God's power to solve it. More powerful than talking to God is the ability to *listen* to the thoughts and images we receive when the mind is quiet. In this respect, prayer is similar to meditation. Our focus can be a word like God, peace, or love, a scripture, or any other word or image that fits our religious beliefs.

- **Visual imagery** uses our imagination to picture a scene that is relaxing or gives us strength. To calm down, we can imagine we are at the beach, mountains, a waterfall, or any other relaxing scene. A scene from nature is usually best, and it is important to imagine all five senses in the scene—what does it look, sound, smell, taste, and feel like? (There are audio tapes that guide listeners through a calming scene with relaxing suggestions or simply provide nature sounds to set the mood.) We can also use visualization to see ourselves calmly and assertively handling an upsetting situation. We mentally rehearse the conversation several times, until we feel comfortable enough to try the approach.

Most people find it difficult to *make* time for relaxation. If we think about how much time we spend feeling upset, tense, or worried, we can choose, instead, to use that time and energy relaxing. The benefits of stress management have been repeatedly proven scientifically: the body releases chemicals that can slow or stop heart disease; regulate sleeping, eating, and digestion; increase creativity, work productivity, and brain power; improve interpersonal relationships; and even slow down or reverse aging.

> ***A Personal Story.*** *Stress management is one area where I have a hard time practicing what I preach. Over ten years ago, when I should have been on a maternity break, I continued volunteering nearly 40 hours a week for the nonprofit organization I had started. A serious conflict arose with a person with whom I had to work very closely. This person refused to resolve the problem with me directly and wouldn't accept mediation. The board of directors was unwilling to enforce the conflict-resolution mandates in the bylaws, so I took a leave of absence. Six months later, nothing had changed, so I resigned.*

*My body couldn't handle the ongoing, intense stress of this unresolved conflict. My adrenaline had been so high for so long, it could no longer regulate itself and I developed debilitating physical symptoms. Stress management was the key to regaining and maintaining my health, but I had great difficulty learning the techniques. Visualization was difficult and I was easily distracted by thoughts of more purposeful activities I could be doing. I finally took a meditation class and completely relaxed for the first time in years. I realized that relaxation **was** a purposeful activity. I also promised myself that I would never again allow any person or event to rob me of my inner peace. **Nothing** is worth sacrificing my health.*

Recharge Styles ☆☆☆☆

When we have too much energy or too little, we need a "recharge." What relaxes or stimulates one person does not necessarily help others, because there are two styles of recharging one's energy supply: internal and external.

Internal rechargers get their energy from within. They need to be alone regularly to regain control or recharge their energy supply or they get irritable. When physical isolation isn't possible, they might tune out for a short time. They are often misunderstood and pressured to be a part of groups when they need time alone. Traditional stress management techniques usually work well for them.

When internal rechargers feel stressed or angry, they need to ask people for space, instead of pushing them away or ignoring them. They need to avoid interruptions when working and take time to think before responding to requests or problems.

Internal rechargers can stop one block from home after work and recharge before going home to their children. If they are stay-at-home parents, they can use nap times or quiet play times to recharge—not to do chores or other work. Otherwise, they'll run out of energy by the bewitching hour—dinner time. If a spouse is an internal recharger, we can give the person about 15 minutes to unwind, before demanding time or attention. If 15 minutes is not enough, negotiate an agreement. For example, agree to immediately give the person some time alone if the person agrees to then spend time with you and/ or the children.

If you are an internal recharger, try some of the following activities during your down time:

INTERNAL RECHARGE ACTIVITIES

- Sing, hum, or whistle.
- Listen to music on headphones.
- Write a poem or song.
- Just sit there.
- Paint a picture.
- Write a letter or in a journal.
- Do a crossword puzzle.
- Wake up before anyone else.

- Daydream.
- Curl up by the fire and read a book.
- Take a rainy-day nap.
- Enjoy a cool glass of juice or warm cup of decaffeinated anything.
- Soak in bubbles, a whirlpool, or sauna.
- Enjoy the beauty and sounds of nature: clouds, sunset, birds, wind, rain.

External rechargers draw their energy from the world around them. They need to interact with other people or activities to get energy, calm down, or work through problems. Without opportunities to talk with others, they get cranky and stir crazy. They usually have a harder time learning the traditional stress management techniques.

External rechargers who work outside the home may not feel as drained at the end of the day as an internal recharger does. If they are stay-at-home parents, they are often chomping at the bit for a spouse to come home so they can interact with an adult. If the spouse is an internal recharger, this can cause a conflict in needs upon his (or her) arrival. One person cannot meet all our recharge needs, so external rechargers need to plan outings with other adults.

External rechargers can get energy from anyone or any *thing* outside themselves, not just a spouse or close friend. They can make time each day (or weekly, at the least) to do one or more of the following external-recharge activities:

EXTERNAL RECHARGE ACTIVITIES

- Attend a support group, class, or workshop.
- Participate in a team/group sport.
- Watch children play or play with them.
- Do something adventurous now and then (skydiving, bungee jumping).

- Hug someone.
- Pet an animal.
- Get a back rub.
- Have a picnic.
- Attend an athletic event.
- Rock a sleeping baby.
- Talk to another external recharger.

Internal/External (Combination) Rechargers can get their energy from within or from others, depending on their activities that day and what they need to reach a centered balance.

> *A Personal Story. When Chris was born, I resigned my full-time job to be home full time with him. I was used to daily interaction with many people. Now I was home alone with a child who couldn't talk. I was starved for adult companionship and found few resources for meeting others during the day. It was difficult, financially and emotionally, to be a full-time mother, but my heart had reasons to stay home that were stronger than my need to socialize. Then, I thought of a compromise. I started a local discussion group for stay-at-home parents. Eight years later, when I returned to part-time work, the group was a non-profit organization with almost 100 members.*

> *During my eight years as an at-home mother, I was an external recharge person. When my husband came home, I had difficulty waiting for him to unwind before I rattled on about my day. Now, I am usually an internal recharger. I teach parenting classes almost every day (or evening) and it takes a lot of energy to discuss and meet everyone's needs. My husband has time to himself while I'm gone, so when I come home, he wants to talk about his work day or a TV show he's watching. I try hard to listen to his stories and share a little about my day, but it's often a short summary. Usually, I just want to relax without talking for a while. It's ironic that we both have opposite recharge styles from what we had years ago.*

There are some recharge activities that serve both needs, depending on whether we do them by ourselves (internal) or with someone else (external). Some can be internal *and* external, because the solitary activity involves an energy source outside us.

INTERNAL/EXTERNAL (COMBINATION) RECHARGE ACTIVITIES

- Go for a walk.
- Watch a thunderstorm.
- Look at the stars, moon, sunrise.
- Listen to night sounds.
- See a play, movie, or concert.
- Climb a tree.
- Window-shop.
- Search for four-leaf clovers.

- Go sailing/paddle-boating.
- Roast marshmallows.
- Do a hobby.
- Look at old photos.
- Watch a comedy or read a funny book and laugh.
- Go for a swim.
- Visit a park or forest.

These lists of recharge activities are just ideas to get you started. Some might not fit your schedule, needs, or interests. There is no right or wrong recharge style; both serve a healthy purpose. They are part of a person's biology and personality makeup. We need to be sensitive to others' needs for time alone or interaction with others. This includes our children.

FLASH FIRES NEED ERUPTION OUTLETS

Flash fires are sudden explosions that can result from single events that push our emotional trigger buttons. Trigger buttons are reactions that were usually programmed at an early age from an upsetting memory. When a similar event occurs, it triggers a quick, extreme emotional reaction.

A Personal Story. Being rushed in the morning and morning arguments were two of my trigger buttons. As a child, I was always running late in the morning. If someone nagged or pushed me to hurry, I'd get a big knot in my stomach. My brother and I would also fight and argue almost every morning before school. My days often started out on the wrong foot and I'd cry as I walked to school. For years, when someone rushed me or picked an argument in the morning, it would spark an emotional, tense, irritated reaction from me. These events triggered memories and childish reactions that, at the time, were the only way I knew how to cope with the situation.

Common Trigger Buttons

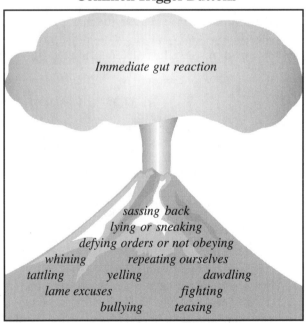

Immediate gut reaction

sassing back
lying or sneaking
defying orders or not obeying
whining   repeating ourselves
tattling   yelling   dawdling
lame excuses   fighting
bullying   teasing

Children do not *program* their parents' buttons, they simply discover them! When children are discouraged, frustrated or hurt, they can use these buttons to serve a purpose. This is PO behavior, a **P**arent problem with **O**n purpose misbehavior. If children can push their parents' buttons, they can get their parents' attention, cause the parents to lose control (which proves the *child* is in control), or get revenge. Although trigger buttons seem to *make* us lose control, we are really the only ones who can control them. We can re-program our buttons and *plan* how we react to similar situations in the future.

> **There are three basic steps in re-programming trigger buttons:**
>
> i. We become aware of the behaviors and situations that set us off.
> ii. Later, when we aren't upset, we examine the steps in our anger cycle, especially how our beliefs are contributing to our feelings and actions. We then *plan* how we *want* to respond to these situations, choosing more helpful beliefs and responses.
> iii. The next time a similar situation occurs (and it probably will), we briefly pause to relieve the pressure of our anger or stress. We follow through with our planned response, instead of emotionally reacting.

At first, this process simply increases the time we pause between the event and our response. As we use our new response more often, it becomes more comfortable and comes to mind more quickly. After a few times, we have de-programmed our trigger button and replaced it with a more helpful response.

Types of Anger Energy

Despite all our efforts to avoid stress and anger, there will still be times we erupt. The energy we experience can be verbal, physical, or both. Our ultimate goal is to replace any automatic, unhealthy reactions with healthier outlets for our anger energy. To do this, we need to first change *how* we release the anger, while we work on the future goal of not getting angry as often.

Verbal anger energy most often comes out as yelling, screaming, or saying something we later regret. If this is our tendency, our goal is to express our feelings in respectful and assertive ways. Simply saying nothing keeps our anger energy inside. Without an outlet, it does not go away. When we feel like yelling or saying something in anger that we might later regret, we need to bite our tongues and take a time-out. We release the anger energy by expressing ourselves through activities like those listed below. Once we've released the anger energy, we can plan a constructive way to express our feelings or resolve the problem using the Universal Blueprint.

> **HEALTHY VERBAL ANGER ENERGY OUTLETS**
>
> - Yell, scream or cry into a pillow.
> - Say "stop" to yourself or out loud.
> - Draw a picture of how you feel.
> - Sing loudly, sing opera, or yodel.
> - Growl (not *at* anyone).
> - Blow up a balloon and set it loose.
> - Go into a room alone, close the door, and let it all out.
> - Talk to someone you know will be supportive.
> - List the positive qualities of the other person in the conflict.
> - Carry on an imaginary conversation with the person with whom you're upset.
> - Write a letter or in a journal.

Physical anger energy builds up in a way that makes it seem almost impossible to control our actions. The physical changes that occur during anger are very real and overwhelming for some people and *must* come out—somehow. It *is* possible to hold back our impulses long enough to get to a safe place and release our energy in healthier ways. We sit on our hands if we have to and then take an immediate time-out. During our time-out, we can do one of the following activities:

HEALTHY PHYSICAL ANGER ENERGY OUTLETS

- Knead and punch dough.
- Rake leaves, then jump in them.
- Play a sport.
- Polish your shoes.
- Clean a closet or dresser drawer.
- Have a pillow fight.
- Mop, vacuum, or dust.
- Skip rope.
- Throw away something you don't like.
- Hit a pillow, punching bag, bop bag, or spring bag.
- Do a job you've been putting off.
- Pound out a dent.
- Rearrange a room.
- Clean out the garage.
- Play kick the can.
- Distract yourself in mindless activity.
- Climb a hill.
- Do a hobby.
- Do an angry dance. (Stomp, jump, flail your arms. There are no directions, each person has a unique dance style.)
- Take a walk. (Stroll if you're stressed. Walk briskly if you're angry.)

Whenever possible, go outside to release physical anger energy. Doing some of these activities inside can make the energy feel like it's trapped and bouncing off the walls.

Physical and verbal (combination) anger energy can surge at the same time. When it does, we can combine some of the activities listed above, or try some of the following activities:

HEALTHY VERBAL *AND* PHYSICAL ANGER ENERGY OUTLETS

- Exercise, blowing out air powerfully (or grunting) when you exhale.
- Blow into a paper bag or balloon then pop it.
- Throw towels into a bathtub (or rolled-up socks into a laundry basket) and grunt (or mumble what you feel like saying to the person you're angry with).
- Throw marshmallows into a sink with a karate yell as you throw.
- Write your feelings. Don't censor yourself. Write whatever comes to your mind. Rip up the letter, as a symbolic way to let go of the feelings and problem.

We may feel silly doing some of these activities, but if we are alone, who cares! It's better to get the anger out in a silly way than to destroy a relationship or hurt someone. Just pick those activities you feel comfortable doing.

A Personal Story. My parents were always nurturing, calm, and skilled, even when they were upset. I experienced emotions strongly, but didn't learn healthy ways to release or express them or the energy they caused. Instead, I would stuff my feelings until I exploded. When my children were young, this scared all of us and I was afraid that even I could be abusive. I had to work very hard to learn how to express emotions appropriately, before I reach my boiling point. I can still lose it if I don't walk away soon enough.

When Amber was about three, we were singing silly songs while I made a snack. I bent down, put my face right in front of hers, and made a goofy face while I sang. In her glee, she clapped my cheeks—so hard it left slap marks on my cheeks. This immediately triggered a button from my childhood memories with my brother and I almost smacked her back. I caught myself as my hand was starting to rise. I backed up against the kitchen counter and leaned on my hands. Tears came to my eyes as the stinging in my cheeks increased. I was ready to yell at her, so I literally bit my tongue. Amber had a shocked look on her face. She didn't mean to hurt me and was just realizing she had. I couldn't control myself much longer and ran out of the room.

I went to my room and cried, but was worried about leaving Amber alone, so I quickly returned. She was crying—she felt so bad that she had hurt me. I was still furious, though, and started to yell at her for crying! "I'm the one who's hurt!" I stopped myself, bit my tongue, and walked away again. I stayed in my room longer, taking deep breaths, trying to calm down. If I returned to the kitchen too soon, I wasn't sure I could control myself. That risk was greater than leaving Amber alone for two minutes. I finally returned when I had calmed down enough to comfort her. I gave her a hug and told her I knew she didn't mean to hurt me. I apologized for yelling at her and told her when I got that angry and left it was because I didn't want to say or do anything mean.

DEVELOP A PERSONALIZED MANAGEMENT PLAN ☆☆☆☆

Once we identify whether we experience verbal or physical anger energy (or both) and need either internal or external recharging, we can plan an individualized anger/stress management plan. If we mix each style of energy and recharging, we have six possible combinations. Here is just one example of what we could do when we are angry or stressed, based on each style combination:

POSSIBLE STYLE COMBINATION PLANS	Internal recharger	External recharger
Verbal anger energy	**V/I.** Go to your room and yell, write, or draw.	**V/E.** Call a friend who will be supportive and talk.
Physical anger energy	**P/I.** Go for a walk/jog by yourself or clean.	**P/E.** Exercise outside or with others.
Verbal/Physical anger energy	**VP/I.** Pull weeds and grunt with each pull.	**VP/E.** Exercise with a friend/group where you can talk, yell, or cheer.

Despite the type of anger energy we experience, there are four acts that anyone can use to regain control. They are the all-time best strategies for managing stress and anger, and each has been proven to have helpful biological benefits.

- **Talk to someone.** When people talk to each other, it reduces their blood pressure. Long-term studies have shown that people with a companion (whether it was a pet or friend), have better long-term health. Those without a companion tend to die younger, even when the presence of disease wasn't apparent.

- **Talk yourself through the anger.** This is internal conversation encouraging ourselves to effectively handle the situation. We can talk ourselves through the various steps of anger control. "Okay, just hold on a second. Count to ten. Take a deep breath. Calm down. That's better. Now, what is it I want to do? I know I can handle this. Take it slow. Remember to listen to what the other person is saying. Breath more, talk less. Think before you speak." If we say these comments aloud, we can openly model healthy anger management for our children.

- **Forgiveness** is more than an ethical principle. It stimulates a release of chemicals that can counteract the toxic chemicals released by anger. Forgiveness is easier said than done. It begins by not taking events and comments personally. Someone may be having a bad day or they haven't learned to control their anger. Just because *they* aren't at peace doesn't mean *we* have to give up our inner peace. We can stop debating who is most at fault and take responsibility for our part. This helps others admit to their part of the problem. We can forgive others whether they admit it or change. It is especially important for us to model forgiveness to our children, although children usually model greater unconditional forgiveness than adults. We can learn a lot from them!

- **Exercise** is widely known to release muscle tension and built-up toxins in the body, while toning the body for total health. Exercise is helpful when we are not yet stressed, already stressed, or ready to explode. It is a healthy way to express the flight or fight response. Internal rechargers can exercise alone, external rechargers can exercise with others.

RESISTANCE TO CHANGE

If we keep doing what we've always done, we'll keep getting what we've always got. To change the effects of our anger, the first step is to make a conscious commitment to change or improve our current anger management skills. Change involves practicing new behaviors that can seem awkward or silly, at first. It also might challenge beliefs we've held since childhood. Awareness is the first step in changing any habit. Once we are *aware* of our unhelpful beliefs, we can *choose* healthier beliefs, feelings, and responses. Below is a list of unhelpful beliefs that can block our willingness to change.

RESISTANT BELIEFS	MOTIVATING BELIEFS
I can't change. It's just the way I am.	Just because I have always been that way, doesn't mean I can't change. It's my choice.
Something (or someone) makes me do that.	Things happen that I can't control, but I *can* control my reaction.
I don't know why I did it; I just did.	If I 'just did it' without thinking, it is a habit—and I can change my habits.
I'd like to do that differently, but it's just too hard to change.	Change *can* be scary and difficult. But what I'm doing now is not helpful nor healthy. I can change that—now.
I've never been able to do that. I can't. (What I really mean is, I won't.)	Just because I've never done it before doesn't mean I *can't* do it. If I put my mind to it, I *can*.

DEALING WITH OTHERS' ANGER AND STRESS

Throughout this chapter, we've only focused on coping with *our* anger—which is an ongoing, lifetime process. We can use most of these same skills to deal with other people who are angry, even if their anger is not directed at us.

Teaching Children Anger Management Skills

Anger and stress management skills are not just for adults, children can learn them, too. Many parents express concerns about their children's temper, disrespectful responses, or inability to control their emotions. When trying to teach children self-control, identify their recharge and anger energy styles. Then suggest they do activities, during their timeout, that fit their styles. (We learn how to use time-outs appropriately in Chapter 13, "Discipline Toolset.")

A Personal Story. When Chris was a toddler, I was concerned about his aggression, especially when he was angry. There was one particular friend who tended to push his buttons and their conflicts had gotten too rough on several occasions. Before this friend came to visit, we did some problem solving. I listened to his feelings and frustrations about how the friend bothered him. Chris and I prepared a three-step plan to handle similar situations in the future. First, he would use words. If that didn't work, he would walk away. If that didn't work, he'd go to his room or ask an adult for help. We rehearsed his words and his plan.

During the friend's next visit, the boy's mother kept talking, oblivious to her son's behavior. Soon, a conflict was brewing at the end of the yard. Knowing Chris had a plan, I simply observed from afar. I could hear Chris using words, although I couldn't tell what he said. Even from a distance, I could see Chris' face getting red, his neck veins bulging, his fists clenched. He walked away, over to the swing set. The friend followed. Chris looked around, then pushed his friend to the ground.

While the other mother tended to her son, I put my arms around Chris, who was still crying and shaking. I said, "I saw you using words! You were angry, but you used words! Then you walked away, but he followed you, didn't he?" My son nodded as he cried. "When he followed, you could have gone to your room or come to me. What happened?" He sniffled and said, "But I didn't know how to get to my room!" He was so flustered, he couldn't figure out how to get to his room from outside! It never occurred to me that we needed a backup plan for outside! I added, "Next time, just open the screen door and go inside the house. Okay?"

Despite the pushing, I was impressed that Chris gave his new skills a valiant try. Our problem-solving session was a major turnaround in his ability to resolve peer conflicts without aggression. Nature had its own timetable and progress was slow. But I was consistent and as he matured, the anger/stress management skills began working—for both of us. By the time he went to preschool, I realized he had progressed from below average in his anger skills to above average. This really reinforced, in my mind, the value of these skills—not just for adults, but for children, too.

Many parents complain about their children's temper tantrums. It's helpful to understand that tantrums are natural and healthy for young children. They provide a nonverbal way of getting their anger energy out, until they become more verbal and learn better anger management skills. Obviously, if they don't learn healthier ways to express their anger, their tantrums continue, in different ways at different ages. (See pages 74–75 in Chapter 3, "The Universal Blueprint," for the different types of tantrums and possible responses.)

When children are upset, we want to avoid getting hooked by the *way* they express it. Instead, we can use the Child Problem Toolbox to learn what's really going on and help them deal with their emotions. We can suggest activities (drawing, painting, clay, etc.) that help them express emotions they cannot verbalize or release their anger energy. The key phrase to use in this situation is, "*Show me* how you feel." The Problem-Solving Toolset is helpful, not only to plan an anger management program for our children, but to explore possible solutions to their problems.

Sometimes our children's anger is a problem for *us,* when it violates our rights, rules, or involves safety. We may need to temporarily move into the Parent Problem Toolbox to set limits and encourage our children to take a self-control time-out.

When we pause to keep our cool, our silence can have a surprising effect. Children look to us for our response to problems. If we take a deep breath, plan what we say, and speak slowly, we can calm down and stay focused. Often, while we are taking a breath, children jump in and take care of the problem!

Sometimes, someone other than the angry person can tell when tempers are about to erupt. At these times, it is helpful to have a family code word that anyone can say to call a time-out. The word can be one small word that is not used often, such as "Break!" Anyone is allowed to say this word; child to parent, parent to child, parent to parent, or child to child. When someone says the code word in the heat of the moment, it means everyone separates, gets out their anger energy and recharges. When everyone calms down, they can come together to resolve the problem more calmly.

A Graduate's Story. During a family council, we actually used one of those silly ideas from brainstorming. Our children chose the word "pickle" for our family time-out code word. Later that week, we were getting into a heated argument about something that really wasn't worth arguing about. My youngest daughter called out "Pickle!" We stopped and looked at her, puzzled, as we tried to figure out what she was talking about. Then we remembered our agreement and started laughing—not at anyone else, but at ourselves. For us, having a silly code word reminds us of what is really important. Every now and then, when the issue **is** *really important, people get a bit irritated having a silly code word. At those times, we don't laugh, but the code word still reminds us to take a time-out to cool off before we hurt someone's feelings or say something we might regret.*

Defusing Another Person's Anger

When someone is angry, defuse the anger before negotiating a solution or problem solving, with the following suggestions:

- **Don't answer anger with anger.** If people make hurtful comments, remember that anger causes people to say things they really don't mean. Don't jump to conclusions or take everything literally, before they calm down. They may be venting. Don't defend yourself by blaming, even if they are blaming you. For example, "Well, I wouldn't have done that if you hadn't . . ."

- **Imagine that you are surrounded by an invisible bubble.** Love and positive thoughts can come through the bubble, from others, and out of the bubble, from you. Negative words and actions bounce right off.

- **Keep your ideas, opinions, and explanations to yourself** *for now*. Stating your opinions and ideas before angry people defuse their emotional energy only slows down the process and frustrates them. At that moment, angry people are *not* ready to listen. If it's necessary to give your side, they will listen better when they are calm. Be patient and wait to take your turn.

- **Try looking at the situation from their point of view.** Tell yourself, "If I saw the world the way they do, I'd feel like them, too." Find a part of what they are saying that is true. You can agree with the facts, their opinion, or the belief involved, such as "I agree, it was inconsiderate of me to be so late without calling."

- **Make what's important to them as important to you as** *they* **are to you.** Use the F-A-X process to let them know you understand how they feel. Restate their views. Focus on their hurt. Remain calm and respectful even if you disagree with them. Avoid the communication barriers listed in Chapter 7, "F-A-X Listening Toolset," which will only enrage them more.

- **Offer a sincere apology for any part you played in the problem or for upsetting them.** Ask for specific suggestions about what they want you to do. Or ask for details about what you did that upset them.

- **Help people discharge pent-up emotional energy by suggesting anger or stress techniques that fit their style of anger** (verbal or physical anger energy and internal or external recharge).

Only move to the negotiation phase after they've worked through their anger. If it is only their problem, use F-A-X communication in the Child Problem Toolbox. If part of the problem belongs to you, also use the Clear Communication Toolset to reach win/win solutions.

A Graduate's Story. My family had some horrendous experiences, affecting every one of our lives. My 11-year-old son was overflowing with anger and resentment, which came out in undesirable ways. He had to be physically restrained for periods up to an hour to keep him from hurting himself or another family member. Thanks to the skills we learned in <u>The Parent's Toolshop</u>, *we learned how to defuse that anger, set safe limits, and create positive outlets for these feelings.* <u>The Parent's Toolshop</u> *taught us to use reflective listening, giving choices, one-liners, and problem solving to create a more open atmosphere that enables us to move on to more creative ways of dealing with feelings in our home.*

My son had a real problem with throwing things, anything, when he was angry. So I figured, "Why not let him throw something he is allowed to throw, like a baseball?" We would go to the backyard and throw a ball when he began to get angry. At first, he could not aim the ball toward me. But as he calmed down, he wouldn't throw the ball as hard or crooked. When the ball was on target, I could use reflective listening and he could verbalize his feelings. Then we could move on to problem solving. But if he began to throw the ball harder or more wildly during the conversation, I knew I needed to slow down or something else was bothering him.

Knowing that it was okay to be angry and finding a safe way to get his anger out helped him break through and resolve the problem. His self-esteem was intact and he was managing his own anger. He was solving his own problems, which helped him feel more in control. When no one is available to throw a ball, he removes himself from the situation and does things such as roller-blading, walking, running, or batting a ball. He finds it helpful to get his angry energy out so he can move on to reasonable thoughts.

Children and Stress

Children experience stress, just as adults do. Obvious times of stress are divorce, moving, or deaths (family members, pets, or others). Other, less obvious, stresses can be recurrent problems with a teacher, with other students, or an unrealistic work load. Parents, too, can sometimes be the source of a child's stress. A parent with unrealistic expectations, unreasonable demands, or perfectionist attitudes causes stress. Parents who are ill or under stress can unknowingly affect their children. When parents try to protect their children by covering up what's going on, children can tell something is wrong. If they don't know the truth, they'll often come to their own (often incorrect) conclusions which are often more damaging than the truth would be.

The best strategy for helping children deal with stress is to be open and honest. Give children the information they need to understand what's going on. They don't need to know *every* detail. Be brief and let them ask questions. Use words and ideas they can understand and tell them in an honest, but reassuring way. (See the list at the end of this chapter for resources that help parents explain difficult topics to children.) Encourage them to express their feelings. If you aren't sure how or when things will work out, reassure them that you love them and will be supportive, regardless of the outcome. Teach children the stress management skills we just learned. Remember, children often *act* out their stress and feelings.[2]

Excessive stress in children can result in the following warning signs:
- A *sudden, dramatic* increase or decrease in effort at school.
- *Uncharacteristic, sudden* changes in attitude, such as irritability, lack of enthusiasm, or being easily distracted from tasks.
- Withdrawal or emotional/behavioral outbursts.
- *Recurrent* complaints of tiredness, illness, stomachaches, or headaches.
- *Sudden* changes in sleeping and eating habits.
- Drug use or abuse.
- *Unexplained* increase in allergic/asthmatic attacks.
- Avoidance of school or tests by direct refusal or convenient illnesses.
- *Excessive* eating, nail biting, or stuttering.

Teenage depression can outwardly appear different among teens. Teens can disguise their feelings through other behaviors that are directed at themselves or others. Although they may not seem to be trying to draw attention to their feelings, many teens are sending a message for help, "I'm hurting! Will someone please see my need and offer me some relief?" Depressed teens believe they cannot solve their problems and have little hope that others can help. We can often trace teenage depression to failed relationships, frequently within the home. Beneath the depression lies built-up frustration, stress, and angry feelings. It is *vital* for teens to know how to use anger/stress management tools, since they may or may not reach out for help when life seems overwhelming.

FINAL COMMENTS

In summary:
1. Admit you are angry and slow down your anger cycle.
2. Deal with your anger as soon as possible, rather than letting it build up to the point that you may explode. Reduce your anxiety by using energy outlets or recharge activities.
3. Identify the source or cause of your anger.
4. Identify and change any unhelpful beliefs you have about the situation.
5. Recognize the situations you can control and those you can't. Don't waste energy on situations you cannot control.
6. Make a conscious choice whether to express your anger. Consider the effects of your response and how others will react. Rehearse how you will deal with their reactions.

It is empowering to know *what* to do with our anger. It can be a great revelation to realize "I can control my own emotions. No one can *make me* feel anything. I can *choose* my reaction, response, and perception in any situation." Such knowledge, however, doesn't bring magical overnight change. These are just tools. Each of us must take these tools and be willing to use them until they are a new way of responding. Like any habit, anger and stress management take time and patience. Our progress may be gradual and slow. At first we notice an increase in our patience, simply because we have more tools at our disposal. With time, we can look back and see how far we've come in our ability to handle stress and anger.

It is not too much to ask that we control our behavior, since that is what we are expecting of our children.

SUMMARY SHEET
KEEP YOUR COOL TOOLSET

Anger is a physical and emotional reaction to a perceived threat. If we don't use the muscle tension and chemicals the body releases in anger, the build-up can lead to serious illness.

STEPS OF CONSTRUCTIVE ANGER/STRESS MANAGEMENT

a. Become aware of your anger cycle ☆☆☆☆

EVENT ———> BELIEF ——-> FEELING ——> RESPONSE
Changing beliefs affects the rest of the anger cycle.
Passive anger = stuffs and denies feelings.
Aggressive anger = takes out emotions on others.
Passive-Aggressive anger = hurts others in passive ways.
Assertive anger = a balanced, honest, respectful response.

b. Relieve the pressure of anger and stress

Smoldering embers need stress management. ☆☆☆☆
Internal rechargers get their energy from within themselves.
External rechargers get their energy from outside themselves.
Flash fires need healthy eruption outlets. ☆☆☆☆
Verbal anger energy = feel like yelling
Physical anger energy = feel like hitting
Change *what* you yell/hit until healthier responses are habits.
Personalize your program: P/I, V/I, P/E, V/E, VP/I, VP/E. ☆☆☆☆
Use an anger log to re-program your response. ☆☆☆☆

c. Plan an assertive response to the problem
(Chapter 10, "Clear Communication Toolset.")

Children experience stress and anger, too. Explain stressful situations in honest and reassuring ways. Be a role model and teach children anger/stress management skills, based on their recharge and anger-energy styles.

PRACTICE ~ USE AN ANGER LOG ☆☆☆☆

An anger log helps us look at the various steps in our anger cycle, identify trigger buttons or symptoms of stress overload, and plan more effective ways of expressing anger in the future. We can use it after an explosion, to understand what happened and re-program a trigger button, or during a time-out to think more clearly and plan an assertive response.

Here are directions for using the anger log that follows. We go through each step twice. First, we go through all four steps of the anger cycle, reliving the angry attitudes, thoughts, feelings, and reactions. Then we go back to step one and rewrite more healthy beliefs and perceptions. Once we do this, we usually have more clarity about our feelings and can plan a helpful response.

1. **Describe the event.** In the Before column, write a description of what happened.

2. **What do I believe about this event?** In the Before column, we write what we told ourselves when this event happened. These are our thoughts, opinions, and interpretations about what happened.

3. **How do I feel?** In the Before column, we write how we felt. If we were calm just before the event occurred, the event might have pushed a trigger button. If we were tense or overwhelmed, we make note of the physical symptoms, so we can catch ourselves the next time, before we blow. (Be careful to catch thoughts we often misinterpret as feelings. For example, "I felt like he was doing it on purpose" is a belief and interpretation, not a feeling.)

4. **What was my response?** In the Before column, we write what we said or did.

Now, move to the After/To Reprogram column.

5. **Am I being objective?** We look at the description of the event we wrote in the Before column. An objective perspective of the problem is factual, the way a camera sees it. Anyone in that situation would see the situation the same way. In the After column, rewrite any judgments or assumptions in a more factual, objective way.

6. **Are my beliefs healthy?** We look at the beliefs we wrote in the Before column. Are they helpful or unhelpful? Rational or irrational? Objective or judgmental? Is there anything about the way we perceived the situation that could have contributed to our anger?

> ***For a belief to be helpful, rational, and objective it must meet at least three of the following four guidelines:***
> a.   The thought is objective and nonjudgmental. It is respectful of me *and* the other person.
> b.   The thought helps me better understand the problem or the other person's perspective.
> c.   The thought helps me think more about how to resolve the problem.
> d.   The thought makes me less upset.

Rewrite each unhelpful belief in the After column, using the guidelines above and those described earlier in this chapter (page 237).

7. **Now, how do I feel?** Now that we've rewritten our beliefs, what are we feeling? List these new feelings in the After column. Look at the feelings we listed in the Before column. We usually find that we are now more in touch with our primary feelings, the ones closer to the core of our onion. We also usually understand the other person's point of view better.

8. **How can I respond?** Once we have rewritten the first three steps, we can plan and write a new response in the After column, using the Universal Blueprint's PASRR formula.

ANGER LOG

BEFORE/DURING ANGER	AFTER/TO RE-PROGRAM ANGER
Describe the event. What happened?	Am I being objective? Look at the Before description. Change biased comments into factual, objective terms.
What do I believe about this event? When the event happened, what did I tell myself?	Are my beliefs healthy? Look at each belief listed to the left. Rewrite unhealthy beliefs using helpful, positive words.
How do I feel?	Now, how do I feel after looking at the healthier beliefs and thoughts above?
What was my response?	How can I respond in a helpful, healthy, rational, and positive way?

SAMPLE ANGER LOG

BEFORE/DURING ANGER	AFTER/TO RE-PROGRAM ANGER
Describe the event. What happened?	Am I being objective? Look at the Before description. Change biased comments into factual, objective terms.
Joey, 12, rode his bike to Jacob's house to play before football practice. He's late and the phone is busy, so they're probably playing on the Internet. Now I have to drive all the way over there just to get him to practice on time.	*Joey **was** late and **had** lost track of time, but the boys weren't the one's trying up the phone line. I don't **have to** drive to Jacob's, but can choose to if I want.*
What do I believe about this event? When the event happened, what did I tell myself?	Are my beliefs healthy? Look at each belief listed to the left. Rewrite unhealthy beliefs using helpful, positive words.
Why is he so irresponsible? Is it too much to ask that he look at the clock now and then? He takes me for granted to remember everything for him. I shouldn't have to drive over there to get him. He'll probably want me to bring his bike home in the van, too. At this point, he's sure to be late.	*When kids are playing, they can easily lose track of time. There was no clock outside, but Joey **was** wearing his watch with an alarm. It would have been nicer if the phone line was free. I could **choose** not to drive there and let Joey experience the natural consequences of being late and the coach's reaction. I can also **choose** whether to pick up Joey and/or his bike. We **might** be late.*
How do I feel?	Now, how do I feel after looking at the healthier beliefs and thoughts above?
Furious, put out and inconvenienced, taken advantage of, rushed.	*Frustrated, rushed, unsure whether to rescue Joey from being late.*
What was my response?	How can I respond in a helpful, healthy, rational, and positive way?
I drove to Jacob's house. Joey was jumping on the outdoor trampoline. I yelled at him to come NOW. I refused to take the bike and followed him home. I stewed while he got his equipment together and lectured him about his irresponsibility the whole way to practice. He was still late and we both were upset.	*Prevent the problem next time, by verifying that Joey has set his watch alarm **before** leaving. Decide up front, **with Joey**, what will happen if he is late. If he is late anyway and I choose to pick him up, I can be calmer and more relaxed. I can simply state the facts and ask Joey how he plans to get to practice on time. I don't can breath deeply while he is getting ready and drive calmly. I still probably won't pick up the bike.*

ADDITIONAL RESOURCES

If you would like to do more work on your anger management skills refer to the resources listed in the endnotes or consult the following resources:

- *Dr. Weisinger's Anger Workout Book*, (William Morrow & Co., 1985).

- *The Dance of Anger*, Harriet Goldhor Lerner, Ph.D., (HarperCollins, 1989).

- *Anger Kills: How to Control the Hostility That Can Harm Your Health*, by Redford Williams, (Random House, 1993.)

- *The Angry Teenager*, Dr. William Lee Carter, (Thomas Nelson Publishers, 1995).

- *Taming the Dragon in Your Child: Solutions for Breaking the Cycle of Family Anger*, Meg Eastman, (Wiley, NY: 1994).

- *Tantrums: Secrets to Calming the Storm*, Ann E. LaForge, (Pocket Books, NY; 1996).

- *When Kids Are Mad, Not Bad: a Guide to Recognizing and Handling Children's Anger*, Henry A. Paul, (Berkeley Books, NY, 1995).

- *The Relaxation Response*, by Herbert Benson (New York: William Morrow, 1975), offers instructions for meditation.

- *How to Talk to Your Kids About Really Important Things: Specific Questions and Answers and Useful Things to Say*, by Charles E. Schaefer, Ph.D. and Theresa Foy DiGeronimo, M.Ed.(1994, Jossey-Bass Publishers, San Francisco.) Topic chapters have suggestions by age groups.

WHAT'S NEXT?

We want to practice stress and anger management skills daily. When we take the time and make the effort, we experience less stress buildup and angry explosions. Once we have our logic back on-line, we can plan a constructive response to the problem. To do this, we move to the Clear Communication Toolset to plan the words we want to say.

Chapter 10, "Clear Communication Toolset," explains Step C1c: Plan an assertive response. Whether we use no words, one word, or several sentences, this chapter provides many tools we can choose. When the prevention tools are working most of the time and we have a positive relationship with our child (thanks to the listening tools), problems can still occur. Since we already took these first two steps of the PASRR formula, we can use the communication tools, immediately and by themselves, to stop the problem before it develops or worsens.

REFERENCES

1. Anger cycle steps are based on a model developed by Albert Ellis, author of *A Guide to Rational Living* (Prentice-Hall, 1961).

2. *The Effective Parent (The NextSTEP)*, by Donald Dinkmeyer and Gary McKay with Donald Dinkmeyer Jr., James S. Dinkmeyer, and Joyce L. McKay (American Guidance Service, 1987) p. 84.

CHAPTER 10
CLEAR COMMUNICATION TOOLSET

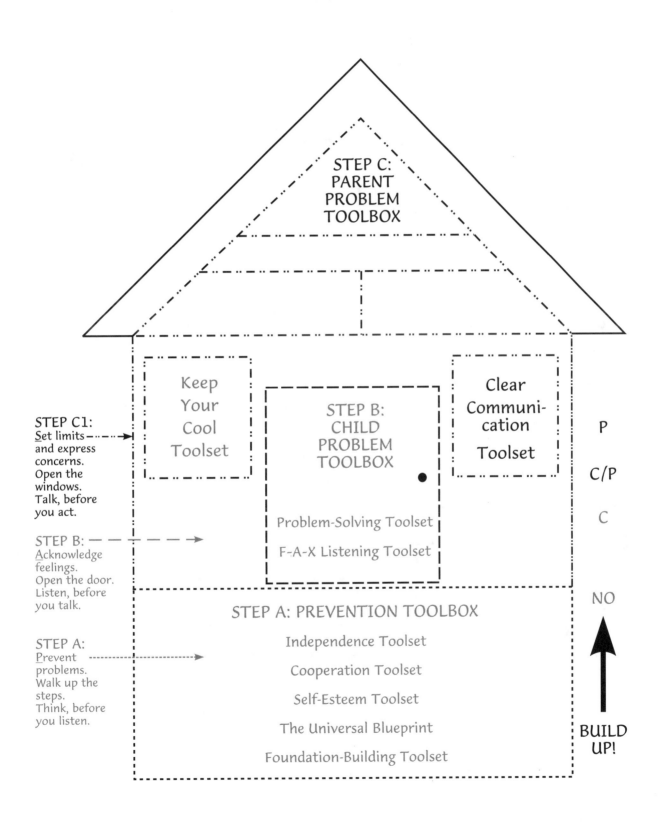

STEP C:
PARENT
PROBLEM
TOOLBOX

STEP C1:
Set limits
and express
concerns.
Open the
windows.
Talk, before
you act.

Keep
Your
Cool
Toolset

STEP B:
CHILD
PROBLEM
TOOLBOX

Clear
Communi-
cation
Toolset

P

C/P

C

Problem-Solving Toolset

F-A-X Listening Toolset

STEP B:
Acknowledge
feelings.
Open the door.
Listen, before
you talk.

STEP A: PREVENTION TOOLBOX

NO

STEP A:
Prevent
problems.
Walk up the
steps.
Think, before
you listen.

Independence Toolset

Cooperation Toolset

Self-Esteem Toolset

The Universal Blueprint

Foundation-Building Toolset

BUILD
UP!

CHAPTER
10 CLEAR COMMUNICATION TOOLSET

If we want to send messages through the windows of our house, the windows must be clean enough to see through. We want the person we are communicating with to clearly see us and understand our message correctly.

When we talk with others, we sometimes send messages we don't mean to send. Our words are only the surface of our total message. Our tone of voice, choice of words, and even the order of our words affect the total message that others receive. We are usually unaware of these hidden messages, but others, including children, pick up on them. These hidden messages are caused by unclear communication and result in others shutting their doors (ears) to what we are saying. If we can send messages clearly, we can better solve problems that arise.

IN THIS CHAPTER

This chapter picks up where the Keep Your Cool Toolset ended, with the last step in anger/stress management, "Plan an assertive response." Together, these two toolsets supply us with the tools for the first step in responding to Parent problems, Step C1 of the Universal Blueprint.

Step C1: <u>S</u>et limits or express concerns.

a. *Become aware of your anger/stress cycle.* (The Keep Your Cool Toolset explained how beliefs about events and people actually cause our feelings.)
b. *Relieve the pressure of the anger/stress.* (The Keep Your Cool Toolset taught us about internal and external recharge styles, verbal and physical anger energy, and activities to help us regain our emotional balance.)

We complete our tour of Step C1 with the Clear Communication Toolset.

c. ***Plan an assertive response to the problem.*** The **Clear Communication Toolset** explains three important points:
   • The four styles of communication and the definition of "assertive."
   • How nonverbal cues send hidden messages that can open or shut down communication.
   • Nearly a dozen tools for communicating *our* feelings, concerns, values and limits.

WHEN TO USE THE CLEAR COMMUNICATION TOOLSET

In Step B, the Child Problem Toolbox, we learned about F-A-X communication when we were *receiving* messages. Step C1, the Clear Communication Toolset, teaches us how to *send* clear messages. We want to remove as many hidden codes as we can and reduce any "static" that can shut down the lines of communication. We can use the Clear Communication Toolset in *any* of the following situations:

• **No problems.** When we need a quick reminder to keep a problem from developing or worsening, we can choose tools from either the Cooperation *or* Clear Communication Toolsets. With these tools, children are less likely to react negatively to our requests.

• **Parent problems.** We can use quick one-word reminders from the Clear Communication Toolset as a first response, if we've taken other steps in the past. When Parent problems persist, we can choose firmer responses from the Clear Communication Toolset.

- **C/P problems.** When children also have a problem, disagree with us, or react negatively to our requests, we *only* use a clear communication statement *after* acknowledging their feelings. Depending on the intensity of children's feelings, we might use several listening responses before shifting to the Clear Communication Toolset.

- **Parent/child problem solving.** When we need to reach win/win agreements, we add a few steps to the problem-solving process we learned in the Problem-Solving Toolset, to account for the parent's part of the problem. Together, the F-A-X Listening, Problem-Solving, and Clear Communication Toolsets provide all the communication tools we need to do back-and-forth problem solving in *any* relationship or with any group of people, including professional and personal adult relationships.

When we are dealing with Parent problems, we don't want to say the same thing five different ways (or five times louder), hoping children will finally listen. If one step in the Universal Blueprint doesn't resolve the problem, we move to the next step. Just remember that as we move through the steps, we can use any of the skills at previous steps. This means we can use the F-A-X Listening Toolset to **A**cknowledge feelings or offer a word of encouragement when we are **S**etting limits or **R**edirecting misbehavior (the next step, which we learn in Chapters 11 and 12).

STYLES OF COMMUNICATION

To begin planning a response, we want to expand on the definitions we learned in the last chapter. There, we learned about the four styles of anger: aggressive, passive, passive-aggressive, and assertive. Communication styles build on these definitions, applying them to our verbal responses.

Aggressive Communication

Aggressive communication has any or all of the following qualities:

- **Aggressive communication is firm, but not kind.** Speakers say what they want, but hurt others in the process.

- **Speakers think they are superior to listeners.** They believe their rights are more important than the listener's rights (just like the over-controlling parenting style).

- **It is controlling and disrespectful.** Any of the following terms could describe aggressive communication: harsh, abrupt, hostile, arrogant, tactless, impatient, inconsiderate, loud, critical, continuous, and dominating.

- **It uses aggressive body language**, such as pointed fingers, pounding fists, hands on hips, and slamming objects.

- **Logical aggressive communication** uses orders, commands, judgments, blame, challenges, and critical remarks.

- **Emotional aggressive communication** is usually the result of stored up anger and involves childish tactics, such as tantrums, yelling, stubbornness, name calling, and arguing.

- **The goal of aggressive communication is to gain power over others**—to win by forcing others to lose. Aggressive speakers want listeners, through sheer intimidation, to give them what they want. In the short-term, aggressive communication can seem to work. In reality, it is a lose/lose outcome, because both people lose respect for each other and it damages the relationship. More problems usually occur, because listeners resent the aggressive speaker for ignoring their feelings and violating their rights. Listeners often become hostile, resistant, and argumentative. Then, aggressive speakers must use increased verbal or physical force to continue getting their way.

Passive Communication

Passive communication has any or all of the following qualities:

- **It is kind, but not firm.** Speakers use a meek, whiny, questioning, or pleading tone of voice. They use indirect hints, hoping listeners will guess their wishes and voluntarily grant them.

- **Passive speakers believe their own rights are less important than the other person's rights** (just like the under-controlling, permissive parenting style).

- **The passive speakers' goals are to please others and avoid conflict.**

- **It allows listeners to take advantage of the passive speakers.** This causes both parties to lose respect for each other. If passive speakers give in, they feel hurt or resentful and often pout or whine about their loss. Other times, passive speakers grow tired of others taking advantage of them and may snap, aggressively lashing out in revenge.

Passive-Aggressive Communication

Passive-aggressive communication has any or all of the following qualities:

- **It is *neither* kind nor firm.**

- **It doesn't assert the speaker's rights *and* violates the listener's rights.**

- **The goal is to hurt others without being obviously hurtful.**

- **Passive-aggressive communication uses passive body language** (silence, frowns, crossed arms) **to send aggressive messages** ("I'm mad").

Sarcasm is a form of passive-aggressive communication. It disguises anger, blame, and criticism with humor. Whether covering little digs with a smile or making someone the center of a joke, sarcastic people are not really being funny; they are attacking. When people see through their sarcasm and get offended by the attack, the sarcastic person often blames the person for being "a poor sport" with no sense of humor. "It was only a joke" is their way of covering up their inappropriate attack on the other person. And if others laugh, they are not only rewarded for attacking someone else, but can shift even more blame, "See, even they knew I was kidding. You're too sensitive, lighten up."

All forms of aggressive communication are destructive to personal relationships. They carry two implied messages, "You are dumb and you are wrong," which is criticism and blame. They shut down communication and make conflicts worse by stirring up more angry feelings. It makes the original problem even harder to resolve.

Assertive Communication

Assertive communication has all of the following qualities:

- **It is both kind *and* firm.**

- **Assertive communication upholds the speaker's rights in ways that respect others' rights.**

- **It uses attentive, responsive, and interested body language.** Speakers have direct eye contact, open arms and hands, a respectful, matter-of-fact tone of voice, and friendly facial expressions.

- **It uses *objective,* factual descriptions that focus on the *present* moment and *solutions* to the problem.**

- **Assertive communication is clear and direct.** Speakers say what they mean to say.

- **The goal of assertive communication is to reach win/win solutions.** Assertive speakers respectfully set limits (their win) while recognizing the feelings and needs of others (their win). Assertive speakers hope that even if the listeners aren't *happy* about their limits, they will consider the speakers' feelings and/or needs. Since assertive speakers address others respectfully, people listen better and are more cooperative. If others don't immediately cooperate, assertive speakers continue responding assertively and respectfully, but more firmly.

THE HUMAN "BILL OF RIGHTS"

A critical part of assertive communication is mutual respect for the rights of the people involved in the communication exchange. Briefly, *all* people have several basic rights in any discussion.

The Human "Bill of Rights"

- *All people have the right to have others treat them with respect*, because all people are unique, valuable, and important. People are no less deserving of respect if they are young or others judge their behavior as worse than others'.

- *All people have the right to have others treat their feelings as important and valid,* even if others *disagree* with those feelings.

- *All people have the right to have personal opinions and values.* With this right comes the responsibility to respect the needs and opinions of others who might disagree.

- *All people have the right to express their feelings*, *if* they do so without violating another person's right to be treated with respect.

- *All people have the right to make and refuse reasonable and unreasonable requests*, with the understanding that others also have this same right.

- *All people have the right to change their minds*, *if* they recognize their responsibility to accept the reactions of others and any negative effects that might result.

- *All people have the right to get what others have promised to give.* If the promise is the result of a *voluntary* agreement, people can assert this right *if* they do so without mistreating the promise-giver in the process.

- *All people have the right to make their own decisions*, with the understanding that they are accepting responsibility for fixing or living with any negative effects that might result from that decision.

NONVERBAL COMMUNICATION

There is scientific proof behind the saying, "Actions speak louder than words." Studies have shown that only 7 percent of the meaning of communication comes from the spoken words. Facial expressions, posture, and gestures account for 55 percent. Thirty-eight percent of the interpretation comes from vocal qualities such as loudness of voice, rate of speech, and intonation[1]. The goal of clear communication is to have our nonverbal and spoken messages match. When verbal and nonverbal information contradict each other, the subconscious mind automatically uses the nonverbal signals to interpret the meaning. It is true that mere words can't hide feelings. So it is important that we not only learn *what* to say but *how* to say it. This prevents us from sending unhelpful hidden messages.

Negative statements can imply hidden messages.   *Positive statements send clear, respectful messages*

Helpful Attitudes

To avoid hidden messages, choose helpful words and present them with the following helpful attitudes:

Mutual respect. We have all been irritated, impatient, or troubled with another person's behavior. Yet, we often make more of an effort to listen and talk respectfully with *them* than we do with our own children, whose relationship we value even more!

> *A Graduate's Story. I was having a garage sale with a friend. She and her son came to our house to help us set up. My son came upstairs with an item that had just been broken. I jumped all over him! I said, "What have you been doing down there? What did you do?" He said, "I didn't break it, Jason did." Jason's mother was sitting right there. Immediately, I said, "Oh well, it's no problem." My son said, "Oh, it's not okay for me to break it but it's okay if Jason did?" The other mother apologized and I apologized to my son. He was right! It made me realize that I am much harder on my own kids when they do something wrong than I am with a friend's child. I love my kids more than anyone else in the world and will have a relationship with them for the rest of my life. So why do I treat them worse than I treat a friend or neighbor?*

We often get more upset with our own family members, because we are more emotionally involved with them. Because we have so much at stake, we let things upset us more. But it is precisely *because* we have so much at stake that we want to make every effort to take care of the relationship.

> **If we treated our friends as we do our children, we'd probably lose some friends. Likewise, if we treated our children as respectfully as we do our friends, our relationships would surely improve.**

Some people react to this statement saying, "But we *aren't* their friends. We are their parents!" This statement does not mean to be friends *instead of* parents. It means we simply conduct ourselves in friend*ly* ways with our children, just as we would with our friends. We may need to set limits, as we do with others who aren't our children. They may not *like* the limits, but at least we aren't being disrespectful in the process.

Another reaction might be, "But friends don't repeatedly do silly, stupid things!" Let's ask ourselves, "What if they did? How would we handle it?" Chances are, we would probably make an extra effort to be tactful and courteous to our friend. We might even overlook or ignore what the friend did, to spare a confrontation over a minor issue. When we are frustrated with our children, let's not throw away our manners, respectful attitude, and effective communication skills.

Allow differences of opinion or respectful disagreement. Differences of opinion don't have to lead to arguments. Discussions can become aggressive arguments, if we are bent on proving ourselves right and the other person wrong. When our attitude is forceful or arrogant, no one will value any opinion we want to share.

When we have a difference of opinion, we want to first listen carefully to the other person. Summarize and repeat the other person's perspective *before* stating our own. This not only shows our objectivity, but opens the door to sharing (Step B, Child Problem Toolbox). Once *we* have listened to others, *others* are usually more willing to listen to us.

We can accept different opinions, even if we disagree. We simply accept them as different views of the facts and respond accordingly. For example, "I see you don't want to lug an umbrella to school, since it doesn't look to you like it's going to rain. The paper said it was going to rain today." Then we wait, to give children a chance to make a voluntary decision. If they choose to assert their will and the effect won't be dangerous (here, the effect is getting wet) one option is to let them learn from their choice (Discipline Toolset). Another option is to suggest a compromise, "What if you take this small one in your backpack, just in case." We want to pick and choose our "battles" carefully. We can often accomplish more by offering choices within limits and backing off than forcefully demanding our way.

> *A Personal Story.* One of my father's best qualities is his willingness to consider other viewpoints and respect others' opinions. I can remember him listening to our records, reading our school books, and watching our television shows to learn more about us and our interests. (Now that I'm a parent myself, I realize he might also have been "screening" them!)
>
> One of our favorite family stories is "The Peanut Butter Taste Test." My dad and I bonded over peanut butter; we shared many heart-to-heart moments over a midnight snack of peanut butter on toast when we couldn't get to sleep.
>
> One day, as I helped unload the groceries, I said I didn't like the generic brand of peanut butter my mother had bought. I liked a name brand better. My dad asked me why. I described how the other brands were too salty and coarse. He proposed the idea of a blind taste test. He said that if I could tell the difference without seeing the jar, he would be willing to switch. He blind-folded me and put three different peanut butters on three saltine crackers. (That's the way they did it in the TV commercials.) All it took was one bite and I named which cracker had which peanut butter on it and described the difference in taste and texture. My dad was amazed and we bought that brand from then on. To this day, as a choosy mother, I still only eat that brand of peanut butter.

Avoid the "blame game." Focus on solutions, instead. The blame game starts when someone asks questions that put others on the defensive, such as "Who did this?" The predictable responses are "Not me," "I don't know," and "He did (pointing to someone else)." If we ask, "Did you do this?" most children answer "No." (This is a set-up question that encourages lying, which we cover in Chapter 12, "PO Toolset.") If we ask, "Why did you do this?" we get a list of excuses. When we go around in circles looking for a target to blame, children can use this to their advantage. If they can confuse us or never let us find out who is responsible, we can't hold anyone accountable. And if they're lucky, we will get so frustrated we'll take care of the problem ourselves. The real point to all these questions is, "There is a problem and the responsible person needs to take care of it." This statement holds others accountable and empowers them to be self-responsible.

The blame game is addictive. Once someone points out another's faults or mistakes, the blamed person waits for a chance to even the score. If a parent yells at a child for leaving dirty dishes in the sink, you can bet the child is just waiting for a chance to point out the *one* time the parent does the same thing! This attitude of "someone has to be blamed for everything that goes wrong" is destructive. People become edgy and defensive. Their self-esteem goes down and they feel incompetent and uncooperative. To avoid or stop the blame game, we want to word our statements in general nonblameful, nonjudgmental ways, using the Clear Communication tools. If we don't accuse or embarrass children, they are usually more willing to take responsibility for their mistakes or the problems that result.

If children don't voluntarily take care of the problem and there are siblings or peers around, peer pressure can work to the parent's advantage. The other children make sure *they* don't have to take care of a problem they didn't create. The key here is to describe the problem and that we expect *whoever* is responsible to take care of it—then walk away. When the parent leaves, the other children say, "I'm not going to clean up your mess!" Don't try to force a confession, since this only leads to power struggles. Don't punish *all* the children, since this breeds resentment and revenge towards the parent and guilty child. If one child repeatedly picks up the slack, notice their efforts to be nice, but explain that rescuing does not help others. People need to learn self-responsibility. The face-saving way out of the situation is for the responsible person to take care of the problem "anonymously." If we are more concerned with solutions than blame, this approach meets our bottom line, too.

Avoid shame and guilt trips. Shame is toxic. It takes a mistake or negative behavior and turns it into one's identity. Just because an action was irresponsible does not mean the person *is* irresponsible. This is how negative labels start.

Shame is also a powerful weapon that causes unhealthy guilt. Unhealthy guilt damages self-esteem with destructive self-talk, "I'm a bad person because I did a bad thing. I'll never amount to anything." Healthy guilt is a feeling of regret, without losing one's self-respect and self-worth in the process. "I'm sorry. I'll do . . . to take care of it." Healthy guilt is usually self-imposed, whereas harmful guilt is imposed by others—to manipulate or control. When people feel unhealthy shame, their motivation and learning stops and avoidance, resistance, denial, and anger take its place. Instead, we want to describe the problem and leave character assassinations out of our comments.

Focus on the present. It is infuriating (and incredibly unfair) when people bring up past failures or predict negative future behavior. For example, "You are always late! Two years ago you made me wait for an hour and a half! You'll never keep a job if you don't learn how to be on time." The real issue is not two years ago. Today, the child was late and the parent needs to count on the child coming home on time. Predictions and criticism have one sole purpose—to hurt and belittle others. They create negative labels and roles, which we learned to avoid and defuse in Chapter 4, "Self-Esteem Toolset."

Be clear and direct. We want to say exactly what we mean and mean what we say. Double messages send two different, inconsistent meanings. Usually, people say the conflicting statements at different times, so they don't realize they presented a no-win situation. For example, a parent says, "Help your sister with the computer. She doesn't know how to get into that program." Later, when the parent sees the helper taking over, the parent says, "Don't do it for her!" The helper gets upset and complains, "But you *told* me to help her!" What the parent really meant was, "*Teach* your sister how to get into the computer program by herself," but the parent wasn't clear and didn't explain the difference between helping and taking over.

"Contradictory" messages begin to say one thing, but end up saying the opposite. For example, "Sure, go to the party. I'll just stay awake worrying about you all night." This statement starts by saying "Yes," but ends with a guilt trip that says, "I don't really want you to go." Direct statements carry one message.

Appropriate Body Language

Sometimes our body language contradicts our words. If our teen asks to borrow the car and we say "Yes" in a hesitant or irritated **tone of voice**, we're implying we have a problem with the request. We can't expect others to read our minds or body language. We shouldn't be surprised or angry if the teen takes our words literally, "Thanks! See ya later!"

We need to pay attention to and control our body language, especially in the following ways:

- **Volume** has a great impact on how others interpret our messages. If our voice is too loud, others think we are being aggressive. Too soft a voice suggests a passive comment. We want our volume to be moderate, with proper changes that express our feelings honestly yet respectfully.

   A Personal Story. My voice is loud, even when I try to whisper. As a child, my loud voice was irritating and got me in trouble at school. Today, as a public speaker, my voice is an asset. When I get excited, I sound like I'm yelling, even if I'm not angry. My kids also have loud voices, so my husband often thinks we are arguing, even if we are simply excited or disagreeing. Because of our own loud voices, we tend to listen more to content than volume.

   A mother, whose child was in my daughter's first-grade class, called me during the first two weeks of school. She is a very soft-spoken woman and I've never heard her raise her voice, not even among a group of wild kids. She said her son was coming home from school upset, because the teacher "yelled" at him all day. Knowing this teacher, I knew she had a loud voice and spoke her mind, but not in disrespectful ways. I thought Amber would have commented if her teacher yelled a lot. I asked this mother whom her son had for a kindergarten teacher. This teacher was a soft-spoken, warm, huggy teacher. I told the mother I suspected that her son wasn't used to being with an adult who had a loud voice. I told her I would check with my daughter and call her back if I found the case was any different. Amber, who had a soft-spoken kindergarten teacher, said this first-grade teacher was nice and didn't yell. Loud voices can intimidate people and seem to be aggressive, even if the person's intentions are warm and friendly.

- **Rate of speech** is how fast we talk. If we talk too fast, it sends the message we are nervous or aggressive. It is also difficult to understand people who talk too fast. (When I'm nervous, I do this, too!) If we talk too slowly, people think we don't care or are unsure of our feelings.

- **Intonation** refers to the words we emphasize. Remember the example of "I didn't say your dress looked silly" in the F-A-X Listening Toolset? Emphasizing different words can change the meaning of the same sentence.

- **Facial expressions** need to match our verbal statements. If we smile and say "I'm furious," people think we are joking. Likewise, if we frown and say, "I'm okay," others will ask, "Are you sure?" Controlling our facial reactions is an important part of keeping our message respectful. We want to keep our faces relaxed, with appropriate facial expressions. We can use our words and a stern tone of voice to emphasize "I'm *furious* right now," rather than screaming it with veins bulging. Mostly, we want our face and tone of voice to be friendly and matter-of-fact. This is how we are both firm *and* kind.

- **Eye contact** is important if we want to "get through." A curious "Are you listening?" look as we seek eye contact is most desirable. Cold glaring stares scare people and cause them to avoid eye contact.

- **Hand motions** also speak volumes. Pointing fingers and pounding fists convey aggression and cause defensiveness. We want to keep our hands open and move them in relaxed flowing ways.

- **Standing** over someone with our hands on our hips is a position of authority and dominance. We are likely to get defiance in return. The ideal stance is to move toward others calmly, while speaking in a controlled way. With young children or someone sitting, it is preferable to kneel or sit at eye level. Just this position, alone, helps them be more open to what we are saying.

- **Timing** is also important to get our message through. Avoid confronting or criticizing others in front of a group. It is embarrassing and humiliating. They will not only react negatively, but will probably seek revenge later for their humiliation. Ask the person to step into a private place. If we can't leave, we can get their attention with a gentle hand on the shoulder as we whisper something in one ear. When we respect others' privacy and confidentiality, they are more likely to respect us by listening and cooperating.

CLEAR COMMUNICATION TOOLS

Notice that when we use the following communication tools, we don't usually tell people what to do. This is not passive communication, because we assertively describe the problem and, sometimes, the solution we prefer. We then wait to see if people will voluntarily cooperate with our request or figure out an equally acceptable solution on their own. When we add an order or command to the end of an assertive statement, it sends a hidden message of "do what I say—now—or else" and can start a power struggle. Instead, simply focus on the problem, and give the person time to respond or act. Our hidden message implies, "I have confidence in your ability to resolve this problem." If we make these statements in a friendly, matter-of-fact way, children usually respond quicker. If they don't, we can select a firmer statement from this toolset before moving to the next level—redirecting misbehavior with the PU or PO Toolset.

Describe What You *See* ☆☆☆☆

Use objective words that create a picture. Instead of labeling ("You're messy"), judging ("You always leave your messes for me to clean") or assuming why children are misbehaving ("You just love making my job harder"), we simply describe the problem as we *see* it. "*I see* books, coats, and papers on the living room floor." If children know where the objects belong, we don't have to give this information again. Without tacking on an order, our description says, "You know where they go and I trust you to put them there, now."

Avoid the word "you"; say "I" instead. Saying "you" is like pointing a finger of blame. People take it personally and defend themselves. Instead of *"You* need to take out the trash," say "The trash needs to be taken out." Try to use "I" whenever you can. Say, *"I see* wet towels laying on the bathroom floor," instead of blaming, *"You* left wet towels . . ." or ordering, "Pick up the wet towels *you* left . . ." Follow the "Don't Say 'Don't'" rule when using this tool. Describe what needs doing ("*I see* the dog needs food") or what you see ("The dog's bowl is empty").

> **When dealing with Child problems, use "you" and avoid "I."** Child problems belong to others, so we talk about how *they* think and feel. Using "I" shifts the focus to us, which causes others to feel we interrupted them, so they stop talking.
>
> **When dealing with Parent problems, use "I" and avoid "you."** Parent problems belong to us, so we talk about how *we* think and feel. Using "you" shifts the focus to others and sounds blameful, which causes others to feel defensive and stop listening.

Use "someone" or "people" when describing behavior, because it would probably bother us if *anybody* acted this way. Instead of saying, "I saw *you* throw sand," say "I see *someone* throwing sand."

The appropriate children know we are referring to them without pointing any fingers. If we say, "I'm sick of *your* smart-aleck attitude," we're not only blaming by using "you," but labeling the behavior as "smart-alecky." We can be just as assertive and more tactful if we say, "I understand you are angry (we can use "you" when noticing *their* feelings), but it's easier to listen to feelings and concerns if they are worded respectfully." This says what we *are* willing to do, within limits. We can also say, "In this family, we treat each other with respect even when we are angry," which teaches a family value.

Use "sometimes" or "when," instead of "always" or "never." ("You *never* return my stuff.") People usually deny or debate exaggerations and blame, "No, I don't do it *all* the time!" Instead, say "Sometimes my _____ is missing when I need it" or "When I go to use my _____, I expect it to be in the _____."

Describe How You *Feel*

We can combine this tool with the previous one to express our feelings about a particular behavior or problem. The description focuses on our feelings about the *behavior*, not the person. "I feel _____ when (describe the problem)." For example, "It's frustrating to say something three times and get no response."

Own your feelings, saying "I feel," instead of, "*You make* me feel . . ." Remember what we learned in the Keep Your Cool Toolset—no matter what another person does, we *choose* how we are going to interpret the event. If we say, "You make me feel . . ." we are *giving away* our personal power. We might as well say, "Look how powerful you are. You *made me* lose my temper." With children, this statement can reinforce the belief that being in power is important, which increases manipulative or rebellious behavior. When we own our feelings, *we* are in control—of *ourselves*.

Avoid overusing *angry* or *upset*. Remember that anger is a secondary emotion. We want to express the emotion we felt *before* the anger. This helps children learn about the emotional effects of their behavior. Also, if we overuse "angry," children simply conclude, "Everything makes you mad!" There are many shades of anger and many words to describe it:

	Alternatives to "I'm angry (or upset)."			
I am/feel . . .	irritated	exasperated	seeing red	stewing
livid	frustrated	provoked	uncomfortable	boiling over
fuming	furious	enraged	displeased	ticked off
annoyed	aggravated	outraged	smoldering	
I'm ready to. . .	explode	have a cow	fly off the handle	I can't see straight.
	blow my top	blow my stack	hit the ceiling	My blood's boiling.

So, what can we do if we keep our cool and respectfully assert our concerns, only to have children reply, "Tough. I don't care. If you're upset, that's your problem."? We can say, "Well, I *do* care—about you. That's why I try to show respect for other people's feelings, even when I disagree. And I do have a problem if others don't treat me respectfully in return."

Express feelings authentically. If it is difficult to control our volume, we can try instead to emphasize certain words to get our point across. For example, we would stress the word "furious" more strongly than we would stress the word "annoyed." We always want to be respectful, even when we're angry. If we do take our feelings out on our children, we can restate ourselves in a more controlled way or say, "I'm sorry I yelled. I (describe the problem or your feelings) . . ." This conditional apology says, "I have a valid reason for being upset, but I regret the way I expressed it." Doing this can help rebuild trust and salvage something good out of the situation.

Avoid the word "embarrassed." "I'm embarrassed" is often misinterpreted as *"You are an* embarrassment." Embarrassment is based on the belief that we must care about what others think or how they will judge us. Therefore, no one *makes* us feel embarrassed, it is a self-imposed emotion. Naturally, things happen that are embarrassing (especially if we have children), but we can choose whether to accept that feeling and let it cause us to lose our self-control. If we cannot avoid the word, use it in a way that takes ownership of our feelings. "When I have to walk through a store with a child hanging on my pants, it's hard not to feel embarrassed." A good way to deal with embarrassment is to use humor. "It would be much easier for me to walk if my pants stayed on my body and your feet stayed on the floor!"

Avoid the word "disappointed." It turns statements into guilt trips. It sends the hidden message, "You *are* a disappointment" or "You could have done better." These comments cause others to feel like failures. Disappointment is usually caused by unrealistic expectations. When parents use guilt trips, children might change their behavior to please others. There is value in every good behavior and a positive sense of self-worth when it's practiced. *This* is the healthy motive for changing behavior.

> *A Parent Group Discussion. In class, a parent asked a valid question about feeling disappointed. Here is our conversation:*
>
> *Parent: If my child is normally a straight "A" student, can't I expect her to get good grades and be disappointed when she doesn't do her best? Can't I just tell her "You have a choice, you can put forth the effort and get good grades or keep sloughing off and fail"?*
>
> *Me: You can **hope** she will do her best and get good grades. But realistically, you can **expect** that there will be times when she feels bored, unmotivated, wants to take a break, or doesn't do her best. Usually these are normal cycles we all experience. It might be premature, however, to present a natural consequence. Remember, that's climbing into the attic of discipline. The truth is that we can never really **make** our children get good grades or do their best. If children feel encouraged, they naturally try harder. If we point out mistakes, children feel **more** discouraged and often give up.*
>
> *Since school problems are mostly Child problems, you want to use the F-A-X Listening and Problem-Solving Toolsets. Detach yourself from **your** disappointment and expectations and find out how your **daughter** feels and what she expects from **herself**. Use the Parent Problem Toolbox only when the problem interferes with the "SHARP RV" issues. Limit your opinions to these issues and quickly refocus on your daughter's feelings and perspective.*

Put them in your shoes. Use this tool when others can't relate to your perspective or how it feels to be in your shoes. This tool uses a point of reference that is familiar to the listener. It puts them in a similar situation in that area of *their* life so they see how they would feel. Then you make a comparison between *that* situation and their feelings and *your* feelings in *this* situation. Here are a few examples to illustrate this tool:

> *Situation:* Your young child runs away from you in a crowded place. You are afraid he'll get lost, but he has no fear.
>
> *Similar situation:* This child has a special stuffed animal, named Scruffy, that he wants to carry everywhere. (It could be *any* toy or object the child deeply loves.) Say, "Imagine that we went to the carnival and you and Scruffy went for a ride on the merry-go-round. When the ride is over, Scruffy is gone and you don't see him anywhere! Imagine how you would feel." If he doesn't use feeling words, continue the description, pausing between questions. "Would you look and look and look? Would you worry you might not ever find him? Would you wonder if someone took Scruffy? Do you think you should wait for Scruffy to find you? When you find him, what would you do when you rode the next ride?" If he doesn't volunteer an answer, add "Would you hold onto him even tighter?" When it seems he is experiencing the feelings in this situation, say, "That's how *I* feel when I can't find you. I love you so much and don't want you to get hurt or have someone else take you home! I look all over and worry I might not be able to find you. When I do, I want you to hold my hand so I can make sure I don't lose you again."

Situation: Your teenager wants to stay out extra late. She knows you will say "no" if she asks you privately, so she asks you in front of her friends, hoping their presence will pressure you to agree. She doesn't understand why it matters *where* she asks you this question.

Similar situation: "Imagine that you are at a party and your friends are in another room. One of them comes to you privately and wants you to play a cruel practical joke on a boy at the party. What would you say?" Wait for her response. Hopefully, she says she won't do it. Then say, "Now, imagine they call you into the other room and ask you in front of your friends. Now what would you say?" If she says she would still refuse to participate, add, "Now, as a group, they try to pressure you to change your mind. How do you feel toward your friends and the way they are using the group to pressure you to make a decision you know is wrong?" After she responds, make the connection to *your* feelings. "When I need to deny people's requests in front of their friends, I feel pressured and resentful, too. I might have even said 'yes,' *if* the person asked me in private!"

Share your values. Although we learned tips for teaching values in the Independence Toolset, many Parent problems are value conflicts. When we try to express our concerns, we often end up preaching and lecturing. Here are some additional suggestions we can follow when we want to share our values:

- *Talk about values before conflicts arise.* Values are best taught when children are young and more easily influenced. Use teachable moments to bring up the subject. Discussing news events, television shows, or advertisements, and telling stories about others' experiences are all ways we can share our values without a sermon.

- *Live by the values you want children to adopt.* Children, especially teens, can easily identify hypocrites. If we simply practice what we are tempted to preach, our children are more likely to imitate and adopt our values.

- *Don't force values on others.* When children raise moral questions, we can state *our* opinions and values, emphasizing that not everyone believes the same way. We can explain the basis for our conclusions and the effects of believing otherwise, but not impose our beliefs on others. Force is usually met with force. A relaxed attitude more often results in children considering and voluntarily adopting our values.

- *Be willing to consider other points of view.* We can admit when our children have a valuable point to consider. We can even change our beliefs, if their values have merit for our lives. If we find their values are right for their lives, but not necessarily right for ours, we can acknowledge their right to choose their own values. Here, we are not compromising our own values nor are we forcing them on others. Value conflicts arise mostly in the teen years. (There are some additional comments about values in the "Tips for Teens" section at the end of this chapter.)

Describe the Negative Effect of the Behavior

This tool combines the description of behavior ("When milk is left out . . . ") with a description of the effect that behavior has (. . . it spoils.") We are giving information so the person understands the reason for our concern. To be most effective, use measurable or visual terms, such as time, money, energy, or emotions. We can use this tool in any of the following circumstances:

- If we aren't sure if children know this information.
- If children might have forgotten the information.
- Before we expect children to follow through with a request.
- Before we assume children's behavior is "on purpose."

Often, once we give information, children figure out what action they want or need to take. We don't usually need to add an order or command, it is implied. For example, if we say, "When someone eats on the couch and food falls under the cushions, it attracts bugs," it implies two things: (1) "We don't want bugs" and (2) "don't leave crumbs in the couch." We want to keep our tone of voice matter-of-fact and avoid blameful statements like, "If you do __, you're going to *make__* happen." If we simply give information, most children prefer to feel responsible and mature by doing something about it. If we nag and order, they resist even more.

Emotional consequences are often less obvious to children. We can help them understand why certain behaviors, such as politeness or tactfulness, are important. For example, avoid saying, "Quit being so bossy" or "If you don't quit bossing your friends around they won't be your friends anymore." Instead, we can say, "When people don't get a turn now and then, they may not want to play any- more." Or "People don't like being told what to do. They stop having fun and might leave."

If we can't find a way to make a connection between the behavior and the negative effect, children can conclude that we want them to do it for no valid reason. If they see no value in the request, they are less likely to take action.

Keep it brief and simple, avoiding long explanations or lectures. The more we say, the less others will want to listen. It is nagging and blameful to say, "Someone didn't hang up the towels. They're all over the floor. They're going to get the carpet moldy." Instead, we can simply say, "Wet towels make carpets moldy."

Describe What You Want, Expect, or What Needs to Be Done

If we have used the previous tools in the past and the behavior occurs again, we want to make a firmer statement. We can also use this tool when children can't figure out a remedy. Rather than telling someone what to do with an order or command, try these firm, but respectful options:

- When (describe the problem), I expect (action we want done).
- I would like (describe positive behavior).
- I want _____ .
- I prefer _____ .

- I expect _____ .
- I need _____ .
- I plan to _____ .
- I'm willing to _____ .
- I'm not willing to _____ .

Be careful about turning this tool into a command or order. We are better off stating *our* limits, what we are and aren't willing to do, than telling children what *they* will or won't do (since we usually start power struggles when we do this). Here are some examples:

➤ *"When* people borrow my tools, *I expect* them returned to the toolbox right away."
➤ *"I want* everyone to rinse their own dishes and put them in the dishwasher."
➤ *"I expect* people to come home when they agree to be home."
➤ *"I plan to* take a nap, so *I would like* everyone to do something quiet for half an hour."
➤ *"I'm willing to* take someone to the library *when* I can schedule the time in advance. *I'm not willing to* take someone the night before a project is due."

A Personal Story. When Chris was in kindergarten, he decided he wanted to wear ten shirts to school—all at once! (Don't ask me why! To this day I don't know!) As he stood before me, looking like the Incredible Hulk, he proudly showed me his layers. I briefly commented that he might get hot and that others might think him strange. He insisted and I decided not to make a big issue out of this. He'd had strange, but innocent, ideas before and they usually didn't last long. I said, "You can wear ten shirts if you want, but **I'm only willing** *to wash the top shirt and the one that touches your skin.* **I expect** *the other shirts to be folded and put back in the drawer.* **I want to see** *zero shirts on the floor." He agreed. He wore ten shirts—and folded eight each night—for a couple of weeks and then went back to the traditional one-shirt style.*

State the Rules or Limits

There are short but effective rules that have stood the test of time. We can call them "Grandma's Rules":

- "Work before play."
- "Say it nicely."
- "Safety first!"
- "Make amends for mistakes."
- "There is always an effect, positive or negative, for every action."

Rules need to be bottom-line statements, not detailed descriptions. (Remember the "Rules for Setting Rules" in the Cooperation Toolset.) Once we state the bottom line, we can then shift the focus to the choices children have within those boundaries. Instead of threatening ("If you don't pick up these dirty clothes, I won't do your laundry), state the bottom line, "I only wash clothes that are in the hampers on laundry day." We state the rule with an implied expectation that dirty clothes are put in hampers. We have also revealed the effect of not putting clothes in the hamper.

Use helpful questions to decide rules. For example, "What would happen if . . . ? (Wait for the response.) What could you do to prevent this?" Use a curious tone of voice, not an angry one.

Don't assume people know the rules, especially those that could vary from family to family. Some examples are "Please remove your shoes at the door" and "We ask permission to be excused from the table." It is unrealistic and unreasonable to expect others to follow unspoken family rules. It is especially important to clarify rules when blending two families after divorce and remarriage.

> *A Personal Story. My parents divorced my first year in college. When I came home to visit, I naturally operated by the family rules and routines we had always followed. For example, each evening I'd check everyone's schedules and move the cars so they could pull out in order. One weekend, I arrived before my mother and parked in the driveway, where I had always parked. My future stepfather came to visit. When he arrived, he scolded me for "taking my mother's parking space." He said it was "disrespectful to park in the garage or driveway. Children are supposed to park on the street."*

> *Surprised by this new rule, I explained that we had never had designated parking spaces. I said I could see the value of his point and explained my parking plan. He insisted that I had "disrespectful disregard" for my mother's needs. Knowing how much I respect my mother and try to consider her needs, I was very offended. We got into a heated argument and I stormed out of the house. (Our first and only big argument.)*

> *From then on, I was careful not to park in their driveway and asked permission first before parking there. I discovered other "hidden" rules over the years, but didn't argue or try to explain myself. I simply memorized them and revealed them to my family.*

"Hidden rules" cause resentment. If we expect others to follow our *preferences* as though they are universal rules we are being unfair and unreasonable. People are not mind-readers and resent it when others accuse them of violating rules they don't know about. Here's the bottom line: *If we expect it, we need to make the expectation realistic, respectful, and clear. Otherwise, we can't expect others to know or comply with our rules.*

Get Eye-to-Eye Agreements ☆☆☆☆

When we want to confirm that someone heard and understood us, eye contact is *vital*. If we ask someone to do something and we hear, "Okay" or "I will," we can add one final word, "When?" If we want to avoid getting a simple, "Later" or "Soon," we need to be specific. "*What time can I expect to see* _____?" Most children (and adults) will choose the latest time possible. When they do, we confirm our expectation. "So at six o'clock, I can expect to see _____, right?"

When we have a commitment, we want to maintain eye contact until we see some form of agreement. This could be as simple as a nod "yes" or something more. Here are some other ways to confirm agreements:

- "Do we have a deal?" (*Shake hands.*)
- "So you will do (task) by (time), right?" *Get eye contact*, so you avoid a "Yeah, whatever" response and later an "Oh, I forgot." People are less likely to forget when they look at our eyes and then agree.
- *Confirm your expectations*, "So when you tell me you're done, I can expect to see the floor clean, with everything where it belongs. Right?"
- *Confirm the agreement*. "So when Saturday night comes and you're tired, I can still count on you to go to the party and not cancel, right?" (This is the one I use with my husband! ☺)

When the agreed time arrives, if the other person forgets or tries to back out of the agreement, we can still avoid a power struggle. Set limits by emphasizing the agreement. "We had an agreement that the leaves would be raked *before* you left for the mall. You can go *after* the leaves are finished." Then don't add any extra nagging or reminders. Instead, use nonverbal cues, such as pointing to or looking at a watch, smile knowingly, or giving a hug. They may not be happy, but they will probably cooperate. Don't make a big deal about under-the-breath grumbling. Shift gears to listening, "I know you don't really feel like doing this. Thank you for keeping your agreement." If the comment is really out-of-line, the child *and* parent need to calm down before discussing the behavior. Otherwise, it's like two volcanoes ready to erupt.

If children have broken agreements in the past, we can add a statement that reveals discipline. Although we haven't learned the specifics of the Discipline Toolset, an example could be, "If the dishwasher isn't running by 6:30, I'll know you've decided to turn off the TV and do the dishes then." Then say nothing, wait for the agreed time to arrive, and follow through.

Mix and Match Tools

We can use all these tools by themselves or with other communication tools. This does not mean we repeat ourselves. We combine the tools to make *one* statement, as in the following examples.

INSTEAD OF SAYING :	SAY:
Don't interrupt me. It's rude.	*I feel* frustrated *when I'm* interrupted. (Describes the feelings and behavior.)
Turn off that TV and listen to me.	*When* I'm talking, *I expect* others to listen. (Describes the behavior and our expectations.)
Stop driving so fast!	*It* scares me *to* go 75 miles an hour. *We could* have an accident. (Describes feelings, the behavior, and the negative effect.)
You're giving me a headache!	*I get* a headache *when* there's so much noise. (Describes the negative effect of the behavior and the behavior itself.)

Shift Gears

When we are talking, we need to remember to shift back to the listening tools if we encounter resistance or an emotional reaction from others. We may need to go back and forth several times to get a clear understanding. Then we can move onto problem solving or redirect problem behavior.

> *A **Parent Group Discussion**. A mother shared the following story and we discussed how she could use a combination of the skills she had already learned to respond more helpfully.*
>
> *My four-year-old son fell asleep in the car after shopping. When we got home, his sister woke him up. He was mad at her for waking him (he wanted me to wake him) and started being mean to her. I said, "I'm not going to wake you up when I'm tired from carrying in stuff from the car and she's right there." He kept saying, "But . . ." I yelled, "If you won't listen I'll yell even louder until you do!" I know he was tired and wanted me to carry him in, but . . ." I interrupted the mother's story, "Wait a minute. Did you tell **him** you understood he was tired and wanted **you** to wake him up, even though you weren't willing to do it?" "Well, no," she replied. I said, "Let's reword this so you can move beyond his emotions and the power struggle, without violating your rights. Let's use the universal PASRR formula. Fill in the blanks: 'I can tell you feel _____.' **Then** say what you're feeling or thinking." She said, "Okay, I know you don't like your sister waking you up, but I'm not willing to carry you in when I'm already tired and you can walk." "Now," I said, "offer him some choices." She thought a few seconds and replied, "You can either keep sleeping in the car or have your sister wake you up." She added, "But what if he fusses at those ideas, too?" I said, "Then you can move into problem solving. This is a problem for him, too! Set your bottom line, 'I'm not willing to carry you in and you don't want your sister to wake you.' Then ask him, 'How else can you wake up?' Put the ball in his court."*
>
> *She did some brainstorming with her son before their next shopping trip. He whined a bit, but followed through with his agreement to have his mother wake him, but walk inside by himself.*

Quick Reminders ☆☆☆☆

We want to avoid nagging and constant reminders. When we have used longer descriptive statements in the past, sometimes we only need a quick reminder.

Human behavior is consistent, despite age. When we tell children something in one or few words, it gets their attention. They don't have time to tune us out. Then, because they are so appreciative that we didn't lecture them or embarrass them in front of others, they *reward our* behavior by cooperating.

Short, clear statements can help us avoid lectures, which cause eyes to roll and ears to close. Here are four short and clear reminders.

 ## NONVERBAL SIGNALS

We have all used nonverbal signals at some time or another, such as putting a finger to our lips to say "Shh." Another is "the look," that knowing glance with a smile that says, "Okay, that's enough!" This look differs from the "evil eye," which conveys a threat or spite. A firm but matter-of-fact look that says "I heard that" or "You know better" is often all that's necessary to get children thinking twice about what they are saying or doing.

These nonverbal signs are fairly obvious, but we can invent more to suit our needs and the situation. These are nonverbal codes that we explain ahead of time. Children like nonverbal codes, because they are fun and spare them embarrassment. Here are a few signals that other graduates and I have used:

➤ Twisting my nose means, "turn down the volume" on your voice.
➤ Using the American Sign Language sign for "thank you" to remind children to show appreciation, instead of saying, "What do you tell the nice lady?"

> ➤ A teenage son and his father came up with the code, "8-3-1," which means "It has eight letters, three words, and means one thing, 'I love you.'"
> ➤ One mother sent her dog into the family room with his bowl hanging from his neck. The kids got the message to "feed the dog."

USE ONE WORD

When children forget something we've explained in the past, we can use one or two words to remind them of the longer explanation we once gave. *Do not* use a child's name as the one word. It sends no information and can cause the child to equate his name with being in trouble. (I always knew when the boy down the street was in *big* trouble. His mother would yell his full name from the front door.) If we use children's names, we only want to use them to get their attention and then add the one word reminder. Also, follow the "Don't say 'Don't'" rule and make the word state what you want the child *to do.*

INSTEAD OF SAYING	USE ONE WORD
Turn off the light.	Light!
Flush the toilet.	Flush.
Pick up your shoes.	Shoes.
You know you're not allowed on the wood pile!	Wood pile or Off!
Don't run.	Walk.
Get out of the street.	Sidewalk.

LEAVE A NOTE

When children have a case of "parent deafness," notes are particularly effective. Notes visually say something without actually talking, so children have no chance to tune us out. We can use notes anytime, with children of all ages. Here are some ideas for using notes:

* Notes can be simple, friendly, or even humorous reminders. For example, I saw this sign hung over a toilet, "We aim to please. You aim too, please."
* We can get creative, giving inanimate objects a voice. For example, attach a note to a laundry basket that says "I'm hungry, please feed me dirty clothes."
* Even if children can't read, they can understand pictures. Just the sight of a note gets their interest and they will probably ask what the note says.

A Personal Story. A friend has little signs posted in her bathroom. They have pictures she and her son cut out of magazines of different tasks in his morning and bedtime routines. All he has to do is look at the pictures and he can remember what to do next. This has prevented a lot of reminding and nagging.

When my son was old enough to take responsibility for feeding the dog, but wasn't old enough to read, I hung this note (to the right) on our family room door.

We can also write notes when we are too upset to trust ourselves to keep our cool. Just the process of writing a note helps diffuse our anger. If our first effort comes off too strong, we can rewrite it, until we say what we want, the way we want to say it. When we put apologies or words of encouragement in writing, they can have a lasting effect:

> *A **Personal Story**. When I was a teen, my brother's behavior had really deteriorated, so our home was always a high-stress zone. My dad would often take a nap after work. One evening, I didn't know he was sleeping and was being loud and silly. He flew out of bed, thinking there was an argument. He was scared and upset and yelled at me. I felt bad, but was hurt by what he said, and gave him the silent treatment the rest of the night. The next evening, on my desk, was a letter of apology. He told me he appreciated my sense of humor and how much I meant to him. He shared his reasons for getting angry and told me how much he loved me. To this day, I still have his letter, although there is a big tear stain on the words.*

When someone writes a letter, whether to apologize or encourage, it often means more than an in-person talk. We know the person took the time to sit and write and it's something we can save for later, to rekindle the warm feelings it brought. Notes are so effective, our children often start using them to communicate with us.

> *A **Personal Story**. When I came home from an evening class, I found a note on the door. Chris, then age 8, must have run out of his favorite clothes. His note said, "Please wash blacks tonight. I'll dry them in the morning. P.S. Good night. Love, Chris."*

FLASH CODES

Flash codes are one-word reminders that parents and children agree on privately before a problem arises. The word means a sentence or idea. The word has special meaning to both of you, but can mean nothing to others. For example, the word "banana" can mean "Quit picking your nose." In public, we can say, "Tommy, do you smell *bananas*?" This spares children from nagging and embarrassment. (I invented flash codes when Chris was three and we did parent/child problem solving. I'll share the whole story in the next section.)

Two-Party Problem-Solving ☆☆☆☆

We learned how to do one-party problem solving with Child problems, "keeping the ball in their court." When a problem also affects us, we both need to be involved in the problem-solving process and agree on a solution that meets both our needs. To do this we add one step, defining the problem from both viewpoints, and expand another step, detailing who will do what to achieve the plan. Although we can use two-party problem solving in any relationship, we will apply it to parent/child relationships. We can do problem solving on the spur of the moment in a condensed form or, if a problem keeps occurring, we can arrange a time to follow the process step-by-step in writing.

The goal of two-party problem solving is to reach a "win/win" agreement. "Win/win" does *not* mean both people get *everything* they want. Usually, it means both people get *some* of what they want, their "bottom line" needs. Both or neither may be happy about doing what they agreed to do, but they know it is a fair agreement and are therefore willing to follow through with it.

These are the basic steps of two-party problem solving:

a. Define the problem.
     i. Introduce the problem topic in one sentence.
     ii. Invite the other person to share his/her perspective.
     iii. Ask if the other person is willing to listen to your concerns.
     iv. Share your perspective.
     v. Summarize the problem for each person.
b. Brainstorm ideas.
c. Evaluate the options.
d. Choose, define, and commit to the solution.
e. Follow-up.

---

a. Define the Problem

Since we use two-party problem solving when *we* have a problem, we usually need to bring the problem to the attention of the other person. Even if the problem is not a C/P problem, we still want to listen to other people's feelings and perspectives. To get off on the right foot, define the problem by following these steps:

    i. ***Introduce the problem topic.*** We *briefly* introduce the topic (without opinions) using one of the Clear Communication tools. For example, "We have been having a lot of arguments about curfew lately."

    ii. ***Invite the other person to share his/her perspective.*** We stress that we *want* to see the situation from the other person's point-of-view and quickly shift to listening mode. "I'd like to hear your thoughts about curfew and any ideas you have for an agreement we can both live with. What are your concerns about the way we currently handle curfew?" To avoid arguments, *stick to the issue*. Keep asking, "What else do you think or feel?" We don't defend our position or disagree. (This can be difficult if we hear blameful statements. If others criticize or blame us, we can use a quick "I" message, "I'm willing to listen to your perspective, but it's hard if I feel criticized. Can you tell me what you don't like with respectful words?") Write their feelings, opinions, and other comments on the "Problem Solving Worksheet" at the end of the Problem-Solving Toolset. Now and then, we clarify and summarize their opinions, "Let me get this straight, you feel _____, because _____."

    iii. ***Ask if the other person is willing to listen to our concerns.*** If we have been listening with respect and ask permission before speaking, most people are willing to listen to us without interrupting. In the remote chance that the other person says, "No, I'm not willing to listen to you," reveal the result. "Well, we can keep arguing about this or we can come up with an agreement that meets both our needs. I'd like to *try* to resolve this. Will you give it a try, too?"

    iv. ***We share our concerns,*** using the Clear Communication Toolset. *Do not* try to *agree* on the same viewpoints or issues. We can agree that we *both* have different concerns. We look for truth on both sides and simply try to understand each other. Then we ask them to tell us what they just heard us say, so we know they understand, even if they don't agree. (This teaches them reflective listening skills.) If, at any point in our sharing, they interrupt us, we can calmly say, "I listened without interrupting. I'd like to have my ideas and opinions heard, too, even if we disagree."

    v. ***Summarize the problem for each person.*** Once we both state our opinions, we summarize the problem in a nutshell, "So for you it's like this . . . and for me it's like this . . ." Or "You'd like _____ and I want _____."

b. Brainstorm Possible Solutions

Introduce brainstorming with a comment such as, "Can you think of some ways that you could (their biggest issue) and I could (your biggest issue)?" In the curfew example, we might say, "Can you think of a way that you could be with your friends longer and I could know where you are and that you're safe?" ***We want to summarize the problem in a way that gives us a win/win goal to focus on.*** This helps us move beyond differences of opinions and needs to focusing on solutions.

We allow the other person to come up with ideas first. This emphasizes that we are not trying to impose *our* solutions. Allowing someone to state an idea is entirely different from accepting that idea for the final agreement. Be patient. Just keep asking, "What else?" and write down every possibility. If we offer an idea, we want to word it as a suggestion, "One possibility is . . ." or "We could . . ." Avoid "We should . . ." ***Do not evaluate any ideas at this point.*** If others criticize *our* ideas, we remind them, "It's just an idea. We don't have to use it."

c. Evaluate the Options

Consider the possible outcome of each idea. Unacceptable options can be altered to make them acceptable to both parties. Use phrases such as, "What would happen if we did this?" And "How do you feel about this one?" Or "Are you willing to . . . ?" If we don't like an idea, we express our concerns without blame or criticism. "I would be concerned about doing that because. . ." Or "I'm not willing to do this because . . ." We want to keep the word "you" out of our comments if possible. Cross off ideas or parts of suggestions one or both parties are unwilling to agree to.

d. Choose, Define, and Commit to the Solution

Choose the solution both parties favor most. It may be a combination of more than one idea. Make sure both parties understand what that plan would involve. Define who will do what and when it needs to be done. Agree not to nag or remind. If it seems appropriate to the situation, also define what will happen if the agreement is broken. This last part may involve revealing discipline (Chapter 13, "Discipline Toolset"). Agree to try the solution for a trial period. Set a time to discuss how the agreement is working—or isn't working. During the trial period, if we notice others aren't following through with their agreements, we can say, "Remember our agreement?" Use a friendly attitude of respect, keeping *our* agreement not to nag.

e. Follow-up

See what happens during the trial period and bring up any problems at the follow-up meeting. Be willing to adjust or change the agreement if it seems unworkable or new information is available. We want to check to see how the solution is working for others, even if it's working for us.

> *A **Personal Story.** When Chris was three-and-a-half years old, he would whine and complain about how long it took to clean his room and got distracted by the toys he was picking up. I knew Chris' behavior was age-appropriate and tried keeping realistic expectations. I had taught him how to pick up items and organize them, but found myself nagging him to stay on task.*
>
> *We sat over a cup of hot chocolate and did problem solving. I started by asking him how he felt about cleaning. He said it was no fun and was afraid he would die of starvation and thirst before he was done. I held back my laughter and remembered how different his sense of time was. I wrote his concerns on paper. I acknowledged how hard it is to get motivated to clean and how easy it is to get distracted (his part of the problem). I told him I was frustrated about how long it took him to clean even a small part of his room (my part of the problem.) I said I was tired of nagging and was sure he didn't like feeling pressured, either. Then I summarized the problem, "So it sounds like we need to find a way to make cleaning more fun, make sure your body is taken care of, and keep you focused on cleaning without me nagging."*
>
> *Then, I moved into brainstorming, "Let's take these one at a time. What could we do to make cleaning more fun?" I was surprised how many ideas he suggested. He suggested roller skating around the room to deliver his toys and playing "Supercalifragilisticexpialidocious" to help him work faster. So far, I didn't have a problem with any of the ideas. He wanted potty and snack breaks. I was concerned he'd use these as excuses not to clean, so I set some conditional limits, ". . . when you finish cleaning one group of toys or one section of the room." These agreements dealt with his boredom and my concern about how long it took to clean. Now I needed suggestions to deal with my part, the nagging. I asked him to suggest a word that, when I said it, would mean "Get back to work." He saw his Flash superhero character on the floor and suggested the word "flash." "Okay," I said, " Whenever you hear the word 'flash,' it means 'Get back to work.' (When I told this story to my class, they named the skill "flash code.")*
>
> *Our problem-solving session was a big turning point. For years he skated to Mary Poppins music. Eventually, Chris didn't need the songs, skates, or "flash" code to complete his tasks. On those occasions when he didn't finish, I didn't nag. The next day, when he asked to play, I'd ask if his room was clean. When he said, "No," I simply said, "You can play as soon as your room is clean." It only took a few times of following through (which I occasionally still need to do) for better cleaning habits to develop.*

PROBLEM SOLVING "ON THE RUN"

"Who has time to sit and figure all this out?" some people ask. If we find we are spending a lot of time reminding, nagging, or arguing, our time is better spent problem solving. We may find that we only do the sit-and-write-it-down version under the following circumstances:

- When we are dealing with recurring problems.
- When we are negotiating ongoing rules and agreements.
- When we and our children have strong differences of opinions or needs.
- When children have seriously violated a rule.

Many times, we can do a quick version of two-party problem-solving. We follow the same steps, except we combine the brainstorming and evaluation steps. Here is a sample conversation with the steps highlighted.

Dad: (*Introduce the problem topic.*) I was expecting you home at six o'clock. (*Invite the other person to share his/her perspective.*) What happened?
Son: I just forgot the time. I'm only half an hour late! What's the big deal?
Dad: (*Acknowledging his perspective.*) I know it's hard to keep track of time when you are having fun, (*Now share your perspective using the Clear Communication Toolset*) . . . but I worry when you are more than ten minutes late and haven't called. I called your friend's house, but the line was busy and I had dinner waiting. (*Summarize the problem in a way that focuses on the solution.*) How could you remember to be on time, even when you are playing? (*Invite brainstorming.*)
Son: You could quit worrying. I can take care of myself.
Dad: (*In quick brainstorming, we can acknowledge their perspective while evaluating the idea.*) You're right, you *can* handle a lot of problems, but I still sometimes worry. My real concern is that I expect to see you walk in the door when you've agree to come home. (*Keep the focus on finding a solution.*) How can you remember what time it is when you are busy?
Son: If I had a watch with an alarm, I could set it.
Dad: (*Evaluate the options.*) Well, the alarm would go off even if you were distracted. (*Choose a solution. Define the details and roles.*) I would be willing to buy a watch if it is less than twenty dollars. If I do that, will you agree to set the alarm each time you leave?
Son: Yeah.
Dad: (*Confirm the agreement and the effects of breaking it.*) And what will happen if you don't set the alarm as you agreed and are late for dinner?
Son: I'll just heat up the food.
Dad: And clean up your dishes and put away the food?
Son: Okay.
Dad: (*Parents can make a value statement if it hasn't already been stated.*) I *really* want to eat together as a family, so I want to know you will make every effort to keep our agreement.
Son: I'll try.
Dad: (*Get a commitment.*) Try?
Son: Okay, I *will* remember.
Dad: All right, I'm holding you to that (Dad pats son on back.)

TIPS FOR TOTS AND TEENS

Be patient during difficult developmental stages, such as the toddler and teen years. We never want to give up or stop showing unconditional love for our children, even when we cannot condone their behavior. Our future relationship is often riding on how we handle these difficult periods.

Tots

Young children *can understand* what we are saying long before they can actually speak themselves. They especially pick up on our tone of voice, attitude, and body language. If we express our feelings and needs assertively, young children learn the value of respecting others' feelings and rights. This helps prevent rude speaking habits.

Young children may have a harder time thinking of ideas during problem solving, but don't jump in and tell them what to do. Be patient and encouraging. Focus on the bottom line and allow any ideas that fit within that limit. Offer simple suggestions and teach skills for carrying them out. If we use problem solving when children are young, they better resolve problems as they grow older.

Teens

Teens are often quite opinionated, outspoken, and question values and rules. (Remember the backpack analogy in Chapter 6, "Independence Toolset"?) These are all positive signs that our teens are maturing. Nevertheless, it can be surprising and difficult when once-quiet, compliant children suddenly speak out strongly and emotionally. We need to work extra hard not to take what they say personally and not to get hooked into arguing over differences of opinions or values. It is vital that we keep the lines of communication open during the teen years. We want to talk less and use F-A-X Listening more.

Many parents worry about teens abandoning family values. Usually, teens only temporarily test values and rules they have not learned firsthand or observed in action. If parents aren't trying to control their teens, teens won't feel such strong needs to push away from their parents' values. When teens are testing and acting out, we want to be careful not to blow things out of proportion. Teens usually need to experience temporary imbalances before they settle into their own unique values and opinions. We need to keep long-term goals (ours and theirs) in mind for teens to become well-balanced independent adults.

> **The way our teens act, think, and feel on a bad day is not usually what they will be like as adults. If we observe them on a good day, when everyone is in the No problem zone, we can predict more accurately what they will be like as adults.**

Parent/child conflicts often increase during the teen years, because of all the above reasons. There are also dangerous safety issues facing our teens and we are no longer with them constantly to protect and guide them. It's tempting to lecture or restrict their independence, but both tactics only result in greater rebellion. If our teens haven't yet learned responsible decision-making skills, we need to use problem solving to teach these skills. We also need to understand teens' points-of-view and be willing to negotiate win/win solutions to problems. When discussion and negotiation have no impact, consider whether the teen's behavior will harm anyone. If so, we can listen first to the teen's perspective and hold firm to our bottom line. We can allow teens to have as much choice or control as the situation allows. If this doesn't work, we can reveal the positive and negative effects of their choices. Our goal is to be a "consultant," listening, offering advice when they ask, or making it clear something is *our* opinion and letting teens choose and experience the lessons. It's more important that we are assertive about our concerns and "keep the ball in their court" as much as possible. They may be testing us or planning to change their behavior later, when we aren't pressing the issue, to "save face."

At times, we need to accept what we cannot change. If our teens have not given us valid reasons to distrust them, we need to demonstrate our trust and have faith—faith in our teens' ability to make responsible decisions and learn from their mistakes, faith in our long-term parenting plan, and faith in a higher power who can protect them when we aren't around.

Most of these suggestions for communicating with teens apply to teens who are not severely troubled or into extremely dangerous behavior. When these factors apply, parents need to access community resources to protect and redirect teens until they can learn better decision-making skills and work through the *real* issues causing their behavior.

CONCLUSION

Many parents keep trying to get through to their children until they tire of nagging and then blow up. If we follow the Universal Blueprint, we usually only need to make our point once or twice, before moving to the next step. We always start at the lowest step and intensity as possible (using prevention tools, for example). We only move to the next step to make firmer statements if children ignore or resist our first attempts. We want to make sure we and our children understand the problem and each other's feelings. It is important to remain assertive, even if we get firmer, and not resort to passive or aggressive tactics.

> *A Personal Story.* On vacation, we went grocery shopping for two weeks of supplies. In the first aisle, my kids asked me to buy an extra item. I calmly said, "We are only buying what we'll use while we are here, the items on this list. Maybe when we get home we can get that."

> The next time they asked, I moved up a level, saying, "I know you really want that. I'd like it, too, if we had enough room in the cooler to bring home the leftovers. Besides, whatever extra money we spend on groceries cuts into our fun money."

> I was sure that last point would curb their demands, but they asked again! I decided to make it short but clear. I said, "Today, we are only getting what's on the list—period!" I couldn't believe they asked yet again! This was very unusual for them and I was getting angry.

> I knew I needed to be firm enough to prevent things from getting worse. I said, "I've heard three requests for extras that are not on this list. I'm getting annoyed and feel like I'm being nagged. I don't want to hear that question again, is that clear?" I even revealed my intentions, "I will ignore any further requests for extras." We were all quiet for a few minutes, which gave me time to cool down.

> We finished our shopping without any further requests. Although my tone of voice and body language increased in intensity, I had to try very hard not to become aggressive.

It is difficult for everyone, at first, to filter their words. As we practice assertive communication, we do a quick double check before we speak. We ask ourselves, "If someone said this to me, how would I take it?" Soon, it only takes a couple of seconds to think about our response and remove the judging, blaming, and criticism. We want our communication to open doors, not put up walls and close doors.

> *A Graduate's Story.* I was tired of blaming and criticizing my young son so often. My negative comments reminded me of the fairy tale "Toads and Diamonds." In this tale, two sisters, one kind and generous and one selfish and critical, are put under an enchanted spell. The kind daughter drops diamonds and other jewels from her lips whenever she speaks. The critical daughter spews toads and snakes whenever she speaks.

> I thought my comments sounded more like toads than jewels—and I couldn't stand listening to myself any longer. I told myself, "If I can't say something respectfully, I won't say anything at all." Still, I found little "digs" slipping from my lips. I read the story to my son and explained how I felt. I told him I had decided to tape my mouth shut for a day, to enforce my commitment to myself. And I did!

> As silly as it sounds, this was a profound learning experience. I learned that I talked more than I needed to and **was** capable of thinking about what I wanted to say. I also found new ways to communicate, without words. When my day was over, I was less talkative and more thoughtful about what I said. My son learned much, too. When he is having a bad day and I comment on it,

he sometimes replies, "Maybe I could put tape on my mouth." (Author's note: I don't think it's necessary to tape our mouths shut, although I had a similar learning experience when my jaw was reconstructed and wired shut for seven weeks.)

A woman listening to one of my presentations leaned over to a friend and whispered, loud enough for me to hear, "Right. Like I have the time to plan all my words!" If you share her sentiments, add up the time you spend repeating yourself, yelling, or saying "no" and "don't." Also think about the long-term messages your present communication style might be teaching. I admit, the language of effective parenting seems awkward and initially takes more time to think of and say. However, in the long run, we find our children become more cooperative and self-disciplined, instead of relying on our constant reminders.

Interestingly, children often learn effective communication skills even quicker than adults. We can get caught off guard when our children give *us* "I-messages." If we assume children are being defiant, just because they are speaking out, we've missed the point! These are the emotional paychecks that let us know we are on the right track. If children are verbal enough to express themselves assertively, we can definitely use problem solving to reach win/win solutions.

Childhood is Like a Long Car Ride

The car trip starts when we become adults. When children are born, our new passengers go everywhere with us. They depend on us and need to be with us constantly. They need to be protected from the dangers of even short car rides, so we make them ride in car seats. They build trust and security in knowing they are safe and we are trustworthy drivers. We experience irritating behaviors that are natural when traveling with infants. They usually spit up or fill their diaper when we're running late.

As our passengers become toddlers we become aware of their individual personalities. They don't understand the limits of a car ride. They want to explore everything! They try to eat the dried french fries that fell into their car seat. They get cranky while we try to find a restaurant. They want to play at rest stops and resist getting back into their restrictive car seat. They seem to fall asleep the last five minutes, after screaming and crying the first hour. They have no sense of time and every five minutes they ask "When will we get there?" They constantly ask "Why," and point to objects we can't see and ask, "What's that?"

As children enter the early school years, they are more used to structured activities and are developing their intellectual and social skills. They better understand the rules of riding in a car and how to behave. They watch how we drive, the decisions we make, how we find directions, and whether we obey the speed limit. They see how we handle conflicts with others, such as rude drivers that cut us off. From the back seat, they have a special vantage point. We aren't always aware of what we are doing, but they surely are! While they can better tolerate close spaces with others, this becomes a challenge if the other person is their sibling. Children still haven't learned how to live with someone who thinks and acts differently than them and often don't use good problem-solving skills when they have conflicts.

By the time our passengers reach their teens, they've seen and done it all. (Or so they think!) They would rather stay home with their friends than be stuck in a car with grownups and siblings. If they have to ride along, they want more say about where we go, who goes, and when we go. They want to take their own side trips, before they are legally old enough to drive. In preparation for that day, they need to build the skills that will be necessary for their solo trips: how to plan ahead for a trip, make a budget and stick to it, read a map, keep the gas tank full, handle unexpected delays and detours, and make split-second decisions that could affect their lives. We know the day is coming when they will begin their own car trip—and we can't always control what exit ramp they get off to explore. The most we can do, is help them learn the skills they need to survive in the car, with other people, and on the road. Then we need to trust, and let go.

SUMMARY SHEET
CLEAR COMMUNICATION TOOLSET

DESCRIBE WHAT YOU *SEE* ☆☆☆☆

Take out the word *you*. Use *sometimes* and *someone*.

DESCRIBE HOW YOU *FEEL*

Own your feelings. Avoid shaming.

DESCRIBE THE NEGATIVE EFFECT OF THE BEHAVIOR

DESCRIBE WHAT YOU WANT, EXPECT, OR WHAT NEEDS DONE

STATE THE RULES OR LIMITS

State the bottom line. Don't assume people know your rules.

GET EYE-TO-EYE AGREEMENTS ☆☆☆☆

QUICK REMINDERS ☆☆☆☆

Use nonverbal signals, one word, flash codes, or notes.

TWO-PARTY PROBLEM SOLVING ☆☆☆☆

a. Define the problem.
   i.   Introduce the problem topic.
   ii. Invite the other person to share his/her perspective.
   iii. Ask if the other person is willing to listen to your concerns.
   iv. Share your perspective.
   v.   Summarize the problem for each person.
b. Brainstorm ideas.
c. Evaluate the options.
d. Choose, define, and commit to the solution.
e. Follow-up.

PRACTICE EXERCISES

A. Identifying Communication Styles. Each of the following statements is an example of one of the four communication styles: Passive (P), Aggressive (Ag), Passive-Aggressive (P/A), or Assertive (As). Match each statement with the type of communication style it represents (P, Ag, P/A, As). If the sentence is not an assertive statement, rewrite it, using the Clear Communication Toolset (or any other appropriate tools you've learned.)

P = Passive   Ag = Aggressive   P/A = Passive-aggressive   As = Assertive

_____ 1.   The parent says, "You kids just go ahead and watch TV while I break my back cleaning up your messes." Rewrite, if not assertive:

_____ 2.   Your child is cracking her gum loudly. Parent says aloud to self, "Gee, I wish I could concentrate on my reading." Rewrite, if not assertive:

_____ 3.   "I'm willing to share the chips, but I'm not willing to let someone eat the whole bag!" Rewrite, if not assertive:

_____ 4.   "Don't interrupt me when I'm talking to you! You said your piece, so you *will* listen to mine!" Rewrite, if not assertive:

B. Use the Clear Communication Toolset. Plan an assertive response to the following situations, using the suggested tool.

1.   You just mopped the kitchen floor and see muddy shoe prints on it. (Describe what you *see.)*

2.   You were ready to leave on time for a wedding, but your children took so long that now you will all be late. (Describe how you *feel.)*

3.   Tony, 10, voluntarily did a load of laundry. When you take the laundry out of the washer to put into the dryer, you find one of your white dress shirts has black dye stains on it because one tiny black sock got mixed in with the whites. (Describe the negative effect of the behavior.)

4.   You walk out of the kitchen into the living room and almost trip over a coat and backpack left on the floor in the doorway. (Describe what you want, expect, or what needs to be done.)

5.   You start to sit at the family computer. You find diskettes, empty pop cans and chip bags strewn around the area. (State the rules or limits.)

6.   Tammy, 7, left her training-wheel bike on the sidewalk while she was playing next door. It was stolen in broad daylight. She wants another bike. (Get an agreement.)

7.   It is Kevin's, 9, responsibility to take out the trash. It's trash night, he's about to go to bed, and still hasn't taken the cans to the street. (Use a quick reminder: a nonverbal signal, one word, or flash code.)

C. Mix and match tools. Use any combination of the Clear Communication Tools or any of the other skills you have already learned to respond to these situations.

1.   Jack, 9, says he's finished cleaning the bathroom. The next time you go in, it doesn't look like he cleaned it at all! There's soap scum and water spots all over the faucet and there's still a ring in the toilet. You've already taught him the proper way to clean the bathroom.

2.   Chrissy, 6, and his mother are shopping for a birthday present for another child. Chrissy keeps pointing out toys he wants you to buy *her.* (Offer *three* responses you could give, assuming Chrissy persists after your first and second response.)

3. Emily, 14, wants to sit with her friends during her younger brother's choir performance at a festival and then walk around the festival with them. Your parents have traveled from out-of-town for this event and you want Emily to spend time with the family.

D. Teach Values. How would you teach values (without preaching) and use problem solving in these situations?

1. John, 4, received from relatives a hat and scarf set he didn't like. He said it was "ugly" in front them. You tried to smooth things over with both him and your relatives, but John just keeps getting louder and ruder.

2. Charlie, 6, read several stories to you last night, to practice his new reading skills. The next day, as he cleans out his backpack before school, you find a book and note from the teacher. It says he was supposed to read a certain story to you last night. You are to sign a paper verifying that he read it to you. Charlie suggests you sign the paper since he did read to you, although it wasn't the exact story he was supposed to read.

3. Bridgette, 13, says she doesn't want to go to church anymore. She says she isn't sure if she believes in God anymore, because science hasn't proven God exists.

Possible Answers

A. Identifying Communication Styles.

1. Passive-aggressive. Possible rewrite: "How can we work together to get this house clean?"

2. Passive. Possible rewrite: "I have a hard time concentrating when I hear gum cracking."

3. Assertive. No rewrite needed.

4. Aggressive. Possible rewrite: "I try to listen to others without interrupting and want to be treated with the same courtesy."

B. Use the Clear Communication Toolset. (These are just possible responses.)

1. "I just finished mopping the floor and now I see muddy shoe prints on it."

2. "I feel frustrated when I'm ready to leave on time but we end up being late anyway. This is a special wedding to me and I want to see *all* of it."

3. "Tony, thanks for taking the initiative to do a load of laundry." (Remember to notice the positive and offer encouragement.) "A black sock accidentally got in with the whites and left black stains on my white dress shirt. Since the shirt is still wet, let me show you how to get the stain out. (Teach skills.) In the future, what can you do as you are putting clothes in the washer to prevent this from happening again?"

4. "I expect coats and backpacks to be put away as soon as people come home."

5. "People who use the computer are responsible for cleaning up the area when they are done." Or "Food and drinks belong in the kitchen, away from the computer."

6. "You really didn't do anything wrong to cause your bike to get stolen. But I am worried about getting another bike if it can get stolen that easily. If we buy another one, we need to have an agreement for where you will park it. Where will you keep it when you are home? Where will you park it when you visit a friend's house?"

7. "Trash!" or sit a trash bag outside his bedroom door or by the outside door as a nonverbal reminder.

C. Mix and Match Tools.

1. In a friendly tone of voice, "Jack, come here. Can you show me exactly what you cleaned?" (Wait.) "I know it's tough to get off soap scum and toilet rings, but they need to be gone before the bathroom is 'finished.'"

2. "It's hard to shop for gifts and not get a toy for yourself, isn't it?" If it happens again, "Today, we are shopping for Susan's gift. If you want to make a list for gifts you want, here are a paper and pen."

3. "I'm sure it would be fun for you to explore the festival with your friends. Grandma and Grandpa can only stay for the festival and I want them to spend some time with you. If you sit with us during the choir performance, I'd be willing to let you walk around the festival with your friends for an hour."

D. Teach Values.

1. Excuse yourself from the relatives. In private say, "I know you're disappointed, but it hurts people's feelings when others criticize their gifts. It's important for us to say "thank you," even if we don't like the gift. Later, you can tell me, *in private*, that you don't like it. We'll figure out what to do then." (Give opportunities to share feelings and listen.) "I want you to apologize to them for saying it's ugly and thank them for picking out something they thought you would like."

2. "I wish I had known about this assignment last night when you read to me. This paper says you read *this* book to me. If I sign it, I'd be lying. I can either write a note telling the teacher what you did read or you can bring the book home again tonight and I'll sign the paper tomorrow. What do you think?"

3. "I'm glad you are thinking seriously about your religious beliefs. That's an important part of being an adult. Having faith in something without proof is a hard thing to do." (Wait for response and listen.) "We don't have to agree about all our religious beliefs, but it means a lot to me to attend church as a family. Can we find a way to meet both of our spiritual needs? Is there something in particular about our church you don't like?" (Wait.) "Would you like to try a different church?" (Wait.) "What about finding information about scientific proof of God?"

WHAT'S NEXT?

Whether we use no words, one word, or several sentences, we want to practice assertive, clear communication daily—in all areas of our lives. Once others know there is a problem, they may voluntarily take action to change or resolve the problem. If not, we can use two-party problem-solving, alternating between the listening, problem solving, and communication skills.

If the problem continues, despite these efforts, and problem behavior is involved, we are ready to use the behavior management tools. The next chapter, Chapter 11: "PU Toolset (Unintentional misbehavior)" describes in more detail how to tell the difference between PU and PO behavior. If the behavior is unintentional, this chapter reviews the tools we've already learned that can redirect misbehavior and offers a few new options we can choose.

REFERENCES

1. *Listening for Heaven's Sake*, by Dr. Gary Sweeten, Dave Ping, and Anne Clippard (Teleios Publishing, 1993) p. 84.

CHAPTER 11
PU TOOLSET (Unintentional misbehavior)

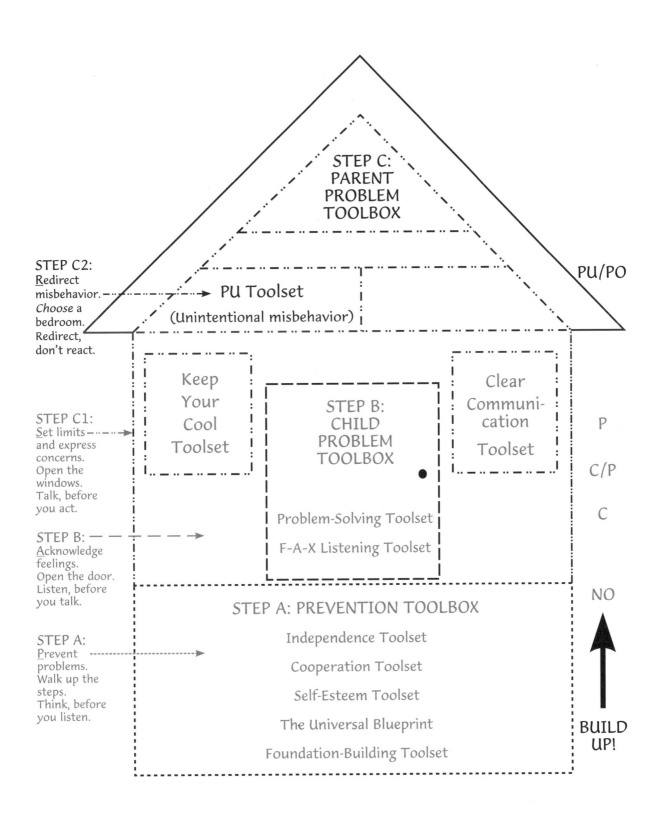

STEP C:
PARENT
PROBLEM
TOOLBOX

PU/PO

STEP C2:
<u>Redirect</u>
misbehavior.
Choose a
bedroom.
Redirect,
don't react.

PU Toolset
(Unintentional misbehavior)

STEP C1:
<u>Set</u> limits
and express
concerns.
Open the
windows.
Talk, before
you act.

Keep
Your
Cool
Toolset

STEP B:
CHILD
PROBLEM
TOOLBOX

Clear
Communi-
cation
Toolset

P

C/P

C

STEP B:
<u>Acknowledge</u>
feelings.
Open the door.
Listen, before
you talk.

Problem-Solving Toolset

F-A-X Listening Toolset

STEP A:
<u>Prevent</u>
problems.
Walk up the
steps.
Think, before
you listen.

STEP A: PREVENTION TOOLBOX

Independence Toolset

Cooperation Toolset

Self-Esteem Toolset

The Universal Blueprint

Foundation-Building Toolset

NO

BUILD
UP!

CHAPTER
11 PU TOOLSET (Unintentional misbehavior)

We can expect some "normal" problems in the life of a house. Paint eventually chips, floors creak as the foundation settles, and roofs need new shingles. We try to make improvements to prevent future problems or prepare a plan when problems occur.

In parenting, we can expect some problems during the different developmental stages in children's lives. If children have certain medical conditions or personality traits, they can exhibit challenging behaviors that are considered "normal" when these factors are present. We do not excuse their behavior. Instead, we teach children the skills they need to achieve developmental milestones, balance negative traits, and compensate for their medical challenges. Until they master these skills and work through these issues, children can unintentionally misbehave.

IN THIS CHAPTER

Our tour has finally arrived at Step C2, **R**edirecting misbehavior—and I have some good news—you have already learned most of the tools you need to use! We often use the same tools to redirect behavior that we use to prevent it. So why do we need separate chapters on PU (**P**arent problem, **U**nintentional misbehavior) and PO (**P**arent problem, "**O**n purpose" misbehavior) problems? Because there are certain tools that are best for redirecting certain types of misbehavior. This chapter encourages us to consider five important ideas about PU behavior:

1. There is a difference between PU and PO behavior. We need to recognize which type of behavior we are facing, so we choose the most effective tools for our response.
2. Some behaviors can be *both* PU *or* PO, depending on the underlying reason for the behavior. This is why it is important to correctly diagnose which type of behavior we are dealing with.
3. PU behavior can result from several factors.
4. PU behavior can turn into PO behavior, if we don't correctly identify it and respond appropriately.
5. There are certain tools we've already learned, and a few new ones, that are particularly effective in redirecting PU behavior. In this chapter, we review and learn these specific tools.

WHEN TO USE THE PU TOOLSET

Whenever we see problem behavior, we need to first stop and ask ourselves, "Is this behavior unintentional or on purpose?" To help us answer that question, we use the information in the PU Toolset. Once we know we *are* dealing with PU behavior, we can use certain tools we've already learned and those in the PU Toolset to redirect it.

IDENTIFYING PU PROBLEMS

Let's review what we learned in Chapter 3, "The Universal Blueprint," and then we will take each point and examine it in detail.

> **Question #2: Is the misbehavior Underlined{U}nintentional or "Underlined{O}n purpose"?**
> To tell the difference between PU and PO behavior, consider the following questions:
>   1. Is this behavior the result of the child's **immaturity** or developmental stage?
>   2. Is this behavior part of the child's **personality** (it doesn't come naturally)?
>   3. Is this an **accident** or is a **medical condition** influencing the child's self-control?
>   (Illness, mental retardation, ADHD, autism, etc.)
>   4. Does the child **lack the information** to know better?
> ★ 5. **Has the child *not consistently shown* that he or she has *mastered* the skills to**
>   **behave properly in this situation?** (This one often covers the first four issues,
>   which might explain *why* the child hasn't mastered the skill.)
>
> **"Yes" to *any one* question   = *PU problem* (P**arent problem, U**nintentional misbehavior).**
>
> **"No" to *all* questions   = *PO problem* (P**arent problem, "O**n purpose" misbehavior).**

1. This behavior *is* the result of the child's immaturity or developmental stage.

It is important to have realistic expectations about children's abilities. If we don't understand what behaviors are age-appropriate, we can easily mistake PU behavior for PO behavior. It is unrealistic to expect infants to sleep through the night or not cry when they are hungry. It's normal for a two-year-old to refuse to share or to be curious about dangerous objects. Most teenagers want more freedom and question values and rules. Each of these behaviors serves a specific developmental purpose.

> **Every human being goes through the same basic developmental process, but each**
> **child has an individual rate and style of development.**

STYLE OF DEVELOPMENT
Children can differ in the number of new skills they learn at once and how much they practice them.

- **All-at-once versus one-at-a-time learners.** Some children practice several different new skills at once. (A toddler might practice walking, toileting, and self-feeding.) Others practice skills in one or a few areas at a time, adding new skills to the ones they've already mastered. (A toddler might practice walking, but not show any interest in toileting.)

- **Trial-and-error versus wait-and-do learners.** Similarly, some children repeatedly try a new skill without getting discouraged. Other children observe and practice skills in their minds, until they know the skill well enough to perform it. It seems that these children aren't progressing in their development and then, one day, suddenly, they do something new!

Children with the two latter styles often have frustrated parents who say, "All the other ___-year-olds are doing ___, but mine isn't even trying!" These children *are* learning and practicing skills, but just aren't showing it outwardly. When these children are ready, they use a new skill right away, without the trial and error period. We want to look at the skills our children *have* learned and trust their own timetable for learning new skills.

A Personal Story. Both my children were late potty trainers. At 2½, neither used a toilet, but could boot-up a computer on their own. Despite my best efforts to teach and encourage, nothing made a difference. Exasperated and desperate, I'd occasionally push, bribe, threaten, and shame them, even though I knew those tactics wouldn't work—and I was right. We just got into power struggles and felt more discouraged. Finally, I decided to trust nature's timetable and neither went to pre-school in diapers.

RATE OF DEVELOPMENT

Children develop at their own pace. Each child has a unique biological timetable. Sooner or later, all children reach developmental milestones, unless there is a medical or emotional problem. As we learned in the Independence Toolset, our rule-of-thumb is to "nudge, but don't push." Our job is to teach skills, give encouragement, be patient, and allow children to experience and learn from their mistakes.

While there are certain ages that most children master certain skills, these are age *ranges*. Some time, usually within that age range, children develop certain skills. For example, most preteens go through puberty between 11 and 14. It is still "normal," however, for the onset of puberty to occur in children as young as 9 or as old as 16. If children have not begun to do certain tasks by certain ages, however, it may suggest they are experiencing difficulty. Knowing what is appropriate at different stages is important, so we know if the child needs professional help.

Developmentally delayed children function below what is considered normal for their age. We use their *functioning* age to identify *emotional* and *intellectual* causes of misbehavior. For example, if we are diagnosing whether misbehavior is PU for a twelve-year-old who functions at a six-year-old level, we base it on what is considered normal behavior for a six-year-old child. What does a six-year-old know and understand? *We still consider the biological age*, however, when diagnosing *physical* factors that influence behavior, such as hormone surges during puberty.

Traumas and poor adjustments to change can cause temporary developmental delays. If children experience great changes, inconsistencies, or traumatic experiences, these issues can sidetrack their development. These issues can include ineffective parenting or teaching styles, abuse, neglect, moving, divorce, or other separation and loss issues. It is difficult for children to deal with these emotional issues *in addition* to their normal developmental issues. If children are unable to resolve these issues in healthy ways, their poor coping skills can cause developmental delays.

Growth occurs in waves. At each major developmental stage, children work through certain issues and tasks. There are natural ups-and-downs as children master these new skills. *It is necessary for children to go through a temporary period of imbalance before moving to a new level.* If they didn't do this, they would have to immediately jump from one developmental stage to the next, with no transition period. This would be unnatural. Children often step back and regroup between their great spurts of learning. In the early years, these difficult periods often come at approximately six-month intervals, but even this time frame is not a hard and fast rule.

If things are going smoothly and suddenly our children's behavior takes a downward dive, we want to consider what is happening with them developmentally. If we can't identify any traumas or mistakes *we* are making, there is a good possibility that these children are getting ready to make a developmental leap and are entering this transition period. Many parents are concerned about these regressions, when children revert to old, outgrown habits. It is particularly helpful, during these times, to review literature about the developmental issues children face at that age.

Developmental Stages

The descriptions in this book are brief summaries of developmental stages. An excellent resource for more detailed information is a series of books, by Louise Bates Ames and Frances L. Ilg of the Gesell Institute of Child Development. The series goes from *"Your One Year Old"* to *"Your Ten to Fourteen Year Old"* (Copyrights 1976–1990). These books are available at most public libraries. Each book explains the physical, emotional, intellectual, and social development of children that age. Usually within the first few pages, we say to ourselves, "Yes! That's what my child is doing! They are describing my child to a tee!" This realization is reassuring. It can help us get on track with a healthy approach to their PU behavior. This series of books is informational, rather than skill-oriented. It explains very well *what* is going on but only gives general suggestions for what to *do* about it. Once we know what issues we are facing, we can refer back to *The Parent's Toolshop* and plan a helpful response.

All children develop in a predictable sequence—but at their own pace and in their own style. Certain kinds of skills must come before others. For example, all children sit up and crawl before they walk. Below are some general descriptions of the major developmental stages and the tools we use most often with children that age. Although children may not show all the PU behaviors listed at the end of the chapter, they are still working on the following developmental issues.

INFANTS

Age: Birth through approximately 12 to 15 months.

Developmental Issues: Their world is very focused—it consists of the infant and caretakers. When infants become mobile, they start working on developmental issues similar to toddlers.

- *Infants are learning to trust.* Since infants are totally dependent, they learn trust by feeling secure that someone will meet their needs. A good parental motto is "A baby's wants are a baby's needs." Contrary to old wives' tales, infants cannot be manipulative or spoiled. Parents cannot hold infants too much or meet their needs too quickly. Human touch and interaction promotes physical, emotional, and intellectual growth. (Remember the brain studies and monkey experiment in Chapter 4, "Self-Esteem Toolset"?)

Tools to use: Infants best understand nonverbal messages, tone of voice, and actions. When infants display PU behavior, we can use the nonverbal tools we've already learned, the Self-Esteem and Independence Toolsets, and tools listed later in the PU Toolset. Practice the language of effective parenting, because infants will understand *you* before they can speak themselves.

TODDLERS

Ages: Approximately 12 to 15 months (when they are toddling and walking well) through 3 years.

Developmental Issues: Young toddlers are aware of the world around them—but their world is still quite small. It consists of the toddler, the caretakers, siblings, and their daily environment (home, day care, and places they regularly visit). The toddler years are a busy developmental stage—for toddlers *and* their parents. Toddlers are learning about many issues all at once, but still don't understand or use communication well, so there are more possibilities for PU behavior. When we understand all the wonderful, exciting things toddlers are learning, we see that the "terrible" twos and threes are really a "terrific" time in a child's life.

- *Toddlers are learning about body control*—eating, sleeping, and bathroom activities. A good parental motto is "We can't *make* them do it," whatever "it" is. We need to be patient and respect each toddler's individual timetable. We can teach skills, establish routines, and encourage their efforts and improvement.

- *Toddlers are striving for independence.* They often want to be in control of themselves and their environment, which often includes other people. Many toddlers insist on doing tasks by themselves, even if parents can do the task quicker. When we do tasks for them, they often rebel through power struggles and temper tantrums. Since most toddlers still don't talk well, this is how they say they don't like what we are doing and exert their independence.

- *Toddlers are learning about ownership.* This is why toddlers don't like to share and say every object in their hands is "mine." Children must understand and experience ownership before they can understand and want to share. This is the age we can start teaching sharing behavior, but not expect children to always practice the skill.

- *Toddlers are learning about cause and effect and how the world works.* They are naturally curious—and curiosity promotes brain development.

Tools to use: Use the Cooperation Toolset, especially "Offering Choices," "Don't say Don't" and "No No's," to prevent power struggles. Use the Independence Toolset constantly, to teach skills and allow children to do tasks for themselves. Since most of their misbehavior is PU, we want to use the PU Toolset before or with the Discipline Toolset.

PRESCHOOLERS

Ages: Approximately 3 (when they might begin preschool) through 6 years (when they begin school).

Developmental Issues: Preschoolers are learning many new skills and refining skills they learned in the toddler years.

- *Preschoolers are near the end of the " transitional period."* This is the time between birth (total dependency) and approximately 4 years, when children become physically independent. If we have been encouraging independence, most children will master basic body-control skills, such as weaning, toileting, self-feeding, and mature sleep patterns. Now, they focus more on increasing their independence and improving their social skills.

- *Preschoolers are very imaginative and interested in learning.* They want to learn as many new skills as they can. Their imaginations are in full bloom and they use fantasy when they play. Some children recognize the difference between fantasy and reality, while others blur the two. Preschoolers are fascinated by the fine details of the universe, so they ask many thought-provoking "why" questions.

- *Preschoolers are learning social skills.* The preschooler's world is expanding even more—they are interested in playing with other children and exploring new environments.

Tools to use: We use the Prevention Toolbox to build self-esteem, independence, and cooperation. We use the Child Problem Toolbox to mediate peer/sibling conflicts. When preschoolers share their opinions, feelings, and problems, we listen to their perspective, keep the ball in their court, and teach them problem-solving skills. We want to use the PU or PO Toolsets before or with the Discipline Toolset, so children *learn* from their behavior mistakes. We can start involving preschoolers in family councils, giving them age-appropriate ways to participate.

EARLY ELEMENTARY SCHOOL

Ages: 6 (kindergarten) through approximately 8 years (third grade).

Developmental Issues: Children are continuing to learn skills and resolve issues from early childhood, while preparing for and coping with many new changes. They can still experience frequent regressions into childish behavior. Children this age may also exhibit some PU behaviors of older children.

- *The new world of school brings many changes.* When children enter school, they enter a new world that may be quite different from what they've experienced. The school's rules might be different from the rules at home, so they must adapt and be flexible. They need to sit still for long periods of time, so they must practice self-control and self-discipline. Teachers might have a different teaching and communication style than their parents, so children must practice effective listening and communication skills.

- *Children meet new people and begin new activities.* Children learn how to make new friends each year, in school and through extra-curricular activities, such as scouts, dance, etc. These activities can teach them important social and personal skills. They can also add stress to children's lives if they are involved in too many activities. A good family policy is to allow no more than two activities per season (i.e., sport season or one complete round of lessons). As children are exposed to other children and adults with different personalities and behaviors, they need to listen to their inner voice and learn responsible decision making and problem-solving skills to resolve conflicts that arise.

Tools to use: We mostly use the Prevention and Child Problem Toolboxes. Using the Cooperation Toolset, we can explain the value of the school's rules and the choices they have within those limits. We can use the Independence Toolset to acknowledge the difficulty of sitting still and being responsible for homework assignments. We can also teach time management skills. We can use the Self-Esteem Toolset to offer encouragement, as children gradually improve these skills. When they have difficulties with teachers or children, we can use the Child Problem Toolbox to teach problem-solving skills so *they* can resolve these problems. When children make poor decisions, we can use the Clear Communication, PU, PO, and Discipline Toolsets to help them learn from their mistakes and make better future choices. At home, we want to use the Maintenance Toolbox and start involving children more in family councils. Since young elementary children are developing their communication, problem-solving, and decision-making skills, family councils provide a safe way to learn and practice these skills. Children this age really enjoy being involved in family councils that offer them opportunities to share their ideas and talents with the family.

PRETEENS (LATE ELEMENTARY)

Ages: Fourth through sixth grades, approximately 9 through 11 years.

Developmental Issues: Preteens are refining the many skills they've already learned. Certain issues become even more important to the preteen.

- *Individuation intensifies.* Individuation is the process of becoming an individual person with unique values, behaviors, personality traits, and sense of identity. Although "individuation" begins at birth, it becomes more intense in the preteen years as children express their independence more strongly. (Remember the backpack analogy in the Independence Toolset?)

- *Peers are becoming more important in their lives, but parents are still quite influential.* Preteens are still limited to socializing with peers at school and close to home. Although adults are usually nearby, preteens must frequently rely on whatever communication, decision-making, and problem-solving skills they have to manage peer conflicts. Peer pressure is more intense than in previous stages and children are still likely to use poor judgment. We use these experiences to teach more skills and reinforce our family's values.

- *Healthy, well-adjusted preteens are often in a coasting stage.* They have usually adjusted to their world of home, school, and friends. Their intellectual skills are developing rapidly, as school teaches them about the larger world around them. For some parents, the preteen years are smooth. This may be nature's way of giving us some rest, before the teen years arrive.

- *Fourth or fifth grade is often a difficult year.* Teachers hold their students more accountable than in previous years, since the students have had four years to understand the school's rules and develop the skills they need to meet these expectations. School discipline becomes firmer and more consistent, older students are no longer offered "the benefit of the doubt."

Tools to use: Since most of the preteen's problems revolve around peers and school, the Self-Esteem, F-A-X Listening, Clear Communication, and Problem-Solving Toolsets are the tools to use. If preteens have not yet mastered the skills they need to succeed at home and in school, we need to back up to the Prevention Toolbox and help them develop these skills before they experience more severe problems. If preteens have experienced many changes or traumatic events, we need to use the Child Problem Toolbox to help them work through their feelings. Unresolved issues can cause more intense problems in the teen years. Outside counseling is often helpful when parents are unable to make an impact or are part of the problem. We want to use the Discipline Toolset and avoid over-controlling punishment tactics. It is vital to hold regular family councils that involve preteens in meaningful ways. Helpful family councils build leadership, decision-making, and communication skills preteens can use at home, at school, and with their peers and siblings.

YOUNG TEENS (JUNIOR HIGH)

Ages: Seventh through ninth grades, approximately 12 through 14 years.

Developmental Issues:

- *Individuation is in full bloom.* Young teens are discovering what they are capable of doing and might test limits. If adults are unreasonably controlling, young teens are more likely to rebel and defy authority.

- *Peers are increasingly important, but parents still have some influence.* Young teens begin trying on identities, to fit in with peer groups. This can lead young teens to "follow the crowd," if they don't feel secure enough in their self-worth to stand their ground. If children are going to experiment with drugs, they usually start by the early teens.

- *While puberty might begin earlier, it most commonly starts during this stage.* Young teens are maturing physically, emotionally, and mentally and have a great need for privacy.

- *The first year of junior high or middle school is a major transitional year.* They change classes often and have many different teachers, each with a different teaching style and list of rules. There is less personalized attention for problems. Many rules are black and white, because teachers don't have time to negotiate gray areas. Students must be totally responsible for their schoolwork. No one will give them stickers for completing their work or frequently remind them. If young teens don't learn good study habits by the end of elementary school, the first year of junior high they will sink-or-swim. If they start to sink, parents need to teach skills (or find someone who can), offer encouragement, and acknowledge feelings.

Tools to use: It is important to use the Self-Esteem, F-A-X Listening, Clear Communication, and Problem-Solving Toolsets daily. They can help us guide young teens through Child and Parent problems without taking over or starting power struggles. We need to use the Independence Toolset to teach skills (social, emotional, and physical tasks) so we can let go and trust. If we use two-party problem solving, we can get win/win agreements and reveal respectful discipline. Young teens like to discuss their ideas and feelings, so family councils are a great way to keep the lines of communication open and to build trust. Family councils can also help parents teach skills, prevent problems, and make family decisions.

TEENS (HIGH SCHOOL)

Ages: Tenth through twelfth grades, approximately 15 through 18 years.

Developmental Issues: Older teens have many of the same issues as younger teens. They may resolve some of these issues in the later teen years, while other issues intensify.

- *Individuation is at its peak,* but completes between ages 25–30 (unless problems like drug addiction or emotional issues delay the process). The teens' job is to decide who they are and who they want to be. Parents start seeing more signs of what their teen will be like as an adult.

- *Long-term consequences of ineffective habits are more obvious.* If parents have used imbalanced parenting tactics, they will now backfire. Teen rebellion (from over-controlling parenting) can become intense, with daily power struggles and revenge cycles. Under-controlling parents probably see spoiled, self-centered, irresponsible teen behavior.

- *Peers are more important and parents have less influence.* Most teens are interested in dating and begin struggling with more adult relationship conflicts: power and control personalities, peer violence, premarital sex, male/female communication styles, cliqués, gossip, and betrayal by friends. *Adults* have difficulty dealing with these issues, so teens especially need good communication and decision-making skills, emotional stability, and a strong sense of self-worth to work through these problems.

- *Independence is a critical issue for teens.* Healthy, well-balanced teens often display maturity and responsible behavior. They begin thinking about future careers and finding jobs to pay for the extras they want.

Tools to use: The Self-Esteem, Independence, F-A-X Listening, Clear Communication, and Problem-Solving Toolsets are the most important tools to use during the teen years, to maintain trust and open communication. Parents need to use two-party problem solving to discuss discipline and responsibility issues. Family councils are crucial—they help teens feel their ideas, opinions, and participation in the family are important and valued.

2. This behavior *is* part of the child's personality.

No two people are the same, however similar they may seem. We all have a unique combination of personality traits. We've already identified several kinds of personality traits: problem-solving, recharge, anger energy, learning and communication styles. Any one of these traits is not right or wrong, healthy or unhealthy; they are just different. Each has positive and negative aspects to it. We cannot *change* someone's temperament, because much of it is determined by genetic factors, but we can influence how they *use* their natural abilities.

Be careful labeling children and adults by their personality traits, such as "overly emotional" or "bull-headed." This implies something is wrong with the trait or person. Remember the skills and suggestions in the "Roles and Labels" section of the Self-Esteem Toolset.

Below is a list of personality traits which can cause PU problems. It includes suggestions for building on the strengths of the trait and managing common problems related to the trait.

- **Children are full of energy, experience strong reactions, and are easily frustrated.** When we see intensity building, we can provide quieting activities (reading, imaginative play) or acceptable ways to release energy (creative activities, such as drawing, singing, or acting). The Keep Your Cool Toolset's recharge activities are helpful for both adults and children with this trait.

- **Children are determined** and stick to tasks and issues. They seem to push limits often. Parents can find positive ways to set limits (Don't Say "Don't," No "No's," and Rules for Setting Rules), allow choices within bottom-line limits, and acknowledge feelings.

- **Children are easily overwhelmed** by senses (touch, smell, etc.) and emotions. (Yes, that shirt label really *does* bother them!) Parents need to be sensitive to the environment and their own moods. They can change the environment (like cutting off the tag) to reduce stimulation and teach children coping skills.

- **Children get easily distracted because they hear or see everything** and have difficulty tuning out unimportant input. They are often accused of not listening. Speak directly, establish eye contact and use gentle touch. Use words, drawings, and *show* children what to do. Limit the number of instructions given at one time and keep them simple and clear. Avoid "don't"; focus on what they *can* do. Help children find ways to remind *themselves* to stay on task.

- **Children have a hard time making transitions between activities.** These children are uncomfortable with change and become upset in new and unfamiliar situations. Limit the number of transitions children must endure. Have consistent routines and as few surprises as necessary. Explain what will happen next and allow time for children to end one activity before moving to the next. Arrive early or visit ahead of time before expecting children to participate. Be encouraging, but don't push too hard. With young children, use tangible time references they can understand. Older children with this trait can have difficulty adjusting to classroom changes if they haven't learned effective coping strategies.

- **Children's natural rhythms are irregular** (sleeping, eating, elimination). All children will have changes in their body rhythms throughout the developmental cycle, like eating more during growth spurts, but these children are regularly irregular. They may have difficulty adapting to consistent routines, so be patient. Show respect for their individual timetables for potty training, weaning, and putting themselves to sleep. Teach skills and nudge, but don't push. Such irregular cycles seem unusual in childhood, but can prove beneficial in the adult years. (We appreciate emergency room doctors who are fully alert at 3 a.m.!)

- **Children need to move a lot** and this need is real. Allow children to move after long sitting periods. Provide safe, acceptable ways to release the energy. Offer frequent opportunities to run, jump, and climb, but make sure they don't get too wound-up. If children are overstimulated or experience too many transitions, their behavior can fall apart.

- **Children are analytical and serious.** They often focus on faults and whine or complain. Help these children find the positive aspects of situations. Appreciate their ability to logically evaluate situations and offer suggestions for improvement. Show children how to have a sense of humor even when things don't go their way.

Adult PU behavior is often the result of unbalanced personality traits. Negative, controlling people who seem "set in their ways" are difficult to be around, if they expect others to adjust to them. Adults have more control over their environment, the jobs they choose or whether they marry, so some people never learn self-regulating skills that could greatly improve their lives and relationships. We can try using some of the same prevention and response skills with adult PU behavior, but usually have less influence. We can try three approaches: (1) unconditionally love and accept people just as they are, (2) learn how to cope with and respond to their behavior without trying to change them, or (3) set limits that protect us from the damaging effects of being around them. (See the "Setting Limits" section in Chapter 15, "Three C's: Consistency, handling Criticism, Confidence" for more suggestions.)

3. This *is* an accident or a medical condition *is* influencing the child's self-control.

If misbehavior is an *accident,* involve children in cleaning or fixing the results of the accident. Teach positive attitudes about mistakes and accidents. Don't shame or blame children; focus on solutions.

If children suddenly behave in uncommon ways, they might be getting sick, but haven't shown any symptoms yet. This is most common when children are tired or hungry.

*A Personal Story. When Amber was young and ran low on energy, her personality completely changed. She couldn't make a decision, cried over little things, picked arguments, and snapped at us. (Of course, I know adults who act the same way if they have to wait too long in a restaurant when they're hungry!) I easily recognized that she needed to eat or sleep, but if I said, "You're just tired" or "You are hungry" she'd yell, "No I'm not!" If I forced the issue, we'd get into a power struggle and she'd fall apart even more. I had to find a way to help **her** be more aware of her body's needs.*

One night at bedtime, I explained how her body was like a car and that food and sleep are like the gasoline that gives a car the energy to go. When cars run out of energy, they stop moving until they get more gas. I described what bodies do when they run out of energy, naming the symptoms she often shows. I suggested that whenever she did those things, her body was telling her it needed more energy and she could choose what kind of energy she wanted to give her body. The fact that we discussed this when there was no problem made a big difference; she understood.

*From then on, we tried preventing the problem by adding an after-school snack to her daily routine. She had to eat something before going outside to play. On the few occasions when she started falling apart, I now said, "**Is your body telling you** it needs some food or sleep?" Because I wasn't trying to force the issue and asked her to listen to her own body, she was more willing to consider the idea. If she resisted, I'd offer a choice, "Do you want a snack or to rest?" She'd usually eat a snack or do something quiet to recharge her energy. By age eight, she automatically got herself a snack when she was hungry and voluntarily took a nap.*

Illness, mental retardation, autism, food allergies, or Attention Deficit Hyperactivity Disorder (ADHD) are examples of *medical conditions* that influence children's behavior. These children might truly have a limit to how much they can control their behavior when these factors are present. We can still use all the tools we've learned, but need to have realistic expectations about how long it might take to see progress. (Remember, a deeper problem is one of the five reasons the tools might not immediately work.) These tools will, at the least, not make matters worse and usually help speed progress. Read as much as you can about the disorder and specific strategies to use. Most are compatible tools to add to the Universal Blueprint (file them in the PU Toolset). If there are recommendations that go against some of the basic principles of *The Parent's Toolshop*, discuss your concerns with a trained professional who can explain whether there is a valid reason for using that approach. While we can't discuss all medical conditions in this book, it is important to focus on one—Attention Deficit Hyperactivity Disorder. Many children are labeled ADHD without proper diagnosis and quickly put on medication to "fix" them.

DIAGNOSING ADHD

True ADHD is a biological condition and there is no single method that accurately diagnoses it. ADHD children are not lazy, defiant, or bad. They often understand what they are told, but have difficulty controlling their impulses to do what they know they should do. Other medical problems (e.g., food allergies, auditory processing problems, or learning difficulties) can cause behavior that looks like ADD or ADHD. Similar behavior can also result when children haven't learned self-control, decision-making or listening skills. All these factors *must* be ruled out, before diagnosing a child with ADHD, so concerned parents want to involve a team of people from four critical areas:

1. *Parents* are a good source of diagnostic information since they are with the child the most.

2. *Teachers* can make observations of the child's behavior in large groups. Children can have a "learning disability" and not be ADHD. Some children have learning difficulties *because* their ADHD is untreated. Often, there are environmental factors (such as too much noise) that make it difficult for children to concentrate at home *or* at school, but they don't have a physical problem.

3. *Medical doctors* can rule out food allergies and hearing/visual problems, which have symptoms that mimic ADHD.

4. ***Psychologists or psychiatrists*** who are specially certified and trained in ADHD assessments can perform psychological testing. Parents can determine whether professional assessment might be necessary by reviewing the standard criteria for diagnosing ADHD:

Standard Criteria for Diagnosing ADHD[1]*

A. Either (1) or (2):

   (1) *six (or more)* of the following symptoms of **inattention** have *persisted for at least 6 months* to a degree that is *maladaptive and inconsistent with developmental level:*

   Inattention
   a. often fails to give close attention to details or makes careless mistakes in schoolwork, work, or other activities
   b. often has difficulty sustaining attention in tasks or play activities
   c. often does not seem to listen when spoken to directly
   d. often does not follow through on instructions and fails to finish schoolwork, chores, or duties in the workplace (not due to oppositional behavior or failure to understand instructions)
   e. often has difficulty organizing tasks and activities
   f. often avoids, dislikes, or is reluctant to engage in tasks that require sustained mental effort (such as schoolwork or homework)
   g. Often loses things necessary for tasks or activities (e.g., toys, school assignments, pencils, books, or tools)
   h. is often easily distracted by extraneous stimuli
   i. is often forgetful in daily activities

   (2) *six (or more)* of the following symptoms of **hyperactivity-impulsivity** have *persisted for at least 6 months* to a degree that is *maladaptive and inconsistent with developmental level:*

   Hyperactivity
   a. often fidgets with hands or feet or squirms in seat
   b. often leaves seat in classroom or in other situations in which remaining seated is expected
   c. often runs about or climbs excessively in situations in which it is inappropriate (in adolescents or adults, may be limited to feelings of restlessness)
   d. often has difficulty playing or engaging in leisure activities quietly
   e. is often "on the go" or often acts as if "driven by a motor"
   f. often talks excessively

   Impulsivity
   g. often blurts out answers before questions have been completed
   h. often has difficulty awaiting turn
   i. often interrupts or intrudes on others (e.g., butts into conversations or games)

B. *Some* hyperactive-impulsive or inattentive *symptoms* that caused impairment *were present before age 7 years.*

C. Some impairment from the symptoms *is present in two or more settings* (e.g., at school [or work] and at home).

D. There must be clear evidence of *clinically significant impairment* in social, academic, or occupational functioning.

E. The symptoms do not occur exclusively during the course of . . . [another mental or physical disorder.] (*Author's paraphrasing.*)

---

*Diagnostic criteria is reprinted with permission from the *Diagnostic and Statistical Manual of Mental Disorders,* 4th ed. copyright 1994, American Psychiatric Association.

There are actually three types of attention deficits: (1) Inattentive (ADD), (2) Hyperactive/Impulsive, and (3) Combined type (ADHD). ADHD can also appear in children who have other neurological (brain and nervous system), psychological, and learning disorders, so **a *thorough* diagnosis process is vital.**

TREATING ADHD

No one approach can "cure" ADHD and treatment must be long-term. Therefore, effective treatment plans should address all the possible factors that influence ADHD. The best treatment plan uses the first four interventions at the same time and may or may not include the last (medication).

A. ***Parent education is the most important part of treating ADHD.*** *The Parent's Toolshop* includes *every* parenting skill that ADHD experts recommend. Most of the strategies are adaptable to school and other settings. If a child does *not* have true ADHD, just problem behavior that mimics it, it is important for parents to spend time teaching children important behavioral skills.

- *ADHD children have a high degree of variability—they are consistently inconsistent.* These children *do* have good days—and it can be their undoing—because the adults around them may expect them to have good days every day.

- *Teach children organizational techniques*, such as making lists, using self-reminders, using a planning calendar, and making desk, drawer, or closet organizers. These skills are also important to teach children who do not have ADHD, but have similar behavior problems.

B. ***Consistent behavior management.*** Parents, educators, and others who work with ADHD children should not feel inadequate for having difficulty managing ADHD children. They must repeat themselves often to make progress or just keep situations from getting worse.

- *ADHD children have a hard time being **self**-motivated toward **long**-term goals.* They have difficulty paying attention or sticking with tasks unless the tasks provide instant gratification, or are novel, stimulating, and fun. This is why they have no difficulty playing video games for long stretches of time. Use positive, creative teaching methods that will maintain their interest. Teach children how to remind themselves to stay on track and find their own way to get the job done. (It is important to consider whether excessive TV viewing and video games have conditioned the child to only pay attention to stimulating events.)

- *ADHD children respond well to external rewards, but also get quickly addicted to them.* Provide frequent, positive feedback, such as nods, descriptive encouragement, smiles, pats, and high-fives. Only add external motivators *if* the internal rewards are long-term. ***If you use external rewards*** (such as extra privileges, games, computer time, or free time), ***always comment on the long-term, internal rewards of a task or behavior and teach children how to set up self-rewards.*** This reduces children's dependency on rewards and praise from others.

- *Effective reprimands are immediate, brief, unemotional, and consistent.* Reprimands are ineffective when they are delayed, long-winded, harsh, critical, or emotional. Selectively ignore attention-seeking, minor behavior that is not aggressive or disruptive.

C. ***Effective classroom environment.*** There are *many* small changes teachers can make in the school environment that greatly benefits ADHD children. Many of these changes will help *every* child's ability to concentrate. For example, face children away from windows and stand in one location when speaking, so all the children can see *and* hear the instructions. Unfortunately, we can't list all the ideas in this resource. (See the list of recommended reading at the end of this chapter.) Parents and educators should at least know about the following factors and incorporate them in their teaching style.

- *There are three steps to the learning process (learning, understanding, and remembering) and four ways people learn best (seeing, hearing, doing, and teaching).* Education commonly presents information through visual aids (books) and uses discussion to explain and practice the information. Some teachers add hands-on learning. If a child cannot learn or understand information until they have an opportunity to do hands-on activities, they may be behind other students who primarily learn through sight and hearing. This is only one example of how someone's learning style affects their ability to learn and retain information. The most effective teaching approach, however, incorporates *all* four learning styles at *each* step of the learning process, to account for the various combinations of learning styles.

- *In addition, **everyone** uses eight different areas of the brain[2] at each step of the learning process, but each person is stronger in some areas than others.*

  1. Words (written or spoken), songs.
  2. Numbers, patterns, and other logical strategies.
  3. Music, sound, rhythm.
  4. Pictures, visualizing, building structures, drawing, doodling.
  5. Physical movement, sports, dance, repetitive movements.
  6. Socializing with others, reading body language.
  7. Internalizing, imagination, self-discipline.
  8. Nature, plants, animals, and outdoors.

  If a child is particularly strong in areas that schools don't happen to use and weak in areas they do use, the child might have difficulty learning. ***Parents and teachers can help children learn by incorporating all three learning styles and a variety of the eight learning centers of the brain.*** It takes far more creativity, time, and energy, but helps *all* children learn.

- ADHD children often participate in special programs, such as tutoring and reading groups, that take place during school hours away from the classroom. While they learn important skills in these programs, they also lose the extra time they need to complete schoolwork, absorb and process information, or simply get a mental break. They may get farther behind in their work and have difficulty adjusting to the transitions.

D. ***Psychological Treatment.*** Locate a psychologist, psychiatrist, or therapist who is knowledgeable and experienced in treating ADHD. They can address the following special issues of ADHD:

- Treat depression and anxiety.
- Explain how the mind/brain works and doesn't work.
- Teach anger control, social, self-motivation, self-reminding, and relaxation techniques.
- Build self-esteem, since ADHD children are often discouraged.
- Provide marital and family therapy. ADHD affects the whole family (the ripple effect). ADHD children should not be labeled "problem children" or blamed for other family problems.

E. ***Medication therapy***

- *Medication is only **one** type of treatment and should **only** be used as a last resort.* Some medications have negative side-effects and most are considered "controlled substances." Some employers (the military for example) will not hire adults who used these "drugs" in childhood. Given these risks, parents must seriously consider whether medication is really necessary. **Above all, *never* use medication alone or as a replacement for *any* of the other treatments.**

- *Medication will not **fix** ADHD; it only manages it.* Medication for ADHD works like eyeglasses on vision problems; glasses don't fix the eyes, they simply help people see better. Poor vision and ADHD are both lifelong problems. As children mature and master self-regulating skills, they can often reduce or eliminate the need for medication.

"NORMAL" ISN'T AN EXCUSE

Some behaviors are considered "normal" for children of a particular age or who have a diagnosed medical condition. **"Normal" doesn't mean parents *excuse* unacceptable behavior.** We need to teach children the skills they need to move beyond their current limitations and develop the maturity and skills they need later in life.

4. The child *does* lack the information to know better.

Sometimes children simply don't know or remember how they are supposed to behave. Rules at home might be different from the school's or a neighbor's rules. "Knowing better" involves a logical understanding *and* an ability to consistently control the behavior. If we teach skills (Independence Toolset) and give information (Clear Communication Toolset) this type of misbehavior often stops or lessens, but this process can take time and practice.

Age alone does not determine if misbehavior is PU or PO. Children can be old enough that we assume they "should know better," but haven't learned or mastered the necessary behavior skills. For example, teens reared in violent homes or communities have learned violence. While we can expect other teens to resolve conflicts peacefully, these teens have not learned these skills. In these cases, our focus is to teach skills, as in PU behavior.

5. The child has *not consistently shown* he or she has *mastered* the skills to behave properly in this situation.☆☆☆☆

This last deciding factor usually accounts for the previous four. Children often haven't mastered skills *because:*

- They are too young and haven't had enough practice or experience.
- It doesn't come naturally to them (personality traits).
- They aren't feeling well or have to compensate for a biological barrier to using the skill.
- They don't know about or fully understand how to use the skill.

The key to accurately answering "true" or "false" to this statement lies in understanding the words of this definition. "Consistent" means repeatedly or many times. "Shown" means we have *seen* the child act appropriately. Still, just because we have "told" children how to behave and maybe even seen them behave this way does not mean children have *mastered* the behavior. "Mastered" skills are behaviors children use *very* well and are almost a habit.

When we see PU behavior, we want to figure out the positive skill we want them to use and then ask ourselves, "Have I *seen* my child *regularly use* this skill, often enough that I am positive he or she is fully capable of behaving properly?" If not, we need to work more on teaching skills and not assume the child is intentionally misbehaving.

When in Doubt, Assume Misbehavior Is PU

Eliminate the possibility that children don't know better, before assuming they are *deliberately* misbehaving. If their behavior is really PU and we react as though it's PO, the behavior won't improve. Children still won't understand and will feel more discouraged, which leads to PO misbehavior.

Give children the benefit of the doubt. Just because their behavior is irritating (such as tapping a foot), it doesn't mean it is "on purpose." Only if we've taught them the skills, they've behaved "better" on a consistent basis in the past, and are behaving negatively in a *deliberate* way, is the behavior "on purpose." **The key to recognizing PO behavior is intent;** *PO behavior is deliberate.*

PU Behavior Can Turn into PO Behavior

Our reactions to PU behavior influences whether children use the behavior later as PO behavior. If we give the behavior negative attention, the child receives a payoff. A classic example of this is when children say a swear word, but don't know what it means. In this situation, their behavior is PU. If children get a big reaction, they may intentionally repeat the behavior later for attention. Then the behavior would be PO. They knew they were not supposed to use the word and normally don't, but to some children, negative attention is better than no attention at all. If we keep in mind that "children usually repeat any behavior we reward," we can consciously control our responses to PU behavior and redirect it, instead of accidentally rewarding it.

*We can **react** to PU behavior and turn it into PO ...*   *... or we can effectively **respond**, preventing PO.*

USING THE UNIVERSAL BLUEPRINT

When responding to PU problems, we want to follow the universal PASRR formula. Here we will find many helpful tools to prevent or respond to PU problems. Let's review some of the tools we've learned that are especially useful with PU behavior and add a couple more tools.

Step A: Prevent the Behavior (Prevention Toolbox)

We can prevent many PU behaviors or, at the least, influence how quickly children learn appropriate behavior skills. We can use the **Prevention Toolbox** *anytime*, to prevent PU behavior or at any time in our response.

FOUNDATION-BUILDING TOOLSET

- **Choose helpful beliefs, attitudes and perceptions** about PU behavior, such as "The child hasn't mastered the skill yet." This can help us stay focused on teaching the child better skills and being patient during their learning process.

- **Model the behavior skills we want children to develop**. If it is a mental process that is difficult to observe, we *openly* model the behavior, a skill we learned in the Independence Toolset.

SELF-ESTEEM TOOLSET

- **Express unconditional love.** Children need to know we love them no matter what. We want to show we understand they aren't perfect and are trying the best they can, even if their best effort is less than desirable.

- **Use descriptive encouragement.** Discouragement can cause PU behavior to turn into PO behavior, so *encouragement can prevent both PU and PO behavior*. Notice positive behavior, describing what we see and how the behavior helps the child or family.

- **Acknowledge any effort or improvement** children make to control their behavior or use new skills.

- **Avoid labeling children by their behavior.** Help them see their potential.

COOPERATION TOOLSET

- **Plan ahead,** to prevent PU behavior. For example, if we know our children don't handle long shopping trips, or get overstimulated in crowds, we can prepare for these times. We can explain what we will be doing, what behavior we expect, and plan frequent breaks. We can bring activities children enjoy, rearrange the order in which we run errands, or arrange child care so we don't have to bring children with us.

- **Use positive words to make requests.** Saying "no," "don't," "stop," or demanding obedience offers no new information and often results in a tantrum or power struggle. When we tell children what they *can* do, they learn positive behavior more quickly.

- **Routines** are especially helpful with children who are still learning skills. We can also fall back on our routines to guide children in appropriate ways, "I know you don't feel like taking a bath, but remember, bath comes before books!"

INDEPENDENCE TOOLSET

- **Nudge, but don't push** children when developmental factors are causing PU behavior. Instead, teach skills, offer encouragement, and trust a child's natural timetable. We need to be extra patient if they regress during the transition from one stage to another.

- **Give information** when PU behavior occurs in children who "don't know any better."

- **Teach skills** one step at a time, give simple directions and many chances to practice the skills. We need to *see* they can behave appropriately on a *regular* basis, before realistically expecting them to do so.

- **Offer quick tips,** let children **be responsible for their own mistakes,** and **notice the difficulty** of tasks and skills children are learning but haven't mastered.

Responding to PU Behavior

When prevention doesn't work, or we need to immediately respond to PU behavior, taking the next steps of the Universal Blueprint's PASRR formula.

STEP B: <u>A</u>CKNOWLEDGE FEELINGS (CHILD PROBLEM TOOLBOX)

PU problems are onions; the outer skin is the PU behavior, the inner layers are the child's feeling or underlying *reason* for the behavior. PU behaviors are often the result of feelings like frustration, lack of control, or inaccurate beliefs. Here are some specific statements we can use at each step of the F-A-X Listening process, although you may have difficulty using the last two steps (A and X) with very young children.

Focus on Feelings

- **Give the feeling a name.** "That's (feeling)!"
- **Connect the feeling with the event.** "Sometimes you feel _____ when (event)."
- **Use wishes and fantasy.** "I bet you wish . . ."

Ask Helpful Questions

- "What can happen when people (misbehavior)?"
- "Do you know why it's important to (behavior you want to see)?"

X-amine Possible Options

- "How can you (what child wants) without (parent's concern)?"
- "What else can you do when you feel like (misbehavior)?"

STEP C1: SET LIMITS AND EXPRESS CONCERNS

Even if PU behavior is normal, we still need to stay calm and respectfully state our concerns, expectations, and limits.

Keep Your Cool Toolset

- If we don't control our anger, our unhelpful reaction will most likely start PO behavior. Avoid getting hooked into the problem *behavior* and deal with the real issue—the child's feelings or lack of skills.

Clear Communication Toolset

- **Describe what you see,** without blaming, shaming, and name-calling. Say, "I see chips all over the floor" instead of "You left a big mess. You are such a slob!"
- **State limits and expectations.** Instead of saying "Don't hit," say, "When people are really angry they need to (appropriate anger energy outlet)."
- **Use quick reminders,** one word, nonverbal or flash codes, and notes.

Usually the first three steps in the Universal Blueprint's PASRR formula (prevention, listening, and communicating) provide enough resources to resolve PU problems. When the problem continues, we move to the PU Toolset to Redirect behavior.

STEP C2: REDIRECT THE PU BEHAVIOR (PU TOOLSET)

Acknowledging feelings (Step B) and Setting limits (Step C1) are what we *say.* Redirecting the behavior (Step C2) is usually what we *do* while we are speaking. We can redirect problem behavior with a verbal statement or by taking action. Here are some extra tools especially helpful in redirecting PU behavior.

Ignore Behavior When Appropriate

This tool is only useful if the behavior is *not dangerous*. It is particularly helpful for irritating PU behavior, such as whining. By not giving the behavior attention, parents prevent giving a payoff that can turn PU behavior into PO behavior.

Ignore the *behavior*, not the *child*. A parent can acknowledge feelings, "I can tell you really want something" or encourage cooperation, "If you can use words I will know what you want and can get it for you." We can also say nothing and only respond when the behavior stops or when the child talks or acts in an acceptable way, possibly unrelated to what they were doing. (We learn more about ignoring behavior in the PO Toolset.)

Offer an Acceptable Alternative ☆☆☆☆

If children are doing something that *isn't* okay, tell them what *is* okay. With younger children, we may need to physically redirect them. This tool is closely related to "offer choices within limits" and "Don't say 'Don't.'" The possibilities for use are nearly endless:

▸ Trade a dangerous object with a toy that's appropriate for a ***baby or toddler***.

▸ When ***preschoolers*** play too rough, say "you can play rough outside or find something quiet to do inside. You decide."

▸ If we have safety concerns about ***school-aged*** children riding bikes around the whole neighborhood, we may approve of them only riding around *our* block several times.

▸ If ***preteens*** want to plan a winter indoor boy/girl party, suggest a springtime outdoor party with acceptable coed activities. Avoid lectures about romantic possibilities that would express distrust.

▸ When ***teens*** resist a visit to relatives, suggest bringing a friend, an activity to do, or make a deal that they don't have to go somewhere else if they go there.

Distraction

Most parents are familiar with the effectiveness of distracting young children, especially those under four years. Because young children are so focused on the present moment, it is easier to change their focus.

> ***A Favorite Story.*** *Many years ago, I read a story in "Welcome Home[3]," a national publication for stay-at-home mothers. As I remember the story, a mother and daughter were at the playground close to their apartment. The toddler resisted leaving. The mother saw a pretty butterfly and suggested they follow it. This got them out of the playground. But the mother didn't stop there. She saw some flowers ahead and they went to look at them more closely. By following the various interesting sites along the way home, she arrived at their front door. Finally, she suggested they go visit their dog and see what he was up to. By using distraction, this mother avoided an argument that could have ended with her carrying the daughter, kicking and screaming, from the playground. Neither would have learned anything constructive and their fun time at the playground would have been spoiled by the way it ended.*

Once children are older than four, distraction takes a different form. With older children, we can try several other techniques:

• Simply change the subject, refusing to argue.
• Add humor that in no way "puts down" the child.
• Give a friendly hug or tousle of the hair, or simply a knowing smile that says "That's inappropriate. Want to try again?"

Environmental Engineering

Parents often fear that unless they control children, the children will take control. When we control a *situation,* we avoid controlling *children* with orders that lead to power struggles (PO problem). The most well known form of changing the environment is "child proofing." By removing dangerous objects or restricting dangerous areas, young children can explore more freely. There are more ways, however, to control the environment that are useful with children of all ages:

• **Add** something interesting to the environment when they are bored.
• **Remove** from the environment, when there's too much going on and they can't filter out distractions.
• **Restrict** the environment, creating special areas for certain activities. For example, have a special homework nook, a specific play-doh area, or one room for all the toys.

- **Enlarge** the environment by moving outside or to a larger room when they need more personal space or room for active play.
- **Rearrange** the environment to make things more accessible, which encourages independence.
- **Simplify** the environment when there are too many changes or activities that overwhelm them.
- **Organize** the environment by establishing routines and rituals.

Identify PU Behaviors and Their Triggers, Then Make a Plan

Changing PU behavior usually takes longer than other behaviors, because the child's maturity and skill development take time to improve. With more severe or disruptive behaviors, we may need to develop a more comprehensive plan.

1. **Identify the PU behavior you want to work on.** Decide what you want children *to* do.

2. **Observe** when the behavior occurs and *doesn't* occur.

   When the behavior occurs, ask yourself, "What is the child doing when it happens? What am I doing? What else is going on? What triggers it? What is the child getting from it?"

   When the behavior does not occur, ask yourself, "What was different? Could this factor prevent the behavior? When *is* it okay to behave this way? What is the child getting from the behavior?"

3. **Control triggering events.** "Triggering" events cause or influence the behavior to occur. Reduce the factors that trigger the PU behavior and strengthen the factors that encourage appropriate behavior.

4. **Break the response chain.** Disruptive behavior can be a habit. One step leads to the next step, which leads to the problem. What *is* the typical pattern? To eliminate PU behavior, we must help the child learn new skills to replace the old habitual behavior.

5. **Give encouragement.** Acknowledge effort toward the positive behavior and any improvements children make. Focus on internal motivators and rewards. "(Friend's name) appreciated it when you (describe appropriate behavior)." If there are external rewards, wean children off of them quickly.

6. **Track the progress.** Notice steps toward the goal and any improvements. Recognize barriers and develop a plan for removing them.

The PU Formula

┌───┐

Using the PASRR Formula with PU Behavior

To use the PASRR response formula with PU behavior, use statements similar to the following examples:

Step A: Prevent the problem. "When people want _____, they (teach skills)."
Step B: Acknowledge feelings. "I can see you want/feel _____ . . ."
Step C1: Set limits and express concerns. ". . . but (explain concerns)."
Step C2: Redirect behavior. "You *can* (offer an acceptable alternative) instead."
Step C3: Reveal discipline. (We'll learn this in Chapter 13, "Discipline Toolset.")

└───┘

Here are a few examples:

▶ "I can tell you're really angry, but hitting hurts! You can hit this pillow instead." (We could substitute hitting pillows with another anger energy release activity.)

▸ "I know you think not wearing a helmet is safe if you ride your bike on the sidewalk. Even though cars might not hit you, you could still wipe out on the cement. When people in our family ride bikes, they do it safely. You can wear a helmet or walk."

▸ "You've said a lot of your friends are getting body piercing. I'm not surprised you want to do it, too, since it's a way to express who you are. I'm worried about the risk of infection and other health risks. I'd be willing to give you permission to do something safer but just as cool. What are some safer options?" (Continue with brainstorming a win/win solution.)

COMMON PU BEHAVIORS

Now lets look at some common PU behaviors that can occur at each developmental stage that we haven't already mentioned. While every possible PU problem isn't listed, *Parent's Toolshop^SM* parenting classes and the next series of books (*T.I.P.S.: Tools for Improving Parenting Skills*) take each age group, tots, tweens, and teens, and apply the universal skills to the topics of interest for that age.

Infants

- **Crying** is the only way infants can communicate, so learn the difference in their cries and meet the need. Reliable responses build trust and security.

- **Fussiness.** If infants are overstimulated and fussy, use soft whispers, low lights, quiet music, rocking, and other soothing motions. Have at least five soothing activities to rotate. Be careful, however, that the soothing activity doesn't contribute to the fussiness. Give infants time to calm down before trying a new round of soothing activities. One activity is to eliminate all stimuli (including the parent) long enough for the child to calm down. An excellent resource is *The Fussy Baby*, by Dr. William Sears (La Leche League, International, 1985.)

- **Putting objects in their mouths.** Infants learn through touch and the tongue has more touch receptors than fingers. Child-proof the home and trade dangerous objects for acceptable items.

- **Sleep problems.** It is normal for infants not to sleep through the night or to need assistance going to sleep. Be careful using any technique that lets children "cry it out." It causes children to eventually give up on parents, which breeds insecurity. We have already discussed some ideas for sleep problems and more follow in the toddler and preschool sections and later chapters. The end of the chapter lists several resources on this subject. (See "Sleeping" in the "Toddlers" section below.)

Toddlers

- **Clinginess.** Older infants and toddlers can be clingy, because they need to feel secure in unfamiliar situations. Be a "home base" that children can come and touch, to reassure themselves you are still there. Pat their backs or stroke their hair, without picking them up. This tells them you know they are there, but are not going to carry them constantly. As their walking skills improve, hold their hands, walk at their pace, and use descriptive encouragement to build independence. (See the "Separation anxiety" and "Delaying" sections below.)

- **Curiosity.** We can discourage our children's natural desire to learn by reacting negatively to their curiosity and exploring. We can encourage children to learn by allowing them to explore safely and child-proofing dangerous areas. Make a game of putting things up and exchange dangerous objects with acceptable alternatives. Use positive words to set limits and physically (gently) redirect toddlers' to other activities.

- **Delaying.** Toddlers can be slow! They seem to take forever walking, coming when called, or doing tasks we want done quickly. Our gut reactions will provide quick fixes, but cause other short- and long-term problems. If we carry children everywhere, they don't get practice walking for themselves and become clingier. If we drag them or swoop them up roughly, they are frightened and cry or resist, kicking and screaming. If we threaten to leave them, when they won't come to us, they believe we love them so little we would actually abandon them. This breeds insecurity. If we do tasks for our young children, simply because we can do them quicker, they don't get experience doing for themselves and are dependent longer. We want to plan ahead and leave extra time for children to do some tasks on their own. We can make deals, "You can put your coat on if you let me zip it up." We can offer choices to walk or carry them. If they continue to dawdle, we can *then* pick them up, saying, "I can see you've decided to be carried this time. Next time, you'll have a chance to walk." They still might kick and scream, but the last sentence teaches them that being carried is a choice *they* have, not a punishment we impose. (This last technique is actually **R**evealing discipline. We'll learn more discipline techniques we can use with PU behavior in Chapter 13, "Discipline Toolset.")

- **Grabbing.** Toddlers usually don't have the verbal skills to say "I want this." They also don't understand ownership. To them, whatever they have (or get), belongs to them. Teach them how to ask and suggest trading objects for something they want.

- **Separation anxiety.** While infants are learning trust, they can feel scared and hesitant when their main source of security, their parents, are gone. Healthy separation occurs periodically, so parents can meet their own needs without sacrificing the infant's needs. *Never sneak away* while someone distracts your child. Although children may cry less, the fact that the parent simply disappears is terribly frightening and actually prolongs separation anxiety. Even if children don't seem to understand words, tell them you are leaving, reassure them you will return, and leave them in a loving way. As they get used to this routine, they will cry less often. With time, you will find children work through their separation in quicker, healthier ways when we handle the situation lovingly and helpfully. (See "Clinginess" and "Delaying" in this section.)

- **Sleeping.** It is still normal for toddlers not to sleep through the night or to need help falling asleep. Establish routines, teach self-comforting, use encouragement, and meet their security needs or the problems will increase. If you let the child cry, start with the shortest time possible, maybe three minutes. Come back to check on the child at the agreed time. Soothe them in quiet ways, but do not pick them up. Do *not* increase the time between your checks until they handle three minutes well. Then increase to five minutes. When they handle five minutes, increase to ten, and so on. The next night, try starting at the time limit the child handled the night before. The key to the success of this approach is that children can rely on parents coming back and the time limit does not become unreasonable.

- **Tantrums.** Figure out what type of tantrum it is and respond accordingly. (See the section on "Tantrums" on page 74–75 in Chapter 3, "The Universal Blueprint.")

- **Throwing objects** teaches cause and effect. Pick up the object *once,* after that say "bye-bye." If toddlers throw food, remove the bowl, saying "I can see you're done" and offer them a towel to help clean up. You can put your hand on top of their's to help.

- **Wants to do tasks "by myself."** Allow extra time, offer choices within limits, teach skills, acknowledge the difficulty, and offer quick tips and encouragement.

- **Whining.** When children are frustrated but can't express themselves well verbally, they will often whine. We need to teach children how to make requests, "When you want something, say 'May I please have a _____.'" Then ignore the whining. Expect it to take some time for children to master the verbal *and* self-control skills they need to express their frustration appropriately. If we give children what they whine for, the whining can turn into a habit or PO problem.

Preschoolers

(See "Infants" and "Toddlers" sections above for behaviors that still remain in the preschool years.)

- **Bragging** and telling fantastic stories are often related to a child's age or moral development and are not necessarily intentional lies. (Since lying is usually intentional misbehavior, there is a section devoted entirely to this topic and its developmental factors in the PO Toolset.)

- **Peer conflicts.** Use the Child Problem Toolbox to mediate and teach peaceful conflict-resolution skills. Instead of saying, "Be nice" or "Use words," be specific. Describe what nice means and suggest specific words they can use. (See the "Sibling Conflicts" section of Chapter 8, "Problem Solving Toolset" for more ideas.)

- **Picky eaters.** Everyone has food preferences and being "picky" can be a personality trait (PU). Do *not* fix special meals. Make foods child-friendly. Involve children in meal planning and preparation; they will take a greater interest in eating what they have helped prepare. Let the child pick some foods to serve themselves. Plan to have one favorite food available, in addition to new or less favored foods. If children are too young to cook on the stove or cut with a knife, let them stir, pour, or wash vegetables. Involving children in gardening is also a great way to spark interest in eating healthy foods.(See Chapter 5, "Cooperation Toolset.")

  Parents can have several *bottom-line* limits: eating nutritious foods before sweets, allowing a reasonable but limited time to eat, and trying foods before rejecting them. Within these bottom line limits, children can choose *how much* they eat, *when* they eat, and *if* they eat. Encourage children to take a little of everything. These are "no thank-you helpings." Children's stomachs are about the size of their fists, so allow small portions. They can always have more. Many small meals are actually better for the body than a few large meals. Appetites vary greatly during and between growth spurts. Focus on well-balanced weeks, not days; nutrition rather than timing or amount. Make mealtime conversation pleasant. Do not criticize or nag about eating habits. Do not use food or dessert as a reward or incentive to eat. If parents become controlling about food issues, pickiness can become a PO problem. (See the index for pages numbers of other advice on picky eaters.)

- **Testing limits.** Be consistent and offer choices within limits. When preschoolers ask a million questions, ask what *they* think is the answer. (See the PO Toolset for suggestions that can prevent this behavior from turning into a PO problem.)

Early Elementary

- **Arguing.** Children enjoy using information they have learned or think others don't know. This is why they correct others, especially parents and younger children. They might pick apart words, arguing about what you really said or meant. Encourage children to share what they are learning. If they use that information to make others feel inferior or stupid, point out the hurt feelings. If they pick apart your words, simply clarify what you *meant* to say and refuse to argue. If they persist, it is PO behavior.

- **Testing limits and rules.** Use the Cooperation Toolset to make requests and reveal rules in positive words. Use the Clear Communication Toolset to set limits and use parent/child problem solving to reach win/win solutions.

Late Elementary

- **More opinionated.** Respect different opinions. Don't force your opinions, just share them. They are testing morals and rules. Ask, "What do you think?" and "What would happen if you did that?"

- **Noticing the opposite gender.** Don't tease. Respect their perspective and feelings. Discuss puberty before age nine. Explain emotional and physical differences between genders to help them understand immature or confusing behavior.

Junior High

- **Criticizing parents.** Don't take this personally or get revengeful. Young teens often think of themselves as all-knowing and invincible. Express your concerns and expectations in private, using the Clear Communication Toolset. When they want more unsupervised time with peers, agree to chaperon but keep a distance.

- **Moodiness.** Young teens can experience sudden and powerful hormonal changes, which influences their behavior and moods. They can be laughing about a situation one minute and crying the next, about the same situation! A junior high principal once described young teens as "chameleons on a roller coaster." Parents need extra patience and understanding during these unpredictable times.

- **Peer Pressure.** Use encouragement (not praise) and internal (not external) approval, which we learned in the Self-Esteem Toolset. Use the Child Problem Toolbox to teach decision-making skills.

- **Puberty.** Respect their individual timetable. Hormones can cause moodiness and confusing feelings (body and emotions). Give them facts, share values, and provide books written *for* young teens.

- **Telephone use.** Telephone privileges are important to teens; it is their second lifeline to their friends (after school). Young teens do much of their socializing and problem solving over the phone, because their conversations are safer and more private than at school. Parents need to find win/win solutions that don't totally cut off young teens from their friends.

High School

- **Asking for more freedom.** Teens feel frustrated, because they are too old for "kid" things, and too young for adult activities. They usually want more freedom to "try out" adulthood. If teens have displayed responsible behavior and their parents don't trust them and allow them to express their independence in healthy ways, teens may simply sneak to do what they want to do (a PO problem). Balance limits and freedom. Make agreements using parent/child problem solving.

- **Dating and involvement in sex** are difficult issues. Teens are told to "wait," but feel nature calling. If lines of communication are not already open, it will be difficult for teens to confide in their parents when facing tough decisions.

- **Dress styles.** Every generation has its own fashion fad. It is a way for teens to identify with each other and feel different from children and adults. Respect their individual tastes. Don't impose your own style, unless it's a rare special occasion. Focus on internal personality qualities, rather than external appearances. Bottom-line limits should relate to safety and health. Extremely provocative styles can invite sexual victimization.

- **Driving.** When teens are ready for drivers education, use two-party problem solving to express concerns about the young driver's safety and to negotiate an agreement for keeping the *privilege* of driving. (It is *not* a "right.") Don't give new cars and unlimited driving privileges to teens on a silver platter; driving is a wonderful opportunity for teens to learn about and practice having adult responsibilities. Have the agreement include maintaining good grades, a job to pay for insurance and repairs, and a good driving record. Agree that if teens break the agreement (poor grades, accidents, tickets) they will give up driving privileges. (We learn more about "Restrictions" in the Discipline Toolset.) This is one agreement parent should get in writing.

ADDITIONAL RESOURCES

In addition to the books mentioned in this and other chapters, there are other resources that address the causes of PU behavior. Here are some possible topics and recommended resources:

Young children:
- *Parenting Young Children*, with James S. Dinkmeyer (American Guidance Service, 1989).
- *Tantrums: Secrets to Calming the Storm,* Ann E. LaForge, (Pocket Books, 1996).
- *Any* book or resource by Doctors T. Berry Brazelton or William Sears.
- *The First Three Years of Life*, Burton L. White, M.D., (Fireside Books, 1995).

Puberty:
- *Changes in You & Me*, by Paulette Bourgeois and Martin Wolfish, M.D. (Somerville House, 1994). A book written *for* children nearing puberty. There is one book for boys and one for girls.
- *Created by God: About Human Sexuality for Older Girls and Boys,* by Dorlis Brown Glass with James H. Ritchie, Jr. (Graded Press, United Methodist Church, 1989).

Teens:
- *The Parent's Handbook: S.T.E.P./TEEN, Systematic Training for Effective Parenting of Teens,* Donald Dinkmeyer, Sr. and Gary McKay, (American Guidance Service, 1983).
- *Between Parent and Teenager,* Haim G. Ginott, (MacMillan, 1969).
- *Positive Discipline for Teenagers : Resolving Conflict With Your Son or Daughter in an Atmosphere of Mutual Respect*, Jane Nelsen, with Lynn Lott, (Prima Publishing, 2000).

All ages:
- *Creative Parenting,* William Sears, M.D., (Everest House, 1982). Explains several developmental issues of all ages, including medical advice.
- *Childswork/Childsplay*, a catalog of therapeutic games/books for parents, teachers, and therapists. An excellent resource for teaching emotional and behavior skills. Call 1-800-962-1141 or write 135 Dupont St., P.O. Box 760, Plainview, NY, 11803. Website: http://childswork.com

Bedtime/Sleep problems:
- *The Family Bed*, by Tine Thevenin. (Avery Publishing Group Inc., 1987).
- *Nighttime Parenting*, by Dr. William Sears (La Leche League International, 1985).

Learning styles:
- *Seven Kinds of Smart: Identifying and Developing Your Many Intelligences*, Thomas Armstrong, (Plume, 1993).
- *How Your Child Is Smart: a Life-Changing Approach to Learning,* Dawna Markova, Ph.D., (Conari Press, 1992).

Personality traits (also called "temperaments"):
- *Raising Your Spirited Child*, by Mary Sheedy Kurchinka (HarperCollins, 1991).

Food allergies:
- *Is this Your Child? Discovering and Treating Unrecognized Allergies*, Doris Rapp, (W. Morrow, 1991).

Attention Deficit Hyperactivity Disorder:
- *The Myth of the ADD Child: 50 Ways to Improve Your Child's Behavior and Attention Span Without Drugs, Labels, or Coercion* Thomas Armstrong, (Dutton, 1995).
- CH.A.D.D. National Headquarters, 8181 Professional Place, Suite 201, Landover, MD, 20785, 301-306-7070, fax 301-306-7090. CH.A.D.D. has parent support groups throughout the United States (call to inquire about international resources) and publishes an "educator's manual" for teachers. For more information, check the CH.A.D.D. Web site, home page address: http://www.chadd.org/

SUMMARY SHEET
PU TOOLSET

CORRECTLY IDENTIFY PU BEHAVIOR ☆☆☆☆

Question #2: Is the Misbehavior Unintentional or "On Purpose"?

"Yes" to *any one* of the following questions means it is PU behavior.

1. Is this behavior the result of the child's immaturity or developmental stage?
   - *Style of Development*: Children learn skills all-at-once or one-at-a-time. Trial-and-error or wait-and-do learners.
   - *Rate of Development*: Children develop at their own pace.
2. Is this behavior part of the child's personality?
3. Is this an accident or is a medical condition influencing the child's self-control?
4. Does the child lack the information to know better?

★ 5. Has the child *not consistently shown* that he or she has *mastered* the skills to behave properly in this situation? ☆☆☆☆

"Normal" isn't an excuse. Don't *excuse* behavior, teach skills that help them move through developmental stages, balance personality traits, or compensate for physical limitations.

When in doubt, assume it is PU.

THE PASRR FORMULA FOR PU BEHAVIOR

Step A. <u>P</u>revent the problem by using the Prevention Toolbox, especially the Independence Toolset. "When people want ___, they (teach skills). You can (offer choices)."

Step B. <u>A</u>cknowledge children's feelings or perspective with the Child Problem Toolbox, "I can see you want/feel _____."

Step C1. <u>S</u>et limits, using the Clear Communication Toolset. "...but (state limits in positive words)."

Step C2. <u>R</u>edirect PU behavior.
   - When appropriate, ignore behavior.
   - Offer an acceptable alternative. ☆☆☆☆
   - Distract by changing the focus or subject.
   - Use Environmental Engineering to control situations, not the child.
   - Target PU behaviors, identify their triggers, and plan a strategy.

PRACTICE EXERCISES

A. PU or PO? Each of the following behaviors can be either PU (unintentional, developmental, personality, lack of skills) or PO (on purpose). Read each explanation and write either "PU" or "PO" in the blank next to each description of the reason for the misbehavior.

1. When Dad tries to play a game with Cassy, 4, and her siblings, Cassy often takes the game pieces and leaves the room.

    a. _____ Cassy has a hard time sitting still for any length of time. She thinks the game pieces are interesting and carries them with her when she moves on to another activity.

    b. _____ Cassy likes to play games and can sit still when she wants. When it's her turn, the other kids tell her to "Hurry up," so when it's their turn, she sometimes takes the game pieces. She likes it when her Dad or sisters run after her to get them back. This is more exciting than the board game.

2. Susan, 9, has her friends visiting her house. When her parent asks her to do something, Susan gives a smart-aleck response.

    a. _____ Normally, Susan is very cooperative. If she doesn't like something, she is usually assertive, but respectful. She only answers this way when her friends are around, as though this might impress them. Is this PU or PO behavior?

    b. _____ Susan has always been outspoken, but since she entered sixth grade, her first year of middle school, she has been a real smart-mouth. It seems no matter how nicely her parent asks, Susan has a flip attitude. The parents have heard Susan's friends talking to their parents the same way. Is this PU or PO behavior?

3. John, 14, punched another young teen, Joe, who was harassing him on the school bus.

    a. _____ John tried to be assertive with Joe and then tried to ignore him. John's friends said, "Are you going to let him get away with treating you like that? If you don't do something, he's gonna keep bugging you." John waited and his friends kept pressuring him, making clucking chicken sounds, and teasing him. So John got up, walked to Joe (who was now sitting and minding his own business), and tapped him on the shoulder. When Joe turned around, John sucker punched him. Is this PU or PO behavior?

    b. _____ John's father always tells him to stand up for himself and never let others get the first punch. When Joe bothered him, he told him to stop or he'd punch him. Joe continued to harass John, so he punched Joe. Is this PU or PO behavior?

4. Teri, 16, wears clothes that are unacceptable to her parents.

    a. _____ Teri has chosen this style of clothing not just to be like her friends, but because she likes it, too. She knows her parents don't like it, but she wants to be able to decide for herself what to wear.

    b. _____ Teri wants to be accepted by her friends and wearing these clothes helps. She is tired of her parents nagging her about her clothes. On days when they *make* her change, she and a friend trade clothes when she gets to school. Now, she won't go shopping with her parents, because they try to force her to change.

B. PU Mutations. The way we respond to PU behavior can cause it to turn into PO behavior. In each of the following situations, identify whether the presenting problem is PU or PO behavior and choose an appropriate response. Depending on your answer, it might "mutate" or change into PO behavior.

1. A toddler is touching a glass clown figurine on Grandma's coffee table.
    Is this behavior PU or PO?
    Which response is most appropriate?

    a. Rush to the toddler. In a loud voice, that emphasizes the danger of this action, yell "No!" Then slap the toddler's hand. Leave the clown there and repeat this response until the child stops touching the clown when visiting.

    b. Kneel next to the child and acknowledge how pretty the clown is. Hold the clown and let the toddler touch it, saying, "This can break. You can touch it now, but then we only look at it when we visit." Then put the clown up on a shelf out of the toddler's reach.

    If you chose response "a," the toddler now looks at you before touching the glass clown that is still sitting on the coffee table. You've said "no" and slapped the toddler's hand several times now. When you are talking to your mother, the toddler tries to get your attention by interrupting you. You ignore the toddler. The toddler goes to the glass clown, picks it up and holds it, looking at you. Now, is *this* behavior PU or PO?

2. A child, age 7, is supposed to be cleaning the toy room, which is littered with toys. The child is sitting in the middle of the floor playing with the toys and occasionally tossing a toy or two into the toy box. Is this behavior PU or PO?
    Which response is most appropriate?

    a. Stand over the child, hands on hips, and say, "You're supposed to be cleaning up the toys, not playing. Now get back to work." The child complains that there are too many toys. You pick up a few toys to help. The child isn't helping, so you say, "I'm not going to help you if you aren't lifting a finger! You can clean it yourself." Then leave.

    b. Kneel next to the child and say, "Wow. There sure are a lot of toys!" The child complains that there are too many toys. Say, "Sometimes it helps if you can make a game of it. Would you like to play a song while you clean? You can see how many books you can put in the bookshelf by the end of the first song. Then you could gather some of the kitchen toys during the next song. Would you like to try that?"

    If you chose "a," the child is now angry and crying. The child starts throwing the toys into the toy box—and against the door you slammed, and against the wall. Now, is *this* behavior PU or PO?

3. A teenager asks for a later curfew on Saturday night, to attend a party.
    Is this behavior PU or PO?
    Which response is most appropriate?

    a. You say, "No, I don't want you going to a party. There will probably be kids drinking there." Your teen says, "My friends don't drink!" You say, "Well, even so, you shouldn't be out that late." Your teen protests even louder, "But . . ." You interrupt, saying, "My answer is final! Now quit arguing!"

    b. You say, "I worry about parties where there might be drinking and then riding home with another teen late at night." The teen says, "But my friends don't drink!" You say, "I know you want to be with your friends. And I trust *you* and the friends I know. Might there be other teens there I don't know who might bring alcohol?" The teen says "Maybe, but I still wouldn't be drinking!" You ask, "How would you respond if they offered you alcohol and tried to pressure you to drink?" The teen explains. "Well, you probably would handle the situation well, but I still worry about those teens being on the road when you are riding home late at night. Is there any other way you can get together with your friends at a safer location or an earlier time?" You explore other possibilities with the teen.

If you chose "a," the teen is angry about missing the party and goes to bed. When you check the teen's bedroom at 11 o'clock, you find the window open. The teen has sneaked to go to the party anyway. Now, is *this* behavior PU or PO?

Activity for Home

List problem behaviors you are experiencing with your child. For each, consider the five diagnosis statements. If the misbehavior is PO, we will learn how to redirect the behavior in the next chapter. If it's PU, answer the questions below for each behavior and apply the PASRR formula to each.

1. Describe the behavior.
   Is it PU or PO? Why?
   If it's PU, can you Prevent it?
   When it happens, how can you respond? (Acknowledge feelings, Set limits, Redirect misbehavior.)

Detailed Answers

A. PU or PO?

1. When Dad tries to play a game with Cassy, 4, and her siblings, Cassy often takes the game pieces and leaves the room.
   a. PU. It is normal for a four-year-old to be antsy, play with objects, and forget she is carrying them. She is simply "in her own world."
   b. PO. The fact that Cassy is capable of sitting still on a consistent basis is one clue this is intentional behavior. The other clue is that she behaves this way when she feels hurt by criticism and is making a game of taking the pieces.

2. Susan, 9, has her friends visiting her house. When her parent asks her to do something, Susan gives a smart-aleck response.
   a. PO. Susan normally isn't disrespectful, only around her friends, to impress them.
   b. PU. Being outspoken is part of Susan's personality, most preteens go through a stage where they test limits and act smart-alecky, which is shown by her friends' behavior. Although it's "normal," Susan's parents should not ignore, accept, or excuse her behavior. They can assertively respond and redirect it.

3. John, 14, punched another young teen, Joe, who was harassing him on the school bus.
   a. PO. John showed he had better conflict-resolution skills, but buckled under pressure to please his friends.
   b. PU. John's father has taught him that he is supposed to respond to harassment by fighting.

4. Teri, 16, wears clothes that are unacceptable to her parents.
   a. PU. Teri is trying to assert her individuality, which is normal for a teen. She chooses these clothes because she likes them, not just to get attention from her friends or to aggravate her parents. As long as her parents don't make an issue out of it or only have bottom-line limits of decency, Teri will probably try other styles, never using clothes as a weapon to control or hurt her parents.
   b. PO. Teri is rebelling against her parents' attempts to control her. She is using clothes, an area her parents can't control, to prove she has power. When they "make her" conform, she complies only until she is out of their sight, then she defies their orders.

B. PU Mutations. In *each* situation, the original presenting problem was PU. The ineffective response (always Option a), either escalated the situation or gave the child a payoff. Then, the situation turned into a PO problem, with the child using a similar behavior later, on purpose.

1. If we let children look at items or maybe touch them *very* carefully while we explain the danger of it breaking, we satisfy their curiosity and give them information. They are *less* likely to be obsessed with touching the item, because they already have. It is no longer forbidden territory. If we forbid them from even exploring them safely, they are even more curious about the item. They might try to touch it when they can't get caught. Or, knowing they can get the parents reaction, they might touch it to get the parent's attention. In this case, the same touching behavior is PO.

2. Cleaning huge messes is overwhelming for *everyone*, especially children who haven't mastered an efficient cleaning system. *If* we help, we want to teach skills or use fun ways to get the job done. If we simply do the job for them, they have little reason to help. If we use the chore as punishment, they are even less motivated to help. Punishment breeds anger and resentment, which often lead to revenge.

3. Being invited to a party makes teens feel accepted, even if they don't know or like everyone who will be there. It is natural for teens to want to go out alone with friends and occasionally stay out later than usual. Parent/teen problem solving does not always result in parents giving permission. Sometimes it helps teens plan for unexpected situations they might face. Other times it results in a plan that meets the teen's needs *and* the parent's concerns. Even when parents' limits must stand, they can use empathy and effective communication tools to prevent the situation from escalating into power or revenge cycles. If teens try the honest approach, asking permission and trying to reassure parents, but they never get a chance to prove themselves trustworthy, they become discouraged. If they know the answer will always be "no," they may stop asking permission and find other, less acceptable, ways to get the freedom they desire. These ways are usually more dangerous than what they originally asked to do.

WHAT'S NEXT?

As we better understand the causes of PU behavior, we more quickly identify it and redirect it. We avoid unhelpful gut reactions that can cause PU behavior to mutate into PO problems.

Chapter 12, "PO Toolset ('On purpose' misbehavior)," explores the purpose behind intentional misbehavior and ways to redirect it. Once we identify a behavior as "on purpose," this toolset helps us answer the next question: "What *is* the purpose?" We learn the four types of purposeful misbehavior and how to redirect each type, using specific tools from previous toolsets. We also learn the motives behind lying and how we can use the PO Toolset in adult relationships. Chapter 12 ties together everything we've learned so far and shows how we can use the Universal Blueprint in any relationship.

REFERENCES

1   ADHD diagnostic criteria comes from the *American Psychiatric Association: Diagnostic and Statistical Manual of Mental Disorders,* Fourth Edition. Washington, DC, American Psychiatric Association, 1994. (pp. 83–85). Underlined emphasis on certain words was added by this author.

Diagnostic criteria is reprinted with permission from the *Diagnostic and Statistical Manual of Mental Disorders*, Fourth Edition. Copyright 1994 American Psychiatric Association.

2   Based on Howard Gardner's multiple intelligence theory, which dozens of other author's have used and written about.

3   *Welcome Home*, a monthly publication of original, inspirational stories. Published by Mothers at Home, Inc., 8310A Old Courthouse Rd., Vienna, VA, 22182. Phone: 703-827-5903, Fax: 703-534-7858, Web site: http://www.mah.org

CHAPTER 12
PO TOOLSET ("On purpose" misbehavior)

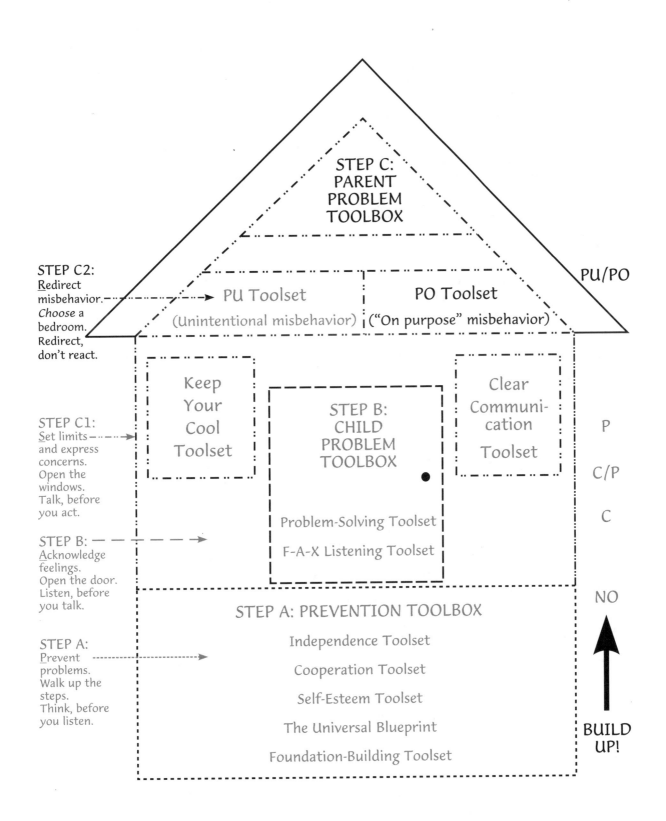

STEP C:
PARENT
PROBLEM
TOOLBOX

PU/PO

STEP C2:
Redirect
misbehavior.
Choose a
bedroom.
Redirect,
don't react.

PU Toolset
(Unintentional misbehavior)

PO Toolset
("On purpose" misbehavior)

Keep
Your
Cool
Toolset

STEP B:
CHILD
PROBLEM
TOOLBOX

Clear
Communi-
cation
Toolset

P

C/P

C

STEP C1:
Set limits
and express
concerns.
*Open the
windows.
Talk,* before
you act.

Problem-Solving Toolset

F-A-X Listening Toolset

STEP B:
Acknowledge
feelings.
*Open the door.
Listen,* before
you talk.

STEP A: PREVENTION TOOLBOX

NO

STEP A:
Prevent
problems.
*Walk up the
steps.
Think,* before
you listen.

Independence Toolset

Cooperation Toolset

Self-Esteem Toolset

The Universal Blueprint

Foundation-Building Toolset

BUILD
UP!

12 PO TOOLSET ("On purpose" misbehavior)

If a furnace rattles or a faucet drips, it's a symptom of a problem. We can tighten the furnace bolts or the faucet handle, but if that is not the cause of the problem, the symptoms will continue and might even get worse. If we figure out the cause of the problem and fix it, the symptoms will disappear.

In parenting, intentional misbehavior is a symptom of an underlying problem. It is the outer skin of the onion. If we react to the behavior, but don't address the real cause, the misbehavior either escalates or gets a payoff. We want to identify what children are trying to accomplish through negative behavior and help them achieve these purposes through positive behavior. When we address the real issue, the symptom (intentional misbehavior) usually stops.

IN THIS CHAPTER

In Chapter 3, "The Universal Blueprint," we learned three questions to ask to identify the type of problem we are facing: (1) Is it a Child problem or Parent problem (SHARP RV)? (2) If there's misbehavior, is it PU or PO? (3) If the misbehavior is PO, *what* is the purpose? This chapter teaches us how to answer the third and final question. We already know the tools we'll use to redirect PO behavior, but we still don't know *which* tools are most effective for specific *types* of PO behavior. The PO Toolset helps us do four very important tasks:

1. Correctly identify the purpose behind PO misbehavior. Misbehaving children give us clues to their purpose. We need to know what clues to look for and what they mean.
2. Avoid reacting in ways that escalate the behavior or give it a payoff, while effectively redirecting the behavior. Each type of PO behavior has a specific strategy for responding effectively, using tools we already know.
3. Use what we learn in the PO Toolset to understand and helpfully respond to intentional adult misbehavior, too.
4. Understand the motives behind lying, how to prevent it, and how to effectively respond to it.

WHEN TO USE THE PO TOOLSET

We *only* choose the PO Toolset when children or adults are misbehaving *on purpose*. If we respond to intentional misbehavior without first correctly identifying the purpose it serves, we will probably choose an ineffective response. If we use discipline without first breaking misbehavior cycles with the PO Toolset, our discipline is less effective and in some cases is even harmful to the relationship.

IDENTIFYING PO PROBLEMS

PO problems are **P**arent problems involving misbehavior that seems to be "**O**n purpose." Parents have seen children *consistently* behave appropriately, but for some reason they *deliberately* misbehave. While their behavior seems intentional, children are usually unaware of their subconscious beliefs and behavior choices. They have an underlying need or purpose and *falsely believe* this misbehavior will help them accomplish that purpose. (Even adult behavior operates on this principle.)

> **People mistakenly believe their PO behavior will help them meet a specific purpose, but are usually unaware of their subconscious beliefs and behavior choices.**

How PU Behavior Turns into PO Behavior

In the PU Toolset, we learned that strong reactions to PU behavior can turn it into PO behavior. Once this occurs, it is difficult to decide if similar future behavior is PU or PO. The clues lie in the child's past behavior and current motive. To be sure the behavior is really PO, consider the following questions.

> **If we answer "yes" to *any* of these questions, we are most likely facing PO behavior.**
>
> • Have we seen *consistent* appropriate behavior in the past?
> • Are we *positive* the child knows better and has *mastered* the skill?
> • Did the child seem to be looking for or *expecting* a reaction?

In addition to strong reactions, PU behavior can also turn into PO behavior if children's positive efforts fail to meet their purpose. It becomes a survival tactic. For example, if children fail to get attention during a family gathering through positive behavior, they feel discouraged and think, "Well, that didn't work! What else can I do?" They remember when they or others *were* able to get someone's attention. If they think misbehavior will work, children are likely to try it. "Hmm, I remember when my cousin burped real loud. *That* got people to notice him!" Others, besides parents, can also reinforce mistaken beliefs or negative behavior. If relatives laugh when children burp the first time (when it's PU behavior) and the parents respond effectively, children *still* might use the behavior again, since *someone* noticed them. If parents don't break PO cycles, they can become habitual problems.

> **PU behavior comes naturally,** as part of the learning and growth process.
> **PO behavior is usually *learned*.** People have often seen or heard the behavior work for someone, somewhere, sometime. People are more likely to repeat any behavior they believe will give them a payoff or quick result.

*A **Personal Story.** As a protective service worker, I had a case involving David, four, and his parents, who were total opposites. David's mother was heavily medicated for depression and very passive. His father was slightly mentally retarded and worked long hours at a minimum-wage job. The few times he was home, he was tired and stressed and physically punished David.*

Whenever David didn't get what he wanted, he would become so out-of-control his mother would eventually give in. Although she complained about David's behavior, she said it was too hard to stand up to him. When she tried to be firmer, he only became more destructive and defiant. He would resort to whatever drastic measures he needed to get what he wanted. I observed him throwing and breaking things, yelling, and even urinating on the carpet just to get his way.

*David only exhibited his demanding behavior and tantrums at home with his parents. With his grandparents, who cared for him frequently, David's behavior was more acceptable. Obviously, David was "in control" of his parents, but could change his behavior when he chose to. Only his grandparents, who were consistent, firm, **and** loving, did not have to endure David's tirades. David had **learned** to behave in certain ways with certain people to get what he wanted—attention and control. David's example is extreme, but shows what can happen when parents reward misbehavior or overreact to it.*

THE IMPORTANCE OF THE UNIVERSAL BLUEPRINT

We can prevent *and* effectively respond to PO behavior if we follow the Universal Blueprint. As we discuss each type of PO behavior, we will dip into toolboxes and toolsets we've already learned. In PO problems, the importance of following the Universal Blueprint becomes crystal clear. If we skip steps, we miss opportunities to prevent PO behavior or we may even accidentally reinforce it.

We will learn exactly what skills to use to prevent and respond to specific behavior goals, but first, let's review some important points we've already learned that will help us respond to *all* PO problems.

Step A: Prevention Toolbox

Planning ahead is an important part of preventing PO behavior. If we follow two major philosophies from the Prevention Toolbox, we can prevent many different types of PO problems.

- **Balanced parenting sets limits without overreacting, which can prevent or break PO cycles.** An over-controlling parenting style usually escalates PO problems. An under-controlling style usually gives a payoff, because the parent gives in.

- *Discouragement is the root cause of intentional misbehavior.* Therefore, it is a logical conclusion that descriptive *en*couragement (noticing or describing positive behavior) can help prevent it.

Step B: Child Problem Toolbox

We can use this toolbox as the main source of tools for our response to *one* specific type of PO behavior and as part of our PASRR response to *any* PO behavior. We can use the F-A-X process to identify the feelings beneath PO behavior, which offer clues to the goal of the PO behavior. When we look at each goal in detail, we learn which feelings usually cause certain types of PO behavior. If we can help children resolve these feelings, it often de-escalates the situation or even stops the behavior.

Step C: Parent Problem Toolbox

- **Step C1: Keep Your Cool Toolset** prevents us from *reacting* to misbehavior instead of effectively redirecting it. *Gut reactions almost always escalate the PO problem or accidentally give the PO behavior a payoff.* We must have enough self-control to be aware of what we *feel like* doing, but *not act* on those feelings and temptations. The Keep Your Cool Toolset helps us maintain our self-control. We can then think logically enough to see the clues we need to identify PO behavior and choose the most appropriate response.

- **Step C1: Clear Communication Toolset** helps us respond assertively to intentional misbehavior. Passive responses do not address the misbehavior or give it a payoff. Aggressive responses escalate the behavior and cause discouragement and hurt—core issues behind almost all PO behavior. Assertive communication addresses the problem *and* prevents escalation.

- **Step C2: PO Toolset** offers reliable guidelines for identifying and responding to PO behavior. Once we use the Universal Blueprint to correctly identify PO behavior, we are ready to take three new steps (which we learn in detail in the next section):
  - Step C2a: Identify the purpose of the misbehavior.
  - Step C2b: Avoid escalating the situation or giving the misbehavior a payoff.
  - Step C2c: Redirect the behavior by showing children how to meet the purpose through positive behavior.

- **Step C3: Discipline Toolset** shows children that PO behavior has a negative effect. We need to be careful, though, not to jump right to this step. If we do, we are simply reacting to the behavior without addressing the real issue children are trying to express. The PO Toolset breaks the PO cycle, which makes our discipline more effective, and prevents repeated PO behavior.

> **When we use discipline as a first response to PO behavior, it can escalate PO behavior or give it a payoff. Therefore, discipline is only effective *after* negative misbehavior cycles are broken.**

When we see problem behavior, we first decide whether the behavior is PU or PO. If we have *consistently seen* that children know how to behave but aren't (PO), we keep our cool and use two or three sentences *at the most* to move through the first four steps of the PASRR formula. (The Prevention and/or Child Problem Toolbox and the Clear Communication and PO Toolsets.) These tools usually stop the behavior. If not, we have broken the PO misbehavior cycle, which is essential before revealing discipline.

PO TOOLS ☆☆☆☆

Let's look at the three basic steps we take *every* time we deal with PO behavior. Then we'll apply these steps by looking at each of the four types of PO behavior, learning the clues that reveal the purpose, and reviewing the best tools for preventing and responding helpfully to that type of PO behavior.

> **The steps in the PO Toolset are always the same, but our response will differ depending on the *type* of PO behavior we identify.**

Step C2a: Identify the Purpose of the Misbehavior

To answer Question 3 of problem identification, "If misbehavior is 'on purpose,' *what* is the purpose?," we ask the following *three questions* to find the clues we need.[1]

   i. **How do *I feel* when I see this behavior?** Since all intentional problem behavior can cause us to feel angry (PO'd), we want to look for the underlying feeling that is *causing* our anger. Different feelings are clues to the different goals of PO behavior.

   ii. **What am I *tempted to do*?** Our feelings and temptations are clues that help us identify the purpose, but we don't want to act on them. Gut reactions usually escalate the situation or give a payoff.

   iii. **If I did this, how would the *child react*?** If we carried out our gut reaction, would we give the behavior a payoff? Would it escalate the situation? How would the child interpret our actions? Would the behavior get better or worse? Would the short term result have long-term negative consequences?

We can also ask, in a curious, respectful tone, "Could the reason you're (action) be that you feel ___?" They probably won't admit it, but their reaction often shows we've guessed correctly. We don't want to *confront* others about their goals, nor do we always need to check it out. If we don't see the clues easily, however, it may be helpful to ask.

Step C2b: Avoid Escalating the Situation or Giving a Payoff

This is a tricky step, because we need to avoid doing the very thing we are tempted to do (the answer to question ii above). This is harder than it sounds! We must keep our cool and resist the urge to react.

> **Hard as it is, we need to get in touch with our feelings and temptations, to learn the clues they hold, without acting on those urges.**

 Step C2c: Redirect the Behavior

In each case, we want to show children how to meet their purpose through positive behavior. Depending on the purpose we identify, we select specific skills we already know for our response. Sometimes we try to meet the need directly, through our response. Other times, we use problem solving to brainstorm more appropriate ways children can meet their purposes.

> **We usually use the same tools to redirect PO behavior that we use to prevent it.**

Now, let's go through each type of PO misbehavior, answering the three questions for each. We will learn which tools (that we've already learned) are best for preventing *and* responding to each type of PO behavior. *One* tool will have a black star next to it (★). This is usually the best all-around tool to use if you want to prevent *or* respond to *that* type of PO behavior. Your goal is to remember three important facts:

- The different clues to look for when identifying the four types of PO behavior.
- What reactions to avoid
- Which tool is usually the best tool to use with each type of PO behavior (the starred tools)

 THE FOUR TYPES OF PO BEHAVIOR

When Rudolf Dreikurs[2] identified "The Four Goals of Misbehavior" decades ago, it explained the *cause* of intentional problem behavior, which led to more effective responses. Several generations have passed and these four goals have been proven to be accurate and the remedies effective.

Each misbehavior goal has a positive and negative side. If people *think* they cannot meet their purpose through positive behavior, they become discouraged and resort to negative behavior to accomplish their goal. Ideally, we want to *prevent* negative behavior by teaching children positive ways to meet their behavior goals. The next page shows the four goals and their positive and negative sides.

Involvement/Attention

Some common negative attention-seeking behaviors are interrupting, silliness, whining, emotionally overreacting, or acting "stupid" so someone will spend more time explaining something.

STEP A: PREVENT THE BEHAVIOR (PREVENTION TOOLBOX)

We want to use the Prevention Toolbox when PO misbehavior first appears, or we will become increasingly frustrated and impatient. Then, our nonverbal language says that we *do* notice them, which gives the child a payoff and escalates the negative attention-seeking behavior.

Meet the positive goal of *involvement*. People feel accepted and important when they can be involved with, included in, and offer meaningful contributions to a group they identify with, such as their family or peers. They want others to recognize their efforts, contributions, and presence.

When children try to gain this approval through positive behavior and no one notices, they feel discouraged and may settle for negative attention. If others *only* notice children when they are making bids for attention, the children may believe they are *only* important *if* they are the center of attention.

THE FOUR GOALS OF MISBEHAVIOR

POSITIVE GOAL/BELIEF   If people believe they have failed to meet this goal, they feel discouraged and change their beliefs and behavior.   NEGATIVE GOAL/BELIEF

✦ **INVOLVEMENT:** "I want to be a part of the group. I belong when I'm involved and noticed." ✦ **ATTENTION:** "They will *only* notice me if I am the center of attention—and negative attention is better than no attention at all!"

✦ **INDEPENDENCE:** "I want to make decisions and do things by myself." ✦ **POWER:** "Someone is trying to take away my power! If I want to keep it, I must be the one in control."

✦ **JUSTICE:** "One good deed deserves another!" ✦ **REVENGE:** "Someone hurt me! I must hurt others the way I've been hurt."

✦ **WITHDRAWAL:** "I can handle conflict and failure appropriately. I want reassurance." ✦ **GIVING UP:** "I *can't* belong because I'm incompetent. Others should expect nothing from me."

★ **Notice and describe children's good behavior.** If we notice children's positive behavior, they are more likely to behave this way in the future. Unexpected descriptive encouragement helps children feel important, without having to go all-out to get our attention. Describe any effort or improvement, no matter how small.

Show unconditional love. If children behave poorly and we send the hidden message, "I don't love you when you misbehave," they become more discouraged. This leads to more misbehavior.

Spend time with children. If we frequently spend quality time with our children, when they are not demanding our attention, we can prevent some negative attention-seeking behavior. Giving children attention whenever they demand it sends the message that they are entitled to special service. Then, if these children don't always receive special treatment, they feel discouraged and disappointed and make stronger, more negative bids for attention.

Focus on internal approval and motivation. Descriptive encouragement allows children to tell *themselves* they are valuable and did a "good job." It prevents dependency on others' opinions. Consequently, they don't need to get constant attention and approval from *us*.

As peer acceptance becomes more important to children, they can misbehave to gain approval from their peer group. If parents have built self-esteem (rather than ego-esteem) through encouragement (instead of praise) children are less susceptible to negative peer pressure.

Build teamwork. When we order children around, they don't feel important, just used. We want to focus on teamwork and cooperation and let children know how their contribution is important to the family. Nagging and reminding with "please" and "don't" can give a payoff through negative attention.

STEP B: ACKNOWLEDGE FEELINGS (CHILD PROBLEM TOOLBOX)

When the goal is attention, people are *usually* feeling lonely, unimportant, rejected, or forgotten. Use the F-A-X process to identify *and* resolve these feelings.

STEP C1: SET LIMITS (CLEAR COMMUNICATION TOOLSET)

In one sentence, we acknowledge feelings (F-A-X Listening Toolset) and state our needs or concerns (with the Clear Communication Toolset). If there is a reason children can't have our full attention immediately, we explain this now (if we haven't already).

STEP C2a: IDENTIFY THE PURPOSE OF ATTENTION

When children try to get *attention* through negative behavior, we usually find the following clues:

i. **We feel** *annoyed* or *irritated,* as though our personal space or rights are being *violated.* We might even feel exhausted from trying to please (or stop) the child.

ii. **We are tempted to** *remind, nag,* tell children to "Stop it," "Quit it," or Leave me alone!" and *push away* emotionally, to get some space or regain our sanity.

iii. **If we do any of these,** we don't break the cycle. The behavior might *stop temporarily,* because children receive the attention they want, but may be repeated later. Sometimes the behavior will *escalate* until we give them attention (the payoff). Children might also choose a *different behavior* to get our attention.

STEP C2b: AVOID ESCALATING OR GIVING MISBEHAVIOR A PAYOFF

When people misbehave and we notice them (even if it's to discipline them or to tell them to stop), we are still giving them our *attention*. **If giving attention is a payoff, we want to give the behavior *no* attention. We can say *one thing* before we ignore the behavior.** Any more attention and we give children a payoff. We want to give quickly use the PASRR formula. "I can tell you feel ___. I feel ___. If you want ___, you can ___ instead." Then *ignore* the behavior long enough (usually 15–30 seconds) to send the message, "This behavior does not affect me." Do not give the silent treatment, roll your eyes, or huff and puff. These are passive-aggressive responses that tell children, "You are getting to me." The effective way to ignore behavior is to act as though children aren't doing what they are doing. If, at anytime, children stop that misbehavior or behave appropriately, we can pay attention to them again. For example, a child is demanding you give them something. Clearly and firmly state, "When people want something, they need to say 'May I please have a ___?'" Then ignore the behavior until they ask appropriately.

Sometimes children escalate their behavior, thinking if they get outrageous enough, we can't possibly ignore them. In the PU Toolset we learned that ignoring behavior is only appropriate *if the behavior is not dangerous.* If we must respond to dangerous behavior, do it quickly with few words until they are safe. (For example, move a child in a head-banging tantrum to a pillow or carpet. Remove a dangerous object without comment and go on with your activity.) Children may still be misbehaving, but we can then ignore the behavior completely. *Once we have completely ignored the behavior long enough to get our point across and break the cycle (usually about 15–30 seconds) we can move to the next step.*

STEP C2c: REDIRECT THE MISBEHAVIOR

Suggest or brainstorm appropriate ways to get attention or to get involved with another activity. Name a specific time when you can be with children—and follow through. Give attention when children are not expecting or requesting it. Involve them in what you are doing or in a activity they can do nearby.

Choose a "meaningful" activity, not just something to keep them busy and out of your hair; kids eventually figure out what you are up to and will continue the misbehavior.

> ***A Graduate's Story.*** *While talking on the phone, I noticed my four-year-old son tormenting the dog. He'd look at me and, when he was sure I was looking, pull the dog's tail. I kept telling him to stop. Instead, he kept getting worse! He kicked the dog and finally grabbed a butter knife and chased the dog. I dropped the phone, chased him, and spanked him when I finally caught him.*

Did this boy get his mother's attention? How extreme did he have to act to get her attention? Since his misbehavior ended with a payoff, how far do you think he'll go the next time he wants her attention? No, he's not destined to be a serial killer or animal mutilator. He probably just believes the phone is his competition or that misbehavior is the best way to get his mom's attention. As the mother reinforces these beliefs, it becomes harder to change his behavior. At four, however, there's plenty of time to reprogram the parent and child in this situation. So let's replay this scene using the skills we just learned.

If you are making a call, plan ahead. Whenever possible, make calls when kids are napping, at school, or busy playing. Let children know you will be on the phone and under what circumstances they may disturb you. (Fire and blood are a minimum bottom line!) If you have young children, take care of their bodily functions (drink, snack, potty, etc.) and get them involved in an independent activity. If they like to be near you, keep a box of quiet toys near the phone. If children are older, let them know they can write you notes.

If you are receiving a call, ask to return the call or ask the caller to hold. Take 30 seconds to 1 minute to do the above activities. Tell children that you *will* spend time with them and make sure you keep your promise. Avoid taking phone calls during your special time with children (that's what answering machines are for).

When children behave appropriately, thank them. Describe what they did and how it was helpful and independent. Don't word it negatively, "Thanks for not ___" This reminds them of misbehavior and gives it attention. Instead, say, "I really appreciate the way you ___." Usually, these preventive measures work if you don't talk for unreasonable periods of time (like an hour). It is especially helpful if you immediately spend time with children when you are off the phone, to ask them about their activity and give positive attention when they weren't asking for it.

If you haven't planned ahead, you are already on the phone, and children interrupt for an unacceptable reason, you can stop *once*. Acknowledge their feelings (Step B). Remind them of the phone rules (Step C1) and their options (Step C2). Reassure them that you will spend time with them when you are done. Some additional options are to let them sit on your lap (if they are quiet) or color with them. (Most of us can handle coloring and talking, if we don't have to stay in the lines.) Make it clear that once you start talking you expect to talk uninterrupted. Explain the value—respect for the caller and your right to talk to others. Acknowledge their rights and suggest alternative activities. Reveal the effect of interrupting—you will ignore them. If the behavior is annoying, but not dangerous, and you have a cordless phone or long extension cord, move out of the room.

> ***A Personal Story.*** *Since I work from home, I get many business calls when my children are home. They had to learn, when they were very young, that Mommy needed to listen to people on the phone. When they fussed, I used all these great ideas and they really worked. Now and then, nothing seemed to help, so I'd sit on the basement stairs to talk. My kids would fuss on the other side, but never opened the door! I have never had a bad problem with this behavior and probably talk more on the phone than many parents.*

Independence/Power

Some common power behaviors are logical arguments and defiance, either aggressive verbal refusals or passive ignoring. People also use emotions like pouting, tantrums, or crying to get their way. "Defiant compliance" is following an order, but doing a lousy job of it or doing it in an aggressive or hurtful way.

STEP A: <u>PREVENT</u> THE BEHAVIOR (PREVENTION TOOLBOX)

Meet the positive goal of *independence*. All people want to feel as though they have some control and independence in their lives. We see this goal of power and independence at every developmental stage of life, adults and seniors included. People assert their independence and personal power in positive ways when they make choices, offer opinions, and do things by themselves.

If people try to exert their independence and personal power, but others resist or try to take their power away, they feel discouraged and frustrated. Rather than give up their control, they may push even harder for control. The toddler and teen years are developmental stages in which achieving independence and a sense of power are primary developmental tasks. Consequently, curious toddlers and teens often experiment with risky behavior and test limits (others' and their own) to prove they have some power, control, and independence.

The best tools for preventing power struggles are in the Cooperation and Independence Toolsets. These skills can prevent *and* redirect power struggles.

Model humbleness. It takes maturity to admit when we are wrong and accept responsibility for our mistakes. Openly model this. Some people, whether by personality or conditioning, believe they must always be right or never to blame. When we insist on pointing out faults or gaining confessions, they become more defensive. Focus on lessons and solutions, not blame.

Avoid bribery. It is manipulative, to control others. Over time, children resent others controlling them and use defiant compliance, logical arguments, and deals to get what they want.

★ **Offer choices within bottom-line limits.** Keep priorities in line by picking and choosing "battles" carefully. When children have choices, they can assert their independence without starting power struggles or violating our bottom-line rules.

Don't Say "Don't." Any time we approach people with negative attitudes or words, we are more likely to get negative responses. "You can't do that" challenges some people to try it, "Oh yeah? Watch me!" They'll test to see if we mean it, what will happen if they do it, and if we follow through with our threats. Instead, we describe what others *can* do or the behavior we want to see.

No No's. "No" often results in logical arguments, "But why?", "But I . . ." Instead, we can give a conditional "Yes, when . . ." or "Sure, if . . ." State the reason or give information in a few words. Acknowledge feelings and offer acceptable alternatives.

Use humor. If children try to bait us into an argument, we can respond in a light-hearted tone of voice. A smile, tilted head, and glance from the corner of the eye says, "I don't think so." If, for example, we ask children to turn off a light and they say "I did," we use humor in several ways. "Light!" With a smile, "I must be crazy! I was just up there and saw it on! The electric elves must have turned it back on!" We can use, "Please," but only once, to be polite.

Routines and family rules prevent many power struggles. When we start routines in the early years, they become habits. When family rules are clear, all we have to do is acknowledge feelings and briefly restate (or ask others to repeat) the rule.

Teach skills. If children are frustrated, angry, or express opinions disrespectfully, we can teach assertive communication skills. We allow children to have their feelings or opinions, but teach them how to express them respectfully.

Let them do things by themselves. Children can become defiant or resistant when they think we are trying to take over. Offer a few quick tips and let go.

Ask their opinion. This prevents power struggles, because we consider their needs when formulating a win/win plan. When children argue, "but . . .," they are trying to express their opinions. We can't always give them exactly what they want, but listening to them with respect, stating our limits, and seeking a win/win solution will usually prevent defiance and resistance.

Nudge, but don't push. It is easy to get into power struggles over PU behavior by pushing children too hard. Many parents find potty training, mealtime, and bedtime are daily battles. It takes practice to know when we are nudging or motivating and when we are pushing. Usually, if we get resistance, we've crossed the line. Get to the bottom line and shift the focus to choices.

STEP B: ACKNOWLEDGE FEELINGS (CHILD PROBLEM TOOLBOX)

If people are challenging *our* power and authority, they are *usually* feeling frustrated, disappointed or out of control of the situation, too. They may not know how to get power in positive ways or have already tried and think their efforts failed. If people want something and can't have it, acknowledge their disappointment and frustration. Sometimes, this alone prevents power struggles.

STEP C1: SET LIMITS (CLEAR COMMUNICATION TOOLSET)

If we follow the Universal Blueprint, we have probably already stated our reasons for not allowing children to do what they want. Children don't have to *like* what we ask them to do, but if we offer them some control or listen to their feelings first, they may cooperate, grudgingly. If they don't, keep your cool and decide whether your limits are too controlling. If they aren't, we can say we are unwilling to argue or debate the issue. We don't want to spend too much time at this step, emphasizing *our* feelings and needs. It easily turns into a lecture, which escalates power struggles and shuts down communication. Use one sentence and move to the next step to stop and redirect the power struggle.

STEP C2a: IDENTIFY THE PURPOSE

When children resist requests, make power plays by testing us, or we've been sucked into a power struggle, we usually find the following clues:

  i. **We feel** as though the person is *challenging our authority* or we are in a battle of wills.

  ii. **We are tempted to** either *exert our authority* with a power play (threats, demands, punishment) or *give in* to their demands to avoid conflict.

  iii. **If we do any of these,** we don't break the cycle. If we exert our authority, it escalates the power struggle. The more we push, the more they resist. If we force a "parent wins/child loses" outcome, children often rebel and feel hurt, which brings on revenge. If we allow a "child wins/parent loses" outcome, we give children a payoff. "It worked!" They will try at least this hard, and two steps more, to get their way the next time.

STEP C2b: AVOID ESCALATING OR GIVING MISBEHAVIOR A PAYOFF

Fighting and giving in are both "win/lose" outcomes. (Actually they are "lose/lose" in the long-run.) *Avoid doing both.* Logical arguments also rarely accomplish much. If there is nothing for others to struggle against, it breaks the cycle. We often feel we are "between a rock and a hard place" and have no other options. You do—a *balanced* approach—choices within limits.

STEP C2c: REDIRECT THE MISBEHAVIOR

Most of the tools listed in the "prevent the behavior" section also help break power struggles and redirect misbehavior. Once we make our point, if children do not cooperate, we first want to shift the focus to the choices (the child's "win") within bottom-line limits (the parent's "win"). If the child persists, we make it clear that we are willing to listen further if they are willing to put forth an effort to solve the problem. "We've discussed this problem for quite awhile. You've come up with several options. I'm sure you'll decide how you want to handle it." Then we may need to emotionally and/or physically disengage by walking away. If they follow, they are now trying to get our attention. Shift to the appropriate strategy—ignore them. (This is why it is so important to control our emotions and keep our logic on-line. **The goal of intentional behavior can shift.** If we aren't on the ball, the situation can mutate into another goal before we realize it!)

Only reveal discipline or follow through with it *after* there has been a break in the power struggle. If we discipline in the middle of the power struggle, it turns our discipline into punishment. When discipline results in a "parent wins/child loses" outcome, children feel hurt, which can *start* revenge cycles.

> *A Personal Story. Chris has particular taste in clothes. He knows what he wants and doesn't like others trying to talk him into buying anything different. My dad and stepmother, after taking him shopping, once joked, "We'd rather throw our money off a cliff than take him shopping." I can usually shop with him, but have to be on-the-ball for power struggles.*
>
> *When Chris was 11, he needed a winter coat. I was willing to go to three stores of his choice in our local area. He would need to agree, however, to pick one coat from those stores. (Step A: **P**revent the problem.) At the first store, we found hundreds of choices, so I said, "With all these coats, I'm sure you can find something you will like." He wanted a particular name-brand and styled coat. (This was a first! I could tell he was nearing the teen years.) We only found a boys' size in an ugly green and a man's size that cost nearly $100. Again, I had to adjust my bottom line. I said, "I'm willing to get any coat in this store that is less than $50."*
>
> *He almost got the $50 ugly green coat, but put it back and started getting resistant. He was trying to bait me into an argument or to make the decision for him. I knew that no matter what I picked, he would complain about it. Things were starting to escalate and he was anxious to go home. I said, "Look, there are plenty of coats to pick from here. I know you won't find the one you really want (Step B: **A**cknowledge feelings), but I bet you can find **something** you like. I'm going to look for a shirt over there. The next time I see you, I want to see a coat that costs less than $50 in your hand. Then we'll go home." (Step C1: **S**et limits with Clear Communication Toolset and Step C2: **R**edirect misbehavior.) As I walked away, he headed back toward the coats, mumbling "I'll pick one out, but I won't wear it." I shopped where I could keep an eye on him, for safety reasons, but stayed out of sight.*
>
> *In a few minutes Chris walked up with a soft, brown coat that cost $40. He acted only somewhat satisfied, so I confirmed his decision and my unwillingness to return it or go somewhere else. He confirmed this was the coat he wanted. The next day was a cool (but not cold) day and, to my surprise, he wore his new coat to his soccer game. The whole team took turns wearing it on the sideline. It ended up being one of his all-time favorite coats.*

Justice/Revenge

Revengeful behavior takes many forms. Aggressive tactics can involve name-calling or physically acting out. Passive-aggressive tactics are the silent treatment or secretly damaging or hiding something of value to the person who hurt them.

STEP A: PREVENT THE BEHAVIOR (PREVENTION TOOLBOX)

Meet the positive goal of *justice*. All people have some sense of justice and fairness. When people receive a kind gesture, they often want to repay the kindness. When people feel wronged, they think something should happen to "balance the scale." Few people have the assertive communication skills to respond respectfully, so they even the score with another unkind word or deed. Some people will even attempt to hurt themselves (drugs, attempted suicide, risky behavior) to hurt others ("They'll be sorry") or to express how much they are hurting inside.

★ **Revengeful behavior is usually the result of hurt feelings or anger over a lost power struggle.** *Acknowledge feelings* before setting limits, to prevent hurt feelings. Use *choices within limits* to avoid win/lose power struggles. ***Teach children assertive communication and problem-solving skills***, so they can express their hurt respectfully. If we defend ourselves, argue, or say they are "mouthing off," they will conclude that assertiveness doesn't work, feel more hurt and discouraged, and resort to stronger revenge tactics.

STEP B: A̲CKNOWLEDGE FEELINGS (CHILD PROBLEM TOOLBOX)

If the goal is revenge, people are *usually* feeling hurt and angry. When we *listen* to the hurt, people may not resort to revengeful behavior to *show* the hurt. When revenge has already occurred, listening rebuilds trust and *problem solving* helps people resolve their hurt and reach healthier solutions without revenge.

STEP C1: S̲ET LIMITS (CLEAR COMMUNICATION TOOLSET)

When people do something mean on purpose, it usually causes an immediate angry reaction. It is *vital* to keep your cool and stop this reaction, but identify the feelings behind it, which are clues to the goal of the revengeful behavior. Not reacting is very different from not asserting our right to be treated with respect. Later in our response, we *will* address the negative effect of hurtful behavior and brainstorm more appropriate, healthy ways to express or resolve the hurt. If we skip Step B, A̲cknowledging feelings, rush through the steps, or spend too much time expressing *our* hurt, we are not addressing or resolving the *real* issue behind the revengeful behavior—the hurt feelings.

STEP C2a: IDENTIFY THE PURPOSE

When someone does something mean to us, we usually find the following clues:

i. **We feel** *hurt* (either physical or emotional), *disgust,* or *disbelief.*

ii. **We are tempted to** *retaliate* or *show our hurt.* We want to punish the person for hurting us or use guilt and shame to make the person feel bad. Verbal or nonverbal responses such as shock, crying, passively withdrawing, or getting angry all say, "You hurt me."

iii. **If we do any of these,** we continue the revenge or give the behavior a payoff. Children interpret immediate discipline as punishing revenge. Children then find a way to match this new hurt, which escalates the revenge cycle. Shame and guilt makes children feel more discouraged, which brings on new forms of intentional misbehavior. Any retaliation will escalate a revenge cycle. When parents show their hurt, they give revengeful behavior a payoff. Since children wanted to even the score by hurting back, they think, "Yes! It worked!" This reinforces the mistaken belief that revenge is an effective way to achieve justice.

STEP C2b: AVOID ESCALATING OR GIVING MISBEHAVIOR A PAYOFF

We must break revenge cycles before we address the misbehavior. Power and revenge cycles take two people. If we don't participate, we can break the cycle. We may need to walk away temporarily to get our emotions and thoughts together. This will prevent children from seeing our hurt. This is a temporary delay, to show the behavior had no effect, not a passive withdrawal that never deals with the problem. Once we get our attitude and logic on-line, we can respond helpfully.

STEP C2c: R̲EDIRECT THE MISBEHAVIOR

We've already learned how to respond to hurt feelings with the F-A-X Listening Toolset. Responding to revengeful behavior with listening is the hardest tool to use in *The Parent's Toolshop*. When someone is mean to us, it is *not* our natural reaction to say, "Wow, you must be really angry with me right now. Tell me how you feel." This tool asks us to "turn the other cheek," which means "return kindness for hurt," not "do nothing" or "invite more hurt." Until we acknowledge and resolve *their* hurt, children will continue to seek ways to express their feelings through revenge.

If we follow the Universal Blueprint, we can rebuild trust. Take Steps B (**A**cknowledge feelings) and C1 (**S**et limits) in one sentence, "I can tell you are really hurt and angry, but I don't appreciate being spoken to like that." If we need to apologize, do so now. Quickly move to the PO Toolset, because the guidelines for revenge remind us to spend more time at the Child Problem Toolbox. **F**ocus on feelings ("Tell me how you feel about what happened."), **A**sk helpful questions ("Do you understand why I did that?"), and **X**-amine possible solutions ("What do you think we can do, instead?"). Model forgiveness. Once we resolve their hurt, children will be ready to listen to us. Then we can assert our feelings or expectations, "It's okay to be angry, but I am more willing to listen if people express themselves respectfully."

If children use dangerous behavior for revenge, we may need to gently restrain young children or temporarily distance ourselves from older children until everyone cools down. If we need to do either of these, we use the statements just outlined *while* taking action. For example, a young child hits a parent. The parent says the statements above *while* firmly but gently taking the child's hands, to keep them away from the parent's body. With older children, the parent acknowledges feelings and sets limits while walking away. "I can tell you are really angry, but I will not subject myself to this treatment. I'm willing to listen when you've calmed down. I'm going to calm down, too. Let me know when you want to work this out." The parent disengages, physically and emotionally, until both have cooled off.

Once we address the hurt that caused the revengeful behavior, we need to deal with the way the child *expressed* the hurt. We can simply point out the emotional consequences of revengeful behavior using the Clear Communication Toolset. "When people feel hurt, they often hurt back, which only creates more hurt and doesn't solve the problem." If children damage something, we can show them how to make amends (Step C3: **R**eveal discipline). If possible, we want to use parent/child problem solving to reach this agreement. If we tell them what they *will* do, we can start a new power struggle or revenge cycle. The trust level is still shaky, so we need to carefully choose our attitudes, words, and actions.

> *A **Personal Story.** Before I decided the best way to set allowances, I proposed a new system to my children. The allowance system was something like one dollar per year of age. The child had to split the money three ways, a third each for savings, spending, and family "taxes," which are used to fund family activities. To pay this much, I concluded, they'd have to do more chores. After calculating the actual dollar figures, Chris realized he would be doing more chores for less spending money. I had regrettably not done the math, but didn't want to give up the idea of trying a good way to teach responsibility. Chris saw my idea as a new way to control how much work he did and how he spent his money.*
>
> *I tried to avoid a power struggle by offering a choice between three allowance options. Amber chose the new system and I was pleased. Chris complained that I rarely paid him his allowance anyway (this was true, we rarely had enough left over after bills). The discussion was dragging on, so I pushed a final decision. It started a power struggle, so I tried to disengage. I stated the bottom line, "You need to pick one of the choices." Chris kept trying to argue. I stopped the discussion at that point and started to walk out of the room. Chris said something like, "Why should I do more chores, you never do anything extra for me." Now I was offended. I decided to get out of this before I got angrier. I concluded, "If you don't want to do chores to help the family, then I'm not willing to do chores for you. You can do your own laundry for a while." I did not say this in an angry way and, in my mind, the discipline made logical sense.*
>
> *Later that week, my kids began packing for a weekend trip to Grandma's. When they needed clean clothes, I offered to wash some for Amber. I thought if I did Chris' laundry I wouldn't be following through. I said, "Chris, since I'm not doing your laundry this week, you'll need to do it yourself."*

No sooner had the words passed my lips than I heard the revenge in my plan. Here it was, a week later, that I realized that I was in a revenge cycle. I was surprised, because I wasn't feeling angry or hurt at that exact moment. I asked myself, "If this is revenge, who felt hurt and why?" I replayed the entire allowance discussion in my mind. Only then did I realize that I had forced a win/lose solution to the power struggle and was using discipline for revenge.

I called Chris into the room. We sat together and I apologized for using the laundry to get back at him. I acknowledged his feelings about the allowance being unfair. I told him my discipline was inappropriate and canceled it and the new system of allowances. We decided to do allowances as we always had. I emphasized that I was willing to do his laundry for the trip, but he insisted on doing it anyway! We hugged each other and confirmed all was okay. While I made several mistakes in this situation, I learned a lot. I recognize revenge almost immediately, now, and know the guidelines for redirecting it really work.

Withdrawal/Giving up

Children who have become deeply discouraged may finally give up. They believe they are helpless and incompetent. They give up so others won't expect anything from them. This behavior is most common when learning a task or managing a responsibility. It can also occur when children have been negatively labeled and give up, believing they are worthless.

STEP A: PREVENT THE BEHAVIOR (PREVENTION TOOLBOX)

Meet the positive goal of *withdrawal.* There are times when it is appropriate and healthy to withdraw from conflict or avoid frustration or disappointment. This withdrawal may be temporary, until the timing is better or an effective response can be planned.

Sometimes, when people feel particularly threatened or discouraged, they withdraw more than necessary—they give up. If a task seems to too demanding or past attempts to resolve a conflict failed, people sometimes simply choose to quit trying. At these times, withdrawal may be unhealthy.

★ **When children are so *discouraged* that they've given up, use descriptive *en*couragement and teach skills.** These are the tools that can prevent *and* redirect "giving up" behavior.

Teach when withdrawal *is* appropriate. It *is* healthy to walk away from fights and arguments where continued involvement will escalate the situation. There are times when it is healthy to accept the things we cannot change and change the things we can (like *our* attitude or behavior). We want to teach this value and skill to our children.

Show unconditional love. Make it clear that children don't have to achieve anything for us to love them. Children need to know we love them, even when they fail or aren't perfect.

Focus on what's right not wrong. Avoid "constructive criticism." Give credit for any effort children make or improvements they show, no matter how small.

Describe, don't praise. Since praise adds pressure, it usually backfires when children are deeply discouraged and have given up. More pressure does not motivate them to try again, but descriptive encouragement can.

Be gentle with mistakes. Focus on what children learn from their mistakes. Avoid perfectionism. Instead, encourage children to strive for their personal best.

Let children do things by themselves. Notice the difficulty of the task and be supportive, but don't rescue them.

Nudge, but don't push. Children give up when we push too hard or their goal can change to power. Just offer choices or quick tips. Don't push children to continue a voluntary activity if they truly aren't interested. They may need to finish a commitment period, but then let them choose whether to continue. If they are still interested but discouraged, give encouraging nudges. This helps them weather the difficult times that naturally occur when learning a new skill.

Teach skills. Break the task into small steps. Let children try to do things their way. Offer descriptive encouragement at every step.

STEP B: ACKNOWLEDGE FEELINGS (CHILD PROBLEM TOOLBOX)

When the goal is giving up, people *usually* feel discouraged, frustrated, or confused. When we acknowledge these feelings, we give the feeling a name. This reassures children that their feelings are normal and it is okay to feel it. Now they can focus on resolving the *cause* of the feeling.

STEP C1: SET LIMITS (CLEAR COMMUNICATION TOOLSET)

When *we* give up, we don't reach *our* parenting goals, to develop courage, self-esteem, and confidence in our children. In one sentence, we want to acknowledge children's feelings, maybe state the negative effect of giving up, and quickly move to the next step to redirect the behavior.

STEP C2a: IDENTIFY THE PURPOSE

When children have given up we usually find the following clues:

  i. **We feel** *discouraged, frustrated,* or *at a loss* about what to do. We may start believing the child really *isn't* capable.

 ii. **We are tempted to** *give up* on children or *do things for them.* "Here, let me show you, it's really easy once you get the hang of it." Sometimes we agree that they aren't up to the task. "Maybe you're not cut out for sports." We might try to motivate them by pointing out what they could be doing differently (constructive criticism) or judge what they've done and reassure them of their potential. "But you're really good at that." "If you try a little harder, I'm sure you'll get the hang of it." This implies they haven't already tried hard.

iii. **If we do any of these**, it sends the message, "You're right, you can't do this." Children feel incompetent and will not try harder. They will continue the behavior until we expect nothing from them and relieve them of their responsibilities. If we pressure with praise or push too hard, it starts power struggles or increases their commitment to give up.

STEP C2b: AVOID ESCALATING OR GIVING MISBEHAVIOR A PAYOFF

Avoid both criticism and praise. Children who have given up usually agree with criticisms and argue with or deny compliments. They insist they are incapable or "no good." If we discipline children who are already so discouraged they've given up, they withdraw even more. These tactics escalate the situation. Payoffs come from rescuing. Rescuing protects children from the possibility of failure— and the ecstasy of success. If we take over, we only confirm their incompetence and give children an easy way out. If we suggest trying something they will be better at, children learn that people should only participate in activities where they can be the best, instead of learning skills or having fun. If we allow them to quit, we teach that it's okay to give up on commitments, responsibilities, or tasks.

STEP C2c: REDIRECT THE MISBEHAVIOR

Use the tools listed in the "prevent the behavior" section. Find an area of strength to encourage. Use descriptive, observable facts and avoid value judgements like "good job." Break tasks into small steps and shift the focus to a different step, one they might find more success with. We can suggest "taking a break and coming back to it," but not imply they can "give up" on the task.

Acknowledge the difficulty of the task and express faith in their abilities. Focus on what they are learning or what they enjoy about the activity, rather than whether they succeed. Allow them to experience mistakes that aren't dangerous. If we help, *ask* if they want a demonstration, then work side by side, doing the task *together*. We do not want to take over or do it completely for them. We also want to be careful not to make the task look easy for us to do. Express the difficulty we have, or had when we first learned how to do the task. Instead of commenting on the quality of their job, we can always point out positive qualities we admire, such as a willingness to try and perseverance.

> *A Personal Story. Chris' teacher called to say he had failed one test because he hadn't studied and was making careless mistakes on homework. She acknowledged this was not a big deal, since his grade was still in the "B" range, but just wanted to bring it to my attention. When I told Chris about the phone call and asked him how he felt about his grades, he said, "I don't care." Chris often talks about schoolwork like it's no big deal, but he's actually quite self-motivated and disciplined, so I asked what he learned from not studying. In a defiant tone of voice, he replied, "Nothing." I was surprised by this uncaring, almost hostile attitude. I was tempted to say, "You'd better start caring!" But his uncharacteristic behavior tipped me off that this was an "onion." I shifted into listening mode. At first, he didn't share anything and gave one-word, "nothing" answers to my questions. I just acknowledged, "So right now you don't care about that, huh?" He was not giving me many clues to work with. As I clarified the few details he did volunteer, I mentioned the teacher's concern for him. He began to cry and poured out details about times when the teacher singled him out and criticized him. She had called him into the hallway (which is normally only done when someone is in trouble) and said, "I'm so disappointed in you. You could have gotten an "A" on this test. If you'd just put a little more effort into studying, you could be doing better work." Chris thought she wasn't giving him credit for his efforts and other good grades. She also moved his seat (which isn't normally done unless someone is causing trouble), because she thought he was having trouble concentrating near several disruptive students.*
>
> *I acknowledged how it could appear as though the teacher was picking on him. I tried to present the teacher's perspective, that she liked him so much that she wanted the best for him. She didn't realize her words were discouraging or that he had misinterpreted her actions. He was unwilling to discuss or work out the problem directly with the teacher, choosing instead to hold a grudge and glare at her during class. We discussed **his** goals and how **he** felt about his grades. His self-motivation was shrinking and he was too angry and discouraged to do anything about it.*
>
> *Since he wasn't willing to meet with the teacher and the problem was continuing, I carefully considered whether to get involved. I made a few phone calls to friends who had children in his class and asked some open-ended questions, without sharing any details that would violate Chris' confidentiality or make the teacher look bad. They were able to get information from their children that confirmed everything **had** happened just as Chris described it. I decided to talk to the teacher, positive that her intentions were caring, but her words were unintentionally discouraging. Once I explained how Chris saw and interpreted her words and actions, she understood how he had misunderstood her intentions. She assured me how much she liked, respected, and admired Chris. I told her **Chris** was the one who needed to hear that from her. She thanked me for bringing the problem to her attention and said she'd learned an important lesson about using positive ways to express concerns in the future. She suggested apologizing, which I thought would help, but I asked her not to do it alone in the hall.☺*

IMPORTANT POINTS TO REMEMBER ☆☆☆☆

The guidelines we've learned and stories we've read emphasize several important points about PO misbehavior:

- *Deliberate* **is the key word in identifying PO behavior.** Children know better and have the skills to behave properly, but *deliberately* misbehave.

- **PU behavior can turn into PO behavior, if it gets a reaction or payoff.**

- **Children can use emotions, rather than behavior, to meet any of the four goals.** For example, children can "turn on the tears" to get attention or their way. They can cry to get revenge, hoping parents will feel bad for "making kids cry." They can cry out of despair and discouragement. Parents need to correctly identify *why* children are crying: to express sadness (a Child problem), communicate needs (PU), or when tears seem forced or insincere (PO). Then they will know how best to respond.

- **Misbehavior might not immediately stop.** It takes time for both parents and children to break the habit of getting hooked in these cycles. Sometimes children may be testing to see if they can get the predictable response or might want a face-saving way to prove *they* stopped the behavior, not us. We can walk away and give children time to think about what we said and change their behavior without an audience.

- **If we don't break power or revenges cycles before we discipline, it turns the discipline into a power play or revenge tactic.** Don't immediately discipline a behavior just for the sake of responding quickly. It can make matters worse. Don't skip steps, just move through them quickly.

- **At whatever point we realize we are facing PO behavior, we begin following the PO a-b-c identification process and PASRR response formula.** It's better to get back on track than to continue in an ineffective direction, just for the sake of following through on what we said when we were hooked into the misbehavior.

- **Giving up behavior *always* involves passive behavior, but passive misbehavior does not always serve the goal of giving up. Passive misbehavior *can also* serve other goals.** We must look at the a-b-c clues ("How do we feel," etc.), to correctly identify the true purpose. Children can get *attention* by acting shy. They can passively exert *power* by procrastinating, forgetting, partially completing a task, or claiming to have forgotten. The silent treatment is a passive form of *revenge*.

- **One behavior can serve more than one purpose.** For example, when children don't clean their rooms, we must first eliminate the possibility that the behavior is really PU. Do they have the skills and consistently shown us they can do the chore? If so, and we are sure it's PO, they might be seeking *attention* to get us involved. They could also be exerting *power,* challenging us to "make them." If parents use power to force the issue, children might stuff things under their beds in "defiant compliance." They might refuse to clean their room as a *pay back* for a hurt. Children may feel so overwhelmed and incapable they *give up*.

> The only way to tell which goal it is in *each* instance is to consider the three clue-finding statements. As we respond, the goal can change and the next time we see the same behavior, the goal might be different. With time, we see the clues more quickly and can respond more helpfully.

- **The purpose behind misbehavior can shift.** If children try to get attention and it doesn't work, they might try to use power. The most common shift is a lost power struggle turning into a revenge cycle. We need to stay in touch with our feelings and how we are *tempted* to react (but not act on them) so we can see the clues that tell us the goal has shifted. When we notice a goal shift, we adjust our response accordingly. (You can see why keeping our cool, staying logical, and regular practice are all so important. That's why we waited so long to learn this toolset! We use every tool we've learned so far!)

- **Each goal represents a deeper level of discouragement.** The revenge and giving up stories are good illustrations of how goals shifted as the child became more discouraged. A child who is seeking attention is less discouraged than a child seeking revenge. Children who have given up are the most discouraged of all. This does not mean, however, that shifts in behavior *always* follow a predictable pattern: attention to power, to revenge, and finally giving up. Sometimes, when we try to walk away from a power struggle, children follow us, trying to get our attention! Again, look for the clues so you know when and how the goal has changed.

PO COMBINATION PROBLEMS

We've been talking mostly about situations that are clearly or exclusively PO problems. What about situations where PO behavior is just one part of the total picture?

C/PO Problems

Whenever there is a Child problem, we always want to address that part of the problem first. The Child problem is often the real issue underlying the PO behavior—if we resolve *it*, the PO behavior might disappear. Other times, there are two different problems in one situation. We still want to resolve the Child problem first, unless we must respond to the PO behavior immediately. If this is the case, move through the Universal PASRR steps quickly, making sure to include Step B: **A**cknowledge feelings (Child Problem Toolbox). Once we've taken care of the immediate PO problem, we want to come back to the Child problem and resolve it.

Some homework and school problems illustrate important points about C/PO combination problems. When children don't do homework *on purpose*, the goal could be any of the four purposes of misbehavior. Children can "act stupid" so teachers (or parents) will pay attention and spend time helping them. Children might also want to prove that they are in control, by doing nothing. "You can't make me do my homework." Power can also be the goal if children want to see if giving up will make us take over and do the work for them. After all, if someone else is willing to take responsibility for remembering homework or thinking of answers, why not let them? Children might believe giving up on homework will "punish" a disliked teacher or hurt parents. If good grades are important to a parent and children want to hurt the parent, getting poor grades is revenge. Most often, however, children do not do their homework because they are extremely discouraged and have given up.

> *A Personal Story. The only "F" I ever got was in fourth grade math. The teacher was grumpy and mean and had flunked my brother five years earlier. Because I was left-handed, she wouldn't help me learn to write in cursive. She showed everyone the right-handed way and told me, "Just do it the opposite way." If I asked for help, she said, "Figure it out."*

> *I was discouraged because I wasn't getting the help (attention) I was legitimately entitled to. I finally concluded that if she was going to treat me this way, I wasn't going to do the homework she asked me to do. This would "show her." I did all my homework—except math.*

> *I hadn't really thought about report card day. When I saw the "F," I thought about changing it to an "A," but knew it would be too obvious. I prepared myself for my parents' reaction. Fortunately, my parents knew how to do effective listening and problem solving by this time. My mom commented on all my As and Bs first. I knew she wasn't blind and actually enjoyed a few moments of pride. She asked me how I felt about the F and what I thought happened. I told her my logic. Instead of lecturing me, she asked open-ended questions such as, "Who really suffered when you didn't do your homework? What other options do you have for dealing with this teacher?" We both knew this teacher wouldn't change, so my plan was just to survive that year.*

> *I realized on my own, without a parental lecture, that I was only hurting myself by failing math. I decided to do the best I could in math—for me. The following grading period, I brought my grade up to a "C." By fifth grade, I was on honor roll. Had my parents punished me for the grade, I might not have learned this lesson. Knowing me, a power and control child who was already discouraged, I might have resorted to another type of misbehavior.*

C/PU/PO Problems

In most cases, problem behavior is *either* PU *or* PO, but rarely both at the same time. Usually, the reason children are misbehaving is because the don't have the skills to express themselves appropriately and choose misbehavior to express their goals. The *real* cause of the behavior is PU, a lack of skills.

> ***A Graduate's Story.*** *Jackie, eight, is my youngest daughter. I admit to spoiling my last child, my "baby." I was planning to be away from home for a week and told Jackie ahead of time so she would have time to prepare for my absence. Jackie was upset about my impending vacation. She became moody, short-tempered, and smart-alecky. She even yelled at me, "You don't love me! You wouldn't leave me if you loved me!"*

What type of problem is this? The core of this onion is a Child problem, Jackie's sense of loss and abandonment. At eight, she doesn't understand why her mother must leave and is taking the decision personally. She feels hurt by her mother's decision, so she uses guilt trips for revenge (PO) *and* to express her feelings the only way she knows (PU). Since Jackie has shown that she can behave properly and has not acted this way before, her behavior seems deliberate. When we look further, however, we see the underlying issues. Instead of reacting to the PO behavior, Karen needs to help Jackie work through her feelings of loss, anger, and hurt (Child Problem Toolbox). If Karen can teach Jackie how to express herself appropriately (PU and Independence Toolsets), then Jackie won't have to use PO behavior to meet her needs in the future.

Always try to resolve the problem that is closest to the center of the onion. If we resolve *this* problem, the more surface behaviors and issues sometimes take care of themselves or are much more manageable.

THE GOALS OF ADULT MISBEHAVIOR

Parental reactions can follow the attention ➔ power ➔ revenge ➔ giving up cycle and can serve all four goals. Some frustrated and angry parents yell or spank to get a child's *attention*, although it doesn't serve any positive purpose. Parents frequently discipline or give orders to exert their *power*. Parents use punishment, which makes children suffer for their mistakes, to get *revenge*. Some parents give in or *give up*, just to avoid conflict. All these approaches escalate the misbehavior cycle or give children a payoff. Instead of repeating unhelpful cycles, we can identify *our* goal and choose healthier responses to meet that goal.

In troubled adult relationships, like unhappy marriages, adults may try to get people's *attention*, to let them know there is a problem. If their polite and positive attempts fail, they may use louder, more negative ways to get attention. If these attempts fail, adults often argue or make threats, to see if they can get their way (*power*). If they lose the power struggle, they feel hurt and seek *revenge*. "You'll see how it feels to be treated the way you treat me." As the revenge cycle continues, both parties resort to more extreme behaviors and the relationship quickly deteriorates. If adults don't heal hurts at this level and use healthier conflict resolution skills, irreparable damage to the relationship can occur. Finally, when adults experience nothing but emotional pain, they *give up*. Couples divorce, but if children are involved, they often use the children to continue their power and/or revenge cycles.

When adults want to get another person's attention, we can use the Cooperation or Clear Communication Toolsets. If they ignore our attempts, we can try to negotiate a win/win agreement. If others use PO behavior with us, recognize what's really going on, avoid escalating the situation or giving a payoff, and respond in ways that break these cycles. Notice positive behavior, no matter how small, when people aren't expecting or demanding it. If others try to argue with us, we can set limits for *ourselves* (what we are willing to do or endure) and disengage. If we recognize revengeful behavior, acknowledge the other person's hurt and rebuild trust. If we are totally discouraged, we need to encourage ourselves and the other person. Positive, encouraging, or empathetic statements can have amazing, almost miraculous, results. Sometimes all efforts fail and we need to end a relationship in the healthiest way possible, for our own safety, self-respect, and inner peace.

LYING

When children lie, parents must first ask themselves "Why?" What purpose did the lie serve? We can avoid giving the lie a payoff or making the situation worse with our reaction. Instead, we show children how to meet this goal without lying. These three steps are consistent with the PO Toolset.

Motives for Lying

Lying is intentional behavior and the motives fit the four purposes of misbehavior.[3] These motives apply to both children's and adult lies. Here is a list of some types of lies and their related goals:

Lying for Attention

- *Getting a reaction.* Exaggerated stories and imaginative stories get people's attention.

- *Acceptance by peer group.* Sometimes, children lie to do something with their peers they know is forbidden. Other times, adults question children about their peers' wrongdoing and children feel pressured by their peers to lie. Research shows that children almost always tell the truth when interviewed alone, but almost none tell the truth when interviewed in pairs! Parents need to acknowledge the difficulty of telling the truth at these times. A quick reminder about the value of honesty and possible effects of lying are helpful, before pressing children further.

Lying for Power

- *Fooling people.* People feel powerful if they tell a false story and the listener believes it.

- *Avoiding punishment/lecture.* When there is a problem, parents may angrily ask, "Did you do this?" If children say "yes," they know they will definitely get in trouble. If they say "no," they have *some* chance of not getting in trouble. Guess which choice most make?

> **Fear of harsh or unjust punishment and long lectures is the main reason people lie.**

- *Protecting privacy.* Children may lie when parents ask prying questions. If lying works, children prove they have the power to prevent parents from knowing everything. (Remember the "Respect Their Privacy" section in Chapter 6, "Independence Toolset"?)

- *Getting something that's forbidden.* When people think a request will be denied, they may sneak or lie to get it. Some examples are shoplifting, having an unchaperoned party, or experimenting with cutting one's own hair. These lies usually need a planned alibi. When parents catch these lies, they are particularly angry, because the child had to plan the misdeed *and* the lie.

Lying for Revenge

- *Getting justice for a hurt.* When people are hurt, they lose respect for and trust in the person who hurt them and may lie to "even the score."

Lying because the person has given up

- *Feeling discouraged with honesty.* When others don't believe truthful statements, people may give up and lie.

Lying and Development

There are five stages of understanding and practicing truth and lying, but age is only one factor. Not everyone reaches the final stage and many adults never go beyond the second stage. When people feel strong emotions, they may revert to an earlier stage.

1. By age 4, children are honest (or lie) to get their own way, get rewards and to avoid punishment.

2. By age 5 or 6, children are honest (or lie) to please adults. Children may tell adults what they think the adults want to hear. If the lies during these first two stages work and children get their way often, they can become manipulative or more chronic liars.

3. Around ages 6–8, children's honesty (and lying) is motivated by what's in it for them. At this stage, if adults around them model lying, children will believe that lying is okay.

4. Around ages 8–12, children are honest (or lie) so others will think well of them. At this age, children also shift their focus from wanting to please parents to wanting the approval of their friends. They may lie if they think their peers expect them to.

5. Ages 12 and older are usually honest because they want to be good citizens or lie because it is a habit.

Two age periods are especially important. One is somewhere around three or four, when children can tell a deliberate lie. Adolescence is the other crucial period, because teens are capable of understanding that lying destroys trust. Whether teens reach the final stage of learning honesty depends on several factors: how well parents handle their teens' need for privacy, whether they grant their teens more responsibility over new areas of their lives, and how they react to the truthful (but difficult to hear) statements their teens share.

Parental Influences on Lying

Children who lie most often have parents who also lie frequently: lying to the traffic cop, asking children to lie for parents ("Tell (the telephone caller) I'm not here."), or not admitting their mistakes. Such commonplace deceits often go unnoticed—by parents, that is.

Parents usually lie to avoid conflict, to protect children from an unpleasant or dangerous situation, to benefit themselves or to be tactful. There *are* ways to be both truthful in these situations. "My dad can't come to the phone right now. Please call later." (Actually, adults should speak for themselves, instead of using children to help them avoid uncomfortable situations!)

It is also important to teach children the difference between "good" secrets and "bad" secrets. "Good" secrets are surprises that make people feel good (as in birthday gifts). "Bad" secrets make the secret-keeper feel uncomfortable or hide something others *should* know (as in sexual abuse).

Parents also lie to their children to protect them from knowing about potentially upsetting situations. Once parents lie about these situations, they must continue lying to answer children's questions and keep the false story alive. (See the "Children and Stress" section of Chapter 9, "Keep Your Cool Toolset," for more information about discussing these topics with children.)

A Personal Story. In 1995, a four-year-old girl was missing. The girl's picture filled television screens and the front pages of newspapers. Children could hardly avoid seeing or hearing about the missing girl and many joined the search effort. Many parents used the situation as a reminder to their children to "never talk to strangers."

After several days, police found the girl's body and within days her mother was charged with the murder. Children who knew about the missing girl still asked about her. Now parents had a dilemma; how could they explain that the cute little girl was dead and it was the girl's mother, not a stranger, who killed her? Some parents made up lies to protect their children from the grim reality. The children's continuing questions about the girl prompted these parents to tell even more lies. The more lies they told, the more guilty they felt about lying.

One neighborhood brought in a panel of experts, of which I was one, to allow parents to discuss their feelings and get advice about explaining this situation to their children. We encouraged parents to tell their children the truth, as difficult as it was, in a factual but reassuring way, saying the mother did something very wrong and the child was not at fault.

Children from bitter divorces lie more than children from intact families or from respectful divorces. Divorce is *always* traumatic for children, but one of the biggest factors in the children's adjustment is their parents' treatment of each other in front of and away from the children. Children of bitter divorces suffer from the lies and half-truths angry parents tell them to gain the child's loyalty. Visitation and custody disputes can divide children's loyalties and disrupt their lives. Children love both parents, but angry parents may criticize an ex-spouse or use the children as pawns in the parents' struggle for control. The emotional damage to children and the relationship between the adults who must still parent them can take decades to heal.

Privacy is especially important to children who are trying to survive the delicate balancing act of living in two worlds and pleasing two separate parents. When parents grill their children about an ex-spouse's activities, children may lie or hide information, knowing it could be used against them (or the other parent) later. To avoid putting children in situations in which lies seem the only way out, parents must develop a short "need to know" list. This list might include whether children are sick while visiting the other parent or if children are physically or emotionally abused. Beyond this, parents can be friendly nonjudgmental listeners, if children feel like talking. It takes enormous self-discipline to suppress questions and criticisms, but parents need to remember *they* are the adults and act like it.

Parents start with their children's trust, but as children grow older, they must earn it.

Preventing and Responding to Lies

- **Model truthfulness.** We want to be clear with our children that we do not accept lying and why—and then practice what we preach.

- **Teach truthfulness.** It is best to teach truthfulness repetitively, not only after children have already lied. Share events from the newspaper and talk with children about the hardships people experience because of their mistakes and lies. Almost every fairy tale poses a moral problem. Parents can use these opportunities to discuss decision-making and the results of truth and dishonesty.

- **Practice balanced parenting and respectful discipline.** Children need to feel safe enough to admit their wrongdoing. When parents use power punishments that are harsh or unfair, children are more likely to lie. When there is too little parental supervision, children can get away with lying often, so they become quite skilled at it. When parents use reasonable, respectful discipline, children are more likely to be truthful. Studies have found that children from balanced families not only lied less, but showed a stronger belief in moral behavior.

- **If you suspect a lie, try not to respond in anger, although you will probably feel hurt and betrayed.** Remember what it was like to be a child and how hard being honest can be. Try to understand the child's motive and use problem solving, instead of only punishing the child.

- **Believe children, unless you have good reason to be suspicious.** Too often, parents presume children are guilty unless the children can prove themselves innocent. If children have lied in the past, don't hold a grudge and suspect lying even when children are being truthful. When we disbelieve truthful children, the damage can be severe. Be willing to forgive and start rebuilding trust.

- **Question children in ways that encourage them to be truthful.** *Don't try to trap children in a lie.* For example, a parent finds an empty bottle of alcohol in the trash and asks, "What did you and John do while you were playing pool in the family room last night?" If you have reason to suspect a problem, maintain self-control, be up-front with what you know, and present it respectfully. "I just found . . . I need to know the truth about . . ."

- **Reassure children that you won't be as angry if they tell the truth**—and then keep your cool as you listen. Deal with the problem and thank them for taking the risk to be honest. Depending on the offense, consider not disciplining or disciplining less, when children are honest about their mistakes. This doesn't mean we "plea-bargain" about more or less discipline.

- **Have separate disciplines, one for the actual misdeed and an additional one for lying.** Children need to understand that these are two separate disciplines for two different offenses. The discipline for lying can reflect the breakdown in trust. For example, when teens miss curfew and lie about why they were late there are two problems. An appropriate discipline for the missed curfew is to give up social privileges for one or a few nights. Teens can rebuild trust by agreeing to call home once or twice during the evening, when their privileges are restored.

A Personal Story. One night, when Amber was six, I saw that her bed sheet had been cut or ripped. I said, "Look at this big rip! Did you do this?" Her nonverbal language said, "Yes," but I could tell she was considering lying, probably because I sounded upset. I quickly changed my tone of voice and approach. I said, "This sheet has been cut. It was either cut a little bit and it tore more or the whole thing was cut. Can you tell me which?" She was still hesitant and whispered, "Will I get in trouble if I tell?" I said, "If you lie, you will be in double trouble, for lying and cutting the sheet. If you tell the truth, you might or might not get in trouble for cutting the sheet. I would need to ask you a few questions first."

She admitted to cutting the sheet by nodding her head "Yes" ever so slightly. I said, "Thank you for being honest. I know it's scary to talk about something that might get you in trouble, but it's important to tell the truth. I won't get as angry about what you did if I know it took extra courage to tell the truth. What were you thinking when you cut the sheet?" She shrugged her shoulders. I said, "You just had the idea and didn't think first?" She nodded. I continued, "How did you feel when you cut the sheet?" "Bad," she replied. "So you realized you did something wrong," I reflected back. She nodded. "What did you learn about using scissors on cloth?" She didn't say anything. I said, "Do you see how scissors ruin cloth forever?" She nodded, "Yes." I asked, "Will you do this again?" She shook her head, "No." "Will you tell me the next time you do something wrong?" She nodded her head, "Yes."

I concluded, "Since you were honest with me, realize what you did was wrong, and promise not to do it again, I won't take the scissors away. But I won't buy a new sheet, either. You'll have to sleep with this hole in it. Just think before you cut something again, okay?" She looked relieved and nodded her head "Yes." While we hugged, I said, "It can be hard to be honest sometimes. But you usually get in more trouble lying. I hope you feel better being honest." She nodded "Yes."

SUMMARY OF LYING

It's hard to lie if . . .	*It's easy to lie if . . .*
• the stakes are high.	• the stakes are low.
• they respect the target of the lie.	• the target of the lie is harsh and unfair.
• they are inexperienced in lying.	• they have successfully lied often.
• the target of the lie is hard to mislead.	• the target of the lie is gullible.
• others who know the truth will witness the lie.	• the person can have time to plan ahead.
• they will be disciplined for lying.	• there is no consequence for lying.
• the discipline for the misdeed is fair.	• they will get punished, not disciplined, for the misdeed.

SUMMARY OF PO PROBLEMS

This chapter has *two* summary pages. The first takes the universal process of handling PO problems and *compares* the goals of PO behavior at each step. The second summary page (with cartoons) lists each goal and the steps of identifying and responding to that type of PO behavior.

COMPARING PO BEHAVIOR GOALS AT EACH STEP

Step A: Prevent the behavior by meeting the positive goal
- *Attention.* Involve child in meaningful ways. Foster a sense of importance and belonging.
- *Power.* Promote independence, offer choices in limits, make requests in positive words.
- *Revenge.* Acknowledge feelings and teach assertive respectful communication.
- *Giving up.* Use descriptive encouragement and teach skills.

Step B: Identify and Acknowledge the feelings beneath the behavior.
- *Attention.* Children are usually feeling lonely, unimportant, rejected, or forgotten.
- *Power.* Children are usually feeling frustrated, disappointed or out of control.
- *Revenge.* Children are usually feeling hurt or angry.
- *Giving up.* Children are usually feeling deeply discouraged, frustrated, or confused.

Step C1: Set limits or state your concerns

STEP C2a: IDENTIFY THE PURPOSE
  i. We feel . . .
     . . . annoyed, irritated, tired, or hounded, when the goal is *attention.*
     . . . others are challenging our authority, when the goal is *power.*
     . . . hurt, shocked, or disgusted, when the goal is *revenge.*
     . . . frustrated, discouraged, or hopeless, when the goal is *giving up.*

  ii. We are tempted to . . .
     . . . remind, nag, and push away, when the goal is *attention.*
     . . . argue, punish, or give in, when the goal is *power.*
     . . . show hurt or hurt back, when the goal is *revenge.*
     . . . rescue, pressure, criticize, praise, or expect less, when the goal is *giving up.*

  iii. If we do any of these, we either escalate the cycle or reward the behavior.
- We still give *attention* when we remind, nag, or show we are bothered.
- We feed the *power* struggle when we argue and reward it when we give in.
- We add to the *revenge* cycle when we hurt back and reward it when we show hurt.
- We discourage children who are *giving up* when we criticize and reward them by rescuing.

STEP C2b: AVOID ESCALATING OR GIVING MISBEHAVIOR A PAYOFF

STEP C2c: REDIRECT THE MISBEHAVIOR
Attention. Stop *once;* use PASRR. Offer positive attention. Ignore the behavior, not the child.
Power. Offer choices within limits. Disengage, emotionally and/or physically.
Revenge. Rebuild trust by resolving the child's hurt *first.* Offer acceptable anger alternatives.
Giving up. Break tasks into smaller parts. Focus on *any* effort or improvement. Express faith in the child's abilities. Use problem solving.

Step C3: Reveal Discipline
Only discipline *after* breaking the PO cycle. Immediate discipline, as a first response, escalates PO behavior or gives it a payoff.
- Immediate discipline gives negative *attention,* which is better than no attention.
- Children interpret discipline as a *power* play punishment and may seek revenge.
- Discipline becomes a *revenge* weapon of punishment. It feeds the cycle.
- Children who are *giving up* feel even more discouraged and incompetent.

RESPONDING TO

ATTENTION

Positive belief: Involvement, belonging, to feel important.
Negative belief: "I only belong if I'm noticed."
Reinforce positive/prevent negative:
Plan ahead. Spend time together. Give attention unexpectedly. Involve child. Recognize efforts.
Identify the goal of attention:
I feel . . . Annoyed, irritated, personal space violated, tired, frustrated.
I'm tempted to . . . Remind, nag, give undue service, "Stop," "Leave me alone."
If I do . . . reactions give negative attention (payoff), behavior temporarily stops, escalates, or new behaviors keep parent involved.
Avoid: Reinforcing negative behavior or giving special service on demand.
Redirect: Stop *once*. In one sentence, use Universal PASRR formula. Offer acceptable activities. Then ignore the behavior, not the child. Involve child, if possible. Give attention for positive behavior. Use prevention tools above.

PO BEHAVIOR

POWER

Positive belief: "I want to make decisions and have some control in my life."
Negative belief: "I only belong if I'm in control."
Reinforce positive/prevent negative:
Offer choices within limits. Ask for their help. Build teamwork. Word limits in positive words. Involve in decisions. Teach skills and let go.
Identify the goal of power:
I feel . . . Provoked, authority is challenged.
I'm tempted to . . . Argue, exert more power, or give in. "I'll show you who's the boss."
If I do . . . Arguing escalates power struggle. Child passively or aggressively defies. Giving in gives a payoff.
Avoid: arguing or giving in. Break the cycle before disciplining.
Redirect: Keep your cool. Be kind *and* firm. Use bottom line limits and offer choices one last time. Decide what you will do, not what you'll make child do. Disengage, emotionally and/or physically. Use prevention skills above.

REVENGE

Positive belief: "Good deeds deserve repayment."
Negative belief: "I must hurt others who hurt me."
Reinforce positive/prevent negative:
Use listening and communication to avoid hurting feelings. Teach assertive, respectful conflict resolution skills.
Identify the goal of revenge:
I feel . . . Hurt, physically or emotionally. Disappointed, disbelief, disgusted.
I'm tempted to . . . Show hurt or hurt back. "How could you do this to me?"
If I do . . . showing hurt gives a payoff. Retaliation escalates revenge cycle.
Avoid: Hurting back or showing hurt. Break cycle before disciplining.
Redirect: Disengage. Cool off. Rebuild trust. Acknowledge child's hurt first, *before* addressing revengeful behavior. Brainstorm acceptable anger alternatives. Suggest child make amends for hurt. Use prevention tools above.

GIVING UP

Positive belief: Withdrawal. "I can avoid conflict when it's healthy to do so." "I want reassurance."
Negative belief: "I don't belong because I'm incompetent." "Don't expect anything from me."
Reinforce positive/prevent negative: Describe any effort or improvement. Teach skills.
Identify the goal of giving up:
I feel . . . Frustrated, discouraged, hopeless.
I'm tempted to . . . Help, rescue, praise, give up, expect less.
If I do . . . Rescuing gives a payoff for giving up. Praise and pressure escalates. Child feels more incompetent and fails to respond.
Avoid: Praise, all criticism and comparisons. Don't rescue, give up, or pity.
Redirect: Break task into smaller parts. Focus on *any* effort or improvement, no matter how small. Express faith in abilities. Build on interests and strengths. Use problem-solving. Use prevention tools above.

PRACTICE EXERCISES

(Detailed answers are at the end of the chapter.)

A. Identifying Positive Goals. Each of the following situations is an example of a child using positive behavior to meet a positive goal of behavior. Write the letter of the positive goal in the left column next to the most appropriate example in the right column.

a. Involvement/Recognition

b. Independence

c. Justice/Fairness

d. Withdrawal from conflict

____ 1. Bonnie's mother bought her a new outfit as a surprise, so tonight she washes the supper dishes and cleans the kitchen floor as a surprise to her mother.

____ 2. Katie, 5, shows her Dad a picture she colored.

____ 3. George, 5, is playing with his little sister, who's two-years-old. When she grabs the blocks he is playing with, he just uses what's left. He doesn't say anything and lets her play with the blocks she took.

____ 4. Toby, 17, saved his money for a used bike. He purchased a broken bike for half the cost of most bikes. He wants to fix it himself, as a hobby.

B. One Behavior, More than One Goal? Each of the following behaviors can serve more than one of the four goals of behavior: Attention, Power, Revenge, or Giving up. Explain how the behavior serves each purpose. Hint: Some don't serve all four purposes. Just write "n/a" if it does not apply.

1. Refusing to talk (not a shy personality trait).
    How can this behavior give the child more *attention?*
    How can this behavior give the child more *power?*
    How can this behavior help the child seek *revenge?*
    How can this behavior show the child has *given up?*

2. Running away.
    How can this behavior give the child more *attention?*
    How can this behavior give the child more *power?*
    How can this behavior help the child seek *revenge?*
    How can this behavior show the child has *given up?*

3. Boredom, "I don't have anything to do."
    How can this behavior give the child more *attention?*
    How can this behavior give the child more *power?*
    How can this behavior help the child seek *revenge?*
    How can this behavior show the child has *given up?*

C. Identifying and Responding to Negative Goals. In each of the following situations, use the PO a-b-c process to identify the goal. Suggest ways to prevent the misbehavior and redirect it.

1. Chelsea, 4, was told she had to play with a girl who came to visit with her mother. She does not like this girl. Chelsea tricked the girl into letting her paint her from head to toe. Now Chelsea has locked herself in the bathroom. She won't come out because she is sure she'll get punished.
    What is the purpose behind Chelsea painting the girl?
    Is there more than one goal involved?
    What is Chelsea's motive for hiding in the bathroom?
    How could her mother have prevented this from happening?
    How can her mother respond helpfully?

2. A teacher accused Paul, 8, of cheating on a test. He says he didn't cheat, which is the truth. The teacher doesn't believe him, because the other child's test answers are so similar and Paul did better on a test than usual. Paul said he studied much harder than usual for this test. The teacher gives him a zero on the test and won't let him retake the test or make up the work. He will get a "D," a failing grade. He figures a "D" is as bad as an "F," so he stops studying and starts cutting this class.

    What is the purpose of Paul's behavior?

    What can Paul and his parents do?

3. Jeff, 11, has a habit of running the heel of his hand up people's backs and through their hair, saying "Zoom!" He laughs, but it irritates and aggravates others. Despite telling Jeff, "Stop it! I don't like that," he continues.

    What is the purpose of Jeff's behavior?

    How could his family prevent this from happening?

    When it does happen, how can they respond helpfully?

4. Shawn, 12, broke his collarbone the weekend before the summer school break. He can't swim for three weeks or play sports for two months. Shawn was looking forward to an active summer. He doesn't want to watch the other kids having fun, so he just hangs around the house. After one week, he's going stir crazy. He walks to a friend's house and rides the friend's bike home—with one arm and no helmet! When Shawn's parents express concerns about reinjuring his collarbone, Shawn argues with them.

    What is the purpose of Shawn's behavior?

    Is there more than one goal involved?

    How can Shawn's parents respond helpfully?

5. Glen, 14, repeatedly ignores his stepfather's requests, such as "Turn out the light before leaving a room." Glen's comment is, "You're standing there, you turn it out." His stepfather stands there with his jaw dropped, in shock. When his stepfather pushes the issue, Glen becomes angry, yells "You're not my Dad," and usually walks out of the house.

    What is the purpose of Glen's behavior?

    Is there more than one goal involved?

    How could his stepfather prevent this from happening?

    When it does happen, how can his stepfather respond helpfully?

D. Breaking Misbehavior Cycles. In the following scenario, the parent is trying to prevent and respond to a situation using effective parenting skills. The child, however, is still trying to get the parent hooked into a PO goal. Answer the questions.

1. Maria, 13, and her mother used to get into a lot of power struggles and arguments before her mom took a parenting class. Now, even when Mom gives her choices or avoids threats, Maria still tries to argue with her. On Wednesday, Mom told Maria, "The laundry needs done by Sunday evening." Maria interrupts her and reacts as though her Mom said it had to be done yesterday! She twists her words around, complaining "I can't go out or do anything all week!"

    What is the purpose of Maria's behavior?

    What can Mom say or do next, without making matters worse?

    Is there anything Mom could have done differently to prevent this?

2. Since George, 12, entered junior high, his friends have changed. Last night, when he came home, his eyes were bloodshot and he was not acting like himself. His parents confronted him, insisting he had been using alcohol or marijuana. After a heated argument, George admitted he had tried both, but only once. His parents forbade him from seeing those friends again. George says his parents are overreacting and that they can't stop him from seeing the friends, since they go to school together.

    What is George's goal?

    Is there anything George's parents could have done differently when they first confronted him?

    What can they do now, to address their concerns?

Detailed Answers

A. Identifying Positive Goals.

1. Answer is c.   Bonnie did the dishes to repay her mother's kindness, which is *justice/fairness*.
2. Answer is a.   Katie is showing her picture to get her father's *involvement/recognition*.
3. Answer is d.   George *withdraws from conflict* with his little sister.
4. Answer is b.   Toby is excited about doing his hobby *independently*.

B. One Behavior, More than One Goal?

1. Refusing to talk can get extra *attention* when people fuss to get them to talk. They can have *power* by getting people to talk for them or by ignoring a request. It can be *revenge*, if it is the silent treatment. It could also be *giving up*, if they are afraid to talk or afraid of criticism if their speech sounds "funny."

2. Running away can be a way to get *attention*, if children feel neglected. It is a cry to "notice me!" Or "Show me you care enough to find me." It can be *power*, if it is a way to refuse to cooperate with rules, defy punishment, or show the child can't be controlled. It can be *revenge*, if done in retaliation for punishment. It can also be *giving up*, if children have tried to resolve the parent/ child problem, but failed.

3. Boredom can be a way to get *attention*, if children want more parental involvement. It can be *power*, if children want the parent to be responsible for entertaining them. *Revenge* doesn't apply here. Boredom can also be used to *give up*, if children don't have skills to entertain themselves or really can't think of anything to do.

C. Identifying and Redirecting Negative Goals.

1. Chelsea, 4, resented that her Mom *made her* play with a girl she didn't like. She decided to get *revenge* on the girl. When she realized she'd be punished, Chelsea exerted her *power* by locking herself in the bathroom. Chelsea's mom can first acknowledge Chelsea's feelings, "I know you are upset and feel bad about what you did to ___. If you come out now and help clean up ___, you won't be punished. If you don't help clean up ___, you'll be in 'double trouble.' We'll discuss your discipline after she leaves." Mom can acknowledge the little girl's feelings and Chelsea's, while cleaning up the girl. She can encourage Chelsea to apologize, but not force the issue. If Chelsea helps clean her at all, she is showing her regret. After the child has left, Mom can discuss Chelsea's feelings further and what options she has when she doesn't want to play with someone. An appropriate discipline would be giving up play privileges for a brief period.

2. Paul, 8, was falsely accused of cheating on a test. Because Paul's teacher had labeled him a "poor student," she didn't believe his explanation. The fact that Paul studied extra hard and *still* can't succeed was incredibly discouraging, so he is *giving up*. Since Paul tried to work out this problem with the teacher directly, the situation is greatly affecting Paul, and the teacher's decision is incredibly unfair, Paul's parents are justified in getting involved. They can meet with Paul and the teacher, to verify that they saw Paul studying for this test. If the teacher didn't actually see Paul cheat and is still unwilling to let him do extra credit work or retake the test, they should talk to the principal. In all these meetings, Paul's parents want to serve as a mediator between Paul and the school personnel. If all attempts are unsuccessful, Paul's parents can write a letter of formal complaint (detailing the *facts*, not making emotional accusations) to put in Paul's record. Regardless of the outcome, the parents need to acknowledge Paul's feelings and encourage his efforts and improvement. They can use the F-A-X process to help Paul get in touch with his *self*-motivation again. They can ask helpful questions to help Paul consider the possible consequences of getting an "F," instead of a "D," and of cutting classes. They can also brainstorm other plans to further resolve this problem or prevent a similar incident in the future.

3. Jeff, 11, is trying to get *attention* with his "zooming." Being 11, he may feel uncomfortable with hugging or other "childish" ways of showing affection. This might be a safer way for him to get the physical contact he wants. There are several options available. Mom can spend time with Jeff in the evenings, offering to scratch or rub his back. Maybe even playing sports would be a way to have physical contact. Mom doesn't want to force Jeff to spend time with her; but can make it clear she is available. She can give positive attention to Jeff when he is not misbehaving or makes other, more appropriate attempts to get her attention. She might even want to say, "Do that again! I liked it!" If he really wants to aggravate her, he might stop if it isn't working. Finally, Mom could just walk away, without saying anything, when she gets "zoomed." No attention is less desirable than negative attention.

4. Shawn, 12, broke his collarbone and argues about taking it easy. Shawn is used to having more *independence* and this injury has unexpectedly ripped it away. He downplays the risks of reinjury and wants the *power* to do more than the doctors and his parents are willing to let him do. Shawn's parents need to keep acknowledging his frustration, discouragement, and boredom, but not coddle or overprotect him. Since serious medical and safety issues are involved, they need to remain firm about the bottom line—following the doctor's orders and wearing safety gear. They need to focus on Shawn's choices within those limits. They can make an extra effort to help Shawn find interesting non-physical activities and help him get together with friends.

5. Glen, 14, ignores his stepfather's requests. Anytime divorce or remarriage is involved, children probably have some underlying hurt feelings. If stepparents exert a parental role too soon or are too controlling, resentment and rebellion often follows. The purpose of Glen's behavior is both *revenge* and *power.* His stepfather needs to build a relationship of trust and open communication before exerting his parental authority. If he uses the F-A-X Listening and Cooperation Toolsets, he can prevent some power and revenge struggles. When these fail, Glen's stepfather needs to back up and acknowledge Glen's perspective. "I know you don't like me telling you what to do" or "It must be hard to feel you have to listen to someone you don't consider your parent." In blended families, more than most others, teamwork, family councils, and a united parental front are important. Autocratic parenting divides blended families and permissiveness prevents the new parent from taking his or her rightful place in the family. Mutual respect and balanced responses are essential if stepchildren are to develop any respect for a new stepparent.

D. Breaking Misbehavior Cycles.

1. Maria, 13, is used to baiting her mom into arguments and having it work. Although Mom isn't biting the bait, Maria is still going to try to start an argument, especially if she can get out of her responsibilities. Mom needs to ignore Maria's dramatic performance. She can restate the choices and limits, "The laundry needs to be done by Saturday. That's three days from now." It's your choice if you stay home until the laundry's done. As far as I'm concerned, you can play all you want, *if* the job gets done." At this point, Mom can ignore any further attempts by Maria to argue. Maria may not get started on the laundry immediately, but she has three days to get it done. Mom has time to wait and see if Maria chooses to accept her responsibility.

2. George, 12, has experimented with drugs and his parents are justifiably concerned. By late elementary school, most children have been exposed to drugs (either directly or they are simply aware of their presence). Experimentation usually begins as a way to gain acceptance from peers. Parents can help children find other ways to feel *accepted* by their peers. When involvement with drugs grows from experimentation to regular use, it is usually one of three reasons (or a combination of them): (1) peer acceptance (*attention*), (2) a way to prove the child has some *power,* or (3) to cope with an overwhelming problem (a Child problem). Drug use is always an indication of an "onion"; it masks some underlying issue.

George's parents recognized the signs of his drug use and were wise to discuss their concerns. Unfortunately, they took an autocratic, controlling approach to the problem. This caused George to shift goals. He originally tried the drugs because he lost his childhood friends (a Child problem) and was seeking peer acceptance (attention). Now, because his parents *forced* an admission and *forbid* him from seeing these friends, George is exerting his power. He might sneak to see his friends and to use drugs, and he will probably get better at hiding the symptoms from his parents. George's parents could have described the physical symptoms they saw and stated their concerns. They could have used the Child Problem Toolbox to determine the real issue behind George's use and help George find more acceptable ways to meet his goal. Drug experimentation and use can quickly become problematic or addictive. It is important for parents to be educated and skillful when they first discuss the issue with their young teens. Their reactions at the early stages greatly determine whether the problem is resolved helpfully or becomes a more serious problem. Parents should seek professional consultation if they have *any* concerns.

WHAT'S NEXT?

We can practice identifying PO behavior daily, with children and adults. As we practice using *all* the tools in *The Parent's Toolshop*, we more easily prevent and redirect PO behavior.

At this point in the book, many parents are already successfully redirecting many problem behaviors. Nevertheless, there are times we still need to go to the next step in the Universal Blueprint—discipline. When children make poor behavior choices, discipline helps them learn from their mistakes. Chapter 13, "Discipline Toolset," defines the difference between discipline and punishment. It outlines the four important parts of effective discipline. The chapter then offers a variety of discipline choices available to us and details each tool's proper use. When we use respectful, effective, healthy discipline tools, we reach two of our most important parenting goals—our children become *self*-responsible and *self*-disciplined.

REFERENCES

1. *Parenting Young Children: Early Childhood S.T.E.P.*, by Donald Dinkmeyer, Gary McKay, and James S. Dinkmeyer (American Guidance Service, 1989) p. 34.

2. For more information about Dreikurs' goals of behavior, see *Children: The Challenge*, by Rudolf Dreikurs, M.D. with Vicki Soltz, R.M. (E.P. Dutton, 1964); *S.T.E.P.: Systematic Training for Effective Parenting*, by Donald Dinkmeyer, Sr. and Gary McKay (American Guidance Service, 1982); *Positive Discipline*, by Jane Nelsen (Ballantine, 1987, Revised 1996); or *Active Parenting*, by Michael Popkin (Harper Row, 1987).

3. The "Lying" section summarizes some of the key points in *Why Kids Lie: How Parents Can Encourage Truthfulness*, by Paul Ekman, Ph.D. (1989, Penguin Books). Dr. Ekman's book is a comprehensive, detailed report. I highly recommend reading this book for more information about lying.

CHAPTER 13
DISCIPLINE TOOLSET

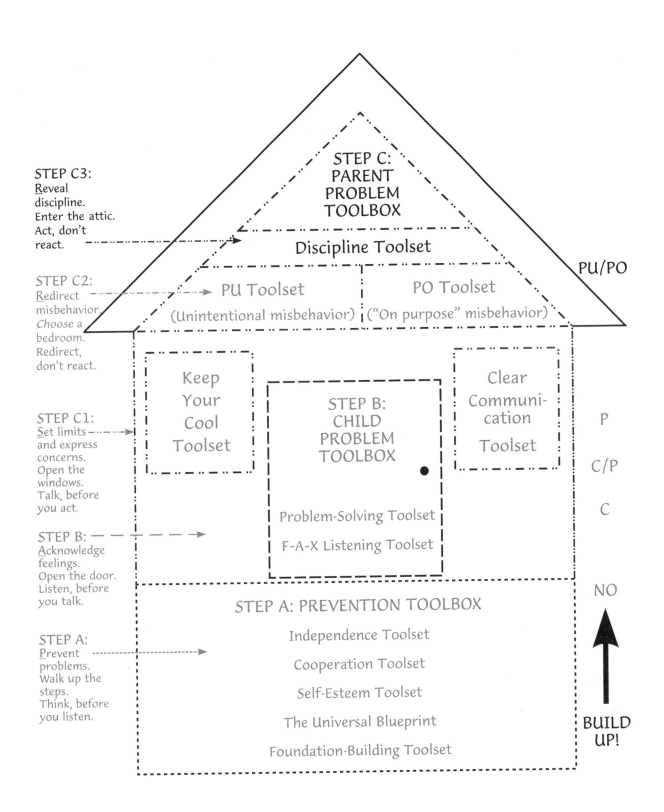

STEP C3:
<u>R</u>eveal discipline. Enter the attic. Act, don't react.

STEP C2:
<u>R</u>edirect misbehavior. Choose a bedroom. Redirect, don't react.

STEP C1:
<u>S</u>et limits and express concerns. Open the windows. Talk, before you act.

STEP B: —
<u>A</u>cknowledge feelings. Open the door. Listen, before you talk.

STEP A:
<u>P</u>revent problems. Walk up the steps. Think, before you listen.

STEP C:
PARENT PROBLEM TOOLBOX

Discipline Toolset

PU Toolset
(Unintentional misbehavior)

PO Toolset
("On purpose" misbehavior)

PU/PO

Keep Your Cool Toolset

STEP B:
CHILD PROBLEM TOOLBOX

Clear Communi-cation Toolset

Problem-Solving Toolset

F-A-X Listening Toolset

STEP A: PREVENTION TOOLBOX

Independence Toolset

Cooperation Toolset

Self-Esteem Toolset

The Universal Blueprint

Foundation-Building Toolset

P

C/P

C

NO

BUILD UP!

CHAPTER
13 DISCIPLINE TOOLSET

We store items in an attic that we don't use daily but occasionally need. Likewise, the Discipline Toolset is in the attic, because we don't use these tools constantly. We use discipline when other efforts have been unsuccessful or when more serious problems arise.

If we are frustrated and don't have the knowledge or skills to properly repair something in our house, we might hit it with the closest tool we can find. Sometimes, this approach can make the item start working again, but we haven't really solved anything and might have caused more damage. Sooner or later, the problem will arise again. It is better to take the time to use the best tool correctly.

*Some parents lack the knowledge or skills to discipline appropriately. When they are frustrated, they get desperate. Thinking a drastic measure will shock children into obedience, they punish them. While punishment might bring some short-term change, the underlying problem still exists and the punishment itself usually creates new problems. When we use discipline appropriately, we can teach children **self**-discipline, **self**-responsibility, and how to learn from their mistakes.*

IN THIS CHAPTER

The Discipline Toolset asks us to consider four important parenting ideas:

1. There is a difference between "discipline" and "punishment." Discipline is the best tool to use if we want to reach our positive, long-term parenting goals.
2. There are four important parts of discipline that must be present for it to be effective. If any parts are missing, it turns our discipline into punishment and/or makes our discipline tools ineffective.
3. There are specific discipline tools we can choose for certain types of problems.
4. With this toolset, we now have all the tools we need to plan the most appropriate response to *any* problem.

WHEN TO USE THIS TOOLSET

Usually, we use the Discipline Toolset as the last of several attempts to resolve a Parent problem. Sometimes, when we are dealing with extreme behavior, we use the Discipline Toolset as the last part of our three-sentence PASRR response formula. If we use the Discipline Toolset too often or misuse it, the tools lose their effectiveness.

THE DIFFERENCE BETWEEN PUNISHMENT AND DISCIPLINE

As with other terms in *The Parent's Toolshop*, "discipline" has a specific meaning, which is different from "punishment."

Punishment

> **Punishment is an over-controlling, autocratic parenting method. One of its basic beliefs is that children must feel bad to "learn their lesson."**

Punishment imposes physical or emotional suffering, such as spanking, slapping, yelling, criticizing, or using guilt trips. It is common to find parenting advice such as "make sure you take away your child's *favorite* activity" or "make the quarreling children sit together in an *uncomfortable* chair until they work out the problem." Why restrict a favorite activity if it has nothing to do with the misbehavior? We want to add suffering! Why *not* let children sit in a comfortable chair or a "heart-to-heart corner" like I have in my house? Adding this extra suffering is sure to cause the children to *dread* problem solving, because it is an uncomfortable, punishing experience! Ideally, we want our children to someday sit together voluntarily to resolve problems. We shortchange our children's abilities when we assume they must suffer to learn.

This idea, that people must feel bad to learn, is illogical. Imagine if every time you sat to read this book, chains whipped around your legs and you could not move from your chair. How would you feel about reading this book? How would you feel about me? Could you concentrate or would you be distracted from the lessons? Any time someone is suffering, it makes learning more difficult and builds resentment toward the person who inflicts the suffering.

Parents most commonly use punishment to exert power or get revenge. Most parents wish they could control their children's behavior and feel angry, hurt, or frustrated when they can't. Punishment can feel satisfying to angry, frustrated parents, but does not help children learn *self*-control and *self*-discipline. Punishment teaches parents, not children, to be responsible for controlling children's behavior. It becomes the parent's job to catch children being good and reward them, then catch them being bad and punish them.

The most extreme punishments impose physical suffering; other punishments are usually the result of parents misusing discipline. Slaps across the face or hands, pushing or shoving, grabbing arms, necks, or ears and dragging are all physical forms of punishment that border on abuse. It's sad, but in many countries, children (and often wives) are viewed as property and parents (or husbands) are allowed, by law, to abuse them.

Spanking is a punishment chosen by many parents of young children. Most parents spank when they are frustrated, either by a situation or because nothing else seems to work. Spanking is usually a reflection of the parent's lack of skill, patience, self-control, or knowledge. Some parents, however, actually believe spanking is a valuable, effective parenting tool—and some parenting resources even offer rules for spanking. (I won't!) Spanking teaches fearful obedience to the person who has the most physical power.[1] While spanking seems to quickly curb misbehavior, long-term research studies have found that the more a parent spanks a child for misbehaving, the worse, over time, that child behaves.[2]

The most common justification for spanking and physical punishment (also known as "corporal" punishment) is the "Spare the rod, spoil the child" quote from Proverbs. In the 23 Psalm, it says, "Thy rod and thy staff, they comfort me." In both instances, the "rod" is a shepherd's cane, which the shepherd uses to *guide* the flock, not beat it into submission. Another ancient definition of "rod" is a standard of measurement, which people use to see whether they are meeting standards. Using these interpretations, the scripture instructs parents to provide boundaries for children and to lovingly guide them or children will become spoiled.

LONG-TERM CONSEQUENCES OF PUNISHMENT

Punishment is an illusion; it only *seems* to work. If children stop misbehaving, parents get an immediate payoff, which reinforces the belief that the punishment worked. Sure, sometimes punished children behave, but they are motivated to *avoid negative* results. We want children to *choose positive* behavior because they understand the value of it.

Punishment reinforces or escalates intentional misbehavior cycles. Punishment gives misbehavior attention, even if it's negative attention. Since punishment is based on power, it escalates power struggles. Punishment is often a parent's way to get   revenge, which escalates revenge cycles. If punishment occurs for even small offenses, children may give up.

Children become immune to punishment. Eventually, children develop a defensive "You can't hurt me" attitude. Parents feel their threats and punishments must become increasingly harsh. This increases the risk of the punishment crossing the line into abuse.

Punishment cancels responsibility. Once the suffering is over, children think they have paid for their mistake. If they are willing to "do the time," they can again choose to "do the crime." The only lessons children learn from punishment are the importance of power, how not to get caught, and that others are responsible for controlling their behavior. Children don't learn *self*-discipline or to make amends for the results of their actions.

> **Before choosing a discipline, ask yourself, "What will this discipline teach?"**

Physical punishment teaches unhealthy lessons:

- Superior people have the right to hurt those who are inferior.
- Physical violence is an acceptable way to resolve conflicts and get revenge.
- It's okay for parents to hit children.
- Parents can do whatever they want, even if it is unreasonable or harmful. Children must do whatever parents say.
- If I hit you because I "love you," then hitting is acceptable in love relationships. That's how people show love.

Physical punishment breeds violence. *All* abusive people witnessed or experienced abuse at some time in their lives. They may not like being violent, but they have not learned other ways to express themselves or resolve conflict. The good news is that not all abused children grow up to be abusive adults. They have free will and can make a conscious choice to break the punishment/abuse cycle and learn healthier skills.

If you say, "I spank, but I'm not *abusive*," consider the effects of milder physical punishments. Many nonabusive parents who once used physical punishment make comments like the following:
- "I always slapped my kid's hand, until he started slapping me back."
- "I used to spank my kid, but he's getting too old for that." (Now these parents must either increase the physical punishment or change their whole approach.)
- "I saw my child spanking her doll and yelling at it, the way I yell and spank her."
- "My child hit another child because he didn't get what he wanted. I realized that's what I do!"

Usually, the children are imitating adults (not just parents) who have made a powerful impression on them. For many parents, these experiences are a wake-up call that what they are doing is unhealthy and ineffective.

Punishment lowers self-esteem. Punishment hurts. It's difficult for children to understand how anyone who hurts them could also love them. Punished children begin to see themselves as unloved and unlovable. They believe they are worthless because they have been told they are bad people.

The emotional scars can last a lifetime. People do not need physical scars to feel abused. Many adults can vividly remember how they felt when they were punished as children. Their obedience was out of fear, not out of respect or from having "learned their lesson." If you ask them *why* they were punished, most cannot remember what they did wrong, only how they felt about the punishment and the punisher.

A Graduate's Story. During a group discussion about discipline, a woman said, "When I was a child, my momma would beat me with a switch until I bled. She was mean and abusive and I hated her for it! I didn't learn nothin' from it. My grandma also lived with us and there were lots of times she whipped me with a switch—and I'm glad she did! She wasn't mean and I always learned my lesson. So isn't it okay to whip kids if we aren't mean about it?"

I was surprised by this mother's comparison and decided to explore it further. I asked her, "When your grandmother whipped you, was it just as hard as your mother's whipping?" She said, "Sometimes. There were lots of times she left marks, too, but I learned from her whippin's." Still confused, I added, "Then what was so different about your grandma's whippings?" She explained, "My grandma would sit me on her lap and explain what I done wrong and why it was wrong. Then she told me I had to get a whippin' for it and had me go outside and pick the switch she would use." Now it was making more sense to me. I asked her, "Is it possible that the reason you learned from your grandma's punishment was that she sat you on her lap and taught you right from wrong?" She thought for a second and I think I might have actually seen a light bulb go off above her head. She said "Yes!" So I added, "Do you also think it is possible that if your grandma had those talks with you without the whipping that you also would have learned a lesson?" She willingly nodded her head in agreement. Then I asked one final question, "Looking back, which do you remember more, your grandmother's lessons or the whippings that came after them?" She thoughtfully answered, "the whippings." "So," I concluded, "if you had learned the same lessons without the whipping, do you think you'd remember them better?" "Definitely," she said cheerfully.

Jane Nelsen, author of *Positive Discipline*, sums up the effects of punishment as "The Four R's of Punishment[3]." When parents use punishment, it can have any or all of the following results.

THE FOUR R'S OF PUNISHMENT

RESENTMENT ("This is unfair.")

REVENGE ("They are winning now, but I'll get even.")

RETREAT: Reduced self-esteem ("I am a bad person.") or sneakiness ("I won't get caught next time.")

REBELLION ("I'll do it anyway, just to prove who's in control.")

Discipline

The basic belief of discipline is that children *can learn* from their mistakes without adding extra suffering. In fact, the more one learns, the less one suffers. The suffering children experience in discipline is usually the natural result of what they did. When someone *else* inflicts extra suffering, it turns the discipline into unhealthy, unhelpful punishment.

The word "discipline" comes from the Greek word " disciple." Disciples follow a leader who guides them. The parent's role in discipline, therefore, is that of teacher and leader, not controller. The focus is on solutions and lessons, not imposing consequences. Discipline teaches several important lessons:

- **Behavior is a choice.** Every action has an effect, positive or negative. (This is a universal law of nature!) Therefore, children's behavior *choices* determine whether they will experience positive or negative outcomes. When children choose irresponsible behavior and it does not reward their goals, they see no purpose in continuing to act negatively. If we show them positive ways to meet their goals, they naturally choose these more effective behavior. Poor behavior choices are mistakes that provide opportunities to learn better behavior.

- **Children are responsible for controlling their own behavior.** Parents are responsible for holding children accountable for their behavior choices and helping them see the lesson each mistake holds. With punishment, parents do something *to* children. When trying to overpower or control children, parents decide the discipline *for* them. If parents use these quick fixes rather than long-range teaching, children miss opportunities to learn *self*-discipline. Ideally, we want to involve children and plan the discipline *with* them. Only then will children fully understand their behavior (and its outcome) are within *their* control.

Discipline has "Four R's[4]" too. For discipline to be effective, it must meet *all* the following criteria.

THE FOUR R'S OF DISCIPLINE

To be effective, discipline must be:

REVEALED ahead of time, whenever possible.

Logically RELATED to the behavior.

REASONABLE in extent and/or time limit.

Mutually RESPECTFUL to children *and* parents.

If *any* of the "Four R's of Discipline" are missing, it can bring on the "Four R's of Punishment."

DISCIPLINE IS *REVEALED*, WHENEVER POSSIBLE

If we want *self*-disciplined children, they need to know their behavior is a *choice*. Revealing discipline lets children know what they can expect from their behavior choices—misbehavior has negative outcomes and positive behavior has value. When we reveal these behavior choices and the outcomes, children can make educated decisions about their behavior.

> *A Graduate's Story. I took my two girls and three other children, all under age five, to swim at a lake. In the car, I realized how difficult it would be to watch so many kids and prevent an accident. As we drove, I revealed my rules for swimming. I said, "It's important that you stay in the shallow water, because you could drown if the water is too deep. You can walk into the lake until the water touches your bellybutton. Then you need to stop. If you choose to go out farther in the water, I'll know you've decided to sit with me on the beach until you are ready to swim safely."*
>
> *When we got to the lake, the kids went into the water. One boy inched his way into the water. He called to me, "Lory! The water's touchin' my bellybutton!" Then he stopped. My daughter and another child went out too far. I called to them, "The water is above your bellybutton!" The girls came out of the water and ran over to my towel. They said, "We've decided to take a break for awhile." I was surprised that they said this and knew they probably wanted to save face, so I didn't add any lectures. They were actually disciplining themselves!*

The most effective discipline is preventive discipline. Use questions to help children figure out and understand the need for a rule. For example, "What could happen if you ride your bike in the street? (Wait.) So where should you ride your bike?" We can reveal discipline with helpful questions. "If you ride in the street, are you showing you are ready to handle bike privileges responsibly?" (Wait.) We can then present discipline as a choice. "So you can ride your bike on the sidewalk or put the bike away."

Revealing discipline differs from making threats. Threats are power plays. "If you don't stop _____, *I'm going to* _____." Threats send the message that it is the parent's responsibility to control the child. Threats challenge children to test the parents' willingness to follow through. ***Revealing***

discipline is most effective if we ask helpful questions such as "What would happen if you did that?" This helps us avoid lecturing or threatening. If children understand the value of positive behavior, have the skills to behave appropriately, understand the results of negative behavior and *still* make a poor behavior choice, they either forgot (PU) or are testing whether the outcome will really happen (PO). Therefore, consistent follow through is vital. If children complain or accuse parents of being unfair, parents can ask children to think about the choices and outcomes they discussed earlier. Poor behavior choices are a normal part of growing up, but children can learn from these mistakes and make improvements for the future.

Sometimes threats are vague, with no realistic consequence. "If you don't stop, you're going to get it!" These are empty threats—parents let off steam, but their words are just hot air. The most common threat is a 1-2-3 threat, "You have until I count to three to do it." Counting teaches children they don't have to do "it" the first time parents ask. Children rarely respond at 1, because they know we won't follow through until we reach 3!

Some threats repeat the same statement in a louder or firmer tone of voice. "Please stop . . . I said, 'Stop!' . . . STOP IT OR ELSE!" These threats condition children not to respond unless parents yell or threaten. We might as well say, "Keep it up. I'm not really angry, yet." Our goal is to have children respond the first time we ask them to cooperate. If we need to say something more than once, we want each statement to make a specific, different, increasingly firm message. Our first sentence invites cooperation (Step A: **P**revent the problem). The second **A**cknowledges their feelings, but **S**ets limits (Steps B and C1). At this point we have made it clear that this behavior is unacceptable. If children misbehave again, they either haven't mastered the proper behavior (PU) or are doing this to serve a purpose (PO). To **R**edirect the misbehavior, without starting or escalating negative behavior cycles, our third statement **R**eveals their choice—a positive way to meet their purpose or experience the effect of continuing the behavior. This last statement lets children know that the next step, should *they* choose to take it, is discipline.

Sometimes, we can't reveal discipline in advance, because we don't always expect a problem. When these situations arise and we want to reveal the discipline for repeated misbehavior, we quickly move through the Universal Blueprint's PASRR formula (detailed above). If the behavior is so severe that immediate discipline is necessary, it is best to use problem solving to discuss the problem and reveal discipline. We learn how to do this later in this chapter.

Threats make parents responsible for children's behavior choices and invite rebellion.

Respectfully reveal children's behavior choices and hold them accountable.

DISCIPLINE IS LOGICALLY *RELATED* TO THE SITUATION

If discipline isn't logically related to the misbehavior or lesson children need to learn, it seems like the parent made up an unfair punishment or is trying to get revenge. This shifts the focus away from the lesson to who is in power. Together, these attitudes can cause or escalate power struggles, revenge cycles, and rebellion.

If the logical connection between a behavior and the effect isn't obvious, state it or ask a helpful question so the child can figure it out. Otherwise, children don't understand the logic of the discipline.

> *A Graduate's Story. This week, I had a situation where my discipline really backfired, but I can't figure out what I did wrong! My son, Chad, said he'd be home at five o'clock. We needed to eat before we left for church at six o'clock. At five thirty, Chad came home. I said, "We had an agreement that you would be home at five. Hurry up and eat." When six o'clock arrived, Chad had finished his meal, but not his dessert. I told him he couldn't have his dessert because he came home late. He became very upset and yelled at me and said I was being unfair. We had an agreement, I was respectful when he broke his agreement, and he didn't have time to finish his dessert, so it seemed like a logical discipline.*

This mother didn't do anything wrong, but she did neglect to state the logical connection between being late and not getting dessert—their need to leave for church on time. She said her son couldn't have dessert because he came home late. Her son didn't see how dessert and being late were logically related. She would have been clearer to say, "We need to leave at six, so you don't have *time* to eat your dessert." Sometimes we need to explain that "Because A (misbehavior) happened, B happened. Therefore, C (discipline) is the outcome (or solution)." We can also ask this as a question, "What happened when A (misbehavior)?" (The answer is B.) "So what do you think will happen now?" (The answer is C, a logical outcome.)

Choose the most logically related discipline tool for the situation. Many parents use one discipline tool for everything—restrictions, grounding, or time-outs. Each of these disciplines, however, are only logically related to certain types of misbehavior. If any of these options become a regular way of disciplining, without any logical connection to the misbehavior, it decreases the effectiveness of the tool. It also brings on one or more of the Four R's of Punishment. Since people can misuse discipline tools, to punish, we will learn when and how to apply each tool, according to the Four R's of Discipline.

DISCIPLINE IS *REASONABLE*

"Reasonable" usually relates to time—how long a discipline lasts.
- If the time is too short, children might not learn the lesson the discipline can teach.
- If the time is too long, children resent that they've learned the lesson but are still being punished. It seems unfair, which causes resentment and rebellion. This shifts the focus from the lesson to our power to make them suffer longer.

Consider the cost and benefit of the discipline. For example, a messy room is less important than the value of participating in a community project. If children plan ahead, they have time to do both. If children don't clean their room and the parent doesn't let the child participate in the community project, the child is missing out on a lesson far more important than cleanliness. Reduced playtime would be more related and reasonable.

Discipline must be enforceable, so we aren't forced to back down. What if we say, "Leave the room" to older children and they refuse to go? It's hard to *make* them leave without physical force, which escalates the situation and borders on punishment or abuse. We *can* say, "I will leave" and still enforce it.

When setting time limits for discipline, consider hours or even minutes, rather than days or weeks. Use times in your regular routine as possible time markers. For example, "I can see you need to come inside until we finish lunch." Or "You'll have another chance to try after school." With young children, start with the shortest time possible (minutes) and make it tangible. ("It will be time to leave when Sesame Street is over.") Remember the child's sense of time and make it age-appropriate. (We discuss time limits further in the "Restrictions" section.)

Focus on the lesson and the "next chance to try," not on the discipline itself. We want to give children a chance to practice what they learn from discipline while the lesson is still fresh. After we decide a reasonable time, focus any further comments on when their "next chance to try" will occur. Express your confidence in their ability to choose more wisely next time. Describe in positive, specific terms the behavior you want to see, ***"You can have another chance (when) to show you can (describe positive behavior)."*** For example, "You can have another chance after dinner to show you can keep your bike on the sidewalk." (Notice, I did not say ". . . not ride in the street." Remember, "Don't say Don't.")

Every time the same behavior occurs, increase the length of time by small increments. (This is called a "progressive" restriction, which we will discuss further in the "Restrictions" section.) If a time is unreasonable, any increase makes it even more unreasonable. If it is short and reasonable, with a chance to improve, any repeated misbehavior can be connected to the lesson. "When someone (behavior), it shows they haven't learned how to (describe positive behavior) yet. During the next (time) you can plan a way to show you have learned this behavior."

"Reasonable" can also refer to the extent of the discipline. Avoid tacking on extra suffering. It shifts the focus from the lesson to the parent's control and desire for revenge. For example, a child was supposed to do the dishes, but some dishes weren't cleaned properly. An unreasonable discipline is to clean *all* the dishes again. The child will ask, "Why should I have to wash a clean dish?" The honest answer to this question is because the parent wants to make the child suffer. There are few, if any, circumstances when "If you don't do the job right, you have to do the entire job again." If my hair stylist misses a lock of hair, I won't ask her to cut all my hair again! If I miss a few leaves when I'm raking, I'm not going to throw the pile of leaves back on the lawn and start over! If the focus of the discipline is on learning, it must be reasonable. Only those dishes that are still dirty need to be washed again. I can ask my stylist to even up the haircut. I can simply rake the remaining leaves. This teaches a much healthier lesson about mistakes: "Mistakes can happen, but we want to fix them or prevent them if possible."

> *A Parenting Class Discussion. A man in my class said, "When I was a child and misbehaved, my parents would threaten to throw away my favorite toy. Several times they followed through with this threat." Clearly, this was not logically related or reasonable, so I asked him, "What did you learn?" He said, "I learned never to get attached to anything, because it could be ripped away, and never to show my love for a favorite toy or friend or **that** would be the first thing I'd lose." The class was stunned. Several people, including me, had tears in our eyes as we sighed, "How sad!" I'm sure his parents had no idea their punishment affected their child so profoundly. It taught him nothing about proper behavior and much about conditional love, rejection, and the risks of attachment.*

> **Reasonable discipline is enough (time or extent) to teach the lesson, without being so much (long or extreme) that it shifts the focus to who is in power or adds extra suffering.**

If we set an unreasonable discipline and children *show* they are ready to change their behavior, follow these suggestions for **canceling discipline:**

1. Admit that you overreacted out of anger or frustration, if you did.
2. Describe the behavior you've seen that leads you to see they are ready to try again.
3. Get an agreement for future behavior.

This process models how to handle mistakes, apologize, and make amends. If we cancel discipline without saying anything, children might think they are "getting away with" something or that we don't mean what we say. They won't know *why* we are letting them off the hook. Also, notice the emphasis on children *showing*, through their behavior, that they have learned their lesson. Another option is to ask children to explain what they learned. These methods prevent children from pleading or making false promises, just to manipulate the parent into giving in.

DISCIPLINE IS *RESPECTFUL* TO CHILDREN AND PARENTS

Discipline is both firm *and* kind. To be firm *and* kind at the same time, our tone of voice is matter-of-fact and friendly, while our words and follow-through show our firmness. Do not interpret kindness as permissiveness, or confuse firmness with strictness or harshness. Strictness deals with controlling the child. "Get to bed now, or else!" Firmness refers to *our* attitude, behavior, and feelings. "Thirty minutes until lights-out! If you get ready quickly, we'll have more time to read books." When we present discipline disrespectfully or in anger, children stew about the way we treated them, instead of learning from the choices they made or making amends for their mistakes.

Discipline does not label or condemn. Punishment implies that children *are* bad when they misbehave. Discipline implies that children are lovable and loved, even when their behavior *choices* are poor. Our nonjudgmental attitude says, "While I don't agree with the behavior choice you made, I still love you. I have faith that you are capable of choosing better behavior (or finding a way to solve this problem)."

Discipline is the *child's* choice. This does not mean we ask children if they *want* discipline. Nor do we imply "It's *your* fault" in a disrespectful tone. If we've taught that behavior choices have results, we can remain calm and matter-of-fact when children make poor behavior choices. We send the message, often nonverbally, that "I see you are facing the results of your choices. I respect you enough not to interfere with those outcomes and will hold you accountable by following through."

> **To teach *self*-responsibility, use helpful questions and word discipline as a choice:**
> "If you *choose* to (negative behavior), what will happen? (Wait.) So if you choose to (negative behavior), I'll know you've decided to (discipline). (Which means the child will be responsible for resolving or experiencing the negative outcome.)

When following through, children might say, "No, I didn't *choose* that!" Our response can be, "I'm not making you (discipline). When you chose to (negative behavior), you knew what would happen. I'm simply following through with your choice." It's important that our tone of voice is kind and matter-of-fact, not punishing, when we say this.

Respectful discipline is not humiliating or embarrassing. When we need to discipline children in a group or in public, speak to them in private, so they don't lose face. If we embarrass or humiliate children, they feel hurt, which often leads to revenge. If we speak to children in private, we are more likely to get their full attention. Children realize we could have embarrassed them, so they reward *our* efforts by quickly cooperating!

DISCIPLINE'S LONG-TERM CONSEQUENCES

Discipline eliminates problem behavior. When parents consistently follow the PASRR formula to discipline, children learn from it and break the misbehavior cycle faster. Soon, all it takes is a quick reminder. Eventually, the problem behavior is eliminated. This keeps discipline where it belongs—in the attic, where we can find it when it is really needed and after using other tools.

Appropriate discipline teaches children self-control, self-discipline, and self-responsibility. Children develop respect for themselves, others, authority, and rules. They are not obedient only when a superior is present, but see the value in rules and learn to respect *all* people. Discipline shows children the results of their behavior and how to make amends, accepting responsibility for the decisions they make.

Discipline maintains self-esteem. Although they may regret their behavior choice, children still feel worthwhile if they learn a valuable lesson or have a chance to make amends.

The benefits last a lifetime. The self-discipline and other lessons children learn through discipline are valuable to them as adults in nearly every setting: work, personal relationships, and parenting. Effective discipline builds trust and children respect and admire their parents.

THE DIFFERENCE BETWEEN PUNISHMENT AND DISCIPLINE

PUNISHMENT	DISCIPLINE
Over-controlling and harsh.	Balanced—kind *and* firm.
Belief: "The more you suffer, the more you learn." The focus is on suffering, which distracts the child from learning.	Belief: "The more you learn, the less you suffer." The focus is on learning from mistakes.
Misbehavior is a crime and children *are* bad.	Misbehavior is a poor behavior choice, which even good children can make.
Parent is responsible for controlling children.	Parent is responsible for teaching children *self*-control and holding children accountable for their actions.
Uses condescending lectures and blame.	Is respectful and focuses on solutions.
Uses warnings and threats, "If you do _____, I'll _____."	Uses choices, "If you choose (behavior), I'll know you have chosen (discipline)."
Respects *only* the parents' rights.	Respects parents' *and* child's rights.
Is arbitrary, based on parents' whims and anger.	Is logically related to misbehavior.
Is usually unreasonable. Parent adds on extra suffering or time.	Is reasonable, suffering is self-imposed and time ends when the child is ready to try again.
Is reactive and revengeful.	Is proactive (revealed).
Reminds child of past mistakes, "I told you so."	Allows a quick return to the normal routine.
Decreases self-esteem.	Maintains self-esteem.
Children develop defensive "I don't care" attitude. The severity of punishments must increase.	Children care about behaving well and correcting their mistakes. The need to discipline decreases.
Builds resentment and rebellion.	Builds respect, responsibility, self-control, and self-discipline.

Discipline in blended families. Give new step-relationships time to develop and emphasize communication and teamwork. Children are usually skeptical of a new stepparent. They feel a new surge of loyalty to the natural parent who is left out of this family. It is foolish for new stepparents to try to take over the role of the left-out parent. It only causes more resentment.

When blending two families with children, family councils are vital. (Chapter 14, "Family Council Toolset," addresses special circumstances of single and blended families). Many experts encourage the new stepparent to take a back seat in discipline issues. This is only necessary if the natural parent or stepparent uses over-controlling power punishments. If the natural parent and stepparent use balanced discipline, including open communication and problem solving, they can participate in discussions more equally.

DISCIPLINE TOOLS

We must use each discipline tool according to the "Four R's" or we will turn it into punishment.

 ## Show Children How to Make Amends ☆☆☆☆

Whenever possible, use this tool, because it is always logically related. We only need to present it respectfully and have reasonable expectations. For example, if a child writes on a wall, ask a helpful question, "How can you get these marks off the wall?" Our question makes it clear it is the child's responsibility to clean the wall and the child's answer will reveal how to do it. If children don't know how, we can give information. This is how children learn self-discipline and resourcefulness. The child does not have to do it all at once or use a toothbrush, since this would be unreasonable and punishing. When children know how to correct mistakes, they often do it on their own in the future—becoming *self*-disciplined.

Ways to Make Amends

- Whoever drops it .... needs to pick it up.
- Whoever spills it .... needs to wipe it up.
- Whoever break it .... needs to fix or replace it.
- Whoever loses it .... needs to find or replace it.
- Whoever left it open......................... needs to close it.
- Whoever left it on .... needs to turn it off.
- Whoever hurt it.................................. needs to apologize and help heal it.

Do not *tell* children what to do; suggest it as an option. Explain how children can make amends in a calm, friendly, matter-of-fact tone of voice. You can even give them choices about ways to make amends. For example, if children break something, they can either fix it or do extra chores to earn the money to replace it. If children are too young or inexperienced to do the activity, they can help *you*. For example, if a toddler spills a drink, the parent can hand the child a towel and put a hand on top of the child's, to show how to wipe the spill.

When another person (rather than a "thing") is hurt, there are several ways to make amends. Look at the wound, get ice, write a letter of apology, give a hug or kiss, or say "I'm sorry." Avoid getting into a power struggle *making them* do any of these things. (See the "Sibling Conflicts" section in the Child Problem Toolbox for details on handling an insincere "sorry.")

A Graduate's Story. My husband and I were both working late one evening and hired Allison to babysit our two children. Isaac, 9, was playing outside when his tennis ball landed on the roof. He asked Allison if he could get the ball and she said "No." Isaac decided to get it anyway. Soon, Isaac's friend, Aaron, showed up and climbed on the roof with Isaac. When Allison saw them both on the roof, she asked them to get down. The boys said they were "stuck" and refused to come down. (It's debatable if this was sincere or a game.) Allison asked nicely, then firmly, and finally demanded they come down. The next-door neighbor came out. She knew the sitter and the boys. She, too, insisted the boys come down. The boys got off the roof only after Allison and the neighbor walked away.

The next morning, my husband told Isaac, "We are aware of what happened with Allison last night. You need to be thinking about what you did. When you come home from school today, be prepared to talk to your mother about appropriate discipline."

When Isaac came home, I went to his room. "We need to discuss what happened last night when Allison was here." Isaac made excuses for why he was on the roof, insisting he was stuck. I listened to his feelings and reasons, but didn't accept any as an excuse. I said, "Isaac, I know you think you are old enough to be allowed on the roof, but when a sitter is here, we expect you to do what she says. Allison told you not to get on the roof and you chose to defy her. Now we need to talk about what happens next."

"There are three issues here," I said. "First, you got on the roof when you weren't supposed to and wouldn't come down. Second, you involved Aaron in this . . ." Isaac interrupted, "But Aaron decided, on his own, to get on the roof!" I calmly asked, "And whose roof was it?" I paused while he thought. Then I continued, "When Aaron is at our house, I expect you **both** *to follow our rules." He nodded in agreement. "Third," I continued, "this behavior is unacceptable anytime, but this incident occurred when a sitter was here. Now, we need to decide what the appropriate discipline is for each part of this problem."*

Isaac suggested restricting himself to the house for three weeks. Normally, I would have thought this was unreasonable, but this was a serious offense. I suggested we break down the time. Since Isaac abused the privilege of playing outside, he would be restricted to the house the first week. The second week, he could play outside by himself. The third week, Aaron could play at our house, if they were supervised. If all went well, the fourth week would be back to normal. (This is called a "regressive restriction," which is explained in the Restrictions section.) This plan also took care of problem number two, the fact that Aaron was involved. Isaac agreed to give up his privilege of being on the roof, even to help his father clean gutters, until late autumn, which was not far off.

Finally, I asked Isaac how he could make amends with Allison. He suggested writing an apology. I agreed and added a firm suggestion, "I paid Allison to supervise you and your sister. What she had to handle was above and beyond the call of duty for a sitter. Since she worked twice as hard, I would like you to pay her extra for the time you spent on the roof. It amounts to $2.00." Isaac agreed.

I also talked to Aaron's mom and we coordinated our discipline. Aaron was restricted to his house for a week and voluntarily wrote letters apologizing to both Allison and me for his part in the incident. Isaac did not complain once while on house restriction. He confirmed our arrangements several times and knew when it was time for the next level of restrictions. It was hard for him to write and deliver his apology to Allison, but he did it anyway.

This mother could have easily turned this discipline into punishment. She could have *demanded* the apologies and payment. She could have blamed and shamed Isaac. Although she was not pleased with what happened, she was pleased with the discipline they arranged.

Children need to learn that *making* mistakes isn't as important as what they can do to prevent or correct them. When we teach children that mistakes are bad, they will spend their energy denying responsibility or covering up. Hiding mistakes prevents someone from fixing them or learning from them. Children can take responsibility for what they have done, whether or not it was a mistake. For example, if children steal something they must give it back in person and apologize. If it was a teen who was old enough to shop alone, the teen could have supervised shopping visits before regaining this privilege.

Offer Choices ☆☆☆☆

Throughout our tour of *The Parent's Toolshop*, we have learned to use choices within limits: to prevent problems, gain cooperation, prevent and redirect power struggles—and now, to reveal and follow through with discipline.

It is important to only offer choices we are willing to allow. If we say, "Eat your peas or leave the table" and the child leaves the table, we can't say, "Get back here and eat those peas!"

Offer a choice between positive behavior and the result of negative behavior. Remember that both choices must be respectful to the child. Unfair choices, like "Do it or get a spanking" are power threats. There are several formulas appropriate for discipline:

1. "(Describe the positive choice and the value behind it). If you choose to (negative behavior), I'll know you've decided to (discipline)."
   - ▶ "To roller blade safely, people need to wear a helmet and pads. If you decide to skate without protection, I'll know you've decided to not play street hockey today."

2. "You can (positive behavior) or (result of negative behavior). You decide."
   - ▶ "You can settle down or leave the room. You decide."
   - ▶ "You can either throw the ball away from the street or go in the back yard. You decide."

Adjust the choices as issues shift. This is tricky, but it can prevent power struggles at each level of your response. Consider the bike example and notice how the focus of the choices changes to avoid power struggles at each step:

1. Reveal the discipline as a choice, "You can either ride your bike on the sidewalk or put it away."

2. When the child goes near the street again, we say, "I can see you've decided to put your bike away." (Do *not* say, "I can see you want *me* to put your bike away." Give the child a chance to be responsible for following through with the discipline.)

3. If the child does not put the bike away, the issue has shifted. Now the issue is *how* the bike is going to be put away. We reveal a *new* choice, "Either you can put your bike away or I can. You decide."

4. If the child refuses or doesn't respond, we can say, "*I can see you want* me to put your bike away." If the child fusses, we can say, as we follow through, "You had the choice to put the bike away yourself. You can have another chance to ride it (time)."

The only exception to this scenario is if the child refuses to come out of the street to have this discussion. A friendly, nonthreatening approach is more likely to result in the child coming out of the street. ("Hey Jon! Come here a second," instead of "Jonathan Michael Jones! Get over here this instant!") We may need to run in the street, get a hold of the handlebar, and say all of the above firmly but respectfully as we guide the bike back up to the sidewalk. This approach is called . . .

Take Action

Any action *must* fit the "Four R's." The action must be related to the behavior. It must be reasonable and done in a respectful way. Usually, we want to reveal our plan so children are expecting it, but there are times when the very act of revealing the plan turns the statement into a threat.

A Graduate's Story. I drive my two teenagers to school every morning. They worked out a plan for who sits in the front seat. Whoever sits in the front gets to pick the radio station. If they argue about seating arrangements or break their agreement, they both automatically sit in the back seat. *Then* they argue about which radio station to play. I've tried saying, "If you two are going to argue, I'll turn off the radio," but they either can't hear me or take it as a power play. This week, I simply took action. When they started arguing I turned off the radio without revealing my plan. They immediately stopped arguing and asked, "Why did you do that?" Now, I had their full attention. I said, "I can't listen to the radio **and** arguing. If you two can't agree, we won't listen to **any** music." So far, it's worked! They are back to their seating agreements and haven't argued about the radio all week.

Taking action involves deciding what *you* will do, not what you will make the *child* do. If you have already revealed a discipline and children test you, simply follow through with what you said you'd do, with as few words as possible. It is perfectly okay to take children by the hand and start walking, turn off a TV, or lock a toolbox if you have revealed your intention to do so.

When you take action you may or may not say anything. We've learned a lot about what to say in various parenting situations. Often, we need to take some action *while* we are speaking. *If* we speak, we want to use all the communication skills we have learned. Sometimes no words are necessary; our actions speak for themselves.

A Personal Story. My husband and I sleep in on Saturdays, when we can, and our kids occupy themselves while we sleep. Before they were teens, they would often get too loud or start arguing and screaming and wake me up. I felt aggravated and resentful when I went downstairs. If it hadn't happened for a while, I would remind them of the discipline for screaming while others are sleeping. "You can watch TV quietly or you can play quietly in your own rooms—you decide."

If they woke me up again, I did one of two things. If I was still calm enough, I'd say, "I can see you two have decided to go to your rooms for a while," as I turned off the TV. If I was fuming, I stumbled down the stairs, walked into the family room, turned off the TV, and left. I didn't say anything. They knew what they did and why I took action. If it happened the next weekend, I would simply take action at the first incident, because the rule and discipline were still fresh in their memories. I only had to do this a half dozen times before the problem stopped for good. Today, many years later, my teens sleep in later than I do!

Allow Natural Consequences ☆☆☆☆

Natural consequences happen if the parent does nothing. They are predictable and always logically related. To follow through with a natural consequence, parents must hold themselves back from rescuing children. We can reveal a natural consequence or our unwillingness to rescue children. If children insist on behaving that way, they are choosing to experience the natural consequence of that behavior. Do *not* say, "I told you so"; Instead, ask, "What can you do now?" or "How can you prevent this the next time?"

A Personal Story. When Chris was three, he wore a superhero sweatsuit with matching winter boots the entire summer! I told him he would get too hot (the natural consequence), but he didn't! My friends still remember this and tease Chris and me (in a friendly way) about how cute he was.

***Only* use natural consequences if they meet the following criteria:**
- ***They are safe.*** Allowing a child to go in the street would be too dangerous.
- ***They are not too far in the future.*** Not brushing teeth results in cavities after several months. This is too long to wait.
- ***There* are *consequences.*** Nothing naturally and predictably happens when someone talks out of turn, although it is inappropriate behavior.

Parents often worry that their children's mistakes could ruin their lives forever. Few mistakes are this serious. Fear encourages parents to control their children's lives, rather than letting go, so the children can learn how to live their own lives. With **teens,** these behavior choices and natural consequences usually occur away from parents. This is an even greater reason to allow teens (and children of all ages) to experience the consequences of mistakes that aren't dangerous, so they will learn sooner rather than later.

In the following examples, the parent probably has a chance to reveal the natural consequence. If the child still chooses that behavior, the parent could use another discipline tool or let the natural consequence occur.

► Dropping an object on the floor from a high chair and letting it stay there.
► Forgetting a school lunch and being hungry.
► Forgetting homework and experiencing the school's consequence.
► Coming home late and missing dinner.
► Not washing a breakfast bowl until later and having a harder time cleaning it.
► Not practicing enough and doing poorly at a recital.

The first time children forget books, homework or lunches, or if they forget only a few times a year, it is less risky to deliver the item. Use problem solving to have children select self-reminders they can use. If they are regularly forgetful, don't rescue them. Let them experience the natural outcome. If the child experiences the result and comes up with a plan for remembering, the problem will usually resolve itself.

> *A **Personal Story.** I have a policy that I am only willing to deliver forgotten lunches, homework or books **three** times each school year. I have the same "three strikes" rule about driving the kids to school if they miss their bus. The first time it happens, I willingly deliver the item or drive the child to school. I remind them that I am only willing to do this two more times the entire school year. We do problem solving so the child has a plan to prevent the problem from happening again. If I have to deliver an item or drive a third time, I reveal my intent to not rescue them again. We do problem solving again. This time, we discuss the school's consequences and what the child can do to solve the problem on their own if it happens again. So far, my kids have reached the "third strike" only once. Most years, they only get one strike.*

Apply Restrictions

Use restrictions sparingly; they are one of the most misused and overused tools of discipline. Restrictions are power plays, because parents have the power to restrict something. Restrictions are best arrived at through problem solving, with the child's involvement and understanding.

Restrictions are only logically related to an abuse of a privilege or right. Most rights and privileges have a responsibility connected. The obvious effect of not accepting the responsibility is to lose the privilege.

► Having toys requires the responsibility of taking care of them. When children don't take care of them, they lose the opportunity to play with the toys they don't take care of. Throwing away the toys, however, would be unreasonable punishment.

► Teens earn a driver's license by passing a test and signing an agreement to abide by the laws. If young drivers break an important law or an accident occurs at their fault, they are showing they might not be ready to have a license. Get a conditional driving agreement between parent and teen before the teen actually has the license.

► If children come home late, there are two options. If it is a chronic problem, they cannot go out the next day or can have friends visit at their house. If it's not a chronic problem, however late the child is, that is how much earlier he or she needs to be home the next time.

Don't restrict responsibilities or children's commitments. Restricting children from an extracurricular activity when the offense has nothing to do with the activity is illogical and unreasonable. If it is a team sport, the entire team suffers and the child is forced to neglect a responsibility. The only time it might be reasonable to restrict an extracurricular activity would be for poor grades or in-game fighting. Grade requirements should be established before the child makes the commitment and are usually a school policy. If children want to take on additional activities, get an agreement that they will maintain their other responsibilities or give up the activity. When children are involved in more than two extracurricular activities, it is probably too much. Allow children to try out different activities, one at a time. If they want to start something new, they must decide which activity they are going to temporarily give up.

If misbehavior occurs during a sport or extracurricular activity, deal with the act, not the place the act occurred. For example, if children fight during a game, the coach is the appropriate person to restrict children from playing. Parents can suggest children make amends with the other player; an apology, written or verbal, for example. If that is not possible, parents can brainstorm what children can do the next time they are tempted to fight. Involve the coach to reveal that, if it happens again, they will sit on the sidelines for one game (to start).

Avoid restrictions from special events, such as school dances or scout/church outings. You especially want to make an exception if the outing would be a positive learning experience or was planned far in advance. A more logical and reasonable discipline can be in effect before and after the activity. Special activities should only be restricted if a severe infraction occurs that is logically related to that specific event. When there is no logical connection between the event and the restriction, it's unreasonable and clearly a parent's effort to make the child suffer.

Negotiate restrictions in direct relation to the severity of what occurred. You want children to have an opportunity to *show* they can behave responsibly. While they are restricted, they can't put the lesson to use.

- *Progressive restrictions* start with the least restriction and increase if the behavior continues. It is best to use progressive restrictions when children are in the process of learning a skill, so they can have another chance soon to practice the lessons and skills. The example of riding a bike in the street illustrated a progressive restriction.

- *Regressive restrictions* start with the most restrictive limits. If all goes well, the next period is less restrictive, and so on, until all privileges are restored. It is most appropriate to use regressive restrictions when the offense involves a severe misuse of a privilege and the child knew *very* well that he or she was breaking an important rule. As the restriction decreases, children can show they can responsibly handle each new level of privilege restoration, which helps parents rebuild their trust. The story about the boys on the roof illustrated a regressive restriction.

When a restriction is over, ask "How can you *show* that you are ready for this responsibility/privilege?" Review agreements or conditions related to the privilege.

Use Problem Solving ☆☆☆☆

We learned in the Clear Communication Toolset how to do parent/child problem solving. We learned that the last step might be to reveal a discipline, if the behavior happens again. Here, discipline is proposed for the future. Sometimes, however, you will want to use problem solving to plan discipline at the time of a severe violation. When used to plan a discipline, you follow the same steps, except the problem to solve is "What discipline is appropriate?" (The story of the boys on the roof illustrated this process.)

Involve children in deciding disciplines. If the child can describe what they did wrong, why it was wrong, and what they plan to do differently, they have probably learned the lesson. There may not need to be any discipline at all. If discipline is needed, we can ask children what they think it should be. Children are often better at suggesting discipline that meets the "Four R's" than parents! When children suggest something that doesn't fit all four R's, simply adjust it until it does.

*A **Personal Story**. When I was 16, I passed my driving test with flying colors. I enjoyed cruising past friends' houses, honking a "Hello." One day, I looked at a friend's house for a brief second, as I honked my horn. When I looked back to the road, it was too late, I hit my friend's father's parked car. Fortunately, it was an old tank and didn't have a scratch. My bumper was so crumpled I couldn't drive it further.*

I had to go to my friend's house, tell them I hit their car, and ask to call my parents. Having to make this call was a natural consequence I couldn't avoid. Fortunately, the friend's family was nice about the accident. My mom was calm and I was impressed that she first asked "Are you okay?" before asking about the car. "We'll discuss this when you get home," she said.

*My dad drove me home. He didn't say a word. Now I knew I was in **big** trouble. I had already thought about what I did and what should be done about it. When I arrived home, my mother first asked me what happened and then listened. I told her and then handed her my driver's license and bank book. I restricted myself to the house for three weeks and gave up my phone privileges.*

She accepted the license, saying, "You can get your license back when you pay for the damages." She looked in the bank book and said, "This is not enough to cover the damage to the car. You'll need to do some extra work to make up the difference." She accepted my restriction to the house, but said it would only last until I had paid for the damages to the car. She then said, "Your phone has nothing to do with driving. Besides, if you are stuck in the house that long, you'll never survive without your phone."

I learned a lot from this experience. This was the worst thing I had ever done, yet my mom treated me with respect throughout our problem solving. I was so impressed that she changed the illogical part of my self-discipline, even though she was disappointed and angry. My parents didn't have to enforce this discipline; I did it myself. Since I came up with the discipline, I couldn't shift the responsibility for what I did to someone else. By the time I had worked through my self-imposed guilt, I had earned the money, repaired the car, and I was ready to drive more safely. I didn't have another accident for 20 years, and that one was the other guy's fault!

Ask questions, instead of lecturing. When parents are faced with disciplining their children, they often *tell* children what happened, how children should feel about what happened, and what they should do next time. They think they are "teaching" them a lesson, but they are really taking on full responsibility for pulling the "lesson" together. The F-A-X process we learned in the Child Problem Toolbox helps children figure out the "lesson." Parents ask questions that draw the information out and help children piece together the puzzle for themselves. This approach helps children learn from their own answers. It prevents parental lectures that children tune

> **Did you know . . .**
> *The original meaning of the word "educate" is "to draw forth" information? Yet, so often we try to teach by cramming information into people.*

out and keeps the ball in the child's court, where it belongs. Acceptable questions avoid the word "why," which puts children on the defensive. Instead, ask "what" and "how" questions, such as the following:

- What can you do to show you have learned _____ and are ready to be responsible for _____?
- What happened?
- What caused this?
- What were you trying to accomplish?
- How do you feel about what happened?
- What did you learn?
- What could you do differently next time?
- What should your discipline be?
- What would that teach you about _____?

Use a matter-of-fact, friendly tone-of-voice and pause between each question, or children feel they're being grilled.

Start with verbal agreements. Written contracts can be disrespectful and send the message that parents don't trust children to keep their agreements. If children forget, simply remind them once of the agreement and follow through with your end of it. Use nonverbal reminders after that. (See problem solving in Chapter 10 for ideas.) Let written agreements serve as reminders, not evidence of guilt.

The following story is a good example of how disciplinary problem solving actually sounds. The story involves the two boys who climbed on the roof—it seems that summer they were into testing limits. The mother said her son had never been in trouble before he climbed on the roof. With great credit to her handling of this situation, she says he has not severely tested limits or gotten into any trouble since then (1993).

> ***A Graduate's Story.*** *My son, Isaac, and his friend, Aaron, asked if they could ride their bikes to a convenience store. Aaron's mother and I both said the store was too far. It was also too dangerous to ride through the woods (and against park rules) and cross a four-lane intersection to get there. So the boys got permission to ride their bikes as far as the park and then sneaked off to the store. When they arrived, Aaron began shaking pop cans. Isaac was not causing any trouble and he repeatedly told Aaron to stop. When Aaron refused to behave, Isaac started to leave—but it was too late. The cashier had already called the police. Both boys had to sit in the back of a police car while he called their parents.*
>
> *As I drove the boys home, I could tell they had been crying. Isaac looked really angry, too. I asked them both, "So, what did you learn?" Isaac didn't answer. Aaron said, "Not to go to the store without permission." I asked him, "What else?" He added, "To treat the stuff in the store with respect." I only added, "Well you'll need to work this out with your parents. I assume you know we won't be seeing you for a while." He nodded. I gave Aaron a hug and wished him luck in telling his parents.*
>
> *I asked Isaac to wait in his room while I pulled my emotions and thoughts together. "Sitting in a police car was already a consequence that imposed suffering," I thought. Since Isaac wasn't the one who was causing the trouble in the store, I didn't think I had to be extra hard on him. Nevertheless, discipline was still in order, since Isaac knew he wasn't supposed to ride his bike through the park or to the store. I went to Isaac's room and sat on his bed. "What happened?" I asked. Isaac didn't say anything. I was determined to listen and not lecture, so I sat quietly and waited—and waited—until Isaac finally told me the story. "What did you learn?" I asked. "Nothing," was Isaac's reply. "That's not the answer I'm looking for!" I said with raised eyebrows and a smile. "Not to go anywhere with Aaron," Isaac added. I summarized, "I guess you learned how you can get in trouble when the person you are with acts irresponsibly. It's important to choose your friends wisely, huh?" Isaac nodded in agreement. I continued, "You know, you showed good judgment in telling Aaron you were going to leave if he didn't stop," I said. "I guess next time you'll do that sooner, huh?" Isaac nodded.*
>
> *I needed to move into discipline. I knew I'd have to be careful not to lecture so I could keep Isaac involved, although he wasn't very talkative. I began, "You knew it was against the rules to go to the store, right?" Isaac nodded, "Yes." "Well, there are a couple issues here," I continued. "You rode your bikes beyond the park, where you told us you would be, to the store where you were not allowed to go. The cashier has said you and Aaron aren't allowed back in the store, so that takes care of that issue. What do you think the discipline should be for abusing your bike privileges?" Isaac suggested a bike restriction for three weeks. I suggested a regressive restriction, "How about no bike at all for one week. If all goes well, the next week, you can ride your bike on our street only. If you are responsible, the next week you can ride around our block, and the next you can ride one block over." Isaac agreed.*
>
> *"How long do you think you should be restricted from going to the park?" I asked. Isaac suggested, "Until Spring break," which was in one month. Although this was a long time, I agreed, adding a few conditions. "When Spring break arrives, you can go to the creek, but still can't go into the park without an adult or older teenager, okay?" Isaac nodded. "Anything else?" I asked.*

Isaac shook his head. Isaac and I gave each other a hug and he chose to stay in his room for a while. When he came out, I didn't say anything more about what happened. Isaac followed through on his discipline without any reminders.

 Reveal Logical Consequences

Logical consequences are the riskiest of all the discipline tools, because it is so easy to violate any one of the 4R's of discipline: The consequence is not logically *related* to the behavior or the logical connection is unclear. It is presented *disrespectfully,* is *unreasonable*, or is not *revealed* ahead of time.

These mistakes usually occur when parents choose or present consequences in anger. Taking time to calm down and plan an effective discipline is far better than rashly reacting and making one of these mistakes. During our think time, children can also be thinking about what they did and an appropriate discipline.

Identify the goal of the misbehavior before using logical consequences. Natural consequences are useful with *any* of the four goals of misbehavior. We aren't involved; we are simply letting nature take its course. When we use *logical* consequences, however, it's important to consider the child's misbehavior goal:

- Logical consequences are *only effective at the time of conflict* if the goal is *attention*. Parents must be careful, though, that their comments or actions don't give attention-seeking children an unintentional payoff. Stay detached and friendly.

- When the goal is *power* or *revenge,* logical consequences are most effective during a problem-solving session *after* a cooling-off period and *after* parents have defused the power or revenge cycle. Otherwise, any logical consequence will be interpreted as a power or revenge tactic. Some consequences make the *parent* suffer more than the child! A child stuck in the house for three weeks might drive parents crazy! Having to leave a restaurant or party deprives parents of their meal or adult company. Maybe, as in the latter example, the child *wanted* to leave! Now who is suffering and who "got their way"?

- Do *not* use natural and logical consequences when the goal is *giving up*. It usually causes more discouragement. Consider other options listed in the "Giving Up" section of the PO Toolset.

Logical consequences are not always appropriate for very young children or teens.

- Logical consequences are rarely appropriate for **babies**, because they cannot think logically. Of course, when there's a problem with a baby's behavior, there can be some kind of discipline. For example, if an infant grabs the parent's glasses or earrings, the parent can hold the baby's hand or place the infant on the floor (taking action).

- *Young children* often don't understand the logic of the consequence but can still learn cause and effect. "When I do ___, ___ happens." Since young children have short memories, the lesson may not last long. This is why we want to use the PU Toolset before or in combination with discipline.

- Logical consequences are usually not effective with *teenagers*. Since teens are in a developmental stage that revolves around power and independence, they see logical consequences as a means of being controlled. A more effective tool is to use problem solving to reveal or decide discipline.

Follow through as soon as possible, even if it is inconvenient for the child. I call this an "inconvenience consequence." If children are upstairs playing and have left the TV on, call them downstairs to turn it off. Yes, we *are* sitting right there, but if they turned the TV on, it is their responsibility to turn it off. Don't go out of your way, however, to *make* a consequence inconvenient.

> *A **Personal Story.** Fall was ending and winter was arriving. I had kept the front door open for months, but had the heat on now and wanted the front door closed. Chris was not used to closing the door behind him. The first time he forgot, I called him in and explained, "I have the heat on now. You need to remember to close the front door when you leave." "Okay, Mom," he replied. The next time I walked through the living room I found the door open again! (I knew it was still PU. Although I had explained, it was still reasonable that he'd forget.) I called to him, saying "Chris, the door is open!" He came running back to close the door. I revealed a consequence, "If you want to play outside, you need to remember to close the door behind you. If I find the door left open again, I'll know you've decided to play inside." "Okay, Mom," he replied. Again, I found the door open. I felt bad having to call him in, but I did anyway. All I said was, "Chris! Door!" He yelled to his friends, "I gotta go inside now!" and he came running. He said, "Sorry, Mom," and went downstairs to find something else to do.*

You may be thinking your children wouldn't be this cooperative. (Remember that I'm already seeing the long-term benefits of using the Universal Blueprint. I am *not* immune, however, to problems!) At first, children might think we are being unreasonable. Don't get into power struggles; acknowledge the inconvenience and the value behind the request. Follow through consistently, or children will try to negotiate exceptions to the rules.

There is never just one possible logical consequence for a problem situation. Logical consequences often take great thought, creativity, and effort, which is why we want to use them sparingly. Here are a few examples of logical consequences:

- Beth runs up and down the aisles of the grocery store and almost ran into another cart. She can either hold on to the cart or ride in it.

- Donna, 14, forgot to lock the house in the morning when she was the last one out. She needs to develop a reminder plan to prevent it from happening again. If it happens again, she will need to wait for the bus outside. She can try being responsible for locking the house again the next day, with the time increased every time she forgets.

Use Self-Control Time-outs

Time-outs are one of the most misunderstood and misused discipline tools around.[5] Myths and inaccurate information thrive among parents and professionals. Most parents are familiar with the ineffective time-out process: *make* children go to a chair, room, or isolated spot *every* time they misbehave. The parent sets a *timer* (one minute for every year in age), and the *parent* makes sure the child has no fun while there. Everything about this time-out is decided and controlled by the parent. This type of "power time-out" is punishment and implies, "You are bad and I'm going to make sure you suffer for what you did." When you think a time-out is needed, ask yourself, "Do I want to give my children a chance to feel better and behave more constructively, or do I simply want to shame them or control their behavior?"

Imagine, for a moment, that *you* are so angry you are ready to lose control. If someone made you sit still in a chair and say nothing one minute for each year of *your* age, could you do it? Who says it should take me 40 minutes to calm down and my son 15 minutes? What if we're calm sooner and still have to sit there? Would you feel better or more angry? Would you feel resentful and think about revenge? Most parents would agree that "power" time-outs wouldn't work for them if *they* were angry. So why do we think this will work with children who usually have poorer anger management skills than we do?

Healthy, effective time-outs meet each of the "Four R's of Discipline."

Since the purpose of healthy time-outs is to regain self-control, they are only logically related to behavior that suggests the child has lost control. (Otherwise, use another, more appropriate discipline tool.) Time-outs are usually only appropriate for very disruptive or aggressive behavior that could possibly be harmful to the child or others, such as hitting, biting, or throwing. Actually, ***time-out is a Keep Your Cool tool, more than a discipline tool.*** (Parents wouldn't look for it there, so I put it here!) Healthy time-outs are useful for parents *and* children. They provide a way to calm down, before anger (or misbehavior) gets out of control.

Reveal the plan in advance. Teach children, during a happy time, about the value of a cooling-off period and the importance of waiting until everyone feels better before trying to solve conflicts. Explain that the purpose of a time-out is to calm down, not to punish or to suffer. It is not a time to sit and think about how bad they are, to do work, to write sentences, or anything else that would be punishing or humiliating. Time-outs are a time to do whatever we need to do to feel better and work through upsetting feelings or bad moods. Our goal is to work through feelings so we can talk calmly about solutions to the problem.

Present time-outs in a respectful way. Time-outs are respectful only when children know the purpose is to help them feel better and work toward solving a problem. Shame and humiliation make them feel more discouraged and more motivated to misbehave. ***Present the time-out as a choice.*** A child can choose to do problem solving or calm down first. Ask, "Do you want to talk about this?" Or "What would help you most right now?" If children resist, change the focus of the choices as you follow through, as in the following example.

1. "Would you like to (positive behavior) or would you like to go to (your room or other place) and (anger energy release activity) until you calm down?"

2. If children continue to resist and are still out-of-control, say, "I see you need to ("go to your room," for example). Are you going to go by yourself, or do you need help?"

3. If children don't go on their own, say "I see you need my help." Kindly and firmly guide them to the room (or other location). If they come out, it is often a sign that the child is an external recharger. (See the next section about choosing time-out locations.) If the child is an internal recharger, but is trying to get attention or power, say, "When you've calmed down, you can join me again and work out a solution."

4. If children cry and plead, "I'm calm! I'll be good," say, "I'll know you are calm and ready to come out when I hear you've ____." Give a mental checklist, such as ". . . stopped crying and are breathing and talking calmly." Stay calm yourself and ignore any attention-seeking behavior. Often, you will hear them doing each suggestion *in order!*

If we fail to present each escalating step as a choice, it turns the time-out into a power play. Ultimately, if we consistently follow through with this plan, children begin to put *themselves* into time-out. This is an excellent sign that they are learning self-control and recognize when they are about to lose control.

Select a location for the time-out. Involve children (if old enough) in selecting the location of time-outs; almost anyplace is appropriate. Remember the different recharge styles you learned about in the Keep Your Cool Toolset, internal and external. Decide whether the child needs a lack of stimulation and isolation (internal) or company and stimulation (external) to calm down and recharge their energy. Select a location according to the needs of the individual child, according to the following categories:"

*   ***Internal recharge*** children will benefit from the privacy of their rooms or any place away from others. They might also benefit from being outside by themselves. If these children don't get enough time alone, their behavior can deteriorate. If they are in a group and can't be alone, teach them to find a quiet corner or sit slightly out of the group. Don't pressure internal recharge children to stay in a group. The interruptions and demands rob them of energy.

*   ***External recharge*** children get their energy from people. Being with people helps them calm down. Traditional time-outs, which isolate children, can make their behavior *worse!* They often

grieve as though they were being rejected, crying even harder when alone. If children won't stay in their rooms, follow parents, or their behavior escalates when they are alone, it is a good sign they are external rechargers. Let these children take a time-out on your lap, a chair in the same room, or outside. If your comfort calms them down, they are surely external rechargers. If they don't calm down, they may be seeking attention. Offer a gentle hug, while ignoring bids for attention. (*Gentle* touch is the key here. Avoid squeezing or using any other excessive force.)

Some parents hesitate to use a child's room for fear the child will view the bedroom as a prison. If the time-out is presented respectfully and the goal is to give the child and parent some quiet space, it will seem like a safe place, not a punishment. If you are in public, a restaurant for example, you can use a progressive time-out, where each step removes the child farther from the action.

A Personal Story. Whenever we waited for a meal when our children were young, we'd pass the time with quiet activities (Step A: Prevent the problem). Sometimes, one of the kids would get too wound-up at the table or begin to throw a tantrum. We Acknowledged their feelings and Set limits, "I know it's hard to wait when you're hungry, but we all need to be quiet so we don't bother others while they're eating." (Steps B and C1). We'd try to Redirect their behavior by focusing on the activities they could do (Step C2). If the tantrum began to escalate, we'd Reveal discipline (Step C2), "If you're too loud, we'll need to leave the table." If the behavior didn't subside, my husband or I would begin our public time-out plan. (I'll use my daughter and me as an example.)

I'd take her by the hand and walk to the bathroom saying, "Let's wash our hands." If she resisted, I'd gently pick her up and carry her quickly. Once in the bathroom, I would talk to her gently and firmly as we washed our hands. If she was having a tantrum, I'd try to soothe her by acknowledging her feelings while setting firm limits. If her tantrum started to echo, I'd offer a new choice, "You can settle down here and go back to the table or we can go outside." She usually settled down. If she didn't, I'd make a hasty retreat out the door.

We'd sit outside, somewhere away from the door. I'd put my arm around her gently, but firmly enough to prevent her from flailing her arms or legs or leaving. I'd say, "When you stop crying and calm down, we can go back inside." I'd take a deep breath, loud enough for her to hear, so I could model calming down. (I usually needed it to keep my cool!) I'd try to ignore her behavior, distracting myself by looking at cars, people, trees blowing in the wind—anything to help me stay calm and detached from her tantrum. If she begged to go back inside or was getting more upset, I'd remind her that we could go back inside, when she calmed down.

Once she had stopped crying, I'd help her wipe her tears and compose herself. I'd give her a hug, acknowledge her feelings, and get an agreement for her future behavior. We'd walk back to the table and get her involved in an activity or her food, if it had arrived. We only had to use this plan several times. Our kids quickly learned the consequence for disruptive behavior in public and chose to be involved in the fun activities or conversation we offered. We have even received compliments from strangers about our children's patience and behavior in public.

Time-out activities. We want to structure time-outs so children can learn to calm down and regain self-control. When discussing time-outs with children ask, "When you feel like you've lost control, what can you do to feel better?" Many parents are upset if their children are happy to go to their rooms or play while in time-out. This is buying into the "kids must suffer" belief of punishment.

If children play during time-out, it shows they have regained some self-control; the time-out worked. Don't worry that children will misbehave so they can go in a time-out. We aren't "rewarding" misbehavior by allowing children to play; we are teaching them anger/stress management techniques to help them regain self-control. Eventually, children will put *themselves* in time-out *before* they lose control. Also, children don't have to come out of the time-out if they don't want to—unless they are trying to avoid problem solving.

Use the Keep Your Cool Toolset to offer suggestions for what children can do while in the time-out to channel their verbal and physical anger energy. Combine the anger energy and recharge style ideas to plan the most appropriate time-out for each child's individual needs. Here are a few examples:

Child's Anger/Recharge Style	Appropriate Time-Out Activities
Verbal anger, internal recharge	Scream in a pillow *in their room*, color, draw, read, write, listen to tapes, sing to self or play quietly.
Verbal anger, external recharge	Talk to a friend, parent, or stuffed animal, *sit on a nearby chair* or a parent's lap.
Physical anger, internal recharge	Hit a pillow or punching bag. Pound an inflatable hammer *in their room*. Outside they can take a walk, run around the yard, or swing *alone*.
Physical anger, external recharge	Swing or play catch *outside* with a parent or friend.

If you think children will be destructive, plan ahead by removing things you don't want destroyed. Suggest physical anger energy activities to channel the energy in an appropriate way. If children destroy their own toys, they'll experience the result of no longer having the toy. Don't buy any new toys (except holiday gifts) until they show that they can respect the toys they have. If parents can stay calm, they can "coach" children through the anger energy activities.

> *A Graduate's Story. When my 12-month-old toddler began to scream and hit, I scooped her up and took her to her room. There, I would find something she was allowed to hit. She particularly liked shaking a pair of maracas. I would help her hold the maracas and show her how to shake them or bang them on her bed. I would reflect her feelings and coach her, saying things like, "That's it! You're really angry, aren't you? Bang those maracas!"*

> *Soon, when I took her to her room, my daughter grabbed the maracas herself. Then I only needed to help her get to her room. Eventually, all it took was a suggestion to "go to your room and get your angry energy out." At 18 months, my daughter was putting herself in time-out! Better yet, she used words (instead of screams) to express her feelings. What shocked me most, was that I started this process before she could talk, so as my daughter began talking, she immediately used the verbal skills I had taught her. I realized that my daughter was understanding and learning before she could put the skills into practice on her own. When she was able, she used the anger management skills I had taught her.*

Plan a reasonable length of time. Avoid using timers and allow children to return when they have regained self-control or show they are ready to act appropriately.

I don't know who thought of the idea of setting a timer for one minute per year of age, but I wish I had a dime for every time someone has repeated that time-out rule. Timers teach children that they don't have to calm down until the timer goes off. Also, if children show they have calmed down and the timer hasn't stopped, it turns the time-out into a power struggle. Timers also make the parent responsible for controlling the child, instead of the child developing self-control.

> *A Personal Story. Before my friend Vickie moved, we tried to have lunch several times. Every time, she had to leave due to her three-year-old son's behavior. One of Vickie's strengths as a parent was her consistency in following through. She had learned that time-outs were to be "one minute for every year of age." When her son didn't settle down, she'd give him a choice: he could either settle down or go in a time-out. When he didn't calm down, she made him sit on a chair and*

set her watch for three minutes. Within about 30 seconds, her son calmly sat there and explained what he had learned and described what he would do differently. He seemed sincere. Since Vickie said the time-out would last three minutes, her son had to wait the full three minutes. He started pleading to get out of the time-out. After two minutes, he was crumbling into a tantrum again, this time from not getting out of the time-out.

Vickie warned him that if he didn't calm down by the end of the three minutes, another three minutes would be added. When three minutes were up, he still wasn't calm. Vickie gave her son a new choice; if he didn't calm down when this three minutes was over, they'd go home. Again, the same thing happened—he calmed down before the time was up and a power struggle developed over whether he could come out of the time-out. This time, when he was crying at the end of the time-out, Vickie left. That was what she said, so that was what she had to do. We never did finish a meal together. Her son smiled as his mother left the boring lunch setting and I stayed and finished lunch with my kids, who had watched the entire spectacle.

I want to emphasize that Vickie is a terrific parent. She, like many other parents and professionals, had heard commonly accepted (but ineffective) information about time-outs and consistency. Her experience shows that even using a power tool in a respectful way will still produce a power struggle.

When a time-out is over:

- ***If the behavior that caused the time-out was serious or is a recurring problem, you can do some brief problem solving when the time-out is over.*** This type of time-out is a step toward discipline; before any further discussion or problem solving occurs, both parties must calm down. This time-out ends when the child is calm enough to do brief problem solving.

- ***If the time-out was simply a matter of calming down, don't discuss the misbehavior further.*** It will only call attention to the behavior you want to stop. This type of time-out is a discipline in itself. Its focus is on learning or practicing anger management and respectful assertive communication skills.

DISCIPLINE CHECKLIST

Before or during discipline, ask yourself the following questions:

- **Is discipline really necessary?** Could I use the prevention, communication, or behavior management skills before or instead of discipline?

- **Have I skipped steps in the Universal Blueprint that could address the behavior?** (If you skip the PO Toolset, your discipline could turn into a power play or revenge.)

- **How will my child interpret the discipline?** (View your words and actions as children do.)

- **Am I focusing on suffering or learning?** Am I adding extra suffering? What do I want to teach? Will this discipline teach this lesson?

- **Am I making a power play or threat?** ("If you . . . I'll . . .") Am I revealing discipline respectfully, as a choice? ("If you choose to . . ., I'll know you've decided to . . .")

- **Am I using positive words?** (Avoid "if you don't stop . . ." Instead, say "You need to . . .")

- **Am I controlling my emotions and tone of voice?** (Volume is as important as the content. Keep your cool and respectfully communicate.)

- **Is my discipline logically related?** Is the logical connection obvious to my child? If not, have I stated it?

- **Is there any natural consequence I can allow to happen that isn't dangerous or too far in the future?**

- **Is this discipline reasonable?** Am I giving my child information about the positive behavior I want to see and another chance, as soon as possible, to change the behavior?

- **Can I use problem solving to either avoid discipline, reveal it for the next time, or decide what discipline is appropriate in this situation?**

- **Am I shifting gears to listening, allowing my child the chance to express feelings?** (Remain emotionally detached and respectful, not defensive. You can acknowledge children's feelings about the discipline, without agreeing or changing the discipline.)

USING THE DECISION-MAKING WORKSHEET

If we really want to eliminate problem behavior, not just simply respond to it, we need to have a plan that uses tools at every step. To help you remember the steps, use the "Decision-Making Worksheet" that follows the summary sheet. Use it to plan a solution to *any* type of problem. If we plan what we want to say and do, it helps us keep our cool and respond consistently and effectively. Refer to the detailed blueprint (house diagram) at the end of the book for individual tools or hints for using the different toolsets. It is the entire book summarized on one page.

In the practice exercises that follow the summary sheet and Decision-Making Worksheet, we will follow the Universal PASRR steps outlined on the worksheet. Feel free to make extra copies of the worksheet, so you don't have to write in your book.

SUMMARY SHEET
DISCIPLINE TOOLSET

- Discipline helps children learn *from* mistakes, not suffer *for* them. Focus on solutions, not blame or shame.

- Children are responsible for controlling their own behavior. Parents are responsible for providing appropriate behavior choices and holding children accountable for their poor behavior choices.

- Discipline is *respectfully revealed*, whenever possible, as a choice. "If you choose to (misbehavior) I'll know you've decided to (discipline)."

- Discipline is logically *related* to the misbehavior. If it's not obvious, state the logical connection.

- Discipline is *reasonable*. The time and extent should be the least restrictive, giving children a chance to change or try again soon.

DISCIPLINE TOOLS

- Show children how to make amends. ☆☆☆☆

- Offer choices. ☆☆☆☆
  Alter the focus of the choices as issues shift.

- Take action. ☆☆☆☆
  Decide what *you* will do, not what you will make children do. Respectfully follow through, with or without words, with reasonable, related actions.

- Allow natural consequences. ☆☆☆☆
  They happen if parents do nothing to rescue. Only use if they are quick and safe. Ask, "What did you learn?"

- Apply Restrictions that are logically related to an abuse of a privilege or right. Don't restrict responsibilities or privileges children already earned.

- Use Problem Solving to prevent, reveal, or decide discipline. ☆☆☆☆
  "I am concerned about (misbehavior). What can we do to make sure this doesn't happen again?"

- Reveal Logical Consequences that meet the Four R's. Use them sparingly.

- Use Self-control Time-outs that teach anger and stress management.
  - ➤ Choose the location based on the child's internal/external recharge style.
  - ➤ Allow children to do calming activities (verbal/physical anger energy).
  - ➤ Time-outs are over when children have calmed down. No timers!
  - ➤ When a time-out is over, it's over, unless problem solving is needed.

PARENT'S DECISION-MAKING WORKSHEET

SITUATION/PROBLEM: _____

_____

_____

WHAT TYPE OF PROBLEM IS IT? (NO, C, P, PU, PO, C/P, C/PU, C/PO)	_____
(Any SHARP RV issues? No = C, Yes = P. Is misbehavior PU or PO? Has child consistently
shown mastery of the skill? No = PU, Yes = PO? Is this a combination problem?)

IF PO, WHAT IS THE GOAL? (Attention, Power, Revenge, Giving up?)	_____

STEP A: <u>P</u>REVENT THE PROBLEM from starting or worsening (Prevention Toolbox: Foundation-Building, Self-Esteem, Cooperation, and/or Independence Toolsets)

_____

_____

_____

PLAN A RESPONSE, USING THE APPROPRIATE TOOLSETS:

STEP B: <u>A</u>CKNOWLEDGE FEELINGS (Child Problem Toolbox: Step B1: Focus on feelings, Step B2: Ask helpful questions, Step B3: X-amine possible options)

_____

_____

STEP C1: <u>S</u>ET LIMITS and/or express concerns (Clear Communication Toolset)

_____

_____

STEP C2: <u>R</u>EDIRECT BEHAVIOR (If PU, what skill do you teach? If PO, break the cycle.)

_____

_____

STEP C3: <u>R</u>EVEAL DISCIPLINE (Must be Related, Respectful, and Reasonable. Use
problem solving to decide?)

_____

_____

PRACTICE EXERCISES

Since discipline is usually the final step in responding to a problem, consider other alternatives first in the following situations. For each situation, apply the Universal Blueprint steps as outlined in the Decision-Making Worksheet:

Identify the type of Parent problem (P, PU, PO, or C/P, C/PU, C/PO). Apply the PASRR formula.

Step A: **P**revent the problem from starting or worsening (Prevention Toolbox: Self-Esteem, Cooperation, and/or Independence Toolsets).

Step B: **A**cknowledge feelings with the F-A-X Listening Toolset.

Step C1:   **S**et limits using the Clear Communication Toolset.

Step C2:   **R**edirect the behavior with either the PU or PO Toolsets. (If it is PO, identify the goal and break the cycle.)

Step C3:   Then **R**eveal an appropriate discipline.

Try to move through all the steps in a total of two or three sentences. (Detailed possible answers are at the end of the chapter.)

1.   Derek, 2, screams and refuses to cooperate when you try to buckle him into his car seat.

2.   Elizabeth, 3, has written her name and drawn on her bedroom wall with a crayon and ballpoint pen.

3.   Nicole, 6, and Kristin, 3, have made a game out of bedtime. They take forever getting ready and make up lame excuses to stay up longer. To keep them moving, their mother can spend nearly an hour reminding them.

4.   Margie, 5, is a picky eater. She eats very little and is unwilling to try new foods. She expects her mother to fix her something special for every meal and refuses to eat if her mother doesn't comply. When she does eat, it takes her hours!

5.   Gene, 8, was playing with a stick, hitting the branches of a neighbor's tree. There are branches all over the ground when the neighbor comes to Gene's father to complain.

6.   Patrick, 7, takes so long getting ready in the morning that he frequently misses the school bus.

7.   Ethan, 10, got a phone call from a girl, but wouldn't tell his mother who it was or what she wanted. He asked if he could take a walk. When his father came home, he said he saw Ethan walking with a girl on the other side of a dangerous four-lane street. Ethan did not have permission to go beyond his neighborhood boundaries. When Ethan returned and was confronted, he said the girl asked him to help her sell candy (which was true). Although he had never been willing to do door-to-door sales himself, he wanted to help this girl friend.

8.   Dustin, 14, went to the state fair with his parents. He wanted to explore on his own and agreed to meet his parents at a certain time. He didn't keep his agreement. After his parents searched for more than an hour, he showed up.

9.   Susan, 14, was caught with drugs at school. She is a straight-A student who has never been in trouble. Susan said: A boy walked past her locker, stuffed a bag of marijuana in her purse, and said, "Just keep this until next period and Joey will get it from you" as he walked away. She was shocked and dumbfounded. She didn't know what to do. The school bell rang and she was afraid to be late to class. She was debating what to do throughout that class period. Another student saw the bag in her purse and reported her. The boy admits giving her the bag and someone else admits he was going to buy it. They both confirm that Susan was simply an innocent victim. Nevertheless, the school policy says she must be referred to Juvenile Court. What should Susan's mother do or say?

Detailed Answers

1. Derek, 2, screams and refuses to cooperate when his parent tries to buckle him into his car seat.

   Type of problem: PU and PO. Derek doesn't understand the purpose or importance of a car seat (PU). He is also exerting his *power* (PO), because he doesn't like being confined. Safety is more important than comfort.

   Prevent the problem: The parent can demonstrate, during a "no problem" time, with a doll or egg and a toy vehicle, what happens when there is an accident and someone isn't using a seat belt or car seat. Ask "What happened? What would have happened if the doll/egg had on a seat belt?"

   Acknowledge feelings, **S**et limits, and **R**edirect behavior: Acknowledge Derek's feelings about being strapped in the car seat, "I know you hate being stuck in that car seat, but it will keep you safe if we ever have an accident. You can climb in on your own or I can put you in the car seat. You decide." Brainstorm ways Derek can have power in the situation. He can learn to buckle himself and can select some special toys to play with.

   Reveal discipline: If Derek resists, say, "I can see you want me to put you in the car seat this time. Next time, you can climb in yourself." Use gentle force to get him in the car seat. Keep a friendly, matter-of-fact tone of voice. Offer toys or songs as a distraction. Briefly acknowledge his wails, but don't give them extra attention. Parents can sing a song to themselves or turn on the radio to help them keep their cool.

2. Elizabeth, 3, has written her name and drawn on her bedroom wall with a crayon and ballpoint pen.

   Type of problem: PU. It is age-appropriate for children to want to draw anywhere and with anything, even though they've been told "a million times."

   Prevent the problem: Try to keep all drawing materials out of reach, although this will be difficult. Make sure she knows what she *is* allowed to color with and on. You may need to repeat quite often, Pens are for paper," and "Keep the crayons on paper." For some kids this is enough to prevent further problems.

   Acknowledge feelings, **S**et limits, and **R**edirect behavior: "I know you really enjoy drawing, but crayons and pens ruin walls. It's going to be very hard to get this off your wall."

   Reveal discipline: "I can see you aren't ready to keep your pens and crayons on paper. We'll need to   put them up until this mess is cleaned—and I'll need your help." Allow her to do as much as she is capable of doing. She might be able to spray the cleanser and use a sponge by herself. Have her work on it a little longer than she wants to. Work together; when she stops, you stop. If you have cleaned all you can and it won't come off (hint: use "white out" on the pen), she will have to live with messy walls until you can paint again. By the time you have the time and money to repaint the room, the child will probably be older. Say, "I bet you are tired of looking at the writing on these walls. If I paint your walls, will you keep them nice and clean?" If the child has had to live with the effects of her actions for a while, she'll most likely remember and follow through.

3. Nicole, 6, and Kristin, 3, make a game out of bedtime.

   Type of problem: PO and PU. Nicole understands the rules (PO), but Kristin is probably imitating Nicole (PU). Nicole makes excuses to keep the parent involved (*attention*) and/or to delay bedtime (*power*).

   Prevent the problem: Make bedtime a positive experience. The routine should allow time to unwind and talk. (See "Bedtime Routines" in Chapter 5, "Cooperation Toolset.")

   Acknowledge feelings, **S**et limits, and **R**edirect behavior: Use any one of these responses to acknowledge feelings: "I know you don't want to go to bed." "I know you don't feel tired." or "It's hard to have to go to bed when you don't want to." Now, set limits, "I know you want to have fun at bedtime, but I don't think either of us has much fun when I'm reminding and nagging you to get ready."

Reveal discipline: "I am willing to spend a half-hour for bedtime. This includes the time it takes you to get ready. You can spend all this time getting ready or you can get ready quickly and have time to play a special game. You decide." Mother can be available during that time, but not remind or nag. Everyone can also brainstorm ideas to make the bedtime routine go smoother.

If children make lame excuses, try putting a limit on how many times they can get up. You can put three ribbons on the doorknob or three balls in a bowl. Each time the child comes out, she delivers one item to the parent. When the items are gone, the parent ignores the child as though she is in bed.

With both of the above plans, the parent can reveal one final discipline—however late the child goes to bed, that's how much earlier she has to go to bed the following night. It is important to reveal this plan in advance. Otherwise, it will turn into a power struggle.

4. Margie, 5, is a picky, slow eater.

   Type of problem: PO. This mealtime battle is *not* about hunger. If Margie's mother caters to her, she feels important (*attention*). Eating (or not eating) is also a way children can feel in control (*power*).

   Prevent the problem: Many mealtime battles are preventable. We've already learned many ideas for making mealtimes smoother. (See suggestions in Chapters 5, 6, and 11, the Cooperation, Independence, and PU Toolsets.)

   Acknowledge feelings, Set limits, and Redirect behavior: If, despite preventive measures, children still complain and resist, parents can remain firm to their bottom-line limits. They could say any of the following: "I know this is not your favorite food, but I expect you to try at least one small bite." "This is what we are having tonight. I'm unwilling to fix separate meals. You can decide whether you want to eat." "I'm willing to prepare some things you like to eat, if you're willing to help me plan menus." "You don't have to like what I fix, but I don't want to hear criticism."

   Reveal discipline: Make it clear that there will be no more food until the next meal. Snacks are only allowed for those who eat healthy meals. If she refuses to eat, allow her to experience the natural effect of hunger.

   Decide if slow eaters are simply taking their time (which is healthy) or are getting distracted. Allow children a reasonable amount of time (no longer than an hour) *if* they concentrate on eating. Once the reasonable, tangible time limit is up, put away the food. Do *all* these disciplines in a matter-of-fact, friendly way. If parents become abusive and domineering about food, eating disorders can develop.

5. Gene, 8, was playing with a stick, hitting the branches of a neighbor's tree. There are branches all over the ground when the neighbor comes to Gene's father to complain.

   Type of problem: PU. Gene meant to hit the tree, but he was just playing. He probably didn't realize he would damage the tree. Once more than a few branches were knocked off, he realized he was hurting the tree and stopped. He probably didn't think about picking up the branches or confessing his wrong. Only if Gene hated the neighbor and was getting revenge would you consider this to be intentional (PO) behavior.

   Prevent the problem: Teach children in a NO-problem time that they are to treat all people and things with respect. They should think about the effects of their actions and make amends for their mistakes. These rules are for life, not just for any particular incident. If children are taught these lessons, it will reduce intentionally destructive behavior. You may not, however, be able to prevent unintentional mistakes like Gene's.

   Acknowledge feelings, Set limits, and Redirect behavior: "I know how much you enjoy playing with sticks, but you need to be thinking about what you are hitting. You need to keep your stick away from people or things that could get hurt."

Reveal discipline: This incident seems to have risen unexpectedly, with no chance to reveal discipline ahead of time. Nevertheless, some discipline is indicated. Say, "You'll need to take responsibility for the damage to Mr. X's tree." Then have Gene pick up the branches and apologize to his neighbor. For the time being, Gene should not play in that neighbor's yard, until he can show he can play with sticks responsibly.

6. Patrick, 7, takes so long getting ready in the morning that he frequently misses the school bus.

Type of problem: PO, Attention or Power. If a child is old enough to go to school, he is old enough to be responsible for getting ready. Younger children will need more time and preplanning. They should still, however, be held accountable for getting ready and the results of being late.

Prevent the problem: Give children an alarm clock and show them how to set it. Have them make their lunch, check their backpacks, and choose clothes the night before. Have children get dressed first and eat last.

Acknowledge feelings, Set limits, and Redirect behavior: "Getting ready in the morning is tough! There are a lot of things to do and remember." "I'm willing to fix breakfast for you, but it's up to you to get up on time, get dressed by yourself, and leave yourself time to eat."

Reveal discipline: Avoid nagging, helping, and reminding. These prevent children from learning how to be responsible for themselves. If the child misses breakfast, allow the natural consequence of hunger. Remind him he'll have another chance to get ready on time and eat breakfast tomorrow. Few children experience this consequence more than once! Another natural consequence is to leave in whatever shape they are in. They may have to tie their shoes or brush their hair on the way to school. Children may also experience consequences at school, such as receiving a tardy mark. Refuse to lie if you are required to write any excuses to the school.

If your children ride a bus, you probably live too far for them to walk to school safely. If children can run to another bus stop, go for this option. Driving a late child raises a dilemma for parents. If we repeatedly drive them, we are rewarding their lateness and are taking responsibility for getting them to school. If we must drive a late child to school, we can do so with certain restrictions or conditions. Children can pay parents a "taxi" fee, wait for the parent to get ready, or be ready that much sooner the next day. Parents can time how long it takes to drive children to school and require them to do a chore for that amount of time when they come home.

7. Ethan, 10, lied so he could help a girl friend sell candy in an area beyond his boundaries.

Type of problem: PO. Ethan lied to protect his privacy; he didn't want his parents to know he was helping a girl friend. Ethan knew how far he was allowed to travel on his own and intentionally defied a rule (*power*).

Prevent the problem: Ethan knew his boundaries, so the parents did what they could to prevent this situation. The fact that Ethan was helping someone else, however, should not go unnoticed. Express admiration for Ethan's willingness to help a friend. Comment on his willingness to do something he is normally hesitant to do (sell door-to-door), but did it to help someone else.

Acknowledge feelings, Set limits, and Redirect behavior: "I understand your hesitancy to tell me you were going to see a girl. I know that can be an embarrassing thing to tell a parent, but you knew how far you were allowed to go. Had you asked me, I probably would have been willing to drive you to her neighborhood." If Ethan says he should be allowed to cross the dangerous street, the parent can say, "I know you feel ready to cross that street. Since it's a matter of life and death, I have to stand firm about the rule. You don't have to like the rule, but I still expect you to follow it."

Reveal discipline: The discipline for going beyond the neighborhood might have already been revealed. Use problem solving to decide discipline for the two issues, violating a rule and lying. Ethan can stay around the house or on his street for a few days. When his travel privileges are restored, he will need to tell his parents where he is and call home frequently. This last part relates to the parents' ability to regain their trust. Ethan's parents might check on him. If revealed ahead of time, this act is not a breach of privacy.

Do not allow Ethan's poor judgement to overshadow his good deed. Finish by summarizing, "What you did for your friend was very kind. Next time, although it's embarrassing for you, please *tell me* you want to go somewhere far. I promise not to tease you or ask you about anything I don't need to know."

8. Dustin, 14, was more than an hour late to meet his parents at the state fair. *(When I was at the state fair, I saw a father yelling at his son about being late. He smacked him across the head a few times. I could understand the father's anger, but was appalled at the violence.)*

Type of problem: Chances are this is a PU problem. Dustin might have forgotten the time or gotten stuck in a long ride. Maybe something really *did* happen to him. There was probably no way for Dustin to let them know he was running late. It is also possible that Dustin didn't care enough to keep his commitment (PO). Either way, discipline is still indicated.

Prevent the problem: When you split up a group in a large public place, cover all the angles in the meeting plan. Most importantly, make the details and the importance of the agreement are clear. (I once waited for my parents for over an hour at an amusement park. They were angry, until they realized *they* were at the wrong location. Now, I worry whenever I go places with my family or a large group and we split up.)

Acknowledge feelings, Set limits, and Redirect behavior: Dustin's angry parents need take a sigh of relief and get in touch with their *primary* feelings—concern and worry—and give Dustin a big hug. Then they can ask, "Do you know what time it is? We were worried something happened to you! What happened?" Hopefully, Dustin will have a good reason for being so late. If he simply lost track of time, the parents can *respectfully* address their concerns *after* Dustin explains himself. "It sounds like you were having a lot of fun and being on time wasn't on your mind. I can understand that, but we were seriously worried." Then they can problem solve.

Reveal discipline: The family should not separate again for awhile and use the experience in setting up future agreements. "If you want to go somewhere different the rest of this trip, one of us needs to be with you."

9. Susan, 14, was caught with drugs at school. The boy who set her up admits she was an innocent victim. *(This situation happened to a graduate's daughter. Fortunately, the mother had taken my parenting class and she and Susan were participating in the "Parents and Teens—Together" class at the time.)*

Type of problem: In *this* situation, it's PU. (See the Chapter 12 answer key for information on PO drug use.) The mother had talked with her about such a hypothetical situation, but neither she nor Susan ever dreamed something like this would really happen. The particular circumstances happened so fast, Susan felt confused and she waited too long, instead of immediately going to the principal herself.

Prevent the problem: Susan's mother can show Susan unconditional love and support. She can give Susan credit for staying "straight" and doing the best she can to stay out of trouble. (The boy got her in trouble more than she got herself into it.) Most importantly, since the boy admitted she was an innocent participant, Susan's mother can reassure her that she trusts her and believes her story.

Acknowledge feelings, Set limits, and Redirect behavior: Susan's mother needs to do a *lot* of F-A-X listening and problem solving with Susan. She can recognize the predicament Susan felt when she was handed the bag and her fears about being referred to court. It is *very* important, however, that Susan's mother not make excuses for her or "bail her out" of the situation. This is *Susan's* problem. Mother's responsibility is to help Susan work through her feelings and help her learn an important lesson from the experience.

Reveal discipline: The police and court system are setting the consequences. Susan's mother doesn't need to add any other discipline. She can point out, in a matter-of-fact, friendly way, that when Susan made the decision not to report the drugs to the principal, she was taking the risk of getting caught, which is what happened. Now she must experience the results of that choice.

The mother in this situation did all these things. She told the principal, police, and judge about the parenting class and teen group she and Susan were attending. The judge understood Susan's predicament, but the law is the law and he had to sentence her. He took all the factors into consideration and put Susan on probation until she was 16. Rather than sentencing her to jail time, he ordered her to do community service. Susan learned a rather hard, but important, lesson. Her mother was **extremely** grateful she had learned these parenting skills, because, she says, she would not have handled the situation nearly as helpfully had it happened before she took the parenting class.

WHAT'S NEXT?

When we use *all* the tools in *The Parent's Toolshop*, we prevent problems and redirect them before they reach the point of needing discipline. Therefore, we usually don't use the discipline tools daily. If this approach is different from what you have done in the past, you might start to punish, catch yourself, and adjust your response accordingly. Practice planning responses and choosing appropriate discipline, so you can respond quickly *and* effectively in the heat of the moment.

We have finished our tour of the Parent Problem Toolbox. We now have all the tools we need to prevent and effectively respond to problems. The last section, "Step D: Maintenance Toolbox," details the last step in the parenting process—maintaining progress. The first chapter in that section is Chapter 14, "Family Council Toolset." It details several council formats and offers a review of the tools we use when planning and holding family councils. Once we learn the basics, we can decide within our individual family the format that works best for our needs.

REFERENCES

1. For more information about the long-term consequences of spanking and other forms of corporal punishment (Some are quite surprising!), read *Plain Talk About Spanking*, published by PTAVE: Parents and Teachers Against Violence in Education. You can read this book, and dozens of other free articles about corporal punishment, on the Internet at www.nospank.org. You can also order a free sample copy by writing P.O. Box 1033, Alamo, CA 94507-7033 or calling (925) 831-1661. A donation is requested for bulk copies.

2. *American Medical Association's Archives of Pediatrics and Adolescent Medicine* (8/15/97). Research/report by Murray A. Straus, University of New Hampshire.

3. *Positive Discipline*, by Jane Nelsen (Ballantine, 1987; Revised Edition, 1996). The "Four R's of Punishment" were originally the "Three R's of Punishment." The third had two points, so I split them and changed the title to "Four R's," with the permission of Ms. Nelsen.

4. The "Four R's of Discipline" is a different title for Jane Nelsen's "Four R's of Consequences." Logical consequences are just one discipline tool, but the "Four R's of Discipline" apply to *all* discipline tools. Consequently, Ms. Nelsen gave me permission to expand on her original idea.

5. For more information about time-outs, read *Time Out: Abuses and Effective Uses*, by Jane Nelsen and H. Stephen Glenn (Empowering People, Inc., 1992).

STEP D
MAINTENANCE TOOLBOX

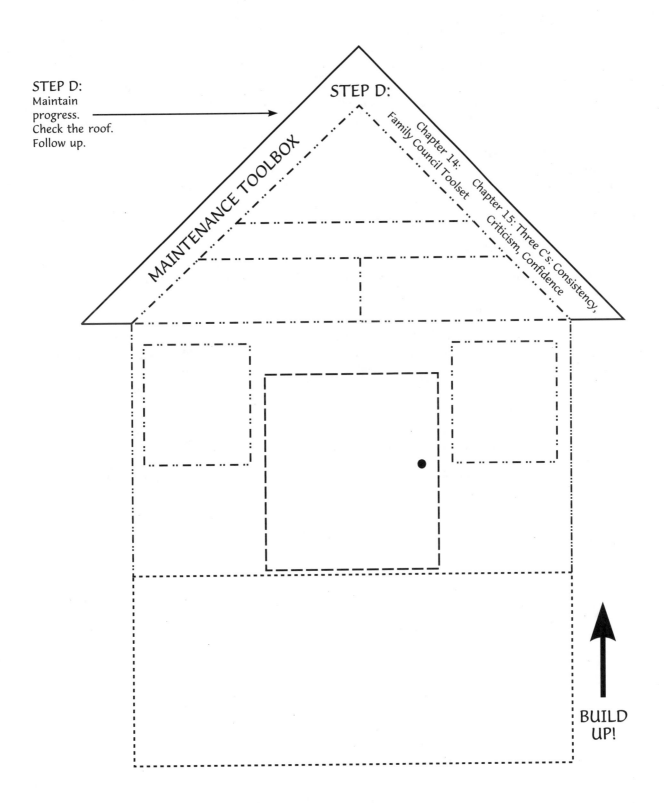

STEP D:
Maintain
progress.
Check the roof.
Follow up.

STEP D:

MAINTENANCE TOOLBOX

Chapter 14:
Family Council Toolset

Chapter 15: Three C's: Consistency,
Criticism, Confidence

BUILD
UP!

D MAINTENANCE TOOLBOX

Every home needs a roof, to protect the dwellers from harsh outside elements. The roof is always present; it doesn't just appear in stormy weather. The roof (and other parts of the house) need regularly scheduled maintenance. We can use all types of tools for these maintenance checks.

In families, we use the Maintenance Toolbox and the many tools we've learned to maintain progress. The Maintenance Toolbox is represented by a roof; it is always there. This reminds us to have family councils regularly, not just when family storms are brewing, and to take care of ourselves. When we maintain our progress, both in the family and in our personal growth, our family becomes a safe haven when the storms of life try us.

IN THIS SECTION

The Maintenance Toolbox contains two chapters:

Chapter 14, "Family Council Toolset," helps us maintain our *family's* progress; it is the last toolset in *The Parent's Toolshop*. While we have most of the tools we need to conduct family councils, there are certain tools and rules for using them that we still need to learn. There are also several ways that family councils can break down, so the tips we learn will help us get started on the right foot and prevent common problems.

Chapter 15, "Three C's: Consistency, Criticism, and Confidence," helps us maintain our *personal* progress. We learn how to maintain our consistency, handle criticism and unwanted or unhelpful advice, and to sustain our confidence. This last chapter gives us a final booster shot to sustain us through the coming years and months—when we have finished reading this book, but are still establishing new habits and growth.

WHEN TO USE THE MAINTENANCE TOOLBOX

We can use the Maintenance Toolbox *anytime*, to prevent or resolve problems that affect the family (Family Council Toolset) or to stay on track with our personal growth (Three C's).

CHAPTER 14
FAMILY COUNCIL TOOLSET

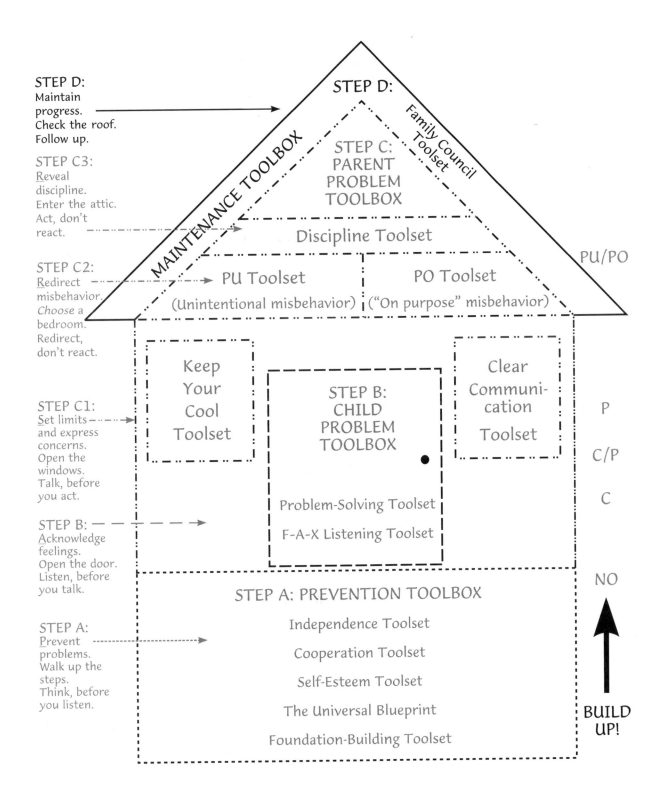

STEP D:
Maintain
progress.
Check the roof.
Follow up.

STEP C3:
<u>Reveal</u>
discipline.
Enter the attic.
Act, don't
react.

STEP C2:
<u>Redirect</u>
misbehavior.
Choose a
bedroom.
Redirect,
don't react.

STEP C1:
<u>Set</u> limits
and express
concerns.
Open the
windows.
Talk, before
you act.

STEP B:
Acknowledge
feelings.
Open the door.
Listen, before
you talk.

STEP A:
<u>Prevent</u>
problems.
Walk up the
steps.
Think, before
you listen.

STEP D:
Family Council Toolset

MAINTENANCE TOOLBOX

STEP C:
PARENT
PROBLEM
TOOLBOX

Discipline Toolset

PU Toolset
(Unintentional misbehavior)

PO Toolset
("On purpose" misbehavior)

PU/PO

Keep
Your
Cool
Toolset

STEP B:
CHILD
PROBLEM
TOOLBOX

Problem-Solving Toolset

F-A-X Listening Toolset

Clear
Communi-
cation
Toolset

P

C/P

C

STEP A: PREVENTION TOOLBOX

Independence Toolset

Cooperation Toolset

Self-Esteem Toolset

The Universal Blueprint

Foundation-Building Toolset

NO

BUILD
UP!

CHAPTER
14 FAMILY COUNCIL TOOLSET

*If we perform regular maintenance on our house, we can sometimes prevent problems or solve them before they get worse. If we don't do regular maintenance, we are always moving from crisis to crisis. In families, we want to have regularly scheduled family councils, not just when there is a problem. If we have ongoing family councils, we can use **all** our effective parenting tools to prevent problems, make family decisions, teach skills, and enrich our family relationships.*

IN THIS CHAPTER

When families hold regular, productive councils, children *and* parents look forward to them and actively participate. There are many pitfalls families can fall into when conducting family councils. That's why it's important to know what to do, and what *not* to do. The Family Council Toolset asks us to consider three important ideas:

1. Family councils are possibly *the* most important factor in building healthy families.
2. When we hold family councils, we use almost all the tools in *The Parent's Toolshop.* We just make a few adjustments to apply the tools to the whole family.
3. There are several myths about family councils and ways they can turn sour. The Family Council Toolset reveals these potential problems and offers suggestions for holding positive, constructive family councils that are a sweet experience for all.

WHEN TO USE THE FAMILY COUNCIL TOOLSET

We use the Family Council Toolset weekly, to hold regularly scheduled family councils. We can also use the ideas and tools in The Family Council Toolset to make any decision or solve any problem that affects the entire family.

THE PURPOSE OF FAMILY COUNCILS

Today, families are so busy, they sometimes stay in touch on the run, only stopping to communicate when there are problems. Listening to children's ideas takes time and energy. It seems faster and easier for parents to make all the decisions and solve all the problems. When families *do* spend time together, many are often in front of the television. Parents might scold children who talk, because they are bothering others. Meeting regularly to talk to each other can seem awkward and unnatural. It's not surprising so many parents resist regular family councils.

Healthy families spend time together regularly to share their joys, frustrations, and daily happenings. Their conversations go beyond superficial issues and scheduling activities. They get to know each other on a deeper level. Parents listen with respect to their children's opinions and involve them in making decisions that affect them. Because they talk often, healthy families avoid many potential problems. When problems do arise, parents involve children in solving them.

A family council is a regularly scheduled time when family members get together to accomplish any or all of the following goals:

- Listen to one another and express joys, feelings, concerns, and ideas.
- Show appreciation and give encouragement.
- Build a sense of family unity, helping family members feel important.
- Make decisions about issues that affect the family.
- Resolve problems and deal with recurring issues.
- Discuss values and teach skills that help each member throughout life, both inside and outside the family.
- Plan and have family fun.

THE BENEFITS OF FAMILY COUNCILS

Effective family councils have many positive short- and long-term results, including the following benefits:

- **A sense of teamwork.** Family members feel they each have a unique contribution to make to the family team. Members work together and support each other.

- **Increased cooperation.** In the family council, parents *and* children take turns planning activities and topics. The family works together to make decisions and solve problems. Because children are involved in setting rules and making decisions, they are more likely to follow through. They complain less, because they've already had a chance to voice their opinions and have them considered in the plan.

- **Increased self-esteem.** Each family member feels important, both as a respected individual and needed member of the family.

- **Decreased rivalry and competition.** Power struggles diminish between parents and children and among siblings. Since family councils have rules of conduct, siblings take a break from teasing and criticizing. (Maybe the only break that week!) They have opportunities to compliment each other and build on the strengths of their relationships. They learn to work together and establish a deeper bond—one that can't be swept away by the winds of competition and jealousy.

- **Improved behavior.** When children feel they belong, can express their feelings, and be respected, they naturally misbehave less.

- **Development of life skills.** This is perhaps the most important benefit. Anyone who participates in a family council learns the following skills, which are useful in the family, in the business world, in adult relationships, and any other relationships:
  - Give encouragement
  - Develop a cooperative leadership style
  - Listen with respect
  - Work together as a team Express feelings respectfully and appropriately
  - Brainstorm and problem solve
  - Reflect and summarize others' thoughts and feelings
  - Make responsible decisions
  - Organize and plan activities
  - Accept responsibility and follow through with commitments
  - Have fun and play with others cooperatively

Any family can hold council meetings. Families with young children can simplify the structure and just focus on fun. Families with teens can discuss issues of concern to adolescents.

Single-parent households can still hold family councils although one parent will not be participating. Families *can* discuss the shared grief and adjustments that can result from the separation, divorce, or death of a parent. Increased teamwork and bonding reduces stress and provides support to each family member. In families affected by divorce, the family council is *not* an appropriate forum for discussing matters that relate to the children's relationship with the absent parent. Those matters are between the children and the absent parent. *If* parents get involved in these issues, they need to handle them individually, using one-on-one problem solving (Child Problem Toolbox)—but only if they can be objective. (No criticizing the ex-spouse!)

Foster families find that family councils are particularly helpful when bringing new foster children into their family. Many foster children come from homes in which fear, anger, withdrawal of love, neglect, or abuse was the norm. The foster child's family rules are usually different from the foster family's. Most importantly, foster children usually have low self-esteem and expect rejection. The positive tone of family councils can give them the encouragement and life skills they might not have learned. The family council experience can make a great impression on a foster child's life.

> *A Personal Story. When I worked at a runaway shelter, we had regular "house meetings." Although there were some set rules, teen residents shared their ideas, concerns, and problems. We jointly planned the menu, grocery list, chore roster, and recreational activities. These teens, who were feeling rejection from their own families, gained a sense of belonging, acceptance, friendship, responsibility, and respect from the house-meeting experience.*

Blended families particularly benefit from family councils. Blended families are two separate families with different expectations, personalities, and ideas who are becoming a new unified family. Rules, roles, and responsibilities need to be redefined. Children resist and rebel if the "new" parent makes these decisions for them. Involving children through family councils creates new, jointly-agreed-upon rules and roles. Just as important, family councils help new parents and step-children get to know each other, providing a safe place to share fears and hopes for the family. Family members develop a feeling of being on a *new* team—one where each member is important to the whole team.

School classrooms and other groups can also modify the family council ideas to fit their needs. (A terrific resource for teachers is *Positive Discipline in the Classroom*, by Jane Nelsen, Lynn Lott, and H. Stephen Glenn; Prima Publishing, Rocklin, CA 1993.)

FAMILY COUNCIL ROLES ☆☆☆☆

There are four roles every family council needs, despite the format or other optional roles families can choose. (If there are less than four family members, someone can take on an additional beginning or ending role.) Have someone in the family be responsible for the following roles:

1. The **Leader** starts and ends the meeting on time, makes sure all points-of-view are heard, and helps keep members focused on the issues. The Leader models mutual respect and effective communication skills. Parents can be the Leader first, to model the skills. Then the family can rotate the responsibility between children and parents. Generally, school-aged children can serve as the Leader with adult guidance. A good way to start is by co-leading with the child. Explain the basics of the Leader's role and the decision-making process. Let the child move through agenda items and problem-solving steps. Only step in to remind the child of procedures.

    It can be tricky for the Leader to shift roles, from leadership responsibilities to a family member with personal opinions, ideas, and feelings. As family members become skilled in respectful communication, they will naturally offer comments and suggestions that a Leader might offer. Also, children who lead a family council become increasingly skilled at shifting gears and keeping the discussion on track.

A Personal Note. Chris suggested the title of "The Big Cheese," for this role. It doesn't matter what you call a position, as long as someone performs the tasks. When Amber was the Leader, at age 3, she sat on my lap. I helped her read the agenda items and whispered comments in her ear to keep the discussion moving.

2. The **Recorder** takes notes during the meeting of ideas generated in problem-solving sessions, issues discussed, and decisions or plans the family makes. Families can have a family council notebook which contains a record of past agendas and decisions. This record is helpful if members need to remember agreements made in the past.

    Amber wanted this role before she could read or write, so she used a tape recorder, which she really enjoyed!

3. The **Icebreaker** decides what opening encouragement activity to use. This starts every family council with people talking, feeling, and thinking positively. There is a list of possible icebreakers at the end of this chapter. For example, "One good thing that happened to me this week is ___." Be creative or draw from group activities you've experienced or read about.

4. The **Anchor** selects a positive closing activity. This ensures that the family council will always end on a positive note. The activities can be similar to the icebreaker's. They might also include something like each person making a commitment to do something in particular the following week. This could be giving a compliment to someone or doing a good deed.

    In our family, we have an activity and end with a family prayer—the kids insisted that we include the dog in our prayer circle.

> **Start and end every meeting on a positive note.** If the family only discusses decisions and problems, members may view the council as a negative experience and resist coming back.

Rotating Roles

One way to rotate roles equally is to make a two-wheeled gadget with each person's name on the outer wheel and roles on the inner wheel. Attach the wheels with a two-pronged brass fastener. Each week, turn the wheel one space, so everyone has a new role.

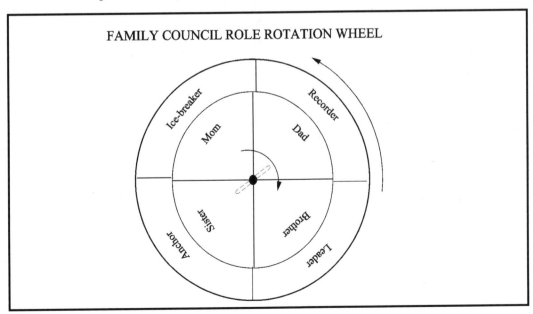

FAMILY COUNCIL ROLE ROTATION WHEEL

If a family has only two members, a single parent and child, one can have a leadership role (Leader or Recorder) and a "fun" role (Icebreaker or Anchor-person.) Besides these four roles, there are other optional roles, based on the format you choose. Read over the following format options and select (in your first family council meeting) those features and roles which suit your family best.

 # FORMAT OPTIONS

If a family follows some basic guidelines, they can decide on their own the structure and details of their family council. Some family councils are formal and structured, almost like a business meeting. Others are informal and less-structured. *Some* structure and flow are necessary, or discussions get side-tracked and people feel frustrated. Each format has additional roles that family members can share or rotate. If young children want a role that seems too difficult, parents can help them with the task. Let the child decide what to do and how to do it. Work side-by-side, teaching skills and only helping with physical tasks that might be too difficult.

Formal Business Meeting Format

This format works well with older children who have good verbal skills, particularly teens. The focus is on communication—sharing opinions, making decisions, and setting rules. The roles and agenda are more business-like.[1]

FORMAL BUSINESS MEETING ROLES

- The **Leader**'s role is the same as described earlier.

- The **Recorder** in a formal meeting writes the "minutes," a summary of what was decided. The Recorder then reads this report aloud at the beginning of the next meeting. If the recorder tapes the meeting, someone needs to write a summary of decisions for the family council folder.

- The **Ice-breaker**'s role is the same as described above.

- **Additional, optional roles:**

    - The **Discussion Topic Leader** chooses a topic to discuss—an important feature for family councils with older children and teens. These issues are not complaints or problems within the family. They are topics about which family members might have different values or opinions. This gives parents and children a chance to practice talking about important values and issues they might not agree on. Each family member voices a nonjudgmental opinion, listens to others' opinions with respect, and maintains a calm, nondefensive attitude. These are time-limited, "third person," general discussions, not discussions about any particular parent, child, or person. There is a list of possible topics at the end of this chapter. Have children add topics of interest to them.

FORMAL MEETING AGENDA

1. Opening icebreaker.

2. The Recorder reads the minutes of the previous meeting.

3. "Old business." Discuss any issues left unresolved from last time.

4. "New Business." Discuss any issues, problems, or decisions the family has listed on an agenda that is posted throughout the week. Usually, families discuss issues in the order they are listed, which motivates children to put their issues on the agenda before the meeting. If there are no issues, the family can discuss a topic.

5. After discussing as many agenda items as time allows, the Recorder summarizes the meeting by reviewing decisions, agreements, and commitments. The Leader confirms everyone's commitment to the decisions they reached.

6. Family members agree on roles for the next meeting and record any issues they didn't get to discuss. A blank agenda is posted for issues members want to discuss at the next family council.

Informal Family Council Format

The informal family council is more fun-oriented, but is still structured. The family talks and takes care of family business, but there are more opportunities for children to have a role in the meeting. The flow is less business-like and more easy-going. There are more optional roles.

INFORMAL FAMILY COUNCIL ROLES

* The **Leader's** role is the same as described earlier.

* The **Recorder** writes brainstormed ideas and decisions the family makes. The Recorder does not, however, have to write and present minutes. Notes, agendas, and decisions from the meeting are filed in the family council notebook for future reference.

* The **Ice-breaker** and **Anchor** roles are the same as described earlier.

* **Additional, optional roles:**

  * The **Topic Discussion Leader** is the same as described earlier.

  * The **Snack Planner** decides what the snack will be and makes it prior to the meeting. Young children can choose a snack and parents can help them prepare it. Snack preparation can also be a family activity.

  * The **Game Planner** decides a fun family activity, such as a game or recreational activity. This person could decide an outing or the whole family could make decisions about outings and this person decides a fun activity only for the meeting. Be creative; don't just select board games. You can use some of the games listed in the "Bedtime Routines" section of the Cooperation Toolset, at the end of this chapter, or make up some of your own.

  * The **Entertainment Leader** picks a song, poem, story, or other form of entertainment for the family council. This could include playing a piece on a musical instrument or organizing siblings to do a play.

  * The **Lesson Planner** shares a lesson that would benefit the whole family. This could be a religious or value lesson, a summary of something learned in school, or teaching the family a new skill.

INFORMAL COUNCIL AGENDA

1. The Ice-breaker leads a compliment activity or other exercise to bring out positive feelings between family members.

2. The Recorder lists any issues left unresolved last time. Discuss and resolve these first.

3. The Leader asks if there are any issues, problems, or decisions the family would like to discuss. The family can decide whether they want preplanned or impromptu topics. (The order of the remaining items can be switched.)

4. The Lesson Planner reads a book or leads an activity that teaches a positive family value. Families with older children can discuss a topic, if they choose. Some examples of lesson activities are listed at the end of this chapter.

5. The Game Planner chooses and leads a game or other fun activity.

6. The Entertainment Leader presents or teaches the family a song, story, poem, play. etc.

7. The Snack Planner serves the snack.

8. Decide roles for the next meeting. Each person plans his or her own activity that week.

Choose whatever optional roles and activities *your* family wants. Help everyone feel involved and let each person contribute something. Make sure there is a Leader to keep things on track and a Recorder to write the decisions you make. The rest is up to the family—be creative!

> *A Graduate's Example. When Paul and Carrie took my parenting class, they had four children (the oldest was six) and had conducted "Family Home Evenings²" since their oldest child was two. They introduced me to new ideas for making family councils less rigid, more fun, and just as effective as formal meetings. Here is how they structured their Family Home Evenings:*
>
> *Each family member over the age of two had a role or responsibility, even if the parent helped. As children became old enough to participate, they added another role, to make sure everyone had something to contribute to the evening. Children had full responsibility for choosing and planning their activity. (They often took pride in making it a surprise.) Younger children chose an activity and a parent helped the child only as much as necessary. One child always chose the same game to play, but that was okay, because it was her turn to pick a game.*
>
> *When Paul or Carrie chose the lesson, story, or game, they would sometimes incorporate an issue they were dealing with in the family. For example, they might read a book about sharing, if the kids had been getting into tug-of-wars that week. They would discuss how people feel when others don't share, why we share, and what to do when someone (including you) doesn't want to share. I thought this approach was a great improvement over "We have a problem with people not sharing" as a business agenda item.*
>
> *This, I thought, is the kind of family council experience everyone needs to have. My kids (three and seven at the time) were bored and resistant to the restrictiveness of our formal family meeting structure. When I included some of these informal ideas, my kids started showing enthusiasm for family councils again.*

Emergency Meetings

Emergency meetings may occur only for decisions that absolutely can't wait for the regular family council. During these meetings, *only* discuss and decide the emergency issue. Postpone other topics until the next regular meeting.

If the family can't agree on a decision and some action is needed, parents can make a temporary decision until the family can more fully discuss the matter. If all family members are willing to abide by a majority vote, **this is the only time that voting is allowed.** If parents make the decision, they can prevent power struggles and resentment by saying, "It appears that we're not ready to make a decision on this yet. Something must be done about it right away, so I will consider your opinions and make the decision. We can discuss it more next week."

Be cautious with emergency meetings and decisions. Closely evaluate whether an issue actually needs immediate attention. If the family is pressured to make an unnecessary quick decision, they might later resent it and rebel. Parents need to reserve their "executive decision-making privilege" for *critical* emergency decisions that cannot wait. If parents choose this option, they need to get everyone's agreement to abide by it until the family can resolve their differences. Often, just this suggestion alone will spur those people who have dug in their heels or are on the fence to make a commitment to a solution.

Maintenance Meetings

Hold maintenance meetings periodically, to discuss how everyone feels the family council is going. Is it too negative, too long, or too structured? Is everyone encouraging equal respect for opinions and ideas? Are people listening and speaking respectfully? If the family council seems problematic, schedule a maintenance meeting. If things are going well, plan one at least once a year, just to make sure the family thinks about progress and improvements. As children mature or schedules change, you may need to review some "first meeting" decisions.

GETTING STARTED—THE FIRST FEW MEETINGS

Parents usually present the idea of having family council meetings and get the meetings started. Here are some issues parents want to consider:

- **Arrange the first meeting.** Discuss the idea of having regular family councils with the children. Children must be involved in deciding whether to have family councils; parents should not force the decision. When children understand the value of family councils, they are usually enthusiastic.

- **Introduce family councils to young children.** When children can talk well, they are ready for the experience of family councils. Keep the meetings brief and simple. Usually, participation in one issue per meeting is all we can expect of young children. Allow younger children to float from the meeting to a quiet activity they can do alone. Parents can briefly interact with young children when they "touch base" and involve them in the meeting. They won't need to misbehave if they feel they belong and aren't being rejected or ignored. As we continue to meet and children mature, we can move to longer, more formal meetings. Have each child be responsible for one aspect of the family fun time.

- **Involve both parents, if possible.** Both parents must have a clear understanding of the meeting goals and be ready to function as *equals* with each other and the children. They must make a conscious decision to work together. If one parent doesn't want to attend, the other can conduct meetings that focus on issues and decisions that only affect the members who are present. Do not use any decision to intentionally hurt or inconvenience the absent member—this will only create more resistance. When the spouse sees the benefits of the meetings, he or she may decide to participate.

- **Have some structure to the meetings.** If children resist structured meetings, we can choose a more casual approach. We might say, "Let's do something together this Sunday. Does anyone have ideas about where we could go?" The family can decide the time, the place, who will make preparations, and so on. Expect the children to carry out the responsibilities they chose. If they forget, do not single them out, criticize, or rescue them. (If we do, they won't volunteer again!) Let everyone experience the consequences and brainstorm possible solutions. Our goal is to teach teamwork and reliance on each other, not to play "supervisor."

  As family members learn to cooperate, we can informally begin to introduce problems or other family decisions. As they become used to working through problems and planning family fun, raise the idea of establishing more formal meetings so decisions can be made in one session each week.

- **Start with those who are willing to attend.** Some family members may not be ready to discuss matters in a group setting, but you don't have to abandon the idea. You can still hold family councils if most family members agree to attend. Those who do not attend the early meetings may decide to attend later, when they see the advantages.

> **Family councils include parents, children, and anyone else who lives with the family and would be affected by decisions about the daily life of the family.** Always leave the "door open" and make it clear that everyone is welcome, but not pressured, to attend family councils.

- **Schedule the first meeting.** During the first meeting, begin planning your format. The first family council needs to be a short one. It's a good idea to have only one item of business at this meeting and plan an outing or fun activity for after the meeting. Later meetings can be longer and follow an agenda. Spend your first few meetings making the following decisions. Start with number one and try to get through number four during the first few meetings, if you can. You can discuss other decisions later.

Decisions to Make ☆☆☆☆

1. **When to meet.** If you discuss nothing else the first meeting, try to decide this. Don't use busy schedules as excuses not to have regular family councils. It is usually possible to find some half-hour period when everyone can come. If mealtime is the only time available, have your meal first, clear the table, and then meet.

2. **How often to meet.** A family council is like any other commitment, such as a new exercise regime or going to religious services. If you make an excuse or exception even once, it's hard to get back into the habit again. Get a commitment from everyone to schedule around this time. Schedule around children's responsibilities and commitments that cannot be changed.

> **Hold family councils *once a week*, rather than once or twice a month or as needed.** This helps prevent the council from seeming like a gripe session. Also, families can discuss issues before they become full-blown problems.

Some parents object to the idea of weekly or regular meetings. "We don't need them," they say, "We discuss things like this all the time." It's great if you talk regularly to your children, but councils can take these discussions to much deeper, meaningful levels.

3. **Where to meet.** Sitting at a cleared table is conducive to staying on task for formal problem solving. Sitting informally in a living room is more appropriate for an informal format. Writing, however, will be difficult. Try to find a setting where everyone is at an equal eye level. If parents sit at the head of the table or in a chair that implies an authority position, it is a nonverbal way of displaying superiority. Instead, set an atmosphere of equality.

    *A **Personal Story.** Chris' fifth grade class held weekly class meetings. When the class was deciding where to meet, they were concerned that Todd, who was wheelchair-bound, would feel different, because his wheelchair was higher than the classroom chairs. The class decided to find another room to hold their class meetings so Todd would feel like an equal participant. It took them several weeks of touring the school building to find just the right setting, but they did. Such consideration for Todd's need was a beautiful illustration of being sensitive to every member's needs during the meeting, even if only one member has a special need.*

4. **How long to meet.** Plan the amount of time you will reserve for family councils. Unless you plan to spend a whole evening full of many fun activities, don't let meetings run longer than 45–60 minutes with older children. Limit the time to about 10 minutes, but no longer than 20–30 minutes, when young children are involved. Start and end on time and stay focused. This shows respect for everyone's time schedules.

5. **What to discuss.** People are always welcome to share news, feelings, problems, concerns, and decisions. They don't have to request input or problem solving. Lessons, topics, finances, chores, and allowances may also be regular topics. (Don't discuss these or other big parent issues until you've had a few meetings to discuss children's issues. Otherwise, family councils will seem like forums only for parents to get what they want.) You'll need to decide how to handle your agenda. Post it throughout the week? In what order will the family discuss issues? Use first-come-first-serve order or based it on priority and urgency? (Priority could be a sticky issue. Younger children's issues are just as important to them as older children's. Parents' issues are not always more important than children's.)

   Issues that effect the entire family are appropriate issues to discuss. Individual issues can only be brought up by the individual involved. Use one-on-one problem solving in private, first. If the two of you get stuck, you can offer the family council as a resource for additional ideas. It is the child's decision, though, whether to bring the issue before the whole family.

   Never handle individual discipline in a family council in front of other family members; it's humiliating. General discussions about consequences for certain rule violations are appropriate to discuss, as are setting up the rules, since this is *revealing* discipline.

6. **Choose a format: informal or formal.** Review the different formats and use problem solving to decide which activities you want the family council to have.

7. **Roles.** Decide which roles you will have in your meeting. Try to make sure everyone has something to contribute at each meeting. Decide whether people will volunteer for roles each week or if there will be a regular rotation schedule. If people volunteer, make sure everyone has an equal chance to have each role so they can develop a variety of skills.

FAMILY COUNCILS USE ALL THE TOOLS

To have effective family councils, we need to use *all* the tools we've learned, especially the communication and problem-solving skills. Establish basic ground rules for discussions that will model and teach others how to communicate respectfully and result in win/win solutions to problems and decisions that need to be made.

Prevention Toolbox

- Use the *Self-Esteem Toolset* to begin *every* council meeting in an encouraging way.
- Use the balanced leadership styles in the *Foundation-Building Toolset* to maintain an atmosphere of mutual respect.
- Use the *Universal Blueprint* to identify who has a problem and use the tools and formulas we've learned to resolve the problem.
- Use the *Cooperation Toolset* to involve everyone in decisions and the tasks to carry them out.
- Use the *Independence Toolset* to teach skills, especially the communication and decision-making skills. (The other toolsets listed below are not in the PASRR order we learned them, but from least-used to most-used.)

Clear Communication Toolset

> *The ground rules for expressing concerns in family councils:* "Express yourself respectfully—no name-calling or blaming allowed. If someone has a concern, complaint, or idea, describe the problem and how you feel about it. Speak for yourself, without blaming or criticizing anyone else."

Use "I"-messages:

- *Concerns:* "I am (feeling) that I . . ." or "I'd like it if . . ." Not, "You make me feel . . ." or "You should . . ."

- *Complaints:* "I've seen (describe the problem, with no names)" or "Sometimes (describe the problem) happens." Not, "You always . . ."
- *Ideas:* "I think we could . . ." or "Can we . . .?" Not, "We should . . ." or "We have to . . ."

When someone violates these rules, suggest a better way to say it or summarize the statement, without the blame.

➤ "Could you try wording that without blaming Susan? Try saying, 'When (describe behavior without blame) happens, I feel _____.'"

➤ "Can you *describe* how you feel, without calling names or labeling?"

This strategy prevents a discussion from becoming a heated argument and teaches family members to express themselves respectfully. You need to be careful to word *your* concerns respectfully, too. Don't fall into these power play traps:

- *Nagging:* "Remember, the meeting is at six o'clock." Instead, make sure the time is clear and then show respect by not reminding.

- *Criticizing:* "You didn't . . ." or "No one does their chores on time unless I remind them." Instead, "I feel frustrated when chores aren't finished on time or without reminders."

- *Threatening:* "Everyone in this house needs to pull his weight or there's going to be no social privileges!" Instead, talk less when revealing discipline and follow through with few words. "Everyone knows their responsibilities. These need to be met before we play or do something social." Then simply follow through on the consequence if people break agreements.

- *Lecturing:* "If I've told you once, I've told you a thousand times . . ." Instead, ask open-ended questions, "What is our agreement about _____? Is there a problem with that time? Is there something you could do to help remind yourself?"

- *Probing:* Listen and allow the child to initiate conversation. "Chad, how was your week? Did anything happen that you'd like to share with the family?"

F-A-X Listening Toolset

> *The ground rules for family council discussions:* **"When someone is speaking, everyone listens with respect without interrupting.** We can summarize what the person is saying to make sure we understand, but we need to wait until the person is finished before giving our opinion."

Everyone's opinions and feelings are okay. When anyone expresses a feeling or complaint, model and teach the listening tools. This is especially important when children complain about parents' actions. Here is an example of unhelpful and helpful responses to such a complaint:

Toby: "I don't think it's fair that you make me go to Uncle Henry's. It's so boring. All he does is tell war stories and watch TV. I'd have more fun getting a root canal!"

Unhelpful response: "Watch it, buddy! That's my brother you're talking about. He's lucky he didn't get killed in the war! If you weren't such a spoiled brat, you'd appreciate all the wisdom and good things he's given you. The least you could do is go and quit groaning about it." A response like this will surely make Toby defensive and increase his resentment toward his parent and uncle.

Helpful response: "I can understand how you would rather do something that is more interesting to you." Wait for a response and reflect more, if needed, before you respectfully express your side of the issue. Then move into problem solving, "Visiting family is important to me. Even if I don't have a lot in common with Uncle Henry, I still love him and want him to know we care. It's important to me—and to him—that you visit with us. Can you think of a way that visits with Uncle Henry could be more interesting for you?"

When people complain, let them know you heard and understand them. Shift the focus to solutions, instead of rehashing complaints or the problem. Identify the issue for both parties. Toby's issue is boredom and the parent's issue is spending time with a valued, though admittedly difficult, relative. The F-A-X process can help parents and children reach win/win solutions.

Problem-Solving Toolset

CONSENSUS DECISION-MAKING ☆☆☆☆

When problems arise or decisions need to be made, the goal is to reach win/win solutions and agreements everyone agrees with. This is called **consensus decision-making.** The word "consensus" means "to think together."

Never use voting as a regular form of decision-making. Every vote has winners and losers—and the losers often try to sabotage the decision.

Some people think consensus means "everyone states opinions and Mom and Dad decide." If everyone agrees to abide by the parents' decision, it's a consensus decision. True consensus, however, considers all opinions.

Consensus decision-making involves several elements:
- Giving everyone an equal chance to be heard, contribute ideas, and influence decisions.
- Working together to reach an agreement to which everyone is willing to commit (even if some members agree not to get their way).
- Everyone understands the decision and is prepared to support it.

Consensus decision-making doesn't mean parents have to go along with whatever the children want. *Parents can present bottom-line limits for decisions and then focus the rest of the discussion on the choices within those boundaries.* This can prevent families from going around in circles and splitting into "sides" of a decision.

It's rare, but sometimes families need to discuss an issue for several meetings before they reach a consensus decision. (Each member thinks of ideas and gathers information between meetings.) While consensus decisions clearly take more time and effort than autocratic decision-making, they are much more effective and lasting. Everyone gets a say in the decision and at least part of the decision meets their needs. There is also little to no resistance or rebellion and those involved in the process usually follow through with few reminders.

To reach consensus decisions, follow the basic problem-solving steps we have learned and reviewed for different types of problems. Since the problem is a "family" problem, everyone can have the opportunity to give input at each step.

1. DEFINE AND SUMMARIZE THE PROBLEM

Ask the person with the complaint or issue to explain it. This step uses I-messages, reflective listening, open-ended questions, and summarizing the problem. Each person has an opportunity to voice a view of the problem and understand what others are feeling and thinking. Here are some tips to remember and pitfalls to avoid at this step:

Give everyone a chance to share feelings. Acknowledge each person's opinion and summarize the problem after everyone has spoken. The Leader or Recorder can say, "So let me get this straight, Mom is really frustrated about (describe the problem). It bothers me a little bit. It's not a problem at all for Joanne, and Bobby is also frustrated and would like the situation to improve. Do I have that right? Does everyone understand *what* the problem is and how each person feels? Okay, then let's discuss what we can *do* about the problem." This leads the family into creative brainstorming.

Limit griping. Reflect the complainer's feelings and summarize the problem. Then shift the focus to solutions, "So what do you think we could *do* about that?"

2. EXPLORE ALTERNATIVES THROUGH BRAINSTORMING

Get children involved in coming up with solutions. Ask them for their suggestions first. Parents can add ideas only if necessary. The more involved the children are in offering solutions, the more likely they will carry them out.

Allow all ideas, no matter how silly. Silly ideas might contain the seed of a workable solution. The Recorder simply lists all the ideas until no one thinks of further ideas.

Ideas don't "belong" to anybody. Once someone offers a suggestion, it becomes a general idea. When people take agreeing or disagreeing with an idea personally, remind them that this is just one idea, not "(name)'s idea." Similarly, just because someone suggests an idea doesn't mean he or she necessarily wants that idea to be the final solution.

Do not permit criticism of ideas. If someone disagrees with an idea or criticizes it, offer a reminder, "All we are doing right now is sharing any idea at all that comes to mind. We are simply listing them; we aren't agreeing to use them. Everyone will have a chance to say how they feel about each idea when we have thought of every possibility."

3. EVALUATE THE SUGGESTED IDEAS

Give everyone a chance to express their opinions about each idea. Express opinions respectfully, "I am concerned about doing that because . . ." or "That idea could work if we did it this way . . ." Do not allow any comments such as "That idea's stupid." Ask *what*, specifically, they don't like about the idea.

Emphasize the difference between details and matters of principle. If someone wants to discard an idea because of a serious concern, this opinion might carry more weight than disagreeing about a detail. You can usually work out details later, in the planning stage, if the family can agree on a general idea.

Deal with minority issues. If some people are unwilling to agree to an option most of the family wants, listen to their feelings and summarize their points of agreement and disagreement. Ask, "What would you need to hear or feel to consider this option?"

Pinpoint the real issues. Don't get sidetracked by personal issues. If people simply want their way, encourage them to think about the entire family's needs, "I'm sure we *all* would like to have our own way. It would be more helpful, though, if we can look for ways we can meet *everyone's* needs. How can we resolve ___ in a way we can *all* agree?"

4. CHOOSE AN AGREEABLE SOLUTION

Mix and match parts of ideas. Modify or combine ideas to reach a solution agreeable to everyone.

Take a survey to see where everyone stands on a possible solution. "Could we all agree to . . .?" Although some people might have concerns about the plan, you might be surprised to find they are still willing to agree to it. Compromise by having a trial period or conditional agreement, "I'd be willing to agree if . . ." If the rest of the group agrees to the conditions, move on.

Plan the details. Decide who will do what, how it will be done, and when it needs to be completed. Get everyone's input, ideas, and agreement on the plan. When appropriate, discuss the effect of broken agreements. Have children offer suggestions, rather than revealing discipline as the parent. If children suggest it and agree to it, they will be more likely to follow through and discipline themselves.

If you can't reach a consensus decision, you have several options:

- *Table the discussion.* Sometimes people need more time to think about ideas or their willingness to agree to the decision. Ask everyone to think of ideas or research information before the next meeting.

- *Make a decision smaller.* Go with the part of the agreement everyone has agreed on and work out the rest of the details at the next meeting.

- *Make a temporary decision, until a more final decision can be reached.* You can probably get people to agree to a temporary conditional decision. The decision might not be final, but it can be a starting place.

- *Agree to a trial period,* with the understanding that the solution can be brought up for discussion later, if it doesn't work.

- *If an urgent decision and action are needed*, you can get a consensus decision for the parent to make an "executive decision." (See the "Emergency Meeting" section for cautions and guidelines on this option.)

5. MAKE A COMMITMENT AND SET A TIME TO EVALUATE IT

Get firm commitments. Summarize the agreement and ask if everyone agrees to it. If you get "I'll try," as a response, seek a more firm commitment. "'I'll try' is not a commitment; it gives you an 'out' if you don't feel like making the effort. We need a commitment from everyone. 'Yes' or 'no'?"

Record the decision. Have the Recorder write down the final agreement and the details of the plan and file it in the family council notebook. If you make a schedule (e.g., for homework, chores, or allowances) or calendar, post it where everyone can see it.

Evaluate the plan. The minimum time to try out a plan is one week, until the next family council. (You might want to talk with younger children within a couple of days.) Then, ask everyone how the plan is working. Are there unexpected problems? Do you need to make adjustments? If all has gone well, agree to review the plan in several months.

> The *process* of making decisions and solving problems is just as important as reaching a final decision. It may seem the prize we gain from problem solving is a win/win solution. The real prizes, though, are the valuable life skills everyone learns.

FAMILY COUNCIL TROUBLE-SHOOTING GUIDE ☆☆☆☆

Establishing new patterns of communicating and making decisions takes time. Developing and teaching cooperative leadership skills takes time and effort. It is natural and expected that difficulties will arise and "sour" meetings will occasionally occur. Don't let this discourage you or cause you to give up on family councils. Instead, review your guidelines again and check this troubleshooting guide. For each suggestion, ask yourself, "Did we do this?"

Always start positively and end positively. Make a "positive sandwich," where problems and more serious discussions are sandwiched between an uplifting beginning and a fun ending.

Keep a balanced, cooperative atmosphere.
- Don't use family councils as a court session or lecture forum. Resentment and resistance will only intensify.
- Avoid an "us and them" attitude, with parents on one side and children on the other, especially when there is an only child.
- Allow everyone to share opinions and feelings without criticism—no teasing or putdowns.
- Make sure children's issues get equal attention during the meetings. If they don't offer opinions or ideas, make a point to ask them for input. When children feel their input is important, they start voluntarily participating more.

Keep out the welcome mat. Welcome everyone at your family councils, even if they have never attended or don't feel like talking. They can simply sit and observe. If someone chooses not to attend a meeting or is unwilling to agree to a decision, they may be affected by decisions made in their absence. These are natural consequences, not intentional punishments for not attending. Make it clear that the decision isn't written in stone and their input is valued and welcome. "We tried to consider what your feelings and opinions might be, but we couldn't check with you first. If you'd like to come to the next family council, we'd be happy to include any ideas you have."

Never throw a decision "in someone's face" as a revengeful payback for not attending or participating in a decision.

A Personal Story. By the time my parents learned about family meetings, my brother and I were teenagers. Our relationship was so bitter, it was difficult to sit in the same room, let alone respect each others' ideas! Family meetings didn't last long in our family, because not much information was available on troubleshooting. One family decision was handled so poorly I swore never to attend a meeting again.

Someone suggested growing a vegetable garden. I was allergic to fresh fruits and vegetables and hated weeding. Everyone else thought the garden idea was great, but I didn't want to participate. "Why should I?" I thought, "I can't even eat what we would grow!" The others tried to sway me to their side, but I wasn't willing to make an honest commitment to the project. They decided to go ahead with the garden anyway, without me. I agreed to this. My parents revealed the consequence for my nonparticipation: "If you don't help grow the garden, you can't eat anything we grow." That was fine with me.

Months passed and one night, during dinner, my mother served some juicy, red, sliced, home-grown tomatoes. I couldn't eat raw tomatoes and didn't plan to try these. She laid them in front of me and said, "Since you didn't help grow these, you can't eat any." Her tone of voice hit me like she was rubbing the tomatoes in my face! I was hurt! Not because I couldn't eat the tomatoes, but because they were used as revengeful punishment! I was so hurt by this incident that I withdrew from the family meetings and never attended again.

*Take my advice: start family councils when your kids are young or after you learn how to do them helpfully. Keep reviewing information about constructive family councils. If someone's feelings get hurt, deal with them. Apologize and make amends. Most of all, **never** use family council decisions to punish those who do not attend or participate.*

Focus on goals and solutions, rather than griping about why things aren't working.

Stay on task. The Leader's job is to see to it that everyone sticks to the point. Set time limits on discussions and refocus the discussion if it wanders from the topic. Break larger problems into smaller parts, focusing on one part at a time. A large family can break into smaller groups to discuss them.

Redirect disruptive behavior. Sometimes a child's personality, energy level, or misbehavior goals can disrupt the family council. Handle misbehavior as you would any other time. Getting a child involved in the task at hand is the most effective way to **P**revent misbehavior in a family council. When problems arise, briefly **A**cknowledge feelings, **S**et limits, and try to **R**edirect the behavior. We can also **R**eveal children's choices; they can participate in the group in a helpful way or they can leave the meeting. They will have to abide by any decisions made in their absence, but are welcome to return to the council any time, when they are willing to conduct themselves appropriately. *Only eject participants from the meeting as a last resort.*

Reserve certain types of decisions for parents. Meeting together does not mean that the parents must always do whatever the children decide. Basic questions of health and well-being are parental responsibilities and the decisions are sometimes theirs alone to make. (Remember our first exercise in the "Parenting Styles" section about a father receiving a promotion that would involve moving?) If a decision has to be made without family input, discuss how everyone *feels* about the decision and how the decision can be made easier for the children. Involve the children in making the necessary plans to put the decision into action.

All decisions hold firm until the next family council. If people complain about decisions between meetings, simply reply, "That was a family decision, so the whole family needs to be involved in any changes. Put it on the agenda so you can bring it up again at the next family council."

CONCLUSION

It may take several weeks or months to establish a comfortable, smooth family council routine. Be patient with your progress and concentrate on what is going well. Don't expect your meetings to be thrilling every week. Expect to run into difficulties. Review the summary sheet before meetings (to prevent problems) and after sour council experiences (to rebuild trust and avoid similar mistakes in the future.) Learn from your mistakes and use what you learn to teach the whole family new skills that will prevent and resolve such pitfalls in the future.

Don't expect solutions to last forever; that's unrealistic. Choose an idea and try it for a week to see how it works. If it doesn't work, put the problem back on the agenda and try again, and again. Remember the long-range benefits you are working toward. They are important enough to weather any short-term frustrations and failures, which are simply part of the growth and learning process.

AGENDA/ACTIVITY IDEA LISTS

You can use the "Problem-Solving Worksheet" in the Problem-Solving Toolset for one-on-one, sibling, parent/child, *and* family council problem solving. Use the following lists to get started and feel free to add, change, or modify them to suit your needs. Get the creative juices flowing!

Lesson Activities[3,4]

Everyone is special. This activity teaches a lesson and builds teamwork at the same time. The family *bakes a cake* as the activity and snack. As you make the cake, each family member takes an ingredient or job to do to prepare the cake. As each ingredient is added, talk about how special and important it is. The ingredients are good all by themselves, but unless they are mixed together, you can't call it a cake. While the cake cooks, discuss how each person in the family is important and adds special gifts the family appreciates. A family is where you can be yourself without worry of criticism. These bonds are created when we serve and help each other. Discuss what the cake would be like if we left out any of the ingredients. Is any one ingredient more important than another? How does this apply to our family?

Secret admirer. Write each family member's name on a slip of paper and fold it. Each person chooses a slip (but not one with their own name). Without revealing the name of the person, have family members tell of an incident in which another family member showed love. "I'm thinking about someone who did _____ to show me love. Have the other family members guess the loving family member.

Help someone outside your family. For young children, choose a service that is small and simple, writing a note or drawing a picture for someone who is sick or for a grandparent far away.

Discussing death. (Use a glove with your hand to describe physical death.) "Suppose my hand represents your spirit. It is alive. It can move by itself. Suppose this glove represents your physical body. A glove cannot move by itself. But when the spirit enters it (put your hand in the glove and move it around), the physical body can move. As we live on earth, each of us is a spirit clothed in a physical body. Someday because of old age, disease, or accident, the spirit will leave the physical body. We then say the person has died (take off the glove and lay it down). So, death is a separation of the spirit from the physical body. Death is not, however, an end of life, for the spirit continues to live (show that your hand still moves)."

FAMILY COUNCIL OPENING ICE-BREAKERS

One new thing I learned this week is . . .

One nice thing someone in the family did for me this week is . . .

(Family member) is special to our family because . . .

One funny thing that happened to me this week is . . .

A good habit I have is . . .

Something I read in the paper or heard this week and how I felt about it is . . .

A good clean joke I heard this week is . . .

What really makes me happy is . . .

The three most important things in my life are . . .

Something (family member) did for me this week that I never thanked him/her for is . . .

Something I do well is . . .

My biggest accomplishment is . . .

Something I did that helped someone this week is . . .

Something I did that took courage is . . .

The funniest thing I've done is . . .

One way I've improved myself is . . .

A good habit I have is . . .

FAMILY COUNCIL DISCUSSION TOPICS

A bad habit I have and what I can do about it

A time when it was the hardest/easiest for me to be honest

The hardest decision I ever made

The worst decision I ever made and what I learned from it

Something I want to do, but am afraid to do. What's the worst that could happen? What's the best?

The hardest thing to deal with at school/work

Expectations of authority figures, dealing with authority

Being accepted by others (cliqués)

Rules, how to deal with unfair rules

Different opinions, how to disagree respectfully

Male/female relationships

What is your "purpose" in life? How do you know?

Drugs/alcohol/smoking, sex and dating (consider parents *and* teens who are attending parties)

Personal/career goals

Dealing with conflicts

Attention—who gets it and why

Honesty and openness with tact

AGENDA (at least do the starred items)

★ ICEBREAKER/COMPLIMENTS:

    MINUTES:

    OLD BUSINESS:

★ NEW BUSINESS:

    FINANCES/ALLOWANCES:

★ FAMILY CALENDAR:

    LESSON/STORY:

    TOPIC DISCUSSION:

    ROLES FOR NEXT COUNCIL:

★ CLOSING "ANCHOR" ACTIVITY:

    ENTERTAINMENT:

    GAME/FAMILY ACTIVITY:

    TREAT:

SUMMARY SHEET
FAMILY COUNCIL TOOLSET

- The purpose of family councils is to have regularly scheduled time together to build a sense of unity, make decisions, resolve problems, and teach values and life skills. Council meetings are useful for any family, school, or group.

- Every member has a role. ☆☆☆☆
  Necessary roles are the Leader, Recorder, Ice Breaker, and Anchor.

  Optional roles are the Discussion Topic Leader and Snack, Game, Entertainment, or Lesson Planner.

- Start with those who are willing to attend; include anyone who lives with the family. Let everyone know they are welcome to attend, when they are ready. Never punish someone for not attending.

- Meet regularly, not just to discuss problems. Don't skip meetings because you are too busy. ☆☆☆☆

- Start positive and end positive. ☆☆☆☆ Keep an atmosphere of equality.

- Start and end on time and set time limits on discussions.

- Discuss issues that affect the entire family. Individuals can ask for family input on personal issues. *Never* handle individual discipline in a family council.

- Hold maintenance meetings to discuss how councils are going.

Ground rules:

- Express yourself respectfully, with no name-calling or blaming.

- Everyone's opinions and feelings are okay; listen with respect.

- Limit griping; turn the complaint into a suggestion.

- Focus on goals and solutions, not problems. Don't get side-tracked.

- Get children involved in suggesting solutions. Allow all ideas.

- Give everyone an equal chance to share feelings and ideas.

- Reach win/win solutions everyone agrees with. Don't vote.

- If you can't reach a consensus, table the issue until you reach a final decision or agree on a trial period. Reserve "executive decision-making privilege" for critical emergency decisions.

- All decisions hold firm until the next family council.

PRACTICE EXERCISES

A. Identify and Correct Mistakes. In each situation, the family makes one or more mistakes in setting up or conducting a family council. For each situation, (a) identify the mistake and (b) offer suggestions to correct or prevent it.

1. Holly says she can come to family councils only every second and fourth Sunday of the month, because she has softball practice on the first and third Sundays. The family decides to meet only the second and fourth weeks so everyone can attend.

2. In the Hoskins family, meetings are attended by Dad, Mom, Hannah, and Seth. Grandpa Hoskins, who has lived in the back bedroom for the last four years, is not invited.

3. The McCann family has decided not to hold family councils because one of their three children, Trevor, said he wouldn't attend. He thinks the idea is stupid.

4. In the Metzger family, meetings are held in Dad's study. He sits behind his desk and everyone else pulls in chairs from the kitchen.

5. Joel is Chairperson this week. On every question he asks for a vote, counts the "yeas" and "nays," and lets the majority rule.

6. Alyssa's parents are divorced, and she lives with her mother and her two brothers. The four of them have regular family councils. This week, Alyssa complains to her mother about her weekend visits with her father. She says she spends most of her time cleaning up his apartment and washing several days' worth of dirty dishes. Mother says, "Well, bring it up at our family council tomorrow."

7. Brandon feels that a decision made at a family council about his bedtime was unfair. He pleads with Mom, who says it's okay for him to stay up until 10:00, instead of 9:00 as the family decided. (There are *two* mistakes here, did you find them both?)

8. Mr. and Mrs. Bowling ask the kids, "Where do you want to go for vacation this year?" The children (ages 15, 10, and 5) want to go to the beach. The parents want to go to the mountains. Since Mother and Dad are paying for the vacation, they decide that the family will go to the mountains anyway, since they dislike the beach.

B. Get Unstuck. The following two families are "stuck." For each situation, answer the following questions:

a. How is this family getting stuck in their problem solving?
b. How could they have approached the decision differently?
c. How can they get unstuck and reach a consensus (win/win) decision?

1. Mr. and Mrs. Evans have three children: Jared, 10, Casey, 9, and Kara, 6. During their first family council, they tried to plan a family outing. Jared and Kara decide they want to go to a movie, but Casey wants to go to a baseball game. Mother would prefer the movie. Father would like to go to the game, but is willing to go to the movie if the rest of the family would rather go there. Casey refuses to go along with the rest of the group.

2. Travis, 8, is a homebody. He'd always rather stay home than go somewhere. Saturday is when the family meets to plan something fun together. Everyone, except Travis, wants to go to the movies. Although Travis says he likes this movie, today he insists that he wants to stay home. All he wants to do is play with his friends and video games. Travis' parents want the family to stay together. Travis is too young to leave him home alone and they don't want to pay a sitter to watch him.

Activity for the Week

Hold a family council this week.

1. Decide which roles you would like members to choose. The necessary roles are already checked.

✓ Chairperson	___ Song selector
✓ Recorder	___ Game planner
✓ Ice-breaker	___ Lesson planner
✓ Anchor-person	___ Snack planner

2. Select items for your agenda. The necessary agenda items are already checked.

✓ Compliments	✓ Calendar planning
___ Reading of the minutes	___ Lesson/topic discussion
✓ Progress on decisions made	___ Roles for next council meeting
✓ New decisions/problems	___ Closing Activity
___ Finances/Allowances	___ Snack/song/poem/story

Detailed Answers

A. Identify and Correct Mistakes.

1. Holly's softball practice is a *responsibility* and she doesn't have practice *all day*. Instead of canceling the council meeting, the family can find a day and time convenient for everyone.

2. The Hoskins family needs to welcome Grandpa Hoskins, since he lives with them.

3. The McCann family can hold family councils, even if Trevor chooses not to attend. They can let Trevor know he is always welcome. They do not punish Trevor for not attending or exclude him from any family activities they plan, just because he didn't help plan them. If he doesn't like the idea, they can invite him to attend the council and offer his ideas.

4. Mr. Metzger is exerting his authority position, nonverbally, by sitting behind his desk. The family needs to meet in neutral territory, where everyone is on an equal level.

5. Effective family councils do not use voting. Joel can guide the family through the problem-solving process, until they reach a consensus decision.

6. Alyssa's problem is with her father, who lives elsewhere, so this problem is not appropriate to resolve at the family council. If Alyssa's mother is not bitter and can remain objective and helpful, she can do one-on-one problem solving with Alyssa. If she cannot remain objective, she can offer Alyssa's siblings as resources. If they visit together, they could suggest holding family councils at Dad's. Or the kids could hold their own "sibling" council to brainstorm ideas.

7. Brandon's bed time is not an appropriate issue to discuss at a family council. If general bedtimes are discussed as they apply to all the children, then it might be appropriate to discuss. In that case, any agreement must hold at least until the next family council. Mom does not have the authority or right to cancel or change a decision the entire family made.

8. Mr. and Mrs. Bowling asked, "Where do you want to go for vacation this year?" This implies the possibilities are endless. If this is truly the choice, they need to work on a win/win decision. They could choose someplace where there are mountains *and* beach, for example. If they are only willing to go to the mountains, they can present the decision as, "This year, we are going to go on vacation to the mountains. What would you like to do while we are there?"

B. Get Unstuck

1. The Evans family has tried to tackle too much for their *first* family council. Instead of deciding *what* to do for their family activity, they might want to start by deciding *how* they will make the decision and what kinds of activities are appropriate. For example, does the activity have to be with the entire family? Can pairs break up and have independent "dates"? Then they could brainstorm ideas for *possible* activities. Could each person have a turn selecting an activity? How do they set priorities? A movie shows for a month at a time, but that particular sporting event might

feature a favorite team only on that date. Under those circumstances, would the sporting event be considered a priority? If the family is split between two options, can there be a conditional agreement that the next activity will be the other choice?

2. Travis is trying to exert his independence. If he feels his opinions are not considered in a decision, he may choose to start a power struggle. Travis' parents have several options that could prevent this. If their bottom line is that Saturdays are for *family* activities, they can point out that Travis can usually stay home other times. They may want to take turns picking a family activity, so Travis gets his way sometimes. They could shift the focus of the choices, "You do have to go, but you don't have to participate." Usually, children come around once they are in the car and see the activity. The parents could also provide one last option, "You may choose to stay home, but *you* will need to pay for a sitter out of your money." Even if he chooses this option, he will be unlikely to follow through with it. If Travis complains or tries to spoil the fun for everyone else, he is trying to get revenge for losing a power struggle or vote. To prevent this, his parents want to acknowledge his disappointment at having to do something he doesn't want to do. They can redirect his behavior by letting him choose some of the activities they do there.

WHAT'S NEXT?

It's always difficult for busy families to set aside time for family councils. Make a commitment to your family and children's future by scheduling weekly family councils. We all can use the practice and the long-term benefits are well worth our efforts.

Chapter 15, " Three C's: Consistency, Criticism, and Confidence," is the final stop on our tour of *The Parent's Toolshop*. We now have all the tools we need to build a healthy family and reach our long-term parenting goals. We have learned many new ideas and made great strides in our growth as parents. Now, our challenge is to nurture ourselves and maintain our progress.

We've dispelled many parenting myths in *The Parent's Toolshop*. The last chapter corrects the last few myths by explaining the true definition of consistency (the first "C"). The second "C" stands for criticism—how to respond (or not respond) so criticism and unhelpful advice do not deter us from our long-term parenting goals. This chapter also gives us a final booster shot of confidence (the third "C") by offering suggestions for self-nurturing, so we continue our upward path of growth. As we end our tour of *The Parent's Toolshop*, we reflect on all we've learned and how much we've grown—and look ahead, to what the future holds for us as we continue our mission of building a healthy family.

REFERENCES

1. For more information about conducting "formal" family meetings, read: *Positive Discipline*, by Jane Nelsen (Ballantine, 1987; Revised Edition, 1996); *S.T.E.P.: Systematic Training for Effective Parenting* (American Guidance Service, 1982) and *The NextSTEP* (American Guidance Service, 1987), by Donald Dinkmeyer, Gary McKay, Donald Dinkmeyer Jr., James S. Dinkmeyer, and Joyce L. McKay; and *Active Parenting*, by Michael Popkin (Harper Row, 1987).

2. "Family Home Evening" is a practice of the Church of Jesus Christ of Latter-day Saints (Mormons).

3. Lesson activity ideas are used with the permission of The Church of Jesus Christ of Latter-day Saints, from their Family Home Meeting publication, which accompanies their video, *"Family First"* (1992). For a free video, call 1-888-537-8433.

4. Another terrific (and inexpensive) resource for family council activities is *Families Creating a Circle of Peace*, published by The Institute for Peace and Justice (1996). To order a copy, contact the Families Against Violence Advocacy Network at 4144 Lindell Blvd., #408, St. Louis, MO 63108 or you can call 314-533-4445 or send e-mail to ppjn@aol.com.

CHAPTER 15
THREE C's: Consistency, Criticism, Confidence

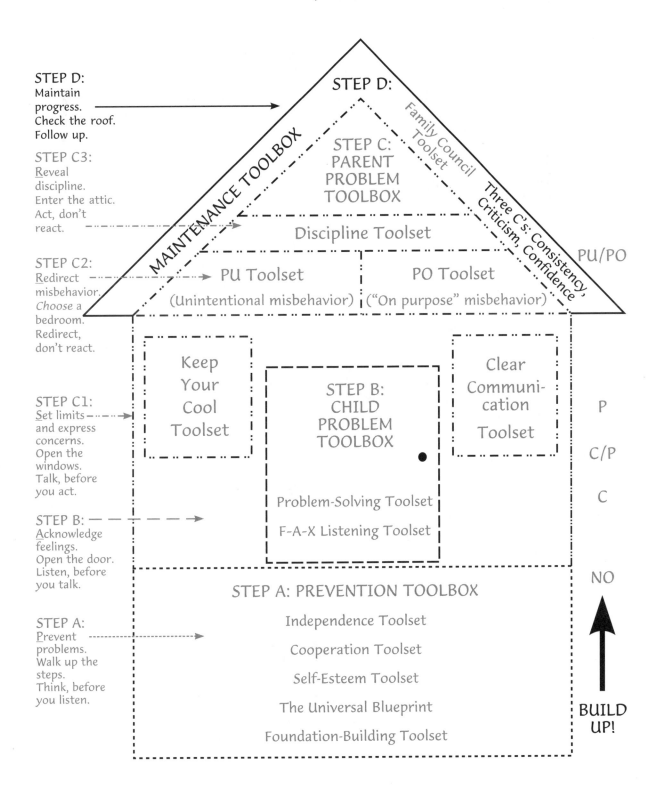

STEP D:
Maintain
progress.
Check the roof.
Follow up.

STEP C3:
Reveal
discipline.
Enter the attic.
Act, don't
react.

STEP C2:
Redirect
misbehavior.
Choose a
bedroom.
Redirect,
don't react.

STEP C1:
Set limits
and express
concerns.
Open the
windows.
Talk, before
you act.

STEP B:
Acknowledge
feelings.
Open the door.
Listen, before
you talk.

STEP A:
Prevent
problems.
Walk up the
steps.
Think, before
you listen.

STEP D:

Family Council Toolset

Three C's: Consistency, Criticism, Confidence

MAINTENANCE TOOLBOX

STEP C:
PARENT
PROBLEM
TOOLBOX

Discipline Toolset

PU Toolset
(Unintentional misbehavior)

PO Toolset
("On purpose" misbehavior)

PU/PO

Keep
Your
Cool
Toolset

STEP B:
CHILD
PROBLEM
TOOLBOX

Problem-Solving Toolset

F-A-X Listening Toolset

Clear
Communi-
cation
Toolset

P

C/P

C

STEP A: PREVENTION TOOLBOX

Independence Toolset

Cooperation Toolset

Self-Esteem Toolset

The Universal Blueprint

Foundation-Building Toolset

NO

BUILD
UP!

CHAPTER
15 THREE C's: Consistency, Criticism, Confidence

Once we learn how to build a house, we follow the same steps and use the same tools to build other houses. The type of house we build might be different, but the basic elements of the blueprint and the tools we use to build it are the same. If we make a mistake, we try to correct it, learn from it, and get back on track. Once we succeed in building different parts of our house, we have greater confidence as a builder. We have to work hard, however, to keep believing in our abilities when we make mistakes, something doesn't turn out right, or someone criticizes our work. At times like these, it is helpful to know how to respond without getting defensive and see if there is any value in the comment.

Once parents have a plan for their parenting, they want to follow the same basic steps using the same types of tools. The individual problems or specific tools they select, however, may vary. Mistakes and ineffective responses will naturally happen. Rather than trying to prove "I'm right," parents can correct the mistake, make amends, and learn from the mistake. The confident parent maintains consistency as much as humanly possible, getting back on track quickly, and handles criticism assertively and respectfully.

IN THIS CHAPTER

The Three C's help us maintain our personal progress with three important ideas:
1. True *consistency* means we stick with our parenting plan and get back on track when we stray. It also means we handle problems the same way in public and around others as we do at home.
2. When others *criticize* our parenting methods or we need to deal with adult "misbehavior," we can use our new tools to respond to adults, too.
3. It can be difficult to maintain our *confidence* as a parent and person, but there are specific attitudes and actions we can use to continue on the positive path we are now on.

WHEN TO USE THE THREE C'S

We use the tools in this chapter constantly, but especially when *we* feel discouraged or under pressure to stray from our parenting plan. The tools we've learned are helpful in *all* relationships, not just with children, so we can begin taking our skills to a higher level. We can return to this chapter (and the rest of the book) as a reference guide anytime in the future—for a quick review, an extra boost of confidence, or for help in solving a problem.

INCREASING OUR *CONSISTENCY*

Children need parents who are consistent. When parents have consistent responses, no matter where or when, children know what to expect if they misbehave. Effective parents work to increase their consistency, but also accept their limitations. It's not humanly possible to *always* be consistent.

The Myth about Consistency ☆☆☆☆

Many people think, "If I said I was going to do this, I have to follow through," and follow this motto even when they make a poor choice or overreact. This is not true consistency. True consistency is staying on the same path or getting back on it when we stray. When we realize we've made a mistake, we can get back on track and model for children how to handle mistakes with this four-step process:

1. Admit that we made a mistake.
2. Apologize for any hurt feelings that resulted from the mistake.
3. Learn what we can from the mistake. Make changes to correct the mistake or avoid it in the future.
4. Work with our children on a fairer solution.

Pressure Situations

When children are at school all day long, they often put a lot of effort into "being good." When they come home, they may not put as much effort into controlling their behavior. Parents often do the same thing. When we interact with other people's children, we have the patience and tact to handle their misbehavior respectfully. We might be yelling at our children, but if we run into someone we know, we immediately put on our smile and talk nicely to them and our children. This is proof that if we make a conscious choice, we *can* handle stressful, pressure situations. While we can't always be alone or have a constant audience, we can "trick" ourselves into behaving as though we do.

> *A Personal Story. Several years ago, there was a television news special about spanking. They took several sets of parents who believed in spanking and followed them around for a month with a video camera. They showed some very upsetting incidents that bordered on abuse. Tears came to my eyes for the children involved.*
>
> *Next, they had an expert in family violence research (my focus area in college) sit with this group of parents to explain why spanking wasn't good. He knew his statistics well on what didn't work, but only told the parents, "Don't ever spank. Do something like time-out instead." He didn't even give them guidelines for effective time-outs!*
>
> *Then they showed these families six months later. One or two of the families had stopped spanking and were being respectful. Several were using time-outs instead of spanking, but were using them in humiliating ways to exert their power. Several said nothing else worked and had returned to spanking. Considering the advice they got, I wasn't surprised! You can't take a tool (even an ineffective one) away from someone, without exchanging it for a more effective tool and giving specific directions for its use.*
>
> *Soon after that report, Amber had a really bad day. No matter what I did, she would whine, fuss, and begin to throw a tantrum. I stayed on track pretty well, but by dinner time I was pressured and hungry, and my brain cells were running on empty. Things escalated to the point that I was trying to make her sit in a time-out chair and she was trying to kick me. As I tried to grab her legs to stop her kicking, I had an almost uncontrollable urge to spank her. At that instant, I thought about the parents in the television report. I thought, "What would I do if the TV cameras were watching* **me** *right now?" I pulled myself together and started talking to Amber respectfully and calmly! I was amazed that I could do it! "If I can pull myself together for a camera (or a neighbor)," I thought, "I can do it at other times, too." Now, when I think I'm about to "lose it," I imagine a television camera is filming me, with all my students watching. It never fails to help me pull out that extra effort to do what I know I can do.*

If you are like me and having an audience helps you stay on track, just imagine "everyone is watching." If, on the other hand, you feel pressured thinking about people watching you and cave in, imagine that you have blinders on. You are the only person there and no one is watching or judging your performance. Neither of these has to be true. They are simply ways to bring out in ourselves what is already there—a competent parent with a helpful response.

MISBEHAVIOR IN PUBLIC

When other adults are watching our interaction with misbehaving children, we often think they are judging us on how well we handle the situation. We may use punishment to satisfy the spectators, since it appears to achieve the *quickest* results. It takes great courage to think clearly during these pressured times to achieve the most *effective* long-term results.

> **It's important to follow the same parenting plan away from home that we use at home.**

If we use one method of parenting at home and another outside the home, children learn there are times when they can get away with misbehavior and test us more often. If we use the same parenting plan wherever we go, our children always know the limits and are better behaved.

If we are somewhere new or anticipate a problem, we can plan ahead (Prevention Toolbox). We explain what we will be doing, what behavior we expect, why that behavior is important, and reveal discipline. Then we follow through, ignoring others and staying on track. If we need to discipline in public, we can go to a private place or whisper in their ear if we can't leave. (Empty aisles and back corners of stores can offer a quiet, private place to talk.) We can avoid feelings of embarrassment by reminding ourselves, "The only person who can make me feel embarrassed is me."

FRIENDS AND EXTENDED FAMILY

Social gatherings and visits to other homes can be stressful. When children misbehave around friends or family, we often feel embarrassed and pressured to respond however *they* expect us to respond. We must remain firm to our long-term goals. If we give in, children learn they can get their way if they embarrass us in front of others. If we overreact and punish children, they feel confused and humiliated in front of a group. These are key motives for revenge, and further misbehavior is a good way to get that revenge. Consistently using effective parenting tools helps children learn *self*-control and *self*-discipline. When others criticize or interfere with our parenting, the best approach is to excuse ourselves and solve the problem with our children privately.

INCONSISTENT PARENTING PARTNERS

I often hear the comment, "When my husband (wife) is home, it's his (her) rules. When I'm there, it's my rules. When we are both there, the kids play us against each other. I've tried telling him (her) what I've learned, but he (she) just gets defensive. How can I make him (her) change?" The answer is, "You can't." That does not mean, however, that the two of you can't have a consistent parenting plan, even if the plan includes different styles of parenting. In addition to the suggestions in the "Parenting as a Team" section in Chapter 2, there are several options available to parents:

- **Agree on a plan for common problems that arise.** Use the problem-solving and decision-making worksheets. Decide what each of you wants to accomplish and find a way to meet both parents' concerns and needs. It is important to listen carefully to your partner and not immediately offer solutions or advice. You can offer information and observations, but don't sound like a know-it-all or criticize your partner's efforts. Offer encouragement and support to enlist your partner's involvement in the solution.

- **Agree not to sabotage each other.** Even if a partner's decision is imperfect, agree to either back up the partner or, at the least, not to interfere, even if you disagree. The parent who makes a decision is the one who has to follow through with the commitment and experience any consequences of that decision. Part of this agreement is that if a parent makes a poor decision, the other parent agrees not to say "I told you so." Pointing out mistakes builds resentment and further divides parents. Simply allow the parent to learn from his or her mistake. This is still an imperfect plan, but one that is often workable until the parents iron out their differences.

- **If the other parent's style is not abusive or does not grossly violate the child's rights, you can back off and not interfere.** If the child's feelings are hurt, acknowledge their feelings without taking sides or criticizing the other parent. (If your partner *does* physically, emotionally, or sexually abuse your child, you must have the courage to contact someone who can help: a counselor, child abuse prevention hotline, or in emergencies, the police.)

- **Agree to disagree respectfully.** If you disagree or argue in front of the children, do so respectfully and fairly. Screaming and yelling scares children. Do your part to calmly work out disagreements and model healthy problem solving. If you argue or disagree in front of children, it's important to show them that you've made up and how you got there (from disagreeing to working together).

- **If you choose to get involved, back up your partner with your skills.** If we can figure out what our partners are trying to accomplish, we can model the effective skills we've learned. If it works, the partner feels supported, without feeling criticized.

If your parenting partner has not learned the skills in this book, the best attitude to take is, ***"Live it, don't preach it."*** No one likes to hear, "You're supposed to do this. You're not supposed to do that!" (And don't use *my* name in vain either! "Jody says to do . . .") Let your example speak for itself. Acknowledge your partner's frustration and be reassuring that you know he or she is trying to make the best choice. They may have old "tapes" that are at the core of *their* onion and resolving their own issues may take time.

GIVING ADVICE

Most parents are interested in doing the best they can, but feel defensive if others present new ideas in a judgmental way. The tools we've learned are to help us improve *ourselves* and our families. Don't use your knowledge to judge or impose advice when others haven't asked for it. Many parents are enthusiastic about their new skills and want to "help" other parents by correcting them, but this *isn't* helpful. The situation is *their* problem, not yours. We can support them with our skills or, if they are open to suggestions, ask helpful questions such as, "What do you want him to learn? Does he understand . . .? How do you think he'd react if you did . . .?" Never push your ideas on others.

Before you say anything, ask yourself, "What do I hope to accomplish by getting involved? Does the person seem open to discussing options?" Only say something if you can say it in a way that makes the person feel supported and better about themselves. Sandwich suggestions between compliments, "I noticed how well you . . . Have you ever considered . . . I'm sure you will . . ."

If you give information about child development or long-term consequences, use general non-judgmental words, "When children hear ___, they often think the parent means ___." Avoid the words "you," "right," and "wrong." Instead, use statements like "more effective" and "less effective" or "more respectful" and "less respectful." These terms are less judgmental. You want to be sensitive without sounding superior.

When you are in public and see another parent in distress, offer a reassuring look and smile. You can sometimes offer them an extra hand, but don't take over. Open the door or ask if they need help carrying packages, for example. If your motive is to be helpful, not critical (as though they can't manage on their own), most parents will appreciate the support and understanding.

A Personal Story. I don't give parenting advice to others, unless they ask for it. It's hard to know a better way to handle a situation and watch someone use ineffective parenting skills. Once, when I was in a store, there was a young mother with a newborn on her shoulder and a toddler in tow. The toddler was going beyond where she could see him. I remembered how hard those first weeks of adjustment were, after having a second child—juggling a newborn again, forgetting to watch the older child, etc. I smiled at her and gave her an "I understand" look. She looked tired and overwhelmed. She kept calling to her toddler, "Dawana! Dawana! Get back here! Stay with me," but her toddler took advantage of his mother's inability to catch him.

This mother and I ended up in the check-out line together. Her toddler was still running around. When she couldn't see him, I told her where he was and what he was doing. She thanked me. When the toddler was near his mother, I bent down and said, "You know, if you stand right here in front of your mommy and give that toy to the lady behind the desk, your mommy will buy that for you. But you need to stand in front of your mom if you want to take it home." This amazing bundle of energy stayed put! His mother thanked me as she left and I said, "Hey, I know what it's like. We mom's need to stick together."

If we interact with other people's children, make sure the parent is present and can see and hear us. Otherwise, the parent or child might worry that we are a "bad" stranger. We need to be cautious not to overstep our boundaries. Just be supportive and encouraging, modeling skills instead of preaching them.

*A Graduate's Story. I was at the playground when another mom come up to me and asked, "Where did you learn to talk like that?" This gave me a chance to tell her about the parenting class, without implying, "You aren't a good parent, you **need** a parenting class." The myth that parenting classes are for bad parents is so widespread, such a suggestion doesn't come off well unless someone asks for more information. I've had several people ask me, "Why did **you** take a parenting class?" It gives me a chance to reinforce the value of learning as much as we can about any commitment or responsibility we take on — and my kids are one of my highest priorities in life. Why **wouldn't** I learn as much as I can to be the best parent I can?*

HANDLING *CRITICISM* AND UNHELPFUL ADVICE ☆☆☆☆

We've learned how to be supportive of others, when they are experiencing problems with their children, but how do we handle people who are less than supportive to us?

Screening Advice

Not all advice is healthy or accurate, even when people tell us "it works." Whenever we hear or read advice, we want to screen it, to make sure it is consistent with our positive parenting plan and long-term goals. Here are a few guidelines for screening advice.

Don't blindly accept parenting advice without double-checking its accuracy. Consider the basis for the advice.

*   *Is it someone's personal opinion or is it based on research, broad experience, and methods that have been proven effective over time?* Don't automatically trust advice just because someone believes "It worked for me and my children, therefore it will work for everyone." There could be other factors that led to the success—or the long-term negative effects are yet to be seen!

*   *Does it reflect personal power, control, or superiority issues?* Don't blindly accept advice from people who think "I am an expert simply because I have a degree and work with families; therefore I know it all and everything I say is automatically accurate."

- *Is the advice based on fear or love?* Be careful if you hear a hidden message that says "If you don't do what I say you're a wimp and will lose control of your kids." Avoid advice that offers unhealthy quick fixes or extreme reactions.

Compare the advice to the proper definitions and guidelines of healthy parenting philosophies and techniques you've learned on this tour. Don't get hung-up on whether the person uses the same terms we use in this book. Look beyond the words to the *qualities* and *philosophy* of the technique. Especially consider the following questions:

- *Is the philosophy positive, balanced, and healthy?* Does an author promote a balanced approach or only see things in black and white; their way and the wrong way. Do they use the correct definitions for healthy parenting techniques? If the definition is incorrect, does the advice still fit the guidelines of healthy, balanced parenting?

- *What is the philosophy of discipline?* Is it really punishment? Does this style promote the parent's power and superiority at the expense of the child's rights and needs?

- *What does the technique teach children?* Are there unhealthy hidden messages?

- *Does the advice say this is the only way to handle a situation or that there are choices to pick from?* The Parent's Toolshop outlines specific steps for responding to problems, but at each step there are several options we can choose and no one response is the only possible helpful response. We can even mix and match these tools, as long as we follow the basic guidelines.

- *Is the advice a commonly accepted idea, but inaccurate, unhealthy, or unhelpful?* Consciously choose advice based on how well it can help you reach your long-term parenting goals.

> *A Professional's Comment. There's so much about The Parent's Toolshop that I like. As a parent, it is easy to react to problems; this offers many healthy alternatives. As a counselor, I like the way I can apply the process to all relationships. There were so many things that even as a therapist, with all the training I've had, that I didn't realize—like the myths about time-outs. I've been giving the same kind of advice lots of other professionals give—and assumed it must be right, because so many people believed it. This was a real eye-opener.*

You will find that you can trust the advice of the authors I've referenced in this book. Since *The Parent's Toolshop* is so comprehensive and references many other books, it could take a lifetime just to master *these* ideas. We don't need to confuse ourselves by reading books where we have to pick and choose ideas with a fine-toothed comb. We can be selective about our future reading, choosing those books and articles that explore balanced parenting techniques in more depth or those that deal with specific issues.

> **Our focus is on establishing a good relationship with our own children. We can ignore any advice that gets in the way of these goals or reduces communication and mutual respect in our family.**

Why People Criticize

Adult behavior can be unintentional or intentional, just like children's. Unintentional criticism usually comes from people who mean well, but express themselves poorly. Seek the value in what they say, instead of reacting to the *way* they say it. People often criticize parents because they are insecure about their own parenting (their upbringing, or how current methods compare to those they used when their children were young). If someone follows their advice, it confirms their way is "right" (PO, power).

Often, people offer advice because they assume others don't know any better, especially first-time parents. It often seems that everyone from the maternity nurse to the stranger in the grocery store thinks new parents need advice. Unfortunately, unsolicited advice is often inaccurate and confuses new parents. When a mother has her second child, the maternity nurse often says, "Oh well, I guess you know all this." Use this to your advantage. The more educated you become, the more confident you will be, and the less criticism and unwanted advice will sway you.

Other people criticize because pessimism and know-it-all-ism are part of their personality (PU). You probably can't change them, but you can learn to protect yourself from their toxic personalities. Refuse to believe their insults. Let comments "roll off your back." If you can do this, you'll reduce your stress and maintain the relationship (if you must, as with relatives). If this doesn't work, you may need to set limits for yourself or the other person. (See "When to Set Limits" later in this section.)

Some people intentionally criticize to get revenge or express jealousy (PO). They might feel guilty about mistakes they made and want to justify their decisions. They might also think that because you read a lot of parenting books or have taken a parenting class, you think you're perfect or your children are perfect. They thrill in pointing out your mistakes or shortcomings. "Did they teach you to do *that* in your parenting class?" "So when does the book tell you to finally give that kid a spanking?" Always try to present yourself humbly, "I'm not a perfect parent and neither are my kids. I don't know it all and still have a lot to learn." If you want to explain your methods, you can say, "This may not be the way for everyone, but from all I've seen, read, believe, and tried, this is the way I want to go. I believe it's worth the investment, but that's my choice. I don't expect everyone to agree with me."

 ## Responding to Criticism

Use the Universal Blueprint. It is best to take the same approach with criticism as we do with parenting problems. Remember, the blueprint is "universal" because it applies to *all* relationships.

A. **First, figure out whose problem it is, theirs or yours**. If it's their insecurity, just listen and be understanding. Is their behavior unintentional or intentional? If it is intentional, what is their goal. Power? Revenge?

   If you are repeatedly criticized by someone you can't avoid, <u>P</u>revent the problem from starting or worsening by planning ahead for the next "attack."

   •   Consider the criticizer's perspective, so you can acknowledge their feelings and reduce their defensiveness. If they feel understood, they might not attack as much. It can also help you better understand their motives.

   •   Imagine the situation and what the person usually says. Plan a respectful response and practice it in your mind or with a person who knows the criticizer and what he or she might say or do. Include in your plan the words you will say, staying calm, positive self-talk, tone of voice, body language, and when to walk away, if needed.

B. **If or when you respond to criticism, start by <u>A</u>cknowledging the other person's feelings** or perspective, "I can understand how you might feel that way . . ." or ". . . how it might seem that . . ."

C. 1. **<u>S</u>et limits or express your feelings respectfully**, "I feel . . ." or "I've decided to . . ." Just speak for yourself, without attacking what they're doing. That causes others to feel defensive or offended.

    2. **Remain firm in your decision**. Don't defend or explain yourself, unless someone is truly interested in your opinion.

If people don't realize how critical they sound and are willing to change, set up a signal. When we use the Universal Blueprint, people who are unintentionally hurting us usually hear our concerns and don't want to hurt us again. They may agree to a hand signal, word, or phrase you can use whenever they blame or criticize, to help them change this habit.

Use a "one-liner." If you react to criticism like me, you stand there stunned with your jaw dropped to the floor. Over the next week, you think of a million things you "should have" said. At these times, it helps to have some are quick, assertive, respectful responses you can choose:

- *"We've researched this and discussed it and we've decided . . ."* Or "I know it might not work for everyone, but we've decided . . ." Once people realize you are making a conscious choice to handle a situation this way, they often back off, even if they disagree with your decision.

- *Say you'll consider their opinion* the next time you and your partner discuss it. You *can* choose to give the idea some thought . . . even if only for one second!

- *Accept your mistakes and faults, without apologizing.* "You're right; I made a mistake. I know better than to do that." Use this when you agree that the other person is right.

- *Calmly acknowledge that there is "probably some truth"* in what they said. You are agreeing in principle only, without making any commitment one way or another to change.

- When asked a "Why do you do ____?" question, respond with *"Why do you ask?"* instead of defending yourself. It may cause the person to think about their motives and whether they want to admit their reasons.

- *Agree to disagree.* Say you're not willing to discuss the issue and *change the subject.*

- *Ignore the cut.* Forgive and forget. If you're not ready for that, let the person know you heard the remark ("Umm-hmm") but don't respond further.

- *Use humor.* If someone says, "You still haven't lost your weight from the baby!" a woman can reply, "Yeah, I'm still trying to pass for pregnant so I can get special treatment." We can also simply agree with no excuse, "Yeah, I'm in no hurry to lose it." One graduate's mother-in-law asked her, "How long are you going to breastfeed him anyway?" Her reply was, "Well, what do you think they have recess for?" Her mother-in-law realized how ridiculous her question was and never brought it up again.

When to Set Limits

If you have consistently used respectful communication skills and the person is intentionally trying to hurt you or undermine your parenting, you may need to set limits. Try setting less restrictive limits first, in the following order:

1. **Remind the person that you need support more than you need criticism.** Reveal that you will not respond to criticism. If your children are the targets of criticism and it hurts their feelings, try to explain to them in nonjudgmental, understanding words that some people don't know nicer ways to say how they feel. Teach your children how to let the comments "roll off their backs."

2. **Set guidelines for your visits with this person,** such as what you are willing to discuss, how you plan to handle situations, or how you expect others to treat you or your children. Set time limits for the visits. If difficult people from out-of-town want to visit, limit the visit to a few days or arrange to have them stay at a nearby hotel. (I know, this is an expensive option, but the alternative—having a nervous breakdown or major blow-up—would make it worth seriously considering.)

3. **If they are unwilling to respect your bottom-line limits, you may need to leave or keep visits on "your turf,"** where your family rules are in effect. If you've revealed your expectations and they criticize you again, say "We need to be going now" and leave (even if it's abrupt). This emphasizes your willingness to follow through with your intentions. If the criticizer wants to visit you, say, "You can come to visit if . . ." Use the assertive communication skills you learned to keep the blame out of your statements. If they violate your family rules, you have every right to say, "I think it's time for you to go."

Even within our own families we sometimes need to set these kinds of limits. The bottom line is to do what you can to resolve these conflicts peacefully and assertively, but be willing to do what is best for you and your children's mental and emotional health. To decide whether you should compromise your rights, ask yourself the following questions:

• How important is this issue to me?
• If I compromise my rights, will I violate my values, principles, or feelings of self-worth?
• How will I feel later if I compromise?
• How much will it cost me if I compromise? (time, energy, self-respect, money.)

Let's practice a few examples of responding to criticism and unhelpful advice. The practice exercises and the answers are in the middle of the chapter this time, so we can end our tour with a final booster shot of confidence.

PRACTICE EXERCISES

A. Correcting Myths about Parenting

Remember the true/false quiz you took in the beginning of the book? Every answer was totally or partially "false." The following exercise lists these myths again. Recall all that you've learned on this tour and rewrite the myths so they are true statements. Possible revisions follow the exercise.

Myth 1   Parents should attend parenting classes when having problems with their children.

Myth 2   Parent educators tell parents what they are doing wrong and how to raise children the right way.

Myth 3   Whenever parents use an effective parenting skill, they should see it work right away.

Myth 4   Children should not be the center of the family; the parent should.

Myth 5   Democratic parenting is too permissive and only works with certain kinds of children.

Myth 6   It is the parent's job to control children's behavior.

Myth 7   Parents need to immediately react to a problem to effectively resolve it.

Myth 8   When parents stop children's misbehavior, the problem usually goes away.

Myth 9   Parents can encourage children by giving them lots of praise and rewards.

Myth 10   When parents let children know they are proud of them, children feel parents are giving them credit for their accomplishments.

Myth 11   Sometimes it's helpful to offer constructive criticism to help children improve.

Myth 12   Children should obey their parents because they are adults in authority. When children ask "Why should I?" parents only need to say, "Because I said so."

Myth 13   Behavior charts with stars or rewards foster internal motivation.

Myth 14   When parents give children choices, children think they should have a choice about everything.

Myth 15   All toddlers go through a "no" stage; it's a normal part of childhood.

Myth 16   Parents should give children more independence when they show they can handle it.

Myth 17   When children struggle with simple tasks, it helps to say, "You can do it if you try harder."

Myth 18   When children have problems, parents should help solve them.

Myth 19   When children aren't doing their homework, parents should set up a homework schedule, make sure they stick to it, supervise their work, and sign off on it every day.

Myth 20   People get angry because other people and events are out of their control.

Myth 21   Children know how to push their parents' buttons because they program and control them.

Myth 22   When children misbehave, parents should show their disappointment so the children will want to change.

Myth 23   When parents repeatedly tell children to stop misbehaving and they don't stop, parents can assume their children know how to behave better.

Myth 24   Children misbehave to get what they want or sometimes just to get on their parents' nerves.

Myth 25   When misbehaving children need to "learn a lesson," parents should make sure they suffer a little, to drive home their point.

Myth 26   When parents want children to behave, they should threaten to punish the children.

Myth 27   Timeouts should be one minute for every year of age. Children should be isolated in an unpleasant or boring place and not allowed to play.

Myth 28   Parents should call a family meeting when there is a problem.

Myth 29   Every family member votes on decisions in family meetings.

Myth 30   Parents should be consistent. If they say they are going to punish their children, they need to follow through, even if they realize later they overreacted.

Myth 31   Inconsistent parenting is damaging. Effective parenting partners do things the same way.

B. Responding to Criticism

1. The Greer's are visiting friends. Five-year-old Jason begins misbehaving at the dinner table. Mrs. Greer, who has learned balanced parenting techniques, disregards those approaches and sternly scolds Jason, "You need to obey me. Now settle down!" The child stops for a few minutes, but begins again. This time, Mrs. Greer excuses herself, takes Jason to another room, and closes the door. She returns to the table and apologizes to Mrs. Payne. Mrs. Payne says, "You ought to just spank him. That would teach him to behave!"
    a. Why might Mrs. Greer have violated her child-rearing principles?
    b. Why was she embarrassed?
    c. What other alternatives, consistent with balanced principles, were available?
    d. How can she respond to Mrs. Payne's advice?

2. Mr. Trent is at a park with a friend and the friend's child, Tony, 7. Mr. Trent's child, Melissa, 7, gets into a tug of war with Tony over the only remaining swing. Although they are having a conflict, no one is really getting hurt. Mr. Trent wants to wait and see if the children will work out the problem

without his interference. Tony's father says, "Aren't you going to do something about Melissa? She's trying to take that swing away from Tony?" What can Mr. Trent say or do?

3. Mrs. Salyer's parents are visiting when the ice cream truck comes down the street. Holly, 8, comes to get money from her mother. Mrs. Salyer reminds Holly that she already chose to spend her allowance on a toy and refuses to give her more money. Mrs. Salyer's father says, "Oh, come on, let her have some ice cream." The mother tells him that she and Holly have an agreement that she is to use her allowance for things such as ice cream. The grandfather pulls a dollar bill from his wallet and gives it to Holly, who hurries out the door to catch the ice cream truck. What can Mrs. Salyer do or say to the grandfather and/or to Holly later?

4. Mr. White and Jesse, 4, are in the grocery store. While Mr. White puts the food on the conveyor belt, Jesse tries repeatedly to climb out of the cart. When Mr. White tries to get him to stay in the cart, Jesse throws a tantrum at the check-out line. Everyone is looking at Mr. White disapprovingly because his child is being so loud and disruptive. What can Mr. White do or say?

5. Mrs. Carson's son, Tommy, 3, isn't potty-trained. When Mrs. Carson's mother-in-law sees her changing his diaper, she says, "You know, if you had been trying to teach him to go on the potty when he was younger, he would be potty-trained by now. All my kids were potty-trained by the time they were two year's old!" What can Mrs. Carson do or say?

6. Mr. and Mrs. Rose and Mark, 6, are having dinner with Mrs. Rose's parents. Mark is a very skinny boy who doesn't eat much. He also doesn't like many foods, but what he eats is nutritious. During dinner, his grandparents tell Mark he doesn't eat enough and tell his parents they are concerned about him. Mrs. Rose explains that she has discussed his weight and eating habits with his doctor, who agrees that there is nothing to worry about. The grandmother says to Mrs. Rose, "*You* are the parent here, it is *your* responsibility to make sure he eats well. If you don't do something soon, Mark's going to be malnourished!" What can Mrs. Rose do or say?

Possible Answers

A. Correcting Myths about Parenting

These are possible "true" revisions and the chapters in which you can find them.

Truth 1   Parenting classes can benefit *anyone*. Ideally, parents take parenting classes *before* serious problems develop. (Chapters 1 and 15)

Truth 2   A parenting instructor points out what parents are doing *right,* the options they have, and information about the positive or negative effects of *all* their choices. (Chapter 1)

Truth 3   Certain parenting skills are most effective *if* parents use them for certain types of problems and present them in specific, effective ways. It may take time to see results. (Chapter 1)

Truth 4   No individual family member or relationship should be the center of the family. Each relationship's needs are equally important, but different. (Chapter 2)

Truth 5   Democratic parenting is a *balance* between choices and limits. Parents set limits, but offer the child choices within those limits. Democratic parenting benefits all children, despite their personality or behavior traits. (Chapter 2)

Truth 6   A parent's job is to teach their children how to be *self*-controlled. (Chapter 2)

Truth 7   It is better to stop and think first, before responding to a problem. (Chapter 3)

Truth 8   Misbehavior is a symptom of a deeper problem; *that* issue needs to be resolved or misbehavior will reappear. (Chapter 3)

Truth 9   Descriptive encouragement is more effective than praise and stimulates *internal* motivation. (Chapter 4)

Truth 10   Parents want to focus on the *child's* feeling by saying, "I bet *you* feel proud of *yourself*" or "I bet it feels good to know you could (describe accomplishment)." (Chapter 4)

Truth 11   Parents want to describe what children do right and ask *them* how or if they could improve. Pointing out faults or mistakes is not encouraging, it is discouraging. (Chapter 4)

Truth 12   Children need to respect *all* people, not just adults and parents. They need to understand the *value* of the rules so they will voluntarily follow them. (Chapter 5)

Truth 13   Behavior charts foster *external* motivation, unhealthy competition and further discourage those who struggle to succeed. (Chapters 4 and 5)

Truth 14   Parents can give choices *within* limits, so children know they do not have a choice about *everything*. (Chapter 5)

Truth 15   *Not* all children go through a "no" stage. It depends on the child's personality and how parents use "no." (Chapter 5)

Truth 16   Parents will see whether children can handle more independence *if* given more freedom— not all at once, but staying one step ahead of their skills.

Truth 17   Parents want to acknowledge the difficulty so children feel excited if they do it and not so bad if they can't. (Chapter 6)

Truth 18   When children have problems, parents can *guide* children to a solution, with F-A-X Listening, without taking over. (Chapter 7)

Truth 19   If children aren't doing their homework, parents can use the Child Problem Toolbox to "keep the ball in their court," brainstorm solutions, and hold children responsible for following through. (Chapter 8)

Truth 20   My *beliefs* and *interpretations* about people and events determines whether I get angry. I have a choice about my beliefs and emotions. (Chapter 9)

Truth 21   Children don't program parents' trigger buttons, they just discover them. I can reprogram my buttons and control my reactions. (Chapter 9)

Truth 22   When we tell children we are disappointed in them, they feel discouraged and *less* motivated to improve themselves. (Chapter 10)

Truth 23   Just because we tell children "a million times" doesn't mean they fully understand and have mastered the skills to behave appropriately. (Chapter 11)

Truth 24   Children misbehave because they are discouraged and confused about a positive way to meet their goals. (Chapter 12)

Truth 25   Children won't learn *if* parents make them suffer. They can learn from discipline, without physical or emotional punishment. (Chapter 13)

Truth 26   If parents want children to behave and follow rules, they can explain the value of the rule, the child's options, and the positive and negative effect of the child's choices. Respectful discipline is the result of the child's negative behavior *choices*. (Chapter 13)

Truth 27   Effective time-outs teach self-control and healthy anger management skills. They are logically related to out-of-control behavior. The location is based on the child's recharge style and the activities they engage in are decided by the type of anger energy they experience. The time-out lasts until the child has regained control. (Chapter 13)

Truth 28   Family councils need to occur weekly, before problems arise. (Chapter 14)

Truth 29   Healthy families use consensus decision-making, because voting has a win/lose solution. "Losers" usually feel discouraged and often resist or sabotage the decision. Consensus decisions are win/win, because everyone agrees to the decision, even if they do not "get their way." (Chapter 14)

Truth 30   If parents are truly consistent, they will "get back on track" when they realize they have overreacted. Rather than just giving in, parents need to admit their mistake and restate the appropriate discipline, making sure it fits the "Four R's." (Chapter 15)

Truth 31   Each parent can have a different, unique personal style of parenting within the balanced range. Only when inconsistencies are harmful, sabotage the other parent, or children can use them to manipulate, do the differences become more damaging to relationships. (Chapters 2 and 15)

B. Responding to Criticism

1. a. Mrs. Greer might have temporarily abandoned her effective parenting because she felt embarrassed and pressured by her son misbehaving in someone's home.
    b. If she believes her son's behavior is a reflection of her abilities as a parent, she will be more likely to react negatively.
    c. She could have used quick reminders or talked to Jason privately before she lost her cool.
    d. Mrs. Greer can either give Mrs. Payne a disapproving, but respectful, look or she can explain her beliefs (which she is not obligated to do). If she chooses to do this, she can be clear that these are *her* beliefs and Mrs. Payne does not have to agree.

2. Mr. Trent can explain that he's been teaching Melissa how to resolve problems and wants to see if she remembers what she's learned. He can assure the other father that if Melissa chooses not to handle the problem respectfully, he *will* say something. If this happens, Mr. Trent can do brief peer mediation, which will model positive skills to the other parent.

3. Mrs. Salyer has two opposite response choices, depending on how important this issue is to her. She can acknowledge her father's desire to "spoil" Holly and set limits, making it clear that she has already given Holly an answer and she expects him to abide by it. If he disagrees with what she is doing, she would appreciate him telling her privately. She can also make it clear to Holly that their agreements and rules apply even when grandparents are there. This is the most likely approach if the grandfather visits regularly and his actions are regularly sabotaging Mrs. Salyer's agreements with Holly. Another possibility would be to let Holly's grandfather enjoy spoiling her. This option would most likely be appropriate if the grandfather rarely visits.

4. Mr. White can ignore the other customers, offer choices within limits, and get Jesse involved in putting the groceries on the conveyor belt. If all his best efforts seem to fail, he can realize Jesse is probably tired from shopping and make the quickest exit he can after paying for his groceries. He may or may not choose to reveal discipline, shopping alone next time, depending on how often this has happened before.

5. Mrs. Carson can say to her mother-in-law, "I know parents were told to do things differently when we were young. Although Tommy isn't completely potty-trained, he's making a lot of progress. He and I both feel better when he accomplishes things independently."

6. Mrs. Rose can change the subject away from Mark's weight. She can also make encouraging comments to Mark. After dinner, she can thank her mother for her concern and make it clear to her mother that Mark's weight and eating habits are not an acceptable dinner topic. She can even point out that Mark eats less when he is upset and that her comments might upset him. If her mother is not willing to agree to curb her comments, Mrs. Rose can suggest that she visit another time, besides dinner, for a while. This, however, would be a last resort measure.

MAINTAINING YOUR *CONFIDENCE*

Throughout *The Parent's Toolshop*, we have learned about children's behavior and effective techniques for improving our relationships with our children. I hope this training has helped you grow as a person and as a parent. By now, after learning so many effective tools, you are probably feeling more confident as a parent. Some people feel discouraged because they realize they are still making mistakes or aren't improving fast enough. "After all I put into this," you may think, "I deserve fewer problems with my children!" Here are some suggestions for maintaining your confidence.

- **Have realistic expectations.** In times of stress, when you're discouraged, or when you are tempted to be hard on yourself for a mistake, look at how far you've come. Learn from your mistakes, make a commitment to your future, and move on.

  > *A Personal Story. The Keep-Your-Cool tools have always been the hardest for me to practice consistently. Once, after I had been doing so well, I was under a lot of stress and getting increasingly irritable. Finally, I blew my stack and yelled. I felt bad and started to put myself down. Then I stopped myself. I realized I lasted a lot longer this time, before finally yelling. What I yelled was different. I was yelling "I" messages, instead of blaming and criticizing. "At least my words were more respectful," I thought, "even though I yelled them." I calmed down, got my brain back on track and apologized to the kids. We worked out a solution to the problem. It's taken years for me to improve my anger management to a level I feel good about, but I still have to keep working at it. At least I can give myself credit for the positive changes I **have** made.*

- **Set realistic goals**. Do not expect the beds to be made perfectly, the dishes to be spotless, or things to run smoothly all the time. Children may choose new behaviors to test you. You are dealing with human beings who are constantly learning (including yourself), and they will make mistakes. Most of all, if many of the tools in this book were new to you, don't expect to master them all at once.

- **Believe in yourself and your children.** Children can change and so can you. When you believe in the value of a tool, you'll try it. When you use it long enough, you'll see results. Don't give up if you don't see immediate results. Make a commitment to the future. With time and practice, you *will* see results and improvement.

- **Take it one step at a time.** Don't expect perfection out of yourself or your children. If your expectations are too high, you and your children will feel more discouraged. If you take small steps, you will move forward and you'll all feel more confident.

It is unrealistic to expect your growth to go ever upwards, like a straight line.

Realistically, growth comes in waves, with occasional dips, but always improving. In a dip, look back at how far you've come.

- **Trust your intuition.** When logic fails you, get in touch with your heart. Intuition is often confused with emotions. Emotions cause us to react with blame and judgment, but intuitive ideas result in inner peace and responses that leave us feeling better about ourselves.

- **Stop worrying and feeling guilty**. Unproductive guilt causes us to focus on the past—an action that no amount of reliving can change. If we condemn ourselves for being less than perfect in the past, we become unproductive and unable to take action in the present.

- **Educate yourself.** Periodically read this book again, taking one toolset or toolbox at a time and working with it at a slower pace. Read complementary books, such as those I've mentioned throughout the book. Attend seminars and support groups that teach healthy, effective parenting skills. As you learn and practice the skills, you will be more consistent and feel more confident. (These don't however, replace the need for counseling for severe behavior problems, troubled relationships, or issues from your childhood you have become aware of. Even healthy individuals may need therapy at a challenging time. It can be a valuable part of the healing process.)

- **Surround yourself with supportive people** who think like you do about parenting. Select people or resources whose opinions and values you respect when seeking advice or information. Join a support group if you are dealing with a special issue like separation, divorce, death, special-needs children, teens, or young children.

- **Balance** fun, work, and rest. Enjoy yourself and your children. Treat yourself with respect and don't allow others to treat you disrespectfully.

- **Have the courage to be imperfect** and grant this right to your children. Say to yourself, "What can I learn from this mistake?" Sometimes we have to learn the same lesson repeatedly (this applies to us *and* our children).

- **Be optimistic.** Instead of assuming children want to be difficult, assume they want positive results and are simply confused about how to achieve them. Try to see the positive in everything. Get into the children's world and understand things from their perspective.

- **Encourage yourself.** Consciously choose how you interpret events and find constructive ways of looking at situations. Have a sense of humor and keep things in perspective. Focus on your strengths and realize that it's not necessary to compare yourself to others. Use affirmations and positive self-talk. Here are two final exercises to keep your confidence soaring.

Practice Exercise

A. List 10 things you do well, positive qualities you have (as a person and/or parent), goals you have, or accomplishments you've reached.

B. Write affirmations for yourself. The rules are to make them positive statements that use words like "I can" or "I will." Periodically read them out loud, especially when you are feeling discouraged. Here are some affirmations to start with, but feel free to add or substitute more.

AFFIRMATIONS

- I have many personal strengths. I strive to be the best parent—and person—I can be.
- My sense of personal worth and identity goes beyond my role as a parent. I will look at *all* my positive qualities to feel good about myself.
- I respect myself and am worthy of respect from others.
- I like being a parent and find ways to enjoy my children every day.
- I am honest with myself about areas I want to improve. I am willing to learn from my mistakes.
- I see my children's positive qualities and show them how much I appreciate them.
- I am willing to let go of caring about what other people think I should do and make decisions based on what's best for my family.
- I am ready to let go of controlling others and will focus, instead, on controlling myself.
- I am more interested in improving my relationships than I am in being a perfect parent or having perfect children.
- When my children misbehave or things don't turn out the way I'd like, I can change my approach if I need to and accept the things and people I can't change.

▶ I want to find ways to improve my relationship with my children and respond so they *want* to cooperate more.

IN CLOSING

You are probably more aware of how you parent, your strengths, and areas you want to improve. You have a conscious plan, supported by new tools, to respond helpfully and effectively to just about any issue that arises in any relationship. When you make mistakes, you may no longer berate yourself, having developed the courage to be imperfect. You can look at the choices you made, learn from them, and choose to handle things differently next time, using the many techniques you've learned.

As you practice what you've learned, your children's behavior will improve, and you will strengthen *all* your relationships. When this happens, you won't have to put as much thought and emotional control into what you do—your new style will be second nature to you.

Completing this book is a priceless gift from you to your children. Not only will you be a better (but imperfect) parent, but you will be teaching and modeling valuable life skills to your children and others. These skills are like a precious heirloom you can pass from one generation to the next. All it takes is one person to break a negative cycle. That one person is you.

I hope, as you reflect back on the day you first started your tour of *The Parent's Toolshop*, you realize how much you've grown. The poem that follows the Three C's Summary Sheet is one we read at the end of the parenting class, because it illustrates the growth process we all go through.

Keep up your hard work. You and your children are worth your investment of time and energy.

SUMMARY SHEET
CONSISTENCY, CRITICISM, CONFIDENCE

Maintaining CONSISTENCY ☆☆☆☆

- True consistency is staying on the same path or getting back on it when we stray.

- It's important to follow the same parenting plan away from home that we use at home.

- Support your partner with your skills.

- Live the skills, don't preach about them.

- Only give advice in a way that makes other people feel supported and better about themselves.

Responding to CRITICISM and Unhelpful Advice ☆☆☆☆

- Screen other parenting resources for advice that is accurate, consistent with your philosophy, and compatible with your long-term goals. Ignore any advice that gets in the way of these goals or reduces communication and mutual respect in your family.

- Adult behavior can be unintentional or intentional, just like children's. Use the Universal Blueprint to respond to problems in *all* your relationships.

- Seek the value in criticism, instead of reacting to the way someone said it.

- If you have consistently tried to use effective communication skills to respond to toxic people, it may be time to set limits.

Maintaining Your CONFIDENCE

- Look at how far you've come. Educate yourself. Surround yourself with supportive people. Encourage yourself.

Autobiography in Five Short Chapters
by Portia Nelson

I

I walk down the street.
there is a deep hole in the sidewalk.
I fall in.
I am lost . . . I am helpless.
It isn't my fault.
It takes forever to find a way out.

II

I walk down the same street.
There is a deep hole in the sidewalk.
I pretend I don't see it.
I fall in again.
I can't believe I am in the same place.
But it isn't my fault.
It still takes a long time to get out.

III

I walk down the same street.
There is a deep hole in the sidewalk.
I see it is there.
I still fall in . . . it's a habit.
My eyes are open.
I know where I am.
It is my fault.
I get out immediately.

IV

I walk down the same street.
There is a deep hole in the sidewalk.
I walk around it.

V

I walk down a different street.

GLOSSARY OF TERMS

ABC-123-D Steps: (A) prevent the problem, (B) acknowledge feelings, (C1) set limits or express concerns, (C2) redirect misbehavior, (C3) reveal discipline, (D) maintain progress.

Aggressive anger: Explodes at targets, hurting people physically or emotionally.

Aggressive communication: Being firm, but not kind. Speakers uphold their rights in ways that violate the listeners' rights.

All-at-once learners: Children who practice several different new skills at once.

All-or-nothing learners: Children who practice skills in only one area at a time, adding new skills to the ones they've already mastered.

Assertive anger: Being honest about feelings without hurting others.

Assertive communication: Being kind *and* firm. It upholds the speaker's rights in ways that respect those of others.

Autocratic parenting: Another name for an Overcontrolling parenting style.

Avoider: The most extreme type of under-controlling parenting style, characterized by an apathetic lack of interest and follow through. Its most extreme form is neglectful.

Balanced independence: As children increase their skills, parents expand the limits, staying one step ahead. Children can handle the freedom responsibly.

Balanced parenting style: A general parenting style that offers limited choices, uses respectful, reasonable parenting techniques, and has positive long-term results.

Behavior modification: Programs that reward subjects for desired behavior and withhold rewards or impose punishments for undesirable behavior. These methods are also called behavior charts, star/sticker charts, and incentive programs.

Blame game: Blaming others for power or revenge, rather than focusing on solutions. The blame game is addictive and escalates into intense defensiveness and revengeful blame cycles.

Bottom line: The basic limits, the minimum that must occur, or the least to settle for. There are usually more choices within bottom-line limits.

Bribe: A tempting reward, designed to manipulate or influence someone to take a particular action. The focus is on external payoffs, instead of the value of the rule or request.

Bribe junkies: People who are addicted to bribes and *only* do something *if* they get a reward.

C (Child problem): The child has a problem that does not directly affect or concern the parent.

Child-friendly: Making tasks or items more appealing to children, by using creative names for items or making tasks easier for children.

Child Problem Toolbox: Contains the toolsets to use when others have problems.

Clear Communication Toolset: Contains the tools for sharing feelings and concerns in simple, clear, respectful, and assertive ways.

Consensus decision-making: Thinking together about a solution and discussing the matter until all agree on a plan.

Conditional apologies: Apologizing for the *way* one expresses a valid reason for being upset.

Conquerors: People who want to reach solutions quickly and logically.

Consistency: Staying with a plan or getting back on track when we stray.

Constructive criticism: Doesn't exist—constructive builds up; criticism tears down.

Contradictory messages: Begin to say one thing, but end up saying the opposite.

Cooperation: Working together as a team toward win/win solutions. Team leaders focus on the value of the request or rule and offer choices within reasonable limits. People are *self-*

motivated to cooperate for the internal payoffs received.

Cooperation Toolset: Contains tools that emphasize teamwork and promote cooperation, rather than demanding blind obedience.

C/P: Part **C**hild problem and part **P**arent problem that does not involve problem behavior.

C/PO: Part **C**hild problem, part **P**arent problem involving **O**n purpose misbehavior.

C/PU: Part **C**hild problem, part **P**arent problem involving **U**nintentional misbehavior.

Defiant compliance: Obeying a command in a hurtful or aggressive way.

Descriptive encouragement: Describing children's feelings, effort, or improvement, the value of the act, or how it was helpful.

Developmentally delayed: Children who function below what is considered "normal" for their age.

Discipline Toolset: Contains the tools for helping children *learn* from their mistakes (discipline), rather than making them *suffer* for their mistakes (punishment).

Don't Say "Don't": Avoiding the word "don't," by describing the behavior we *want* to see.

Double messages: Sending two inconsistent messages.

Double standards: Rules that apply to children, but not to parents. Children usually follow the parents' example.

Duping delight: The excitement of fooling someone.

Ego-esteem: Believing we are *better than* others. People compete with others, trying to be the best or always win.

Encouragement: Descriptive, non-judgmental comments that cause others to say positive things to themselves.

External-rechargers: People who draw their energy from the world around them. They need to interact with other people or activities to get energy, calm down, or work through problems.

External Problem Solvers: People who work out their problems with others.

Family Council Toolset: Contains tools for holding regularly scheduled family get-togethers to build self-esteem, discuss issues, make decisions, and solve problems that affect the family.

Family goals: The qualities we want our family to have.

F-A-X Listening process: **F**ocus on feelings, **A**sk helpful questions, and **X**-amine possible solutions.

F-A-X Listening Toolset: Contains tools that open the door to communication and acknowledge others' feelings.

Flash fires: Anger caused by events that push an emotional trigger button that sets off a sudden eruption.

Foundation-Building Toolset: The beliefs and attitudes that affect our parenting style.

Healthy competition: Doing one's best, having fun, and learning skills in the process.

Healthy guilt: A self-imposed feeling of regret that does not reduce one's self-respect or self-worth.

Healthy paranoia: Becoming aware of one's words, thoughts, actions, and habits.

Healthy pride: An *inner* sense of accomplishment and satisfaction that is not boastful or conceited.

Inconvenience consequence: Follow through on discipline as soon as possible, even if it is inconvenient for the child, without adding suffering.

Indecisive children: Children who are afraid that if they choose one thing, they'll miss out on the other option.

Independence Toolset: Contains tools that teach children life skills so they can handle more freedom responsibly.

Individuation: The natural, necessary process of becoming an individual, with ideas, identity, beliefs, and values all one's own.

Individual goals for children: The skills and qualities we want children to develop.

Individual needs: The different personalities and needs of each individual member of each individual family.

Internal problem solvers: People who prefer to do their problem solving alone.

Internal rechargers: People who need time to be alone on a regular basis. They go within to regain control or recharge their energy supply.

Keep Your Cool Toolset: Contains anger and stress management skills both parents and children can use.

Learning styles: How people learn, remember and recall new information and skills.

Maintenance Toolbox: Contains toolsets that maintain family and personal progress.

Mediation: Taking turns, between two people, at each step of problem solving.

NO (No problem): There is no problem or a problem is expected, but has not yet occurred.

No "No's": Setting limits with positive words.

"No thank you" helpings: Taking a small serving of each food, just to try it.

Nudging is a firm and gentle encouragement to take the next step.

Obedience: When an inferior person unquestioningly follows orders or commands from a superior. Superior wins/inferior loses. Motivation is usually from fear, not respect, and there is little or no choice for the inferior. It is a temporary solution that creates resentment and rebellion.

Openly modeling behavior: Making internal (logical or emotional) processes something children can observe, usually by talking our way through the steps we normally take in our mind.

Over-compensation cycle: One parenting partner thinks the other is too strict, so he or she becomes more lenient to counteract the other (or vice versa).

Over-controlling independence: Children have the skills, but little freedom to use them. Children resent limits and push for more freedom.

Over-controlling parenting style: A general parenting style that uses power tactics to control children's behavior and has mostly negative long-term consequences.

Over-Indulger: The less extreme under-controlling parenting style, characterized by doting, rescuing, offering unnecessary service to children, few rules, and even less enforcement.

P (Parent problem): The parent is experiencing a problem that does not bother the child. No problem behavior is involved.

Parallel conversation: A low-pressure, nonchalant conversation that occurs during a side-by-side activity with no eye contact.

Parenting myths: Inaccurate, but commonly accepted parenting information.

Parenting style: A general set of beliefs, attitudes, and techniques parents use with their children.

Parent Problem Toolbox: Contains the toolsets parents use to respond to problems or concerns that affect them, including misbehavior.

PASRR formula: **P**revent the problem, **A**cknowledge feelings, **S**et limits or express concerns, **R**edirect misbehavior, **R**eveal discipline.

Passive anger: Stuffing angry feelings or hinting at them.

Passive-Aggressive anger: Hurting others (aggressive) in passive ways.

Passive communication: Being kind, but not firm. Speakers believe their rights are *less* important than the listeners' rights.

Perfectionistic Supervisor: The less extreme type of over-controlling parenting style, characterized by unrealistic expectations, rigid organizational structure, and correcting techniques.

Permissive parenting: Another name for Under-controlling parenting style.

Personal responsibility: Being responsible *for* and *to* oneself.

Play fighting: When both children agree to play rough and no one is getting hurt.

PO (Parent problem, "On purpose" misbehavior): The parent has a problem with misbehavior that seems intentional, to serve a purpose.

PO misbehavior: Misbehavior that results when children *mistakenly believe* the behavior will help them accomplish a specific purpose. Children are unaware of their subconscious beliefs and behavior choices.

PO Toolset (**P**arent problem, "**O**n purpose" misbehavior): Contains tools for identifying and redirecting misbehavior in children who have the skills to behave properly but choose not to.

Power-and-control children: Children who debate and argue, so they can have some power or control in a situation.

Power Patrol: The most extreme type of over-controlling parenting style, characterized by harsh, critical, power tactics. Its most extreme form is abusive.

Power time-outs: *Make* children go to a chair, room, or isolated spot every time they misbehave. The parent sets a timer and the parent makes sure the child doesn't have any fun while there. Everything about the timeout is decided and controlled by the parent. This is a form of unhelpful punishment.

Praise: Comments that use judgmental labels that can accidentally cause discouragement or put negative pressure on others.

Praise junkies: People who must get praise and approval from others to feel good about themselves or who won't do something unless they get recognition or rewards.

Prevention Toolbox: Contains toolsets that can prevent problems from developing or worsening.

Problem-Solving Toolset: Contains tools that teach independent, responsible problem-solving and decision-making skills without taking over and solving problems for others.

Progressive restrictions: Start with the least restriction and increase as the behavior continues.

PU (**P**arent problem, **U**nintentional misbehavior): The parent has a problem with misbehavior that is the result of the child's lack of maturity, skills, or knowledge.

PU/PO mutations: When PU behavior gets a strong reaction, it can change (or mutate) into PO behavior. Because of the reaction, children believe the misbehavior can help them achieve a specific goal.

Pushing is an unrealistic pressured expectation to reach the final goal all at once.

PU Toolset (**P**arent problem, **U**nintentional misbehavior): Contains tools that redirect misbehavior resulting from children's lack skills.

Rebellion: A reaction to control. Every child individuates, but *not* all rebel. Individuation turns into rebellion when parents try to control children's independence and individuality.

Regression: When children revert to old, outgrown habits.

Regressive restrictions: Start with the most restrictive but still reasonable limits. If all goes well, the next period is less restrictive, and so on, until all privileges are restored.

Response-ability: The ability to accept the consequences of the choices we make.

Ripple effect: When pebbles drop in a pond, the ripples start at the middle and expand outward. When one person in a family changes, it has some effect, usually small at first, but more obvious over time.

Role model: One who sets an example.

Routines: A regular, consistent way of doing a task or handling a situation.

Sarcasm: A form of passive-aggressive anger. It disguises anger, blame, and criticism with humor.

Secondary emotions: An emotion that comes *after* another feeling. The first feeling, which is closer to the real issue, causes the second feeling.

Self-esteem: How we *feel* about our *inside qualities.* This includes our worth as a human being, sense of purpose in life, and how lovable we think we are.

Self-Esteem Toolset: Contains tools that build self-esteem, encourage positive behavior, and stimulate internal motivation.

Self-image: What we *think* about our *outside appearance,* what we think others see. This includes our looks, talents, popularity, or accomplishments.

SHARP RV: The six problem areas that concern parents: **S**afety, **H**ealth, **A**ppropriateness, **R**ights, **P**roperty, **R**ules, **V**alues.

Smoldering embers: Slow buildups of stressful situations that eventually spill over or erupt.

Tattling: Telling an adult about another child's behavior simply to get that child in trouble.

Taunting: Severe teasing that borders on cruelty.

Teasing: Mean-spirited and hurtful treatment that often involves put-downs or name-calling.

Telling: Letting an adult know that another child is doing something dangerous or someone is hurt.

Transitional period: The time between birth (total dependency) and approximately 4 years, when children become physically independent.

Three C's: Contains tools for maintaining Consistency, handling Criticism, and boosting Confidence.

Toolbox: Group of toolsets that deal with a particular type of problem. Each of the four major steps in the Universal Blueprint contains a toolbox, and each toolbox deals with a different type of problem.

Tools: Individual parenting techniques, located within the toolset of the purpose they serve.

Toolsets: Groups of skills that serve a common purpose, located at the appropriate step in which parents use them.

Trial-and-error learners: Children who are willing to repeatedly try a new skill without getting discouraged.

Trigger buttons: Conditioned reactions to events, usually due to unresolved childhood issues.

Tweens: Elementary school-aged children through preteens.

Under-controlling independence: Children have few skills and too much freedom. They can't handle the freedom responsibly.

Under-controlling parenting style: A general parenting style that offers great freedom to children with few limits and has mostly negative long-term consequences.

Unhealthy competition: Focuses on winning at others' expense, being the best, or being better than others.

Unhealthy guilt: Guilt that causes people to feel they are worthless. It may be imposed by others, to manipulate or control, or be self-imposed.

Unhealthy pride: Thinking we are *better than* others.

Universal Blueprint: A guide for identifying types of problems and planning an effective response to each.

Unique personal style: The way individual parents express themselves while using the Universal Blueprint and its tools in individual ways.

Venters: Emotional people who need more time to work through their feelings before thinking logically about solutions.

Wait-and-do learners: Children who observe others and practice skills in their minds, until they think they know the skill well enough to perform it well.

INDEX

Parent's Toolshop Products

★ Full-color pictures and detailed descriptions of products listed below *and* additional or new products are at www.parentstoolshop.com.)

☐ *The Parent's Toolshop: The Universal Blueprint for Building a Healthy Family* (Second Edition, ©2000, ISBN: 1-929643-34-9, 456 pgs.)
> *Item #: PT-99002* $24.95

☐ *Shared Blessings: Creating and Facilitating Stay-at-Home Parent Discussion Groups* (Revised Edition ©1999). Are you a stay-at-home parent who would like to meet other like-minded parents? This manual will offer you tips for finding other parents, organizing groups and activities, leading topic discussions, and stimulating ownership of the group among its members.
> *Item #: PT-99001* $5.95

☐ **Parent's Toolshop T-shirt.** Long-sleeve pre-shrunk natural cotton. State size when ordering: (Adult M-XX, supplies limited).
> *Item # PT-98004* $14.95

☐ *Pocket-sized Hintbook* guides the reader through the Universal Blueprint's decision-making steps. Take any situation and use the hintbook to quickly plan your ideal response—anywhere, anytime.
> *Item #: PT-20002* $5.95

☐ *11" x 17" Full-color Poster* of the detailed house on the book's last page. Large enough to list more tools, but small enough to hang on a refrigerator. Great for quick reference.
> *Item #: PT-20001* $4.95

☐ *Parent's Toolshop Correspondence Study Guide.* (© 1998, ISBN: 0-9659119-5-0) The best way to learn *The Parent's Toolshop* is to graduate from a full-length (10+ hour) Parent's Toolshop program. When this isn't possible, the correspondence study guide helps readers focus on information that is critical to understanding, using, and even teaching the tools in *The Parent's Toolshop*. Throughout the training process, a Parent's Toolshop liaison will assess your understanding of the teachings and provide a certificate when you "graduate." Packet includes hard copies and a PC-compatible diskette of the study guide in three software formats: ASCII, WordPerfect, and Word97.

★ **All Tour Guide applicants** *must* complete the correspondence study program before Tour Guide training and certification.

★ **Discounts available** if you have attended *any* Parent's Toolshop training program. Submit your receipt for the training you attended and deduct training fees (up to $70) from the cost of the correspondence training program.
> *Item #: TG-98001* (A tax-free service) $70.00

☐ *Interactive Activity Packet* (First Edition, © 1998.) Twenty-five (25) activities, including cooperative games, partner activities, role plays, and dramatic demonstrations that help participants of parenting classes or other communication-skill-training programs have fun *while* learning.
> *Item #: PR-98001* $19.95

☐ *Tour Guide Standards & Practices Manual.* (©1998, ISBN: 0-9659119-4-2) If you are interested in *teaching* programs based on *The Parent's Toolshop*, you must receive training and certification by the author to use this copyrighted resource. The information booklet explains the process—from pre-certification requirements to recertification.
> *Item # FR-98004* .... FREE

The author welcomes your stories and suggestions. Feel free to write her, Jody Johnston Pawel, c/o Ambris Publishing, P.O. Box 343, Springboro, OH, 45066, or send her an e-mail at pawel@parentstoolshop.com.